Stief/Matschke

Infringement of Second Medical Use Claims

# Infringement of Second Medical Use Claims

## A global study focusing on skinny labels

edited by

Marco Stief

Tobias Matschke

2024

C.H.BECK

**beck.de**

ISBN 978 3 406 81753 3


Wilhelmstraße 9, 80801 München
Druck und Bindung: Beltz Grafische Betriebe GmbH
Am Fliegerhorst 8, 99947 Bad Langensalza

Satz: Fotosatz Buck
Zweikirchener Str. 7, 84036 Kumhausen
Umschlag: Druckerei C.H.Beck Nördlingen

myclimate
shape our future

chbeck.de/nachhaltig

Gedruckt auf säurefreiem, alterungsbeständigem Papier
(hergestellt aus chlorfrei gebleichtem Zellstoff)

# Preface

The number of patent applications in Europe, the United States, and Asia covering second medical use claims has been increasing steadily over the past few years. While only 250 patent applications containing an European Patent Convention (EPC) 2000 claim were published by the European Patent Office (EPO) in 2009, by 2017 this number had already risen to over 1,500 and has consistently stayed at this level in Europe.[1] Similar trends can be observed all over the world.

This significant increase is concomitant with a rise in the number of patent infringement cases in the field of second medical use claims. In such actions, courts all over the world had and have to determine the legal requirements for claims for patent infringement. A major bone of contention in this respect is the infringement of second medical use claims in the case of 'skinny label products', i.e. drugs approved for non-patented indications. A skinny label application permits a generics manufacturer to seek market approval solely for the unpatented uses of the drug by excluding or carving out the patented use from the Summary of Product Characteristics (SmPC) and the product leaflet (or from its label). Against this background, the question arises whether a mere *infringing prescription practice,* i.e. the fact that the generic or biosimilar drug is also used for a patented indication (outside the indications mentioned in the SmPC, the leaflet or any similar documents), can be sufficient to presume patent infringement of a skinny label product.

While in most European countries a skinny label might not be sufficient to rule out infringement if an infringing prescribing practice has occurred, in almost all European jurisdictions there remains legal uncertainty surrounding the precise legal preconditions and the factual threshold to be fulfilled. Likewise, recent rulings from the US Federal Circuit and other countries outside Europe have raised questions about what actions a generic or biosimilar company can take once it has excised patented indications from its label.

With contributions from highly qualified and experienced patent litigators all around the world, this book provides a comprehensive legal study on the current legal situation in Europe (Part I), the United States (Part II), Australia (Part III) and Asia (Part IV), whereby a plurality of European jurisdictions (Austria, Denmark, France, Germany, Ireland, Italy, the Netherlands, Poland, Portugal, Spain, Türkiye, and the United Kingdom), and several Asian jurisdictions (China, Japan, Singapore, and Taiwan) will be subject to the present analysis. This book aims to serve as a guide to generics and biosimilar manufacturers as well as originator companies concerning the enforcement of second indication patents in the context of skinny labelling.

Marco Stief
Tobias Matschke

---

[1] Aboy et al, Mapping the European Patent Landscape for Medical Uses of Known Products (November 2021) available https://bioengineeringcommunity.nature.com/posts/mapping-the-european-patent-landscape-for-medical-uses-of-known-products.

# Authors

**Søren Chr. S. Andersen** *[Denmark]* is Partner in the IP & Life Science Department at Accura Law Firm – one of the largest commercial law firms in Denmark. He is a Representative before the Unified Patent Court. Søren has approx. 20 years of experience advising on all subjects within IP and other matters of particular relevance to businesses within life sciences and other regulated industries. Søren has solid experience as a patent litigator, having taken part in many of the most significant cases before the Danish courts. Some of the cases he has litigated has broken new ground in Danish jurisprudence, including by finding for the first time the existence of a right of prior use and by finding, also for the first time, litigated patents and utility models invalid in the context of PI proceedings before the Danish courts. Through the years, Søren has also extensively been involved in litigation before the Danish and European courts relating to IP in other fields, such as the cases that led to the referrals to the European Court of Justice in *Infopaq* (C-5/08) – a seminal case on European copyright law in the digital age. His field of expertise also extends to drafting and advising on contracts relating to e.g. IP and to regulatory matters in e.g. the pharmaceutical industry. Søren is an accomplished teacher, and his teaching experience has included a position as an Associate Professor of Intellectual Property Law at Copenhagen Business School (CBS). Søren studied law at the University of Copenhagen and received his Master of Laws (LL.M.) degree in 2004, finishing first in the class of that year.

**Filipe Baptista** *[Portugal]* is one of the founding partners and head of the patent litigation department with Baptista Monteverde & Associados (BMA), a leading IP law firm in Portugal. Filipe has more than 25 years of experience in advice and litigation in all types of IP matters and on unfair competition, with particular focus on patents, life sciences and regulatory pharmaceutical law. Filipe regularly assists multi-national companies in different sectors of industry, with particular focus on life sciences, automotive, clothing and IT. He completed his Law degree from the Lusíada University of Lisbon in 1995 and subsequently completed a post-graduation degree in Intellectual Property at the Law School of the University of Lisbon. Subsequently, Filipe qualified as a lawyer and joined the Portuguese Bar Association. Filipe has been recognised by numerous organisations in the IP practice, including The Best Lawyers, IAM-1000, WTR, MIP, The Legal 500 and Chambers. Filipe is a former vice-president of the Portuguese Consultants IP Association (ACPI) and is currently serving as member of the Supervisory Board (former Council) of ECTA, representing Portugal, and as a member of the Patent Committee of ECTA. He is also serving as member of the Unfair Competition Committee of INTA.

**Carly van der Beek** *[The Netherlands]* is active in the practice of pharmaceuticals and life sciences with a strong focus on European and domestic regulatory matters and patent law. Carly's practice covers advising and litigating in domestic and European (cross-border) matters relating to the launch of (generic) medicinal products, the combination of incentives and rewards for pharmaceutical research such as data and market exclusivity and SPCs. Further, Carly advises and litigates in national and international patent cases in the field of pharmaceuticals, chemistry and mechanical engineering. Carly is an active member of various professional associations including Farmacie & Recht, EPLAW, AIPPI and VAR.

**Matthew S. Bodenstein** *[United States]* is a director in the Biotechnology & Chemical Practice Group at Sterne, Kessler, Goldstein & Fox where he advises a diverse range of clients in the chemical, pharmaceutical, food science, material science, and biotechnology spaces. He has been recognised by his clients and peers as a leading patent strategist and is well-known for his thoughtful and creative approaches to obtaining business-critical patents. Matt's practice includes assisting clients with creating and managing strategic patent portfolios, managing complex and high priority patent prosecution (including 'Track 1' applications), conducting and managing complex due diligence investigations in connection with potential investments, acquisitions, and licensing opportunities, and rendering freedom to operate, validity, and non-infringement opinions. In addition to his focus on pure patent matters, he regularly helps clients negotiate term sheets, license agreements, and other strategic transactions. Prior to joining Sterne Kessler, Matt was Intellectual Property Counsel for the former Medicis Pharmaceutical Corp., and an associate and patent agent in the IP Group of an 'AmLaw 100' law firm. Before becoming a lawyer, he worked in the CNS Medical Chemistry group at Pfizer, Inc. and the Process Research and Development Group at Merck & Co., Inc. Matt earned his J.D., *cum laude*, from Temple University Beasley School of Law, and his M.S. and B.A. degrees in Chemistry, from the University of Pennsylvania.

**Álvaro de Castro** *[Spain]* joined Pérez-Llorca as Counsel in September 2021, after practising since 2008 at two other prestigious Spanish law firms as a lawyer specialising in intellectual property and unfair competition. He is an specialist in advising and representing clients in litigation concerning the acquisition, exploitation, infringement and validity of intangible assets such as patents, trademarks, industrial designs, copyrights and trade secrets, in all sectors of economic activity. His core speciality is patent litigation, especially in the pharmaceutical and life sciences fields. Over all these years Álvaro has contributed as author or co-author in publications by institutions like the European Patent Academy, international legal publishers like Wolters Kluwer, professional associations' journals like LESI's Les Nouvelles, financial journals like Financier Worldwide or leading sectorials publications like CEFI's for the pharmaceutical sector in Spain. In recent years, Álvaro has been invited to provide sessions for some of the leading and most prestigious Master's degrees and courses specialised in intellectual property in Spain, such as the Magister Lvcentinvs of the University of Alicante, the WIPO Summer Schools, and the European Patent Law Course organised by the School of Industrial Organisation (EOI) and the Spanish Patent and Trademark Office (OEPM). Álvaro studied law and business administration at Madrid's Autonomous University (UAM), followed by a Master's Degree in Intellectual Property and New Technologies at ESADE. He is a member of the Madrid Bar Association (ICAM), EPLAW and LES, and has been individually recognised in various legal directories including Legal 500, IP Stars, Best Lawyers, Who's Who Legal or Leaders League.

**Katrina Crooks** *[Australia]* is a Principal and Head of Spruson & Ferguson Lawyers. Dual qualified as a lawyer and patent attorney, Katrina has over 25 years' experience in intellectual property law. Her practice now focuses on intellectual property litigation, with a particular interest in the life sciences sector. Katrina has a wealth of international experience, having practiced in IP for many years in major full service firms in Dublin and New Zealand. She has been recognised by a range of ranking publications including MIP Stars, IAM Patent 1000, The Best Lawyers in AustraliaTM, WIPR Australian Patent and Trade Mark Leaders and Doyles Guide New South Wales. Katrina maintains a strong interest in intellectual property policy and education. She currently sits on the IP Committee of the Law Council of Australia, and as Treasurer in the Executive of the Intellectual Property

Society of Australia and New Zealand. She has guest lectured on IP topics at UTS Sydney and regularly writes on IP issues, including as author of the 'Patents in New Zealand: A Comparison with Australian Patent Law' chapter of LexisNexis' Lahore's Patents, Trade Marks and Related Rights. Katrina holds a Bachelor of Commerce and Bachelor of Laws with First Class Honours from the University of Canterbury in Christchurch, New Zealand, where she received the Gold Medal in Law. In 2001 she received a Masters in Law with First Class Honours from the University of Cambridge, graduating as a Tapp Scholar of Gonville & Caius College and an Honorary Cambridge Commonwealth Trust Scholar.

**Nevyn Fournel** *[France]* is a lawyer at the Paris Bar. Working at specialist patent litigation firm Schertenleib Avocats in Paris, France, Nevyn's practice is focused on complex cross-border disputes, principally in the area of life sciences. She has experience at every stage of litigation, from preliminary injunction to final hearing and appeal. Nevyn holds several degrees, including a Masters in Private Law from University Pantheon-Sorbonne, where she graduated first in her class, a Masters in IP Law from University Pantheon-Assas, a Masters in International Law and Management from HEC Paris, where she won the prize for best thesis, and a Masters in Law from Columbia Law School in New York.

**Luca Giove** *[Italy]* is the Founding Partner of the Italian IP law-firm GR Legal. Since the beginning of his career, almost 25 years ago, Luca has dedicated himself exclusively to Intellectual Property with a focus on litigation particularly on patent and trade secrets also before the Italian Supreme Court. He has regularly taken part in proceedings involving parallel actions in other jurisdictions related to patents. He also has a significant experience in other fields of IP litigation in the most diverse industrial and commercial sectors as well as on IP contracts related to technology. He is the author of many articles in English and Italian published in journals such as 'Il Diritto Industriale', 'La Giurisprudenza Italiana' and the Oxford Journal of Intellectual Property Law and Practice, as well as essays such as 'The SPC in Italy' in the 'European Handbook on Supplementary Protection Certificates'. He was an adjunct professor at the University of Padua for 'Patent and Biotechnology Law' for many years. He still regularly lectures in patent law at this University for post-graduate students. After having graduated from the University of Padua, Luca obtained an LL.M. from the University of London (School of African and Oriental Studies) in 2000. Subsequently, he worked in the intellectual property departments of Freshfields Bruckhaus Deringer's Milan office and of Bonelli Erede.

**Dominik Göbel** *[Austria]* is a partner at GASSAUER-FLEISSNER Rechtsanwälte GmbH, Attorney at Law, in Vienna, Austria. He studied at the University of Vienna (Mag. iur. 2003, Dr. iur. 2006) and holds an LL.M. in International Intellectual Property Law from the Illinois Institute of Technology Chicago – Kent College of Law (2007). Dominik has more than 15 years of experience as an IP lawyer and regularly advises and represents national and international companies in all areas of IP law (patents, trademarks, designs and copyrights) and unfair competition law (UWG), including the protection of know-how and trade secrets. His expertise in these areas includes both the enforcement of IP rights and the defence of claims in contentious proceedings, representation before public authorities as well as contract drafting and strategic advice. He has particular experience in patent litigation for the life sciences industry, where he has acted for leading pharmaceutical and biotechnology companies in several high-profile cases. He regularly publishes and lectures on IP matters and is a member of numerous organisations active in the field, including as a board member of EPLAW, a board member of LES Austria and an AIPPI delegate.

**Bethan Hopewell** *[United Kingdom]* is a partner at Powell Gilbert LLP, a specialist IP law firm based in London. She has a BSc in Molecular Biology from Imperial College and a D. Phil in Molecular Physiology from the University of Oxford. She has 19 years of experience of advising clients on patent disputes in the life sciences sector. This includes successfully acting for clients in some of the most high-profile patent cases to come before the UK courts in recent years, including the landmark UK Supreme Court decisions in *Warner-Lambert v Actavis* and *HGS v Eli Lilly* (in relation to the validity and infringement of second medical use patents and the law of industrial application). Bethan's recent work includes cases in the areas of DNA sequencing, molecular diagnostics and pharmaceutics. Bethan represents clients before the UK Patents Court, Court of Appeal and Supreme Court, as well as before the European Patent Office at opposition and appeal proceedings. She has particular expertise in co-ordinating complex multi-jurisdictional patent disputes in the life sciences sector. Bethan frequently lectures on IP law and is a tutor on the Oxford University IP Law and Practice diploma course.

**George J. H. Huang** *[Taiwan]* is the Director and Founder of Wisdom International Patent & Law Office. He is the first Attorney at Law with a solid technical background who qualified as a Patent Attorney in Taiwan. Having over 27 years of experience in the intellectual property field, George is skilled at handling patent, trademark and design matters, and has been individually ranked and recognised as 'Recommended Individual – Silver' in the IAM Patent 1000, the WTR 1000 and the ASIA IP rankings. George has substantial experience in pharmaceutical and chemical patent prosecution, disputes and infringement proceedings. His clientele includes leading international pharmaceutical and chemical companies. Being fluent in English and Japanese, George demonstrates his strengths by assisting notable overseas and Japanese corporate clients from diverse industries to obtain IP protections and enforce their rights. He is also the author of the two Japanese books: 'Taiwan Patent Practice Guide' and 'Taiwan Trademark Practice Guide', which are highly praised by in-house counsels and critics. George actively participates in professional associations and is a member of FICPI, a member of Anticounterfeiting Committee of International Trademark Association (INTA) and is a Councillor & Supervisor for the Asian Patent Attorneys Association (APAA) Taiwan Group. Before beginning his career as an IP attorney, George worked for the multinational pharmaceutical company Eisai Co., Ltd, where he gained hands-on experience in clinical research and regulatory affairs. George studied Biochemistry and Law at the National Taiwan University, and he received his Master's Degree in Biotechnology and Biochemistry from The University of Tokyo.

**Lichen Jia** *[China]* is an attorney-at-law at Liu Shen & Associates. She focuses on dispute resolution and consulting in the field of intellectual property and has handled a couple of intellectual property infringement and unfair competition cases in the past years. Lichen contributes regularly practical articles regarding enterprise intellectual property management and has published several articles on service inventions, and intellectual property compliance management. Before joining Liu Shen & Associates, she had worked as an intern in a government agency and a domestic law firm. She obtained her master's degree in International Economic Law at East China University of Political Science and Law in 2020.

**Erdem Kaya** *[Türkiye]* studied electronic engineering in Türkiye and qualified as a Turkish and European Patent Attorney in 2001. He is the founder of Erdem, Kaya & Partners, one of the most respected full service IP firms in Türkiye with a team of more than 50 IP professionals. Throughout his professional life, he has provided patent counseling services in almost all relevant aspects, including but not limited to patent drafting and prosecution, FTO studies, IP disputes, strategic IP managements, licensing agreements and valuation. Erdem also headed a national patent union called UPB for four years where he provided awareness or advanced level IP training to more than 20,000 people. He is currently one of the most active IP profiles in Türkiye and regularly speaks and writes on many platforms. He is a member of the world's leading IP organisations such as EPI, LES, AIPPI, INTA, GRUR and I3PM and is ranked among the top patent professionals in Türkiye by respected rating agencies. Finally, Erdem is a licensed angel investor and has invested in several start-ups with strong patent portfolios and software companies providing IP and technology transfer related solutions.

**Kian Hoe Khoo** BSc(Hons), Ph.D, Grad Dip IP Law *[Singapore]* is a registered Singapore patent attorney who is experienced in the drafting and prosecution of patent applications in the areas of life science-related disciplines including molecular biology, protein engineering, immunotherapy, antibody therapeutics, vaccines and medical diagnostics. He is also experienced in providing patent validity and infringement advice. Kian Hoe was previously a Research Fellow at the p53lab of A*STAR, where he worked on deciphering the molecular basis of drug resistance in acute myeloid leukaemia cancer cells, in a collaborative project with Roche Pharmaceuticals. He also worked on the development of novel antibody diagnostic and imaging tools for the early detection of cancer at A*STAR. Kian Hoe obtained a Bachelor of Biochemistry (1$^{st}$ Class Hons) from Imperial College London and a Doctor of Philosophy (Protein Engineering) from the University of Cambridge.

**Cathal Lane** *[Ireland]* is a Partner at Tomkins & Co. in Dublin. He has over 25 years of experience, and is a former Managing Partner. Cathal's practice concentrates on helping clients realise new opportunities by leveraging IP. He has acted for some of the world's leading companies, universities, semi-state companies and SMEs in the pharmaceutical, medical devices, machinery, composite materials and adhesive sectors. Cathal adopts a multi-disciplinary approach to intellectual property and regularly works with clients' tax advisors and lawyers in order to develop and execute business focused IP strategies. Cathal has an honours degree in Science, majoring in chemistry. Coupled with an agricultural background, a lot of his work has spanned from pharmaceutical/biomedical to machinery. Cathal worked for Bristol Myers Squibb before joining Tomkins. Cathal has acted for and advised many well-known (and not so well known) entities including Henkel, GSK, NUIG, TCD, UCD, Nogra/Giuliani, Novartis, Coillte (SmartPly/Medite,) Tanco, Ball Corporation, Celgard, DaramicKingspan, SMEs and private individuals. With a farming background, a mechanical mind and his life sciences, Cathal has dealt with many technologies: (electro)mechanics including agricultural machinery and control systems, medical devices including stents, valves, intravascular devices, composite materials, new molecules, new processes, formulation chemistry including pharmaceutical, drug delivery and polymer chemistry, electrochemical treatment and sensing, and has established patentability based on new applications of pre-existing molecules or formulations, and uses including the treatment of medical conditions/diseases, new physical properties including insulative properties, and/or product composition, food technology, packaging etc. One speciality is adhesive chemistry. Cathal is a prominent speaker on IP issues including New Frontiers, Massachusetts Continuing Legal Education (MCLE); Orange County Patent Law Association; Universities etc. and continues to lecture regularly on IP. In addition, he is a contributor to the book 'New Venture Creation in Ireland'.

**Jason Liu** *[China]* is a partner of Liu Shen & Associates. He is a patent attorney, attorney-at-law, M&A dealmaker, and intellectual property management system auditor. Jason Liu focuses mainly on intellectual property strategic consulting, patent portfolio management, patent infringement, validity, and freedom-to-operate opinions, and due diligence; representing multinational pharmaceutical companies, small and medium-sized innovative companies in handling intellectual property, especially in the field of pharmacy, chemistry, material science, chemical engineering and medical device. Dr. Liu obtained his B.S. in Chemistry and Ph.D. in Organic Chemistry, both from Fudan University (China, 2001 and 2007 respectively), and obtained his Master of Laws in Intellectual Property Law from John Marshall Law School (the U.S., 2016). He also received training on US patent practice from Myers Wolin, LLC in New Jersey, USA (2018).

**Mathew A. Lucas** BSc(Hons), Ph.D, M IP Law, FIPTA *[Singapore]* specialises in the preparation and prosecution of patent applications in the areas of general organic and inorganic chemistry including the pharmaceutical sciences, mining and petrochemical industries as well as food technology and nanotechnology. He has experience in patent oppositions and providing patent related validity and infringement advice. Mat conducted post-doctoral research at the University of Illinois – Chicago (UIC), working on low-temperature radical initiators and aryl selenide radical induced polarity reversal catalysis. Mat was also involved in a joint project between the University of Adelaide and Flinders Medical Centre, in which he designed and prepared various heterocyclic compounds for the treatment of precancerous adenomas of the colon. During his Ph.D. he prepared novel classes of selenium containing carbohydrates and explored the homolytic chemistry of some new tellurium functional groups. Mat has published in many areas including surfactant chemistry, mechanistic organic chemistry and free-radical methodology.

**Tobias Matschke** *[Germany]* advises international and national companies on all aspects of intellectual property law, in particular patent law (pharma/life sciences and engineering) and represents clients in transnational patent and utility model infringement and validity proceedings. As well as preparing infringement analyses and negotiating and drafting IP-relevant contracts (e.g. license and research agreements, assignments of IP rights, settlements), he also specialises in German employee invention law. His work in this area comprises assisting clients in reviewing and/or setting up internal remuneration systems as well as the general enforcement of claims under the German Employee Invention Act before the Arbitration Board of the German Patent and Trademark Office (DPMA) and the ordinary courts. He also advises clients on competition law matters. Tobias was admitted to the German Bar in 2016 and is a Certified IP Lawyer. He is a member of the German Association for the Protection of Intellectual Property and Copyright (GRUR). He regularly lectures on IP-related topics and is a lecturer for intellectual property law at the Technical University of Dresden.

**Jacek Myszko** *[Poland]* is Partner and Head of the Life Sciences department at Sołtysiński Kawecki Szlęzak, one of the largest and most prestigious law firms in Poland. With more than 20 years of experience in a variety of IP and regulatory cases, including pharmaceuticals, foodstuffs, medical devices, tobacco, veterinary products, and cosmetics, his expertise covers all aspects of introducing regulated products to the market, licensing patents and know-how, complex intellectual property and unfair competition disputes, M&A and restructuring of pharmaceutical companies, and creation of distribution systems for pharmaceutical wholesale in Poland. Jacek represented both Polish and international clients in all levels of court, including the Supreme Court of Poland. A speaker who frequently presents at legal training courses on regulated products, intellectual property, and unfair competition issues. He has authored or co-authored several publications, including 'The Life Sciences Law Review – Polish chapter' – [Law Business Research], 'Treatment upon request – a few words about hospital tenders for medicinal products' and 'Legal models of biosimilar medicines' – [The Cardinal Stefan Wyszynski University Publishing House (Wydawnictwo Naukowe UKSW)]. He also wrote the gloss for the administrative court's landmark decision regarding switching from reference products to biosimilars and its impact on patient rights, which was published in 'Państwo i Prawo' ('The State and the Law'), – [Wolters Kluwer]. Jacek earned his Master of Laws degree from the University of Toruń, Poland. He also completed a program in English and EU law organised by Cambridge Law School, a Business and Trade Law Summer Program organised by Catholic University of America's Columbus School of Law, and post-graduate studies in Intellectual Property law at Jagiellonian University in Cracow, Poland. Additionally, Jacek is a graduate of the European Studies Centre at the University of Toruń, Poland.

**Harald Nemec** *[Austria]* is an Austrian and European Patent Attorney as well as European Patent Litigator. Harald has been a partner in the IP firm Schwarz & Partner Patent Attorneys (based in Vienna, Graz and Innsbruck) since 2003. Holding a degree in chemical engineering from the Vienna University of Technology, Harald first worked as in-house patent counsel before moving to private practice. His technical expertise includes organic and inorganic chemistry, pharmaceutical chemistry and chemical engineering. He is active in both patent prosecution (before the European and the Austrian Patent Offces) and patent litigation matters, and has been involved in some of the most prestigious pharmaceutical litigation cases in Austria.In addition to advising clients in litigation matters, Harald acts as a lay judge in the patent benches of the Vienna Commercial Court, the Vienna Higher Regional Court and the Austrian Supreme Court.

**Philippa Owens** *[Ireland]* obtained a PhD in Chemistry from the University of Strathclyde, Glasgow, in 2017. Her PhD research focused on the synthesis of novel iridium–NHC complexes and their application in organic synthesis. During her doctoral studies, Philippa participated in collaborations with a number of industrial partners and regularly advised colleagues from international pharmaceutical companies on the adaptation of her group's deuteration methodology for use in industrial lab settings. Philippa obtained her undergraduate degree in Chemistry from Imperial College London and also holds an MSc (by Research) from the University of York. Before joining Tomkins, Philippa worked as a postdoctoral researcher at the Max-Planck-Institut für Kohlenforschung in Mülheim an der Ruhr, Germany. Philippa was awarded the Professor David MacMillan Prize for the best PhD thesis in synthetic organic chemistry at the University of Strathclyde, and in 2015 won the International Isotope Society's Young Scientist Award for her contributions to the field of isotope chemistry, delivering the award lecture to an international audience at Princeton University. She finds that patent law offers the perfect environment to combine her passion for science and her love of technical writing. Since joining Tomkins in 2020, Philippa has worked with local and international clients of all sizes, from universities and start-ups to large multinationals. She advises on a range of patent issues, including drafting, prosecution, freedom to operate, and contentious matters.

**John Christopher 'J.C.' Rozendaal** *[United States]* is a director and chair of the Trial & Appellate Practice Group at Sterne, Kessler, Goldstein and Fox. His practice is focused on representing clients in complex business and intellectual property litigation, principally in federal court, and he regularly tries patent-infringement cases to juries. Mr. Rozendaal frequently briefs and argues cases at the U.S. Court of Appeals for the Federal Circuit and has represented clients in the U.S. Supreme Court, both at the certiorari stage and on the merits. J.C.'s practice includes counseling generic pharmaceutical companies on matters related to generic pharmaceuticals and biosimilars, as well as assisting international companies as they navigate the U.S. patent system. A seasoned litigator, J.C. is particularly adept at explaining complicated technical concepts to juries and judges who have no background in science or technology. Since 2019, he has been named an 'IP Star' by *Managing Intellectual Property.* In 2021, he became a Fellow of the American Bar Foundation, where membership is limited to just one percent of lawyers licensed to practice in each jurisdiction. He has twice been named 'Hatch Waxman Litigator of the Year' by *LMG Life Sciences*. Prior to becoming a practicing attorney, J.C. served as a clerk for Judge Douglas H. Ginsburg, U.S. Court of Appeals, District of Columbia Circuit, and Justice Anthony M. Kennedy, U.S. Supreme Court. J.C. earned his J.D. from the University of Texas School of Law with highest honors. He received a B.A. and M.A. from Oxford University, Brasenose College, with first-class honors and a B.A., Plan II, from the University of Texas at Austin with highest honors and with special honors in Zoology.

**Armin Sarvan** *[Denmark]* is a Director in the IP & Life Science Department at Accura Law Firm. With his already many years of experience dealing with intellectual property rights with a particular emphasis on patent litigation, Armin is one of the most experienced young IP lawyers in Denmark. Throughout his career, Armin has been involved in many of the most significant patent cases before the Danish courts. Armin also frequently assists on transactional matters, including drafting and negotiating business critical technology-related agreements, with a particular focus on the needs of clients within life sciences, tech and renewables. Armin's expertise also extends to matters within pharmaceutical law and other aspects of life science regulatory law. Armin studied law at the University of Copenhagen and received his Master of Laws (LL.M.) degree in 2017.

**Denis Schertenleib** *[France]* is a partner of Schertenleib Avocats. Having run more than 50 patent cases, he has an established reputation in this area. Denis's practice is focused on complex cross-border disputes, principally in the area of life sciences but also in other technical fields such as chemistry, mechanics, telecommunications, and physics. Denis's experience includes cases before French, English, and European courts and tribunals, as well as arbitral tribunals, across the lifecycle of proceedings, from preliminary injunction through to final hearing on the merits and appeal. Denis holds a Bachelor of science in physics from the Imperial College London where he graduated with first class honors and a Ph.D. in molecular neurobiology from King's College London. Prior to establishing Schertenleib Avocats, Denis worked at an international law firm in London and was also a partner at a specialised intellectual property law firm in Paris for several years.

**Yoshinori Shimizu** *[Japan]* is the Vice President of SOEI PATENT & LAW FIRM. He has been involved in patent prosecutions and litigations, opinions, and intellectual property consulting for 25 years. He has experience as a board member of the Japan Patent Attorneys Association, a member of the Japan Intellectual Property Strategy Headquarters, and an external advisory member of the European Patent Office (SACEPO). He is the author of publications in Japanese and English, including 'Introduction to Intellectual Property Rights – From System Overview to Litigation', 'Pharmaceutical Test Data Exclusivity: A Multi-Jurisdictional Survey', 'Use inventions – Issues in the establishment and enforcement of rights', and 'Considerations on the extension system for pharmaceutical patent protection in Europe'. He was involved in intellectual property education at Kyoto University's Center for iPS Cell Research and Application, and supported the laboratory of Professor Shinya Yamanaka, who later received the Nobel Prize. Before joining Soei, he conducted polymer research at 3M Company (Japan and the US) for over 10 years, and was awarded the Technical Circle of Excellence Corporate Award, which is given to only a few researchers from around the world. He studied polymer synthesis at the University of Tokyo, received an MBA from Bond University in Australia, and a Juris Doctor degree from Toin Yokohama University Law School.

**Marco Stief** *[Germany]* is a Partner and Head of the legal department at the IP law firm Maiwald. With 25 years of experience in national and international patent infringement litigation, his expertise also includes advising on a broad range of IP law issues that include complex contracts and technology transfer agreements. He is the editor and author of numerous publications in German and English, including the German '*Handbuch des Patentrechts*', the 'European Handbook on Supplementary Protection Certificates', the 'Handbook Pharmaceutical, Biological and Chemical Patents', and the '*Vertragshandbuch Pharma and Life Sciences*'. Marco lectures in patent law at the Ludwig-Maximilians University in Munich, on intellectual property law at the University of Dresden and on patent, pharmaceutical and international contract law at the University of Marburg. Before joining Maiwald, Marc was a lawyer with the law firms Clifford Chance, Freshfields Bruckhaus Deringer and Baker & McKenzie as well as Global Director Legal for the Fresenius Group. Marc studied law at the universities of Bayreuth and Tübingen graduating in the top one percent of his class. After further law studies at the University of Chicago, where he graduated with the highest-grade score of his class, he received his Master of Laws (LL.M.) degree in 2001. Marco earned his doctoral degree in patent law from the University of Basel. His academic achievements were rewarded with scholarships from, among others, Fulbright International, Rotary International, the German Academic Exchange Service.

**Otto Swens** *[The Netherlands]* is a patent litigator and co-founder of Vondst Advocaten. Otto litigates in the field of pharma & biotech, chemistry, medical devices and mechanical engineering. Also, Otto is active in the life sciences regulatory practice. He advises about marketing authorisations, (orphan) medicinal products, paediatric indications, and incentives and rewards for pharmaceutical research, such as data exclusivity, market exclusivity and patent term extensions (SPC's), Otto represents clients before the Dutch national courts, the General Court / European Court of Justice in Luxembourg and the Unified Patent Court. Otto is recognised internationally as patent and life sciences specialist in guides such as Chambers (Europe/Global), Legal500, IAM Patent, Juve and Managing IP. Otto also regularly lectures and publishes on patent law and life sciences topics, at conferences and in national and international journals.

**Tom H. Wittop Koning** *[The Netherlands]* is European and Dutch patent attorney and has been partner of several Dutch and international IP firms. Tom started his own boutique firm Biopatents IP Consultancy in 2018. The clients are biotech companies, universities, research institutes, chemical and pharmaceutical companies, food and dairy industries, but also start-ups in the Netherlands and abroad. Tom has extensive experience in Dutch and Belgian patent litigation and coordinates multi-jurisdictional cases for international clients. His patent prosecution work covers International (PCT) applications, European application and national applications in the Netherlands, Germany, Belgium and Luxembourg. Tom studied biology in Groningen, Netherlands and received his Ph.D. at the University of Berne, Switzerland in 1993 and until 1998, he was a post-doctoral fellow at the Max Planck Institute in Berlin, Germany.

**Jie An Yang** BSc(Hons), Ph.D, Grad Dip IP Law *[Singapore]* is a registered Singapore patent attorney who is experienced in the drafting and prosecution of patent applications in the areas of chemistry-related disciplines including pharmaceutical sciences, nanotechnology, polymers and food technology. He is also experienced in providing patent validity and infringement advice. Jie An completed his BSc at the National University of Singapore, and his PhD at the University of Illinois at Urbana Champaign. He then spent about two years at Mitsui Chemicals undertaking polymer and nanoparticle research. His work has cumulated in the publication in several peer-reviewed scientific journals and he is an inventor of an international patent application (PCT/JP2017/036687).

**Stephen Zou** *[China]* is a partner and head of life science at Liu Shen & Associates. He assists clients in matters involving patents, trade secrets, and unfair competition, and focuses mainly on intellectual property strategic consulting, patent portfolio management, patent infringement, validity, freedom-to-operate opinions, due diligence and dispute resolution. He represents multinational pharmaceutical companies, and small and medium-sized innovative companies in handling intellectual property, drug regulatory matters, technology transfer and market access-related legal affairs. The wide variety of technical areas in which Dr Zou has obtained and enforced patent protection for clients include pharmacy, chemistry and biotechnologies, as well as mechanical systems and medical devices. In recent years, Dr Zou has handled hundreds of IP due diligence works in biotechnology, pharmaceutical and medical device areas, and has been invited as an IP expert to issue IP legal opinions in helping dozens of bio-companies successfully listed with Hong Kong & New York stock markets. He also represented brand companies in defending their patents in China and led a series of significant pharmaceutical patent disputes against local generic companies, either via administrative or via civil action. Dr Zou received a PhD in pharmaceutical chemistry and a LL.M. in intellectual property. He started his IP career with Liu Shen in 2003, and prior to his legal profession, he has been engaged in research in pharmaceutical research and diagnostic method development.

**Maciej Zwoliński** *[Poland]* is Senior Counsel, attorney-at-law at Sołtysiński Kawecki & Szlęzak – specialises in intellectual and industrial property law, represents parties in disputes in this field. Maciej is affiliated with SK&S since 2010. He has worked as a lawyer at top law firms since 1998 including as the manager of the intellectual property law team of the Polish branch of one of the big international firms. Maciej represents entrepreneurs before common courts and arbitration courts in civil law and commercial law disputes, in particular in corporate disputes involving shareholders of commercial companies. He has also advised on transactions and other non-contentious matters.

# Table of contents

## § 4. France



## § 5. Germany



## § 6. Ireland

## § 7. Italy



## § 8. The Netherlands



## § 9. Poland

## § 10. Portugal



## § 11. Spain



## § 12. Türkiye

## § 13. United Kingdom



## § 14. European Unified Patent Court and Unitary Patent



# PART II
# UNITED STATES OF AMERICA

## § 15. United States of America

## PART III
## AUSTRALIA

### § 16. Australia

## PART IV
## ASIA

### § 17. China



### § 18. Japan

## § 19. Singapore



## § 20. Taiwan

# PART I
# EUROPE

## § 1
## Overview

### A. Skinny labelling of generic and biosimilar products in the European Union

1 In Europe, generics[1] and biosimilar[2] manufacturers can only submit a marketing authorisation application for their drug once the period of data and market exclusivity of the reference medicine has expired, usually from 10 to 11 years from the date of first authorisation of the reference product. EU data and market exclusivity currently follows an '8+2+1' year approach;[3] since 2005, the period of 'data exclusivity' has been fixed at eight years from the date of first authorisation in Europe. However, the EU Pharma Package as currently discussed opts for a shorter general '6+2+1' year approach, while the period of data exclusivity can be extended to a maximum of eight years as in the current legal regime if further criteria are met, e.g. launch in all EU Member States, addressing an unmet medical need.[4] During this period, the pre-clinical and clinical trials data of the originator may not be referenced in the regulatory filings of the generics or biosimilar manufacturer for the same drug substance.

2 In parallel, there is currently a 10-year period of 'market exclusivity' during which the generics/biosimilar manufacturer may not market its product but is entitled to make use of the pre-clinical and clinical trial data of the originator in their application for authorisation. Unless the originator product qualifies for one further year of market protection, the market exclusivity terminates at the end of the 10th year from the date of first authorisation in Europe. It is also worth mentioning that the EU Pharma Package discusses a

---

[1] A *generic medicinal product* is defined as a medicinal product that has: (i) the same qualitative and quantitative composition in active substance(s) as the reference product, (ii) the same pharmaceutical form as the reference medicinal product, (iii) and whose bioequivalence with the reference medicinal product has been demonstrated by appropriate bioavailability studies.

[2] A *similar biological medicinal product*, also known as 'biosimilar', is a product which is similar to a biological medicine that has already been authorised, the 'reference medicinal product'. The active substance of a biosimilar is a known biological active substance similar to that of the reference medicinal product.

[3] Article 14(11) Regulation (EC) No 726/2004: '(…) medicinal products for human use which have been authorised in accordance with the provisions of this Regulation shall benefit from an eight-year period of data protection and a ten year period of marketing protection, in which connection the latter period shall be extended to a maximum of 11 years if, during the first eight years of those ten years, the marketing authorisation holder obtains an authorisation for one or more new therapeutic indications which, during the scientific evaluation prior to their authorisation, are held to bring a significant clinical benefit in comparison with existing therapies.'

[4] European Commission, Proposal for a Directive Of The European Parliament and of the Council on the Union code relating to medicinal products for human use, and repealing Directive 2001/83/EC and Directive 2009/35/EC, 26.4.2023, COM(2023) 192 final.

tiered system of market exclusivity for orphan medical products (OMPs) depending on the degree of the 'unmet need': for example, a 10-year market exclusivity with the possibility of extension would be available only for OMPs that address a high unmet medical need; five years of market exclusivity will be granted to AM with known substances with well-established use; nine-year market exclusivity will generally apply to all other OMPs with possible extensions. A one-year extension may be granted to small and medium sized enterprises (SMEs), for launch in all EU countries or contingent on approval in another OMP indication (maximum twice).

3 Nevertheless, it remains to be seen, what exact provisions the EU Pharma Package. At present, the draft Pharma Package presented by the Commission is being scrutinised by the other EU institutions (the Council of the EU that comprises Member States' government ministers – whose national healthcare systems will have to adapt accordingly – and the European Parliament), not to mention the highly sceptical generics industry, the originators and of course, civil society, especially patients organisations.

4 Consequently, once data exclusivity has expired, generics or biosimilar manufacturers may apply for market authorisations. In the EU, Regulation (EC) No 726/2004 creates a 'Centralised Procedure' for the authorisation of medicinal products, with a single application, a single evaluation and a single authorisation by the European Medicines Agency allowing direct access to the EU market. This procedure coexists with other alternative non-centralised procedures conducted at the national medicines agencies, and regulated by means of Directive 2001/83/EC; namely: national procedure (whereby an authorisation is sought for a single EU Member State), mutual-recognition procedure (whereby a marketing authorisation granted in one Member State can be recognised in other EU Member States) and decentralised procedure (whereby a medicine that has not yet been authorised in the EU can be simultaneously authorised in several EU Member States). Although there are different rules to determine which procedure must be followed in each case, broadly speaking, biosimilar medicines must generally be authorised through the centralised procedure at the European Medicines Agency (EMA), whilst generic medicines are generally approved by the competent national bodies through the non-centralised procedures regulated by means of Directive 2001/83/EC.

## I. Generics

5 The legal requirements and the application procedures for a marketing authorisation are set out in Directive 2001/83/EC and in Regulation (EC) No 726/2004. For generics, the legal basis can be found in Article 6 Regulation (EC) 726/2004 and Article 10 Directive 2001/83/EC. If the applicant can demonstrate that the medicinal product is a generic medicinal product of a reference medicinal product which is or has been authorised under Article 6 Directive 2001/83/EC for not less than eight years in a Member State or in the European Union, the applicant is not required to provide the results of pre-clinical tests and clinical trials. The reference medicinal product is a medicinal product, which has been granted a marketing authorisation on the basis of a complete dossier (submission of quality, pre-clinical and clinical data). By demonstration of bioequivalence (usually through bioavailability studies), the generic product refers to such dossier. For understandable reasons, this simplifies the authorisation process of a generic drug significantly and is a major game changer in the development of generic products.

6 Even when data exclusivity, or even market exclusivity, of the reference medicinal product has ended, generics manufacturers often face further obstacles due to existing (second medical use) patents on the originator product. In such case, a generics medicine

still cannot be marketed for the protected indication or pharmaceutical form, even though the period of data and market exclusivity of the reference medicine has expired.

However, Article 11 Directive 2001/83/EC and Article 3(3)(b) Regulation No 726/2004 allow applicants as well as marketing authorisation holders to exclude from their proposed product information those parts of the Summary of Product Characteristics (SmPC) of the reference medicinal product that refer to indications or dosage forms still covered by a valid patent: information directly related to the patented indication can be deleted from sections 4.1. (therapeutic indications), 4.2. (posology and administration method) and 5.1. (pharmacodynamic properties) of the SmPC. On the other hand, for public health reasons, safety-related information in sections 4.3 to 4.8. SmPC should be retained. 7

## II. Biosimilars

Article 6 Regulation 726/2004/EC in conjunction with Article 10(4) and Annex I Part II No. 4 Directive 2001/83/EC form the legal basis for the regulatory approval of biosimilar products. Under these provisions, additional documentation must be submitted for biological medicinal products that do not fulfil the requirements for a generic medicinal product.[5] The type and scope of this additional documentation depends on the extent of the difference between the biosimilar and the reference product. This ranges between a purely analytical comparison and an extensive clinical comparison in (usually) one indication. To obtain authorisation for a biosimilar the product must be an 'exact copy' of the reference product, not counting differences in content resulting from the biosimilar itself (e.g. cell origin, cell line, excipients, storage conditions, shelf life; this may also include contraindications, warnings and side effects). 8

This means that the marketing authorisation for a biosimilar product automatically includes any indications of the reference product (thus also patent-protected indications). However, as in the case of generics, a biosimilar manufacturer is entitled to remove the patent-protected indication(s) and related information from the SmPC and product information. 9

# B. Protection of second medical use claims under the European Patent Convention

As can be seen, coverage of therapeutic indications by second medical use claims already has a significant impact on the regulatory filing process for a generic or biosimilar product. Hence, the scope of protection conferred by second medical use claims is of utmost importance when applying for marketing authorisation. 10

Over the past decades, the European Patent Office (EPO) has continuously adjusted its requirements for patent protection of second medical use claims. Starting in 1984 with its decision G5/83[6], the EPO had allowed second medical use claims in the 'Swiss-type' form, i.e. claims formulated as 'Use of a substance X in the manufacture of a medicament for the treatment of disease Y'. The patent claim had to be limited to the 'manufacturing' of the substance since a broader use claim was not considered susceptible of protection 11

[5] Step 1: comparative quality studies; step 2: comparative non-clinical studies; step 3: comparative clinical studies.

[6] EPO Enlarged Board of Appeal G5/83, dated 5 December 1984.

pursuant to Article 52(4) of the European Patent Convention (EPC) 1973 (prohibiting patent protection of methods for treatment of the human body). Following a comprehensive revision of the EPC in 2007, Article 54(5) EPC 2000 then expressly allowed second medical use claims. Pursuant to Article 54(5) EPC 2000, where a substance or composition is already known to have been used in a 'first medical use', it may still be patentable under Article 54(5) for any second or further use in a method according to Article 53(c), provided that said use is novel and inventive. However, it was only three years later that the EPO abolished the practice of the Swiss-type claims in its decision G2/08[7]. Since then, claims on second medical use will only be granted in the form of 'EPC 2000 claims', i.e. purpose-related product claims such as 'Product X for use in the treatment of disease Y'.[8] Depending on the EPO's granting practice pertaining at the time of grant of a given patent, infringement courts thus have to deal with different claim forms in the field of second indication patents:

1. Swiss-type claims accepted under the EPC 1973 ('use of compound X for the manufacture of a medicament to treat disease Y'),
2. use claims accepted by the German Patent Office and courts ('use of compound X for the treatment of disease Y'),
3. product claims limited by purpose / EPC 2000 claims ('Compound X for use in the treatment of disease Y').

**12** Consequently, this part also aims to analyse the different approaches taken by the European courts towards such different claim formulations. This part will also provide an overview of the available European case law regarding the infringement of second medical use claims in the case of skinny label products.

---

[7] EPO Enlarged Board of Appeal G2/08, dated 19 February 2010.

[8] An overview on the currently admitted claim forms by the EPO can be found here: https://www.epo.org/law-practice/legal-texts/html/guidelines/e/g_vi_7_1.htm.

# § 2
# Austria

## A. Executive summary

Second medical use claims are directly infringed if the product is purposefully prepared (*'sinnfällig hergerichtet'*) for the protected indication. Generally, this is established by reference to the Summary of Product Characteristics (SmPC). It is irrelevant if the claim is formulated as a Swiss-type or EPC 2000 claim. 1

There is no Austrian case law regarding skinny labels. However, if the statutory provisions of the Austrian Patent Act (*Patentgesetz*) do not deviate from the German Patent Act with regard to a particular scenario and Austrian case law has not yet developed, Austrian courts tend to adopt German case law, due to the similarity of the patent systems and legal traditions. Therefore, infringement in skinny label cases may potentially be established using the criteria set out in the German case law since 2017, i.e., a generic or biosimilar pharma company may be held liable for infringement if (→ mn. 19 et seq.): 2

1. The product is (objectively) suitable for the patented purpose.
2. The potential infringer takes advantage of circumstances which, in a manner similar to an active purposeful preparation, make it highly likely that the product being offered or marketed is / will be used for the specified therapeutic purpose.
3. There is sufficient and not only occasional use of the product for the patented indication.
4. The potential infringer knows of these circumstances or disregards such knowledge, i.e. acts in bad faith.

However, there is no guarantee that Austrian courts will adopt the German approach. Thus, the legal situation regarding skinny labels is uncertain. 3

## B. Scope of protection and interpretation of second medical use claims

Under Austrian case law, both Swiss-type and EPC 2000 claims are considered purpose-limited product claims.[1] Thus, both claim categories must be treated equally in the infringement proceedings. 4

Claims protecting a substance for use in a therapeutic treatment method are explicitly exempt from the prohibition of the patentability of therapeutic treatment methods (§ 2(1) 5

[1] Austrian Supreme Court (OGH) 9.2.2010, 17 Ob 35/09k – *Isoflavone;* → mn. 34. Of historical note (only), the Austrian Supreme Patent and Trademark Panel (OPMS), then competent for final decisions regarding patent validity matters, had held in its decision dated 28.9.2005, Op 3/04 that Swiss-type claims are to be interpreted as purpose-limited process claims. Only by way of this interpretation, patents containing Swiss-type claims and filed before the end of the so-called product protection prohibition (*Stoffschutzverbot*) in Austria (1984) could be exempted from a non-patentability objection under this regime.

no. 2 Patent Act; → mn. 30). Also, since 2007, Austrian law has explicitly allowed claims to a substance for use in a novel therapeutic treatment method, even if the use of this substance was already known in the state of the art, for a different therapeutic treatment, i.e. second-medical use claims (§ 3(3) Patent Act); → mn. 31.

6 Austrian statute law contains no further specific provisions for second medical use claims. Thus, like all other patents, the scope of protection of the second medical use patent is defined by the claims (whereas the description and drawings serve to interpret the claims).

7 The central feature of second medical use claims is that they do not protect the use of the compound during therapeutic treatment as such. Rather, they protect the product itself, with the limitation that the active substance is intended to treat a specific medical indication.[2]

8 The scope of protection of a purpose-limited substance protection claim is thus narrower than the scope of protection of a pure substance protection claim. However, acts of infringement are not limited to the final therapeutic use. Rather, infringement occurs if a product intended for the protected purpose enters the commercial sphere, e.g. is offered for sale or put on the market. Otherwise, the scope of protection of second medical use claims would remain largely toothless. If direct infringement were limited to the use of the product in a therapeutic method, the 'actual' use would in general only occur when a patient takes the preparation. Apart from the fact that there are various reasons not to enforce a patent against a patient, the patient as the 'end user', however, does not act commercially and thus cannot infringe a patent under Austrian law.[3]

9 Any effective scope of protection of second medical use claims hinges on the question of which acts and circumstances, attributable to the company therefore offering the product for sale/placing it on the market, are sufficient to consider the product as intended for the protected use.

10 Under current Austrian case law, this is the case if the product is purposefully prepared ('*sinnfällig hergerichtet*') by the infringer for the protected use (→ mn. 34).[4] Whether there can be an infringement without such purposeful preparation, e.g. in skinny label cases, has not yet been decided by Austrian courts.

## C. Direct and indirect infringement of second medical use claims

### I. Direct patent infringement

11 A patent entitles the patentee to exclude others from making, offering for sale, placing on the market or using the subject matter of the invention or importing or possessing it for the said purposes (§ 22(1) Patent Act, → mn. 32).

12 As mentioned, the subject matter of a second medical use claim is a product intended for a specific use.

13 In determining if such a product is present, it first has to be established if the product in question is suitable for the protected use; meaning that the product can achieve the protected purpose to a practically significant extent. Infringement is ruled out if, for

[2] Vienna Higher Regional Court 24.2.2021, 33 R 116/20a (→ mn. 37).
[3] Adocker/Wildhack/Petsche/Strobel in: Koller/Stadler, PatG, Vienna 2019, § 22 mn. 95 et seq.
[4] Austrian Supreme Court (OHG) 9.2.2010, 17 Ob 35/09k – *Isoflavone* (→ mn. 34).

example, the protected active substance is contained in the product in such a small quantitative amount that the protected therapeutic effect cannot be achieved. In the pharmaceutical sector, this will rarely be the case in pharmaceutical products due to regulatory requirements. However, as an Austrian Supreme Court decision demonstrates, this can be relevant, for example, regarding food supplements where the effect was unclear, and a therapeutic effect was even disputed by the defendant.[5] In such cases, the patent proprietor bears the burden of proof for the suitability of the potentially infringing product for the protected therapeutic effect.[6]

Besides being suitable for the protected purpose, the product must also be intended for this purpose. Under current Austrian case law, this requires purposeful preparation ('*sinnfälliges Herrichten*') for the protected use. The product must be prepared so that it is foreseeable that it will be used for the protected purpose. This preparation can be established in a variety of ways. The most common way is by reference to the SmPC or package leaflet.[7] However, the formulation, dosage, packaging or repackaging, labelling or advertising claims may also establish purposeful preparation. In general, the Austrian Supreme Court emphasises that a practically reasonable standard must be applied in answering whether the product is purposefully prepared. In case of a food supplement without a SmPC it was held that the fact that a product is – also – suitable for the protected purpose does not mean that it is also intended for such use (in dosage, formulation and packaging). It was stated in that case that the burden of proof for showing 'purposeful preparation' resided with the plaintiff.[8] **14**

There are no decisions where infringement of second medical use claims was recognised in the absence of purposeful preparation. However, there is no case law that explicitly states that such preparation is necessary in any case. It is therefore not improbable that the Austrian courts may apply the concept of a preparation-free liability (*herrichtungsfreie Haftung*) as established by recent German case law in skinny label and similar cases. **15**

## II. Indirect patent infringement

Indirect infringement prohibits any third party from offering or supplying means relating to an *essential element* of the invention for its use, to persons other than those entitled to use the invention if the *third party knows* or it is obvious from the circumstances that these means are *suitable and intended* to be used for the use of the invention (§ 22(3) Patent Act). **16**

Correctly applied, indirect infringement has little significance with regard to second medical use claims. This is because supplying a product under circumstances that make it clear that it is *suitable and intended* for the protected use constitutes purposeful preparation and thus results in direct infringement of second medical use claims as per the above. **17**

However, in a recent decision, the Higher Regional Court Vienna departed from these principles and found indirect infringement of a second medical use claim. The central issue of this case was that the purpose for which the active substance in question was protected included the combination with a second active substance, i.e. the claim was structured as follows: 'Compound X for use in combination with compound Y for the treatment of Z'. The infringing product contained only the first compound, but its SmPC and package leaflet required the combination with the second compound. The Higher **18**

[5] Austrian Supreme Court (OHG) 9.2.2010, 17 Ob 35/09k – *Isoflavone* (→ mn. 34).
[6] ibid.
[7] Vienna Higher Regional Court 24.2.2021, 33 R 116/20a (→ mn. 37).
[8] Austrian Supreme Court (OHG) 9.2.2010, 17 Ob 35/09k – *Isoflavone* (→ mn. 34).

Regional Court Vienna denied direct infringement arguing that it would require the physical presence of both compounds in the infringing product. Thus, the court only found indirect infringement.[9] Since the ruling on indirect infringement was obviously considered sufficient for the patent proprietor in the present case, the question was not debated further in proceedings before the Austrian Supreme Court. In previous Austrian case law, direct infringement had been found irrespective of whether both compounds were physically present in the infringing product (in that decision, however, the question was not discussed in detail).[10] Such decisions in any event depend on the circumstances of the individual case. A clear line of jurisprudence has not yet been established.

## D. Infringement of second medical use claims and skinny label products

**19** Due to a lack of case law, establishing infringement in the case of a skinny label product is challenging. In the absence of evidence to the contrary, Austrian courts will generally assume that a medical product will only be used for the indication stated in the SmPC, and the package leaflet. Thus, patentees will have to overcome this initial assumption and will bear the burden of proof for any circumstances necessary to prove infringement beyond the contents of the label.[11]

**20** What those circumstances could be is unclear. However, due to the largely identical provisions and similar legal tradition, Austrian courts will, quite probably, orient themselves on the criteria established by German case law, i.e. may assume infringement if:

1. The product is (objectively) suitable for the patented purpose.
2. The potential infringer takes advantage of circumstances which, in a manner similar to an active purposeful preparation, make it highly likely that the product being offered or marketed is/will be used for the specified therapeutic purpose.
3. There is sufficient and not only occasional use of the product for the patented indication.
4. The potential infringer knows of these circumstances or disregards such knowledge, i.e. acts in bad faith.[12]

**21** The question of the extent to which the infringing product is prescribed in practice for the protected indication will most probably play a significant role in a skinny label case before an Austrian court. Such evidence may be difficult to obtain, at least in the period before the generic/biosimilar product is on the market, which is the time the patentee needs to initiate proceedings in order not to lose their price and market share. There is no easily accessible public data published by health insurance providers or similar institutions could be used to show cross-label use. An alternative may be expert statements from practitioners familiar with the prescribing practice.

**22** The other requirements may pose fewer challenges. The infringer's knowledge of the relevant circumstances, and acts in bad faith may be established through sending warning letters or even the serving of a legal complaint from the patentee. After such measures,

[9] Vienna Higher Regional Court 24.2.2021, 33 R 116/20a (→ mn. 37).
[10] Vienna Higher Regional Court 12.4.2018, 133 R 15/18f – *Pemetrexed*.
[11] Adocker/Wildhack/Petsche/Strobel in: Koller/Stadler, PatG, Vienna 2019, § 22 mn. 111 et seq.
[12] → § 5 on Germany; Düsseldorf Higher Regional Court (OLG), I-2 W 6/17, GRUR 2017, 1107 – *Östrogenblocker*.

the infringer will usually not be able to plausibly deny knowledge of the relevant circumstances.

## E. Infringement of second medical use claims and biosimilar products

Again, there is no Austrian case law in this regard. However, Austrian courts would most probably not differentiate between generics and biosimilars in the context of skinny label cases. If it can be established that the biosimilar is used to a significant degree cross-label for the protected indication, and other criteria are also met, the above conclusions that this may lead to infringement should apply equally. 23

Nevertheless, skinny label cases may be rarer in practice. Due to the complexity of biological molecules and their manufacturing methods, a biosimilar will not be exactly the same as the reference product. Thus, healthcare providers may be more reluctant to use such pharmaceutical products outside their label. On the other hand, due to the higher price of biologics, healthcare providers may be under stronger economic pressure to switch to cheaper biosimilars. Thus, it remains to be seen if skinny label biosimilar cases will be subject to litigation before Austrian courts in the future. 24

## F. Strategies and considerations

Active precautionary measures may include communicating to physicians and other healthcare providers that the pharmaceutical product may not be used for the protected indication. However, such communication may often be of limited use. Healthcare providers are not limited in their prescribing practice by the recommendations of the respective pharmaceutical company. Furthermore, such communication may even be counterproductive – i.e. actually making physicians aware of the possibility of using the product off or cross-label. The same applies to active warnings on the label, which in addition, may not even be possible due to regulatory requirements. 25

Any behaviour which would make a cross-label use more likely or could even be regarded as in support of cross-label use, e.g. actively promoting the product for the protected indication, seeking reimbursement status, covering the protected indication or offering the product in tenders, also for the protected indication, should be avoided. 26

## G. Legal remedies

Austrian patent law provides for permanent and preliminary injunctions. Preliminary injunctions are a powerful enforcement tool since they require neither urgency[13] nor – according to current case law – balance of interest. Thus, only validity and infringement of the patent must be evidenced for a preliminary injunction. Generally, preliminary 27

[13] In contrast to the situation in Germany, → § 5 mn. 37.

injunctions are granted *inter partes*, after one or two rounds of written briefs but without a hearing. However, *ex parte* preliminary injunctions are possible in cases of particular urgency (e.g. if infringement takes place shortly before the end of the patent's term).

28 Permanent injunctions are available in main proceedings, which may be initiated together with or after preliminary injunction proceedings. In main proceedings, the patentee is also entitled to claim recall (with limitations), destruction, publication of judgment, rendering of accounts and damages. Concerning damages, the patentee may choose between three different methods of calculation: reasonable royalty, compensation for damages actually suffered, and surrender of profits. A double royalty can be claimed in a case of gross negligence. The most common form of payment claim is to request a reasonable royalty since it neither requires fault nor disclosure of information by the plaintiff. However, damage proceedings in patent cases are rare in Austria and case law is limited.

29 Additionally, reimbursement of legal fees is awarded in a judgment. However, as reimbursable costs are calculated under the Austrian Attorneys Tariff (RATG), the amount is usually lower than the actual cost incurred.

## H. Statutory provisions

## Patent Act 1970[14]

### Exceptions to Patentability

30 **§ 2(1)**

Patents are not granted for:

[...]

2. procedures for the surgical or therapeutic treatment of the human or animal body and diagnostic procedures carried out on the human or animal body; this does not apply to products, in particular substances or mixtures of substances, for use in one of these procedures.

[...]

### Novelty

31 **§ 3(3)**

The patentability of substances or mixtures of substances belonging to the state of the art shall not be excluded by paragraphs (1) and (2) if they are intended for use in a process under § 2, subsection (1), item 2, and their use in one of these processes does not belong to the state of the art. Similarly, the patentability of the said substances or mixtures of substances for specific use in one of the said processes shall not be excluded by subsections (1) and (2) if such use does not belong to the state of the art. The patentability of substances or mixtures of substances belonging to the state of the art shall not be excluded by subsections (1) and (2) provided that they are intended for use in a process according to § 2, subsection (1), item 2, and their use in one of these processes does not belong to the state of the art. Similarly, the patentability of the said substances or mixtures of substances for specific application in one of the said processes is not excluded by paragraphs (1) and (2) if such application does not belong to the state of the art.

[14] As amended BGBl. I No. 51/2023.

**Effect of the patent**

**§ 22(1)** 32

The patent shall entitle the patentee to exclude others from manufacturing, placing on the market, offering for sale or using the subject-matter of the invention or importing or possessing it for the purposes mentioned. The effect of the patent shall not extend to studies and tests and the practical requirements resulting therefrom, insofar as they are necessary for obtaining a marketing authorisation or registration under medicinal product law.

**§ 22a(1)** 33

The scope of protection of the published application and the patent is determined by the claims. However, the description and the drawings shall be consulted for the interpretation of the claims. The Protocol on the interpretation of Article 69 of the European Patent Convention shall apply mutatis mutandis.

# J. Extracts from court decisions

## I. Supreme Court (OHG) – *Isoflavone*[15] 34

The Supreme Court, as a court of appeal, by the President Hon.Prof. Dr. Griss as President and by Dr. Vogel, Dr. Jensik, Dr. Musger and Dr. Schwarzenbacher as further Judges in the case of the plaintiff N***** Limited, *****, represented by Gassauer-Fleissner Rechtsanwälte GmbH in Vienna, with the assistance of Dr. Daniel Alge, Patent Attorney in Vienna, against the defendant A***** GmbH, *****, represented by Dr. Andreas Manak, Attorney at Law in Vienna. Daniel Alge, Patent attorney in Vienna, against the Defendant A***** GmbH, *****, represented by Dr. Andreas Manak, Patent attorney in Vienna, with the assistance of DI Peter Itze, Patent attorney in Vienna, for injunction (value in dispute EUR 250,000 EUR), removal (amount in dispute 50,000 EUR), rendering of accounts (amount in dispute 50,000 EUR) and publication of judgment (amount in dispute 10,000 EUR), on the extraordinary appeal of the Defendant against the judgment of the Vienna Higher Regional Court as Court of Appeal of 24 September 2009, Z 5 R 35/09t-83, by which, as a result of the appeal of the Defendant, the partial judgment of the Vienna Commercial Court of 13 January 2009, GZ 19 Cg 178/05f-64, was confirmed, the decision was made in closed session:

**Judgment**

The appeal is allowed.

The decisions of the lower courts, which remain unaffected with regard to their decisions dismissing the action, which have become final, are otherwise set aside and the case is referred back to the court of first instance for a new decision after supplementing the proceedings to the extent that it remains pending.

The costs of the appeal proceedings constitute further procedural costs.

**Justification:**

The Plaintiff is the proprietor of the European patent EP 0 656 786 B1 (priority 19. 5. 1993) with the following claims:

[15] 9.2.2010, 17 Ob 35/09k.

1. Use of an isoflavone phytoestrogen extract of soy or clover for the manufacture of a medicament for administration in unit dosage form for the treatment of premenstrual syndrome, symptoms associated with menopause or prostate cancer.
2. Use as claimed in claim 1, wherein the medicament further comprises at least one food-grade excipient.
3. Use as claimed in claim 1 or 2, wherein the isoflavone phytoestrogen is extracted from soy.
4. Use as claimed in claim 3, wherein the isoflavone phytoestrogen is extracted from soy hypocotyls.
5. Use as claimed in claim 1 or 2, wherein the isoflavone phytoestrogen is extracted from clover.
6. Use as claimed in any one of claims 1 to 4, wherein the isoflavone phytoestrogen extract comprises one or more members selected from the group consisting of genistein, daidzein or glycosides thereof, or metabolites or derivatives thereof.
7. Use as claimed in claim 1 or 2, wherein the isoflavone phytoestrogen comprises genistein and/or biochanin A: daidzein and/or formononetin present in a ratio of about 1:2 to 2:1.
8. Use as claimed in any one of claims 1 to 7, wherein the isoflavone phytoestrogens are present in an amount of from about 20 mg to 200 mg per dosage unit, the amount optionally being from 50 mg to 150 mg.
9. Use as claimed in any one of the preceding claims, wherein administration of the medicament is at least daily for a period of at least one month.
10. Use as claimed in any preceding claim, wherein the extract includes coumestans, lignans and flavones.
11. Use as claimed in any one of the preceding claims, wherein the dosage unit form is a tablet or capsule.

In the patent specification (p 21 f), as example 1 for carrying out the invention, the production of the red clover product is described in more detail. After harvesting the raw plant material, it is dried and extracted in a solvent mixture of water and organic solvent, whereby the isoflavones are extracted from the material. After concentration of the liquid (typically by distillation), the extracted natural product is then transferred into capsules, tablets or other convenient forms for integration.

[...]

The Defendant markets a product called 'Vita Lady Vitalkapseln' (Vita Lady Vital Capsules) in pharmacies, namely a food supplement which, according to the description, is supposed to provide relief from menstrual or menopausal complaints as a result of the red clover isoflavones contained therein, among other things. It contains 8 % red clover extract = 150 mg per capsule and is supplied in capsule form. It is recommended to take one capsule daily for an unlimited period of time. The isoflavones it contains are ononin, sisstorin, biochanin A and formononetin.

The Plaintiff seeks an order requiring the Defendant to cease and desist from marketing in Austria (in accordance with claim 1. of its patent) an isoflavone phytoestrogen extract of clover for the manufacture of a medicament for administration in unit dosage form for the treatment of premenstrual syndrome, symptoms associated with menopause or prostate cancer, in particular a use according to claims 6, 7, 8, 9 and 11 of the Injunction Patent, and/or offering for sale, putting on the market, using, importing or possessing articles directly manufactured according to these claims, in particular 'Vita Lady' capsules. It also filed a request for removal, rendering of accounts and publication of the judgment. The Plaintiff's patent was a process patent within the meaning of § 22(2) Patent Act and related to medicines, which for the purposes of the patent also included food supplements. The Defendant infringed the Injunction Patent, in particular claims 5 to 9 and 11, by marketing a food supplement containing red clover isoflavones under the name 'Vita Lady'.

The Defendant objected that its product 'Vita Lady' was not a medicine, but a food supplement without therapeutic effect, so that there was no patent infringement for this reason

alone (written statement of 23 October 2006, Vol. I/ON 33). The Defendant did not use the Plaintiff's special extract for its product, but a combination product. [...] The Plaintiff's patent, a Swiss claim, was invalid because of the circumvention of the prohibition of patentability of therapeutic treatments within the meaning of § 2(2) Patent Act.

In the partial judgment under appeal, the court of first instance granted the request for injunctive relief with the exception of the claim relating to claim 7 of the Injunction Patent, which was reserved for the final decision, and the claim relating to the use of the isoflavone phytoestrogen extract of clover for the treatment of prostate cancer (which was dismissed with final effect), as well as the claim for removal and rendering of accounts relating to the part of the claim that was granted, and the claim for publication of the judgment (with a minor partial dismissal that became res judicata). The patent claims concerned a medicament for the treatment of health disorders. The amendment of the claim wording in the application procedure did not mean a limitation of the scope of protection. [...]. A food supplement could also infringe the patent. The scope of protection 'food supplement' and 'medicament' were not mutually exclusive; the concept of medicament in European patent law did not coincide with that of the Austrian Medicines Act.

The Court of Appeal confirmed this judgment and declared that the value of the subject-matter of the decision exceeded EUR 30,000 and that the ordinary appeal was not admissible. [...] The Defendant's use of the protected substance fell within the scope of protection of the patent in suit. [...] Claim 6 of the Injunction Patent was also infringed: This only requires that the isoflavone phytoestrogen extract comprises one or more representatives from the group genistein, daidzein or glycosides or metabolites or derivatives thereof. The HPLC analysis of the 'Vita Lady' capsules (Annex to the expert opinion of patent attorney DI Beer ./G) showed that the isoflavone phytoestrogen extract contained in the Defendant's product comprised representatives from the group genistein, daidzein. Claim 8 was also infringed because the intervention product contained 150 mg of red clover extract per capsule.

### Legal assessment

The appeal is admissible because the Court of Appeal did not deal with the objection of the lack of therapeutic healing effect of the intervention product; the appeal is also justified in terms of its motion to set aside.

[...]

**2.1** The Defendant draws the conclusion from the fact that in the application procedure the Plaintiff restricted its claim for protection via several intermediate stages to the now registered use claim for the manufacture of a medicament that the protection of claim 1 cannot extend to food supplements – such as the Defendant's product; namely, the Plaintiff had 'renounced the general supplements originally claimed by restricting it to a medicament' (Statement of Defence p 5 f = AS 59 f). This line of argument cannot be accepted.

**2.2** According to Article 69(1) EPC, the scope of protection of the European patent and the European patent application is determined by the content of the claims. However, the description and the drawings shall be taken into account for the interpretation of the claims.

**2.3** It follows that what matters for determining the content of the patent claim is how the wording of the granted patent, explained by the description and drawings, is to be interpreted. Whether or not the files of grant speak for a narrower scope is not decisive. This is because the files of grant in no way guarantee to reflect the entire event that actually led to the grant of the patent in the respective version, and taking their contents into account would in many cases create new problems of interpretation. Accordingly, a proposal providing for such consideration did not find a majority at a diplomatic conference on the revision of the EPC held in November 2000 (Scharen in Benkard, EPÜ Article 69 mn. 27).

**3.1** The Defendant alleges a violation of the law of reasoning in affirming infringement of claim 1 of the Plaintiff's patent. It is only established that its product is composed of red clover extract; however, such an extract contains 'natural isoflavones in small quantities' and only

becomes an isoflavone phytoestrogen extract as protected by claim 1 after 'enrichment' of the isoflavones. On the merits, the Defendant repeats its objection of lack of patent infringement already raised at first instance and maintained on appeal, which it bases on the fact that its product is not a medicament but a food supplement without therapeutic effect, especially since it does not use the Plaintiff's special extract for its product but a combination product. The Defendant's further objection that the Plaintiff's product 'does not correspond to the description according to the main action', but to the analysis according to Annexes ./28 and ./29, was countered by the Plaintiff, who stated that it was clear from the said Annexes that the product contained isoflavone phytoestrogen extracts from clover and therefore infringed the patent (AS 438/Volume I). However, this reply does not go far enough because it focuses solely on the ingredients and does not take into account the intended purpose covered by the patent.

**3.2** Protected according to claim 1 of the patent is the use of an isoflavone phytoestrogen extract of, inter alia, clover for the manufacture of a medicament for administration in unit dosage form for the treatment of premenstrual syndrome, symptoms associated with menopause or prostate cancer.

**3.3** According to this wording of the patent claim, it is a matter of purpose-limited substance protection for use in a (here:) therapeutic process (Article 54(5) EPC in conjunction with Article 52(4) EPC). Such purpose- limited substance protection is available – exceptionally (Article 52(4) EPC) – for substances and mixtures of substances (in particular medicaments) which already belong to the state of the art, but whose use for (inter alia) therapeutic procedures is new (Spangenberg in Singer/Stauder, Europäisches Patentübereinkommen Article 54 mn. 87). The novelty is based on the effect (medical purpose); composition, structure or form of preparation are irrelevant for the examination of novelty (Melullis in Benkard, EPÜ Article 54 mn. 226; Reich, Materielles Europäisches Patentrecht mn. 583).

**3.4** The concept of therapeutic treatment within the meaning of Art 52(4) EPC essentially covers the restoration of health by curing diseases and the alleviation of suffering, but also methods of maintaining health by prophylactic treatments. The therapeutic character of a treatment presupposes that a pathological state or a disorder with pathological value is to be restored to a normal state or a pathological state is to be prevented. The term therapy is not to be interpreted narrowly: The alleviation of pain or discomfort and the restoration of physical performance, even if their reduction is not caused by disease, must also be regarded as therapeutic treatment within the meaning of this provision. Even if the disorders of well-being have natural causes (e.g. menstruation, pregnancy, old age), they coincide with symptoms of illness and injury and are often hardly distinguishable from them. It is difficult and inappropriate to distinguish between therapies for causes and therapies for symptoms. Below the borderline of medical prophylaxis are methods which only serve to improve general well-being, such as the use of healthy food (health food) or the administration of vitamins not specifically indicated by a doctor (Nack/Moufang in Beier/Haertel/Schricker/Straus, Europäisches Patentübereinkommen, Münchner Gemeinschaftskommentar, Article 52 mn. 371 et seq; Singer/Stauder in Singer/Stauder, Europäisches Patentübereinkommen 4 Article 52 mn. 55, each with reference to the case law of the European Patent Office).

**3.5.1** In cases of protection of a substance for a specific purpose with indication of the intended use in the patent claim (Article 54(5) EPC in conjunction with Article 52(4) EPC), the patent protection covers only those products and articles which are suitable for the indicated purpose (Spangenberg in Singer/Stauder, Europäisches Patentübereinkommen Article 54 mn. 86). The final element of the intended use limits the scope of protection of the patent. The proprietor is (only) entitled to those acts which relate to the manufacture and use of substances of the same nature and intended purpose as medicaments in the field of the claimed indication (Melullis in Benkard, EPÜ Article 54 mn. 238; cf. BGH GRUR 1987, 794 – *Antivirusmittel*). Whether a third party makes use of the teaching of such a patent depends primarily on whether the same substance is used for the same purpose (Melullis in Benkard, EPÜ Article 54 mn. 238).

**3.5.2** In answering the question whether the purpose stated in the patent or another purpose is pursued and achieved, a practically reasonable standard is to be applied which leaves no room for overly sophisticated approaches. The fact that an active ingredient is – also – suitable for the purpose stated in the patent in suit does not mean that it is also designed for such use (in dosage, formulation, packaging). Rather, in order to use the teaching protected in the 'purpose-limited claim', it must be added that the purpose inherent in the invention is achieved (realised) to a practically significant extent in the sense of the concrete objective of the patented teaching (BGH GRUR 1987, 794 – *Antivirusmittel*).

**3.6** Whether these conditions of an infringement of patent rights (use of the same substance which achieves the same purpose to a considerable extent) apply to the Challenged Products of the Defendant 'Vita Lady Vitalkapseln' cannot yet be conclusively answered on the basis of the findings to date. The contested decision must therefore be set aside and the case referred back to the court of first instance for a new decision after supplementing the proceedings in the sense indicated.

**4.1.** In the continued proceedings it will have to be determined in particular whether a red clover extract containing 8 % isoflavones (according to the undisputed composition of the Defendant's product) is used according to the Defendant's intended purpose as an isoflavone phytoestrogen extract of clover for the treatment of premenstrual syndrome, symptoms, associated with menopause, and whether the Defendant's product achieves the purpose inherent in the Plaintiff's patent within the meaning of the specific aim of the patented teaching (limited to use for the treatment of premenstrual syndrome and symptoms associated with menopause) to a practically substantial extent.

**4.2** The evidence topics mentioned are facts relevant to the alleged infringement of patent rights, for which the plaintiff is obliged to prove according to general principles. However, under certain conditions – to be described in more detail below – it is also possible to obtain these facts relevant to the facts by using conclusions based on experience in the sense of prima facie evidence.

**4.3** The prima facie evidence has been developed by jurisprudence and doctrine in order not to let the enforcement of rights fail due to difficulties of proof (RIS-Justiz RS0040281 [T4]). The prima facie evidence is based on typical sequences of events, the realisation of which is probable. It serves as a facilitation of proof for the person who has to present facts giving rise to a claim, enables a shift of the subject of proof and the burden of proof and can be invalidated by the opponent by the evidence of an atypical course of events to be seriously considered (RIS-Justiz RS0040266 [T8]). The prima facie evidence is considered appropriate in cases where concrete evidence cannot reasonably be expected from the party obliged to provide evidence (2 Ob 167/07h mwN = RIS-Justiz RS0123919). As a rule, this is the case if the circumstances are solely in the sphere of the opponent and therefore only known to him and only provable by him (RIS-Justiz RS0040266 [T12]; RS0040281 [T6]).

**4.4** In the present proceedings, there are no findings as to how the Defendant presented the efficacy and indication of its intervention product in its advertising to consumers and/or doctors or pharmacies. In the case of conformity of the advertising presentation of the intervention product with the patent-protected purposes – for which the Plaintiff would be obliged to prove – this circumstance, in the sense of prima facie evidence according to life experience, leads to the conclusion that the intervention product has a purpose in accordance with the patent and also achieves the effect of the patent to a practically significant extent. Of course, in this case it would be open to the Defendant to rebut the prima facie evidence, for example by proving the serious possibility that its product is ineffective. In this case, the Plaintiff would then have to provide full evidence of the alleged patent infringement.

[…]

## 35 II. Vienna Higher Regional Court – *dexmedetomidine*[16]

The Vienna Higher Regional Court, as the court of appeal ***** for invalidity of patent AT E 347 359 T1, on the appeal of the applicant against the decision of the Cancellation Division of the Patent Office of 8.6.2016, N 2/2015-6-9, in closed session

[…]

rightly recognised:
The appeal is not upheld.

[…]

**Reasons for decision**

The defendant is the proprietor of patent AT E 347 359 T1 (Austrian part of EP 1 069 893 B1, published on 6.12.2006), which was filed on 31.3.1999 and claims priorities of 1.4.1998 and 4.12.1998. The patent 'Use of dexmedetomidine for sedation in intensive care' comprises 12 claims with the following wording:

1. Use of dexmedetomidine or a pharmaceutically acceptable salt thereof for the manufacture of a medicament for sedating a critically ill patient who is under intensive care, wherein the patient remains excitable and oriented.
2. Use according to claim 1, wherein the dexmedetomidine or a pharmaceutically acceptable salt thereof is substantially the only active ingredient or the only active ingredient.
3. Use according to claim 1 or 2, wherein the dexmedetomidine or a pharmaceutically acceptable salt thereof is administered in an amount such that a plasma concentration of 0.1 to 2 ng/ml is achieved.
4. Use according to claim 3, wherein the dexmedetomidine or a pharmaceutically acceptable salt thereof is administered intravenously.
5. Use according to claim 4, wherein a loading dose and the maintenance dose are administered.
6. Use according to claim 5, wherein the loading dose and the maintenance dose are administered to a human.
7. Use according to claim 6, wherein the loading dose of dexmedetomidine is 0.2 to 2 µg/kg.
8. Use according to claim 7, wherein the loading dose is administered within about 10 minutes.
9. Use according to claim 8, wherein the loading dose of dexmedetomidine is 1 µg/kg.
10. Use according to claim 6, wherein the maintenance dose of dexmedetomidine is 0.1 to 2.0 µg/kg/h.
11. Use according to claim 10, wherein the maintenance dose of dexmedetomidine is 0.2 to 0.7 µg/kg/h.
12. Use according to claim 11, wherein the maintenance dose of dexmedetomidine is 0.4 to 0.7 µg/kg/h.

The patent in suit relates to the use of dexmedetomidine or a pharmaceutically acceptable salt thereof for the manufacture of a medicament for sedating a critically ill patient who is under intensive care. In addition to actually sedating a patient in the intensive care unit (ICU), the word sedation in the context of the ICU also includes the treatment of conditions that affect the patient's well-being, for example pain and anxiety.

The applicant seeks a declaration of invalidity of the Austrian part of the European patent. She disputes novelty and inventive step and also alleges deficient disclosure.

[…]

[16] 11.5.2017, 34 R 113/16m.

## Legal assessment

The appeal is not justified.

[...]

## Re II. Ad sufficiency of disclosure

It can be stated in advance that dexmedetomidine was known as a sedative agent for patients long before the application for the patent in suit was filed. The patent claim in its wording is formulated as a further medical use/indication ('second medical use'), namely as a substance protection for a specific purpose in a therapeutic procedure, and is to be examined under this aspect.

[...]

## Ad Novelty

2.1 Since the EPC 2000 Amendment 2007 (Federal Law Gazette I 2007/81), the fiction of novelty for the substance or mixture of substances under § 3(3) second sentence Patent Act (cf. Article 54(5) EPC) also applies to further surgical, therapeutic or diagnostic methods of treating humans or animals (Weiser, PatG GMG, § 3 PatG mn. 135).The assessment of novelty and/or inventive step of a second medical indication is difficult in many cases; however, a clear and unambiguous demarcation from a discovery not eligible for protection must be made. The EPO's case law on Art 54(5) EPC, which is also followed by the Supreme Court (cf. for the patent infringement proceedings 17 Ob 35/09k, Isoflavon), is as follows (§ 3(3) second sentence Patent Act is modelled on this provision):

2.2 In order to safeguard the second medical indication, protection of a substance for a specific purpose can be considered even if the application does not belong to the state of the art. If the substance has already been used in medicine, only a use that differs from known uses can be new; the same specific therapeutic effect can no longer be treated as new, even under the fiction of § 3(3) second sentence Patent Act (cf. Article 54(5) EPC).

The subject matter is the suitability of a known substance or mixture of substances for a specific medical purpose and thus ultimately an inherent property of the substance/mixture of substances. Thus, the application is not limited to indications for the treatment of further clinical pictures (Busse/Keukenschrijver, Patentgesetz § 3 mn. 171; Haedicke/Timmann, Handbuch des Patentrechts, § 7 mn. 59).

Both the use of a substance or mixture of substances for the preparation of a medicament and a process for the preparation of a medicament characterised by the use of the substance in question can be claimed (T 958/94); likewise the definition of a new patient group by indicating a new clinical situation (T 836/01) as well as a different mode of administration (subcutaneous instead of intramuscular, G 2/08). A new dosage instruction as the only claim feature not contained in the state of the art may also establish patentability (G 2/08; cf. Heusler in Singer/Stauder EPÜ Art 54, mn. 131 ff.). In this case, novelty is given if, on the basis of a known substance already used for application in a therapeutic method relating to a specific disease, a different temporal administration pattern for the treatment of the same disease is filed (BGH GRUR 2007, 404, 405, Carvedilol II, takes at least a critical view of this possibility; Haedicke/Timmann, Handbuch des Patentrechts, § 7 mn. 59).

A new (second) medical indication cannot be seen in the fact that for the first time the known effect of a known therapeutically active composition is attributed to the presence of one of the components of this composition. Such a teaching concerns the scientific explanation of the known effect, but not a new use of the known composition (T 254/93). Nor does the discovery of a further mechanism of action in the context of a known therapeutic use lead to a further new medicinal use (T 486/01).

2.3 Patent protection under § 3(3) second sentence Patent Act is often indication-related. It is granted for showing possibilities for the treatment of diseases, not for the knowledge of the

cause-effect relationships. The medical suitability and the specific applicability of a substance for therapeutic treatment are determined on the one hand by the disease to be treated and by the dosage, and on the other hand also by all other parameters which have an influence on the effect of the substance and can thus be of essential importance for the achievement of the success aimed at by the application.

The novelty is based on the effect; composition, structure or form of preparation are irrelevant, as are the medical-pharmacological causes on which this effect is based (cf. Melullis in Benkard, PatG § 3 mn. 379; Melullis in Benkard, EPÜ Article 54 mn. 226).

2.4 The concept of therapeutic treatment covers in its essence the restoration of health through the cure of diseases as well as the alleviation of suffering, but also procedures for the preservation of health through prophylactic treatments. The therapeutic character of a treatment presupposes that a pathological condition or a disorder with disease value is thereby restored to a normal state or that a pathological condition is to be prevented.

The term therapy is not to be interpreted narrowly: Also the alleviation of pain or discomfort and the restoration of physical performance are to be considered therapeutic treatment (cf. 17 Ob 35/09k, Isoflavon, with further references).

[...]

36

## III. Supreme Court (OHG) – *Isoflavone II*[17]

The Supreme Court, as appellate court, by the President of the Senate, Dr. Vogel, as Chairman, and the Court Counsellors Dr. Schwarzenbacher and MMag. Matzka, as well as the expert lay judges DI Dr. Gerda Cunow and MR DI Dr. Sabine Rödler as further judges in the patent case of the plaintiff K***** Pty Limited (formerly N***** Limited), *****, represented by Gassauer-Fleissner Rechtsanwälte GmbH in Vienna, against the Defendant A***** GmbH,*****, represented by Dr. Andreas Zahradnik, Rechtsanwalt in Vienna, as procedural aide, who is represented by Dorda Rechtsanwälte GmbH in Vienna, on the ordinary appeal against the judgment of the Court of First Instance of the European Communities in the case of K***** Pty Limited. Andreas Zahradnik, attorney at law in Vienna, as an intervener in the proceedings, represented by Dorda Rechtsanwälte GmbH in Vienna, for rendering of accounts (§ 151 Patent Act), on the ordinary appeal of the Defendant against the judgment of the Vienna Higher Regional Court as the Court of Appeal of 13 September 2017, GZ 133 R 78/17v-191, by which the judgment of the Vienna Commercial Court of 26 April 2017, GZ 19 Cg 178/05f-188, was amended as a result of the appeal of the Plaintiff, and found in favour of the Defendant:

### Judgment

I. The name of the applicant party shall be corrected to 'K***** Pty Limited'.

II. the appeal is allowed.

The contested judgment is amended to the effect that the judgment of the court of first instance is restored with the proviso that also the claim to rendering of accounts regarding the Defendant's activities in Austria which would involve the use of the Plaintiff''s patent EP 0 656 786 (in Austria E 275 959), namely the product 'Vita-Lady Vitalstoff-Kapseln', within 14 days, setting out all relevant circumstances for the calculation of the statutory claim for payment, and – at the unilateral request of the Defendant – to have this rendering of accounts examined by an expert, with the costs to be borne by the Defendant, insofar as this results in a higher amount than that resulting from the rendering of accounts, is dismissed.

[...]

[17] 29.5.2018, 4 Ob 232/17x.

**Reasons for decision:**

[...]

The Plaintiff was the proprietor of European patent EP 0 656 786 B1 (in Austria E 275 959; priority 19 May 1993), which expired on 19 May 2013, with the following claims – remaining after a decision of the Technical Board of Appeal of the European Patent Office of 22 October 2013, T0987/11-3.3.02:

1. Use of an isoflavone phytoestrogen extract of soy or red clover, said isoflavone phytoestrogen extract comprising isoflavones selected from genistein, daidzein, biochanin A or formononetin, for the manufacture of a medicament for administration in unit dosage form, which unit dosage form is a tablet or capsule, for the administration of isoflavone phytoestrogens in an amount of about 20 mg to 200 mg per day, optionally in an amount of 50 mg to 150 mg, for the treatment of premenstrual syndrome or symptoms associated with menopause.
2. use as claimed in claim 1, wherein the isoflavone phytoestrogen comprises genistein and/or biochanin A: daidzein and/or formononetin present in a ratio of about 1:2 to 2:1.
3. use as claimed in claim 1 or claim 2, wherein the administration of the medicament is at least daily for a period of at least one month.

The Defendant distributed and advertised – in addition to 'Vita-Lady Meno-Kapseln (Tages- und Nachtkapseln)' and 'Vita-Lady Meno Tag/Nacht'-capsules, which are not subject to appeal – 'Vita-Lady Vitalstoff-Kapseln' with herbal hormones and nutrients, including the active ingredient red clover, to be taken once a day during menstruation and menopause. The ingredients listed on the package include '150 mg stand. Red clover extract'. The product information mentions, among other things, red clover isoflavones (= plant hormones) and menstrual and menopausal symptoms as indications. [...]

In the magazine 'Apotheker-Krone', an advertisement promoting this product informs that red clover contains all four isoflavones known so far, namely biochanin A, formononetin, genistein and daidzein; the product contains isoflavones (150 mg red clover) against premenstrual and menopausal complaints.

The extract used by the Defendant for 'Vita-Lady Vitalstoff-Kapseln' contains 8 % isoflavones, so that one capsule (= daily dose) contains a total of about 12 mg red clover isoflavones.

In contrast to the complete natural product, an extract consists of isolated substances and is enriched compared to the latter. A certain proportion of characteristic ingredients is obtained by extraction. From the term 'red clover extract' it cannot be deduced whether it contains isoflavone phytoestrogens; the same applies to 'red clover special extract'. From both it is clear that certain ingredients have been enriched or that accompanying substances have been separated, but not which ones. However, it is obvious that isoflavone phytoestrogens are enriched, as these are the ingredients of red clover that are of importance to experts because of their efficacy.

The Plaintiff requested

a) a declaration that the Defendant infringed the said patent until 19 May 2013 by operationally using substances corresponding to the patent claims and/or by offering for sale, putting on the market, importing or using or possessing for these purposes articles directly manufactured in accordance with these claims, in particular 'Vita-Lady' capsules, in particular 'Vita-Lady Vitality Capsules' and/or 'Vita-Lady Meno Capsules' and/or 'Vita-Lady Meno Day/Night'; and
b) to oblige the Defendant to rendering of accounts with regard to its activities in Austria involving the use of the said patent, setting out all relevant circumstances for the calculation of the statutory claim for payment, and, at the Plaintiff's unilateral request, to have this rendering of accounts examined by an expert, the costs of the examination to be borne by the Defendant, insofar as this resulted in a higher amount than the rendering of accounts.

Furthermore, the Plaintiff c) filed a claim for publication.

The Defendant contested a patent infringement with regard to the 'Vita-Lady Vitalstoff-Kapseln' (Vita-Lady capsules) and argued that they contained only 12 mg of isoflavones.

The court of first instance dismissed the claims for declaratory judgment and for publication because the Plaintiff no longer had a legal interest in them more than three years after the expiry of the patent. The court granted – unchallenged – the claim for rendering of accounts with regard to the defendant's activities concerning the products 'Vita-Lady Meno capsules (day and night capsule)' and 'Vita-Lady Meno day/night' capsules, because the defendant had used the patent unlawfully in this respect. However, the 'Vita-Lady Vitalstoff-Kapseln' were not patent-infringing because they did not reach the minimum amount of isoflavones as required by the patent; an explicit dismissal of this part of the accounting claim in the award was omitted – recognisably by mistake.

The Court of Appeal upheld the Defendant's appeal against the partial dismissal of the accounting claim to the extent that it obliged the Defendant to rendering of accounts also with regard to its offers concerning the product 'Vita-Lady Vitalstoff-Kapseln'.

[...]

The Defendant's ordinary appeal seeks the restoration of the first judgment in its part rejecting the accounting claim concerning the product 'Vita-Lady Vitalstoff-Kapseln' (Vita-Lady Vital Substance Capsules); in the alternative, a motion to set aside and refer back the case is filed.

The Plaintiff requests that the appeal be dismissed or, in the alternative, that it be disallowed.

The appeal is admissible to clarify the legal situation; it is also justified.

The Defendant argues that, according to the objective facts, there was no patent-infringing 'offering for sale'. Moreover, this would require that the Defendant had been prepared to manufacture and supply an object of infringement, which was not the case.

**Legal assessment**

To this end, it was considered:

The principles of evidence in patent proceedings are the same as in any other civil proceedings. The norms of patent law are also within the framework of the usual rules of evidence of the Austrian Civil Procedure Code (4 Ob 280/98z). Accordingly, the basic rule that each party has to prove the actual conditions of the legal norm favourable to it also applies in patent proceedings (RIS-Justiz RS0037797, RS0039939).

Accordingly, if the Plaintiff asserts claims based on a patent infringement, it has to prove its patent right and an act of infringement by the Defendant (cf. RIS-Justiz RS0111375).

(2) Insofar as the admissibility of prima facie evidence (cf. RIS-Justiz RS0123919) was affirmed in the first instance (17 Ob 35/09k), this was done against the background of the purpose-limited substance protection at that time under specification of the purpose of use in the patent claim within the meaning of Art 54(5) in conjunction with Art 52(4) EPC, whereby primarily the final element of the purpose of use limited the scope of protection of the patent. In such a case, the Plaintiff must first prove the conformity of the advertising representation of the infringing product with the purposes protected by the patent. If this evidence succeeds, the question arises whether the Defendant's product achieves the purpose inherent in the Plaintiff's patent to a practically substantial extent in the sense of the specific aim of the patented teaching. The concordance of the advertising presentation leads to the conclusion, in the sense of prima facie evidence according to life experience, that the infringing product has a purpose in accordance with the patent and also achieves the effect of the patent to a practically significant extent (17 Ob 35/09k).

(3) Whether prima facie evidence is admissible at all, i.e. whether it is a matter of facts with a typical course of events that allows a shift of the subject of evidence and the burden of proof, is a question of the burden of proof and thus a question of legal assessment that is reviewable in the revision proceedings (cf. RIS-Justiz RS0022624).

The present situation is characterised by the fact that there is now (no longer) any pure protection of a substance for a specific purpose with an indication of the intended use in the patent claim. Rather, the claim – as the court of first instance correctly pointed out – is delimited by concrete minimum amounts of isoflavones. In such a constellation, there are no reasons for shifting the subject matter of the evidence and the burden of proof from the factual circumstance that actually has to be proved to auxiliary facts that are easier for the Plaintiff to prove and that are typically linked to each other in a formulaic way (RIS RS0040274, RS0040287; cf. RS0040266, RS0040272).

It was therefore incumbent on the Plaintiff to prove according to general rules that the Defendant had infringed the patent. In concrete terms, the plaintiff had to primarily prove that the product was offered for sale by the Defendant in a patent-infringing manner, i.e. that the advertising representation of the infringing product – which did not actually infringe the patent – corresponded to the patent.

4 According to the findings, on the packaging – next to the depiction of a red clover flower – the indication '150 mg stand. Red clover extract', from which it cannot be deduced that this product contains isoflavone phytoestrogens, but only that certain ingredients have been enriched or accompanying substances have been separated, but not which ones.

However, according to the objective explanatory value, no infringement of the patent can be deduced from this, which covers the administration of isoflavone phytoestrogens in a concrete amount of approximately 20 mg to 200 mg per day, possibly in an amount of 50 mg to 150 mg. The same applies to the advertisement in Apotheker-Krone, from which no specific advertising statement of a patent-infringing content of isoflavone phytoestrogens in the product can be inferred. However, since – as explained – the burden of proof in this respect is on the Plaintiff, any ambiguities fall on it.

This applies to all three patent claims, since the content of each of them was delimited by concrete minimum quantities, as the trial court also already assumed. The Plaintiff did not show any deviation from this either in the appeal or in the appeal proceedings.

In summary, the Defendant did not infringe the Plaintiff's patent by actually manufacturing the product in question (undisputed), nor was it demonstrable that its advertising statements suggested that the infringing product was in conformity with the patent. It was therefore not relevant to the question of admission under which further conditions a product that did not actually infringe the patent was offered for sale in a way that infringed the patent, contrary to § 22(1) Patent Act.

Therefore, the original judgment had to be restored with the clarifying proviso that the claim for invoicing was expressly rejected with regard to the product 'Vita-Lady Vitalstoff-Kapseln'.

[…]

## IV. Vienna Higher Regional Court – *Everolimus*[18] 37

The Higher Regional Court Vienna, as the court of appeal, by the President of the Senate, Dr. Hinger, as Chairman, as well as Judge Janschitz and the expert lay judge, patent attorney Dr. Alge, in the patent law case of the plaintiff parties 1. *****, 2. *****, represented by Gassauer-Fleissner Rechtsanwälte GmbH in Vienna in cooperation with Schwarz & Partner Patentanwälte OG, against the Defendant *****, represented by Kletzer Messner Mosing Schnider Schultes Rechtsanwälte OG in cooperation with Wildhack & Jellinek Patentanwälte OG, for (in provisional proceedings) injunction (EUR 30,.000) on the appeals of the plaintiff (appeal interest EUR 100,000) and the Defendant (appeal interest EUR 300,000) against the

[18] 24.2.2021, 33 R 116/20a.

preliminary injunction of the Commercial Court of Vienna of 18.9.2020, 58 Cg 55/20a-9, in closed session:

## Judgment

A.

The appeal of the Defendant is not upheld.

The value of the subject matter of the decision exceeds EUR 30,000.

The ordinary appeal is not admissible.

B.

The appeal of the plaintiff parties is not upheld.

The preliminary injunction is confirmed with the proviso that it reads:

'I.

1. In order to secure the claim of the Defendants for an injunction against the Defendant's infringement with the Injunction Patent, which is the subject of the application, the Defendant is prohibited from using 40-O-(2-hydroxyethyl)rapamycin for use in combination with an aromatase inhibitor in the treatment of hormone receptor positive breast tumours, wherein the aromatase inhibitor is atamestane, exemestane, formestane, aminoglutethimide, roglethimide, pyridoglutethimide, trilostane, testolactone, ketoconazole, vorozole, fadrozole, anastrozole or letrozole, in particular 'E***** r***** 5 mg tablets' (marketing authorisation number 137785) and/or 'E***** r***** 10 mg tablets' (marketing authorisation number 137786), in Austria.

2a. [unchanged as in the contested decision].

2b. [unchanged as in the contested decision].

II.

Dismisses the application to prohibit the Defendant from marketing 40-O-(2-hydroxyethyl)rapamycin for use in combination with an aromatase inhibitor in the treatment of hormone receptor positive breast tumours, wherein the aromatase inhibitor is atamestane, exemestane, formestane, aminoglutethimide, roglethimide, pyridoglutethimide, trilostane, testolactone, ketoconazole, vorozole, fadrozole, anastrozole or letrozole, in particular 'E***** r***** 5 mg tablets' (marketing authorisation number 137785) and/or 'E***** r***** 10 mg tablets' (marketing authorisation number 137786), to place them on the market, to use them or to import them for the purposes mentioned;

III.

Dismisses the application to order the Defendant to prove to the plaintiff parties that the application under point 2b. of the ruling has been withdrawn'.

The value of the subject matter of the decision exceeds EUR 30,000.

[...]

## Justification

The first plaintiff is the owner of the Injunction Patent (EP 3 351 246 B1), which is validated for Austria (E 1 135 249) and is in force. The term of protection runs until 18.2.2022 upon regular payment of the renewal fees. The German translation of the Injunction Patent was published by the Austrian Patent Office as AZ AT-E 1 135 249.

The second plaintiff is the exclusive licensee of the Injunction Patent and, according to the licence agreement, is entitled to enforce the Injunction Patent. It distributes the products protected by the Injunction Patent in Austria under the name 'Afinitor'.

The claims of the Injunction Patent are:

'1. 40-O-(2-hydroxyethyl)rapamycin for use in combination with an aromatase inhibitor in the treatment of hormone receptor positive breast tumours.

2. 40-O-(2-hydroxyethyl)rapamycin for use according to claim 1, wherein the aromatase inhibitor is atamestane, exemestane, formestane, aminoglutethimide, roglethimide, pyri-

doglutethimide, trilostane, testolactone, ketoconazole, vorozole, fadrozole, ansatrozole or letrozole.'

On 3.8.2017, the Defendant received marketing authorisation for the generic medicines 'E***** r***** 5 mg tablets' (marketing authorisation number 137785) and 'E***** r***** 10 mg tablets' (marketing authorisation number 137786) for the treatment of hormone receptor-positive, HER2/neu-negative, advanced breast carcinoma.

The instructions for use (./H) for 'E***** r***** 5 mg tablets' and 'E***** r***** 10 mg tablets' contain the following information:

'1. What is E***** r***** and what is it used for?

E***** r***** is an anti-cancer medicine that contains the active ingredient E*****. E***** reduces the blood supply to the tumour and slows down the growth and spread of cancer cells.

E***** r***** is used to treat adult patients with:

Hormone receptor-positive advanced breast cancer in postmenopausal women in whom the disease can no longer be controlled by other treatments (so-called 'non-steroidal aromatase inhibitors'). It is given together with the medicine exemestane, a so-called 'steroidal aromatase inhibitor', which is used as hormone therapy against cancer.'

The active substance of 'E***** r*****' is E*****. E***** is 40-O-(2-hydroxyethyl)rapamycin.

Exemestane is an aromatase inhibitor (mentioned in patent claim 2). 'E***** r*****' is used in combination with exemestane for the therapy of hormone receptor-positive, HER2/neu-negative, advanced breast carcinoma in postmenopausal women without symptomatic visceral metastasis, following recurrence or progression after treatment with a non-steroidal aromatase inhibitor. It is administered together with the drug exemestane, which is used as hormone therapy against cancer.

The Defendant has been offering 'E***** r***** 5 mg tablets' and 'E***** r***** 10 mg tablets' in Austria since June 2019 and has achieved inclusion in Index of Goods I of the Austrian Pharmacy Tariff.

With effect from 3.6.2019, the inclusion of the products 'E***** r***** 5 mg tablets' and 'E***** r***** 10 mg tablets' in the Red Box and with effect from 1.9.2019, the inclusion in the Green Box of the Austrian Reimbursement Code was approved.

[...]

From a legal point of view, the court of first instance assessed the facts of the case as showing that the interventional preparation E***** r***** contained the active substance 40-O-(2-hyroxyethyl)rapamycin and thus exhibited feature 1 of the Injunction Patent. An aromatase inhibitor was not contained in the interventional preparation itself. The acts of use therefore did not directly infringe the patent. However, the SmPC contained instructions for the combination with Exemestan for the treatment of adult patients with hormone receptor-positive breast cancer, so that there was an indirect infringement of the patent within the meaning of § 22(3) Patent Act. Therefore, in the injunction, the infringing act was to be limited to offering.

The Plaintiffs appeal against the dismissing part of the preliminary injunction on the grounds of incorrect legal assessment, incorrect findings of fact based on incorrect legal assessment and incorrect findings of fact based on incorrect assessment of evidence. They apply for the grant of the preliminary injunction sought; in the alternative, for the dismissing part of the order under appeal to be set aside.

The following appeal is directed against the granting part of the preliminary injunction.

The Defendant appeals on the grounds of nullity, procedural irregularity and incorrect legal assessment. It seeks the annulment of the contested order and the dismissal of the entire application for security.

Both parties request that the opposing appeal be dismissed.

### Legal assessment

Both appeals are not justified.

[...]

**I. On the appeal of the Plaintiff:**

In their appeal, the Plaintiffs contested the decision to the full extent of the dismissal [...]

**2) The legal complaint:**

[...]

**2.3** With regard to the Plaintiffs' argument that the 'use' to be prohibited also includes the 'purposeful (meaningful) preparation' of the active ingredient, it should be noted:

**2.3.1** Pursuant to § 22(1) Patent Act, the patent holder is entitled to exclude others from manufacturing, putting on the market, offering for sale or using the subject matter of the invention or from importing or possessing it for the aforementioned purposes.

Pursuant to subsection 3, the patent also has the effect of prohibiting any third party from offering or supplying means relating to an essential element of the invention for the use of the invention to persons other than those entitled to use the invention, without the consent of the patentee, if the third party knows or it is obvious from the circumstances that these means are suitable and intended to be used for the use of the invention.

**2.3.2** According to § 22a Patent Act, the scope of protection of the patent and the published application is determined by the content of the patent claims. The description and the drawings shall be consulted for the interpretation of the claims. The Protocol on the Interpretation of Article 69 of the European Patent Convention, Federal Law Gazette 1979/350, as amended, shall apply mutatis mutandis.

The Injunction Patent can be divided into the following features:

1. 40-O-(2-hydroxyethyl)rapamycin
2. for use in combination with an aromatase inhibitor
3. in the treatment of hormone receptor-positive breast tumours.

**2.3.3** A prerequisite for direct infringement is that the medicinal product is 'purposefully prepared' for the protected therapeutic purpose or is directed towards such use, i.e. if it is foreseeable that the medicinal product will be used for the protected purpose. This preparation or purposefulness can be achieved in various ways, for example by means of a corresponding marketing authorisation or package leaflet (cf. Adocker/Wildhack/Petsche/Strobl in Stadler/Koller, PatG, § 22 mn. 103 et seq.).

Only the substance is protected, namely its suitability and usability for a specific purpose, namely the treatment of a specific disease, but not its use in the treatment (Mellullis in Benkard, EPÜ Article 54 mn. 306; BGH, X ZR 29/15, mn. 83, *Pemetrexed*).

In the present case, the Plaintiffs fail to take into account that the 'obvious preparation' can only refer to the substance in question, the protection of which is not covered by the prohibition to patent therapeutic methods (earmarked substance protection under Article 54(5) EPC and § 3(3) Patent Act). This protection, which is granted for the 'second (and further) medical indication', is not 'toothless', as assumed by the Plaintiffs, but may – in addition to the actual indication – also include other features usually not recognisable on the substance itself, which may relate to the use of the substance itself, but also to the formulation of this substance as a medicament. This protection is, however, limited to exactly this substance (or to the mixture of substances) and finds its limit in Art 54(5) EPC and § 3(3) Patent Act. Therefore, the protective effect conferred by such a claim cannot be subsumed under the facts of the protectability of active substances and extended beyond this legal framework by claim formulations seemingly aiming at the inclusion of further substances.

The preparation of a combination therapy is not yet 'obvious' by the fact that only one substance (E*****) is present in the product, but not the other (exemestane). Therefore, if – as in the present case – in the case of one (actually purposefully prepared) substance (E*****) there are only instructions to additionally provide another substance (here: exemestane) in a

form prepared for the claimed use, patent protection cannot extend directly and immediately to the combination (here: of E***** with exemestane).

It must also be taken into account that – especially in view of the prior art, which identifies both substances (E***** and Exemestan) as tumour treatment agents – the patent claim (and thus the scope of protection) cannot concern an obvious preparation of (only) E***** for a monotherapy, but that the present patent claim concerns (only) the obvious preparation for a combination therapy with Exemestan. Accordingly, such a claim cannot extend protection for the ocular preparation to other – not ocularly present – products (here: exemestane). In the present case, a direct patent infringement would only occur, for example, by offering or selling a specific combination (e.g. in the form of a set), which the Plaintiffs have not alleged at all.

The court of first instance therefore rightly assumed an indirect patent infringement.

3) According to the relevant facts, it could not be established that the Defendant uses the product 'E***** r*****'.

If the Plaintiff asserts claims based on patent infringement, it must assert and prove its patent right and the Defendant's act of infringement (RS0111375).

Due to the indirect patent infringement, only the 'offering' and 'supplying' is to be prohibited according to § 22(3) Patent Act (cf. in this respect Kühnen, Handbuch Patentverletzung10 Chapter A mn. 414 ff., p. 187 f).

The application for inclusion of a medicinal product in the Reimbursement Code of the Main Association of Austrian Social Insurance Institutions, which has to be combined with the announcement of the price and the confirmation of availability, constitutes offering for sale (RS0125407). The same applies to the inclusion of the Defendant's product in the Index of Goods of the Österreichischer Apotheker-Verlag (see 4 Ob 54/12p).

With regard to the Defendant's acts of intervention, the court of first instance found that the Defendant had obtained the inclusion of 'E***** r***** tablets' in the Index of Goods I of the Austrian Pharmacists' Tax since June 2019. With effect from 1.9.2019, the inclusion in the green area of the Reimbursement Code of the Austrian Social Insurances took place. Thus, the Defendant fulfilled the offence of offering for sale (offering for sale) according to § 22(3) Patent Act.

The term 'supplying' essentially corresponds to 'putting into circulation' in § 22(1) Patent Act, but expresses the transfer of the power of disposal to specific purchasers (cf. Adocker/Wildhack/Petsche/Strobl in Stadler/Koller, PatG, § 22 mn. 183 f).

The Plaintiffs did not allege the act of infringement 'deliver'.

[...]

**II. On the Defendant's appeal:**

[...]

**2.3** The Defendant also argues that the obligation to cease and desist is excessive because there is no risk of infringement with regard to the aromatase inhibitors listed in point 1.2 of the contested decision.

The wording of the injunction must primarily be based on the right of exploitation which is affected by the specific act of infringement (RS0037645).

However, in the case of injunctive relief, a certain general wording of the demand in connection with individual prohibitions is usually necessary in order not to make it too easy to circumvent the prohibition. A cease-and-desist order also covers similar or similar types of conduct. It is also practically impossible to describe all conceivable acts of infringement (RS0000845). Therefore, it is permissible to prohibit the infringer not only from a specifically described act, but also from similar ones.

The prerequisite for the assertion of a claim for injunctive relief is an obligation to cease and desist and the danger that this obligation to cease and desist will be violated (RS0037660, RS0012064). With regard to the risk of infringement, a distinction has to be made whether the person obliged to a certain omission has already infringed once or whether he has acted lawfully so far. In the first case, it is presumed that he will act contrary again (risk of rep-

etition). It is therefore up to the Defendant to allege and prove circumstances which make the danger of a repetition of his act appear to be completely excluded or at least extremely improbable (RS0037661, RS0080065, RS0079652). The decisive factor for the existence of the danger of repetition is that a continuing condition does not offer the plaintiff any security against further encroachments on his property (RS0010497 [T3]).

In the present case, the injunction also covers the aromatase inhibitors listed in claim 2. To limit the injunctive relief only to Exemestane would be too narrow because it would not completely exclude the risk of repetition. When examining the danger of repetition, a narrow-minded approach must not be taken. This already lies in the continuation of a condition that offers no safeguards against further infringements. Therefore, the danger of repetition is also to be assumed if the party sued for injunctive relief does not realise that he has done wrong (RS0010497). The risk of commission is not doubtful in the present case, as the Defendant insists even in the appeal proceedings that it has not infringed the patent in suit.

[...]

V.

The ordinary appeal was to be allowed with regard to the decision of the appellate court on the Plaintiff's appeal in connection with the question of direct patent infringement by 'purposeful preparation', because there is no case law of the Supreme Court on this issue.

With regard to the legal questions concerning the decision on the Defendant's appeal, the ordinary appeal was not admissible. Here, there were no legal questions of the quality mentioned in § 528 (1) of the Civil Procedure Code and of importance beyond the individual case to be resolved.

The appeal court adheres to the cited case law. Moreover, whether a security measure is reasonable and necessary always depends on the circumstances of the individual case (RS0078150).

[The Supreme Court did not render a decision in this matter anymore].

## § 3
## Denmark

### A. Executive summary

The provisions of Article 54(4) and (5) of the European Patent Convention (EPC) have been incorporated into Section 2(4) and (5) Danish Patent Act (*patentloven)*[1]. Hence, first and further medical use claims are available under the Danish Patent Act. The Danish Patent and Trademark Office (DKPTO) still allows for the grant of Swiss-form claims, and EPC 2000-form claims are also available for national Danish patent applications. No specific guidance on the proper interpretation of second medical use claims is, however, given in the preparatory works for the Danish Patent Act. Under Danish case law, it should be assumed that Swiss-form claims will be interpreted to be purpose-limited process claims, whereas EPC 2000-form claims will be interpreted to be purpose-limited product claims. 1

There is only limited case law relating to the effect of 'skinny-labelling' a medicinal product in relation to a second medical use claim covering other approved uses of the active ingredient. The case law at hand may suggest a somewhat narrower scope of protection for second medical use claims of the Swiss-form than for such claims of the EPC 2000-form in the sense of a requirement of some form of 'outward presentation' for infringement of a Swiss-form claim. It should be assumed, however, that Danish courts will not consider for there to be any significant distinction and will likely apply similar criteria when determining whether there is direct or indirect infringement of second medical use claims of the Swiss-form as well as EPC 2000-form. 2

In the absence of case law, it is difficult to make specific predictions about which criteria would be decisive. It should be assumed that actual prescribing practices will be given significant weight. On the one hand, the currently applicable substitution rules relating to dispensation at Danish pharmacies should mitigate the risks of infringing second medical use claims relating to some categories of medicinal products. In the Danish public healthcare system, biosimilar medical products, on the other hand, are sold, dispensed and used under different circumstances, which require specific analyses of risks on a case-by-case basis. 3

### B. Scope of protection and interpretation of second medical use claims

In the leading Danish case on infringement of a second medical use claim of the Swiss-form type,[2] the dispensation of generic pregabalin for the treatment of neuropathic pain by Danish pharmacies according to the rules on generic substitution in Danish law at the 4

[1] Consolidated Act no. 90 of 29 January 2019 as amended by Act no. 243 of 7 March 2023; → mn. 37 et seq

[2] The decision of the Danish Maritime and Commercial High Court of 25 June 2015 in *Pfizer v Krka and the Association of Danish Pharmacies (pregabalin)*, case A-6-15; → mn. 61.

time was considered to be an act of infringement according to the provisions on indirect product protection in Section 3(1)(3) Patent Act[3]. Danish pharmacies were accordingly enjoined from dispensing the generic pregabalin product. This result indicates that the court considered the Swiss-form claim to be a purpose-limited process claim.[4]

5 In a decision of 12 August 2014 in *Novartis v Orifarm Generics (rivastigmine)*[5], the Maritime and Commercial High Court stated that an EPC 2000-form claim was for a new medical use, 'and not a purpose-limited product claim'. The decision is difficult to follow on this point, and the statement was not expressly endorsed by the High Court on appeal.[6] It should be assumed that EPC 2000-form claims will be interpreted to be purpose-limited product claims in Danish patent law.

## C. Direct and indirect infringement of second medical use claims

### I. Direct patent infringement

6 As purpose-limited process claims, Swiss-form claims are infringed by using the claimed process or by offering the claimed process for use if the offeror knows, or it is obvious in the circumstances, that the process may not be used without the patentee's consent.[7] The offering, distribution, and use of a product, or importing or possessing the product for such purposes, manufactured in accordance with a patented process is an infringement of the process patent (indirect product protection).[8]

7 Direct infringement of a Swiss-form claim accordingly requires that there is an act of manufacture of a medicinal product *for* the claimed second medical use. In the *esomeprazole* case, the High Court held that the scope of protection of a Swiss-form claim is for the use of the active ingredient in the pharmaceutical process (the manufacture of a medicinal product) as opposed to the chemical process (the manufacture of the active ingredient itself).

8 As purpose-limited product claims, EPC 2000-form claims are infringed by manufacturing, offering, distributing, or using the claimed product, or by importing or possessing the product for such purposes.[9] There is no Danish case law establishing the requirements for direct infringement of EPC 2000-form second medical use claims, but considering the rationale for allowing second medical use claims, it must be the case that more is required than that the product be suitable for the claimed second medical use. In a decision from

---

[3] → mn. 38.

[4] This finding would also seem to underpin the High Court's decision of 17 October 2018 in *AstraZeneca v Krka (esomeprazole)*, case B-528-16. In a decision of 20 December 2018, i.e. shortly after the decision in the *esomeprazole* case, the High Court held in *Eli Lilly v Fresenius Kabi (pemetrexed)*, case B-2735-17, that a patent with a Swiss-form claim had been infringed pursuant to the doctrine of equivalence that forms part of Danish patent law. The High Court stated that the patent concerned a treatment regimen and not a process for the manufacture of the medicinal product in a specific pharmaceutical formulation. However, this statement does not necessarily imply that the High Court considered the claim as something other than a purpose-limited process claim, as the statement was made in the context of establishing the scope of protection of a Swiss-form claim in relation to equivalence.

[5] Case A-6-14.

[6] Decision of 23 February 2015, case B-2504-14.

[7] See Section 3(1)(2) Patent Act; → mn. 38.

[8] See Section 3(1)(3) Patent Act.

[9] See Section 3(1)(1) Patent Act.

the Maritime and Commercial High Court of 18 May 2021 in *Novartis v Orifarm (everolimus)*[10], it was accordingly held that a preliminary injunction under a second medical use claim in EPC 2000-form had to specify that the defendant was enjoined from offering, distributing, and using the product-in-suit *for* the claimed use(s).[11]

It must be assumed that the manufacture, offering, distribution, and use, as well as the import and possession for such purposes, of a medicinal product, in respect of which the claimed second medical use is 'on-label', will be an act of direct infringement of a Swiss-form claim as well as an EPC 2000-form claim under Danish patent law. If the manufacture takes place outside Denmark, only the provisions on indirect product protection should be applicable in relation to Swiss-form claims and the generic manufacturer must be assumed not to have committed any act of direct infringement by virtue of the act of manufacture itself.[12] Applying for and obtaining marketing authorisation for a generic medicinal product with effect for Denmark has been held not to be an act of direct infringement under Danish patent law.[13] Conversely, listing a medicinal product in the official Danish price register[14] or placing a bid in tenders organised by the purchasing entity of the Danish public healthcare sector (Amgros I/S) must be assumed to be acts of offering, and accordingly capable of being acts of direct infringement of second medical use claims. **9**

## II. Indirect patent infringement

Supplying and offering means to carry out an invention can be indirect (contributory) infringement if those means relate to a material element of the invention and the supplier or offeror knows, or it is obvious in the circumstances, that the means are suitable and intended for such use.[15] **10**

As the process is formally the invention in relation to a Swiss-form claim, it must be assumed that it is possible to commit indirect infringement of such a claim by supplying or offering to supply means that are used in the process of manufacturing. In the *pregabalin* case, the patentee had also applied for a preliminary injunction against the manufacturer of the generic medicinal product. It was not in dispute between the parties that the manufacturer of the generic medicinal product did not intend for the products to be used in the treatment of neuropathic pain, and the patentee was bringing proceedings against the manufacturer of the generic medicinal product based on a theory of indirect infringement. This application for a preliminary injunction was, however, unsuccessful as the manufacturer of the generic medicinal product had already taken certain precautionary measures required by the patentee. The case was accordingly decided on a procedural point in relation to the question of the liability of the manufacturer of the generic medicinal product. It cannot therefore be ruled out that there is room for applying the provision **11**

---

[10] Case BS-41864/2020-SHR.

[11] The product-in-suit was 'on-label' in relation to the claimed medical uses, and validity and infringement were not in dispute in the case. The court accordingly only had to decide on the scope of the preliminary injunction.

[12] In the *pemetrexed* decision, the Danish courts did, however, hand down a preliminary injunction enjoining Fresenius Kabi also from manufacturing their generic medicinal product in Denmark, but it does not seem to have been a point in dispute between the parties whether the requirements for a finding that it had been rendered probable that Fresenius Kabi would commit such an act of infringement (in Denmark) in the absence of a preliminary injunction were fulfilled.

[13] The Danish Supreme Court's decision of 9 June 2011 in *Novartis v Teva (valsartan)*, case 266/2009.

[14] https://www.medicinpriser.dk/.

[15] See Section 3(2) Patent Act.

on indirect infringement in Danish patent law in the context of Swiss-form claims, even when there is no subsequent act of manufacture of a medicinal product, including such acts as relabelling, repackaging etc.

12 For EPC 2000-form claims, the claimed use of the product is part of the invention according to the claim. Supplying or offering a product, which can have the claimed use, can accordingly in some circumstances be an act of indirect infringement.

## D. Infringement of second medical use claims and skinny label products

13 In the grounds of the decision of the Danish Maritime and Commercial High Court in the *pregabalin* case, the court emphasises that the Danish pharmacies had applied a label on the packaging indicating that the generic medicinal product was being dispensed to treat neuropathic pain before handing it over to a customer. It is not clear whether this labelling was decisive, or indeed a prerequisite, for the court's finding of direct infringement of a Swiss-form claim by the Danish pharmacies. However, it is possible that the decision in the *pregabalin* case is based on the court considering direct infringement of a Swiss-form claim under Danish patent law to require some form of outward presentation that the generic medicinal product is or has been manufactured *for* the claimed second medical use and that the court considered the labelling to form part of the process of manufacture of the generic medicinal product. This implies that 'skinny-labelling' could mitigate against the risk of direct infringement of Swiss-form second medical use claims under Danish patent law.[16]

14 There is no Danish case law establishing criteria for determining when a medicinal product is *for* a claimed second medical use in the context of an EPC 2000-form claim. The prevailing view in the Danish legal literature is that it should be assumed that 'skinny-labelling' is not in itself sufficient to pre-empt a finding of direct or indirect infringement of an EPC 2000-form second medical use claim. It seems clear enough that it will be an act of infringement of an EPC 2000-form second medical use claim to offer and distribute a 'skinny-labelled' medicinal product in circumstances where it can be proven to form part of the alleged infringer's intent that the generic medicinal product will or should be used for the claimed second medical use.

15 Danish courts generally seek to strike a fair balance between the competing interests when determining the scope of protection of patent claims. In light hereof, Danish courts will likely also find an EPC 2000-form claim infringed if it is sufficiently foreseeable to the alleged infringer that the generic medicinal product will be used 'cross-label' or 'off-label' for the claimed second medical use. Danish courts will likely not distinguish sharply between direct and indirect infringement in such circumstances, at least not in the typical situations that arise in practice. If Danish courts ultimately do establish that 'skinny-labelling' a product is not in itself sufficient to avoid direct (or indirect) infringement of a Swiss-form second medical use claim, the same criteria are also likely to be applied.

16 In the absence of case law, it is difficult to predict with any accuracy which criteria would be decisive. However, on the basis of case law in other types of patent cases and

[16] An unpublished decision of 24 July 2008 from the Copenhagen Bailiff's Court in *Sanofi-Aventis v Merck Generics (fexofenadine)*, case F3-7418/2008, also supports this conclusion. The decision was made in preliminary injunction proceedings in the time before the Maritime and Commercial High Court became the competent venue for all Danish patent cases and should be afforded only supportive weight.

general experiences in relation to how parties in Danish pharmaceutical and biotech patent cases have generally argued their case, the Danish courts' decisions in second medical use claim cases are likely to revolve around the following factors:

1. the degree to which the allegedly infringing medicinal product is in fact used 'cross-label' or 'off-label' for the claimed second medical use;
2. the ratio of 'cross-label' or 'off-label' use for the claimed second medical use to use for a non-patented indication(s);
3. whether the 'cross-label' or 'off-label' use for the claimed second medical use was foreseeable to the alleged infringer, with actual use that can only be said to be incidental likely being afforded limited weight; and
4. the steps taken by the alleged infringer to avoid the 'cross-label' or 'off-label' use for the claimed second medical use.

An effect of the above is that actual prescribing practices will likely be key to the resolution of many cases relating to allegations that the offering or distribution of a 'skinny-labelled' medicinal product represents direct or indirect infringement of a second medical use claim. The point of departure in this regard is that medical doctors are free to prescribe any medicinal product for any indication, and that 'cross-label' or 'off-label' use of a 'skinny-labelled' medicinal product is accordingly theoretically possible. **17**

Danish general practitioners generally prescribe medicine with reference to the brand name, possibly in connection with and may possibly name the active ingredient. Substitution rules in Danish law have had the potential of leading to 'skinny-labelled' generic medicinal products being dispensed from Danish pharmacies even for claimed second medical uses. However, the *pregabalin* case has had a significant impact on the situation in Denmark in this context as the case resulted in these rules being changed by the legislator: under the currently applicable substitution rules,[17] the Danish Medicines Agency must notify pharmacies when a medicinal product is covered by a patented indication, and 'skinny-labelled' medicinal products are not placed in the same substitution group as the branded medicinal product. Pharmacies are obligated to dispense the cheapest amongst 'synonymous' medicinal products for non-patented indications. There not having been more cases after the *pregabalin* case relating to claims of infringement of second medical use claims in Denmark suggests that the substitution rules have had the intended effect and are to a sufficient degree preventing prescriptions from leading to infringement. **18**

## E. Infringement of second medical use claims and biosimilar products

It is likely that the findings set out above will apply also to biosimilar medicinal products. There are, however, practical differences in the way in which biosimilar medicinal products will be sold, dispensed and used in Denmark that can have a significant impact on whether infringement of a second medical use claim is likely in case of a 'skinny-labelled' biosimilar medicinal product. **19**

The Danish Medicines Agency classifies a group of medicinal products as being reserved for dispensation through hospital pharmacies (reserved medicinal products). All biosimilar medicinal products marketed so far on the Danish market are classified as reserved medicinal products, and all use of these biosimilar medicinal products will **20**

[17] The currently applicable substitution rules in Danish law took effect as of November 2015.

occur in the context of treatments being administered at Danish hospital clinics operated by the five Danish Regions – a Region being a tier of local government.

21 The purchasing entity of the five Danish Regions, Amgros I/S, organises tenders for all substantial supplies of reserved medicinal products. The general practice of Amgros I/S has been to organise tenders for the supply of medicinal products containing the active ingredient on a generic level, which creates the potential for allegations of infringement of claims for the use of the active ingredient for a second medical use if a bid to supply a 'skinny-labelled' biosimilar medicinal product is made. Recently, Amgros I/S has been organising tenders with 'multi-awards', which means that multiple bidders can be awarded supply contracts, thereby creating the potential for hospital clinics to choose between suppliers in order to avoid 'cross-label' use. However, even if Amgros I/S were to modify its practice even further and implement indication-specific tenders, there would still be a potential for 'cross-label' or 'off-label' use of a biosimilar medicinal product that has been supplied and is being stored at a hospital clinic that treats patients within the indication of the second medical use claim. It should be noted in this connection that the Danish Medicines Council[18] ('the Council') has determined that, as of 26 January 2023, biosimilar medicinal products should, as the general rule, be deemed interchangeable with their reference biologic medicinal product. Actual prescription practices are thus likely to play a significant, or even decisive role, also in relation to biosimilar medicinal products.

22 Notwithstanding the practitioner's theoretical freedom to prescribe any medicinal product for any indication, almost all use of medicinal products in Denmark occurs in conformity with one or both of the following types of nationally sanctioned treatment guidelines:

1. guidelines laid down by the Council in the form of (a) treatment guidelines for specific therapeutic areas and (b) recommendations for use of specific medicinal products; and/or
2. treatment guidelines laid down by national clinical societies.

23 The recommendations of the Council in relation to uses of specific medicinal products may take the form of either prioritising between a number of available therapies within a treatment area or being a recommendation on whether or not to commence use of a specific medicinal product for a specific indication. The Council makes an overall assessment where a clinical risk-benefit analysis is combined with economic considerations, including the pricing of medicinal products competing within the same clinical indication.

24 It is, however, voluntary for the pharmaceutical company marketing a medicinal product whether to request the Council to make a specific assessment in relation to a specific medicinal product. If the pharmaceutical company prefers to market a medicinal product without an assessment from the Council, the Council will only consider the medicinal product in connection with laying down general treatment guidelines within the therapeutic area in question.

25 The absence of any recommendations from the Council in relation to the use of an active biological ingredient is therefore not conclusive evidence that the active ingredient is not used in clinical practice in Denmark for any relevant indication, but it might be argued that such absence is indicative that such use can be sporadic or only incidental.

26 An assessment of risks associated with marketing a 'skinny-labelled' biosimilar medicinal product in Denmark must accordingly necessarily involve analyses of available relevant treatment guidelines as well as any sources with information about such factors as the size of patient populations and trends in actual prescribing practices.

[18] https://medicinraadet.dk/om-os/in-english.

## F. Strategies and considerations

Only the steps already taken by the manufacturer of the generic medicinal product in the context of the *pregabalin* case serve as guidance for the precautionary measures that the manufacturer of the generic or biosimilar medicinal product can take. In the *pregabalin* case, the manufacturer of the generic medicinal product had: 27

1. informed all pharmacies in Denmark in writing that the generic medicinal product was only to be dispensed for the approved indications;
2. notified the Danish Medicines Agency in writing about the matter and requested the Danish Medicines Agency to ensure that applicable substitution rules were implemented in a way that respected patent rights;
3. informed all general practitioners in Denmark in writing that the product was only to be prescribed for the approved indications;
4. notified the two main wholesalers in Denmark in writing that the product was only to be sold for the approved indications; and
5. contacted the operators of all websites that described the use of the generic medicinal product and asked them to delete any references to the generic medicinal product being used to treat neuropathic pain.

In light of the currently applicable substitution rules for dispensation through Danish pharmacies, it must be assumed that it is not necessary to take any precautionary measures in relation to 'skinny-labelled' generic medicinal products, unless there is some particular reason why it is foreseeable that the substitution rules will not be adhered to or that the substitution rules will have the unintended effect of leading to patent infringement. In such circumstances, the relevant precautionary measures would likely need to be rather tailor-made to meet the specific circumstances. 28

For 'skinny-labelled' biosimilar medicinal products, it will similarly be necessary to take account of the specific circumstances of the tender organised by Amgros I/S and other relevant factual circumstances. It will, for instance, be necessary to consider any implications under Danish tender law in relation to precautionary measures taken prior to making a bid or prior to being awarded a supply contract by Amgros I/S. In some cases, it will probably make sense for the manufacturer to inform the relevant hospital clinics in writing that the biosimilar medicinal product is not to be used for 'cross-label' indications and to inform the hospital clinics of their options in terms of using the biological active ingredient in question. 29

## G. Legal remedies

From a practical perspective, the primary legal remedy available in Danish law in the event of patent infringement is the possibility of applying for a preliminary injunction. Preliminary injunction proceedings are a comparatively effective and reasonably fast means of stopping infringing acts. The patentee may also apply for the grant of a preliminary order compelling the alleged infringer to do certain acts, such as recalling supplies of an allegedly infringing product. The average duration of preliminary injunction proceedings in the first instance relating to patent infringement varies between four to 30 eight months depending on the complexity of the case and the court's docket. It should be assumed that *ex parte* proceedings are not available in patent infringement cases.

31 To obtain a preliminary injunction the applicant must prove or at least render probable that the following conditions are met:

1. that the applicant has the right that is to be protected by the preliminary injunction or order;
2. that the behaviour of the alleged infringer renders it necessary to grant a preliminary injunction or order (a purely hypothetical risk is not enough); and
3. that the applicant's rights will be prejudiced if the applicant has to await the conduct of proceedings on the merits.[19]

32 There are certain further conditions for the grant of a preliminary injunction or order requiring an assessment of the proportionality of granting a preliminary injunction or order, including in relation to the competing interests of the applicant and the alleged infringer.[20] The question of the proportionality of granting a preliminary injunction or order in cases relating to infringement of intellectual property rights has not figured largely in Danish case law, as it has in almost all cases been considered to be relevant and necessary to protect intellectual property rights by granting preliminary injunctions or orders. In the few cases where the alleged infringer has made submissions on lack of proportionality, the courts have generally dismissed such submissions by referring to the fact that a preliminary injunction or order is the primary legal remedy available in Danish law in the event of infringement of intellectual property rights. It is possible, however, that the requirement of proportionality and proportionality assessments may come to play a larger role in preliminary injunction proceedings relating to infringement of second medical use claims.

33 The burden of establishing that the conditions for granting a preliminary injunction or order are met lies, as a general rule, with the applicant (the patentee). In Danish preliminary injunction proceedings, there is, however, a rather strong presumption that a granted patent is valid,[21] meaning that, in practice, the alleged infringer bears the burden of proving any invalidity defence.

34 The grant of a preliminary injunction or order will usually be conditional upon the provision of security by the applicant (typically in the form of a bank guarantee or a cash deposit) to cover an eventual claim for damages by the alleged infringer should it subsequently be established by means of proceedings on the merits that it was unjustified to grant the preliminary injunction or order.[22] Once the decision to grant a preliminary injunction or order is final, it must be followed up by proceedings on the merits within two weeks.[23] If no proceedings on the merits are initiated, the preliminary injunction or order can be vacated.[24]

---

[19] See Section 413 of Consolidated Act no. 1655 of 25 December 2022 as amended by Act no. 1786 of 28 December 2023 (retsplejeloven: 'the Administration of Justice Act'); → mn. 41 et seq.

[20] See Section 414 Administration of Justice Act; → mn. 44.

[21] Most recently, in a decision from the High Court of 11 July 2023 in *Novartis v Zentiva (fingolimod)*, case BS-13247/2023-OLR, the court stated that due to the presumption of validity of granted patents it is for the party raising an invalidity defense to prove that the basis on which the EPO has decided to grant the patent is 'so clearly deficient or erroneous', or that the examination of the conditions for patentability made by the EPO is 'so clearly erroneous', that the applicable presumption of validity cannot be upheld. The High Court also stated that the presumption of validity of a granted patent can be weakened if, e.g., the alleged infringer is able to prove that relevant prior art was not before the EPO during examination. However, the mere fact that certain prior art was not before the EPO does not relieve the alleged infringer from the burden of proving that the decision to grant the patent was erroneous.

[22] See Section 415 Administration of Justice Act; → mn. 45.

[23] See Section 425 Administration of Justice Act; → mn. 55.

[24] See Section 426 Administration of Justice Act; → mn. 56.

A patentee also has the possibility of commencing (infringement) proceedings on the merits, which will provide the possibility for entering pleas for a permanent injunction, recall, destruction and/or damages.[25] Damages are intended to be compensatory, but there is as yet no case law deciding how to take the specific circumstances of the marketing of a 'skinny-labelled' generic or biosimilar medicinal product into account when determining the loss suffered by a patentee. Proceedings on the merits usually take between 18–24 months in the first instance. **35**

The Maritime and Commercial High Court is the specialised venue that has jurisdiction to hear all Danish patent cases.[26] In almost all cases, the court will be composed of a legal judge and two technically qualified judges (often European Patent Attorneys). An appeal from all decisions of the Maritime and Commercial High Court lies with the High Court. **36**

## H. Statutory provisions

### I. Patents Act[27]

#### Section 2 **37**

(1) Patents shall be granted only for inventions which are new in relation to the state of the art prior to the date of filing of the patent application and which, moreover, differ essentially therefrom.

(2) The state of the art shall be held to comprise everything made available to the public by means of a written description, lecture, exploitation or in any other way. The content of a patent application filed in this country before the filing date of the patent application shall also be regarded as comprised in the state of the art if such applications are made available to the public in accordance with the rules in Section 22. The same applies to the content of an application for registration of a utility model filed in this country before the filing date of the patent application if this application are made available to the public in accordance with the rules for utility models. The requirements in subsection (1) hereof to the effect that the invention shall differ essentially from the state of the art shall, however, not apply in relation to the contents of such applications.

(3) Provisions to the effect, that for the purposes of subsection (2) hereof applications provided for in Chapter 3 shall in certain cases have the same effect as patent applications filed in this country, are laid down in Sections 29 and 38.

(4) The requirement under subsection (1) hereof that inventions shall be new shall not prevent the grant of patents for known substances or compounds for use in the methods referred to in Section 1(3), provided that the use of such substance or compound is not known for any of those methods.

(5) The requirement under subsection (1) hereof that inventions shall be new shall also not prevent the grant of patents for the substances or compounds for use in the methods referred to in subsection (4) in accordance with the methods under Section 1(3), provided that there is a specific use of the substance or compound, and this specific use is not known for any of those methods.

(6) A patent may, however, be granted for an invention irrespective of the fact that it has been made available to the public within the last six months prior to the filing of the application, if this is a consequence of

---

[25] See Sections 57 and 58 Patents Act; → mn. 39 et seq.

[26] See Section 225(2)(4) Administration of Justice Act.

[27] Consolidated Act no. 90 of 29 January 2019 as amended by Act no. 243 of 7 March 2023.

1) evident abuse in relation to the applicant or his legal predecessor; or
2) the fact that the applicant or his legal predecessor has displayed the invention at an official, or officially recognised, international exhibition falling within the terms of the Convention on International Exhibitions, signed at Paris on 22 November 1928.

38

### Section 3

(1) The exclusive right conferred by a patent shall imply that no one, except the proprietor of the patent, may without permission exploit the invention by

1) making, offering, putting on the market or using a product which is the subject-matter of the patent, or by importing or possessing the product for these purposes; or
2) using a process which is the subject-matter of the patent or by offering the process for use in this country, if the person offering the process knows, or it is obvious in the circumstances, that the use of the process is prohibited without the consent of the proprietor of the patent; or
3) by offering, putting on the market or using a product produced by a process which is the subject-matter of the patent or by importing or possessing the product for these purposes.

(2) The exclusive right shall also imply that no one, except the proprietor of the patent, may without permission exploit the invention by supplying or offering to supply any person who is not entitled to exploit the invention with means for working it in this country, if these means relate to a material element of the invention and the person supplying or offering to supply the means knows, or it is obvious in the circumstances, that these means are suitable and intended for such use. This provision shall not apply when the means are staple commodities, except when the person supplying or offering to supply the means induces the person supplied to commit acts as referred to in subsection (1) hereof. For the purpose of the first and second paragraph, persons performing acts as referred to in subsection (3), No. (1), (3) (4) or (5) hereof shall not be considered entitled to exploit the invention.

(3) The exclusive right shall not extend to:

1) acts conducted for non-commercial purposes;
2) acts concerning products put on the market in this country or in another country within the European Economic Area (EEA) by the proprietor of the patent or with his consent;
3) acts conducted for experimental purposes relating to the subject-matter of the patented invention;
4) acts that are limited to the subject-matter of the claimed invention, which are necessary to obtain a marketing authorisation for a medicinal product for human or veterinary use in the EU, in an EU Member State or in other countries; or
5) preparation in a pharmacy of a medicinal product according to a prescription in individual cases or acts concerning the medicinal product so prepared.

39

### Section 57

(1) If any person infringes the exclusive right conferred by a patent (patent infringement), and the infringement is committed intentionally or by gross negligence, he shall be punished by a fine. This also applies to infringements of patent rights pursuant to Regulation No 1257/2012 of the European Parliament and of the Council of 17 December 2012 on implementing enhanced cooperation in the area of the creation of unitary patent protection.

(2) If the infringement is committed intentionally and under aggravating circumstances, the sentence may be increased to imprisonment up to one year and six months, except when a higher sentence is imposed in accordance with Section 299b of the Criminal Code (straffeloven). Aggravating circumstances shall be deemed to exist in particular if by the infringement a significant and manifestly unlawful gain is intended.

(3) Companies etc. (legal entities) may be held criminally liable to penalties according to the rules of Chapter 5 of the Criminal Code (straffeloven).

(4) Infringements covered by subsection (1) shall be brought by the aggrieved party. Infringements covered by subsection (2) shall only be brought by the public prosecutor at the request of the aggrieved party unless public interest requires prosecution.

### Section 58 40

(1) Any person who intentionally or negligently commits patent infringement shall be liable to pay a

1) reasonable compensation to the aggrieved party for the exploitation of the invention; and
2) damages to the aggrieved party for the further injury which the infringement may have caused.

(2) When determining the damages pursuant to subsection (1) (2), account must be taken of, among other things, the aggrieved party's lost profits and the infringer's unjustified profits.

(3) In cases covered by subsection (1), compensation may also be determined to the aggrieved party for non-economic damage.

## II. Administration of Justice Act[28]

### Chapter 40. Decisions on preliminary injunctions and orders in civil proceedings

### Section 411 41

(1) On application, the court may by way of a preliminary injunction or order under the provisions of this chapter order private individuals and representatives of the Danish State, regions and municipalities in their capacity as parties to private legal relationships to temporarily do, refrain from doing or tolerate certain actions.

(2) If the purpose of an application under subsection (1) is to obtain security for the payment of a money claim, an application to this effect must be filed and heard under the provisions of Chapter 56 on attachment.

(3) If the purpose of an application under subsection (1) is to preserve evidence of an infringement of intellectual property rights etc., an application to this effect must be filed and heard under the provisions of Chapter 57a on preservation of evidence.

(4) With regard to aircraft, vessels of foreign states and cargoes belonging to foreign states, injunctions or orders will be available only in accordance with the provisions of other legislation to this effect.

(5) The provisions in this chapter are not applicable to cases filed before the Unified Patent Court pursuant to Section 225a(1).

### Section 412 42

(1) Application for a preliminary injunction or order must be submitted to the court which has substantive competence pursuant to Section 224 or subsections (1) and (2) of Section 225 and territorial jurisdiction pursuant to Chapter 22 to deal with such case. Section 225(3) and section 227 apply correspondingly. If the application concerns an EU trade mark or a Community design, subsections (2) and (3) of section 225 apply correspondingly if the use of the EU Trade Mark Regulation or the Community Design Regulation is of material significance,

[28] Consolidated Act no. 1655 of 25 December 2022 as amended by Act no. 1786 of 28 December 2023 (*retsplejeloven*).

but see Sections 43c and 43d of the Trademarks Act (varemærkeloven) and Section 43(2) and (3) of the Designs Act (designloven).

(2) If the dispute concerning the right for which protection is sought by way of a preliminary injunction or order is to be settled by arbitration or a foreign court, the application for the grant of an injunction or order must be filed with the court which would have had the substantive competence and the territorial jurisdiction pursuant to subsection (1).

43

### Section 413

(1) A preliminary injunction or order may be granted if the party applying for the grant of the injunction or order proves or renders probable:

1) that the applicant has the right sought to be protected by the preliminary injunction or order;
2) that the behaviour of the alleged infringer renders it necessary to grant a preliminary injunction or order; and
3) that the applicant's rights will be prejudiced if the applicant has to await the conduct of proceedings on the merits.

44

### Section 414

(1) No preliminary injunction or order may be granted if the general provisions laid down by law on penalty and compensation and any security offered by the opposing party are deemed to provide adequate protection to the party.

(2) The court may refuse to grant a preliminary injunction or order if this would cause the opposing party to suffer a detriment or disadvantage which is clearly disproportionate to the party's interest in obtaining the injunction or order.

45

### Section 415

(1) The court may order the party, as a condition for the granting of a preliminary injunction or order, to provide security for the damage and inconvenience that may be caused to the other party by the injunction or order.

(2) The court decides the nature and amount of such security.

(3) If the court has required the party to provide security, the injunction or order will not be granted until such security has been provided. The court will notify the parties of the date when the injunction or order will be granted if the parties have not already been informed of the date at a court hearing, see Section 162.

(4) The parties may agree, after the dispute has arisen, that any injunction or order may be granted without security being provided. In proceedings between businesses concerning matters relating to the parties' businesses, such agreement may also be concluded before the dispute has arisen. For present purposes, the performance of public services is to be considered conduct of business. The court may, upon request, exceptionally disregard an agreement as mentioned in the second sentence if the interests of one of the parties so warrant.

46

### Section 416

(1) An application for an injunction or order must satisfy the requirements of Section 348. Section 349 applies correspondingly.

47

### Section 417

(1) The application for an injunction or order is heard at a court hearing where the necessary evidence must be produced. The court may cut-off evidence which is deemed to be incompatible with the interest of proceeding with the application. Section 344 applies correspondingly.

(2) The court sets the time and place of the hearing mentioned in subsection (1) and notifies the party who has applied for the injunction or order.

(3) Where possible, the court will notify the opposing party of the time and place of the hearing. Notification may be made by a summons, see subsections (4) and (5). Notification may be omitted, however, if the court has no reservations about holding the hearing without prior notification of the opposing party or if the purpose of the injunction or order will be lost if the opposing party is notified.

(4) Subject to a notice fixed by the court, the court may summon to the hearing the person whom the application for an injunction or order concerns if the hearing is held in the judicial district in which the party resides or is staying or from which the party carries on business, or in a neighbouring district. If the hearing is held in the court building of the Maritime and Commercial High Court or in the City Court of Copenhagen or the Courts of Frederiksberg, Glostrup or Lyngby, the party may be summoned if it has such ties to one of those districts. In the summons, the party may be ordered to attend in person. The summons must contain information about the notice and about the consequences of non-attendance.

(5) If the party whom the application for an injunction or order concerns is an association, a company or the like, the managing director or business manager of the association, company, etc. or, if necessary, a member of the board of directors may be summoned under subsection (4) if the person in question resides or is staying in the judicial district or a neighbouring judicial district or if the home court of the association, company, etc. is in one such district or the association, company, etc. carries on business from one such district. The second sentence of subsection (4) applies correspondingly.

### Section 418 48

(1) If the party applying for an injunction or order fails to attend, the application will be denied.

(2) If the party whom the application for an injunction or order concerns does not attend, the application may be granted if it is sufficiently justified by the statement of facts and any other information available to the court and the party has been duly summoned or notification has been omitted under the third sentence of Section 417(3). The court may postpone the hearing if the court finds the party's attendance desirable.

(3) Subsections (4) and (5) of Section 365 apply correspondingly during the hearing.

### Section 419 49

(1) The court may stay proceedings if:

1) a legal issue the determination of which will affect the outcome of the case is being heard by a court or an administrative authority; or
2) there are other special reasons.

### Section 420 50

(1) A third party may intervene as a party in the hearing of the application for an injunction or order with regard to the question of whether the injunction or order will conflict with the rights of such third party. Intervention takes place by submitting a notice of intervention to the court.

(2) A third party having a legal interest in the outcome of an action may join the proceedings in support of one of the parties. Subsections (2)-(4) of Section 252 apply correspondingly.

### Section 421 51

(1) The court decides on the payment of the costs involved in the decision of whether to grant an injunction or order. The decision of the court is made in accordance with the provisions of Chapter 30. If proceedings concerning the right which is allegedly being infringed

have already been commenced before a Danish court, the court may postpone its decision until the order on costs in the pending proceedings.

52

### Section 422

(1) To the extent necessary, the court will give guidance to any person who is not represented by counsel on his legal position.

(2) The court may grant free legal aid to a person who fulfils the financial conditions under Section 325 if the person is in need of legal representation.

(3) The court will give guidance on the legal effects of the decision to the person whom the injunction or order concerns, including that breach of the injunction or order may lead to criminal liability, see Section 430.

53

### Section 423

(1) If the court grants an injunction or order, the court may, if requested by the party applying for the injunction or order, decide at the same time to seize movable property if there are specific reasons to assume that it will be used to breach the injunction or order. If the court finds that the application for a seizure order should be heard separately, the court may transfer the issue for a separate hearing in the enforcement court in accordance with the provisions of Chapter 57.

(2) The seized property is stored at the party's expense by the court, or any person so authorised by the court.

(3) The court may make a seizure order subject to security being provided by the party for the costs mentioned in subsection (2). The seizure order may also be made subject to an increase in any security required by the court under Section 415.

(4) During the hearing of an application for a seizure order, Sections 491(3), 494(2), 495(2), 497 and 498 apply correspondingly.

54

### Section 424

(1) Assistance to maintain or enforce an injunction or order granted is provided by the enforcement court in accordance with the provisions of Chapter 57.

55

### Section 425

(1) If proceedings concerning the right which is allegedly being infringed have not already been commenced in a Danish or foreign court or before an arbitral tribunal, the party applying for an injunction or order must take or commence such proceedings within two weeks of the decision to grant the injunction or order becoming final. If the proceedings are commenced in a Danish court, the proceedings must be commenced in the court which heard the application for the injunction or order in the first instance or in the Maritime and Commercial Court under Section 225(2). Sections 225(3), 226 and 227 apply correspondingly.

(2) Subsection (1) applies correspondingly where an injunction or order has been avoided by security being provided.

(3) Subsections (1) and (2) can be derogated from by agreement between the parties. Such agreement may be concluded only after a final decision to grant an injunction or order has been rendered.

56

### Section 426

(1) An injunction or order applies until it is vacated under subsection (2) or (3) or ceases to have effect under subsection (4).

(2) An injunction or order may be vacated in whole or in part if:

1) the conditions for the court's decision to grant the injunction or order are no longer fulfilled;

2) the party having obtained the injunction or order unduly delays the matter; or
3) proceedings under Section 425 are not initiated or commenced in time or are withdrawn or dismissed.

(3) An injunction or order in a case where the case concerning the right which is allegedly being infringed is to be decided by a foreign court or by arbitration may be vacated when the decision in the case concerning the right which is allegedly being infringed is final.

(4) An injunction or order in a case where the case concerning the right which is allegedly being infringed is to be decided by a Danish court will cease to have effect where the injunction or order has not already been vacated under subsection (2), when judgment has been rendered in the case concerning the right which is allegedly being infringed and an appeal has not been initiated within the period allowed for appeal or an appeal which has been initiated in time has subsequently been withdrawn or where the judgment directs otherwise.

(5) An application to discharge an injunction or order must be submitted in writing to the court which heard the application for an injunction or order in the first instance.

(6) Before an injunction or order is vacated, the court must allow the party which applied for the injunction or order an opportunity to comment.

### Section 427 57

(1) The city court's decisions concerning injunctions or orders, including a decision to vacate injunctions or orders or a separate decision ordering the payment of legal costs in relation to the issue, are made by a court order, which can be appealed under the provisions of Chapter 53. An appeal will not have suspensive effect with regard to the decision of injunction or order.

(2) The Maritime and Commercial Court's decisions to grant injunctions or orders, including a decision to vacate injunctions or orders or a separate decision ordering the payment of legal costs in relation to the issue, are made by a court order, which may be appealed to the high court of the district in which the case should have been brought pursuant to the provisions of Chapter 22, if the case had not been brought before the Maritime and Commercial High Court. Chapter 53 applies correspondingly. An appeal will not have suspensive effect with regard to the decision of injunction or order.

### Section 428 58

(1) Any person having obtained an injunction or order on the basis of a right which is later held not to exist must pay damages to the opposing party for any loss and compensate the opposing party for the pain and suffering. The same applies where the injunction or order ceases to have effect or is vacated on account of subsequent circumstances if the right must be assumed not to have existed.

(2) If the rightsholder's right is later held to exist only to a lesser extent, the rightsholder must pay damages to the opposing party for the loss resulting from the injunction or order having been too broad in its scope.

(3) If the injunction or order is unlawful for other reasons, the rightsholder must pay damages to the opposing party for any loss and compensate the opposing party for the pain and suffering if the rightsholder should have refrained from applying for injunction or order.

(4) Claims under subsections (1)–(3) may be entered as counterclaims during the proceedings, if such proceedings are already pending in a Danish court, or in a separate action. Separate actions, which may not be brought until the injunction or order has been vacated or ceased to have effect, see Section 426, must be brought within three months of such discharge or cessation.

(5) Subsections (1)-(4) apply correspondingly where an injunction or order is avoided by provision of security, see Section 414(1).

(6) If an injunction or order is vacated in an appeal, the decision in the appeal may award the opposing party damages and compensation under subsections (1)–(3).

59 **Section 429**

(1) If the proceedings concerning the right which is allegedly being infringed are decided by a Danish court, the court will direct in its decision how seized movable property, including property seized by the enforcement court pursuant to Chapter 57, is to be treated. Such direction may also be given when an injunction or order is vacated under Section 426 or in the judgment in an action brought under Section 430. The decision may direct that the seized property is to be returned to the party whom the injunction or order concerns, surrendered to a rightsholder or confiscated. In the case of confiscation, the confiscated property may on request be used to cover any claim for damages to which the party having obtained the injunction or order is entitled.

60 **Section 430**

(1) Any person intentionally acting in breach of an injunction or order may be liable to a fine or imprisonment of up to four months and in that connection be ordered to pay damages. Proceedings under the first sentence must be brought by the party having obtained the injunction or order.

(2) Subsection (1) applies correspondingly to any person who intentionally aids the person whom an injunction or order concerns in breaching the injunction or order.

(3) The issue of imposition of penalty or compensation may be postponed until the proceedings concerning the right allegedly being infringed have been settled.

## 61 J. Extract from court decision

## *Pregabalin*[29]

### Grounds for the decision

*Krka*

The principal plea, under which Krka is enjoined from selling Pregabalin 'Krka' without 'ensuring' at the same time that the medicinal product is not distributed and/or dispensed for the treatment of the indication pain, is, according to its content, not sufficiently clear to be enforced by the enforcement court pursuant to Section 424 of the Administration of Justice Act (retsplejeloven) or to provide basis for punishment pursuant to Section 430 of the Administration of Justice Act. Therefore, the plea cannot form the basis for a preliminary injunction.

Krka has already carried out the acts referred to in the alternative plea. Accordingly, and as this order also imposes a preliminary injunction against the pharmacies, see below, it has not been proved that Krka's behaviour renders it necessary to grant a preliminary injunction, see Section 413(2) of the Administration of Justice Act.

The injunction pleas are therefore dismissed.

*The pharmacies*

The pharmacies are self-employed persons who do not exercise public authority, also not when they dispense prescriptions. Section 411(1) of the Administration of Justice Act therefore does not prevent an injunction against the pharmacies.

Pfizer is holder of a valid patent, DK/EP 0 934 061 T6, which is a so-called 'second medical use' patent with a 'swiss type' claim. The patent-in-suit concerns a new use of the already

[29] Maritime and Commercial High Court of 25 June 2015, case A-6-15: *Pfizer v Krka and the Association of Danish Pharmacies.*

known substance pregabalin, which is sold by Pfizer in Denmark as the medicinal product Lyrica. The patent-in-suit covers according to claim 1 the use of pregabalin for the manufacturing of a medicinal product for the treatment of pain.

Krka legally manufactures and markets Pregabalin 'Krka' in Denmark for the treatment of epilepsy and generalised anxiety disorder. Pregabalin 'Krka' and Pfizer's Lyrica have been determined to be substitutable by the Danish Health Authority, and when Pregabalin 'Krka' is the cheaper of the two medicinal products, the pharmacies must, pursuant to the substitution rules, dispense Pregabalin 'Krka' if the doctors have prescribed Lyrica, including when the medicinal product is prescribed for the treatment of the indication pain. The question is whether this dispensing infringes Pfizer's right under the patent-in-suit.

The Danish Patent and Trademark Office concluded the following in a memo of 26 January 2015, which was prepared at the request of the Danish Health Authority:

'When medicinal products are listed as substitutable, and pharmacies therefore are obligated to dispense the cheapest of the two preparations, this will immediately lead to a patent infringement if generics are sold/placed on the market for use for the second indication (use) protected by a patent.'

Taking into account that the patent-in-suit is a 'second medical use' patent with a 'swiss type' claim, which aims to protect the use of an already known active ingredient for the treatment of a new indication, the Court acknowledges that the pharmacies' supply of Pregabalin 'Krka' with a label stating that the medicinal product is intended for the patented treatment of the indication pain constitutes an infringement of the patent-in-suit, see Section 3(1)(3) of the Patents Act.

Neither Section 61 of the Medicines Act, the preparatory works thereto nor the Prescription Order contain a clear and limited exception to the exclusive rights granted to Pfizer as the patent holder under the Patent Act, such that other parties without Pfizer's consent may commercially exploit the patent-in-suit. This is also supported by Annex 1C, Articles 28 and 30 of the TRIPS Agreement. Accordingly, the Court finds it rendered probable that Pfizer has the right sought to be protected by the injunction plea, see Section 413(1) of the Administration of Justice Act, and that the behaviour of the pharmacies renders it necessary to grant an injunction, see Section 413(2) of the Administration of Justice Act.

The Court assumes, on the basis of the evidence, that it would be possible for the pharmacies to comply with an injunction. The practical difficulties for the pharmacies in this regard are not found to be manifestly disproportionate to Pfizer's interest in the grant of a preliminary injunction

On this background, and as the other conditions for an injunction are fulfilled, Pfizer's principal pleas (A) in plea 2 is granted.

As the case appears before the Court, the Court concludes that granting a preliminary injunction is of no significance to the pharmacies' income, and for this reason alone, there is no basis for making an injunction conditional on the provision of security, which the pharmacies have not claimed.

*Costs of the proceedings*

Following the outcome of the case, Pfizer must pay legal costs to Krka. Considering the value, nature, conduct and scope of the case, including the fact that the oral hearing lasted three days, the amount is determined to a total of DKK 500,000, including VAT, which includes coverage of Krka's reasonable expenses for legal assistance.

With reference to the special and fundamental nature of the case, the Court finds that none of the other parties to the case, including the intervener, must pay legal costs to any other party.

# § 4
# France

## A. Executive summary

1 Depending on their formulation as *product* or *use* claims, second medical use claims have different legal effects under the French Intellectual Property Code (*Code de la propriété intellectuelle* – IPC).

2 French courts have considered both *use* claims accepted under the EPC 1973 (Swiss-type claims such as: 'use of compound X for the manufacture of a medicament to treat disease Y') and *product* claims allowed under the European Patent Convention (EPC) 2000 ('compound X for use in the treatment of disease Y'). To date, however, French courts have only considered skinny labelling in relation to Swiss-type claims. In such circumstances, the question is whether a generic company infringes the patent owner's right by commercialising a product for which certain uses are free of rights while other uses are still under patent protection.

3 Even 50 years after second therapeutic application claims were endorsed by the EPC, there remains little French case law in this area to draw upon. However, in several cases, French courts have appeared to be convinced by the efficiency of skinny labelling practices to reject patent owners' claims of infringement. In addition, under the French legal framework, patent owners attempting to obtain damages on the basis of an infringing medical prescription practice are faced with the difficulty of proving this practice.

## B. Scope of protection and interpretation of second medical use claims

4 Current French law makes no formal distinction between second medical use claims and other types of claims. As to their validity, the French Supreme Court held in a case of 6 December 2017 ('Finasteride') that where a claim relates to a subsequent therapeutic application of a substance or composition, the achievement of that therapeutic effect is a functional technical feature of the claim.[1] In consequence, while it is not necessary to demonstrate clinically the new therapeutic effect in order to satisfy the requirement of sufficiency of disclosure, the patent application must nevertheless directly and unambiguously reflect the claimed therapeutic application, so that a person skilled in the art could understand that the results reflect that therapeutic application.

5 In terms of infringement, the provisions applicable under French law apply equally to all types of claims, including second medical use claims. Members of the French Parliament discussed the scope of protection of second medical use claims at the parliamentary session preceding the adoption of Law of 4 August 2008 on the Modernisation of the

[1] Supreme Court, Commercial Section, 6 December 2017, n°15-19.726; → mn. 49.

Economy[2]. This law amended the last two paragraphs of Article L.611-11 IPC to adopt a word-for-word transposition of Article 54 EPC into national law. In response to concerns relating to the impact of second use claims protection on the generic products market, the French Ministry of Economy made clear that 'the introduction of the second therapeutic innovation has no effect on the deadline for putting generic drugs on the market in *their first indication*, nor their inscription in the repertoire of generic medicines, enabling the use for the substitution right by the pharmacist for this indication'[3] (emphasis added).

Following adoption, Article L.611-11 IPC (→ mn. 40) allows patent owners to assert new medical uses claims, but prevents them from extending the patent protection to the product or its uses that have already entered the public domain and consequently constitute prior art. 6

# C. Direct and indirect infringement of second medical use claims

## I. Direct patent infringement

### 1. Direct infringement of second medical use claims in general

As French law does not distinguish between second medical use claims and other claims, the same requirements apply to both. Article L.613-3 IPC enumerates different situations constitutive of direct infringement (emphasis added): 7

> The following shall be prohibited, but for consent of the patent owner:
>
> a) Manufacturing, offering, putting on the market, using, importing, exporting, transhipping or holding for the aforementioned purposes the *product* which is the subject of the patent;
>
> b) Using the *process* which is the subject matter of the patent or, when the third party knows, or where the circumstances make it obvious that the use of the process is prohibited without the consent of the patent owner, offering the process for use on French territory;
>
> c) Offering, putting on the market, using, importing, exporting, transhipping or holding for the aforementioned purposes the *product* obtained directly by the *process* which is the subject matter of the patent.

French courts have ruled on several cases involving direct infringement of Swiss-type claims, defining the contours of the application of Article L.613-3 IPC to such claims. 8

In a preliminary injunction proceeding on 26 October 2015 (the 'First Pregabalin Case'), the Paris Trial Court stated that Article L.613-3(a) IPC does not apply to Swiss-type claims since this provision relates to *product* claims, whereas Swiss-type claims refer to a *use*[4]. In another preliminary injunction case decision of the Paris Trial Court on 15 March 2016, the Court found that Swiss-type claims imply that a product is already known and therefore cannot be protected as such[5]. 9

---

[2] Parliamentary session of 10 July 2008 preceding the adoption of Law n°2008-776 of 4 August 2008 (extract).

[3] Transcript of the session dated 10 July 2008 at the Senate, Christine Lagarde, p. 4540: 'I wish to avoid any ambiguity, which can be a source of concern regarding the development of generic drugs, by stating that the introduction of the second therapeutic innovation has no effect on the deadline for putting generic drugs on the market in its first indication, nor its inscription in the repertoire of generic medicines, enabling the use for the substitution right by the pharmacist for this indication.'

[4] Paris Trial Court, 26 October 2015; → mn. 51.

[5] Paris Trial Court, 15 March 2016; → mn. 52.

10 In both cases, the Paris Trial Court held that Article L.613-3(b) IPC, which relates to *process* inventions, can only be enforced against a manufacturer using a patented process. A generic company that uses a product to manufacture a drug therefore only commits an act of infringement in so far as the manufactured drug corresponds to the product's new therapeutic application. In addition, if a plaintiff files a complaint against a defendant who distributes or imports a pharmaceutical product that they did not manufacture, a claim on the ground of Article L.613-3(b) IPC cannot prevail.

11 Article L.613-3(c) IPC is better suited to characterising the infringement of Swiss-type claims. For example, in a case on the merits of 25 March 1998[6], the Paris Trial Court had to decide on the infringement of a Swiss-type claim relating to the use of a compound (AZT) in the manufacture of a pharmaceutical product for the treatment of human retroviral infections. The Court held that under Article L.613-3(c) IPC, the defendants committed acts of infringement by offering to supply a medicinal product for the treatment of human retroviral infections in the manufacture of which the AZT was used. The Paris Trial Court adopted similar reasoning in the First Pregabaline Case of 26 October 2015, but ultimately rejected the infringement claim because the plaintiff could not demonstrate that the generic company was offering the product obtained directly by a process still under patent protection.[7]

12 In any event, Article L.613-5(c) IPC provides for an important exemption to direct infringement. Under this provision, the preparation and delivery to the patient of a drug based on second medical use claims by a pharmacist does not constitute infringement as long as the pharmacist performs these acts specifically for the patient, by unit and on medical prescription.

## 2. Direct infringement of second medical use claims by equivalence of means

13 The doctrine of infringement by equivalence of means relates to a type of direct infringement. It arises when the disputed product is technically different from the product subject to the second medical use, but both are deemed equivalent.

14 In a decision dated 11 September 2020 ('Pemetrexed'), the Paris Trial Court held that the defendant infringed a second medical use claim by equivalence of means.[8] This case is a rare illustration of the situation where, because of specific circumstances, the second medical use claim encompasses the whole product, and not only a separate new use.

15 The facts were as follows: the plaintiff obtained a patent on the pemetrexed molecule as an active pharmaceutical ingredient. However, due to its severe side effects on patients, the patent owner could not exploit the product. Later, the patent owner found that administering pemetrexed in combination with vitamin B12 would mitigate the side effects. They therefore applied for and obtained a patent on a new use of pemetrexed to manufacture a pharmaceutical product for the treatment of cancer to be administered in combination with vitamin B12.

16 After the first patent entered the public domain, but while the second patent was still under patent protection, a generic company started to commercialise pemetrexed, though in a different form than the one provided for in the second patent. The generic company contended that they were entitled to do so since the first patent had already lapsed. The patent owner claimed that since pemetrexed's only therapeutic indication was its adminis-

[6] Paris Trial Court, 25 March 1998; → mn. 50.
[7] Paris Trial Court, 26 October 2015; → mn. 51.
[8] Paris Trial Court, 11 September 2020 (on the merits); → mn. 54.

tration in combination with vitamin B12 in the treatment of cancer, the generic company necessarily infringed the second patent covering such combination.

This case is significant with regard to the practice of skinny labelling because even though the generic company did not mention the administration with vitamin B12 in the Therapeutic Indications section of their pemetrexed's SmPC, the administration of pemetrexed in combination with vitamin B12 still had to figure in the Posology and Precaution for Use sections. This means that a proper skinny label was not possible in that case: the defendant could not completely carve out the use of pemetrexed in combination with vitamin B12 from the SmPC. The court found for the patent owner, and held that the fact that the generic company used a different form of pemetrexed was irrelevant since, because of the vitamin B12 mention in the Posology and Precautions for Use sections, the generic company had in fact reproduced the combination of the second patent. **17**

## II. Indirect patent infringement

Just as Article L.613-3 IPC prohibits direct infringement, Article L.613-4 IPC applies to indirect infringement of second medical use claims and provides (emphasis added): **18**

1. It shall also be prohibited, but for consent of the patent's owner, to supply or offer to supply, on French territory, to a person other than those entitled to exploit the patented invention, the *means of implementation*, on that territory, of that *invention* relating to an essential element of the latter, where the third party knows or where the circumstances make it obvious that the *said means* are suitable and intended for such implementation.
2. Paragraph 1 shall not apply where the means of implementation are *staple commercial goods*, except where the third party *induces the person to whom they supply these goods to commit acts prohibited under Article L.613-3.*
3. Persons carrying out the acts referred to in items (a), (b) and (c) of Article L.613-5 shall not be deemed persons entitled to work the invention within the meaning of paragraph 1.

Case law on this provision applying to second medical use claims is limited. However, the few cases involving new uses of products which were already patented for uses no longer under patent protection show that the judges took skinny labelling into account. This will be further discussed below. **19**

It is already worth noting that under Article L.613-4(2) IPC, there is no contributory indirect if the means supplied are staple commercial goods (→ mn. 43). This supports the view that if a product is no longer under patent protection, the supply of this product without mention of a second medical use claim still covered by a patent in force may not constitute an act of infringement. **20**

# D. Infringement of second medical use claims and skinny label products

## I. Significance of skinny labelling in the assessment of second medical use claims' infringement

In two cases where French courts had to assess direct and indirect infringement, the courts appeared convinced by the defendant's practice of skinny labelling the medical uses still under patent protection. **21**

22 In the First Pregabalin Case[9], the Paris Trial Court had to decide whether a company commercialising a product (pregabalin) indicated for a new medical use claim (formulated as a Swiss-type claim) infringed the rights of the patent owner. The patent indicated the use of pregabalin for the manufacture of a medicament to treat three different disorders: epilepsy, general anxiety, and neuropathic pains. The patent protection had lapsed for the first two use claims, relating to the treatment of epilepsy and general anxiety disorder, whereas the third was still under protection, as a new medical use claim. The patent owner turned to the French emergency jurisdiction to obtain a preliminary injunction against a generic company that started commercialising pregabalin products. The patent owner argued that this commercialisation constituted infringement acts of the third medical use claim still under patent protection. The generic company replied that there was no infringement for several reasons. First, they took care to carve out the new third medical use (use of pregabalin in the treatment of neuropathic pains) from their marketing authorisation (even though in France, neither an application for a marketing authorisation nor its issuance constitute infringement acts[10]). Second, the leaflet only mentioned the first two medical uses. Third, the company circulated an information notice to healthcare professionals (physicians and pharmacists) and to wholesalers indicating that the generic product should not be prescribed for neuropathic pains.

23 In response to the *direct* infringement claim, the Court held that the obligations imposed on a generic company in order to commercialise the product had been complied with, and therefore no infringement could be characterised on this basis. To reject the infringement claim, the Court took into account the fact that the leaflet only mentioned the two indications (epilepsy and GAD) for which the generic company had obtained marketing authorisations. Moreover, the Court had regard to the letter of information sent to healthcare professionals indicating that the generic drug should not be prescribed for neuropathic pains.

24 The Court also rejected the plaintiff's *indirect* infringement claim. First, the Court held that on the basis of the debates and the fact that Swiss-type claims were at stake, Article L.613-4(1) IPC did not apply.[11] The reasoning behind this finding is unclear. Indeed, the Court only held that the defendant did not allow any third party to exploit the protected process in France, without providing any deeper explanation. Rather, the Court focused on Article L.613-4(2) IPC.[12] The Court stated that since drugs are goods that are commonly found in the market, in order to demonstrate indirect infringement, the plaintiff would have had to show that the generic company *induced* the purchasers of their products (namely: physicians and pharmacists) to commit infringing acts within the meaning of Article L.613-3(c)[13]. From there, the Court considered several factors to conclude that the generic company did not commit acts of inducement. First, the Court observed that, consistent with the parliamentary debates cited above (→ mn. 5), the French legislative framework relating to prescription and substitution of generic

---

[9] Paris Trial Court, 26 October 2015; → mn. 51.

[10] Article L.5121-10 Public Health Code; → mn. 48.

[11] Article L.613-4 IPC: 1. It shall also be prohibited, but for consent by the owner of the patent, to supply or offer to supply, on French territory, to a person other than those entitled to exploit the patented invention, the *means of implementation*, on that territory, of that *invention* relating to an essential element of the latter, where the third party knows or where the circumstances make it obvious that the *said means* are suitable and intended for such implementation. (emphasis added).

[12] Article L.613-4 IPC: 2. Paragraph 1 shall not apply where the means of implementation are staple commercial articles, *except where the third party induces the person supplied to commit acts prohibited by Article L613-3.* (emphasis added).

[13] By offering, putting on the market or using the product obtained directly by a process which is the subject matter of the patent or importing or stocking for such purposes.

drugs for reference medicinal products could not be regarded as automatically leading to the infringement of the patent owner's rights. The Court stated that it was not the generic company's responsibility to notify health authorities of the new medical use claimed by the patent owner. Therefore, the failure to do so had no consequences. Third, the Court held that the fact that the generic company published its market share in an advertisement could not be considered as an act of infringement nor as inducement of healthcare professionals to substitute the generic product with the reference medicinal product, including for the new medical use. Second, Court concluded that the defendant adequately informed physicians and pharmacists of the limited therapeutic indications associated with their product. Furthermore, the defendant agreed during the hearing to release additional information to healthcare professionals, as demanded by the plaintiff company and at their own expense. The Court thus found that the generic company did not induce healthcare professionals to prescribe their product for the new medical use claim still under patent protection.

The Court reached the same conclusion in a preliminary injunction case decided on 2 December 2016 also involving the pregabalin and the same plaintiff but filed against different generic companies ('Second Pregabalin Case').[14] This case diverges slightly from the earlier case as the Court did not find that Article L.613-4(1) IPC (relating to *indirect* infringement) could not apply to Swiss-type claims. On the contrary, the Court found that the defendant could have been held liable for infringement on that ground, had they supplied or offered to supply the means of implementation of the invention on French territory. However, in that case, the defendant was importing a drug that had already been manufactured in a foreign country. Apart from this slight divergence, the Court followed the same reasoning as in the First Pregabalin Case of 26 October 2015 to reject the claim based on Article L.613-4(2) IPC. The Court confirmed that drugs qualify as staple commercial goods and that generic companies had not induced infringement as they carved out the protected indication from both the SmPC and the leaflet, and voluntarily and faithfully notified healthcare professionals of the limited uses for which their product should be distributed to patients. Further, this second case involving the pregabalin molecule introduced a new element to consider when assessing the infringement of a second therapeutic indication. The Court took into account the negligence of the plaintiff who did not sufficiently warn the authorities of the existence of their rights to reject their argument that the French regulatory framework necessarily lead to infringement of second medical use claims. The patentee's attitude was criticised in so far as they only addressed a small number of letters to the three French health authorities. 25

## II. Significance of a prescribing practice in the assessment of second medical use claims' infringement

Both the First and the Second Pregabalin Cases raise the question of the generic companies' liability for infringing prescribing practices. 26

In the First Pregabalin Case, the patent owner claimed that the generic company's advertisement in a specialised newspaper mentioning a market share of 144 million euro for the litigated product demonstrated acts of direct infringement. They sustained that this market share exceeded the sales of the pregabalin for the authorised uses only and showed that healthcare professionals were prescribing the generic product in the treatment of neuropathic pains (the use under patent protection), and not only in the 27

[14] Paris Trial Court, 2 December 2016; → mn. 53.

treatment of epilepsy and GAD (the uses free of rights). However, the Court rejected this argument and held that while the generic drugs' market share is generally high, it does not necessarily mean that they commit infringement acts nor prove that healthcare professionals prescribe generic products for the patented indication. This decision is significant because it tends to show that a generic company can hardly be held liable for an infringing prescribing practice.

28 In the Second Pregabalin Case, the Court reached the same conclusion and held that the information sent to healthcare professionals would be enough to prevent the latter from prescribing the generic product in relation to the third medical use claim. The Court also reasoned that physicians can indicate to pharmacists that the prescribed drug is not substitutable, and that generic products are eligible for reimbursement by the French social security system only if they are prescribed for the authorised uses.

29 In practice, it should be noted that, pursuant to Article L.5121-1-2 Public Health Code, practitioners prescribing a medication should, except in specific cases, list the name of the molecule and not of a branded pharmaceutical product. This could lead to the prescription of a generic product for a use under patent protection and for which no marketing authorisation has been delivered. However, in France, the medical secrecy rule set out in Article L.1110-4 Public Health Code makes it difficult for the patent holder to establish an infringing prescription practice.[15] Moreover, even if a physician prescribes a drug using its branded name, the pharmacist does not know the indication for which this drug is prescribed. Thus, the pharmacist could easily substitute a generic product to the branded one even though the generic product is not indicated for use in the treatment that is at stake.[16]

30 Accordingly, even though the volume of sales of a generic product may be demonstrated, the specific indication for which this product is used cannot be known with certainty. This may explain why the courts seem reluctant to admit the existence of acts of infringement on the basis of an infringing prescription practice.

## E. Infringement of second medical use claims and biosimilar products

31 There is no difference between generic and biosimilar products in terms of legal requirements to characterise infringement. However, unlike generic drugs, the pharmacist cannot *automatically* substitute a biosimilar for the medicine prescribed by the doctor. In principle, only the physician authorised to prescribe the reference product may prescribe the corresponding biosimilar drug. Pursuant to Article L.5125-23-2 Public Health Code, the pharmacist can substitute a prescribed product with a biosimilar product on their own initiative only under restrictive conditions and if they do so they must inform the patient and the prescriber of the substitution.[17]

---

[15] → mn. 46.

[16] Article L.5125-23 Public Health Code indicates: I. The pharmacist may only dispense a medicine or product other than the one prescribed, or with a common name different from the common name prescribed with the express prior agreement of the prescriber, except in an emergency and in the interest of the patient. II. *If the prescription under a common name can be fulfilled by dispensing a medicinal product included in a generic or hybrid group mentioned in Article L. 5121-1, the pharmacist must dispense a medicinal product belonging to this group* in accordance with the provisions of Article L.162-16 of the Social Security Code. (…)' (emphasis added).

[17] Article L.5125-23-2 Public Health Code, the pharmacist *may* dispense, (emphasis added). In particular, the biosimilar product must be included in a list set up by a joint order of the ministers responsible

Since the conditions for substitution of a biosimilar product to a reference product are more restrictive than for generic products, infringement of biosimilar products is likely to be even harder to prove. 32

## F. Strategies and considerations

The above-mentioned cases show that the French courts place particular emphasis on the defendant's behaviour in assessing whether they infringe a second medical use claim or not. This includes but is not limited to skinny labelling the SmPC and the leaflet of their products. 33

The First and Second Pregabalin Cases suggest that mere compliance with regulatory obligations by the generic company, i.e. the deletion of protected indications in the SmPC and the leaflet, is necessary but not sufficient to rule out the risk of being convicted of infringement. Generic companies should also send letters to healthcare professionals informing them that the products they supply should not be prescribed outside the indications listed in the SmPC and the leaflet. More generally, generic companies should be able to prove that they have acted proactively to avoid committing acts of infringement. For example, in the Second Pregabalin Case, one of the generic companies had sent information letters to more than 170,000 healthcare professionals. Another had sent more than 145,000 letters and almost 100,000 emails stating that the generic version of pregabalin had been granted with a marketing authorisation only for the therapeutic indications in the public domain. The generic companies urged physicians not to prescribe and dispense the generic product for the treatment of neuropathic pain still under patent protection. Further, in case of doubt about the use that a patient would make of the product, the letters invited healthcare professionals to prescribe the originator's version of the pregabalin product. In consequence, before launching a product covered by a new medical use claim under patent protection, companies should consider sending similar letters to inform the relevant healthcare professionals (the ones most likely to prescribe the product) that the generic product should not be prescribed outside its listed indications. For the same reasons, replies to tenders of hospitals should be carefully drafted and include a disclaimer that the indications do not comprise the patented use. 34

However, it is up to the patent owners – who receive notification when a generic company applies for a marketing authorisation for the same product – to alert the French health authorities with a view to obtaining institutional information from official bodies.

## G. Legal remedies

The types of remedies available to the patent owner depend on the type of proceedings initiated. 35

In the context of preliminary injunction proceedings, a court which finds that there are imminent or actual acts of infringement may typically grant preliminary injunction orders to prevent commercialisation, or to recall and/or destroy infringing products. 36

for heath an social security issued after consultation with the National Agency of Medicine and Health Products Safety (ANSM).

However, these remedies are not suitable for second medical use claims, since certain uses of a product are free of rights while other uses remain protected by a patent. Other measures should then be considered. During the First Pregabalin Case, the defendant voluntarily undertook to address additional information at their own expense to health-care professionals. A court could order a defendant to comply with this type of measure if they refused to execute it voluntarily.

37 On the other hand, if the trial is on the merits, pursuant to Article L.615-1 IPC, the infringing acts will be dealt with in a civil lawsuit. As a reminder, in terms of entitlement to damages, second medical use claims are not considered any different from other types of claims. Accordingly, the burden of proof of the extent of infringing sales lies with the patent owner. However, according to Article L.615-2 IPC the courts may assist the plaintiff in proving the alleged facts by ordering the other party to provide documents that may relate to the acts of infringement – provided there is no legitimate impediment, such as medical secrecy which constitutes a limit in assessing the amount of damages that should be awarded to the plaintiff.

38 If a patent owner is entitled to damages, Article L.615-7 IPC sets out the different types of prejudices to be considered (→ mn. 45). In most cases, the calculation of the amount of damages takes into account the negative economic consequences of the infringement for the patent owner (i.e. loss incurred and profit lost). In cases where this ground of prejudice is not sufficient to make the infringement financially detrimental for the infringer, the court may also have regard to the profits made by the infringer (i.e. savings in intellectual, material and promotional investments that the infringer has made from committing the infringement). Alternatively, the injured party may request a lump sum as damages. This sum shall be greater than the amount of the royalties or fees that would have been due if the infringer had requested authorisation to use the right infringed. In both cases, the injured party is entitled to moral damages if they can demonstrate that the infringement acts harmed their credit or reputation.

39 In any event, the specific nature of second medical use claims may raise practical issues as to the calculation of the amount of damages awarded. The difficulty mainly lies in the assessment of the negative economic consequences of the infringement and, where applicable, the profits made by the infringer. Indeed, it is not possible to calculate the amount of damages on the basis of the totality of the generic company's market share (assuming this can be determined through reliable data) as it would encompass sales for authorised uses that do not constitute infringement. Not only this would not be accurate, but it would also likely characterise an abuse of their patent rights by the patent owner. Not to mention that this would contradict the objectives of Article L.611-11 IPC and the guarantees discussed in the parliamentary debates mentioned above (→ mn. 5).

## H. Statutory provisions

### I. Intellectual Property Code

40

#### Article L.611-11

An invention is novel if it is not included in the state of the art.

The state of the art consists of everything that has been made available to the public before the filing date of the patent application by written or oral description, use or any other means.

The contents of French patent applications and European or international patent applications designating France, as filed, which have a filing date prior to that mentioned in the second paragraph of this Article and which have not been published until that date or a later date, are also be deemed to be included in the state of the art.

The second and third paragraphs do not exclude the patentability of a substance or composition included in the state of the art for the implementation of the methods referred to in Article L. 611-16, provided that its use for any of these methods is not included in the state of the art.

Nor do the second and third paragraphs exclude the patentability of a substance or composition referred to in the fourth paragraph for any specific use in any method referred to in Article L. 611-16, provided that such use is not included in the state of the art.

### Article L.611-16 41

Methods of surgical or therapeutic treatment of the human or animal body and diagnostic methods applied to the human or animal body are not patentable. This provision does not apply to products, in particular substances or compositions, for the implementation of one of these methods.

### Article L.613-3 42

In the absence of the consent of the proprietor of the patent, the following are prohibited:

a) manufacturing, offering, placing on the market, using, importing, exporting, transshipping, or holding for the aforementioned purposes the product which is the subject of the patent;
b) The use of a process covered by the patent or, where the third party knows or where circumstances make it obvious that the use of the process is prohibited without the consent of the patent owner, the offer of its use on French territory;
c) offering, placing on the market, using, importing, exporting, transshipping or holding for the aforementioned purposes the product obtained directly by the process covered by the patent.

### Article L.613-4 43

1. It is also prohibited, in the absence of the consent of the proprietor of the patent, to deliver or offer to deliver, on French territory, to a person other than those entitled to exploit the patented invention, the means of implementing, on that territory, that invention relating to an essential element thereof, where the third party knows or where the circumstances make it obvious that those means are suitable and intended for such implementation.
2. The provisions of paragraph 1 shall not apply where the means of implementation are products that are commonly available on the market, unless the third party induces the person to whom they deliver to commit acts prohibited by Article L. 613-3.3. Those who perform the acts referred to in a, b and c of Article L. 613-5 are not considered to be persons entitled to exploit the invention, within the meaning of 1.

### Article L.613-5 44

The rights conferred by the patent do not extend to:

[…]

c) the preparation of medicinal products extemporaneously and per unit in pharmacies, on medical prescription, nor to acts concerning medicinal products so prepared;

[…]

45 **Article L.615-7**

In fixing damages, the court takes into consideration distinctly:

1° The negative economic consequences of the infringement, including lost profits and losses suffered by the injured party;
2° The moral damage caused to the injured party;
3° And the profits made by the infringer, including the savings on intellectual, material and advertising investments that the infringer has made as a result of the infringement.

However, the court may, as an alternative and at the request of the injured party, award a lump sum compensation for damages. This sum is greater than the amount of the royalties or fees that would have been owed if the infringer had requested authorisation to use the right infringed. This sum is not exclusive of compensation for moral damage caused to the injured party.

## II. Public Health Code

46 **Article L.1110-4**

I.-Any person under the care of a healthcare professional, an establishment or service, a professional or organisation involved in prevention or care whose conditions of practice or activities are governed by the present code, the military health service, a professional in the medico-social or social sector or a social and medico-social establishment or service mentioned in I of Article L. 312-1 of the social action and family code is entitled to respect for their private life and the confidentiality of information concerning them.

Except in cases of derogation expressly provided for by law, this confidentiality covers all information concerning the person that comes to the knowledge of the professional, any member of the staff of these establishments, services or organisations and any other person who, by virtue of their activities, has connections with these establishments or organisations. It is binding on all professionals working in the healthcare system.

47 **Article L.5121-1-2**

The prescription of a pharmaceutical product mentions its active ingredients, designated by their international common name recommended by the World Health Organization or, in the absence of such a name, their name in the pharmacopoeia. In the absence of such names, the usual common name is given. It may also mention the invented name of the pharmaceutical product.

48 **Article L.5121-10**

For a generic or hybrid medicinal product defined in 5° of Article L. 5121-1, the marketing authorisation may be granted before the expiry of the intellectual property rights attached to the reference medicinal product concerned. The applicant for this authorisation informs the holder of these rights at the same time as the application is submitted.

# J. Extracts from court decisions

## I. Supreme Court, Commercial Section, 6 December 2017 49

Where a claim relates to a subsequent therapeutic application of a substance or composition, the achievement of that therapeutic effect is a functional technical feature of the claim, so that while, in order to satisfy the requirement of sufficiency of description, it is not necessary to demonstrate clinically that therapeutic effect, the patent application must nevertheless directly and unambiguously reflect the claimed therapeutic application, so that the person skilled in the art understands, on the basis of commonly accepted models, that the results reflect that therapeutic application.

## II. Paris Trial Court, 25 March 1998 50

### I – DECISION

Claim 1 covers: 3'-azido-3'-deoxythymidine for use in the treatment or prophylaxis of a human retroviral infection.

Claim 12 relates to the use of 3'-azido-3'-deoxythymidine in the manufacture of a medicament for the treatment or prophylaxis of a human retroviral infection;

Claim 13 covers the use of 3'-azido-3'-deoxythymidine in the manufacture of a medicament for the treatment or prophylaxis of AIDS;

Claims 14 to 21 are worded as follows:

C 14: – use of 3'-azido-3'-deoxytymidine in the manufacture of a medicinal product for the treatment or prophylaxis of progressive generalised lymphodenopathy.

C 15: – use of 3'-azido-3'-deoxythymidine in the manufacture of a medicinal product for the treatment or prophylaxis of manifestations accompanying AIDS.

C 16: – use of 3'-azido-3'-deoxythymidine according to claim 12, wherein the infection is an HTLV-III infection.

C 17: – use of 3'-azido-3'-deoxythymidine according to claim 12, wherein the infection is a human T-cell lymphotropic virus infection.

C 18: – use of 3'-azido-3'-deoxythymidine according to claim 12 in which the infection is an HTLV-I infection.

C 19: – use of 3'-azido-3'-deoxythymidine according to claim 12, wherein the infection is HTLV-I-positive leukaemia or lymphoma.

C 20: – use of 3'-azido-3'deoxythymidine in the manufacture of a medicinal product for the treatment of HTLV-III carriers.

C 21: – use of 3'-azido-3'deoxythymidine in the manufacture of a medicinal product for the treatment of a human subject with anti-HTLV-III antibodies.

### II – INFRINGEMENT

The documents seized show that :

- APOTEX France sent letters to various public bodies offering to supply a pharmaceutical product called APO ZIDOVUDINE, the active ingredient of which is AZT, for the treatment of AIDS,
- on 10 September 1992, it applied for marketing authorisation for this product, which was refused by letter dated 2 February 1993; it lodged an appeal against this refusal on 20 April 1993,
- that APOTEX Inc sent a letter to the Director of the Central Hospital Pharmacy on 28 October 1992 in which it offered to supply APO ZIDOVUDINE, and undertook to com-

pensate it and Assistance Publique for the costs and damages it might have to bear if it were sued for this;

By proposing to use AZT for the treatment or prophylaxis of human retroviral infections, and more particularly AIDS, APOTEX France and APOTEX Inc have infringed claims 1 and 2 of patent no. 291 633, as well as claims 3 to 10;

They have also infringed claims 12 and 13 of this patent, as well as claims 14 to 21;

Importing and offering for sale a product obtained by a patented process constitutes an infringement under Article L 613-3 of the French Intellectual Property Code;

It follows that by offering to supply a medicinal product for the treatment or prophylaxis of human retroviral infections, and more particularly AIDS, in the manufacture of which AZT is used, the defendants have committed acts of infringement of those claims, even if that medicinal product is not manufactured on French territory;

## 51 III. Paris Trial Court, 26 October 2015 (PI proceeding)

### The dispute

Patent EP 061 was filed on July 16, 1997 by WARNERLAMBERT, under the priority of U.S. Patent Application No. 19960022337 P filed by Mr. Singh. It will expire on 16 July 2017.

This is a second therapeutic application patent, as it discloses the use of pregabalin, already known for treating convulsions, in the preparation of a pharmaceutical composition for treating pain.

The EP061 patent includes 14 claims covering many types of pain, the first 3 of which are worded as follows:

Claim 1: 'Use of (S)-3-(aminomethyl)-5-methylhexanoic acid or a pharmaceutically acceptable salt thereof for the preparation of a pharmaceutical composition for treating pain.'

Claim 2: 'Use according to claim 1 wherein the pain is inflammatory pain.'

Claim 3: 'Use according to claim 1 wherein the pain is neuropathic pain.'

Only claims 1 and 3 are invoked by LAMBERT WARNER.

LYRICA® was first authorised by the European Commission on 6 July 2004 (centralised marketing authorisation no. EU/1/04/279). The marketing authorisation for LYRICA® was initially granted for two indications, namely the treatment of peripheral neuropathic pain in adults, and in combination in adults for the treatment of partial epileptic seizures with or without secondary generalisation.

The marketing authorisation was subsequently extended twice, for the treatment of generalised anxiety disorder (also known as GAD) in adults on 20 March 2006, and for the treatment of central neuropathic pain on 7 September 2006.

To date, the Summary of Product Characteristics for LYRICA® contains the following three indications:

*Neuropathic pain (which is an indication that has been included on the list of reimbursable specialities): 'Lyrica is indicated for the treatment of peripheral and central neuropathic pain in adults';

*Epilepsy (which is also an indication that has been included on the list of reimbursable specialities): 'Lyrica is indicated in combination in adults for the treatment of partial epileptic seizures with or without secondary generalisation'; and

*Generalised anxiety disorder (not included on the list of reimbursable specialities): 'Lyrica is indicated for the treatment of Generalised Anxiety Disorder (GAD) in adults'.

LYRICA® is available as 25 mg, 50 mg, 75 mg, 100 mg, 150 mg, 200 mg, 225 mg and 300 mg capsules, and as a 20 mg/ml oral solution.

These three indications for pregabalin are included in the same 'global' MA for LYRICA®, as each new indication must be authorised as a 'variation' of its MA in accordance with EC Regulation 1234/2008.

Variations are classified according to their importance and the need for an in-depth examination of the application: the addition of a new therapeutic indication is classified as a 'type II major variation', which requires an in-depth examination by the competent authorities, in this case the European Medicines Agency (EMA).

The starting point for the periods of regulatory data protection, which prohibits the filing of generic marketing authorisation applications, and market exclusivity, which prohibits the marketing of generic specialities, is the date of issue of the initial marketing authorisation in the EU.

LAMBERT WARNER estimates that prescriptions of LYRICA® for the treatment of pain represented approximately 88 % of total sales of LYRICA® (including 72 % for the treatment of neuropathic pain) in 2014. Prescriptions of LYRICA® for the treatment of epilepsy and generalised anxiety disorder each accounted for approximately 1 % of LYRICA® sales.

SANDOZ GmbH obtained two marketing authorisations on 19 June 2015, one for a generic of the reference product LYRICA® under the name PREGABALINE SANDOZ, which includes the three indications of LYRICA®, and the other – in dispute – for a product under the name PREGABALINE SANDOZ GMBH for which the indication for the treatment of neuropathic pain has been removed (or 'carved out') from the SPC.

The company therefore only has authorisation to market PREGABALINE SANDOZ GMBH for the treatment of epilepsy and generalised anxiety disorder.

It only mentioned these two indications in the package insert.

PREGABALINE SANDOZ GMBH has been included on the list of specialities reimbursable by social security and approved for use by local authorities and various public services, and was issued with a price and reimbursement rate by order dated 27 August 2015.

Numerous exchanges of letters took place between Pfizer and SANDOZ between April 2015 and October 2015.

LAMBERT WARNER noted that the speciality PREGABALINE SANDOZ GMBH was being marketed in pharmacies in France by having two purchase reports drawn up on 8 October 2015; a prescription for pregabalin having been presented to a pharmacist and the pharmacist dispensing a box of PREGABALINE SANDOZ GMBH.

They also found that the Sandoz companies had published advertisements in the daily newspaper Le Quotidien du pharmacien stating that the potential market they intended to reach was 144 million euro.

LAMBERT WARNER, PFIZER Limited and PFIZER PFE France took the view that this reference to a market that exceeds the market share available to generics, i.e. excluding prescriptions for the treatment of neuropathic pain, brought an interlocutory injunction against SANDOZ GmbH and SANDOZ France, SANDOZ GmbH and SANDOZ France to obtain measures to inform healthcare professionals, measures to limit sales of PREGABALINE SANDOZ GMBH and publication measures.

**DECISION**
**[L613-3 French Intellectual Property Code]**

It is common ground that the conditions set out in paragraphs a and b of Article L 613-3 of the French Intellectual Property Code do not apply in this case, since paragraph a) relates to a product claim and paragraph b) relates to a process invention that can only be asserted against the manufacturer.

With regard to subparagraph c, it must be ascertained whether the offer for sale by SANDOZ FRANCE of the product obtained by the process and manufactured outside French territory and the import by SANDOZ GmbH contravene the conditions set out in subparagraph b.

It is not disputed that SANDOZ GmbH has obtained a 'carved out' marketing authorisation issued by the European Medicines Agency for the marketing of the two indications epilepsy and GAD, with the exception of the treatment of neuropathic pain, that SANDOZ France has been marketing PREGABALINE SANDOZ GMBH in France since the end of September 2015, that it has sent the following information letter to doctors (more than 30,000) and pharmacists (more than 19,000) by means of an e-mailing:

'sandoz will shortly be marketing the generic drug Prégabaline Sandoz GmbH ® following the granting of its marketing authorisation.

Pregabalin Sandoz GmbH ® is indicated for:

- in adults in combination in the treatment of partial epileptic seizures with or without secondary generalisation.
- in the treatment of Generalised Anxiety Disorder (GAD) in adults

Please note that Pregabalin Sandoz GmbH ® is not indicated for the treatment of neuropathic pain as this indication is protected by a patent held by Warner-Lambert Company LLC (part of the Pfizer Group).

For patent protection reasons, Sandoz has decided not to market a pregabalin-based product for the treatment of neuropathic pain. This indication is therefore not included in the Summary of Product Characteristics of Sandoz GmbH® pregabalin.

Sandoz will inform you if this position changes.

The products concerned are:

Pregabalin Sandoz GmbH ® 25 mg, capsule
Pregabalin Sandoz GmbH ® 50 mg, capsule
Pregabalin Sandoz GmbH ® 75 mg, capsule
Pregabalin Sandoz GmbH ® 100 mg, capsule
Pregabalin Sandoz GmbH ® 150 mg, capsule
Pregabalin Sandoz GmbH ® 200 mg, capsule
Pregabalin Sandoz GmbH ® 300 mg, capsule

These specialities have generic marketing authorisations for Lyrica ® 25 mg, 50 mg, 75 mg, 100 mg, 150 mg, 200 mg, 300 mg, capsule, dated 19/06/2015, pending inclusion in the ANSM register of generic specialities.

In order not to infringe the rights of the patentee, it is your responsibility to prescribe / dispense Pregabalin Sandoz GmbH ® only for indications that do not include the treatment of neuropathic pain'.

Nor is it disputed by the plaintiff companies that the marketing of PREGABALINE SANDOZ GMBH for the only two indications mentioned in its package leaflet does not infringe its patent EP061.

With regard to the share of the market that is 'free in law', it should be remembered that while freedom of trade is the rule, the market for medicinal products is governed by regulatory provisions that authorise marketing, and that Pfizer companies are entitled to a monopoly conferred on them by their EP061 patent.

Neither party disputes the data provided by the IMS.

These data come from data collected from 1,190 general practitioners (400) and specialists (790 not including geriatricians); the doctors on the panel code their prescriptions according to the International Classification of Diseases.

However, the documents regularly put forward for discussion by Pfizer are the result of work carried out by their departments, which transform the raw IMS data assigned a specific code for each disease treated with pregabalin into data assigned to the various indications of the global marketing authorisation.

The IMS document defines the following level 1 categories: epilepsy, other illnesses, pain, psychiatry and unspecified, followed by a more detailed table of pain sub-categories.

In this case, it is not possible to understand how the ICD categories have been integrated into the general category of neuropathic pain, with certain indications relating to pain appearing to be inappropriate.

So the figure of 86 % to 88 % for the level 1 category applies to pain in general.

However, while Pfizer only has marketing authorisation for the treatment of neuropathic pain, the present action is based on the EP061 patent and in particular on claims 1 and 3, which relate to the preparation of pregabalin for the preparation of a pharmaceutical composition for treating pain and more specifically for treating neuropathic pain.

PFIZER Limited's patent EP061 covers the treatment of pain in a broad sense, even though only a marketing authorisation has been issued for the treatment of neuropathic pain, so that PREGABALINE SANDOZ GMBH cannot be marketed to treat any pain whatsoever.

If Lyrica has been used by practitioners to treat a wider range of pain conditions, and therefore off-label, this is not a criterion to be taken into account in a debate on counterfeiting (this is a public health debate).

Consequently, the reference market to be taken into account with regard to the opposing claims is indeed the overall pain treatment market, i.e. 86 % of the pregabalin market, without ignoring at this stage the SANDOZ companies' contestation that the patent cannot protect all pain treatments.

According to GERS data, the value of which is not disputed, PREGABALINE SANDOZ GMBH achieved a market share of 16.96 % in week 41, i.e. 3 weeks after its launch, i.e. 2.96 % above the authorised market share.

As a result, doctors and pharmacists prescribed and dispensed PREGABALINE SANDOZ GMBH in excess of the market share reserved for treatments other than pain treatment, and therefore for an unauthorised indication.

However, in order to assess whether SANDOZ FRANCE can be accused of infringement, it is necessary to verify whether it has complied with its obligations, since it has marketing authorisation for two indications not protected by a patent.

In fact, only an offer for sale or marketing and, for SANDOZ GmbH and SANDOZ FRANCE, an import of PREGABALIN SANDOZ GMBH manufactured by SANDOZ (LEK) in Slovenia, infringing claims 1 and 3 of patent EP061 can constitute an act of infringement in accordance with the provisions of Article L 613-3 c) cited above.

As stated above, the obligations imposed on a generic company that markets a medicinal product for which it has obtained marketing authorisation only for indications that have fallen within the public domain, while the molecule is still protected for another speciality, in this case the treatment of pain, in a very broad sense by a patent, in this case patent EP061, were complied with, since the package leaflet only mentions the two indications (epilepsy and GAD) for which SANDOZ GmbH obtained its marketing authorisation, and an information letter was sent to doctors and pharmacists.

The plaintiff companies criticise SANDOZ for not having asked the French health authorities to publish a press release on their website or for doctors and pharmacists to alert them to the fact that PREGABALINE SANDOZ GMBH cannot be prescribed or dispensed for neuropathic pain or pain in general.

However, although they provide the debate with the information disseminated in other European countries on health authority websites or in information letters sent to healthcare professionals, they do not provide any information on the process that led to the publication of such information letters and, in particular, whether they were put online or sent following a positive approach by the SANDOZ companies or whether the health authorities did so of their own accord or at the express request of the Pfizer companies.

In the present case, it has not been demonstrated that the Sandoz companies are in a position to ask the ANSM to distribute such a message to doctors and pharmacists, but that it is up to the Pfizer companies, having been notified of the Sandoz companies' marketing authorisation applications, to alert the French health authorities with a view to obtaining the distribution of institutional information.

[...]

It can thus be seen that SANDOZ only marketed the indications for which it had received marketing authorisation, included a package leaflet referring only to the two indications of epilepsy and GAD, and provided extensive information to doctors and pharmacists at the same time as the launch of PREGABALINE SANDOZ GMBH by means of an email sent at the beginning of October.

As regards the messages to be sent to the health authorities, it appears that the Pfizer companies did so to alert them to their rights and the need to protect them, so that there was no point in the SANDOZ companies themselves sending a letter.

It should also be noted that the SANDOZ companies have agreed to send a more explicit message to doctors and pharmacists in towns and hospitals detailing how to prescribe or dispense PREGABALINE SANDOZ GMBH so as not to infringe the patentee's rights.

In this respect, there is no act of infringement on the basis of direct infringement.

With regard to the advertisement that appeared in the daily newspaper Le pharmacien on 1er October 2015, it appears that it was approved by the ANSM; that the authorised indications are specified at the top of the page, and that at the bottom of the page it is stated that PREGABALINE SANDOZ GMBH have generic marketing authorisations for Lyrica.

The terms of this message are not disputed by Pfizer, which criticises SANDOZ FRANCE, the advertiser of this advertisement, for mentioning in the insert 'potential: € 144 million', which represents the entire pregabalin market and which would mean that it intends to market pregabalin for the treatment of pain.

As Sandoz France rightly points out, infringement cannot be assessed subjectively but only objectively, especially as the Intellectual Property Code does not recognise the concept of good faith in this area.

The fact that SANDOZ FRANCE added the reference to a 'potential market of 144 million euro', which is in fact the value of this market, does not imply that the company infringed claims 1 and 3 of the EP061 patent, since in this advertisement the indications for treatment are clearly mentioned.

This indication of market value is of no interest to pharmacists who are not necessarily aware of the size of the pregabalin market and does not constitute an incentive to substitute PREGABALIN.

SANDOZ GMBH to Lyrica, which in any event is not a relevant criterion for assessing an infringement that the Pfizer companies call direct, i.e. by marketing or offering for sale their generic within the meaning of Article L 613-3 of the French Intellectual Property Code.

While the advertisement as it stands, announcing the arrival of this new generic, can certainly be analysed as an offer for sale to the pharmacists to whom the advertisement is addressed, the fact remains that it does not contain any element enabling it to be considered that this offer for sale relates to the treatment of pain by PREGABALINE SANDOZ GMBH.

While SANDOZ certainly intends to conquer a large share of the pregabalin market, a market valued at 144 million euros and for which each point is worth 1.5 million euros, and also the share allocated to the treatment of pain, there is no objective evidence to suggest that it intends to do so before the patent expires or is cancelled, since cancellation proceedings initiated by MYLAN are pending on the merits before the 2nd section of the 3rd chamber of the Paris Tribunal de Grande Instance.

As a result, infringement on the basis of Article L 613-3 c) of the French Intellectual Property Code has not been plausibly established, especially since throughout the period before the product was placed on the market and after the hearing, Sandoz agreed to send a message to healthcare professionals and to send an even more explicit message, drafted in agreement with Pfizer, to the same professionals and to others in towns and hospitals.

**On contributory infringement**
**[L613-4 of the French Intellectual Property Code]**

In the present case, although the Pfizer companies do not specify which paragraph of Article L613-4 of the Intellectual Property Code they are referring to, it is clear from a reading of their pleadings and the debates and from the Swiss form of the claims that the provisions of paragraph 1 are inapplicable because the Sandoz companies in no way give a third party the means to exploit the protected process in France.

Only paragraph 2 of this Article could possibly be applicable, as medicines are products that are commonly found on the market.

It must therefore be shown that the Sandoz companies have encouraged third parties, in this case doctors and pharmacists, to supply the product resulting from the process and the provisions of Article L 613-3 c) of the French Intellectual Property Code.

It cannot be argued that the French regulatory system relating to prescription and substitution automatically leads to infringement of the patentee's rights in the event that a second therapeutic use of a given molecule is protected when the previous indications for the same molecule are in the public domain.

Indeed, the present dispute concerns precisely the assessment of the measures to be taken to prevent possible infringement in this case and in the present case taken by the SANDOZ companies to prevent any infringement of the Pfizer companies' patent EP061 as a result of the authorised marketing of PREGABALINE SANDOZ GMBH for the unprotected indications of that speciality.

It has already been stated above that it was not up to SANDOZ FRANCE to approach the health authorities directly to alert them to PFIZER Limited's rights to pregabalin for the treatment of neuropathic pain, but that this could only be done by the company holding the rights, that, moreover, this is the reason why the holders of the rights are notified of the granting of marketing authorisation to a generic company, so that the request that the information letter be sent to the medical and pharmacy associations is devoid of purpose.

As regards the alleged manoeuvres of SANDOZ FRANCE in mentioning the potential market in the first advertisement, it has also been stated above that they constituted neither an act of infringement nor an incitement to pharmacists to substitute PREGABALINE SANDOZ GMBH for Lyrica, so that the request to amend the advertisement published in the Quotidien du Pharmacien is also without object.

Lastly, it was found that the generic's share of the market cannot currently exceed 14%; that the measures taken by Sandoz to prevent counterfeit prescriptions and deliveries had been taken with healthcare professionals likely to commit counterfeiting, i.e. doctors and pharmacists; that these measures were not sufficient, since the market share acquired by Sandoz was less than the market share of the generic.

SANDOZ FRANCE exceeded the share available to generic drugs; that on the date of the summons the parties were still in discussion and that during the hearing the SANDOZ companies proposed and agreed to remedy these shortcomings by paying for new mailings of the corrected information message to an even wider professional audience, including by using a database suggested by the plaintiff companies; that they even voluntarily complied with part of the demands contained in the plaintiffs' summons.

Although the SANDOZ companies agreed to provide more precise information to the healthcare professionals concerned, they did so while denying that they were committing any act of infringement.

And in the present case, at no time has it been shown that the SANDOZ companies had encouraged doctors or pharmacists to sell PREGABALINE SANDOZ GMBH for the treatment of pain; on the contrary, the conduct of the latter establishes that they informed doctors and pharmacists and that they agreed during the hearing to supplement this information at their own expense and following the advice of the plaintiff companies.

Consequently, the claims of PFIZER Limited, WARNER LAMBERT and PFIZER PFE France will be rejected, as the facts of infringement by supply of means were not established in a plausible manner.

## 52 IV. Paris Trial Court, 15 March 2016 (PI proceeding)

### Likelihood of infringement

Claim 1 reads: 'Use of an anti-PD-1 antibody that inhibits the PD-1 immunosuppressive signal for the preparation of a medicament for the treatment of cancer.'

This Swiss form implies that the product is already known, but not for this use, and that it is only protected for the manufacture of the medicinal product in its new use.

Schering-Plough, which is located in France, is designated as the manufacturer of the drug and does not demonstrate that any other company manufactures the product.

Consequently, it is difficult to dispute that the likelihood of infringement of claim 1 is established against Schering-Plough. This is not the case for MSD France, which is merely a distributor.

## 53 V. Paris Trial Court, 2 December 2016 (PI proceeding)

### Infringement by supply of means [L613-4 French Intellectual Property Code]

Infringement cannot be assessed subjectively but only objectively, especially as the Intellectual Property Code does not recognise the concept of good faith in this area.

In this case, claims 1 and 3 of the EP 061 patent are drafted in the only authorised Swiss form due to the prohibition on patenting a molecule already known under the EPC 1973.

These claims are considered to be process claims and not product claims, so that the only claim that could be made against the defendant companies would be the delivery of the means enabling the process to be implemented on French territory.

However, it must be noted that the defendant companies import the medicine already prepared, i.e. manufactured, and do not deliver the means of preparing the medicine. Moreover, they are not accused of manufacturing the medicine on French territory.

Contrary to the alleged case law of the EPO, which has no jurisdiction to rule on acts of infringement that are not submitted to it, since its sole task is to grant or not to grant patents, any act of marketing a medicinal product protected by a second therapeutic use patent cannot be analysed as a supply of means.

Even supposing that supplying pharmacists, the only persons authorised in France to dispense medicinal products [since even websites selling medicinal products online must be backed by a pharmacy J], could constitute the supply of the means enabling pregabalin to be used for the treatment of neuropathic pain, it is established for all the defendant companies that they limited their marketing authorisation to the two unprotected indications, clearly indicated this on the package leaflet and, last but not least, provided extensive information to pharmacists and prescribing doctors, who were informed each time a new generic pregabalin was marketed of the precautions to be taken when dispensing this speciality.

And if the pharmacist were to be considered as a third party, it would appear that he knows perfectly well from the information provided, because he is a particularly well-informed professional third party, that he can only dispense generic pregabalin for the two indications of epilepsy and generalised anxiety disorder.

It is even easy to assume that, given the flood of information about these generics, pharmacists are taking precautionary measures by dispensing only the originator, so as not to be accused of counterfeiting.

Consequently, the conditions of Article L 613-4 1 are not met.

With regard to the second paragraph, it can be accepted that a medicine is an everyday consumer product, even if its distribution is regulated because certain molecules are dangerous, particularly in combination with others.

On the other hand, it cannot be accepted that the defendant companies encouraged pharmacists or doctors to substitute generic pregabalin for the originator when prescribing it for neuropathic pain, even though they spontaneously and honestly informed pharmacists that their marketing authorisation was limited to the two indications of epilepsy and GAD and that this broad information had a significant cost for them.

The conditions of Article L 615-4 2° are not met either, without it being necessary to define the market share 'reserved' for generic pregabalin, a percentage that would in fact require discussions on the merits as to its calculation, the panel of doctors used and the references made to capsules or boxes.

In addition, the Intellectual Property Code does not define collective infringement, and it is up to the person alleging infringement to establish the acts that he or she attributes to each of the parties in causing not the damage but the act of infringement.

This means that several people may be involved in the same act of counterfeiting if they are involved at different stages in carrying out the counterfeit.

In the case of direct counterfeiting, the manufacturer, then the wholesaler, then the person who stores the products and therefore holds them, and then the seller may all contribute to the same counterfeit through positive acts.

In the present case, the defendant companies holding the marketing authorisation each imported the drug pregabalin for which they had obtained marketing authorisation and a price.

SANOFI FRANCE, for example, imports the product manufactured outside France and distributes it through its own network of sales representatives and wholesalers.

BIOGARAN manufactures its own pregabalin, for which it has received marketing authorisation, and does not obtain supplies from SANOFI FRANCE. It also sells its pregabalin through its own network.

It cannot therefore be claimed, nor has it been demonstrated, that these companies, which are competitors in the pharmaceutical market, are involved in the same act of counterfeiting.

And it is not enough to assert the same patent against different independent economic players in order to establish that they have all contributed to the same damage.

Moreover, in this case, no joint and several judgment could be handed down.

In the present case, WARNER LAMBERT, after having defined a market share for generic pregabalin based on figures collected by GERS, sometimes in capsule units and sometimes in box units without taking into account the different dosages, and based on a panel of doctors whose composition is questionable to say the least, is content to assert that all sales of generic pregabalin constitute an infringement, which does indeed constitute an accusation of collective infringement.

Nor can it be argued that the French regulatory provisions on prescription and substitution automatically lead to infringement of the patentee's rights where a second therapeutic use of a proprietary molecule is protected even though the previous indications for the same molecule are in the public domain.

WARNER LAMBERT has the means to notify the administrative authorities in accordance with the provisions of Article 51211-14-3 of the French Public Health Code, which states that: The company which markets a proprietary medicinal product shall contribute to the proper use of the latter by ensuring in particular that the product is prescribed in compliance with its marketing authorisation referred to in Article L.5121-8 and, where applicable, the temporary recommendations for use referred to in Article L.5121-12-1, its temporary authorisation for use referred to in Article L.5121-12, its registration referred to in articles L.5121-13 or L.5121-14-1, its authorisation referred to in Article L.5121-9-1 or its parallel import authorisation referred to in Article L.5121-17.

It will take all the information measures it deems appropriate for healthcare professionals covered by Part Four of this Code when it observes prescriptions that do not comply with the proper use of this medicinal product as defined in the first paragraph and will notify the Agence nationale de sécurité du médicament et des produits de santé without delay.

However, the documents submitted for discussion show that Pfizer, representing WARNER LAMBERT, confined itself to writing a few letters to the ANSM, the CESP and the HAS:

* PFIZER PFE France wrote to the ANSM on 27 July 201,5 expressing its concern about the forthcoming marketing of PREGABALINE SANDOZ GMBH alone and the risk it considers real of seeing this product prescribed and dispensed for the compound's protected indication; it recalled its rights and asked the ANSM to keep it informed of the actions it intended to take to prevent the supply of generics for the patented indication by setting out the measures taken in other countries; it referred in its letter to the letter of 12 June 2015 from SANDOZ FRANCE.

* PFIZER PFE France wrote to the COMITÉ ECONOMIQUE DES PRODUITS DE SANTÉ on 23 October 2014 to recall the rights it holds to patent EP061 in relation to the reference speciality marketed under the brand name LYRICA.

It produced the information letter of 16 July 2015 sent to it by that body stating that the laboratory SANDOZ before PFIZER Limited had requested an application for its speciality PREGABALINE SANDOZ GMBH and that the latter had confirmed that it was authorised to market it without infringing the company's rights :

* On 12 October 2015, PFIZER, PFE France wrote to the HAUTE AUTORITE DE LA SANTE and the COMITE ECONOMIQUE DES PRODUITS DE SANTÉ in similar terms to the letter of 27 July 2015 sent to the ANSM.

Pfizer France, representing Warner Lambert, wrote to the ANSM on 7 December 2015 and 15 January 2016, but did not contact the ANSM, the CESP or the HAS again when the other generic pregabalin drugs were placed on the market.

It did so with the ANSM only after a period of 6 months on 29 June 2016 and just before launching the summary proceedings in August 2016.

On 8 December 2015, it wrote to the HAS, which replied on 18 December 2015 that the information provided was sufficient in terms of existing texts.

It sent a letter to the CEPS, whose remit is to set drug prices, which replied on 3 November 2015 that it had no jurisdiction in this area.

All the letters sent to the HAS and the ANSM refer only to the dispute with the SANDOZ companies.

By letters dated 7 December 2015, it sent a copy of the interim injunction of 26 October 2015 to the Ordre national des médecins and the Ordre national des pharmaciens to obtain wider dissemination of the information provided by the SANDOZ companies; it sent further letters on 25 January and 4 April 2016 to the Ordre des pharmaciens, which replied that it considered the information already disseminated to be sufficient, and on 10 December 2015 and 3 February 2016 to the Ordre national des médecins, which indicated that it would put the matter on the agenda for a forthcoming meeting.

Similarly, while the possibility of substituting a generic drug for the originator is encouraged by law, it is nonetheless regulated and provides for the possibility for doctors to indicate that the drug prescribed is non-substitutable and for pharmacists, depending on the circumstances, not to substitute the generic drug for the originator drug.

Lastly, an indication not included in the repertory does not allow reimbursement, so pregabalin prescribed by a doctor for the protected indication is not reimbursable.

These provisions applied by medical professionals are sufficient to protect the indication protected by a patent.

If pregabalin is prescribed as an anti-epileptic treatment in combination with another epileptic treatment, the pharmacist will be able to substitute the generic for the originator.

If pregabalin is prescribed for GAD, a non-protected indication that is not reimbursable, the pharmacist will also be able to substitute the generic for the originator.

Finally, if pregabalin is prescribed on its own (without any other anti-epileptic treatment and without the words 'not reimbursable') or with the words 'not substitutable', the pharmacist will not be able to substitute the generic for the originator.

In case of doubt, the pharmacist is authorised to ask the patient a question to find out the reasons for the prescription and, if he fears breaching medical confidentiality, he may receive the patient in the confidential area that every pharmacy must have.

In this case, WARNER LAMBERT merely assumes that doctors are prescribing generic pregabalin to treat neuropathic pain when the use of pregabalin for this indication is still protected, and similarly assumes that pharmacists are not complying with the regulations in force and are dispensing generic pregabalin for the protected indication.

It does not provide any evidence that healthcare professionals are not complying with the legislation in force other than by asserting collective infringement, which is not provided for in the legislation and has not been established.

## VI. Paris Trial Court, 11 September 2020 54

### FACTS AND PROCEDURE

Eli Lilly and Company, an American pharmaceutical company founded in 1876, has developed a drug marketed under the brand name Alimta® for the treatment of two types of lung cancer (malignant pleural mesothelioma and non-small cell lung cancer). The active ingredient is a compound called pemetrexed, which belongs to the antifolate class of therapeutic agents against cancer.

Antifolates are used in the chemotherapy treatment of cancerous tumours to inhibit tumour growth by affecting the cells' ability to divide and by interfering with certain enzymes involved in cell replication, which are part of the folate metabolic pathway that accelerates tumour growth. However, antifolates do not distinguish between cancerous and healthy cells and affect both, causing serious side-effects for patients, including lethal ones. Although considered promising anti-cancer agents and the subject of research since the 1950s, few have been brought to market, due to their high toxicity and the difficulty of controlling it.

The active ingredient pemetrexed (an antifolate which is not at issue in these proceedings) was developed by Eli Lilly and was the subject of a patent application (EP 677) on 10 December 1990 as a component of the medicinal product Alimta®, but has been little exploited, given its severe undesirable effects.

On 15 June 2001, Eli Lilly filed a patent application, EP 508, under the US priorities of 30 June 2000, 27 September 2000 and 18 April 2001, granted on 18 April 2007, entitled 'composition comprising an antifolate and a methylmalonic acid reducing agent'. Patent EP 508 will expire on 15 June 2021. The patent relates to the combined administration of Alimta®/pemetrexed with vitamin B12 and, optionally, folic acid, to treat two types of lung cancer, making it possible to reduce the toxicity of the active ingredient while preserving its therapeutic efficacy.

It constitutes the first and only authorised therapeutic use. The patent was maintained as granted by the EPO on 27 December 2010, following opposition from TEVA.

To be administered, the drug is presented in acid or salt form (neutral pharmaceutical forms of the active part of a drug), composed of the active part of the compound pemetrexed or pemetrexed anion, combined with two sodium counterparts (cation) or 'pemetrexed disodium'.

Lilly France, a subsidiary of Eli Lilly, markets Alimta® in France.

Fresenius Kabi France markets the generic version of Alimta® in France under the name 'Pemetrexed Fresenius Kabi', presented in the form of a pemetrexed diacid (the sodium cations are replaced by hydrogen cations) for which Fresenius Kabi Oncology Plc obtained a marketing authorisation issued by the European Medicines Agency (EMA) on 22 July 2016.

Taking the view that this generic medicinal product infringed their rights, Eli Lilly and Lilly France brought proceedings before this court on 29 March 2017 against Fresenius Kabi France and Fresenius Kabi Groupe France for infringement of the French part of European patent EP 1 313 508, in addition to other measures.

## REASONS FOR THE DECISION

**III – On infringement**

**- direct counterfeiting by reproduction or equivalent**

Direct infringement presupposes the use of the essential means of the invention, i.e. those which are necessary and sufficient to ensure the primary function of the means invented, and is permitted when the essential similarities are reproduced notwithstanding secondary differences.

In the present case, given the scope of the patent, and whereas the formal modification during the grant procedure does not confer any essential character on the modified element, because it was not a condition for the grant of the patent, as stated above, the essential means of the invention consists of the combined application of the active principle pemetrexed, in whatever form, with vitamin B12 or its other derivatives, and possibly with folic acid or its other derivatives.

Frésenius' generic drug is composed of the same active ingredient pemetrexed, and its administration must be combined, as recommended in EP 508, with vitamin B12 and folic acid. It is therefore irrelevant that the allegedly infringing compound uses a diacid solution to enable it to be administered, since this does not provide any particular technical effect, it being understood that the formulator is capable of proposing a certain number of possible counter-ions, other than sodium, in the form of free acid or in the form of a certain number of well-known acceptable pharmaceutical salts. The selection of the salt form is therefore of no interest whatsoever, the only thing that counts being the therapeutic effect of the pemetrexed anion combined with the other substances. The lack of obviousness relied on by the defendants in using this particular salt, ranked 10th among frequently used salts, which is a criterion of validity of an invention and not of characterisation of infringement, or the fact that Frésenius has obtained patents (EP 768 and US9,421,207) on this form of salt, are irrelevant.

The variant involving the use of a different salt is totally secondary.

Pemetrexed Fresenius Kabi is administered according to the intended use of the invention, and is designed to treat the same cancerous conditions, with the same technical effect. It has been authorised as a generic of the reference drug.

Infringement by reproduction is characterised.

Once direct infringement by reproduction has been established, having regard to the scope of the patent as determined, there is no point in determining whether infringement by equivalence has occurred.

- infringement by supply of means

These claims are moot once direct infringement has been established.

# § 5
# Germany

## A. Executive summary

Starting in 2017, German courts began developing additional liability criteria with a view to closing a potential liability gap caused by the use of skinny labels. Even if there is no manifest arrangement present (i.e. the patented indication is *not mentioned in the Summary of Product Characteristics (SmPC))*, a generic company can be held liable for direct patent infringement if the following four criteria are met (→ mn. 12 et seq.): 1

1. The product is (objectively) suitable for the patented purpose.
2. The manufacturer/distributor takes advantage of circumstances which, in a manner similar to an active manifest arrangement, make it highly likely that the product being offered or marketed is / will be used for the specified therapeutic purpose.
3. There is sufficient and not only occasional use of the product according to the patent.
4. There is corresponding knowledge or at least disregard of such knowledge by the supplier acting in bad faith.

Although the German court decisions have so far dealt with generic products only, we assume that a biosimilar product (despite its differences) will presumably be treated in a similar manner. This all the more so since the German legislator has indicated its intention to align the statutory, regulatory provisions on generic and biosimilar products (→ mn. 26 et seq.). 2

## B. Scope of protection and interpretation of second medical use claims

In its *Pemetrexed* decision[1] of 14 June 2016, the Federal Court of Justice (*Bundesgerichtshof* – BGH) once again confirmed the equivalence of the aforementioned different claim formulations and stated that, irrespective of the wording of the patent claim, all three types of claims grant purpose-limited substance protection based on an inherent characteristic of the underlying substance (pursuant to § 3(4) Patent Act (*Patentgesetz*) and Article 54(5) of the European Patent Convention (EPC)). In 2020, the German Federal Patent Court (Bundespatentgericht – BPatG) has blocked more 'creative' interpretations of the law by reaffirming that that the exception in Article 54(4), (5) EPC applies exclusively to substances and mixtures of substances, not to other products.[2] 3

However, the Federal Court of Justice did not specify the liability hurdles for such purpose-limited substance protection. Treating all three claim formulations as being 4

---

[1] BGH GRUR 2016, 921 – *Pemetrexed*, → mn. 54: with this decision, the German Federal Court of Justice confirmed its decision '*Kollagenese I*' from February 2014 (GRUR 2014, 461).

[2] BPatG GRUR-RS 2020, 35046 – *Wundreinigungstuch*. Cf. Loth in: BeckOK PatR, 32nd edn. 15.4.2024, PatG § 14 mn. 305c.

equal inevitably has consequences for the scope of protection: Since all claims relating to a further medicinal indication must be regarded as purpose-limited product claims, § 9 No. 1 Patent Act applies to all three formulation types. According to § 9 No. 1 Patent Act, any third party is prohibited from offering and distributing the protected active substance for the protected therapeutic indication (→ mn. 44). Hence, direct infringement of a second medical use claim can only be deemed to occur if the offered (generic or biosimilar) product inherently serves the required purpose, i.e. the patented indication.

5 Following the above interpretation, the actual act of use of the invention protected by a second medical use patent is *no longer* limited to the final therapeutic use of the product since such interpretation would greatly narrow the scope of patent protection. Rather, the act of infringing use already occurs upon entry of the infringing product into the commercial sphere, i.e. the market launch, provided that that it takes place for the specific, patent-protected therapeutic purpose.

6 The German courts have thus shifted the goalposts as regards the scope of protection: the actual (prohibited) act of use already begins with the *preparation* and *delivery* of the active substance or product, and is not limited to the actually infringing therapeutic use.

## C. Direct and indirect infringement of second medical use claims

### I. Direct patent infringement

7 Pursuant to § 9 No. 1 Patent Act, the infringing acts encompassed by this provision include producing (i.e. making), offering, putting on the market or using a product, which is the subject matter of the patent. The required purpose limitation can be actively achieved by 'purposeful preparation' ('*sinnfälliges Herrichten*'). However, according to recent case law, it is also conceivable by other means, namely 'preparation-free liability' ('*herrichtungsfreie Haftung*'), i.e. liability in the absence of purposeful preparation. German case law is thus moving away from a narrow interpretation of the scope of protection conferred by second medical use claims.

#### 1. Purposeful preparation

8 For many years, German case law required a 'purposeful preparation' ('*sinnfälliges Herrichten*') when considering the existence of a direct patent infringement.[3] The purposeful preparation of an object for use presupposes that the object as such is prepared in such a way that it is *foreseeable* that it will lead to the protected use.[4] This particular approach to second medical use claims has a practical reason: the offending commercial activity usually does not take place during the actual use of the drug (for the protected indication), e.g. by the physician or patient, but rather beforehand, i.e. when offering the drug on the market.

9 In pharmaceutical cases, a purposeful preparation can occur by preparing the pharmaceutical composition prior to its distribution with the patented use specifically in mind,

---

[3] See e.g. BGH, GRUR 1983, 729 et seq. – *Hydropyridin*; Düsseldorf Higher Regional Court (OLG), GRUR-RS 2018, 2410, 34 et seq. – *Sedativum*.

[4] Kühnen, Handbuch der Patentverletzung, 16th edn, Cologne 2024, chapter A, mn. 512 et seq.

namely in such a way that the protected therapeutic use can be foreseen. This can for example be realised by a formulation, dosage, packaging or repackaging, labelling and/or SmPC of the medicinal product, which are specifically designed for the intended use, provided that the suitability for use in accordance with the patent is sufficiently clear for the relevant recipient.[5] It can thus be seen that for prescription-only medicinal products, the specific indications in the SmPC are of crucial importance.

In the absence of specific indications, e.g. in the SmPC, case law has for a long time denied a purposeful preparation and thus a direct patent infringement. 10

## 2. Preparation-free liability

Due to a perceived insufficient protection of the patentee, a rethink has taken place in the recent past as to whether it would be desirable to deviate from the concept of purposeful preparation (‘*herrichtungsfreie Haftung*’). In a series of important decisions starting in 2017, the Düsseldorf Higher Regional Court has begun to redefine and concretise the existing liability criteria and to extend them to a preparation-free liability in exceptional cases. 11

For the first time, new liability criteria were formulated in its *Östrogenblocker* decision of 5 May 2017.[6] The Court developed a further ground for *liability in the absence of a purposeful preparation*; namely, a sufficient extent of use (in the patented way) coupled with the infringer’s knowledge (or negligent ignorance) of such use (i.e. a subjective element). In this context, the Court formulated the new liability criteria as follows[7]: 12

1. The product must be (objectively) suitable for the patented purpose.
2. The distributor must take advantage of circumstances which, in a manner similar to an active purposeful preparation, make it highly likely that the product being offered or marketed is / will be used for the specified therapeutic purpose.
3. This requires a *sufficient and not only occasional use* of the drug according to the patent, as well as the *respective knowledge or at least disregard* of such knowledge by the supplier acting in bad faith.

In the opinion of the Court, a purposeful preparation is not required if external conditions, such as those commonly present in the case of cross-label use, already lead to a patented therapeutic use of the product.[8] The previously mentioned criteria were developed in relation to and are primarily fulfilled in the case of cross-label use, but also apply to off-label use and in-label use. Depending on the facts of the particular case, it can be justified and appropriate to hold the supplier of the medicinal product liable under patent law if they are aware of or should have been aware of the patent-infringing prescription and substitution practice. 13

The most recent decision of the Düsseldorf Higher Regional Court was rendered in proceedings on the merits concerning the active substance ‘Fulvestrant’.[9] The decision elaborates on the new liability criteria previously formulated in *Östrogenblocker*. The Court for the first time addressed the question of the exact extent to which prepara- 14

---

[5] Düsseldorf Higher Regional Court, GRUR 2017, 1107, mn. 39–40 – *Östrogenblocker*; → mn. 55.

[6] ibid.

[7] ibid. mn. 39.

[8] See Stief/Zorr, ‘Pregabalin and Fulvestrant – a comparison of German and English liability regimes for Swiss-type claims in light of current case law’, Journal of Intellectual Property Law & Practice 2019, 487 (488).

[9] GRUR 2019, 279.

tion-free usage must take place in order to give rise to liability. It also emphasised the *exceptional nature* of such (extended) liability of the distributor.[10]

**15** The Court pointed out that (again in the case of cross-label use) the mere use of a product exclusively or almost exclusively for the patented use would not necessarily be sufficient to establish liability. Rather, the decisive factor must be the certain knowledge, or disregard of knowledge, on the part of the alleged infringer that the marketing of the medicinal product will actually lead to patent infringing prescribing and use of the product.[11] The three basic requirements for a preparation-free liability as presently applied by the Düsseldorf Court can be summarised as follows:

1. The product must be *objectively suitable* for the patented purpose.
2. There is an *actual prescription practice according to the patented invention.*
3. There are circumstances that reveal *knowledge of that practice and exploitation* of such knowledge by the supplier.

**16** In the case of prescription-only medicines, the Court highlighted the importance of the prescription practice and the crucial role of the SmPC since the physician usually complies with the instructions therein.[12]

## II. Indirect patent infringement

**17** The indirect use of patents the subject of § 10 Patent Act is intended to give the owner of a property right the possibility to take legal action against a supplier even before the types of use enumerated in § 9 Patent Act take place. This is relevant in the field of use patents. However, in view of the liability criteria outlined above and the related significant expansion of direct protection for second medical use patents in the context of a preparation-free liability, indirect (or contributory) infringement is limited to only a few liability issues.

**18** First of all, an act that is regarded as direct infringement of the protected invention through purposeful preparation or due to preparation-free liability can no longer, as a matter of principle, constitute an indirect infringing act.

**19** Accordingly, indirect infringement can only be discerned in the corresponding (remaining) preliminary acts, i.e. (i) offering or delivering a neutral item that still has to be processed and subsequently distributed, or an active component from which the patented active ingredient is to be manufactured and then used in accordance with the patent, or (ii) the offering or delivery of a neutral active component, from which the protected product is to be manufactured if its intended therapeutic use is to be expected.[13]

**20** In addition, also the other requirements of § 10 Patent Act, namely, what is known as 'double domestic nexus' (offering / delivering the product in Germany for use in Germany) for use in Germany and several subjective elements (knowledge or obviousness from the circumstances that it is intended to use the means in an infringing manner) would need to be met.

---

[10] Düsseldorf Higher Regional Court, GRUR 2019, 279, mn. 42 – *Fulvestrant*; → mn. 56.
[11] ibid., mn. 44.
[12] ibid., mn. 45.
[13] Kühnen, Handbuch der Patentverletzung. 16th edn, Cologne 2024, chapter A, mn. 556 et seq.

# D. Infringement of second medical use claims and skinny label products

The above-discussed shift in thinking had a significant impact on the risk assessment of skinny label products. For many years, a skinny label product was a safe recourse to avoid (direct) patent infringement in Germany. However, since the *Östrogenblocker* decision in 2017, the newly implemented construct of a preparation-free liability changed the game. Now there is a risk of infringement if the patentee is in a position to prove (i) that the product is objectively suitable for the patented purpose, (ii) that there is an actual prescription practice in the market and (iii) circumstances that reveal knowledge of infringing practice and exploitation of such knowledge by the supplier. Hence, even if the infringing use is not indicated in the SmPC (or other marketing documents) there can still be a risk of infringement. Assessment of this risk will of course be on a case-by-case basis. Nevertheless, in its *Fulvestrant* decision, the Düsseldorf Higher Regional Court provided some helpful insights: 21

The Court held that the plaintiff did *not* show that the substance in dispute was used, or had been used to the required sufficient extent, on the basis of an actual infringing prescription practice. According to the plaintiff's submission, less than 7 % of all female cancer patients treated with Fulvestrant (the patent in suit covered the use of Fulvestrant for the treatment of a specific cancer after unsuccessful palliative pre-treatment with tamoxifen and an aromatase inhibitor) had previously been treated as claimed in the patent. The Court was of the opinion that given this *clearly single-digit figure*, the prescription practice leading to the use of the invention was intermittent and had by no means been employed to such an extent that it could not have remained hidden from the defendant.[14] In view of this clearly single-digit use, the Court rejected all claims.[15] 22

However, it is important to point out that the Presiding Judge, Dr. Kühnen, later clarified this statement. Dr. Kühnen emphasised that this statement was open to interpretation and would not mean that a single-digit use would be insufficient in each and every case to prove a preparation-free liability. Instead, such statement would have to be seen in the context of the *Fulvestrant* decision and in particular in view of the fact that the claimant was not able to prove any infringing use at the date of the oral hearing (0 %). Hence, whereas a single-digit use would of course lead to a higher threshold for the claimant, there is no guarantee that a single-digit use will necessarily exclude any liability in the future. 23

In *Fulvestrant*, the Düsseldorf Higher Regional Court made helpful and substantive findings on the required sufficient scope of use: 24

1. The probability of a finding that the alleged infringer could not have been unaware of the infringing use would increase with the number of patent-infringing uses that have demonstrably occurred.[16] Merely occasional cases of use could not generally give rise to preparation-free liability. 25

---

[14] Düsseldorf Higher Regional Court, GRUR 2019, 279, mn. 49 – *Fulvestrant*; → mn. 56.

[15] ibid.: '(…) Given this *clearly single-digit numerical value*, the prescription practice leading to the use of the invention occurs intermittently and by no means to such an extent that it could in no way have remained concealed from the defendant. (…) With regard to the claim for injunctive relief going forward, liability of the defendant is a fortiori out of the question because – based on the date of the oral hearing (9 January 2019) – *not a single case* of a Fulvestrant prescription in accordance with the patent after unsuccessful palliative pre-treatment with tamoxifen and an aromatase inhibitor can be proven for the last four years. Therefore, for the relevant point in time, a prescription practice leading to patent-protected use cannot be established at all.'

[16] ibid.

2. A clearly single-digit percentage of use in accordance with the patent is likely insufficient to establish a prescribing practice relevant to liability.
3. A further liability scenario could result from the particular outstanding benefits of the patented use compared to other therapeutic uses that would have to almost certainly require use of the medication in accordance with the patent.[17]
4. An injunction based on preparation-free liability could only be considered if a prescribing practice relevant to liability could still be established at the time of the oral hearing.

It is important to emphasise that even a single-digit infringing use of a product will certainly become critical once the generic or biosimilar company has received a warning letter or even a legal complaint from the patentee. From this date, the patentee will be in a very strong position to prove the factual knowledge of the alleged infringer that its product is used in an infringing manner.[18]

## E. Infringement of second medical use claims and biosimilar products

26 The construct of a 'preparation-free liability' has been developed on the basis of cases where the alleged infringing product was a *generic* product. However, it appears at least likely that this case law will also be applied to other situations in the context of second medical use patents, e.g. to biosimilar products. The potential infringement risk for generic and biosimilar products appears to be rather similar:

27 Since November 2020, accredited physicians have been able to find information on the 'adequate, expedient and economical' prescription of biotechnologically produced biological drugs (biologics) in the Drug Guideline of the German Federal Joint Committee ('G-BA') for medicinal products (§ 40a Guideline on Medicinal Products; → mn. 52). The regulations must be observed when prescribing reference drugs and their respective imitation drugs (biosimilars). In the interests of economical prescribing, physicians are encouraged at the beginning of a therapy to select a low-cost product based on the active ingredient in biotechnologically manufactured drugs. According to the G-BA, this is usually a biosimilar, if available. If patients are already being treated with a certain biologic, physicians should (according to G-BA guidelines) check whether they could be switched over to a less expensive biosimilar. A prerequisite for the switch in the case of an already ongoing drug therapy is, in particular, that there are no patient-specific medical reasons contraindicating the switch to a different, 'biosimilar' preparation.

28 On 19 November 2021, the G-BA adopted a new Annex VIIa[19] of the Medicinal Products Guideline with information on the approval status of biologics as reference drugs and their biosimilars. According to the G-BA, the new Annex VIIa is intended to be an

> [o]verview of active ingredients that are available on the market in the form of at least one biosimilar or in more than one original drug. The compilation serves as a basis for information and is not conclusive

---

[17] ibid.

[18] ibid.

[19] https://www.g-ba.de/downloads/40-268-7590/2021-06-08_AM-RL-VIIa_Stellungnahmeverfahren_Erstfassung_TrG.pdf, p. 4 et seqq.

In other words, it seeks to provide the physician with information on available biosimilar products whereby solely the market authorisation will be of relevance. As explicitly stated by the G-BA, when listing the drugs in Annex VIIa, there is no review of the extent to which the drugs are approved for the same indications.[20] Hence, the current version of Annex VIIa does not provide any information that certain therapeutic indications are in fact exempted according to the SmPC, which could constitute a quite relevant infringement risk. This risk appears all the greater since the G-BA adopted a partial 'automatic substitution approach' for biosimilar products in late 2023[21]. In the field of generics, it is longstanding practice that a prescribed drug will be replaced by the pharmacist if discount contracts have been concluded with the respective health insurance company. Hence, even if the physician describes the originator product, the pharmacist will replace this prescription automatically. Since the automatic substition of biosimilars will solely apply in particular cases and also provides for exemption provisions, the impact of this regulatory switch remains to be seen. **29**

Notwithstanding the above, there are nevertheless differences between generic and biosimilar products, which might justify a different legal approach regarding biosimilar products: A key difference could be the significantly higher development costs for biosimilars when compared with generics. In consequence, also the retail prices for biosimilar are often higher than those for generics. In such a scenario, there is usually no threat of price erosion for the originator products, which is an often-cited argument when justifying the broad protection conferred by the preparation-free liability. Hence, it remains to be seen how the German courts will handle the infringement of second medical use claims for biosimilar products. **30**

The *Fulvestrant* criteria have in the meantime also been applied and commented on in other decisions. For example, in its *Transportriemen* decision, the Mannheim Regional Court concurred with this case law of the Düsseldorf courts, at least in part, albeit imposing much stricter requirements than Düsseldorf.[22] According to the Court, the supplier must have positive knowledge of the fact that the supplied product – in the vast majority of deliveries – will be used by the customers in accordance with the patent and he must have chosen the concrete technical design of the product precisely for this purpose.[23] This shows a narrower interpretation of the required knowledge element on part of the supplier compared to how this has been interpreted by the Düsseldorf Higher Regional Court, which accepts purposeful preparation even when the supplier willfully disregarded positive knowledge of patent-infringing potential. Based on the decision by the Mannheim Regional Court, it is unclear whether grossly negligent ignorance could suffice for purposeful preparation on part of the supplier. It can be derived from the facts of the case that the broad knowledge criterion as set by the Düsseldorf Higher Regional Court cannot be dismissed altogether. The Mannheim Regional Court actually examined circumstances that reveal knowledge of that practice and exploitation of such knowledge by the supplier.[24] Since the circumstances in that case pointed at positive knowledge, the Mannheim Regional Court did not need to address the criterion of 'willful disregard of knowledge' as required by the Düsseldorf Higher Regional Court. However, as the wording of the decision shows, the Mannheim Regional Court certainly did not embrace **31**

---

[20] https://www.g-ba.de/downloads/83-691-877/AM-RL-VIIa-Biosimilars_2024-03-15.pdf.

[21] For more information, see: https://www.g-ba.de/beschluesse/6045/.

[22] Mannheim Regional Court (LG), BeckRS 2019, 27104; → mn. 57.

[23] ibid., mn. 49.

[24] Similarly to Düsseldorf Higher Regional Court, GRUR 2019, 279, mn. 44 – *Fulvestrant* and Düsseldorf Higher Regional Court, GRUR 2017, 1107, mn. 39 – *Östrogenblocker*; → mn. 56 and → mn. 55, respectively.

this broader knowledge element.[25] It also remains true that the preconditions for the preparation-free liability of suppliers for the infringement of second medical use patents have not yet been definitively established and will no doubt be the subject of future court decisions. The courts' findings so far also indicate that stringent requirements are placed on the patent owner with regard to proof of the infringing act and the risk of repetition.

32 Due to this shift in the recent decisions of the German courts, a skinny label of a generic (or biosimilar) product might not be sufficient to rule out the risk of a direct patent infringement. While the infringement risk will be lessened and the threshold for the patentee will of course be increased if the patented indication is not mentioned in the SmPC, the overall liability risk will depend on the specific circumstances of each case.

## F. Strategies and considerations

33 The options available to the generic or biosimilar manufacturer are limited insofar as they cannot dictate to the physician the future prescribing practice. However, there are other ways of communicating with the relevant addressees, e.g. through the pharmaceutical sales representatives, and increasingly, by means of digital consulting tools maintained by the pharmaceutical companies, from which the prescribing physicians can access information. However, since the preparation-free liability criteria are still quite fresh, there is an ongoing debate in Germany as to which preventive measures are permissible, in particular from a regulatory standpoint.

34 Active countermeasures (going beyond mere non-mentioning of the indication according to the patent) could be considered, such as a notice that the preparation must not be used for the therapy provided for in the patent ('do not use in …'). Quite apart from regulatory issues, such warnings always carry the risk that the warning could encourage the addressee to use the product in an infringing manner. In each case, the notice should be carefully worded since the Federal Institute for Drugs and Medical Devices (*Bundesinstitut für Arzneimittel und Medizinprodukte*) is usually very restrictive if the mentioning of an indication could create the impression that the product is in fact suitable for this very specific indication. In principle, there is an ongoing conflict between regulatory bodies and patent courts in Germany: whereas regulatory authorities usually conclude that a specific warning notice in a skinny label SmPC is neither necessary nor possible (and also prohibits any kind of notice in the package leaflet or on the product packaging), the German patent courts seem to require such kind of notifications.

35 Hence, whereas any explicit mention of the patented indication should of course be avoided (in the SmPC, the package leaflet, on the packaging, on the internet, in statements made by supplying company's representatives or pharmaceutical sales persons), the legitimacy of warning notices in the SmPC or the package leaflet (that advise against the use of the product for a specific patented indication) appear to be particularly critical from a regulatory perspective.

36 Against this background, it will be particularly important to (i) avoid any infringing prescription practice in advance (e.g. by 'priming' the sales representatives) and (ii) keep a close eye on the market (data acquisition) and react if an infringing prescription practice is observed. As regards the latter, particular caution is called for by the generic/biosim-

---

[25] Mannheim Regional Court, BeckRS 2019, 27104, mn. 49; → mn. 57. *'Dem folgt die Kammer jedenfalls insoweit, als'* translated as 'the Court agrees with this (the knowledge criterion as established by the Düsseldorf Higher Regional Court) at least in so far as'. Cf. GRUR-Prax 2019, 556, case note by Widera.

ilar manufacturer if the sales volumes of their product exceed the market share of the non-patented indication. Moreover, when bidding on discount contracts, the indications covered by the discount agreement are to be duly noted. As soon as a discount contract also includes the patent-infringing indication, the risk of infringement of course increases significantly.

## G. Legal remedies

German patent law provides the remedy of a *preliminary injunction* in patent infringement cases. Preliminary injunctions can make cease and desist orders, and in some cases accede to a claim for information and rendering of accounts. In Germany, it is even possible to apply to the district court for a preliminary injunction *ex parte* (i.e. without oral hearing). Premilinary injunction proceedings can thus be very fast in Germany (in some cases it is possible to get a PI title within 1–2 days). A court is only likely to grant a preliminary injunction if the validity of the patent, as well as the fact of infringement, is beyond doubt. In case of a preparation-free liability, the patentee must thus meet these criteria to the court's satisfaction. Since the application must also contain evidence of the (allegedly) infringing prescription practice in the market, an *ex parte* injunction seems mostly possible where the infringing prescription practice is obvious (e.g. rather high percentage share of the infringing use). As interim relief is granted only if urgency is a factor, applications must be brought quickly. Practice varies from court to court, but generally, applications should be made within four to six weeks of the claimant acquiring knowledge of the underlying facts. 37

To reduce the risk of an *ex parte* injunction, German law allows for the filing of 'protective letters' (*Schutzschriften*), i.e. a written statement to be filed by the generic or biosimilar company outlining why (i) no patent infringement has taken place, (ii) the validity of the patent is questionable and/or (iii) the case is not urgent. Protective letters can be filed with the Central Protective Letter Register (pursuant to § 945a Code of Civil Procedure; → mn. 51) and all German judges are obliged to check such registers before issuing an injunction. 38

A patentee is of course also entitled to file proceedings on the merits, which would then (in general) also allow for an additional claim for recall, claim for destruction and – most important – claim for damages. Proceedings on the merits usually take between 12–16 months. 39

The availability and scope of the claims for an injunction, for information and rendering of accounts, for recall, for destruction or for damages depend on the actual form of infringement (direct versus indirect infringement, as well as 'purposeful preparation' versus 'preparation-free liability'). 40

In its *Fulvestrant* decision, the Düsseldorf Higher Regional Court also commented on the legal consequences of a preparation-free liability and stated that it makes a very significant difference whether the medicinal product has been prepared in a purposeful way or not: For an injunction to be granted in the absence of purposeful preparation, the recurrence risk would need to be credibly demonstrated. In the case of a purposeful preparation, every single case of infringement, even an initial and single infringement, would generally hold the threat of future recurrence. However, if the distributor has not carried out any preparatory measures and if its liability is only tied to an actual prescribing practice corresponding to the protected mode of use, a cease and desist injunction will only be 41 considered if *at the time of the oral proceedings a liability-relevant prescribing routine can still be determined.*[26] In the case of a change in prescribing practice, an injunction would be ruled out, since in such a case the reference point is not the infringer's behaviour, but rather the prescribing practice as an *external condition*.

## H. Statutory provisions

### I. Patent Act

42 **§ 2a**

(1) Patents are not granted for

1. plant and animal varieties and essentially biological processes for the production of plants and animals and the plants and animals produced exclusively by such processes;
2. methods for the treatment of the human or animal body by surgery or therapy and diagnostic methods practised on the human or animal body. This does not apply to products, in particular to substances or compositions, for use in one of these methods.

(2) [1]Patents can be granted for inventions which concern

1. plants or animals if the technical feasibility of the invention is not confined to a particular plant or animal variety;
2. a microbiological or other technical process, or a product obtained by means of such a process other than a plant or animal variety.

[2]§ 1a(3) applies accordingly.

(3) For the purposes of this Act,

1. 'biological material' means any material containing genetic information and capable of reproducing itself or being reproduced in a biological system;
2. 'microbiological process' means any process involving or performed upon or resulting in microbiological material;
3. 'essentially biological process' means a process for the production of plants or animals consisting entirely of natural phenomena such as crossing or selection;
4. 'plant variety' means a variety as defined in Council Regulation (EC) No 2100/94 of 27 July 1994 on Community plant variety rights (OJ L 227, 1.1.1994, p. 1), as amended.

43 **§ 3**

(1) [1]An invention is deemed to be new if it does not form part of the state of the art. [2]The state of the art is held to comprise all knowledge made available to the public before the date governing the filing or priority date of the application by means of a written or oral description, by use or in any other way.

(2) [1]The content of the following patent applications having an earlier filing or priority date which were made available to the public on or after the date governing the filing or priority date of the later application is also deemed to be comprised in the state of the art:

1. national applications as filed with the German Patent and Trade Mark Office;
2. European applications as filed with the competent authority if the application seeks protection in the Federal Republic of Germany and the designation fee has been

[26] Düsseldorf Higher Regional Court, GRUR 2019, 279, mn. 46 – *Fulvestrant.*

paid for the Federal Republic of Germany pursuant to Article 79(2) of the European Patent Convention and if, in the case of a Euro-PCT application (Article 153(2) of the European Patent Convention), the requirements laid down in Article 153(5) of the European Patent Convention are fulfilled;

3. international applications under the Patent Cooperation Treaty as filed with the receiving Office, provided the German Patent and Trade Mark Office is the designated Office in respect of the application.

[2]If the earlier filing or priority date of an application is based on the claim to the priority of an earlier application, sentence 1 applies only to the extent that the version of the application in question does not extend beyond the version of the earlier application. Patent applications pursuant to sentence 1 no. 1, in respect of which an order has been made in accordance with § 50(1) or (4) are deemed to have been made available to the public after the expiry of a period of 18 months following their filing.

(3) Subsections (1) and (2) do not exclude the patentability of any substance or composition, comprised in the state of the art, for use in a method referred to in § 2a(1) no. 2, provided that its use for any such method is not comprised in the state of the art.

(4) Subsections (1) and (2) also do not exclude the patentability of any substance or composition referred to in subsection (3) for any specific use in a method referred to in § 2a(1) no. 2, provided that such use is not comprised in the state of the art.

(5) [1]For the application of subsections (1) and (2), a disclosure of the invention is not taken into consideration if it occurred no earlier than six months preceding the filing of the application and if it was due to, or in consequence of

1. an evident abuse in relation to the applicant or the applicant's legal predecessor, or
2. the fact that the applicant or the applicant's legal predecessor has displayed the invention at an official, or officially recognised, international exhibition falling within the terms of the Convention on international exhibitions signed at Paris on 22 November 1928.

[2]Sentence 1 no. 2 applies only if the applicant states, when filing the application, that the invention has been so displayed and files a certificate to that effect within four months after the filing. [3]Exhibitions referred to in sentence 1 no. 2 are notified by the Federal Minister of Justice and Consumer Protection in the Federal Gazette.

### § 9 44

[1]Patents have the effect that the proprietor of the patent alone is entitled to use the patented invention within the scope of the law in force. [2]In the absence of the consent of the proprietor of the patent, any third party is prohibited from

1. producing, offering, putting into circulation or using a product which is the subject matter of the patent, or from either importing or possessing such a product for the purposes referred to;
2. using a process which is the subject matter of the patent or, if the third party knows or if it is obvious from the circumstances that use of the process is prohibited in the absence of the consent of the proprietor of the patent, from offering the process for use within the territorial scope of this Act;
3. offering, putting into circulation or using a product which is produced directly by a process which is the subject matter of the patent, or from either importing or possessing such a product for the purposes referred to.

### § 10 45

(1) Patents further have the effect that any third party is prohibited, in the absence of the consent of the proprietor of the patent, from supplying or offering to supply, within the territorial scope of this Act, persons other than those entitled to exploit the patented invention with

means relating to an essential element of the invention for use within the territorial scope of this Act if the third party knows or if it is obvious from the circumstances that those means are suitable and intended for using that invention.

(2) Subsection (1) does not apply if the means are generally available commercial products, except where the third party induces the person supplied to perform any of the acts prohibited under § 9 sentence 2.

(3) Persons performing the acts referred to in § 11 nos. 1 to 3 are deemed, within the meaning of subsection (1), not to be persons entitled to exploit the invention.

46 **§ 139**

(1) [1]Any person who uses a patented invention contrary to §§ 9 to 13 may, in the event of the risk of recurrent infringement, be sued by the aggrieved party for cessation and desistance. [2]This right may also be asserted in the event of the risk of a first-time infringement. [3]This right is ruled out if asserting it would, based on the particular circumstances of the individual case and the principle of good faith, lead to disproportionate, unjustified hardship for the injurer or third parties which is not justified by the exclusive right. [4]In such cases, the aggrieved party is to be granted reasonable monetary compensation. [5]The claim for compensation under subsection (2) remains unaffected thereby.

(2) [1]Any person who performs such act intentionally or negligently is obliged to compensate the aggrieved party for the damage caused. [2]When assessing the compensation, consideration may also be given to the profit which the infringer has obtained by infringing the right. [3]The claim for compensation may also be calculated on the basis of the amount which the infringer would have been required to pay as equitable remuneration if the infringer had obtained permission to use the invention.

(3) [1]If the subject matter of the patent is a process for manufacturing a new product, the same product produced by someone else is, until there is proof to the contrary, deemed to have been produced using the patented process. [2]In taking evidence to the contrary, consideration is to be given to the defendant's legitimate interests in protecting his or her manufacturing and trade secrets.

47 **§ 140**

[1]Where, prior to the grant of a patent, rights resulting from an application whose files may be inspected by any person (§ 31(1) sentence 2 clause 2 and (2)) are asserted by judicial proceedings and where the decision on the proceedings depends on whether a claim in accordance with § 33(1) exists, the court may order that the proceedings be suspended until a decision is delivered on the grant of the patent. [2]Where a request for examination pursuant to § 44 has not been made, the court is, upon motion by the opposing party, to set the party asserting rights resulting from the application a time limit to make the request for examination. [3]Where the request for examination is not made within the time limit, rights resulting from the application may not be asserted in the proceedings.

48 **§ 140a**

(1) [1]Any person who uses a patented invention contrary to §§ 9 to 13 may be sued by the aggrieved party for destruction of products held or owned by the infringer which are the subject matter of the patent. [2]Sentence 1 also applies in the case of products which have been produced directly by means of a process which is the subject matter of the patent.

(2) Subsection (1) applies accordingly to materials and implements which are owned by the infringer and were predominantly used for manufacturing these products.

(3) [1]Any person who uses a patented invention contrary to §§ 9 to 13 may be sued by the aggrieved party for recall of the products which are the subject matter of the patent or for definitive removal of the products from the channels of commerce. [2]Sentence 1 also applies

in the case of products which have been produced directly by means of a process which is the subject matter of the patent.

(4) [1]Claims under subsections (1) to (3) are ruled out if their assertion is disproportionate in an individual case. [2]When examining proportionality, consideration is also to be given to the legitimate interests of third parties.

## § 140b 49

(1) Any person who uses a patented invention contrary to §§ 9 to 13 may be sued by the aggrieved party for provision of information, without delay, regarding the origin and the channel of commerce of the products used.

(2) [1]In cases of an obvious legal infringement or in cases where the aggrieved party has brought an action against the infringer, the claim may also be asserted, without prejudice to subsection (1), against a person who, on a commercial scale,

1. had possession of infringing products,
2. made use of infringing services,
3. provided services used for infringing activities, or
4. according to the information provided by a person referred to in no. 1, 2 or 3, participated in manufacturing, creating or distributing such products or participated in the provision of such services,

unless that person would be entitled under §§ 383 to 385 of the Code of Civil Procedure to refuse to give testimony in proceedings against the infringer. [2]In the event of assertion of the claim under sentence 1 in judicial proceedings, the court may, upon motion, suspend the proceedings pending against the infringer until the proceedings on the claim concerning the provision of information have been concluded. [3]The person obliged to provide the information may demand from the aggrieved party reimbursement of the expenditure for the provision of the information.

(3) The person obliged to provide the information must provide particulars of

1. the names and addresses of the manufacturers, suppliers and other previous holders of the products or of the users of the services, as well as of the intended wholesalers and retailers, and
2. the quantity of the products manufactured, delivered, received or ordered, as well as the prices paid for the products or services concerned.

(4) Claims under subsections (1) and (2) are ruled out if their assertion is disproportionate in an individual case.

(5) If the person obliged to provide the information, while acting intentionally or gross negligently, provides false or incomplete information, then that person is obliged to compensate the aggrieved party for the damage caused.

(6) Any person who provides true information without having been obliged to do so in accordance with subsection (1) or subsection (2) is liable to third parties only if they knew that they were not obliged to provide the information.

(7) In cases of an obvious legal infringement, the obligation to provide the information may be imposed by means of an injunction in accordance with §§ 935 to 945 of the Code of Civil Procedure.

(8) In criminal proceedings or in proceedings under the Act on Regulatory Offences (Ordnungswidrigkeitengesetz) the findings may be used against one of the persons obliged on account of an act committed prior to the provision of the information or against a relative referred to in § 52(1) of the Code of Civil Procedure only with the consent of the person obliged.

(9) [1]Where the information can be provided only by using traffic data (§ 3 no. 70 of the Telecommunications Act (*Telekommunikationsgesetz*)), a court order regarding the admissibility of the use of the traffic data is first to be obtained upon motion by the aggrieved party. [2]For issuance of this order, that regional court in whose district the person obliged to provide the information has his or her residence, principal place of business or an establishment has

exclusive jurisdiction, irrespective of the value in dispute. [3]The civil division decides. [4]The provisions of the Act on Proceedings in Family Matters and in Matters of Non-Contentious Jurisdiction (*Gesetz über das Verfahren in Familiensachen und in den Angelegenheiten der freiwilligen Gerichtsbarkeit*) apply to the proceedings accordingly. [5]The costs of the court order are borne by the aggrieved party. [6]An appeal from the regional court's decision is an available remedy. [7]The notice of appeal is to be lodged within a time limit of two weeks. [8]The provisions concerning the protection of personal data otherwise remain unaffected.

(10) The basic right to privacy of telecommunications is restricted (Article 10 of the Basic Law (*Grundgesetz*)) by subsection (2) in conjunction with subsection (9).

50

### § 140c

(1) [1]Any person who with sufficient likelihood uses a patented invention contrary to §§ 9 to 13 may be sued by the rightholder or by another entitled person for production of a document or inspection of an item of which he or she has disposal or of a process which is the subject matter of the patent if this is necessary for the purpose of establishing the claims of the rightholder or another entitled person. [2]Where there is sufficient likelihood of a legal infringement being committed on a commercial scale, the claim extends to the production of bank, financial or commercial documents. [3]If the alleged infringer asserts that the information concerned is confidential, the court takes the measures necessary to ensure the specific protection required in an individual case.

(2) Claims under subsection (1) are ruled out if their assertion is disproportionate in an individual case.

(3) [1]The obligation to produce a document or to acquiesce to the inspection of an item may be imposed by means of an injunction in accordance with §§ 935 to 945 of the Code of Civil Procedure. [2]The court takes the measures necessary to ensure the protection of confidential information. [3]This in particular applies to those cases where the injunction is issued without giving a prior hearing to the opposing party.

(4) § 811 of the Civil Code and § 140b(8) of this Act apply accordingly.

(5) If there was no infringement or no risk of infringement, the alleged infringer may claim compensation for the damage caused to him or her by the production or inspection sought in accordance with subsection (1) from the person who sought the production or inspection.

## II. Code of Civil Procedure

51

### § 945a

(1) [1]The State Justice Administration of Hesse shall maintain a central, cross-Länder electronic register for protective letters (protective letter register) for the Federal German States. [2]Protective letters are precautionary letters of defence against anticipated applications for arrest or temporary injunction.

(2) [1] A protective letter is deemed to have been filed with all ordinary courts in the federal states as soon as it has been entered in the protective letter register. [2]Protective letters are to be deleted six months after being entered in the register.

(3) [1]The courts have access to the register via an automated retrieval procedure. [2]The use of the data shall be limited to the use required for the fulfillment of the statutory functions.[3]Retrieval procedures shall be documented.

## III. Guidelines on Medicinal Products

**§ 40a** 52

(1) [1]When prescribing biotechnologically produced biological medicinal products, the attending physician should follow an economic prescribing practice, in particular by transitioning patients to an inexpensive medicinal product. [2]Patients should also be switched over in line with an economic prescribing practice; this applies both to the switching of the reference medicinal product to one of its essentially identical biotechnologically produced biological medicinal products within the meaning of Article 10(4) of Directive 2001/83/EC (biosimilars) and vice versa.

(...)

## IV. Social Code, Book V

**§ 129** 53

(1) [1]When dispensing prescribed drugs to insured persons in accordance with the framework agreement pursuant to paragraph 2, pharmacies are obliged to

1. dispensing an inexpensive medicinal product in cases where the prescribing physician
   a) prescribes a drug only under its active ingredient name or
   b) has not excluded substitution of the drug by a drug with the same active ingredient,

(...)

[2]When dispensing a medicinal product in accordance with sentence 1 number 1, pharmacies must dispense a medicinal product that is identical to the prescribed one in terms of active strength and package size, is approved for the same indication and has the same or an interchangeable dosage form; (...). [3]The substitution shall be made by a drug with the same active ingredient for which there is an agreement in accordance with § 130a (8) with effect for the health insurance fund, unless otherwise agreed in contracts in accordance with (5).

(...)

# J. Extracts from court decisions

## I. Federal Court of Justice (BGH)[27] – *Pemetrexed* 54

**82.** The Appellate Court (BerGer.) also erred in law in denying an indirect patent infringement.

**83a)** According to the case law of the Senate, the subject matter of a patent claim directed towards the use of a substance for the treatment of a disease, is the suitability of the substance for a specific medical purpose, and thus ultimately an intrinsic property of the substance (BGHZ 164, 220 = GRUR 2006, 135 – *Arzneimittelgebrauchsmuster*). In substance, this corresponds to purpose-limited substance protection, as expressly provided for in § 3 IV Patent Act and Article 54 V EPC, in the version in force since 13.12.2007. This applies regardless of whether the wording of the patent claim is directed towards purpose-limited substance pro-

[27] 14.6.2016 – X ZR 29/15.

tection, to the use of the pharmaceutical substance or to its preparation for a specific purpose (BGHZ 200, 229 mn. 17 = GRUR 2014, 461 – *Collagenase I*).

**84.** The same applies to claims directed towards the use of the substance in the manufacture of a medicinal product, in accordance with the EPO's previous legal practice. This particular version of a claim, known as the Swiss-type claim, took account of the fact that in the opinion of the EPO, the use of a substance for the treatment of a disease was not amenable to patentability. The solution chosen instead, i.e., to extend the protection to the use, to the manufacture of a medicinal product, does not alter the fact that a particular property of the substance, which is also inherent in the manufactured medicinal product is essentially protected.

**85.** The assessment would be no different, even if Swiss type claims were according to their wording, to be interpreted as claims aimed at the protection of a manufacturing process. Based on this interpretation, a medicinal product manufactured according to the protected process would have to be regarded as a direct process product, which may also only be offered, placed on the market, and used by the patent proprietor for the protected purpose pursuant to § 9 No. 3 Patent Act. As a result, this also led to substance protection limited to the intended use.

## 55 II. Düsseldorf Higher Regional Court (OLG) – *Östrogenblocker*[28]

**38.** The considerations to be made by the applicant in the event of a dispute were extraordinarily straightforward, because the case law of the Federal Court of Justice discussed above, already largely prescribes the handling of patents for the use of medicinal products in the event of infringement, so that only a few logical conclusions were needed to identify the liability criteria applicable to purpose-limited substance patents. An initial important finding already follows from the Federal Court of Justice's qualification of patents for the use and manufacture of medicinal products as 'purpose-limited substance protection patents'. It lies in the fact that, as with any other patent in kind, the provision of § 9(1) Patent Act applies to them, according to which, if the subject matter of the patent is a product, it is prohibited for all third parties to manufacture, offer, place on the market or use that product or either import or possess it for the purposes mentioned. In contrast to regular substance patents, which confer absolute material protection on their owner, and therefore, intervene completely independently of the specific purpose for which the patent-protected object is offered or distributed, the peculiarity of purpose-limited substance patents is that – as an inevitable consequence of the purpose-limitation of the property protection granted – the acts referred to in § 9 No. 1 Patent Act must be carried out to achieve a very specific therapeutic purpose. Purpose-limited substance patents (also in the form of manufacturing use patents) therefore impose the prohibition on any third party from offering and/or distributing the protected active substance for the patent-protected purpose (sic: the patented medical indication). In this classification, the actual act of use no longer takes place in the ultimate use of the object for therapeutic purposes (as an act similar to a procedure), but rather, in its transmission into business transactions by offering and distribution, which is not prohibited under all circumstances, but – to a limited extent – only when it takes place for the specific, patent-protected therapeutic purpose. Due to the limited substance protection, because of the purpose limitation, direct use of the patent for use/purpose-limited substance patent therefore only exists if the item offered or distributed has the requisite therapeutic purpose to which patent protection is limited.

39. Firstly, this can be actively accomplished by preparing the pharmaceutical composition specifically for the patented purpose, prior to its distribution. Namely by preparing it in such a way that it is foreseeable that it will result in the protected therapeutic use. This can be done by means of a formulation, packaging, dosage, outer packaging or instructions for use enclosed

[28] 5.5.2017 – I-2 W 6/17.

with the item, tailored to the specific intended use. Since, in the opinion of the Federal Court of Justice, the focus of the protection conferred by a manufacturing use patent is the objective suitability of the medicinal product in question, for use in accordance with the patent, liability on the part of the distributor of the preparation is also conceivable without their own obvious preparation measures. With regard to the fact that substance protection is not all-encompassing, but limited, i.e., purpose-limited, only conditions which otherwise ensure the required purpose limitation for the protected active substance must be fulfilled. Firstly, the product must be suitable for the patented purpose, and secondly, the distributor must take advantage of circumstances which – in a manner similar to an active obvious preparation – ensure that the product offered or distributed, is used for the intended therapeutic purpose. The latter requires a sufficiently extensive, not merely isolated scope of use in accordance with the patent in suit, as well as knowledge to this effect or at least an unlawful concealment by the supplier of their knowledge of this. Where the external framework conditions for the offer and distribution of a product already amounts to its patent-protected therapeutic use, there is no need for separate preparations by the supplier, which is why it cannot be considered as the decisive aspect for liability. Furthermore, there is no justifiable reason to demand it, given the background of the fact that, according to the case law of the Federal Court of Justice, patent protection – regardless of the specific formulation of the claim – 'refers to the suitability of the known active substance for the specific medical purpose, and thus ultimately to a property inherent in the active substance. Given that, patent protection is interpreted in this way, it is almost beside the point to limit the liability requirements for the claim arising from a manufacturing use patent, to situations in which the therapeutic use in question arises as a result of an obvious preparation measure by the distributor, but to deny patent protection when, the said object of the patent-protected therapeutic use, has the same degree of suitability, because other circumstances (such as a common cross-label use) brings it about.'

## III. Düsseldorf Higher Regional Court (OLG) – *Fulvestrant*[29] 56

**42.** b) According to the case law of the Senate (GRUR 2017, 1107 – *Östrogenblocker*), however, since the objective suitability of the medicinal product in question for use in accordance with the patent is at the centre of the protection conferred by a patent for use (BGHZ 211, 1 = GRUR 2016, 921 – *Pemetrexed*) – liability on the part of the distributor of the preparation is conceivable in exceptional cases even without their own obvious preparation measures.

**43.** aa) With regard to the fact that substance protection is not all-encompassing, but limited, i.e., purpose-limited substance protection, only the following conditions must be fulfilled:- firstly, the product must be suitable for the patented purpose, and secondly, the distributor must make use of circumstances which, in a manner similar to an obvious preparation, ensures that the preparation is used for the intended therapeutic purpose. The latter requires a sufficient, not merely isolated scope of use in accordance with the patent in suit, as well as knowledge to this effect or at least the supplier's unfair concealment of their knowledge in this respect (Senate, GRUR 2017, 1107 – *Östrogenblocker*). If the generic pharmaceutical company is aware, or at least should have been aware of the prescribing practice favourable to it, and nevertheless exploits this practice for their own benefit by supplying its wholesalers, it is appropriate to make the generic manufacturer liable under patent law for this.

**44.** (1) The Senate has not yet decided on the exact extent to which the use, without preparation, must take place in accordance with the patent in suit, in order to give rise to liability. The following considerations, which are based on the situation regarding preparation, are decisive: The obvious preparation does not have to specify the use in accordance with the patent as the sole and exclusive purpose of use; rather, it is only a matter of whether the use

[29] 1.9.2019 – 2 U 27/18.

according to the invention – possibly in addition to other uses – is at all part of the use to which the preparation instructs. Therefore, both the situation in which the instructions for use themselves mention several possible uses, including patent-protected use, and the case that the instructions for use relate only to the protected use, but in addition, it is obvious that there are other, competing areas of application, are relevant. As this is the case, even in cases of non-conventional cross-label use, it is not only such use that can be relevant to liability if it relates exclusively, or almost exclusively to the patent protected use. Rather, the decisive factor is the certain knowledge (which is equivalent to closing one's eyes to the knowledge) that the medicinal product being marketed will actually lead to it being prescribed and used in compliance with the patent. This is because the person who acts in the said knowledge must allow themself to be treated with regard to the consequences, as if they had brought about the condition free from preparation, which they had exploited for business purposes, by means of a corresponding preparatory measure. In fact, it must therefore be established by a court of law – firstly – that there has been a sufficient amount of patent-compliant use, and secondly that the generic pharmaceutical company cannot have been unaware of this fact. With the number of verifiable cases of patent-compliant use, the chance of a finding of fact to this effect naturally increases, which is why only isolated cases of use generally cannot give rise to liability. An additional scenario where liability might arise, can result from the particular, outstanding advantages of patent-compliant use compared to other therapeutic purposes, which virtually demand that the preparation be used in accordance with the patent – and not otherwise.

**45.** (2) If – as in the present case – the medicinal product is only available on prescription, the use of which can only be expected to be taken in accordance with the physician's prescription on the indications for use and dosage, the prescribing practice that is to be invoiced according to the content of the funds available to the physician for their prescription shall be decisive. In this respect, the summary of product characteristics (SmPC), which is an integral part of the marketing authorisation for medicinal products, and conclusively defines the characteristics of its version approved for distribution, is of central importance. This is because the approved version of the medicinal product must correspond to the version of the medicinal product placed on the market, it is clear based on experience that the physician will only prescribe the individual medicinal products in accordance with its respective specific summary of product characteristics, so that a generic medicinal product which – unlike the originator's preparation – does not have a specific (patent-protected) indication/dosage, e.g., for patent reasons, will not be prescribed to a patient for this purpose either, which is why the generic medicinal product – subsequently – will not be used therapeutically in this sense.

**46.** (3) Nevertheless, it makes a very significant difference to the liability for injunctive relief, whether the medicinal product has been obviously prepared or not. If the liability of the generic company (or other distributor) is based on an obvious preparation of the product for the patent-protected use, then according to general rules every singular case of infringement (= obvious preparation with subsequent offer/distribution); even the very first and only one, would give rise to a risk of future repetition (the distribution of obviously prepared products and their subsequent use in accordance with its purpose), which automatically results in a cease and desist order, unless the infringer submits a declaration of submission with a sufficient guarantee of penalty, before the court. The situation is completely different in the case of a distributor who has not undertaken any preparatory measures, and whose liability is to be based solely on an actual prescribing practice corresponding to the protected use. Even if sufficient actual use has been practiced in the past (which leads to the distributor's obligation to pay damages, and provide information for the period in question), an injunction can only be considered if there was current liability i.e., at the time of the oral hearing a prescription practice relevant to liability could still be established. If this is not the case because the preparation was used cross-label in the past, but the prescribing practice had changed in the meantime (e.g., due to new active substances that had increasingly replaced the medicinal product in question as a therapeutic agent), a conviction for injunctive relief is ruled out. This is because it is not linked – as is liability for obvious preparation – to a specific conduct on the part of the infringer, the causality-establishing repetition, which is to be expected based on empirical evidence, but it is based solely on certain underlying conditions (sic.: an actual prescribing practice), which, if it no longer exists due to the passage of time, can no longer form the basis for an obligation to cease and desist on the part of the distributor.

[…]

**49.** Therefore, a maximum of less than 7 % of all cancer patients treated with fulvestrant had previously been treated palliatively with tamoxifen and an aromatase inhibitor unsuccessfully. Even in view of this clearly single-digit numerical value, the prescribing practice leading to the use of the invention takes place sporadically, and by no means to such an extent that the defendant could have been unaware of it. Nor does the plaintiff, who relied on the total palliative and adjuvant use of fulvestrant to justify their claims, which averaged 45.7 % over the years, also failed to specifically demonstrate whether and why a (single relevant) palliative use, which occurred in a completely different order of magnitude, at less than 7 %, should have been obvious to the defendant. For this reason alone, all claims are excluded. With regard to the claim for injunctive relief directed towards the future, the defendant's liability is a fortiori out of the question because – based on the date of the oral proceedings (9.1.2019) – not a single case of a patent-compliant fulvestrant prescription, after unsuccessful palliative pre-treatment with tamoxifen and an aromatase inhibitor could be proven over the last four years. For the relevant current point in time, therefore, it absolutely cannot be established that a prescription practice led to patent-protected use. Since the initiation of the legal proceedings, the defendant, based on the special evaluation presented to it, may have been aware of the prescribing practice in accordance with the patent, which from that point on could have resulted in the accusation that the defendant had deliberately taken advantage of the cross-label use practised by its consistent supply of customers and had therefore given rise to liability. However, the plaintiff's data, which showed a zero value for the years 2015 and 2016, which were long before lis pendens, did not show that such deliveries undertaken by the defendant. with knowledge of the facts of the case, resulted on at least one occasion, in a patient compliant prescription and use.'

## IV. Mannheim Regional Court (LG) – *Transportriemen*[30] 57

**49.** Even in cases in which a use other than the patented use can obviously be considered, the case law of the Düsseldorf Higher Regional Court (GRUR 2019, 279, 282–283 – *Fulvestrant*; see also OLG Düsseldorf, GRUR 2017, 1107, 1110 – *Östrogenblocker*; PharmR 2018, 306, 311), for an infringement of the patent for use, it is sufficient to have certain knowledge of it or to have turned a blind eye to the knowledge that the product sold will actually be used in accordance with the patent (to a sufficient extent and not only in isolated cases). In any case, the board concurs with this to the extent, that there is an obvious preparation at least if the supplier is aware that the product will be used by the customers, even in the vast majority of deliveries, in accordance with the patent and that its technical design has (also) been chosen by the supplier precisely for this purpose.

[30] 8.10.2019 – 2 O 35/16.

# § 6 Ireland

## A. Executive summary

1 In Ireland there has been no direct case law on second medical use claims and accordingly one must look to other jurisdictions for precedence. The UK, with its similar common law, has been a common reference source in Ireland. So too has the EPO in respect of interpretation (though of course EPO case law does not deal with infringement).

2 It is thought that the Irish courts will treat a Swiss-type claim as a process claim limited to a specific end use and that an EPC 2000 claim will be treated as a product claim limited to a specific end use. As such, infringement considerations for these two types of claim are likely to be different under the Irish Patents Act, 1992.

3 Consideration of direct infringement of second medical use claims by 'skinny label' products is likely to follow principles such as those considered in the UK Supreme Court decision *Warner-Lambert v Generics*[1] (→ § 13 mn. 19 et seq.). Indeed, in the matter of plausibility the Court of Appeal in Ireland has already considered *Warner-Lambert* decision and adopted a similar approach.[2]

4 In line with this case law, it is likely to be that the sole criterion of infringement is whether the product as it emerges from the manufacturing process, including any labelling or accompanying leaflet, is presented as suitable for the uses which enjoy patent protection – the 'outward presentation' test. In rare cases, the context may make it obvious that the outward presentation is not to be taken at face value.

5 If this UK Supreme Court decision in *Warner-Lambert v Generics* is followed in Ireland then for Swiss-type claims the designated use, and not the subsequent use of the product for treating patients is to be considered, making indirect infringement difficult to show.

6 It is assumed that biosimilar products would be treated the same as any small molecule. While similarity may be an additional factor in determination of infringement, it is not a factor specific to second medical indications.

## B. Scope of protection and interpretation of second medical use claims

7 Methods of treatment of the human or animal body by surgery or therapy and diagnostic methods practised on the human or animal body are excluded from patentability in Ireland. These inventions are treated similarly under the EPC 2000. However, Section 11(4) of the Patents Act, 1992[3] does allow for the patenting of a known substance or

[1] *Warner-Lambert v Generics* [2018] UKSC 56.

[2] *Norton (Waterford) Limited t/a Teva Pharmaceuticals Ireland v Boehringer Ingelheim Pharma GmbH & Co. KG* [2022] IECA 58.

[3] As amended by the Patents (Amendment) Act 2006 [31/2006]. All references to the Patent Act, 1992 refer to the amended version. For the text of the provision → mn. 38.

composition for use in a method for treatment, provided that its use for any such method is not comprised in the state of the art. Accordingly, second medical use claims are allowed in Ireland under Section 11(4).

As with all claims for a new use of a known product, a second medical use claim should reflect a new technical effect, which can then be considered a novel technical feature, rendering the invention patentable. 8

While there is no specific case law on the interpretation of second medical use claims, it is believed that the Irish courts would follow practice elsewhere as discussed above. It is thought that the Irish courts will treat a Swiss-type claim as a process claim limited to a specific end use and that an EPC 2000 claim will be treated as a product claim limited to a specific end use. It is expected that the claimed end use will be taken into account when adopting an interpretation following the Protocol on the Interpretation of Article 69 EPC. 9

## C. Direct and indirect infringement of second medical use claims

The Irish Patents Act, 1992 has the same infringement provisions for all patents and so second medical indications are not treated differently. As noted above, and discussed further below, Swiss-type claims and EPC 2000 claims are likely to be considered to have different scopes of protection because of their different wording. 10

### I. Direct patent infringement

Section 40 of the Patents Act, 1992 governs direct infringement: 11

**Prevention of direct use of invention.**

40.—A patent while it is in force shall confer on its proprietor the right to prevent all third parties not having his consent from doing in the State all or any of the things following:

(a) making, offering, putting on the market or using a product which is the subject-matter of the patent, or importing or stocking the product for those purposes;

(b) using a process which is the subject-matter of the patent, or, when the third party knows, or it is obvious to a reasonable person in the circumstances, that the use of the process is prohibited without the consent of the proprietor of the patent, offering the process for use in the State;

(c) offering, putting on the market, using or importing, or stocking for those purposes, the product obtained directly by a process which is the subject-matter of the patent.

It is thought that as EPC 2000 claims are product claims limited by purpose then Section 40(a) may apply. 12

On the other hand, Swiss type claims, being process-limited claims, might not have Section 40(a) available for consideration and might then only be considered under Section 40(b) and 40(c). 13

Section 40(c) extends to offering, putting on the market, using or importing, or stocking for those purposes, the product obtained directly by a process which is the subject-matter of the patent. Where manufacture of a product which would constitute an infringement of a Swiss-type claim takes place outside Ireland, it will be an infringement to import the product into Ireland. 14

15 A skinny label may allow avoidance of direct infringement. Consideration of what would be sufficient on such a label (and indeed other packaging) would likely be determined under the 'outward presentation' test mentioned above.

## II. Indirect patent infringement

16 Section 41 of the Patents Act, 1992 governs indirect infringement:

**Prevention of indirect use of invention.**

41.—(1) A patent while it is in force shall also confer on its proprietor the right to prevent all third parties not having his consent from supplying or offering to supply in the State a person, other than a party entitled to exploit the patented invention, with means, relating to an essential element of that invention, for putting it into effect therein, when the third party knows, or it is obvious in the circumstances to a reasonable person, that the said means are suitable and intended for putting that invention into effect.

(2) Subsection (1) shall not apply when the means referred to therein are staple commercial products, except when the third party induces the person supplied to commit acts which the proprietor of a patent is enabled to prevent by virtue of section 40.

(3) Persons performing acts referred to in paragraph (a), (b), or (c) of section 42 shall not be considered to be parties entitled to exploit an invention pursuant to subsection (1).

17 Putting the invention of Swiss-type claims into effect involves a process and thus, if Irish courts follow the reasoning of the UK Supreme Court in *Warner-Lambert v Generics*, there may not be indirect infringement by reason of the supply of the generic product to third parties.

18 However, EPC 2000 claims may have the benefit of Section 41: Section 41 allows a patentee to take action against a party who supplies or offers to supply any means, relating to an essential element of the invention, for putting that invention into effect. Section 41 is based on Article 26 EPC and has a double territorial requirement wherein both the supply (or offer thereof) and end use must occur within the state of Ireland. There is no requirement for inducement of direct infringement, except in cases where the means are staple commercial products (there is no accepted definition of 'staple commercial product' but this is unlikely to apply to medicinal products).

19 There is, however, a requirement to show knowledge that the means are suitable and intended for the infringing purpose. In cases where it would be 'obvious in the circumstances to a reasonable person', the knowledge requirement can be inferred. It is expected that both knowledge and intention would need to be proven on the balance of probabilities. It would seem likely that, in the case of generic and biosimilar manufacturers, the threshold for knowledge of suitability would be lower than that of intention, which would require assessment of the end users' intentions.

# D. Infringement of second medical use claims and skinny label products

20 Following on from the above, it appears that consideration of a product sold under a 'skinny label' will be likely determined by the 'outward presentation' test. Other than in rare cases where the context may make it obvious that the outward presentation is not

to be taken at face value, a 'skinny label' should avoid infringement. It could be expected then that prescribing practices will not normally be taken into account.

## E. Infringement of second medical use claims and biosimilar products

It would be expected that the findings above would also apply to biosimilars. It would be expected that that the Irish courts would apply the same legal approach used to assess direct or indirect infringement of a generic product. 21

It is noted that prescribing guidelines and practices vary between generics and biosimilars. Under the Health (Pricing and Supply of Medical Goods) Act 2013, pharmacists are permitted and indeed obliged to offer to substitute a branded medicinal product with a generic medicinal product, with the agreement of the patient. Biologic medicines, however, are not considered interchangeable under current legislation and the Health (Pricing and Supply of Medical Goods) Act 2013 explicitly excludes the inclusion of biologics to the List of Interchangeable Medicinal Products maintained by The Health Products Regulatory Authority. Accordingly, pharmacists are prohibited from substituting a reference biologic medicine with a biosimilar. 22

Since substitution of biosimilars by pharmacists is prohibited, it is recommended that any biological medicine is prescribed using both the brand name and international non-proprietary name (INN).[4] Healthcare professionals are also encouraged to consult the Summary of Product Characteristics (SmPC) when prescribing biosimilars and not to deviate from the listed indications, paying attention to the fact that a biosimilar is not identical to the reference drug and that it might not be authorised for use in all indications approved for the reference medicine.[5] As such, while it is not expected that the courts would treat infringement regarding biosimilars differently to generics, the differences in prescribing practice may mean that off-label prescription of biosimilars is less likely to occur than that of generics. 23

## F. Strategies and considerations

Other than in rare cases where the context may make it obvious that the outward presentation is not to be taken at face value, a 'skinny label' should avoid infringement. Care should therefore be taken not to move toward a presentation that cannot be taken at face value. Suppliers of generics and biosimilars should avoid actively encouraging prescription or supply of their products for patented indications. In cases where the market for the non-patented indication(s) is small, it would be prudent to avoid manufacturing or supplying 'skinny label' drugs in much larger quantities than the non-patented market justifies. 24

---

[4] HSE Guidance for Biological Medicines in Acute Hospitals, V1 (April 2019).

[5] Health Products Regulatory Authority, 'Guide to Biosimilars for Healthcare Professionals' (August 2020).

## G. Legal remedies

25 The remedies available include:

1. an injunction restraining the defendant from any apprehended act of infringement;
2. an order requiring the defendant to deliver up or destroy any product covered by the patent in relation to which the patent is alleged to have been infringed or any Article in which the product is inextricably comprised;
3. damages in respect of the alleged infringement;
4. an account of the profits derived by the defendant from the alleged infringement;
5. a declaration that the patent is valid and has been infringed by the defendant.

26 Infringement proceedings must be brought by the patent proprietor or an exclusive licensee.

27 Injunctions can be sought on differing timelines depending on the circumstances. For example, preliminary injunctions may be sought in cases where launch of a product is imminent. In very rare cases an interim injunction can be granted *ex-parte*. Such a scenario would require full disclosure by the applicant of all material information, regardless of whether it is favourable to them or not.

28 In considering a petition for an interlocutory injunction, the Irish courts use the *Campus Oil*[6] test, which is based on the *American Cyanamid*[7] test developed in the English courts. The *Campus Oil* test requires the applicant to establish that:

1. a fair/serious issue to be tried;
2. that damages would not be an adequate remedy at trial; and
3. the balance of convenience favours the granting of an injunction.

29 A 2003 ruling in *Smithkline Beecham v Genthon B.V.*[8] found that if damages are considered to be an adequate remedy, a petition for injunctive relief should be refused without consideration of where the balance of convenience would lie. As a result, it has since been difficult to obtain interlocutory injunctions in patent infringement cases, where damages have generally been considered to be an adequate remedy.

30 More recently, however, in *Merck Sharp & Dohme Corp v Clonmel Healthcare Ltd*[9] the Supreme Court in Ireland found that a more flexible approach should be taken to the tests set out by *American Cyanamid* and *Campus Oil*. The Supreme Court expressed the view that the adequacy of damages should be considered as part of the overall balance of convenience and should not automatically preclude the grant of an interlocutory injunction:

> While the adequacy of damages is the most important component of any assessment of the balance of convenience or balance of justice, a number of other factors may come into play and may properly be considered and weighed in the balance in considering how matters are to be held most fairly pending a trial, and recognising the possibility that there may be no trial.[10]

31 While the judgment noted that in commercial cases courts should be 'robustly sceptical' of a claim that damages would not be an adequate remedy, it was noted that any potential difficulty in assessing damages can be considered, particularly in cases where such difficulty would mean damages were imprecise or imperfect.

---

[6] *Campus Oil v Minister for Energy* [1983] EPC 88.
[7] *American Cyanamid Co v Ethicon Ltd* [1975] UKHL 1.
[8] *Smithkline Beecham plc. & ors v Genthon B.V. and Synthon B.V.* [2003] IEHC 623.
[9] *Merck Sharp & Dohme Corp v Clonmel Healthcare Ltd* [2019] IESC 65.
[10] ibid., para. 64(7).

This decision is anticipated to make it easier for patent holders in Ireland to obtain interlocutory injunctive relief, particularly in pharmaceutical cases where damages have generally been considered adequate and calculable. 32

A perpetual or permanent injunction may be granted at the final determination of the case. In general, where infringement is found to have occurred, an injunction against further infringement is likely to be granted. 33

Under Section 47(2) Irish Patents Act, 1992, a patentee (or exclusive licensee) bringing an infringement action may claim damages or an account of profits, but cannot be awarded both (→ mn. 42). 34

Damages are compensatory rather than punitive and are typically awarded at a level to put the patentee in a financial position that is the same as they would have been in had an infringement not occurred. 35

This would be a complicated assessment in the case of second medical use claims, as there is already product on the market. 36

## H. Statutory provisions

## Patents Act, 1992

#### Section 10: Exceptions to patentability. 37

10.—A patent shall not be granted in respect of—

(1) (a) an invention the commercial exploitation of which would be contrary to public order or morality, provided that the exploitation shall not be deemed to be so contrary only because it is prohibited by law;

(b) a plant or animal variety or an essentially biological process for the production of plants or animals other than a micro-biological process or the products thereof;

(c)[11] a method for treatment of the human or animal body by surgery or therapy and a diagnostic method practised on the human or animal body.

(2) Subsection (1)(c) shall not apply to products, in particular substances or compositions, for use in any such method.

#### Section 11: Novelty.[12] 38

11.—(1) An invention shall be considered to be new if it does not form part of the state of the art.

(2) The state of the art shall be held to comprise everything made available to the public (whether in the State or elsewhere) by means of a written or oral description, by use, or in any other way, before the date of filing of the patent application.

(3) Additionally, the content of a patent application as filed, of which the date of filing is prior to the date referred to in subsection (2) and which was published under this Act on or after that date, shall be considered as comprised in the state of the art.

(4) The provisions of subsections (2) and (3) shall not exclude the patentability of any substance or composition, comprised in the state of the art, for use in a method referred to in section 10(1)(c) provided that its use for any such method is not comprised in the state of the art.

---

[11] As amended by the Patents (Amendment) Act 2006 [31/2006].

[12] As amended by the Patents (Amendment) Act 2006 [31/2006].

(5) The provisions of subsections (2) and (3) shall also not exclude the patentability of any substance or composition referred to in subsection (4) for any specific use in any method referred to in section 10(1)(c), provided that such use is not comprised in the state of the art.

39 **Section 40: Prevention of direct use of invention.**

40.—A patent while it is in force shall confer on its proprietor the right to prevent all third parties not having his consent from doing in the State all or any of the things following:

(a) making, offering, putting on the market or using a product which is the subject-matter of the patent, or importing or stocking the product for those purposes;

(b) using a process which is the subject-matter of the patent, or, when the third party knows, or it is obvious to a reasonable person in the circumstances, that the use of the process is prohibited without the consent of the proprietor of the patent, offering the process for use in the State;

(c) offering, putting on the market, using or importing, or stocking for those purposes, the product obtained directly by a process which is the subject-matter of the patent.

40 **Section 41: Prevention of indirect use of invention.**

41.—(1) A patent while it is in force shall also confer on its proprietor the right to prevent all third parties not having his consent from supplying or offering to supply in the State a person, other than a party entitled to exploit the patented invention, with means, relating to an essential element of that invention, for putting it into effect therein, when the third party knows, or it is obvious in the circumstances to a reasonable person, that the said means are suitable and intended for putting that invention into effect.

(2) Subsection (1) shall not apply when the means referred to therein are staple commercial products, except when the third party induces the person supplied to commit acts which the proprietor of a patent is enabled to prevent by virtue of section 40.

(3) Persons performing acts referred to in paragraph (a), (b), or (c) of section 42 shall not be considered to be parties entitled to exploit an invention pursuant to subsection (1).

41 **Section 42: Limitation of effect of patent.**

42.—(1)[13] The rights conferred by a patent shall not extend to—

(a) acts done privately for non-commercial purposes;

(b) acts done for experimental purposes relating to the subject-matter of the relevant patented invention;

(c) the extemporaneous preparation for individual cases in a pharmacy of a medicine in accordance with a medical prescription issued by a registered medical practitioner or acts concerning the medicine so prepared;

(d) the use on board vessels registered in any of the countries of the Union of Paris for the Protection of Industrial Property or in any of the members of the World Trade Organisation, other than the State, of the invention which is the subject of the patent, in the body of the vessel, in the machinery, tackle, gear and other accessories, when such vessels temporarily or accidentally enter the territorial waters of the State, provided that the invention is used in such waters exclusively for the needs of the vessel;

(e) the use of the invention which is the subject of the patent in the construction or operation of aircraft or land vehicles of countries of the Union of Paris for the Protection of Industrial Property or of members of the World Trade Organisation, other than the State, or of such aircraft or land vehicle accessories when such aircraft or land vehicles temporarily or accidentally enter the State;

[13] As amended by the Patents (Amendment) Act 2006 [31/2006].

(f) the acts specified in Article 27 of the Convention on International Civil Aviation, where those acts concern the aircraft of countries, other than the State, benefiting from the provisions of that Article,

(g)[14] acts done in relation to the subject matter of the relevant patented invention which consist of:

(i) acts done in conducting the necessary studies, tests and trials which are conducted with a view to satisfying the application requirements of paragraphs 1, 2, 3 and 4 of Article 10 of Directive 2001/83/EC of the European Parliament and of the Council of 6 November 2001 (as last amended by Directive 2004/27/EC of the European Parliament and of the Council of 31 March 2004) for a marketing authorisation in respect of a medicinal product for human use, or

(ii) acts done in conducting the necessary studies, tests and trials which are conducted with a view to satisfying the application requirements of paragraphs 1 to 5 of Article 13 of Directive 2001/82/EC of the European Parliament and of the Council of 6 November 2001 (as last amended by Directive 2004/28/EC of the European Parliament and of the Council of 31 March 2004) for a marketing authorisation in respect of a veterinary medicinal product, or

(iii) any other act which is required as a consequence of the acts referred to in subparagraph (i) or (ii) for the purposes specified in those subparagraphs, as appropriate.

(h)[15] insofar as paragraph (g) does not apply, acts done in relation to the subject matter of the relevant patented invention which consist of—

(i) acts done in conducting studies, tests, experiments and trials (including clinical trials and field trials) with a view to satisfying the application requirements for a marketing authorisation or similar instrument (howsoever described) that is required by the law of the State or of any other state in order to sell or supply or offer to sell or supply—

(I) a medicinal product for human use, within the meaning of subsection (2), or

(II) a veterinary medicinal product, within the meaning of subsection (2),

or

(ii) any other act done which is required as a consequence of the acts referred to in subparagraph (i) for the purposes specified in that subparagraph, as appropriate.

(2)[16] In this section (other than paragraph (g) of subsection (1))—

'medicinal product for human use' means—

(a) any substance or combination of substances having or purporting to have properties for treating or preventing disease in human beings, or

(b) any substance or combination of substances which may be used on or be administered to human beings with a view either to restoring, correcting or modifying physiological functions by exerting a pharmacological, immunological or metabolic action, or to making a medical diagnosis;

'substance' means any matter of—

(a) human origin (including human blood and human blood products),

(b) animal origin (including micro-organisms, whole animals, parts of organs, animal secretions, toxins, extracts and blood products),

(c) vegetable origin (including micro-organisms, plants, parts of plants, vegetable secretions and extracts), or

(d) chemical origin (including elements, naturally occurring chemical materials and chemical products obtained by chemical change or synthesis);

'veterinary medicinal product' means—

(a) any substance or combination of substances having or purporting to have properties for treating or preventing disease in animals, or

---

[14] SI 50/2006 European Communities (Limitation of Effect of Patent) Regulations.

[15] Intellectual Property (Miscellaneous Provisions) Act 2014 [36/2014].

[16] Intellectual Property (Miscellaneous Provisions) Act 2014 [36/2014].

(b) any substance or combination of substances which may be used on or be administered to animals with a view either to restoring, correcting or modifying physiological functions by exerting a pharmacological, immunological or metabolic action, or to making a medical diagnosis.

42 **Section 47: Action for infringement of patent.**

47.—(1) Civil proceedings for infringement of a patent may be brought in the Court High Court by the proprietor of the patent in respect of any act of infringement which he alleges he is entitled under sections 40 to 43 and section 45 to prevent and (without prejudice to any other jurisdiction of the High Court) in those proceedings a claim may be made—

(a) for an injunction restraining the defendant from any apprehended act of such infringement;

(b) for an order requiring the defendant to deliver up or destroy any product covered by the patent in relation to which the patent is alleged to have been infringed or any Article in which the product is inextricably comprised;

(c) for damages in respect of the alleged infringement;

(d) for an account of the profits derived by the defendant from the alleged infringement;

(e) for a declaration that the patent is valid and has been infringed by the defendant.

(2) The High Court shall not, in respect of the same infringement, both award the proprietor of a patent damages and order that he shall be given an account of the profits.

43 **Section 49: Restrictions on recovery of damages for infringement.**

49.—(1) In proceedings for the infringement of a patent damages shall not be awarded, and no order shall be made for an account of profits, against a defendant who proves that at the date of the infringement he was not aware, and had no reasonable grounds for supposing, that that patent existed, and a person shall not be deemed to have been so aware or to have had reasonable grounds for so supposing by reason only of the application to a product of the word 'patent' or 'patented' or any word or words expressing or implying that a patent has been obtained for the product, unless the number of the relevant patent accompanied the word or words in question.

(2) In proceedings for infringement of a patent the High Court may, if it thinks fit, refuse to award any damages or make any order in respect of any infringement committed during an extension period specified in a request under subsection (3) of section 36 but before the payment of the renewal fee and any additional fee prescribed for the purpose of that subsection.

(3) Where an amendment of a specification of a patent has been allowed under this Act, no damages shall be awarded in any proceedings for an infringement of the patent committed before the date of the decision allowing the amendment, unless the High Court is satisfied that the specification of the patent, as originally published, was framed in good faith and with reasonable skill and knowledge.

44 **Section 51: Proceedings for infringement by exclusive licensee.**

51.—(1) Subject to the provisions of this section, the holder of an exclusive licence under a patent shall have the like right as the proprietor of the patent to take proceedings in respect of any infringement of the patent committed after the date of the licence, and in awarding damages or granting any other relief in any such proceedings the Court High Court shall take into consideration any loss suffered or likely to be suffered by the exclusive licensee as a result of the infringement or, as the case may be, the profits derived from the infringement, so far as it constitutes an infringement of the rights of the exclusive licensee as such.

(2) In any proceedings taken by the holder of an exclusive licence by virtue of this section the proprietor of the relevant patent shall, unless he is joined as plaintiff in the proceedings, be added as defendant; provided that a proprietor added as a defendant in pursuance of this

subsection shall not be liable for any costs unless he enters an appearance and takes part in the proceedings.

## J. Extracts from court decisions

No applicable case law. **45**

# § 7
# Italy

## A. Executive summary

1 Although decisions on second medical use issues are rather scant, over recent years Italian courts have nevertheless handed down some decisions on skinny labels. Based on case law available so far, it appears that in order to rule out the risk of infringement, generic companies need to take additional preventive measures to minimise the risk that the generic product will be used for the patented indication.

2 In particular, Italian courts have ordered generic companies to inform all the stakeholders (pharmacists' associations, hospitals, local health authorities, etc.) that the generic may not be used for the patented indications. It still remains to be clarified if such steps are always mandatory in cases where the generic supplier has carved out the protected indications from the SmPC and the leaflet before market entry. However, in light of the available case law and according to the rules on indirect infringement, it is reasonable to conclude that informing the stakeholders will be required when the prescribing practice of the infringing product is primarily for the protected indication.

3 Italian decisions have so far only addressed the issue of generic products, but it appears reasonable to assume that infringement by a biosimilar product of second medical use patents would be treated in a similar manner.

## B. Scope of protection and interpretation of second medical use claims

4 Article 46 of the Italian Intellectual Property Code (*Codice della proprietà industriale* – IPC) concerning novelty – analogous to Article 54 EPC – explicitly provides for the possibility of patenting substances or compositions already known/patented if they claim a new use (i.e. the second medical use).[1] Thus, in principle, it is possible to argue that pursuant to Article 46 IPC, product claims limited by purpose may have been granted well before the reform of the EPC 2000 and that Swiss-type claims may have been unnecessary under Italian law. However, since there is no data available on the approach adopted by the Italian Patent and Trademark Office, such an argument is a mere hypothesis.[2]

5 Accordingly, second medical use patent protection will be limited to the claimed use, consistent with the general rules applicable to any kind of patent for defining the scope of protection.

[1] It should be noted that the possibility of patenting a new use of a substance or composition already known regardless of the technical sector was introduced in Italy on the implementation of the EPC in 1979 when Article 54 EPC in its original formulation allowed the patentability of a known composition with specific reference to pharmaceutical compounds only. For the text of Article 46 IPC → mn. 42.

[2] Cuonzo/Ampollini, Generic Medicines and Second Medical Use Patents: Litigation or Regulation? An Overview of Recent European Case Law and Practice, IIC 2018, 895 (906).

Thus, like all other patents, the scope of protection of the second medical use patent would be defined by the claims (whereas the description and drawings, if any, will be used to interpret the claims). When interpreting the scope of patent protection, it will be necessary to balance the fair protection of the patent owner with a reasonable degree of legal certainty for third parties. 6

## C. Direct and indirect infringement of second medical use claims

### I. Infringement of second medical use claims – direct patent infringement

Pursuant to Article 66 IPC (→ mn. 43), patent claims are infringed whenever an unauthorised third party produces/manufactures, uses, markets, sells or imports into the Italian territory a product, which is the subject matter of a patent or a patent application. It is therefore necessary to consider how this rule applies to patents for second medical use. 7

First, it should be noted that Italian case law has never specifically addressed the issue whether the infringing activities of second medical use patents would constitute direct or indirect infringement. Courts have indeed examined under which circumstances the manufacturing or sale of the relevant drug product constitutes infringement of a second medical use patent, but without exploring whether such infringement was direct or indirect. On the one hand, this could be interpreted as an indication that courts consider the manufacture and sale of the drug in violation of a second medical use patent as a direct infringement. On the other hand, establishing the nature of the infringement (whether direct or indirect) does not appear to have had a material impact on the assessment of the liability of the generic manufacturer.[3] 8

The same applies to scholars with one notable exception (→ mn. 16 et seq.). Rather than considering the nature of the infringement, they have identified some circumstances, which can be considered as establishing the presence of an infringement, or not. Such circumstances can be inherent factors (dosage, quantity, etc.), extrinsic factors (type of packaging, commercial channels, etc.) or specific factors (therapeutic indication in the leaflets).[4] 9

In recent years, case law has outlined some important principles with respect to the circumstances under which infringement of second medical use patents may occur. 10

First, Italian courts rejected the argument that the use as such of an active ingredient for a medical use different from the patented one constitutes patent infringement.[5] Infringement was ruled out in that case since there was no reference to the patented use in the SmPC/leaflet.[6] 11

---

[3] Indeed, indirect infringement is established when the party who supplied the means relating to an essential element of the invention knew or should have known using ordinary diligence that the means were suitable and intended for putting the invention into effect in a country where the invention is protected. Assessment of 'ordinary diligence' is carried out by examining the objective circumstance of the case (→ mn. 16 et seq.).

[4] See Sena, I diritti sulle invenzioni, 4th edn, Milan 2014, p. 323 et seq., Musso, Libro quinto: Lavoro Art. 2563-2574 Art. 2584-2601, Bologna 2012, p. 712.

[5] Court of Milan, 17.12.2010, docket no. 79818/06 – *Alanerv*; → mn. 48.

[6] More precisely, the decision differentiated between the conducts carried out by the alleged infringers prior to the commencement of the proceedings and those carried out after the commencement of

12 In 2020, the Court of Milan held that if the market authorisation (MA) of the generic drug is clearly limited to patent-free indications, the marketing of the generic drug does not infringe the second medical use patent.[7] Said decision also pointed out that even if the generic drug can in principle be administered for the claimed use by virtue of the MA, infringement would nonetheless still be ruled out if the patented indication is not contained in the SmPC. It should be noted however that the reasoning of this decision did not delve into the issue of infringement because the relevant patent was held invalid, and so the direct or indirect infringement was not an issue to be decided. Still, the Court did state that in order to establish infringement by the generic manufacturer it is necessary that the SmPC includes the patented indication. Further, since the Court cited the decision of the Düsseldorf Higher Regional Court,[8] it can once again be argued that the Court considered (albeit without expressly saying so) that the manufacture and sale of the generic may amount to direct infringement.

13 A more recent decision on skinny label required the generic manufacturers to remove the patented indication not only from the SmPC and the leaflet but also from the MA. However, that decision concerned a case where not only the generic's market authorisation but also SmPC and package leaflet indicated inter alia the suitability of the product for the use claimed by the patent. Accordingly, the obligation to remove the protected market authorisation was a remedy to the infringement rather than a pre-requirement upon the generic company to exclude infringement.[9]

14 On 10 January 2022, the Court of Milan in interim proceedings on second medical use patents of Everolimus again implicitly confirmed previous case law. The Court in fact found there had been an infringement where the generic company (which had originally specified the patented indications in the SmPC and in the package leaflet) participated in various tenders for the supply of Everolimus for which there was no specific limitation on its use. The injunction was granted even though, in April 2021, the generic company had submitted a request to the Italian Medicines Agency (*Agenzia Italiana del Farmaco* – AIFA) to remove the relevant patented indication from both the SmPC and the package leaflet. It should be noted that the decision was issued before the requested change was implemented by AIFA (a crucial factor for the outcome of the urgent decision).

15 From the reasoning of the decision, it could be argued that had the generic company adopted all the necessary and appropriate measures to rule out the possibility that the drug would be used for patented indications before its entry onto market and in particular, before taking part in tenders, then infringement would have been ruled out.

---

proceedings. On the one hand, the patent owner was unable to demonstrate whether there had been any infringement of the patent prior to the commencement of the proceedings. Indeed, from the evidence submitted, it was not possible to assess if the package leaflets and brochures bearing the patented therapeutic indications have ever been made available to the public. On the other hand, the package leaflet (and the related SmPC and MA) of the generic product Alanerv manufactured and marketed after the commencement of the proceedings contained no indication of the product's use as an adjuvant for neuropathies of diabetic origin. Hence, the Court stated that there was no patent infringement.

[7] Court of Milan, 3.12.2020 – *Fulvestrant*; → mn. 44. It should be noted that the Court used the phrase 'clear limitation' to describe a situation in which the generic company included in the MA only patent free indications.

[8] For details → § 5 mn. 14 et seq.

[9] The decision (Court of Milan, 13.7.2021 – *Everolimus Ethypharm*; → mn. 47) was rendered in the framework of urgent proceedings and then confirmed in urgent appeal. Proceedings on the merits is, according to our information, still pending.

## II. Indirect patent infringement

16 Italian patent law does not expressly address the issue of indirect patent infringement for second medical use inventions. Furthermore, as stated above, Italian case law on second medical use has not explicitly considered the nature of infringement of second medical use patents by the supplier of the drug.

17 Pursuant to Article 66 ICP (→ mn. 43), patent claims are infringed whenever a third party supplies any person (other than a party authorised by the patentee to exploit the invention), means relating to an essential element of the invention and necessary for putting it into effect within the territory of a State in which the invention is protected, when the third party knows or should have known through ordinary diligence, that those means are suitable and intended for putting that invention into effect. Such rule is applicable inter alia also when the means are supplied to a person making private use of the relevant invention. Further, Article 66 ICP stipulates that in the case of staple commercial products, inducement by the third-party supplier will be necessary to establish infringement by the latter.

18 Scholars consider that the rules on indirect infringement are applicable to the manufacturer/seller of generics and biosimilars of a drug protected by a second medical use patent. According to authoritative Italian literature,[10] if an active ingredient or a composition is capable of two or more uses, only one of which is patented, the manufacture or the sale of the composition as such are lawful and only the purchaser may commit direct infringement by using the patent for the protected use.[11] Consistently, there will be indirect infringement of the patent by the generic manufacturer only when there is knowledge that the product is going to be used for the implementation of a third-party patented invention (whether or not it is for non-private purposes). Such knowledge is derivable from objective circumstances. As mentioned by scholars, this is the case, for example, when the composition is sold in doses, in packages, with instructions, with additives or in physical states that are exclusively functional with respect to the patented use.

19 The above reasoning appears consistent with recent case law: indirect infringement occurs if, from the objective circumstances of the relevant case, it can be inferred that the alleged indirect infringer knew or should have known that an unauthorised protected use of the product was going to occur. In one of the first applications of Article 66(2bis) IPC, the Court of Milan confirmed such approach in denying contributory infringement.[12] The Court reasoned that to recognise indirect infringement, it is necessary both to provide third parties with means relating to an indispensable element of the invention and the third parties' knowledge of the destination of such means to implement the invention; the presence of precautions for the administration of the drug in the SmPC which – if followed – excluded direct infringement, was held sufficient to exclude contributory infringement (in the case in question with reference to the administration of the drug). Indeed, a different use by the pharmacist was not foreseeable (note, however, that in this case the medicine was an oncological drug for which hospital pharmacists and doctors would unlikely depart from the prescriptions of the SmPC).

20 Although the case examined by the Court did not relate to second medical use, this ruling provides some interesting insights, which are arguably applicable also to second medical use. Indeed, if second medical use is not foreseeable, absent any patented indications in the MA and/or at least in the SmPC and leaflet package before market entry of

---

[10] Vanzetti/Di Cataldo/Spolidoro, Manuale di diritto industriale, Milan 2021, p. 463.

[11] To the extent the purchaser does not use the invention for private purposes or other exceptions to exclusive patent rights set forth by the ICP (such as the Bolar exemption) apply.

[12] Court of Milan, 12.9.2017 – *Pemetrexed – Fresenius Kabi – Eli Lilly*; → mn. 46.

the generic, also indirect infringement should in principle be ruled out. Conversely, from the same decision it cannot be ruled out that other particular circumstances making the second medical use foreseeable may be sufficient to establish indirect infringement even if the MA, SmPC and leaflet did not mention any patented indication (e.g. the prescribing practice → mn. 21 et seq.).

## D. Infringement of second medical use claims and skinny label products

21 There is to the best of our knowledge as yet no publicly available case law on the impact of the prescribing practice of second medical use indications in Italy. However, based on the aforementioned decisions on second medical use patents infringement and on the rules applicable to indirect infringement, it is reasonable to conclude that if there is evidence of a very considerable prescribing practice which departs from the SmPC indications of the generic/biosimilar product, there would be room for the originator to argue indirect infringement of the second medical use patent on the basis that the generic manufacturer should have foreseen the use of its drug for the patented use.[13]

22 However, in the absence of clear guidance based on case law, it could be reasonable to exclude even indirect infringement notwithstanding considerable prescribing practice if appropriate additional precautions were adopted by the generic manufacturer before market entry of its product (i.e. written notice to stakeholders not to use the product for the patented indications → mn. 23 et seq.).

## E. Strategies and considerations

23 In light of the remedies ordered by Italian courts in the case of SmPCs and leaflets originally mentioning the protected use, at least in cases when a significant prescribing practice contradicted the indications in the SmPC of the generic drug or in cases where the originator drug is used mostly for the protected indication, specifying only patent free uses in the SmPC (and package leaflet) could be deemed insufficient to avoid indirect infringement. Indeed, taking further precautionary steps, such as informing stakeholders that the biosimilar cannot be used for patented indications and including a disclaimer with the same information in the skinny label, might be highly desirable.

24 Indeed, the Court of Milan in its decision issued on 13 July 2021 on the infringement of a patent on Everolimus – enjoined the generic company to also inform in writing all stakeholders (including databases providing information on medicines on the market) that the generic should not be used for the patented use.

25 The Court drew up a list of parties, to whom the generic manufacturer must notify said information, considering the nature of the drug (oncological drug). Such list included

[13] Indeed, the Court of Milan – in denying the interference – explicitly agreed with the defendant's argument that Teva's drug is not 'suitable' for the claimed use, neither from a regulatory (not having been authorised for such a use) nor from a practical point of view (such a use not being envisaged or practised in current oncological practice) (Court of Milan, 3.12.2020; → mn. 44). *Argumentum e contrario*, it may be concluded that a significant prescribing practice may be a relevant factor to establish – indirect – infringement.

medical associations, pharmacists' associations, hospitals, local health authorities and organisations that manage databases providing information on medicines on the market.

Further, the Court of Milan ordered the generic company to provide a similar statement in writing on the use of the drug each time the generic company participated in a tender/submitted a commercial offer. 26

Again, however it should be noted that such obligation was imposed in a scenario where the SmPC originally did not carve out the patented indications and thus the approach of the Court was arguably particularly strict for such reason. 27

## F. Legal remedies

Articles 128–133 IPC provide several remedies available on an urgent basis to patent holders and/or licensees. In the case of infringement, the main remedy is the injunction by which the court prohibits the infringer from continuing or resuming the activity that constitutes patent infringement. 28

An injunction may be granted either *ante causam* or during proceedings on the merits. The judge may also set a penalty for each day of delay in complying with the injunction or for each breach of the relevant order. 29

In case of infringement of second medical use claims, it would be crucial that the injunction set out in sufficient detail which specific conduct (or rather, use) is prohibited, to avoid overly broad orders that could impair legitimate uses of the generic product in patent-free indications. 30

Further available urgent remedies include the seizure of generic products (especially if the infringer had not adopted the so-called skinny label approach) to prevent their circulation, as well as the withdrawal from the market of the infringing products. 31

The above-mentioned remedies are available also to patent applicants. Indeed, pursuant to Article 53 IPC, patent protection starts on the date on which the application is made available to the public (i.e. 18 months after the filing date or 90 days from the filing date if the applicant has requested the immediate publication of the application or if the patent applicant has directly served the application upon the infringer), and with regards to European patents starts on the date on which the owner has filed with the IPTO a translation of the claims of the application into Italian or has directly served upon the infringer such translation. Accordingly, it is not uncommon in Italy to enforce published patent applications on an urgent basis. 32

Granting urgent measures under Italian law requires that the court assesses both the *prima facie* case and the urgency requirement (a risk of irreparable harm if remedies to infringement are delayed until a first instance judgment on the merits is rendered). It should be noted that Italian case law does not evaluate the urgency requirement rigorously, and thus it would still be possible to file a motion for an interim injunction after few months from the discovery of the infringement. Injunctions and seizures can in principle be granted *ex parte*. However, in patent cases, *ex parte* orders are extremely rare (except for search orders, the '*descrizione*'). 33

Unlike some European jurisdictions and the UPC system, Italy does not allow generic companies to file 'protective letters' before the court.[14] However, the generic company shall be entitled to bring urgent proceedings seeking a declaration of non-infringement if there are circumstances indicating that an infringement action could be brought by the 34

---

[14] For example, Germany → § 5 mn. 38, the Netherlands → § 8 mn. 59, and Spain → § 11 mn. 49.

originator (e.g. a cease and desist letter sent to the generic company or actions brought by the originator against the generic company whether in Italy or in other jurisdictions).

35 Patent holders can also initiate proceedings on the merits in which, in addition to the measures mentioned above that could be also granted on an urgent basis, they can seek reimbursement of damages.

36 Finally, both in urgent and ordinary proceedings, the patentee can request that the decision be published in newspapers and/or websites at the cost of the losing party.

## G. Infringement of second medical use claims and biosimilar products

37 Although in Italy there are no decisions available concerning the infringement of a second medical use patent by a biosimilar product, we assume that Italian courts would apply the same legal approach used to assess direct or indirect infringement by a generic product, and so the potential infringement risk for generics and biosimilars appear to be similar.

38 Nevertheless, there are factors that may play a role in the assessment of infringement and of the diligence of the supplier of the drug and which would render the prescription of a biosimilar for the protected indication less plausible than in the case of a generic.

39 Indeed, generics and biosimilars present a significant difference with reference to the issue of substitutability, i.e. the practice of replacing one drug with another (the replacement drug being usually cheaper for the health service and/or the patient).

40 Unlike the case in which, if the physician prescribes the branded product, the pharmacist may replace this prescribed product automatically with a generic,[15] the pharmacist cannot replace the reference biological medicine with one of its biosimilars, as substitution by the pharmacist should only take place after consultation with the prescribing physician.[16]

41 This difference could reduce *ab initio* the possibility of a prescribing practice for the patented indication of the potential infringing product. Indeed, it is unlikely that the physician will prescribe the drug for a protected use that departs from the therapeutic indications of the SmPC and the package leaflet, especially taking into account inter alia that unlike generic equivalents, biosimilars are not identical to the originators drug (there are differences in content resulting from the biosimilar itself). Such circumstance may exclude the liability of the supplier for lack of predictability of the use of the biosimilar for the implementation of the second medical use invention. However, such assessment should be made on a case-by-case basis.

---

[15] Unless the physician has provided specific medical reasons or the patient agrees to pay the difference between the price of the originator drug and its generic version.

[16] https://www.aifa.gov.it/documents/20142/808717/2_Position-Paper-AIFA-Farmaci-Biosimilari.pdf.

# H. Statutory provisions

## Code of Industrial Property

### Article 46 – Novelty 42

1. An invention shall be considered novel if it does not form part of the state of the art.

2. The state of the art shall be held to comprise everything made available to the public in the territory of the Country or abroad before the date of filing of the patent application, by means of a written or oral description, by use or by any other means.

3. Prior art is also considered to include the Italian patent applications or European patent applications designating Italy, as filed, which have a date of filing prior to the one mentioned in paragraph 2 and that have been published or made available to the public on that date as well or later.

4. The provisions of paragraphs 1, 2 and 3 shall also not exclude the patentability of any substance or composition of substances already included in the prior art, provided that they are for the purpose of a new utilisation.

### Article 66 – Patent Rights 43

1. The patent rights for an industrial invention consist of the exclusive right to put into effect the invention and profit from the same in the territory of the Country, within the limits and at the conditions established by this Code.

2. In particular, the patent grants its owner the following exclusive rights:

a) where the subject matter of the patent is a product, the right to prevent third parties, not having the owner's consent, from manufacturing, using, putting on the market, selling or importing such product for these purposes;

b) where the subject matter of the patent is a process, the right to prevent third parties, not having the owner's consent, from applying the process, and using, putting on the market, selling, or importing the product directly obtained by such process for these purposes.

2-bis. The patent shall also confer on its owner the exclusive right to prevent third parties, not having the owner's consent, from supplying or offering to supply any persons other than those entitled to use the patented invention means relating to an essential element of that invention and necessary for putting it into effect in the territory of a State where it is protected, where the third party has knowledge of the suitability and purpose of those means for putting the invention into effect or is able to obtain it with ordinary diligence.

2-ter. Paragraph 2-bis shall not apply when the means consist of products which are commonly marketed, unless the third party induces the person supplied to perform the acts prohibited pursuant to paragraph 2.

2-quater. For the purposes of paragraph 2-bis, persons performing the acts referred to in Article 68(1) shall not be considered to be parties entitled to use the invention.

# J. Extracts from court decisions

44 
## I. *Astrazeneca v Teva (Fulvestrant)*[17]

### 4. Interference

In light of the invalidity of the patent, the defendant's action for a declaration of infringement of Teva's generic drugs must be rejected.

In any event, this Court Judge notes that infringement would still be excluded, even if EP 195 were valid, considering that:

i. the patent enforced is a second medical use patent, aimed at protecting the use of an already known substance, limited to the claimed use;
ii. in such a case, interference cannot be found should the generic drug in its marketing authorisation already contain a clear limitation to patent-free uses (omissis);
iii. to find interference by a third party's product, it is necessary that the latter is not only suitable in the abstract for the claimed use, but also that the package leaflet indicates the use claimed in the patent.

This assessment is supported by several decisions issued in other jurisdictions ruling in favour of non-infringement[18].

The defendant's considerations that Teva's drug is not 'suitable' for the claimed use, neither from a regulatory (not having been authorised for such a use) nor from a practical point of view (such a use not being envisaged or practiced in current oncological practice), nor has the defendant offered any evidence to the contrary, are therefore correct.

Hence, all plaintiff's alternate claims are likewise rejected, including:

(a) Insertion – in the SPC and the Package Leaflet – of the specification that the drug cannot be used for the use protected by EP '195 with subsequent request for modification of the MA;
(b) indication in the informational, promotional and marketing material that the generic drug cannot be prescribed/used for the use covered by EP '195;
(c) disclosure to all stakeholders that the generic 'Fulvestrant Teva' cannot be used for the population of patients as per EP '195.

45 
## II. *Novartis v Medac (Everolimus)*[19]

With respect to infringement, the [Court-appointed expert's] opinion highlights that – with reference to patent EP '246 (breast cancer), Medac removed from the Everolimus' package leaflet the indication for the treatment of hormone receptor-positive breast cancer, while the parts of the package leaflet still referring to this indication should be removed soon, as requested by Medac to the Italian Medicines Agency (AIFA) on 14 April 2021.

With reference to patent EP '411 (pancreatic cancer), it is underlined that in the documentation provided by Medac the indication for the treatment of pancreatic neuroendocrine tumors is still present (and in any event, is not excluded). Hence, this Court finds the infringement by Medac's Everolimus of EP '411.

As regards EP '246 patent, the issue appears more blurred.

---

[17] Civil Court of Milan, 3 December 2020, docket no. 1186/2018.

[18] See the decision of Düsseldorf Higher Regional Court on 9 January 2019 (→ § 5 mn. 56), which has become *res judicata* (annex no. 24 to the first technical brief and document no. 41 of the defendant); the ruling by the Swiss Federal Patent Court with *obiter dictum* in the Preliminary Opinions.

[19] Civil Court of Milan, 10 January 2022, docket no. 11933-1/2020.

Indeed, while it is true that Medac removed the indication for the treatment of hormone receptor-positive breast cancer and that a new request of carve-out has been filed with AIFA, nevertheless the drug could still be used by recipients even for the discontinued treatment.

Medac was already awarded tenders to supply the drug to the regional health system without a specific restriction on the use of everolimus, and Novartis reports that it has not received requests for additional supplies to cover the needs that should be unmet by the inability to use Medac's drug for the discontinued treatment.

These considerations lead to the conclusion that, as a precautionary measure, and without prejudice to any different assessment in the proceedings on the merits, the circulation of Medac's drug shall be limited also in this respect.

**Now therefore**

Pursuant to Article 700 of the Civil Procedure Code,

this Court:

1) prohibits with immediate effect Medac Pharma s.r.l. from producing, marketing, advertising, promoting also through websites, importing, exporting, possessing, using, distributing and offering, in any form, including specifically taking part in public tenders concerning the supply of products containing everolimus, of Everolimus Medac and of any other medicinal product of the defendant containing everolimus, in any way named and/or marked, for use in the treatment of pancreatic neuroendocrine tumors and breast cancer;
2) prohibits with immediate effect Medac Pharma s.r.l. from producing, marketing, advertising, promoting also through websites, importing, exporting, possessing, using, distributing and offering, in any form, including specifically taking part in public tenders concerning the supply of products containing everolimus, Everolimus Medac and any other medicinal product of the defendant containing everolimus, in any way named and/or marked, without having taken all necessary and appropriate measures to prevent that such products are used in the treatment of pancreatic neuroendocrine tumors and breast cancer, in particular without having taken the following measures:
   (i) ensure that any MA and related SmPC and package leaflet of any Medac product containing everolimus, in any way named, does not contain any reference to the treatment of pancreatic neuroendocrine tumors and breast cancer;
   (ii) in the case of products already authorised with inclusion of the breast cancer in the MA, SmPC and Package leaflet, initiate and complete the process of amending the Marketing Authorisation to remove all references to the treatment of pancreatic neuroendocrine tumors and breast cancer, specifically requesting to publish the amended MA in the Official Journal, also implementing such changes in the SmPC and the product Package leaflet;
   (iii) inform in writing all interested parties and entities, including medical associations, pharmacist associations, hospitals, local health service, procurement bodies and organisations managing databases that provide information on drugs on the market, including at least:
   FARMADATI;
   CODIFA – The medical rep;
   AIOM (Italian Association of Medical Oncology);
   CIPOMO Primari Oncologi Clinici (Italian College of Chief Medical Oncologists Hospital Oncologists);
   SIFO (national and regional sections) Hospital Pharmacists (Italian Society of Hospital Pharmacy);
   SIFACT (Italian Society of Clinical Pharmacy and Therapeutics);
   FARE (Federation of Regional Associations of Bursars and Providers of Health);
   of the fact that Medac's products containing everolimus, in any way called, are not indicated, and should not be used, in the treatment of pancreatic neuroendocrine

tumors and breast cancer, therefore asking these entities and bodies to inform their members accordingly and to include a corresponding note or footnote in the relevant databases;

(iv) communicate in writing whenever they make a commercial offer, submit a bid to participate in a tender or otherwise supply any product containing everolimus, in any way named – to the recipient of that offer, bid or supply that such product is not indicated, and shall not be used, for the treatment of pancreatic neuroendocrine tumors and Breast Cancer Indications, and that such offer, application or supply does not and cannot concern populations requiring everolimus in the treatment of pancreatic neuroendocrine tumors and/or breast cancer;

3) injuncts Medac Pharma S.r.l. from transferring and/or licensing the MA of Medac Everolimus or any other MA for everolimus-containing medicinal products in any way named, to any third party, unless such third party has committed in writing to comply with the measures described herein;
4) orders Medac Pharma s.r.l. to withdraw and recall products already put on the market and stocked at wholesalers, distributors, pharmacies, local health service and hospitals without adopting the measures under point 2 above, and/or request its wholesalers and distributors to withdraw and recall such products;
5) imposes on Medac Pharma s.r.l. a penalty of € 10,000.00 for each day of delay in implementing the above measures starting from the thirtieth day from the communication of this order, and of € 2,000.00 for each unit of product marketed in breach of the above measures starting from the same date.'

46

## III. *Fresenius v Eli Lilly (Pemetrexed)*[20]

6. On indirect infringement.

In its statement of defense, the defendant also counter-claimed indirect infringement since PEMETREXED FRESENIUS would provide pemetrexed anions, an indispensable element of the invention necessary for its implementation according to the defendant. Pemetrexed anions are obtained by dissolution in glucosate solution, it being according to the defendant, irrelevant that the means consisted of pemetrexed diacid instead of pemetrexed disodium.

Moreover, according to the defendant, the marketing of Fresenius's product would represent indirect infringement even if the use of a compound based on pemetrexed disodium were required to find infringement, since the manufacturer's prescriptions would not be followed by the oncologist doctor and pharmacist to whom they were addressed to. Likely, they would use a saline solution instead of the glucosate solution prescribed in the Fresenius product, also using for that purpose the stability data set out in the patent. Law 214/2016 amended Article 66 of the Italian Industrial Property Code, by introducing paragraph 2-bis, which prescribes: 'the patent also confers on the owner the exclusive right to prohibit third parties, except with his consent, from supplying or offering to supply to third parties other than those entitled to use the patented invention, the means relating to an indispensable element of that invention and necessary for its implementation in the territory of a State in which it is protected, if the third party has knowledge of the suitability and purpose of those means for implementing the invention or is able to obtain such knowledge with ordinary diligence'.

The provision essentially transposes the conclusions reached by case law on indirect infringement, requiring, for the recognition of indirect infringement, on the one hand, the supply to third parties of the means relating to an indispensable element of the invention and, on the other hand, the third party's awareness that said means implement the invention. The Court appointed expert, after examining the components of the patent and of the Fresenius

[20] Civil Court of Milan, 12 September 2017, docket no. 54470/2016.

product, the manufacturer's therapeutical prescriptions, as well as the patent referred to by the defendant during the discussion, as requested in the technical question, also excluded indirect infringement, observing, in summary:

- the anion of pemetrexed cannot be considered a mean relating to an indispensable element of the invention, since the invention is limited 'to the use of sodium pemetrexed' which is a different active ingredient from the one used by the Fresenius product (Court appointed expert's report p. 45, 47, 48);
- as to the solution in which to reconstitute and dilute the two products, pemetrexed disodium is indicated, in the description and examples of patent EP '508, as 'ALIMTA®'. The SmPC of ALIMTA® only describes a saline solution (i.e., a 10 0.9 % aqueous sodium chloride solution) in which to reconstitute and dilute the product, and no mention is made of possible reconstitution and dilution in other infusion liquids. The SmPC of the Fresenius Product only mentions reconstitution and dilution in 5 % glucose solution, which is a chemically different, and not equivalent, infusion fluid compared to saline. In the presence of contrary prescriptions of the manufacturer, it is not foreseeable that the operator in charge of preparing the solution for the infusion of the Fresenius product would replace it with a solution having a completely different chemical composition and, 'even considering a diabetic patient, the risk of administering to such a patient a composition containing a potentially unstable and ineffective anti-cancer drug would certainly be a more serious possibility compared to the risk of causing him a modest hyperglycaemia' (Court appointed expert's report p. 44–48). In the light of these coherent observations, indirect infringement cannot be established on a urgent basis.

## IV. *Novartis v Ethypharm and Avas (Everolimus)*[21] 47

### 4.1.5. Infringement

With respect to infringement, the Court-appointed expert examined the scope of protection of the claims highlighting their essential features. Dr. Pallini Gervasi identified the following essential features of claim 1:

- everolimus;
- the combination with an aromatase inhibitor; and
- the use for the treatment of hormone receptor-positive breast cancer.

As to claim 2, it is directly dependent on claim 1 and limits the definition of aromatase inhibitor to the following compounds: atamestane exemestane, formestane, aminoglutethimide, rogletimide, pyridoglutethimide trilostane, testolactone, ketoconazole, vorozole, fadrozole, anastrozole and letrozole.

Secondly, the Court-appointed expert analysed the indications in the Marketing Authorisation, in the Summary of Product Characteristics (SmPC), and in the Package Leaflet of the medicines called Everolimus Ethypharm and Linevero, and then proceeded to a comparative analysis between the scope of protection of the claims and those medicines.

From an analysis of the therapeutic indication in the MA and the SmPC submitted, the Court-appointed expert drew the information that the Everolimus Ethypharm contains the active ingredient everolimus and is indicated for the 'treatment of advanced hormone receptor positive breast cancer , HER2/neu negative, in combination with exemestane, in post-menopausal women in the absence of symptomatic visceral disease after recurrence or progression following treatment with a non-steroidal aromatase inhibitor.'

Furthermore, in paragraph '1. What is Everolimus Ethypharm and what is it for' of the Package Leaflet it is stated that Everolimus Ethypharm is an anti-cancer medicinal product containing an active ingredient called everolimus and is used to treat adult patients with ad-

[21] Civil Court of Milan, 13 July 2021, docket no. 52794-1/2019.

vanced positive hormone receptor status breast cancer in post-menopausal women, for whom other treatments can no longer keep the disease under control. The medicinal product must be administered in combination with the aromatase inhibitor exemestane.

As regards the medicinal product Linevero, from an analysis of the therapeutic indication in the MA and the SmPC submitted, it appears that it includes the active ingredient everolimus and is indicated for the treatment of 'advanced breast cancer with hormone receptor status, HER2/neu negative, in combination with exemestane, in women in postmenopausal in the absence of symptomatic visceral disease after recurrence or progression following treatment with a non-steroidal aromatase inhibitor'.

From the comparative analysis between EP'246 and the drugs Everolimus Ethypharm and Linevero, based on the documentation examined by the Court-appointed expert, it can be concluded that Everolimus Ethypharm and Linevero infringe claims 1 and 2 of EP '246.

The conclusions reached by the Court-appointed expert, preceded by the careful and scrupulous analysis of the documentary evidence submitted, are fully sharable insofar as they are supported by adequate and articulate reasoning, capable of overcoming the objections raised by the defendants.

***

**Now therefore**

Pursuant to Article 700 of the Italian Civil Procedure Code,

the Court:

1) prohibits – with immediate effect – Ethypharm SA and Avas Pharmaceuticals S.r.l. from manufacturing, marketing, advertising, promoting also through websites, importing, exporting, possessing, using, distributing and offering, in any form whatsoever, including specifically participating in public tenders concerning the supply of products containing everolimus, of Everolimus Ethypharm, Linevero and any other applicants' drug products containing everolimus, in any waynamed and/or labelled, for use in the breast cancer indication mentioned above;
2) prohibits – with immediate effect – Ethypharm SA and Avas Pharmaceuticals S.r.l. from manufacturing, marketing, advertising, promoting also through websites, importing, exporting, possessing, using, distributing and supplying, including specifically taking part in public tenders concerning the supply of products containing everolimus, of Everolimus Ethypharm, Linevero and any other medicinal everolimus-containing product of the claimant, in any wayr named and/or labelled, without having taken the following steps:
   (i) ensuring that any Marketing Authorision and related SmPC and Package Leaflet of any Ethypharm and/or Avas products containing everolimus, in any way named, do not contain any therapeutic indication for breast cancer;
   (ii) in the case of products already authorised with the therapeutic indication for Breast Cancer in the MA, SmPC and Package Leaflet, starting and completing the process of amending the Marketing Authorisation to remove all references to the breast cancer claim, requesting in particular that the amended MA be published in the Official Journal and that these changes be implemented in the SmPC and the Package Leaflet of the product;
   (iii) inform in writing all interested stakeholders and entities, including medical associations, pharmacist associations, hospitals, ASLs procurement bodies and organisations managing databases that provide information on medicines on the market, including at least:
   FARMADATA;
   CODIFA – The medical rep;
   AIOM (Italian Association of Medical Oncology);
   CIPOMO Primari Oncologi Clinici (Italian College of Chief Medical Oncologists Hospital Oncologists);

SIFO (national and regional sections) Hospital Pharmacists (Italian Society of Hospital Pharmacy);
SIFACT (Italian Society of Clinical Pharmacy and Therapeutics);
FARE (Federation of Regional Associations of Bursars and Providers of Health);
that medicinal product containing everolimus from Ethypharm and/or Avas, however named, are not indicated, and should not be used, for breast cancer, therefore asking these entities and bodies to inform their members and to include a relevant note or footnote in the relevant databases;

(iv) advise in writing – whenever they make a commercial offer, submit a bid to participate in a tender or otherwise supply any product containing everolimus, in any way named – to the recipient of such an offer, bid or supply that such product is not indicated, and must not be used, for the Breast Cancer Indication, and that such a tender, application or supply does not and cannot relate to populations in need of everolimus for the Breast Cancer Indication.

## V. *Giellepi v Meda Pharma and Alfa Wasserman (Alanerv)*[22] 48

12) Moving to the non-infringement claim of Giellepi's and the counterclaim of infringement brought by Meda Pharma, it must be reiterated that for the patent claims deemed to be valid, insofar as provided with the aforementioned disclaimer, the claimed medical use has been acknowledged as patentable. Such use relates to the treatment of diabetes, insulin resistance and complications of diabetes. Therefore, such use is the discriminating element in assessing possible interference in the activities of third parties.

Whereas the product manufactured by Giellepi and marketed by Alfa Wassermann under the name Alanerv contains two active ingredients (gamma linoleic acid and lipoic acid) – which were described in Meda's patent claims as preferably combinable with each other to obtain the desired effect, it must be stated that, from a chemical composition standpoint, there are no differences between Alanerv and the products under the defendant's patent.

However, and this is common ground between the parties, a different use, both in relation to actual use and in relation to the therapeutic indications proposed by the third company, could be sufficient to exclude infringement.

The therapeutic indication which Meda Pharma considers infringed is diabetic neuropathy, indicated in its patent as a preferred example of a diabetic complication. Given that the burden of proof of infringement should have been on the defendant, the latter should have proved that Alanerv was and is actually suggested for diabetic neuropathy or polyneuropathy diabetic neuropathy.

Since Alfa Wassermann's technical expert stated that since December 2006 the Alanerv package leaflet no longer contains any indication on the use of the product as an adjuvant for neuropathies of diabetic origin, it could be inferred that such an indication had previously existed. The deletion of such indication, however, prevented any interference from the time of the filing of the writ of summons in this proceedings. It should be noted that the interruption of the infringing conduct entails the rejection of requests for injunctions, for seizure and withdrawal from market, which were also formulated by the defendant Meda Pharma.

With respect to the past, however, the infringement was still not sufficiently proven, as it was not possible to assess the timing nor demonstrate if the package leaflets and brochures found bearing (inter alia in an absolutely secondary position) the above-mentioned therapeutic indications (see p. 40 of the Court appointed expert's report) were actually available to the public. Both these arguments were disputed by Giellepi and Alfa Wassermann. On the other hand, Meda Pharma did not submit the necessary evidence. It is significant that Alfa

[22] Civil Court of Milan, 17 December 2010, docket no. 79818/06.

Wassermann submitted copies of the external labelling of Alanerv in the period 2004/2007 by submitting the corresponding update notes sent to the Ministry of Health, and that from these documents no therapeutical indications interfering with the patent at stake could be found.

Hence, there is no concrete evidence – based on documents produced by or invoked against Giellepi and Alfa Wassermann – to confirm the date of the documents, their possible availability to the public and the coincidence of the recommended use of the product with that claimed by Meda Pharma's patent. Moreover, regarding Giellepi, there is no evidence that it had been informed of the use promoted by Alfa Wassermann in the claimed diabetic conditions. The data provided with the Abacam research, based on a survey carried out in 2006 (submitted by Giellepi itself under document 9), are too meager: according to such research, few doctors (at the time already contacted by the scientific informants) recalled the indication of Alfa Wassermann's food supplement also for diabetic polyneuropathy or diabetic neuropathy. Indeed, only 4 doctors out of the 110 interviewed recalled such indication, and they also recalled that it was an indication suggested as occasional. It is even more doubtful that there could have been any interference, since Alanerv is presented as a dietary supplement 'adjuvant to strengthen the body's ability to fight oxidative stress and altered nervous trophism', while the products under the Meda Pharma patent are proper drugs, medicines for the treatment or prevention of diabetes.

# § 8
# The Netherlands

## A. Executive summary

In the Netherlands, the Dutch Supreme Court (*Hoge Raad*) provided guidance for assessing infringement of second medical use patents in two landmark decisions: *Sun/Novartis*[1] and *MSD/Teva*[2]. 1

The question regarding the possibility of indirect infringement of a Swiss-type claim in the Netherlands arose for the first time in the *Sun/Novartis* case. After *Sun/Novartis* came the Dutch Supreme Court decision in which the Supreme Court considered that Swiss-type claims, like EPC 2000 claims, can be indirectly infringed, thereby following the German *Bundesgerichtshof* and the UK Supreme Court in the *Pemetrexed* cases. The Dutch Supreme Court also decided on the evidentiary threshold for proving direct infringement on a second medical use patent. The test is the same for indirect infringement, meaning that the same conduct can be both direct and indirect infringement. 2

According to the Supreme Court, a manufacturer or seller is only liable for infringement if: 3

1. the skilled person will consider that the product is (also) intended for or suited to the treatment covered by the second medical use patent.
2. the manufacturer or seller foresees or ought to foresee that the product they manufacture or offer will intentionally be used for that treatment. For this, it is required that there are circumstances, such as the content of the SmPC or package leaflet, on the basis of which it can be held that the pharmaceutical composition is (also) suitable and intended for the patented treatment.
3. and finally, that the manufacturer or seller does not take effective steps to prevent the product from being dispensed for the patented second medical use.

Since *MSD/Teva*, the Dutch case law has not yet crystallised what exactly constitutes sufficiently effective measures. In any case, there must be a carve-out and/or carve-in, but the Dutch Supreme Court made clear that a carve-out alone is not sufficient to meet the requirement for effective measures. Case law has provided some guidance, and practitioners have debated on what could constitute 'effective measures', both of which will be addressed in this Chapter. 4

## B. Scope of protection and interpretation of second medical use claims

In the Netherlands, Swiss-type claims are considered purpose-bound process claims; EPC 2000 claims are considered product claims. Nevertheless, in its landmark decision of 5

[1] Supreme Court (HR), 14 April 2017, ECLI:NL:HR:2017:692 (*Sun/Novartis*); → mn. 67.
[2] Supreme Court (HR), 3 November 2017, ECLI:NL:HR:2017:2807 (*MSD/Teva*); → mn. 66.

3 November 2017 in the dispute between MSD and Teva, the Dutch Supreme Court equated the scope of protection of a Swiss-type claim with that of a purpose limited product claim. The Supreme Court considered that the reasons for accepting the patentability of Swiss-type claims should be taken into account when deciding whether indirect infringement of a Swiss-type claim is legally possible. According to the Court, the application of a medicinal product is an 'essential element of the patented invention'[3]. If a Swiss-type claim were to be read to the letter, it could be argued that an intermediary dealing in a pharmaceutical composition does not indirectly infringe. After all, this intermediary does not deliver means that can be used in the claimed process 'use of a substance for the manufacture of a pharmaceutical composition for the treatment of a disease'. This goes against the rationale of the Swiss-type claim according to the Supreme Court. In the end, the rationale of these claims is to protect the application of a medicinal product.[4] Given the rationale for allowing Swiss-type claims, namely to circumvent the exclusion of patentability of therapeutic treatment methods, and given that EPC 2000 has created the possibility to claim a second medical use in the form of a purpose-bound product claim, the reasonable protection that must be awarded to a patentee under Article 1 of the Protocol on Article 69 EPC justifies the entitlement to sue for indirect infringement on a Swiss-type claim in the same manner as on an EPC 2000 purpose bound-product claim.[5] With this reasoning, the Dutch Supreme Court followed the German Federal Court of Justice in its decision of 14 June 2016[6] and the UK Supreme Court in its decision of 12 July 2017[7] in the *Pemetrexed* cases.

## C. Direct and indirect infringement of second medical use claims

6 In accordance with Article 53 Dutch Patent Act (*Rijksoctrooiwet 1995* – DPA), any natural person or legal person who manufactures, uses, brings on the market, sells, rents, supplies or in any other way trades in patented products (falling within a patent's scope of protection) may be held liable for patent infringement (→ mn. 61). In addition, a person may also be held liable for direct patent infringement if they apply a patented method in or for their business or use in their business, bring on the market, sell, rent, supply or in any other way trade in products, which are created through the use of a patented method.

7 Besides bringing an action for direct infringement, patentees can also sue for indirect infringement in accordance with Article 73(1) DPA (→ mn. 62). This Article provides patentees with the possibility to bring an action against third parties (such as suppliers of parts of patented products). For indirect infringement, it is required that a person, in or for their business, supplies or offers to supply, means relating to an essential element of the invention for putting the invention into effect, provided that this person knows or that it is obvious that those means are suitable and intended for that use.

8 Recent developments in the assessment of direct and indirect infringement of second medical use patents revolved around two Supreme Court cases: *Sun/Novartis* and *MSD/Teva*. These will be discussed below (→ mn. 16 et seq.).

---

[3] ibid., para. 3.6.4.
[4] ibid., para. 3.6.3.
[5] ibid.
[6] BGH 14.6.2016 – X ZR 29/15 (*Pemetrexed*); → § 5 mn. 54.
[7] UK Supreme Court, *Actavis UK Limited and others v Eli Lilly and Company* [2017] UKSC 48.

## I. Direct patent infringement

In *MSD/Teva*, the Supreme Court provided guidance for assessing direct infringement of a second medical indication.[8] 9

The main question in *MSD/Teva* was whether Teva had infringed MSD's patent which claims, in the form of a Swiss-type claim, the use of ribavirin in the preparation of a medicament for the treatment of chronic hepatitis C, for a duration of about 40–50 weeks, and where the patient is a naive patient with a HCV genotype 1 infection. The patent thus covered a dosage regimen and a subgroup indication. Teva's generic tablets had a skinny label whereby the carve-out excluded the patented group of patients. 10

The Court of Appeal had found that, since the patent indicates a certain subgroup of patients who had been treated with the claimed substance (ribavirin) before, the scope of protection of this so-called subgroup indication patent should be smaller than that of other second medical use patents. 11

The Supreme Court disagreed. It found that a Swiss-type claim is directly infringed by a manufacturer or distributor if they foresee or should have foreseen that the product will be used for the purpose that is the subject of the Swiss-type claim. This would be the case if the skilled person, based on the SmPC, the product information leaflet or any other circumstances, would find that the generic product is intended or suitable for the claimed indication. According to the Supreme Court, the system of the EPC does not allow a distinction to be made between different kinds of second medical uses.[9] 12

The manufacturer and/or distributor can nevertheless avoid an injunction if they have taken all measures that can be reasonably required of them to prevent the product from being dispensed downstream for the patented second medical indication; otherwise, there will be direct infringement. A mere carve-out in the SmPC and the package leaflet are insufficient for this purpose.[10] 13

As will be further explained below, the same test applies for indirect infringement of second medical use patents (→ mn. 15 et seq.). 14

## II. Indirect patent infringement

The question regarding the possibility of indirect infringement of a Swiss-type claim in the Netherlands arose for the first time in *Sun/Novartis*.[11] 15

### 1. *Sun/Novartis*

Novartis owned a patent with a Swiss-type claim for use of zoledronic acid in the preparation of a medicament for the treatment of osteoporosis, with intravenous administration with a period between administrations of at least about a year. Zoledronic acid was also indicated for Paget's disease, which indication was patent-free. Sun marketed a zoledronic acid product with a carve-out for osteoporosis, but had entered a tender of a health insurance company which did not distinguish between indications for the product. Novartis instituted PI proceedings for indirect infringement. The PI judge rejected 16

---

[8] *MSD/Teva* para. 3.4.4.

[9] ibid.

[10] ibid.; *Sun/Novartis*, para. 3.5.2.

[11] *Sun/Novartis*, para. 3.3.

Novartis' claim, but in appeal an injunction for indirect infringement was granted. Sun appealed this decision.

17 The Supreme Court ruled that the PI Court of Appeal correctly held that under the pertaining circumstances the requirements of indirect infringement had been met.[12] Notably, whether indirect infringement of a Swiss-type claim is legally possible had not been a point of debate in PI, so according to the Supreme Court this was taken correctly as a starting point by the PI Court of Appeal. In the meantime, however, in proceedings on the merits it was expressly considered by the District Court that indirect infringement is impossible since the means were not supplied for the preparation of the medicament, but that Sun had committed direct infringement. However according to the Supreme Court this was of no relevance to the outcome of the appeal before the Supreme Court.

18 With regard to indirect infringement, the Supreme Court ruled that the Court of Appeal correctly held that a manufacturer needs to make an effort to prevent their product being prescribed for the patented indication, even if it is not within their power to prevent infringement in the distribution chain in its entirety. According to the Supreme Court, the Court of Appeal had thereby not attributed acts of downstream users to Sun, but had judged, with sufficient reasoning, that Sun had not taken the effective measures which it could and should have taken to prevent downstream infringement.[13]

19 Notably, the Supreme Court reasoned that it is not required for the PI Court of Appeal to state precisely what measures Sun should have taken. Instead, it is for that party to show what measures it had taken to prevent downstream infringement. The circumstances of the case justified the conclusion by the PI Court of Appeal that Sun had insufficiently used the measures, which were available to it to prevent downstream infringement.[14]

20 These circumstances were as follows. In addition to the carve-out, Sun had sent an email to wholesalers and hospital pharmacies informing them about the patented indication. However, this letter started with the sentence 'this information is a formality'. The Court of Appeal considered this insufficient to prevent its product from being sold to third parties for the treatment of osteoporosis. On the contrary, the sentence suggested that in practice the patented indication was not important and did not require any measure.[15] Sun also failed to provide sufficient evidence that it had made an effort to convince the insurance company that it should organise its tender differently in order to make it possible for Sun to tender while respecting Novartis' patent rights, for instance by separating the tender for zoledronic acid for the application of osteoporosis on the one hand and for the application for Paget on the other hand. If the health insurance company had been insensitive to that argument and the manner of structuring the tender would have made it impossible for Sun to bid for it, then that is a circumstance that Sun would have to take up with the health insurance company. However, it does not give Sun a licence to infringe Novartis patent rights.[16]

### 2. *MSD/Teva*

21 After *Sun/Novartis* came the Supreme Court decision in *MSD/Teva* in which the Supreme Court considered that Swiss-type claims, like EPC 2000 claims, can be indirectly infringed. The Supreme Court noted that if one followed the literal wording of the claim,

---

[12] ibid., para. 3.5.2.
[13] ibid.
[14] ibid.
[15] Court of Appeal, The Hague, 27 January 2015, ECLI:NL:GHDHA:2015:1769 *(Novartis/Sun)* para. 4.34–4.35; → mn. 68.
[16] ibid., para. 4.36.

indirect infringement (for example by a distributor) of a Swiss-type claim would not be possible as the alleged infringer does not offer means to put the claimed method into effect downstream. However, the Supreme Court found there were policy reasons for a finding of infringement, such as the fact that Swiss-type claims were an accepted means to provide reasonable protection for the patentee and the fact that indirect infringement of second medical use patents (in the form of a purpose limited product claim) was made explicitly possible with the revision of the EPC 2000.[17]

The Supreme Court also decided on the evidentiary threshold for proving (direct) infringement on a Swiss-type claim. The test is the same for indirect infringement, meaning that the same action can be for both direct and indirect infringement.[18] 22

First, according to the Supreme Court, a manufacturer or distributor is only liable for direct infringement if they foresee or ought to foresee that the pharmaceutical composition that is manufactured or offered by them will intentionally be used in the treatment to which the second medical use claim relates, i.e. the 'foreseeability criterion'.[19] For this it is required that there are circumstances, such as the content of the SmPC or package leaflet, on the basis of which it can be held that the pharmaceutical composition is (also) suitable and intended for the patented treatment. 23

If it is foreseeable that a pharmaceutical composition is (also) suitable and intended for a patented treatment, the manufacturer or distributor must take all effective measures that can reasonably be asked of them, to prevent their product being dispensed for the patented second medical indication. A carve-out as such is not sufficient in this respect.[20] 24

## D. Infringement of second medical use claims and skinny label products

As discussed, the Dutch Court will assess infringement of second medical use claims in two steps. First, it will assess whether the manufacturer or distributor foresees or should foresee that a (generic) medicinal product will intentionally be used for a patented second medical use. If the requirement of foreseeability is met, the court will assess whether the manufacturer or distributor of the medicinal product has taken effective measures that could be reasonably required of them to prevent their medicinal product from being dispensed for the patented second medical use; otherwise there will be infringement. A mere carve-out in the SmPC and the package leaflet are insufficient for this purpose.[21] Notably, what are (or could be) considered effective measures is not elaborated in the Dutch case law. This will be further discussed below (→ mn. 49). 25

Foreseeability will be easily assumed if a generic advertises or suggests that its product is suitable for both the free and the patented indication.[22] The same goes if a company enters a tender with a medicinal product that has free uses and patented uses, and which tender does not distinguish between indications for the product.[23] However, foreseeability can also be assumed if the generic company does not actively promote its medicinal 26

[17] *MSD/Teva*, para. 3.6.3–3.6.4.
[18] ibid., para. 3.6.4.
[19] ibid.
[20] ibid., para. 3.5.
[21] *Sun/Novartis; MSD/Teva.*
[22] *MSD/Teva*, annotation Schutjens in JGR.
[23] *Novartis/Sun*, para. 4.34.

product for the patented medical indication because of the off-label prescribing practice in the Netherlands.

## I. Off-label prescribing in the Netherlands

27 In the Netherlands, physicians have prescriptive freedom and may prescribe off-label based on their expertise and professional responsibility.[24] Pursuant to Article 68 Dutch Medicines Act (*Geneesmiddelenwet*; → mn. 63), prescribing medicinal products outside of the indications registered by the Medicines Evaluation Board (*College ter Beoordeling van Geneesmiddelen* – hereinafter 'MEB'), the Dutch medicines authority charged with issuing marketing authorisations, is only permissible when protocols or standards have been developed within the profession for this purpose. Article 68 was introduced in 2006 after research showed that about 50 % of medicinal products were prescribed and used outside the marketing authorisation. The provision aims to ensure that prescribing outside of this registration text remains possible, but if standards or protocols exist these should be followed.[25] If these protocols or standards do not exist, consultation between the treating physician and the pharmacist is necessary for off-label use. The Dutch Medical Association (*Artsenfederatie* – KNMG), takes the position that in several situations extensive treatment protocols do not need to be present and that documented data from the professional group will suffice. This is the case, for example, if the indication refers to a different patient group or if the indication excludes use by children. The KNMG does consider national guidelines desirable when prescribing for a completely different indication. If there is no such indication, the physician should consult with the pharmacist before prescribing.[26]

28 The current practice of prescribing generics is related to the policies of health insurers. In the Netherlands, health insurers can pursue a preference policy, reimbursing only the cheapest (generic) medicinal product. Agreements insurers conclude with healthcare providers include the principle that healthcare providers prescribe medicinal products on the basis of the active substance.[27] The Guideline Effective Prescribing of the Federation of Medical Specialists, which applies to physicians,[28] also prescribes effective prescribing, i.e. based on the active substance in the medicinal product and not on the brand name. Thereafter pharmacists can dispense the cheapest (generic) medicine, which is reimbursed by the health insurer based on the preference policy.[29] Furthermore, pharmacists themselves do not see for which indication a drug is prescribed. Pharmacists are therefore often unaware of off-label prescribing.[30]

29 This leads to a practice in the Netherlands for physicians to prescribe not by indication, but by active ingredient. It is thus possible that a pharmacist dispenses generics for patented indications. This leads to the foreseeability requirement being quickly met. After all, the court will consider that the skilled person will be aware of this practice and will

---

[24] See Tekst & Commentaar Gezondheidsrecht, 10th edn, Aalphen aan den Rijn 2023, Off-label voorschrijven bij: Geneesmiddelenwet, Artikel 68.

[25] See https://zoek.officielebekendmakingen.nl/kst-29359-57.html.

[26] See https://www.knmg.nl/advies-richtlijnen/dossiers/off-label-voorschrijven.htm#.

[27] See also Court of Appeal The Hague, 4 July 2017, ECLI:NL:GHDHA:2017:1935 (*WLC/State of the Netherlands*), para. 2.4–2.4.3; → mn. 69.

[28] See https://demedischspecialist.nl/sites/default/files/Leidraad_Doelmatig_Voorschrijven.pdf.

[29] See https://www.iqhealthcare.nl/media/124487/factoren-van-invloed-op-voorschrijfbeleid-artsen-afleverbeleid-apothekers.pdf, p. 25.

[30] See p. 52 of the 2017 report RIVM (available via https://www.rivm.nl/bibliotheek/rapporten/2017-0110.pdf).

thus easily assume that a medicinal product is (also) intended or suitable for the treatment of a patented indication.[31]

**30** Finally, the MEB has a specific policy on the publication of labels that arguably contributes to the foreseeability aspect.

**31** In the Netherlands, until a few years ago the policy of the MEB was to publish in the online versions of the SmPC and package leaflet all indications without any warning or announcement that some indications are patented, i.e. 'full label'. In 2015, Warner-Lambert Company LLC (WLC) instituted PI proceedings against the MEB claiming that the full label SmPC of its generic pregabalin be replaced by the version with the carve-out. By decision of 15 January 2016, the PI Judge held that MEB had to replace the online versions of the full label SmPC and package leaflet for the generic pregabalin product with skinny label versions of these documents, from which the patented indication was carved out.[32] The PI judge considered that there was no legal obligation to publish full label information, and moreover this policy was contrary to the request of WLC as generic applicant for the marketing authorisation in question. Even though this policy did not infringe WLC's patent, according to the PI Judge, the policy was irreconcilable with the MEB's duty of care and hence unlawful.

**32** The MEB changed its policy, but only slightly. The online versions of SmPCs and package leaflets for generic medicinal products for which a skinny label version had been requested still disclosed all information (including the patented indications), although this information was now accompanied by an asterisk which referred to the following text: '*This indication is protected by a patent of another marketing authorisation holder. Please see for more information the MEB website: www.cbg-meb.nl.*' In addition, the MEB filed an appeal against the PI decision.

**33** The Dutch Court of Appeal saw reason to refer questions to the Court of Justice of the European Union (CJEU) on the legality of the MEB's policy, and specifically on the interpretation of Article 11 of Directive 2001/83/EC. Pursuant to this provision a marketing authorisation for a generic medicinal product does not, in principle, need to contain those parts of the SmPC of the reference medicinal product that refer to patented indications or dosage forms. This is a specific, patent-related exception to the general rule that a marketing authorisation for a generic product should be identical to the marketing authorisation of the (originator's) reference medicinal product. According to the CJEU, this exception establishes a limitation of the scope of the marketing authorisation application. By making use of this limitation, an applicant (or holder of a MA) thus limits the scope of his application, and the responsible national authority does not have any discretion in that respect.[33] The CJEU states that this limitation must also follow from the publicly available (online) information regarding the marketing authorisation, including the SmPC and the package leaflet.[34]

**34** As a result of this judgment, the MEB changed its policy. The MEB now only publishes skinny labels. However, if a patented indication is not included in the label, the company has to include the following standard sentence in the package leaflet: '*<Product name> contains the active substance <material name>, which is also used in the treatment of conditions not listed in this leaflet. Please contact your doctor or pharmacist if you have any questions.*'[35] This suggests that there is the possibility of off-label use and may con-

---

[31] *MSD/Teva*, para. 3.4.4.

[32] PI Judge, The Hague, 15 January 2016, ECLI:NL:RBDHA:2016:334; → mn. 70.

[33] CJEU, 14 February 2019 – case C-423/17, ECLI:EU:C:2019:125 *Warner-Lambert Company*, para. 43.

[34] ibid., para. 45.

[35] See www.cbg-meb.nl/actueel/nieuws/2019/03/28/beleidsaanpassingpatientinformatie-door-uitspraak-europees-hof.

tribute to a lower threshold for assuming foreseeability of patented second medical use for generic products.

**35** As explained, if a court considers that a manufacturer or distributor foresees or ought to foresee that the pharmaceutical composition that is manufactured or offered by them will intentionally be used in the treatment to which the second medical use claim relates, i.e. fulfils the 'foreseeability criterion',[36] this does not mean that infringement is immediately assumed. The supplier of a generic product can try to take measures in order to prevent infringement. These measures are discussed below (→ mn. 49).

**36** Notably, if the patients to which the second medical use claim relates only form a small portion of the total patient group, this does not change how the Dutch court will apply the foreseeability criterion. A *de minimis* defence is generally not accepted by Dutch courts. Dutch case law shows that, actually, a quantitative *de minimis* non-infringement defence has an even lower chance of succeeding than a qualitative *de minimis* non-infringement defence.[37]

## E. Infringement of second medical use claims and biosimilar products

**37** In the case of biosimilars, prescribing practice differs from that of generics. Since biological molecules have, by their nature, a variability and because biological medicinal products have complex manufacturing methods, a biosimilar will not be exactly the same as the reference product. Therefore, a biosimilar is not considered a generic. Generally, there is a reluctance among physicians to switch patients treated with the reference product to a biosimilar, although this is allowed.[38]

**38** The MEB has published its position on biosimilars on its website.[39] The MEB considers that new patients can be treated with a biosimilar without question. However, according to the MEB, uncontrolled substitution of medicinal products should be avoided by the healthcare provider, and in the case of substitution of biologic medicinal products, the healthcare provider should adequately monitor the clinical situation and give clear instructions to the patient.

**39** The National Health Care Institute (*Zorginsituut Nederland*) takes a similar position: biosimilars are fully therapeutically exchangeable for new users, which means that new patients can be treated with a biosimilar and existing users can also be switched to a biosimilar, provided this has been discussed with the treating physician.[40] Currently, for example, several Dutch health insurers have a preference policy regarding biosimilar insulins.[41]

**40** Overall, it can be concluded that foreseeability that a product is being used for a patented indication may be less likely for biosimilars because physicians will be more reluctant to substitute an innovator product with a biosimilar. For new patients, a pharmacist may

---

[36] *MSD/Teva*, para. 3.6.3–3.6.4 ; → mn. 66.

[37] Maas/Santman, 'De minimis in het octrooirecht', Bijblad Industriële Eigendom 2007/4, 224.

[38] Jonker-Exler/Lisman/Vulto, 'Regulering van biosimilars op Europees en nationaal niveau', Tijdschrift zorg & recht in praktijk 2015, SDU / no. 5.

[39] See https://www.cbg-meb.nl/onderwerpen/medicijninformatie-originele-biologische-medicijnen-en-biosimilars/extra-medische-informatie-voor-zorgverleners.

[40] See https://www.zorginstituutnederland.nl/binaries/zinl/documenten/standpunten/2011/09/29/preferentiebeleid-biologische-geneesmiddelen/Preferentiebeleid+biologische+geneesmiddelen.pdf.

[41] See https://mediq.nl/nieuws/2021/preferentiebeleid-insulines.

dispense a biosimilar. For patients substituting their current medicine for a biosimilar, the treating physician still has to be involved.

## F. Strategies and considerations

Since *MSD/Teva* was handed down, case law has not yet crystallised what exactly constitutes sufficiently effective measures. In any case, there must be a carve-out, but the Dutch Supreme Court made clear that a carve-out alone is not sufficient to meet the 'effective measures' requirement. Case law has provided some guidance. In addition, practitioners have debated what could constitute 'effective measures'. We will first discuss carve outs. **41**

### I. Carve out

Generic companies can have patented uses removed from the SmPC and the patient information leaflet via carve-outs. This is laid down in, among other places, EMA guidance document 'European Medicines Agency procedural advice for users of the centralised procedure for generic/hybrid applications'[42], and is adopted and implemented by the MEB in the Netherlands.[43] **42**

However, the regulatory authorities have a policy that only information from specific parts of the SmPC and patient information leaflet can be removed. Information related to a safe use of the medicinal product can in any case not be removed by means of a carve-out. **43**

The MEB (and also the EMA in its Guidance) has left open the possibility of an exemption to the rule that no safety information may be deleted. If the marketing authorisation holder wishes to remove or amend information in the sections regarding safety information, such as, for example, the removal of text, which can be traced to the patented indication, reasons/justification for this, must be provided. However, there is no case law or further guidance available on this subject in the Netherlands, so it is unclear what would constitute convincing reasons according to the MEB. Moreover, how this exemption to the carve-out rules is applied by the relevant authority may differ from country to country. This is not completely unproblematic. **44**

In recent years, generics are increasingly faced with '*patent thickets*' created around compound patents that have already expired, where innovators deliberately and specifically target the patenting of safety aspects of a medicinal product. These companies realise that generic companies are, in principle, not allowed to 'carve out' information in the SmPC and package leaflet regarding safety aspects (unless permitted on the basis of a substantiated request). Generics confronted with such a situation then face the choice of either starting (costly) invalidity proceedings or trying, by means of a reasoned request, to get the patented information removed from the excluded sections of the SmPC/package leaflet. However, there is currently no known policy or assessment framework other than submitting a reasoned request for removal. **45**

[42] European Medicines Agency procedural advice for users of the centralised procedure for generic/hybrid applications dated 11 January 2021, mn. 2.9 on p. 18.

[43] See https://english.cbg-meb.nl/topics/mah-patented-indication.

46 Finally, a relevant factor to take into account when applying for a carve-out is that the patentee may be able to get access to the exchanges between the generic supplier and the MEB regarding the carve-out via a FOI request. If the generic supplier does not succeed in fully carving out an indication because it also includes information in the sections that are exempted from carve-outs, the patentee may use the exchange between the generic supplier and the MEB to argue that the generic supplier apparently also felt that it might infringe without the carve-out, because otherwise it would not have tried to delete text relating to the patented indication. On the other hand, if a generic supplier does *not* try to delete text in a section concerning safety information, the patentee may argue that the generic has only itself to blame because it did not even try, even though the regulatory laws have created this option.

## II. Carve in

47 Information can also be *added* in the SmPC to exclude a patented use, i.e. a 'carve in'. The MEB allows generic companies to propose the addition of a disclaimer that excludes the patented use from the indicated patient group in the SmPC and patient leaflet. The fact that these proposals are taken into consideration by the MEB follows already from the form that the MA holder must fill in when requesting a carve out / carve in. This form is entitled 'statement on the modification of information in the SmPC and PIL in view of patented indications'. Further, the MEB has a policy, which says that the MA holder can remove a patented indication from the SmPC and PIL (it does not say 'remove *information in relation to* a patented indication'). *MSD/Teva* is the only known case (which was also explicitly discussed in Dutch case law) where the generic successfully applied for a carve-in.

48 Whether or not a carve-in is effective depends on the clinical practice. For example, if the carve-out relates to a patient group with specific characteristics, adding a disclaimer that patients with these characteristics should not be treated with the medicinal product will only be effective if the prescribing physician actually identifies the specific characteristics in patients before prescribing the medicinal product. A disclaimer that has no application in clinical practice will not be considered an effective measure by the court.

## III. Effective measures

49 As mentioned, the case law and literature on infringement of second medical use claims gives some examples of measures that a generic company may take to prevent a product from being marketed for the patented indication:

1. Actively informing prescribers about the patented indication. For this to be effective, in addition to the information that there is a patented indication, the letter or email must also make clear that prescribing the product in question for the patented indication has infringement implications, and that the product should not be sold for the patented indication. As explained above, in *Sun/Novartis,* the letter sent by Sun informed the prescriber about the patented indication but with the disclaimer that the letter was just a formality. This took away the effectiveness of the measure according to the Supreme Court. It is therefore advisable to avoid such a statement.[44]

[44] *Sun/Novartis* para. 3.5.2; → mn. 67.

2. Putting information on packaging (to the extent allowed under the applicable regulatory regime).[45] This is considered to be in the best interest of both the patentee and the generic company and can also be useful in demonstrating that effective measures have been taken.[46]
3. Monitoring market share after the launch. If the market share of the generic product exceeds the patient population in the non-patented indication, the measures taken may be considered not (or no longer) to be effective.[47] It is unclear, however, how this measure would prevent a patentee from starting PI proceedings, as the criterion for granting an injunction is not whether the patentee can demonstrate that it is losing market share to the generic product.
4. Ensuring participation in tenders that are restricted to the non-patented indication.[48] If the health insurer's tender does not want to differentiate between patented and non-patented indications, the generic company cannot participate without infringing.[49] It follows from the Appeal Court's decision in *Sun/Novartis* that if such a situation occurs, the generic company should 'challenge' the healthcare provider. The Supreme Court explicitly stated that this finding by the Appeal Court was not incorrect. It is not entirely clear what it means that the generic company should 'challenge' the decision not to make a distinction between patient groups in the tender. Possibly, the generic company should consider legal action against the healthcare provider for not organising the tender in a lawful way.

## G. Legal remedies

Above we discussed the precautionary measures that generic suppliers may take to avoid infringement (→ mn. 49). However, there is the difficulty that (i) it is not entirely clear what 'effective measures' are, and that (ii) it may be impossible, given the market situation, to take 'effective measures' if other parties in the market, such as hospitals, are unwilling to cooperate. The measures discussed, therefore, at most reduce the risk of a PI, but they are not a checklist that if followed would rule out the possibility of infringement. Below we will discuss the circumstances that usually lead to a patentee initiating proceedings, as well as the legal remedies that are available to the patentee. **50**

### I. Trigger for (threat of) infringement

The patentee will likely initiate PI proceedings when it finds evidence that there is a threat that a company will launch a generic product in the Netherlands. Recent case law shows that the mere *application* for a (full label) market authorisation (MA) does not constitute a sufficient threat of patent infringement without the presence of additional **51**

[45] To the effect that the patentee and generic (have negotiated and) are in agreement on the information communicated to the market. See also Korsten/Bisschop, 'Inbreuk op nieuw-gebruik octrooien – in redelijkheid te vergen effectieve maatregelen', IER 2020, mn. 5.1.5.
[46] ibid., mn. 5.1.6.
[47] ibid., mn. 5.1.7.
[48] *Sun/Novartis*, para. 3.5.2.
[49] ibid., para. 4.36.

circumstances.[50] And actually *having* MA does not create sufficient threat of infringement in order for a patentee to have standing in PI proceedings either. It is after all not unusual for a company to have a marketing authorisation without actually having a product on the market. According to the court, there must be additional circumstances present before accepting that a threat of infringement exists.[51] It follows from case law that listing in the G-Standaard is sufficient evidence that there is a threat that a generic product will be launched.

52 The G-Standaard, the monthly updated list of medicinal products available in the Netherlands, usually alerts the patentee to a forthcoming launch. The patentee generally checks the G-Standaard immediately upon publication to see if relevant new generic products have been listed for the next month by a generic company. If so, the patentee can be expected to take immediate legal action to prevent this generic product being actually launched on the 1st of the next month.

## II. Legal remedies available to patentee

53 In the Netherlands, the patentee has the possibility to commence action for infringement in preliminary injunction proceedings or in proceedings on the merits. For patent cases, specifically there is an accelerated regime in place ('VRO-procedure'). In addition, there is the possibility of *ex parte* proceedings.

### 1. Preliminary injunction proceedings (*inter partes*)

54 An urgent interest is required in order to obtain a preliminary injunction. It follows from NL case law that the urgent interest of a patentee is, in principle, more or less presumed in an action for an injunction aimed at putting an end to a (alleged) continuous infringement of patent rights or to a genuine threat of infringement. Nevertheless, whether a claimant in PI proceedings has a sufficient degree of urgency in the requested remedy is still determined by a PI judge weighing all the facts and circumstances. It may be considered that there is a lack of urgency if the patentee has 'sat still' for a relevant period of time and there are no (new) facts or circumstances which suggest that imposing the requested remedy is (still) justified after that time lapse. A relevant factor is in any event the length of time that the alleged infringing product is already on the market, and whether or not the patentee could have been aware of that and could have acted sooner.

55 Damages can only be claimed in proceedings on the merits. Once PI proceedings have been instituted by the patentee, proceedings on the merits must be commenced within a period set in the dictum of the PI decision, usually six months.[52] If the patentee fails to do so, the preliminary injunction lapses.

### 2. Proceedings on the merits

56 Patent proceedings on the merits are usually conducted in accordance with the so-called 'accelerated regime'. The claimant must apply to the Court to litigate under this

[50] Court of Amsterdam, 16 July 2021, ECLI:NL:RBAMS:2021:4049 (*AbbVie v Alvotech en Stada*), para. 4.2; → mn. 71.

[51] District Court of The Hague, 7 April 2008, KG ZA 08-63 (*Olanzapine*), para. 4.5; → mn. 72. District Court of The Hague, 27 March 2012, 412750 / KG ZA 12-138 (*Efavirenz*), para. 4.7; → mn. 73.

[52] Art. 1019i Dutch Code of Civil Procedure; → mn. 64.

regime by sending a draft writ of summons. If this application is granted (which it usually is) the District Court of The Hague presents a fixed schedule for the proceedings. A first instance decision is thus usually obtained within 12–20 months.

### 3. *Ex parte* injunction

In very urgent cases – in particular where any delay would cause irreparable harm to the patentee – the preliminary relief judge can also grant an injunction without hearing the defendant.[53] The urgent interest must be so strong that the outcome of *inter partes* PI proceedings cannot be awaited. The *ex parte* injunction is usually granted within 1–7 days after receipt of the request. An *ex parte* injunction is furthermore only granted when there is a clear-cut infringement of a valid IP right. In patent cases, this means that the patent must either have been upheld in first instance proceedings on the merits and/or in opposition proceedings. This high threshold can be explained by the fact that *ex parte* measures have a tremendous impact and the party against whom the measures are taken has little or no possibility to defend itself.[54] 57

Apart from an injunction, also seizures can be allowed on an *ex parte* basis, such as seizures of evidence, descriptions of infringing products and seizures on assets. The urgent interest requirement for allowing seizures is less strict. All other types of relief, such as a recall, orders to provide information about the source of infringing products etc. can only be obtained in *inter partes* PI proceedings or in proceedings on the merits. 58

Although the alleged infringing party is not heard in *ex parte* proceedings, this party can file a protective letter if he anticipates an application for *ex parte* relief by a patentee.[55] Protective letters may be filed at any given time. They are sent to the relevant court only (in the Netherlands this is the District Court of The Hague) and are not made public. The preliminary relief judge that receives an application for an *ex parte* injunction against the parties mentioned will take the content of the protective brief into account when assessing whether or not to grant the *ex parte* injunction. It should be noted that the preliminary relief judge may forward the protective briefs to the party applying for the *ex parte*. 59

A party against whom *ex parte* relief has been granted can initiate *inter partes* PI proceedings to claim the 'lifting' of this *ex parte* relief. 60

## H. Statutory provisions

## I. Patent Act

#### Article 53 61

1. Subject to the provisions of Articles 54 to 60, a patent shall confer on its owner the exclusive right:

---

[53] Art. 1019e Dutch Code of Civil Procedure ; → mn. 65.

[54] PI Judge, The Hague, 24 July 2009, *GSK v Pharmachemie*, para. 2.2 'Because of the deviation from the fundamental principle of hearing both sides of the argument, the *ex parte* order in the sense of Article 1019e DCCP is a drastic measure. That is why such a measure only qualifies for application if it can be assumed that other, less drastic measures will not be effective.'

[55] See https://www.rechtspraak.nl/SiteCollectionDocuments/reglement-grijsmaken-octrooi-en-kwekersrechtelijke-maatregelen.pdf.

a. to make, use, put on the market or resell, hire out or deliver the patented product, or otherwise deal in it in or for his business, or to offer, import or stock it for any of those purposes;
b. to use the patented process in or for his business or to use, put on the market, or resell, hire out or deliver the product obtained directly as a result of the use of the patented process, or otherwise deal in it in or for his business, or to offer, import or stock it for any of those purposes, with the exception of any product excluded from the grant of a patent pursuant to Article 3.

2. The exclusive right shall be determined by the contents of the claims in the patent specification, and the description and the drawings shall serve to interpret those claims.
3. The exclusive right shall not extend to acts solely serving for research on the patented subject matter, including the product obtained directly as a result of using the patented process. The exclusive right shall likewise not extend to the preparation of medicines in pharmacies for immediate use in individual cases on medical prescription, or to acts related to medicines prepared in this manner.
4. If a product as referred to in paragraph (1)(a) or (b) has been put on the market lawfully in the Netherlands or the Netherlands Antilles, or, where a European patent is concerned, in the Netherlands, or if it is put on the market lawfully in one of the Member States of the European Union or in another State that is party to the Agreement concerning the European Economic Area by the patent proprietor or with his consent, the person who obtains or later holds the product shall not contravene the patent by using, selling, hiring out or delivering the product or by otherwise dealing in it in or for his business, or by offering, importing, or stocking the product for any of those purposes.
5. A product as specified in paragraph (1)(a) or (b) which was manufactured by a business prior to the grant of a patent or, where a European patent is concerned, prior to the date of publication of the mention of the grant of the European patent in accordance with Article 97(4) of the European Patent Convention, may continue to be used on behalf of that business notwithstanding the patent.

62

### Article 73

1. The proprietor of the patent may institute the claims at his disposal in enforcing his patent against any person who, in the Netherlands or Netherlands Antilles or, where a European patent is concerned, in the Netherlands, supplies or delivers to or for his business, in respect of an essential part of the invention, to persons other than those who by virtue of Articles 55 to 60 are empowered to work the patented invention, the means for the application of the patented invention in the Netherlands or Netherlands Antilles, or where a European patent is concerned, in the Netherlands, provided that that person knows, or that it is evident considering the circumstances, that those means are suitable and intended for that application.
2. Paragraph (1) shall not apply if the supply or delivery takes place with the consent of the proprietor of the patent. That paragraph shall likewise not apply if the means delivered or offered are products which are generally available in commerce, unless the person involved incites the third party to whom he delivers to perform acts specified in Article 53(1).
3. Article 70(5) shall apply mutatis mutandis.

## II. Medicine Act

63

### Article 68

1. Prescribing medicines outside the medical indications registered by the Medicines Evaluation Board is only permissible if protocols or standards have been developed within the

profession on this subject. If the protocols and standards are still in development, consultation between the attending physician and pharmacist is necessary.
2. In cases to be determined by ministerial regulation, the prescription states the reason for prescribing.

## III. Code of Civil Procedure

### Article 1019i 64

1. In cases concerning actions for the ordering of provisional measures referred to in Article 50(1) of the Agreement on Trade-Related Aspects of Intellectual Property Rights, annexed as Annex 1C to the Agreement establishing the World Trade Organisation (Trb. 1995, 130), the preliminary relief judge shall, when granting a provisional measure, determine a reasonable time for the bringing of the main action. The provisional measure loses its force if a claim in the main action is not filed within that time limit and the defendant files a statement to that effect with the Registry. If the statement is filed after the expiry of the stipulated time limit, the provisional measure loses its force with the filing of the statement.
2. If the preliminary relief judge has not set a time limit as referred to in the first paragraph, the provisional measure shall lose its effect by a statement as referred to in the first paragraph, if after at least 31 days, of which at least 20 working days, no claim in the main action has been filed.
3. A statement as referred to in the first paragraph shall be accompanied by a copy of the judgment. If an appeal has been lodged against it, this shall be stated in the statement. The defendant shall send a copy of his statement to the plaintiff as soon as possible.

### Article 1019e 65

1. In cases of urgency, in particular if delay would cause irreparable damage to the holder of the intellectual property right, the preliminary relief judge shall have the power to grant an immediate provisional injunction on an application to issue an order against the alleged infringer to prevent imminent infringement of the holder's intellectual property right, without summoning the alleged infringer. Under the same conditions, an immediate injunction may be granted against an intermediary whose services are used by a third party to infringe an intellectual property right.
2. The preliminary relief judge may grant the request subject to the provision of security up to an amount to be determined by him.
3. The alleged infringer and the intermediary whose services are used by a third party to infringe an intellectual property right may claim that the preliminary relief judge who issued the decision containing the order referred to in the first paragraph review the decision, ruling in preliminary relief proceedings.

# J. Extracts from court decisions

## 66 I. *MSD/TEVA*[56]

**3.4.4:** In the case of a patent with a Swiss-type claim, which by its nature is formulated as a process patent (see 3.4.2), the difficulty arises that, as a result of the operation of Article 64(2) EPC or Article 53(1) opening words and under b, respectively, DPA 1995 (cf. above in 3.4.2), the scope of protection would also extend to the manufacture or use of the substance for the first medical indication, once that patent has expired. That would be incompatible with the principle underlying patent law that anyone is free to apply the doctrine of a patent no longer in force, as well as with the principle expressed in Article 69 EPC that the scope of protection of a patent should not go beyond what the invention justifies. It must therefore be assumed that a manufacturer or distributor directly infringes a patent with a Swiss-type claim only if he foresees or should foresee that the generic medicine produced or offered by him will be knowingly used for treatment covered by the second medical indication patent. This requires that the average skilled person will believe, based on the SmPC and/or the package leaflet, or other circumstances, that the medicine is (partly) intended or suitable for that treatment. The manufacturer or distributor will then have to take all effective measures reasonably required of him to prevent his product from being supplied for the patented second medical indication. The mere presence – as in the present case – of a carve-out in the SmPC and package leaflet of the generic medicine is generally not sufficient to exclude direct infringement. (cf. Supreme Court 14 April 2017, ECLI:NL:HR:2017:692, NJ 2017/296, para 3.5.2).

**3.5:** Against the background of all the above, parts 1.1, 1.2 and 1.3 rightly complain that the distinction made by the court of appeal in the scope of protection of patents for the 'classic second medical use' and the 'subgroup indication' referred to in paragraph 4.2 of the judgment under appeal is incorrect. As follows from the above in 3.4.4, in all cases of Swiss-type claims for (direct) infringement it is necessary, but also sufficient, that the average skilled person will believe that the product is (also) intended or suitable for treatment to which the second medical use patent relates, that the manufacturer or distributor foresees or should foresee that the generic product manufactured or offered by him will be used knowingly for that treatment and that he omits the measures mentioned above in 3.4.4. There is no place in the EPC system for a categorical, abstract distinction between the two types of second medical use as made by the court of appeal at the end of paragraph 4.4 – regarding the specifically stated purpose. The other complaints of part 1 do not require further consideration. The same applies to part 2.

[…]

**3.6.3:** As considered above in 3.4.2, Swiss-type claims have been recognised for the purpose of protecting a second medical use patent and take the form of purpose-bound process claims. It can be argued that, taken to the letter, such a patent cannot be indirectly infringed by, for example, an intermediary dealer, as the latter does not offer or supply any means that could serve the process, consisting in the use of the substance mentioned in the claim for the preparation of a pharmaceutical product, in the manner referred to in Article 73(1) DPA 1995. Against the background of the reason that gave rise to the recognition of the Swiss-type claims, as well as in view of the possibility, introduced into the EPC since the 2000 revision, of attaching a product-specific product claim to a patent for the protection of a second medical use (Article 54(5) EPC, incorporated in the DPA 1995 as Article 4(6)) – in which revision the intention was not to break with the patentability of substances or mixtures by means of a Swiss-type claim developed in the case law (see EBA 19 February 2010, G 0002/08, para 5.10.1-4 and Preparatory Documents MR/18/00 and MR/24/00 cited therein) – justifies accepting the

[56] ECLI:NL:HR:2017:2807.

reasonable protection of the patentee prescribed by Article 1 of the Protocol that a Swiss-type claim may be subject to indirect infringement on the same footing as a claim under the current Article 54(5) EPC. The same view was held by the *Bundesgerichtshof* (BGH 14 June 2016 – X ZR 29/15, GRUR 2016/921 (Eli Lilly/Actavis), paragraphs 83–85). The possibility of indirect infringement of a Swiss-type claim has also been recognised by the UK Supreme Court (UKSC 12 July 2017, [2017] UKSC 48 (Actavis/Eli Lilly), para 103-112).

**3.6.4:** Thus, as is the case with a patent with a claim as Article 54(5) EPC allows, indirect infringement of a Swiss-type claim may occur. After all, in the case of a product-related product claim, the use to be given to the product (the medicine) is 'an essential element of the invention' as referred to in Article 73 DPA 1995. The above implies that the manufacturer of a generic medicine may also indirectly infringe a patent for a second medical use, namely if he offers or supplies the medicine to persons who are not entitled to use the invention and he knows or it is clear to him, given the circumstances, that the medicine is suitable and will be intended for the patented second medical use patent. That it can then therefore infringe such a patent both directly and indirectly is not an objection. The United Kingdom Supreme Court (UKSC) also held, according to its judgment referred to above in 3.6.3, that the same conduct could constitute both direct and indirect infringement.

## II. *Sun/Novartis*[57] 67

**3.3:** In assessing the ground of appeal against the contested judgment, the following is predominant.

a. This patent is concerned with the protection of a second medical use, to which end the patent has so-called 'swiss-type claims', in which connection reference is made to what is stated in note 1 of the opinion of the Advocate General where it concerns the situation applicable here prior to the revision of the EPC 2000. The question whether it is legally possible to indirectly infringe such a patent claim – which the court of appeal assumed – is not at issue in the present cassation appeal.
b. Proceedings on the merits are also pending between the parties on the present dispute, in which the court, pending this appeal in cassation, ruled in an interlocutory judgment (dated 25 November 2015, ECLI:NL:RBDHA:2015:14337) that indirect infringement of a 'swiss-type claim' is not possible as a matter of law and announced further investigation as to whether Sun directly infringes the patent. In its final judgment (dated 5 April 2017, ECLI:NL:RBDHA:2017:3430), the court held that there was direct infringement of the patent. Contrary to what Novartis argued in its written explanation, the court's judgment in the interlocutory judgment does not entail that the Supreme Court in these preliminary relief proceedings should align its decision in cassation with that judgment. Nor does this apply to the court's opinion in its currently pronounced final judgment. The rule invoked by Novartis that the court in preliminary relief proceedings should align its judgment with that in the proceedings on the merits (cf. inter alia HR 24 April 2015, ECLI:NL:HR:2015:1128, NJ 2015/266) does not apply in cassation proceedings. It applies only to the court ruling on the facts. After all, that rule is not compatible with the nature of cassation proceedings, which means that the investigation therein is limited to the application of the law in and the reasoning of the contested judgment against the background of the documents of the proceedings as referred to in Article 419(2) DCCP, on the basis of submitted complaints.

**3.5.2:** The court of appeal held, uncontested in cassation, that it was virtually impossible that Sun's product would not also be supplied and used for osteoporosis and it therefore had to know that its product would also be supplied for the patented indication at the end of the

[57] ECLI:NL:HR:2017:692.

vertical chain of marketing. The court correctly held that – assuming that indirect infringement of a 'swiss-made claim' (read: 'swiss-type claim') is legally possible – the requirements of indirect patent infringement as referred to in Article 73(1) DPA 1995 were met under those circumstances. The court of appeal did not rule that Sun could be held liable for the conduct of third parties over which it had no control, so that to that extent the section cannot lead to cassation in the absence of a factual basis. According to the Court of Appeal, the accusation that can be made against Sun is that it did not do anything – except for the 'carve-out' mentioned above in 3.1 under (viii) and the sending of the e-mail to wholesalers and hospital pharmacies, mentioned in paragraph 4.35, which the Court of Appeal (understandably) deemed insufficient – to prevent its product from being supplied for the treatment of osteoporosis (paragraph 4.34). It is not for the court to point out measures that a litigant such as Sun should have taken in a case such as the present, but, on the contrary, for the litigant itself to show what it has done to prevent infringement, notwithstanding the fact that the court of appeal in this case (in paragraphs 4.35 and 4.36) has given examples of conceivable measures. The impossibilities alleged by Sun to prevent the use of its product for the treatment of osteoporosis were not disregarded by the court of appeal. The court of appeal only charged Sun with insufficient use of the possibilities that were available to it.

The ground for cassation therefore fails.

68

## III. *Novartis/Sun*[58]

**4.34:** Sun argued that it cannot be blamed for this, because these are the consequences of the preference policy applied by VGZ and the tender issued by VGZ that did not allow registration under conditions (only for use in the indication of Paget's disease). The court's preliminary view is that this does not exonerate Sun. Under the given circumstances, in which it was clear to Sun beforehand that VGZ's conduct would inevitably lead to the Generic Product also being used for osteoporosis and thus for the indication protected by the patent, it was incumbent on Sun to do everything possible to prevent the Generic Product from being supplied for the treatment of osteoporosis, which would infringe Novartis' patent. In this, Sun has failed.

**4.35:** After being summoned by Novartis, Sun sent an email to wholesalers (and hospital pharmacies ordering directly from it) with the following content:

Dear [...],

This information concerns a formality.

On the advice of our legal counsel, please note that our product Zoledronic Acid SUN 5 mg/100 ml, Z-index number: 15958264 marketed by us, is currently intended only for the treatment of Paget's disease. This is also the indication stated in the package leaflet Zoledronic Acid SUN 5 mg/100 ml.

For the time being, the indication osteoporosis is not included, as this indication is still protected by a Novartis patent.

By accepting the shipment of Zoledronic Acid SUN 5 mg/100 ml solution for infusion, you indicate that you were aware of the above.

In the circumstances, this was insufficient. It should have at least (also) made it clear that the Generic Product should not be prescribed and supplied for the treatment of osteoporosis, as this would infringe Novartis' patent rights. It had to make sure that effective measures would be taken to ensure that this would not happen either. Instead, by starting the e-mail with 'This communication concerns only a formality', it has instead suggested that the fact that the Generic Product is only intended for the treatment of Paget's disease and that the indication osteoporosis is still protected by a Novartis patent did not need to be given any practical importance and did not require any action.

[58] ECLI:NL:GHDHA:2015:1769.

**4.36:** Sun has also failed to provide sufficient reasoning to argue that it made an effort to convince VGZ that it needed to design its tender differently to allow Sun to bid while respecting Novartis' patent rights, for example by separating the tender for zoledronic acid for the osteoporosis application on the one hand and for the Paget application on the other. If VGZ would (have been) insensitive to that argument and the way the tender was organised made it impossible for Sun to bid for it, then that is a circumstance that Sun has to object to VGZ. However, it does not provide Sun with a licence to infringe Novartis' patent rights.

## IV. *WLC/State of the Netherlands*[59] 69

**2.4:** To answer the preliminary questions, the following undisputed data on Dutch prescribing practice are relevant.

**2.4.1:** The 'Leidraad doelmatig voorschrijven van geneesmiddelen' of the Dutch Order of Medical Specialists (published in March 2011) states – as far as relevant here – the following:

(...) Being efficient also means being cost-conscious: following guidelines, deviating from them where necessary and by prescribing the cheapest variant of medication where possible. (...) This is achieved by prescribing by substance name instead of brand name: the pharmacy can then dispense a generic variant where possible.

(...)

To save costs, for more than 15 years general practitioners have been actively encouraged to prescribe by substance name so that pharmacists can dispense generic drugs. Incidentally, health insurers' preference policies may also have played a role in this.

(...)

In principle, prescribing is done by substance name. The idea is that the pharmacist can dispense generic versions of the drug without any problems if they are available. However, this should follow the recommendations as laid down in the drug substitution guide drawn up by the KNMP in January 2010 (...). For drugs with a limited therapeutic width and for conditions where even minor variations in bioavailability or equivalence cannot be accepted, brand name prescriptions can be made. A brief explanation on the prescription can then show the prescribing doctor's intention.

**2.4.2:** Agreements between insurers and healthcare providers also include the principle that healthcare providers prescribe medicines based on the name of the active ingredient (such as pregabalin) rather than a brand name (such as Lyrica®).

**2.4.3:** In the Netherlands, healthcare providers generally do not state the therapeutic indication for which a medicine is prescribed on the prescription. That principle is departed from for substances that, due to safety risks, are on the list included in the appendix to Article 6.11 Medicines Act Regulations. Pregabalin is not on that list.

## V. *GSK/Pharmachemie*[60] 70

[this consideration is also included in the text in fn. n]

**2.2:** Because of the deviation from the fundamental principle of hearing both sides of the argument, the ex parte order in the sense of Article 1019e DCCP is a drastic measure. That is why such a measure only qualifies for application if it can be assumed that other, less drastic measures will not be effective.

---

[59] ECLI:NL:GHDHA:2017:1935.

[60] PI Judge The Hague, 24 July 2009.

## 71 VI. *AbbVie/Alvotech en Stada*[61]

**4.2:** It is not entirely clear whether AbbVie is now arguing that there is imminent unlawful conduct because Alvotech c.s. will use the yet-to-be-granted full-label MA to facilitate infringement, or whether Alvotech c.s. is already acting unlawfully now because it has not applied for a carved-out MA and the threat is concrete that it will (later) enter the market and not respect the Patents. For both positions, however, it will have to be considered whether the threat is sufficiently concrete that Alvotech c.s. will indeed disrespect the Patents. After all, according to established case law, a prohibition or injunction can only be imposed to prevent infringement or unlawful acts if there is a serious threat to do so. The mere application for a (full-label) MA, without additional circumstances that make it plausible that Alvotech et al. have the concrete intention of introducing a biosimilar onto the European market in violation of a patent right accruing to AbbVie, does not constitute a sufficiently serious threat of patent infringement or unlawful acts. In preliminary view, in the present proceedings there are no additional circumstances that would make this threat nonetheless exist. To this end, it is considered as follows.

## 72 VII. District Court of The Hague – *Olanzapine*[62]

**4.5:** In addition, Ratiopharm correctly argues that, according to established case law, the mere possession (or application) of a marketing authorisation for a medicinal product without additional, concrete circumstances that make it plausible that Ratiopharm intends to place infringing generic products on the market during the period of validity of the patent and the SPC does not constitute a sufficient threat of infringement, so that, if that is the case, an injunction in preliminary relief proceedings cannot be obtained on the mere circumstance of an existing marketing authorisation. Simply having or applying for a market licence is not an act reserved under patent law.

## 73 VIII. District Court of The Hague – *Efavirenz*[63]

**4.7:** The mere fact that Teva has a market authorisation for a product covered by the protection of a patent or SPC is, according to established case law, not sufficient to assume a real threat of infringement. The fact that, according to Merck, the market authorisation was applied for by Teva unusually early, so that it is plausible that Teva intends to enter the market early, has been refuted by Teva with reasons. Moreover, the fact that a market authorisation was applied for (and obtained) long before the end of the patent protection does not automatically create such a threat either. Indeed, applicants should take into account possible delays in the granting procedure.

## 74 IX. *Warner Lambert/State of the Netherlands*[64]

**5.1:** orders the State to replace, within four weeks of service of this judgment, the full-label SmPC and package leaflet of generic pregabalin products destined for the Dutch market that are accessible via the website of the MEB with versions of these documents that include a carve-out, similar to the paper versions of the SmPC and package leaflet for the pregabalin products.

[61] ECLI:NL:RBAMS:2021:4049.
[62] 7 April 2008, KG ZA 08-63.
[63] 27 March 2012, 412750 / KG ZA 12-138.
[64] ECLI:NL:RBDHA:2016:334.

# § 9
# Poland

## A. Executive summary

1 Currently, patents protecting second medicinal use inventions both in the form of Swiss-type claims and purpose-limited product claims co-exist in Poland, although new patents applied for after 2015 may only claim protection for second (or further) medicinal use through the purpose-limited product claim formula.

2 From the practical perspective of enforcing patent claims in Poland, both claim formulae should provide similar protection, requiring in each case proof that the defendant has engaged in an activity legally reserved for the patent holder in relation to the patented product and for the patented purpose. The proof required is comparable to the German proof of 'purposeful preparation'[1].

3 So far, in Polish jurisprudence there has been no attempt to substitute a more objective test in lieu of the purpose criterion as in the German *Östrogenblocker* case.[2] However, in fact there may not be much practical difference. Polish courts would: (i) review proof of purpose by way of its external manifestations using their discretionary power to assess evidence; and (ii) apply presumptions of fact to reconstruct a mental state. The three elements of the infringement test from the German *Östrogenblocker* case could well lead a Polish court to a finding that purpose has been established, and a finding of infringement. As discussed below, a skinny label approach does not eliminate the risk of infringement entirely, and depending on the factual circumstances surrounding the marketing of a particular medicinal product under a skinny label, the court may still decide that a patent was infringed.

4 Polish patent law does not protect against indirect patent infringement as defined in § 10 German Patent Act. In such situations, the patent holder may rely on other provisions of Polish law. In particular, such actions could qualify as unfair competition or accessory liability under the Polish Civil Code.

## B. Scope of protection and interpretation of second medical use claims

5 In Polish law, second medical use claims used to be registered both as Swiss-type claims and (since December 2015) as purpose-limited product claims (EPC 2000 claims[3]). Even though the Polish Industrial Property Law of 30 June 2000 (*Prawo własności przemysłowej* – IPL) still contains provisions pertaining to Swiss-type claims, the Polish Patent Office (*Urząd Patentowy* – PPO) no longer accepts such claims after 2015. For that rea-

---

[1] → § 5 mn. 8 for details.
[2] → § 5 mn. 12 for details.
[3] Art. 54(5) EPC.

son, any new patents filed with the PPO may only include second medicinal use claims formulated as purpose-limited product claims.[4]

6 Article 29 Sec. 1(3) IPL disallows patents for therapeutic and diagnostic methods for the treatment of the human or animal body; however, products, including substances and mixtures used for such purpose are exempt from this prohibition (→ mn. 50). Both Swiss-type claims and EPC claims do not directly relate to therapeutic methods, but medicinal products and methods of productions of same and therefore fit well within that exception. The Swiss form is also expressly mentioned in Article 65 IPL (→ mn. 17; → mn. 52). On the other hand, use claims, as accepted in the German practice ('use of compound X for the treatment of disease Y'), are problematic under Polish law as, nominally, they do not qualify for an exception to the prohibition of patenting therapeutic methods under Article 29 Sec. 1(3) IPL (literally, use claims are protecting a method of treatment). However, in light of the availability of both Swiss-type claims (until 2015) and purpose-limited product claims, there has been a little practical need to allow such alternative third formulation and therefore only the first two are discussed.

7 Since the introduction of EPC 2000 claims to the IPL in December 2015, the PPO (following the example of the EPO) has stopped granting patents on Swiss-type claims, and now treats purpose-limited product claims as the sole proper way of drafting patent claims protecting second medicinal use in Poland. However, previous considerations regarding Swiss-type claims have practical relevance for the patents applied for prior to 2015. The latest such patents should expire sometime around 2035.[5]

8 The availability of purpose-limited product claims in Polish law is not restricted to second medicinal use, but also extends to all further medicinal uses, provided all other patentability criteria are met. Most of the comments below made in respect of second medicinal use patents would also apply to patents granted for further medicinal uses.

## C. Direct and indirect infringement of second medical use claims

### I. Product limited by purpose

9 For purpose-limited product claims, the object of the invention is a product with a precisely defined purpose, i.e. intended for a precisely defined use. Other uses are not covered by patent protection.[6] Such patent is a product patent. Under the IPL, a product patent is infringed whenever a third party, in the absence of the patent holder's authorisation, undertakes any of the actions reserved for the patent holder under Article 66 Sec. 1(1) IPL in relation to the patented product for a commercial or professional purpose. Those reserved actions comprise manufacturing, using, offering, marketing, storing, or warehousing products which are the subject matter of the invention, or exporting or importing them for such purposes.

[4] General Guidelines of the President of the PPO with respect to inventions and utility designs, https://uprp.gov.pl/pl/przedmioty-ochrony/ogolne-wytyczne-prezesa-uprp/wytyczne-w-zakresie-wynalazkow-i-wzorow-uzytkowych-/farmacja-i-biotechnologia/nowe-zastosowania-medyczne.

[5] Supplementary Protection Certificates are not available for the patents protecting second medicinal use (see CJEU, 9 June 2020 – case C-673/18, ECLI:EU:C:2020:531 *Santen SAS vs Directeur général de l'Institut national de la propriété industrielle*).

[6] See, e.g. Ożegalska-Trybalska in: Osajda/Żelechowski (eds), Prawo własności przemysłowej. Tom VIIIA. Komentarz, Warsaw 2022, Art. 65 IPL.

Additionally, since the claims under consideration must contain an additional qualification of specific medicinal (second) purpose, the patent holder will have to establish that the product is intended for such purpose. 10

Under Polish law, the purpose of a product is a matter of fact, which must be established by the claimant using any and all evidentiary methods available under the relevant procedures. There are no legal presumptions and no express guidance in Polish law to show what proof could be used for such purpose; this being left entirely for legal practice to define. 11

Currently, there are only few judgments where the protection afforded by second medicinal use claims has been tested by Polish courts. In light of the still-evolving jurisprudence, only comments of a general nature can be provided. 12

To successfully enforce claims arising from the infringement of a purpose-limited product claim, the claimant must prove that the defendant has engaged in an activity legally reserved for the patent holder in relation to the patented product, and for the patented purpose.[7] Regarding the purpose criterion, that proof, strictly read, pertains to a mental state (the infringer's intent). As in all such matters, in the absence of the infringer's explicit admission (e.g. in advertisements or correspondence), this criterion is mostly satisfied by presenting external manifestations of such state,[8] e.g. observable activities of the infringer which could be interpreted as manifestations of an intent to use the product for the protected purpose, in circumstances where it would be difficult to find other explanations leading the infringer to taking such action. What such manifestations would be depends to a large extent on the contemplated category of infringing action, i.e.: 13

1. for manufacturing, it could be a specific dosage, storage of a manufactured product in a particular way, connected only with such purpose and otherwise not necessary, presence of packaging or leaflets on the premises of the manufacturer indicating the protected use, etc.;
2. for offering, in addition to the elements discussed above, the packaging and leaflets would have great importance, as well as advertising accompanying the offering; or
3. for selling, factors concerning the customer could also be taken into account, i.e. their diseases, if purchasing for themselves; or for further resale (in the case of B2B transaction), the reseller's current and future clientele. Among these potential factors, the content of SmPCs would be of particular importance.

Generally, proof of purpose under Polish law would be similar to the evidence of purposeful production in German law, possibly with a lower threshold of specificity required to satisfy the court as to the fulfilment of such criterion. 14

So far, Polish jurisprudence has not produced a direct equivalent of the German *Östrogenblocker* decision,[9] which extended the protection by objectifying the test of infringement and replacing the 'purpose' criterion with a less subjective one. However, the actual difference between Polish and German practice may not be so significant, as Polish courts would review proof of purpose by way of its external manifestations within their discretionary power to assess evidence, and may use presumptions of fact to reconstruct a mental state. In our view, the three elements of the infringement test from the *Östrogenblocker* case could well lead a Polish court to a finding that sufficient evidence of 15

[7] See, e.g. Regional Court in Warsaw, 7 March 2014, docket no. XX GCo 39/14; Regional Court in Warsaw, 2 February 2015, docket no. XX GCo 8/15; Court of Appeals in Warsaw, 17 May 2016, docket no. VI ACa 640/15; Regional Court in Warsaw, 29 January 2015, docket no. XX GC 284/14; Regional Court in Warsaw, 29 January 2015, docket no. XX GC 311/14. For extracts from these decisions → mn. 61 et seq.

[8] See, e.g. Polish Supreme Court, 19 April 2019, docket no. III CSK 273/18; → mn. 64.

[9] Düsseldorf Higher Regional Court, GRUR 2017, 1107, mn. 39, 40 – *Östrogenblocker*. → § 5 mn. 12 for details.

proof of purpose exists by applying presumptions of fact. The difference may lie in the fact that, in Polish practice, under the doctrine of presumptions of fact, such three-element test would not automatically result in the finding of infringement but would be one of the elements weighted by the court against other evidence to approximate the infringers' purpose, insofar as it is perceptible to others (e.g. a skinny label approach).

## II. Swiss-type claims

16 Under the IPL, a Swiss-type claim formally is a process claim. Thus, it is infringed by actions of unauthorised persons, acting for a commercial or professional purpose, in the scope of the reserved actions under Article 66 Sec. 1(2) IPL. Such actions consist of applying the process that is the subject matter of the invention and using, offering, marketing, storing, or warehousing products obtained directly from that process, and exporting or importing them for these purposes. Having said that, the matter is not entirely clear. For example, some authors claim that the Swiss-type formula, even though formally linked with the mode of product manufacturing, in fact results in the indirect protection of a product limited by its new, specific use (purpose limited patent protection). As a result, it would be more appropriate to rely on Article 66 Sec. 1(1)[10] IPL (which governs product patent protection) when reconstructing the scope of exploitation of an invention restricted for a patent holder.[11]

17 The Swiss form patent also covers products specially prepared according to the invention for such use (Article 65 IPL[12]). Thus, products must be specifically prepared for the patented purpose. Contrary to the similar provision regulating 'regular' process patents (Article 64 Sec. 1 IPL), the wording of the law does not expressly require that the product has to be obtained directly by the patented process. The lack of this requirement is explained by the essence of the Swiss-type claims, i.e. a formal indication of a manufacturing process allowing an emphasis on the use of a known substance during the manufacturing of a certain product (and not specific elements characterising the manufacturing process itself). As a result, each instance of use of such substance for the product manufacturing for the claimed use will be tantamount to obtaining a product directly by such process.[13]

18 The potential clash with Article 64 IPL[14] (designed for 'regular' products resulting from a patented method) is resolved by the general understanding that Article 65 IPL is *lex specialis* in relation to Article 64 IPL. Thus, Article 64 Sec. 2 IPL providing for a presumption that goods capable of being manufactured in the patented process have been manufactured in accordance with it does not apply, and is overridden by the requirement to prove that the potentially infringing products have been specially prepared for the protected purpose, as set out in Article 65 IPL.

---

10 → mn. 53.

11 Ożegalska-Trybalska in: Osajda/Żelechowski (eds), Prawo własności przemysłowej. Tom VIIIA. Komentarz, Warsaw 2022, Art. 65 IPL.

12 Article 65 IPL is not correlated with the amendments to Article 25 Sec. 4 IPL (which, now, is in line with Article 54(4)(5) EPC) and, as a result, strictly speaking covers only substances, not compositions. However, it is interpreted as also covering compositions (Ożegalska-Trybalska in: Osajda/Żelechowski (eds), Prawo własności przemysłowej. Tom VIIIA. Komentarz, Warsaw 2022, Art. 65 IPL).

13 Pacud, 'Naruszenie patentu na drugie zastosowanie medyczne' in: Ożegalska-Trybalska/Kasprzycki (eds), Aktualne wyzwania prawa własności intelektyualnej i praw konkurencji, Warsaw 2015, p. 507.

14 → mn. 51.

## III. Swiss-type and product-by-use claims – scope of protection

*Prima facie*, with the Swiss-type claims resulting in a process patent, and a product-limited-by purpose patent being eponymously a product patent, one would expect their scope of protection (in other words, the class of actions which result in patent infringement) to differ accordingly. In its decision G2/08,[15] the Enlarged Board of Appeal admitted that it appears that the rights conferred on the patentee by the claim category under Article 54(5) EPC are likely broader, and could, in particular, lead to possible restrictions on the freedom of medical practitioners to prescribe or administer generics. Similar reasoning was applied in other decisions, where it was emphasised that it was generally accepted as a principle underlying the EPC that a claim to a particular physical activity (e.g. method, process, and use) conferred less protection than a claim to the physical entity per se (see decision G 2/88). It followed that a purpose-limited process claim also conferred less protection than a purpose-limited product claim.[16] 19

However, as mentioned above, under Article 65 IPL the protection of a Swiss-type claim is extended to products specifically manufactured for the patented purpose. And the patentee's legal monopoly arising from an EPC 2000 product patent includes their manufacture. In fact, despite the nominally different type of the claim, the actual scope of protection of a Swiss-type patent is quite similar to the patent incorporating product claims limited by purpose.[17] Generally, in the case of process patents for methods of manufacturing, the difference between them and product patents lies mostly in the necessity to prove by which method the product was obtained (which is irrelevant for product patents), and thereby prove or disprove the infringement. However, with purpose-limited product claims, the need to prove the specific purpose usually overrides the criterion of proof of process. 20

Therefore, the above comments pertaining to the patents incorporating product claims limited by purpose and their protection in Polish law mostly apply to the protection of patents with Swiss-type claims as well. 21

## IV. Direct v indirect infringement. Indirect/supplementary protection under general civil law/unfair competition law

Under Polish law, there is no equivalent of § 10 of the German Patent Act and the concept of indirectly infringing a patent by making available an essential part of the protected product.[18] Occasionally, in older Polish jurisprudence, judgments were given which tried to apply such concept under the guise of a purposeful interpretation of patent law;[19] however, this tendency is not repeated in newer judgments. In particular, since the doctrine of equivalents has gained a wider acceptance in Poland,[20] patent holders try to supplement the gaps in their patent protection by reference to such doctrine rather than the concept of infringement by realisation of an essential part of invention. 22

---

[15] EPO Enlarged Board of Appeal G2/08 dated 5 December 1984, p. 6.5.

[16] See, Case law of the Boards of Appeal of the European Patent Office, 10th edn, 2022, p. 632 and the case-law cited therein.

[17] Pacud, 'Naruszenie patentu na drugie zastosowanie medyczne' in: Ożegalska-Trybalska/Kasprzycki (eds), Aktualne wyzwania prawa własności intelektualnej i praw konkurencji, Warsaw 2015, p. 504, 505.

[18] → § 5 mn. 17 for details.

[19] See, e.g. Polish Supreme Court, 3 February 1970, docket no. II CR 615/69.

[20] See, e.g. the Polish Supreme Court, 10 December 2015, docket no. V CSK 149/15.

23 However, the factual situations covered by the German concept of indirect infringement are not necessarily legally indifferent in Poland. Instead, indirect infringement could be challenged based on other existing legislation. One may be the Polish Unfair Competition Counteraction Act of 16 April 1993 (UCCA) which, in addiction to definitions of specified activities deemed unfair, sets out a blanket formula whereby any activity harming interests of a competitor, if illegal or contrary to good morals, constitutes a tort of unfair competition. Arguably, an attempt to knowingly and purposefully circumvent patent protection, depriving the rightful patent holder of their duly deserved profits deriving from their patent, contains a sufficient element of bad faith to fall within the scope of the above formula. The remedies available to a patent holder as a victim of unfair competition are generally similar to those for patent infringement.

24 Alternatively, the patent holder could rely on Article 422[21] of the Polish Civil Code (CC) which relates to situations where a party knowingly benefits from another party's illegal act (here: the infringer's), and makes such benefiting party liable for the loss. However, this provision only applies where the partial realisation of patented invention is ultimately connected to a full infringement and requires proof of the benefitting party's knowledge of same (willful misconduct) which, in practice, is difficult. Notably, it does not apply where the partial embodiment of an invention protected by a Polish national patent is exported to another jurisdiction and is used there to reconstruct the whole invention outside of the geographical scope of the Polish right. Moreover, under Article 422 CC, the patent holder can pursue the claim for damages, and no other remedies usually arising from patent infringement.

25 The above protection, under the UCCA or the Civil Code, which can be called indirect or supplementary, could be applied to patents protecting second medical use in, generally, the same way as to other patents. Thus, we will not discuss it in more detail.

26 Moreover, in the context of secondary medical use patents, it seems possible that, in certain cases, the patent holder could potentially seek protection under the provision of the IPL concerning a threat of infringement (Article 285 IPL[22]). Actions taken in the process of manufacturing or marketing a product, even if not sufficient to satisfy the full infringement test, could create a threat of infringement, based on which the patent holder could obtain an injunction prohibiting them.

## D. Infringement of second medical use claims and skinny label products

27 In principle, under Polish law a skinny label is evidence that the product is not intended for the protected purpose and therefore, is a part of the affirmative factual defences on which the potential infringer can rely to avoid liability.

28 As discussed above, under Polish law, the purpose of a product is purely a question of fact and therefore, the evidence, e.g. a skinny label, is directly pertinent to the court's finding whether all elements of the infringement test have been fulfilled. From a practical perspective, such evidence is likely to be assessed as particularly important as it contains the right holder's direct and clear declaration of the purpose, which excludes the patented purpose.

[21] → mn. 55.
[22] → mn. 54.

In a case heard at the Regional Court in Warsaw,[23] it was, inter alia, briefly explained that since the SmPC does not include protected indications, there was no infringement. However, the reasoning given was not very nuanced. The case was dismissed mostly based on the finding that the patent in question did not cover that particular medicinal use for which the defendant marketed it; the 'skinny label' argument was discussed in the alternative. 29

Even with the current state of jurisprudence and without the Polish courts going further in the direction of the *Östrogenblocker* case, the skinny label cannot be considered as an entirely conclusive defence. This is because, when making findings of fact, the evidence in the form of a skinny label would be weighed against other pieces of evidence, and Polish courts would expect to apply legal principles to it, e.g. *falsa demonstratio non nocet* or *venire contra factum proprium*, allowing for the possibility of the infringer making a verbal pretense of disconnecting the product from the protected purpose, while actually relying on such use to create demand for the product. Therefore, if the skinny label, when weighted against evidence, e.g. packaging, advertisements, behaviour of sales representatives, batch size, is considered by the judge as having been made in bad faith, it may legitimately be disregarded within the judge's discretion. In the case XX GC 1117/16, the other evidence supported the finding of no infringement, so the skinny label was not tested against contrary evidence. 30

## E. Infringement of second medical use claims and biosimilar products

It is probable that the conclusions of the above discussion will apply in a very similar way to biological medicines (biologics). However, due to very limited number of judicial decisions in this regard on the one hand and the particularities of the biologics on the other, there may be some deviations. 31

In theory, when comparing an actual situation of generic medicinal products and bioequivalent (biologic) medicines, it is very similar. In Poland, there is a complicated system of reimbursement of medicinal products; the entry of a new generic / biosimilar medicine impacts the algorithm of the price calculation of the already reimbursed products and new generic / biosimilar medicines yet to be entered into the reimbursement list. Therefore, each entry of a new generic / biosimilar medicine is very closely monitored. 32

However, there are certain subtle differences, which become clear during the actual use of the generics and biosimilars. Whereas, in terms of switching onto generic medicines there are no significant disagreements anymore, there is a complex and difficult discussion when it comes to switching from reference to biosimilars. A very important voice in this discussion is the Patient's Ombudsman (PO) proceedings opened at the request of patients' association and resulting decision issued by the Supreme Administrative Court in 2019[24]. The case concerned the use of two medicines with the same active substance (etanercept). Drug A (the reference biologic) had previously been used within the reimbursed program in Poland. For the tender procedure, the hospital described the criteria for the selection of bids without mentioning the trade name of the drug, i.e. only by indicating the international name of the active substance. Drug B (bioequivalent) was selected in the tender, which led to it replacing drug A in the hospital's therapies. Patients 33

[23] See, Regional Court in Warsaw, 16 June 2020, docket no. XX GC 1117/16 → mn. 66.
[24] See, Supreme Administrative Court, 28 May 2019, docket no. II OSK 1114/19.

at the hospital were therefore started on the new drug purchased in the tender (drug B), discontinuing the existing drug (drug A). This practice was considered by the PO to be a violation of patients' collective rights.[25] This is because patients have the right to health services corresponding to the requirements of current medical knowledge.[26] Additionally, public procurement should be carried out under the principles of rational spending of public funds and the protection of competitiveness, but should also guarantee the right of the contracting authorities to choose such products or services that will meet their real needs. In the PO's view, the hospital was not entitled to switch to the new medicine based solely on financial criteria.[27]

34 After the above decision, despite incentives offered by the public payer, there is no automatic switch to biosimilars (and, in general, switching in different possible scenarios between biologics and biosimilars, as switching from a biosimilar back to a reference product is also common). Such decisions cannot be made based solely on financial reasons and each time switch must also factor in the actual needs of the patients (e.g. the medical history of a given patient precluding from switching to a given bioequivalent medicine).

35 The above limitations applicable to biosimilars usually do not arise in the case of generic medicines. The already discussed particularities of the biologics (limitations regarding switching and price erosion of lesser degree, if at all) as against generics will most probably impact also patent disputes regarding biologic medicines. Again, since currently the number of relevant judicial decisions is still very limited, it is premature to speculate on the actual implications regarding the above.

## F. Strategies and considerations

36 From a practical point of view, a party manufacturing or trading in a product under a skinny label would do well to additionally verify whether other elements accompanying its product could be used by a hostile right holder to support contrary findings in a dispute, and to introduce as many other elements as possible distancing its product from the protected purpose.

37 Generally, countermeasures adopted by German parties to protect themselves against the risk of infringing second use patents under broadened protection arising from the *Östrogenblocker* case (e.g. inclusion of suitable wording on labels, leaflets, in advertisements, written instructions to sales representatives, etc.) would be helpful also in Poland, despite the differences in law.

---

[25] See, the PO decision of 11 June 2018 No. RzPP-WPR.45.95.2017.MMA.

[26] See, Article 6(1) of Act of 6 November 2008 on patients' rights and the Patient Ombudsman , → mn. 58; § 5 of the Annex to the Regulation of the Minister of Health of 8 September 2015 on the general terms and conditions of contracts for the provision of healthcare service, → mn. 59 and § 3 Sec. 1 of the Regulation of the Minister of Health of 6 November 2013 on guaranteed services of health programs, → mn. 60.

[27] Myszko/Skrzydło-Tefelska, 'Zbiorowe prawa pacjentów w procesie zakupu leków przez szpital. Glosa do wyroku NSA z 28 maja 2019 r., II OSK 1114/19', Państwo i Prawo 9/2020, 149.

## G. Legal remedies

38 In principle, in Poland a patent holder may seek legal redress not only when an infringement actually takes place but also when the infringement is merely threatened.

39 The activities that are covered by a patent monopoly in Poland are as follows: manufacturing, using, offering, marketing, storing or warehousing products which are the subject matter of the invention, exporting or importing them for these purposes, or using the process that is the subject matter of the invention, as well as using, offering, marketing, storing or warehousing products obtained directly from that process, exporting or importing them for these purposes. Claims for patent infringement will only be justified when there is proof that an unauthorised party has undertaken the above activities.

40 Patent holders may also demand that an unauthorised third party ceases activities that only threaten to infringe the patent. Such a threat should be real and serious. The legal doctrine indicates, that e.g. the purchase of a machine for the production of infringing goods or the conclusion of a contract for the manufacture of a given product, may indicate a risk of infringement. However, all the circumstances surrounding such preparatory activities must be taken into account before reaching conclusion that there is a threat of an infringement under Polish law.[28]

41 A request to cease patent infringement or activities only threatening to infringe patent is possible only during the term of the patent – after the expiry of the patent, only a claim for compensation for damage or loss and return of unjustly obtained benefits during the time when the patent was in force may be pursued.

42 Depending on the circumstances of each case, different activities may substantiate a claim of patent infringement or a threat of such. In principle, regulatory actions aimed at obtaining market authorisation (MA) for a medicinal product are not considered a patent infringement in Poland (even if samples of products must be submitted to the authorities). A broad definition of the Bolar exemption allows for any such actions to be undertaken without a risk of patent infringement (also by third parties mandated by the market authorisation holder (MAH) – the clear result of an amendment introduced some time ago after a fierce dispute regarding third party manufacturing mandated by the MAH for the purpose of regulatory proceedings). The conclusion may be different where the obtained MA is granted long before the expiry of patent protection, so that the period of validity of the MA is shorter than the remaining period of patent protection (if the product covered by the MA is not placed on the market within three years of obtaining the MA, then the MA expires[29]).

43 Despite some court decisions addressing this issues, it is still not unequivocally settled whether an application for reimbursement of medicinal products is sufficient to justify a claim of patent infringement or a threat of a patent infringement; usually all circumstances of the case must be taken into consideration before coming to such a conclusion.[30] However, in more finely differentiated cases (e.g. skinny label) it cannot be ruled out that already at the stage of obtaining regulatory permit there is enough evidence to claim that there is a threat of a patent infringement. Again, this must be evaluated on a case-by-case basis.

---

[28] See: Stefańczyk-Kaczmarzyk in: Kondrat (ed.), Prawo własności przemysłowej. Komentarz, Warsaw 2021, Art. 285.

[29] Art. 33a Sec. 1(1) of the Pharmaceutical Law of 6 September 2001; → mn. 57.

[30] Court of Appeals in Warsaw, 17 May 2016, docket no. VI ACa 640/15; also Stefańczyk-Kaczmarzyk in: Kondrat (ed.), Prawo własności przemysłowej. Komentarz, Warsaw 2021, Art. 285.

**44** Under Polish law, the remedies available to a patent holder, whose rights are infringed by a skinny label medicinal product are similar to those applicable in other patent infringement cases. There is no specific regulation, nor separate established practice.

**45** As a first preliminary step to an infringement action, the patent holder may demand a preliminary injunction. This usually consists of a court order prohibiting the alleged infringer from trading in the infringing goods for the duration of legal dispute, sometimes combined with seizure of goods or devices/materials used in the process. The preliminary injunction generally ought to be decided at an open hearing, although it may be granted *ex parte*, in cases of particular urgency or if the injunction is to be executed by a bailiff (i.e. seizure of infringing goods). Instead of an open hearing, the court may request the defendant to respond to a motion for preliminary injunction in writing. The preliminary injunction, if granted, may be enforced e.g. by way of *per diem* penalties levied on the non-compliant defendant.

**46** The requirements for a preliminary injunction are that the underlying claim is shown to be plausible and that the preliminary injunction is necessary to achieve the purpose of the legal action (legal interest). Making the claim plausible usually involves providing evidence of trade in infringing goods, coupled with a privately obtained expert opinion confirming that the goods are embodiments of the patented medicinal product, plus proof of circumstances evidencing their use for the patented purpose. The second requirement (legal interest) is usually met in patent infringement cases, as long as the plaintiff acts reasonably urgently (the statutory urgency threshold being rather generous six months from learning about the infringement, however, it cannot be excluded that in particular cases, a shorter delay may be argued to be a sufficient indication of absence of legal interest).

**47** If a preliminary injunction is obtained, the patent holder is obliged to file the main action on the merits within a period specified by the court, no longer than two weeks from the grant of injunction. In the main action the patent holder can request the usual range of remedies, including a permanent injunction prohibiting trade in infringing products, publication of the judgment in media at the infringer's cost, destruction of infringing goods/devices used for production of same as well as of ancillary materials, payment of damages (either calculated as loss evidenced by the plaintiff, e.g. lost sales, or as equivalent of reasonable licence fees), transfer of profits derived from the infringing action. The kind of evidence necessary to prove infringement is similar to the proof in preliminary injunction proceedings, except it is more rigorously reviewed by the court and in lieu of a battle of expert opinions provided by parties, a court-appointed expert would opine on technical matters. The parties have a broad range of measures at their disposal, allowing them to obtain evidence in possession of the other party.

**48** The duration of proceedings in the first instance is usually not less than one year and may take several years, in particular due to the length of time required for the court expert to prepare the opinion or opinions (in practice usually there are several, as the parties may require supplementary opinions).

# H. Statutory provisions

## I. Industrial Property Law[31]

### Article 25 Sec. 4 49

The provisions of sections 1 to 3 shall not exclude the patentability of any invention concerning substances or compositions comprised in the state of the art, for use or for specific use in treatment or diagnostic methods referred to in Article 29(1)(3), provided that such use is not comprised in the state of the art.

### Article 29 Sec. 1(3) 50

Patents shall not be granted for: [...]

(3) methods for the treatment of the human or animal body by surgical or therapeutic methods and methods of diagnosis applied to the human or animal body; this provision does not apply to products, in particular substances or mixtures used in diagnosis or treatment.

### Article 64 51

1. A patent for an invention concerning a manufacturing process also covers products directly obtained by this process.
2. As regards new products or if the patent holder demonstrates that they were unable to establish, despite having made reasonable efforts, the product manufacturing process actually applied by another person, it is presumed that the product that can be obtained by the patented process was manufactured by this process.
3. In the case referred to in section 2, when admitting evidence to the contrary, the defendant's legitimate interest in protecting their production and trade secrets should be taken into account.

### Article 65 52

A patent for an invention concerning the application of a substance that forms part of the state of the art to obtain a product that has a new use also covers products prepared according to the invention specifically for such use.

### Article 66 Sec. 1 53

1. The patentee may prohibit a third party, acting without their consent, from exploiting the invention in a commercial or professional manner involving:
   1) manufacturing, using, offering, marketing, storing, or warehousing products which are the subject matter of the invention, or exporting or importing them for such purposes, or
   2) using the process that is the subject matter of the invention and using, offering, marketing, storing or warehousing products obtained directly from that process, and exporting or importing them for these purposes.

### Article 285 54

The proprietor of a patent, supplementary protection right (certificate), protection right, right in registration, or a person permitted under the Act may request that the actions posing a threat of infringing his right be ceased.

---

[31] Act of 30 June 2000, see Journal of Laws 2023 item 1170.

## II. Civil Code[32]

55 **Article 422**

Not only a person who has directly inflicted damage but also the person who has induced another person to inflict the damage or who has assisted them, as well as the person who consciously benefited from the damage inflicted to another person shall be liable for the damage.

## III. Act on Combating Unfair Competition[33]

56 **Article 3 Sec. 1**

1. An act of unfair competition is any activity in violation of law or good morals if it threatens or infringes the interest of another entrepreneur or customer.

## IV. Pharmaceutical Law[34]

57 **Article 33a Sec. 1(1)**

1. An authorisation shall expire if:
   1) the responsible entity does not place the medicinal product on the market within 3 years from the date of receiving an authorisation;

## V. Act on Patients' Rights and the Patient Ombudsman[35]

58 **Article 6 Sec. 1**

1. A patient has the right to health services that meet the requirements of current medical knowledge.

## VI. Annex to the Regulation of the Minister of Health of 8 September 2015 on the General Terms and Conditions of Contracts for the Provision of Healthcare Services[36]

59 **§ 5**

The healthcare provider is responsible for prescribing medicines, foodstuffs for particular nutritional uses and medical devices to recipients in accordance with the applicable regulations and current medical knowledge.

[32] Act of 23 April 1964, see Journal of Laws 2023 item 1610.
[33] Act of 16 April 1993, see Journal of Laws 2022 item 1233.
[34] Act of 6 September 2001, see Journal of Laws 2022 item 2301.
[35] Act of 6 November 2008, see Journal of Laws 2023 item 1545.
[36] Journal of Laws 2023 item 1194.

## VII. Regulation of the Minister of Health of 6 November 2013 on Guaranteed Services within the Scope of Health Programs[37]

**§ 3 Sec. 1** 60

1. Guaranteed services shall be provided in accordance with the indications of current medical knowledge, using diagnostic and therapeutic methods other than those used in unconventional, folk or oriental medicine.

# J. Extracts from court decisions

## I. Regional Court in Warsaw (2014)[38] 61

The obliged party's infringement of the exclusive use of the invention, resulting from the [...]

patent granted to the patent holder, is supported by both: the characteristics of the products with the trade names R. (1) transdermal system patch and R. (2) transdermal system patch, and the indication by [...].V. of the medicinal product E. transdermal system as the reference medicine for them. Its documentation served to register the obliged party's products, authorised for marketing by the decision of the President of the Office for Registration of Medicinal Products, Medical Devices and Biocidal Products, without the obligation to submit clinical and non-clinical studies. The fact that the obliged party's generic medicinal products have fulfilled the patent claim is confirmed by the expert assessment provided in the expert report attached to the application.

## II. Regional Court in Warsaw (2015)[39] 62

In order to make plausible an infringement consisting of an encroachment by the obliged party on the scope of patent exclusivity reserved for the patent holder, the patent holder should have demonstrated that the obliged party was using the invention, in the sense of taking steps to manufacture, import, apply, offer and market medicinal products with the trade names R. T., (...) h, transdermal system patch and R. T., (...) h, transdermal system patch or having any other trade name, containing the active substance (...) for application in a method of preventing, treating or slowing the progression of dementia or disease (...), where (...) is administered in a transdermal therapeutic system (T.) and the approved starting dose is that of a medicinal product called 'E. (...)4 h transdermal system', because this is supposed to be the content of future claims.

The evidence offered shows that the company (...) has obtained a marketing authorisation (MA) in the territory of Poland, where the patent for the invention (...) is protected. Its medicinal products R. T., (...) h, transdermal system, patch, and R. T., (...) h, transdermal system, patch have been entered on the reimbursement list for use in (...) disease. However, this does not mean that it manufactures, imports, applies, markets and offers products specifically formulated for the application and mode of administration protected by the patent. At this stage of the proceedings, it cannot be concluded that the company (...) is actually exploiting

[37] Journal of Laws 2023 item 916.
[38] 7 March 2014, XX GCo 39/14.
[39] 2 February 2015, XX GCo 8/15.

the invention (...) in such a way that belongs exclusively to the patent holder, as provided for in Article 66 in conjunction with Article 287(1) Industrial Property Law.

## 63 III. Court of Appeals in Warsaw[40]

'Turning to the merits of the statement of claims, one has to agree with the Court of First Instance that, in bringing a claim for patent protection to court, the claimant was required to jointly demonstrate three circumstances:
1) the existence of his right,
2) infringement of the patent by the defendant in any if the forms set out in Article 66(1) Industrial Property Law
3) performance of an obligation exhausting the patent claims.

(...)

Thus, while one may agree that the mere submission of marketing and reimbursement applications does not constitute patent infringement, marketing [of the products] does.'

*(Similar holdings in the judgments of the Regional Court in Warsaw of 29 January 2015, XX GC 284/14 and XX GC 311/14)*

## 64 IV. Polish Supreme Court (2019)[41]

It should be noted that when establishing the intention to harm, as a circumstance of a subjective nature, related to a certain state of will (consciousness) of the debtor, the court may resort to inferences based on external, objective and verifiable premises, if they are justified in the light of principles of life experience, general knowledge and logic (Article 231 of the Code of Civil Procedure) (cf. the judgment of the Supreme Court of 9 February 2017, III CSK 60/16, unpublished).

## 65 V. Polish Supreme Court (2015)[42]

The strict interpretation adopted by the Court of Appeal regarding the scope of rights under the patent (Article 63(2) IPL), the consequence of which is the thesis that infringement of these rights (Article 237(1) IPL) occurs only when the solutions covered by the patent and applied by another person are completely identical, is one of those presented in the literature. However, that Court did not consider the comparison presented in the doctrine and case law referred to as the theory of equivalents or the doctrine of equivalent means. This was developed on the basis of the application of the rules of the Convention on the Grant of European Patents (EPC), drawn up in Munich on 5 October 1973, as amended by the Act amending Article 63 of the Convention of 17 December 1991 and by the decisions of the Administrative Council of the European Patent Organisation of 21 December 1978, 13 December 1994, 20 October 1995, 5 December 1996 and 10 December 1998, together with the Protocols forming an integral part thereof (Journal of Laws 2004 No. 79, item 737). The reason for developing this theory was to prevent the possibility of circumventing the patent by making obvious modifications to the patent not expressly provided for in the patent claims, while modifications that are not obvious and that require independent creative input being outside the extended scope of the patent.

[40] 17 May 2016, VI ACa 640/15.
[41] 19 April 2019, III CSK 273/18.
[42] 10 December 2015, V CSK 149/15.

This comparison involves determining the scope of patent protection for a given solution in order to check whether the technical solution of another entity, or its particular features, can be considered equivalent to those claimed by the patent. Its essence lies in the possibility of extending the scope of protection granted to an invention by extending this protection also to all those solutions in which certain elements have been replaced by others performing the same functions and leading to the same result as the patented solution. The equivalence of technical means is determined by the function they perform in the solution, the objective they allow to be achieved in that solution and the result they contribute to. The equivalent means will therefore be such that lead to the same solution of the technical issue that underlies the patent.

The comparative examination should consist of the following steps:

- determining the subject matter of the patent on the basis of its claims, description and drawings, taking into account the technical problem underlying the invention in question and the essence of the solution, as well as the type of invention protected;
- determining the technical features of the invention in dispute, including the underlying technical problem and the nature of the invention as a whole;
- determining which technical features of the solution in dispute functionally reflect solutions already existing in the state of the art (determination of the closest state of the art for the solution in dispute);
- comparing the determined subject matter scope of the patent with the technical features of the contested solution in order to verify which features of the protected solution are reflected in the contested solution in the form of their obvious equivalents;
- determining, where the technical features (obvious equivalents) reproduced in the contested solution constitute the essence of the technical solution protected by the patent, whether those features could have been developed by a [so-called] specialist in the field without knowledge of the patent.

The use of this comparison has an advantage over a formalistic approach, which may not reflect the true scope of the solutions under comparison. The differences between the solutions should relate to the essential features of a concept changing the existing state of the art.

## VI. Regional Court in Warsaw (2020)[43] 66

In the Court's view, both the conclusions presented by the experts' opinions and the above findings confirm that the defendant's medicinal product, in terms of the disputed use in adjuvant treatment, does not infringe the claimant's exclusive rights under the patent. In addition to these arguments, it should be pointed out that, according to the leaflet for (...) and the SmPC of this medicinal product, this drug was not intended for the treatment of inoperable tumors (...), but for application in patients after surgical removal of tumors for preventive purposes, and such use was indicated by the defendant in the above-mentioned documents. As indicated by the experts and confirmed by the positions in the articles on (...), adjuvant treatment means 'complementary', 'preventive', 'prophylactic' therapy after complete removal of the tumor and aims to reduce the likelihood of metastatic recurrence. The defendant could not, for the above reasons alone, infringe the plaintiff's patent, which resulted in the dismissal of the claims covered by the lawsuit.

[43] 16 December 2020, XX GC 1117/16.

# § 10
# Portugal

## A. Executive summary

1 The case law in Portugal on second medical use patents is scarce, difficult to find and still pretty unclear due to the particularities of the patent landscape in Portugal concerning pharmaceutical patents until 2019, when a mandatory arbitration procedure was introduced to be the sole forum to solve disputes concerning IP rights related to medicines of reference and generic medicines. We are aware of only a few decisions on the subject, issued by arbitral tribunals in 2016 and 2017 (essentially regarding pregabalin and zoledronic acid). After the creation of the IP Court in 2019, the forum handling patent disputes, there are no decisions on the subject.

2 It appears that in order to rule out the risk of infringement, generic companies need to 'carve out' the protected indication from the marketing authorisation and also take additional preventive measures to minimise the risk that the generic product will be used for the patented indication, such as recommendations to health professionals.

3 Court decisions have so far only addressed the issue of generic products, but infringement by a biosimilar product of second medical use patents is likely to be treated in a similar manner.

## B. Scope of protection and interpretation of second medical use claims

4 Like Article 54 EPC, Article 53 of the Portuguese Intellectual Property Code (*Código da Propiedade Industrial* – IPC) explicitly provides for the possibility of patenting substances or compositions included in the state of the art for use in a method of treatment provided that its use for any such method is not comprised in the state of the art.[1] The patentability of such substances or compositions for any other specific use in a method of treatment is also allowed, provided that such use is not comprised in the state of the art.

5 Regarding the scope of protection of medical use patents, there is no case law on this matter. However, in line with jurisprudence and EPO guidelines (which are strongly followed by Portuguese courts), the specifically claimed therapeutic use is considered to be an essential element of the invention and an integral part of the scope of protection of this type of patent. Second medical use claims are construed as a 'purpose-limited product claim' and are only infringed when the compound is used for the treatment of the patented indication.

---

[1] → mn. 30.

## C. Direct and indirect infringement of second medical use claims

Portuguese law does not contain a specific regulation regarding the infringement of second medical use patents, so the general rules apply. 6

The relevant Portuguese legal provision regarding the rights conferred by a patent is Article 102 IPC, which states the following: 7

1. The patent confers the exclusive right to exploit the invention on any part of the Portuguese territory.
2. The patent also confers on its holder the exclusive right to prevent third parties, without its consent, from:
   a) manufacturing, offering, storing, placing on the market or using a product object of a patent, or importing or possessing such product, for any of the ends referred to;
   b) using the process covered by the patent or, if the third party has, or should have, knowledge that the use of the process is forbidden without the consent of the patent holder, the offer for its use offering such use of the process;
   c) offering, storing, placing on the market and using, or importing or possession for those ends, of products obtained directly by means of the process covered by the patent.
3. Moreover, the patent confers on its holder the right to prevent third parties, without the holder's consent, from offering or making available to any person who is not entitled to exploit the invention the necessary means to execute it in what concerns its essential element, provided that the third party knows, or should know, that such means are capable of and aimed at said exploitation.

According to the examined case law from the arbitral tribunals, there is no direct infringement when the SmPC does not contain the protected therapeutic indication or when the SmPC is carved out of the protected therapeutic indication, as the product will then will not legally qualify as being 'used' for the protected therapy. However, it should be noted that the only available case law on the infringement of second medical use patents dates from before 2019, in a period where indirect infringement was not foreseen in Portugal. Article 102 IPC, quoted above, was only introduced in July 2019. So, the decisions of the arbitral tribunals known to us only addressed the issue of direct infringement. 8

As far as indirect infringement is concerned, there is still no case law regarding the enforcement of Article 102(3) IPC. 9

From a Portuguese perspective, the risks of infringement of medical use patents (in cases of both direct or indirect infringement), are in any case low when the alleged infringer uses a skinny label product and does not take any steps to promote or incentivise the off-label use of the product during distribution and marketing. The risk of infringement can be further and greatly minimised if the marketing of the product is accompanied by instructions or express recommendations that it be used in accordance with the specific medical use indicated in the SmPC. 10

## D. Infringement of second medical use claims and skinny label products

11 We are aware of the following decisions that have addressed medical use patents in Portugal:

Decision of 13.5.2014 from an arbitral tribunal in a dispute regarding Zoledronic Acid, where it was decided that the use of a skinny label product was sufficient to avoid infringement. No measures were imposed on the generic company (→ mn. 47).

Decision of 18.6.2014 from an arbitral tribunal in a dispute regarding Zoledronic Acid, where it was decided that the use of a skinny label product was sufficient to avoid infringement. No measures were imposed on the generic company.

Decision of 31.12.2014 from an arbitral tribunal in a dispute regarding Zoledronic Acid, where the generic company was ordered not to market packages of the product in numbers exceeding the percentage they were entitled to distribute as free samples (→ mn. 48).

Decision of 6.7.2017 from an appeal court upholding a decision from an arbitral tribunal of 26.4.2016 in a dispute regarding Pregabalin, where it was decided, under the regimen of collision of rights, to order the generic company not to market packages of the product in numbers exceeding the percentage they were entitled to distribute as free samples.

Decision of 1.7.2021 from an arbitral tribunal in a dispute regarding Everolimus, where it was decided that the use of a skinny label product was sufficient to avoid direct infringement. No measures were imposed on the generic company. The arbitral tribunal stated that it seems excessive to impose on the Defendant a behaviour in the sense of being the guarantors of the protection of Claimant patent rights before third parties, imposing notices or instructions to regulatory authorities, hospitals or others that the generic medicine cannot be used for the claimed therapy (→ mn. 50).

12 To our knowledge, aside from carving out the protected therapy from the SmPC, no additional measures have been imposed so far by the Portuguese courts on generic companies intending to sell a skinny label product, such as notices, instructions or recommendations to regulatory authorities, hospitals or health professionals.

13 However, Portuguese scholars are divided on the question of infringement of medical use patents. Prof. Remédio Marques appears take the view that there will only be direct infringement of second medical use patents if the generic medicine can be legally marketed for the claimed therapy and the SmpC or PIL includes such specific medical use. By contrast, Dr. Magalhães Cardoso, following the legal trends set by the decisions from the Dutch Supreme Court of 3.11.2017 (*MSD v Teva*)[2], from the Higher Regional Court Düsseldorf of 5.5.2017 (*Östrogenblocker*)[3] and of the UK Supreme Court of 14.11.2018 (*Warner Lambert*)[4] supports the view that removing the therapeutic indications from the SmPC, PIL and packaging ('carve out') is not enough to avoid infringement, and that additional reasonable and appropriate measures should be taken by the generic company, such as including notices and information in all marketing and promotional literature that the generic products cannot be used for the claimed therapy.

14 In view of the recent case law developed by the Dutch, German and UK courts on this matter, it is reasonable to assume that the Portuguese Court will adopt a similar approach considering that the use of a skinny label product is not enough to avoid the (direct or

[2] → § 8 mn. 66.
[3] → § 5 mn. 55.
[4] → § 13 mn. 36.

indirect) infringement of a medical use patent and imposing some additional measures on the generic company.

In Portugal, the off-label use of medicines is not specifically regulated, is not subject to special authorisation procedures and constitutes a routine clinical practice in several medical areas, particularly in pediatrics, oncology, hematology, psychiatry, obstetrics, rheumatology, ophthalmology, and rare diseases. In any case, as a general rule, the off-label prescription of medicines is accepted when the patient expresses in advance and in writing his informed and free consent after full and clear explanation, and provided that certain requirements are met: 15

1. there is no alternative medicine available on the market approved for the patient's particular clinical condition;
2. the off-label use is supported by scientifically convincing results;
3. the off-label use provides therapeutic results with a favourable benefit/risk ratio for the patient;
4. adequate monitoring (active pharmacovigilance) of the patient is in place.

However, as far as we know, there is no case law on the impact of the prescribing practice of second medical use indications in Portugal. 16

Notwithstanding the prescribing practice, the use of a skinny label product, accompanied by instructions or recommendations that it be used in accordance with the SmPC, and the absence of promotional activities for the patented indication, seems sufficient to avoid risk of infringement of medical use patents. 17

## E. Infringement of second medical use claims and biosimilar products

All of the cases dealt with so far on the infringement of a second medical use patent in Portugal relate to generic medicines. However, it seems reasonable to assume that the infringement of a second medical use patent by a biosimilar product is likely to be treated in a similar manner. 18

However, from a regulatory perspective, there are factors which would render the off-label prescription of a biosimilar for the protected indication less plausible than in the case of a generic. 19

As regards hospital medicinal products, which applies to be vast majority of biosimilars, the off-label prescription must be validated in advance by the pharmacy and therapy and/or ethics committees of the respective hospital. Also, the pharmacist, as a rule of conduct must refrain from dispensing a medication for purposes not foreseen in the SmPC, under penalty of civil, criminal, disciplinary and ethical liability for breach of the information duty. So, a pharmacist who detects an off-label has a legal duty to inform the patient of this fact and of the risks it entails, particularly when it relates to biosimilars, despite having been prescribed by a physician. 20

## F. Strategies and considerations

In light of the developments in the foreign case law, it is advisable to use a skinny label product and to take, voluntarily and preemptively, mitigation risk measures, such as 21 sending information letters, notices and warnings to health professionals that the product cannot be prescribed and dispensed for the patented indication.

## G. Legal remedies

22 Two different proceedings are available to the patent holder in case of infringement: proceedings on the merits and preliminary injunctions.

23 Preliminary injunctions may be filed to stop an ongoing infringement or to prevent any imminent infringement. In case of imminent infringement, the patentee must prove the expected infringing act the urgency of the remedy and the expected damages (*periculum in mora*). In this case, the balance of convenience may also be evaluated by the Court. In case of an ongoing infringement, the *periculum in mora* condition is not required, and patentee is only required to prove the infringement.

24 Preliminary injunctions can be petitioned *inter partes* or *ex parte*. Typically, in patent litigation, the Portuguese IP Court rejects preliminary injunctions *ex parte* and the defendant is served to file the statement of defence before the court making the final decision. Protective briefs are not foreseen in Portugal.

25 The usual remedies in IP proceedings are the following: a court order to stop the infringement, a penalty sanction in case of breach of the court order, seizure of the infringing goods, recall of the infringing goods from the market, collection of evidence and/or information.

26 In proceedings on the merits the remedies available are typically the following: injunctions (seizure and destruction of infringing goods); penalty for non-compliance with a court order; damage compensation (lost profits, infringer's profits, or a lump sum as a royalty fee); non-material damages; the costs incurred in the investigation of the infringement; and the legal costs (but subject to a statutory limit).

27 However, regarding second medical use patents, we anticipate that additional remedies may be available to the patentee, such as orders for the generic/biosimilar companies to take certain measures/steps to avoid the risk of an off-label use of the product, including the sending of notices and information letters to the health professionals prescribing the particular product that it cannot be used for the patented indication.

28 The burden of proving the extent of infringing sales lies with the patentee, but upon a duly substantiated request the alleged infringer may be ordered to provide documents and financial information regarding the alleged infringement.

## H. Statutory provisions

### I. Intellectual Property Code

29 **Article 52: Limitations regarding patentability**

1. Inventions whose commercial exploitation is against the law or contrary to public policy, public health or morality are not patentable and their exploitation may not be considered as such due to the simple fact that it is forbidden by law or regulations.
2. Under the previous paragraph, the following are not patentable:

a) Processes for cloning human beings;
b) Processes for modifying the germinal genetic identity of human beings;
c) The use of human embryos for industrial or commercial purposes;
d) Processes for modifying the genetic identity of animals which may cause them suffering without any substantial medical benefit to man or animal and also animals resulting from such processes.

3. The following are also not patentable:
   a) The human body, at the various stages of its formation and development and the simple decoding of one of its elements, including the discovery of a sequence or partial sequence of a gene, without prejudice to (1)(c) of the following article;
   b) Plant and animal varieties and essentially biological processes for obtaining plants or animals;
   c) Surgical or therapeutic methods for treating the human or animal body and diagnostic methods used on the human or animal body, but the products, substances or compositions used oin any of such methods may be patentable.

**Article 53: Special cases of patentability** 30

1. The following may be patented:
   a) A substance or composition included in the state of the art for use in a method referred to in paragraph (3)(c) of the previous article, on the condition that this use for any method mentioned therein is not included in the state of the art;
   b) The substance or composition referred to in the previous paragraph for any other specific use in a method mentioned in paragraph (3)(c) of the previous article, provided that this use is not included in the state of the art;
   c) A new invention that involves an inventive step and is susceptible of industrial application relating to any isolated element of the human body or produced in any other way by a technical process, including a sequence or partial sequence of a gene, even though the structure of this element is identical to that of a natural element, provided that the industrial application of a sequence or partial sequence of a gene is expressly observed and specifically described in the patent application;
   d) Without prejudice to what is mentioned in paragraph (3)(b) of the previous article, an invention relating to plants or animals, if its technical feasibility is not confined to a particular plant variety or breed of animal;
   e) A biological material isolated from its natural environment or produced on the basis of a technical process, even if it pre-exists in a natural state;
   f) An invention relating to a microbiological process or other technical processes or products obtained by means of these processes.
2. An essentially biological process for obtaining plants or animals is any process that consists wholly of natural phenomena, such as crossing or selection.
3. A microbiological process is any process involving or performed upon or resulting in microbiological material.
4. Biological material is any material that contains genetic information and is capable of reproducing itself or being reproduced in a biological system.

**Article 98: Scope of protection** 31

1. The scope of the protection conferred by a patent shall be determined by the content of the claims and the description and drawings shall serve to interpret them.
2. If a patent concerns a process, the rights conferred by it shall cover the products obtained directly by the patented process.
3. The protection conferred by a patent on a biological material possessing specific characteristics as a result of the invention shall extend to any biological material derived from that biological material through propagation or multiplication in an identical or divergent form and possessing those same characteristics.

4. The protection conferred by a patent on a process that enables a biological material to be produced possessing specific characteristics as a result of the invention shall extend to biological material directly obtained through that process and to any other biological material derived from the directly obtained biological material through propagation or multiplication in an identical or divergent form and possessing those same characteristics.
5. The protection conferred by a patent of a product that contains or consists of genetic information shall extend to any material in which the product is incorporated, contained and performs its function, save as provided for in Article 52(3)(a).
6. By way of derogation of paragraphs 3 to 5 of this
   a) The sale or other form of commercialisation of plant propagating material to a farmer by the holder of the patent, or with his consent for agricultural use, implies authorisation for the farmer to use the product of his harvest for propagation or multiplication by him on his own farm;
   b) The sale or any other form of commercialisation of breeding stock or other animal reproductive material to a farmer by the holder of the patent or with his consent implies authorisation for the farmer to use the protected livestock for an agricultural purpose. This includes making the animal or other animal reproductive material available for the purposes of pursuing his agricultural activity but not sale within the framework or for the purpose of a commercial reproduction activity.

32

### Article 102: Rights granted by a patent

1. The patent confers the exclusive right to exploit the invention on any part of the Portuguese territory.
2. The patent also confers to its holder the exclusive right to prevent third parties, without its consent, from:
   a) Manufacturing, offering, storing, placing on the market or using a product object of a patent, or importing or possessing such product, for any of the ends referred to.
   b) The use of the process covered by the patent or, if the third party has, or should have, knowledge that the use of the process is forbidden without the consent of the patent holder, the offer for its use.
   c) The offer, storing, placing on the market and use, or importing or possession for those ends, of products obtained directly by means of the process covered by the patent.
3. The patent confers moreover to its holder the right to prevent third parties, without its consent, to offer or to make available to any person who is not entitled to exploit the invention the necessary means to execute it in what concerns its essential element, provided that the third party knows, or should know, that such means are adequate and aimed to said execution.
4. The provisions of the previous number do not apply if the means are products that are currently on the market, unless the third party induces the person to whom the delivery is made to practice the acts provided for in paragraph 2.
5. For the purposes set out in paragraph 3, persons who carry out the acts set out in subparagraphs a) to d) of the following Article are not considered qualified persons to exploit the invention.
6. A patentee may oppose all acts constituting a violation of his patent, even if they merge with another patent with a later priority date, with no need to impugn titles or request annulment of patents with which this right merges.
7. The rights conferred by a patent shall not exceed the scope defined by the claims.
8. A patentee may ask the Portuguese Patent Office, on payment of a fee, to limit the scope of protection of the invention by amending the claims.
9. If upon examination it is concluded that the request for limitation can be granted, the Portuguese Patent Office shall promote the publication of a notice of the amendment of

the claims, otherwise the request for limitation shall be refused and the decision communicated to the patentee.

### Article 339: Measures to obtain evidence 33

1. Whenever evidence is in the possession of, held by, or under the control of the opposing or a third party, the interested party may request of the court that it be presented, provided that, to justify its intentions, it presents sufficient indication of a violation of industrial property rights.
2. When the acts in question are practised at the commercial scale, the claimant may also ask the court for the presentation of banking, financial, accounting or commercial documents that are in the possession of, accessible to or under the control of the opposing or third party.
3. In compliance with the provisions in the preceding paragraphs, the court, while guaranteeing protection of confidential information, notifies the respondent that it must present the evidence in its possession within the designated period, implementing the necessary actions in the event of non-compliance.

### Article 340: Measures to preserve evidence 34

1. Whenever industrial property rights are violated, or there are grounds to believe a third party may cause serious, difficult-to-repair harm to said rights, the interested party may request urgent and effective provisional measures aimed at preserving evidence of the alleged violation.
2. These evidence preservation measures may include a detailed description, with or without samples, or the effective seizure of the goods suspected of violating industrial property rights, as well as, whenever considered appropriate, of the materials and instruments used in producing and distributing said goods, as well as documentation pertaining to them.

### Article 341: Follow up and adversarial proceedings 35

1. Whenever a delay in implementing the measures may cause irreparable damages to the claimant, or whenever there is a serious risk of destruction or concealment of evidence, the measures provided for in the preceding paragraph may be applied without a prior hearing of the respondent.
2. When the measures for preserving evidence are implemented without a prior hearing of the respondent, the latter is immediately served of this order.
3. Following the notification provided for in the preceding paragraph, the respondent may request a review of the implemented measures within a period of ten days, providing evidence and presenting arguments not yet taken into account by the court.
4. When the respondent has been heard, the court may decide on the change, revocation or confirmation of the implemented measures.

### Article 342: Causes of extinction and expiry 36

1. The causes of extinction and expiry provided for in Article 389 of the Code of Civil Procedure apply to the measures for obtaining and preserving evidence, except where they function as preliminary measures for the lodging of preventive orders in accordance with Article 345.
2. In addition to the causes for extinction referred to in the previous number, when the alleged breach of a trade secret is at stake, the measures cease to produce effects, at the request of the respondent, if they fail to meet the requirements set out in Article 313 due to reasons not attributable to that party.

37 **Article 343: Applicants responsibility**

1. The implementation of the measures for preserving evidence may depend on the provision of a bond or other guarantee by the applicant aimed at guaranteeing the compensation provided for in paragraph 3 herein.
2. For determining the value, the economic capacity of the applicant should be taken into account, amongst other relevant factors
3. Whenever an implemented measure for preserving evidence is considered unjustified or ceases to produce effects due to a fact imputable to the applicant, as well as in cases where it has been requested abusively or in bad-faith, it is verified that there was no violation or that the fear that another party may cause serious and difficult-to-repair harm to an industrial property right or trade secret is unfounded, the court may order the applicant, if the respondent so requests, to pay appropriate compensation for repairing any damage caused by implementation of the measures.

38 **Article 344: Obligation to provide information**

1. The interested party may request the provision of detailed information on the origin and distribution networks of the goods or services it suspects violate industrial property rights or trade secrets, namely:
   a) The names and addresses of producers, manufacturers, distributors, suppliers and other prior holders of the goods or services, as well as the targeted wholesalers and retailers;
   b) Information on the quantities produced, manufactured, delivered, received or ordered, as well as the price obtained for the goods or services.
2. Provision of the information provided for in this Article can be demanded from the alleged infringer or any other person which:
   a) Is found in possession of the goods or is found using or providing the services on the commercial scale that are suspected of violating industrial property rights or trade secrets;
   b) Is indicated by a person referred to in the preceding subparagraph as having participated in the production, manufacture or distribution of the goods or in the provision of the services suspected of infringing industrial property rights or trade secrets.
3. The provisions of this Article are without prejudice to the application of other legislative or regulatory provisions, namely those which:
   a) Confer upon the interested party the right to more extensive information;
   b) Regulate its use in civil or criminal proceedings;
   c) Regulate responsibility for abuse of the right to information;
   d) Confer the right not to make any statements that may oblige any of the persons referred to in paragraph 2 above to admit to their own participation or that of their immediate family members;
   e) Confer the right to claim professional secrecy, protection of the confidentiality of information sources or the legal system of personal data protection.

39 **Article 345: Preliminary injunctions**

1. Whenever there is violation of, or justified fear that another party may cause serious and difficult-to-repair harm to an industrial property right or a trade secret, the court may, if the interested party so requests, order the appropriate measures to:
   a) Rule out any imminent violation; or
   b) Prohibit continuation of the violation.
2. The court will demand that the applicant provide proof that it is the holder of the industrial property right or trade secret in question, or that it is authorised to use it and that a violation exists or is imminent.
3. The measures provided for in paragraph 1 may also be ordered against any intermediary whose services are used by third parties to violate industrial property rights or trade secrets.

4. The court may, as a matter of procedure or at the request of the aplicant, decide on a compulsory monetary penalty with a view to guaranteeing execution of the measures provided for in paragraph 1.
5. The provisions of Articles 341 to 343 apply to this article.
6. At the request of the respondent, the implemented measures referred to in paragraph 1 may be substituted by a bond, whenever, after hearing the claimant, said bonds proves adequate for guaranteeing compensation to the holder of the right.
7. In determining the measures provided for in this article, the court shall take into account the type of industrial property rights or trade secret in question, safeguarding, in particular, the possibility of the holder of the right continuing to enjoy its rights without any restriction.

### Article 346: Seizure 40

1. In the case of an infringement at the commercial scale, whether existent or imminent, and whenever the interested party can prove the existence of circumstances that may compromise the collection of the compensation for losses and damages, the court may order the preventive seizure of the movable and immovable assets of the alleged infringer, including the balances of its bank accounts. The judge may also order communication of or access to banking, financial or commercial data and information relating to the infringer.
2. Whenever there is infringement of industrial property rights or trade secrets, the court may, if the interested party so requests, order the seizure of the goods suspected of infringing those rights or of the instruments that may merely serve for the execution of the unlawful act.
3. For the purposes of the preceding paragraphs, the court may demand that the applicant provide all reasonably accessible evidence to prove that it is the holder of the industrial property right or trade secret in question, or that it is authorised to use it, and that an infringement exists or is imminent.
4. The provisions of Articles 341 to 343 apply to this article.

### Article 347: Compensation for losses and damages 41

1. Whoever illegally infringes the industrial property rights or trade secrets of another person, be it with criminal intent or by mere blame, must pay compensation to the injured party for the damages resulting from the infringement.
2. In determining the amount of compensation for losses and damages, the court shall take into account, in particular, the profit obtained by the infringer and the resulting damages and lost profits suffered by the injured party. It shall also take into consideration the costs borne with the protection of the right in question and the investigation and termination of the harmful conduct.
3. In calculating the compensation to be paid to the unlawful conduct shall be taken into account.
4. The court shall also take the moral damages caused by the conduct of the infringer.
5. If, under the preceding paragraphs, it is impossible to quantify the losses effectively suffered by the injured party, the court may, provided this is not opposed by the injured party, alternatively define a fixed amount under equity, that is based, as a minimum value, on the remuneration that the injured party would have received if the infringer had requested authorisation to use the industrial property rights or trade secrets in question and the costs borne with the protection of the industrial property right or trade secret and the investigation and termination of the harmful conduct.
6. When, in relation to the injured party, the infringer's conduct constitutes a repeated practice or proves to be particularly burdensome, the court may determine the compensation due to him by resorting to the combination of all or some of the aspects provided for in paragraphs 2 to 5.

7. In any case, the court shall fix a reasonable amount aimed at covering the duly documented costs borne by the injured party in investigating and terminating the infringement of its rights.

42 **Article 348: Additional penalties**

1. Without prejudice to fixation of compensation for losses and damages, the decision on the merits by the court should, on request of the injured party and at the cost of the infringer, decide on measures relating to the destiny of the goods that have infringed the industrial property rights or trade secrets.
2. The measures provided for in the preceding paragraph must be adequate, necessary and proportionate to the gravity of the infringement. They may include destruction or withdrawal or definitive exclusion from commercial circuits without any compensation to the infringer.
3. In applying these measures, the court shall take into account the legitimate rights of third parties in particular consumers.
4. The instruments used in producing the goods that infringe the industrial property rights or trade secrets shall also be the object of the additional penalties provided for in this article.

43 **Article 349: Inhibitory measures**

1. In the decision on the merits the court may also impose to the infringer measures aimed at preventing the continuation of the infringement.
2. These measures may include:
   a) Temporary prohibition of certain business activities or professions;
   b) Loss of the right to take part in fairs or markets;
   c) Temporary or definitive closure of the establishment.
3. The provisions of this Article apply to any intermediary whose services are used by third parties to infringe industrial property rights or trade secrets.
4. In decisions determining the termination of an unlawful activity, the court may include a compulsory monetary penalty aimed at ensuring the execution of the decision.

44 **Article 350: Publication of the decisions**

1. At the request of the injured party, and at the expense of the infringer, the court may order public notification of its final decision.
2. Said public notification may be made through publication in the Industrial Property Bulletin or disclosure in any media outlet considered appropriate.
3. Public notification will take the form of a statement containing elements of the decision and sentence, as well as identification of the parties involved.

## II. Law on the prescription of medicines[5]

45 **Article 2**

1. For the purposes of reimbursement by the National Health Service (SNS), the prescription of medicines must include the common international name of the active substance, the pharmaceutical form, the dosage, the presentation and the posology.
2. When technically indicated, the prescription of medicinal products may include the indication of the commercial name, by brand or name of the marketing authorisation holder, in the cases of:
   a) Prescription of medicine with active substance for which there is no reimbursed generic medicine or for which there is only original brand name and licenses.

[5] Law 14/2000.

   b) Technical justification of the physician as to the inability to substitute the prescribed medication.
3. For the purposes of paragraph b) of the previous number, only the following technical justifications are admissible:
   a) Prescription of medication with a narrow therapeutic margin or index, according to information provided by INFARMED, I. P.
   b) Founded suspicion, previously reported to INFARMED, I.P., of intolerance or adverse reaction to a medicine with the same active substance, but identified by another trade name.
   c) Prescription of medication intended to ensure the continuity of a treatment with an estimated duration of more than 28 days.

**Article 3** 46

1. When dispensing medications, the pharmacist, or his duly qualified collaborator, must inform the user of the existence of generic medications with the same active substance, pharmaceutical form, presentation and dosage of the prescribed medication, reimbursed by the SNS and about that which has the lowest price available on the market.
2. Pharmacies must have available for sale at least three medicines with the same active substance, pharmaceutical form and dosage, among those corresponding to the five lowest prices of each homogeneous group, and must dispense the lowest price, unless it is another the user's option.
3. The user has the right to opt for any medication with the same active substance, pharmaceutical form and dosage contained in the medical prescription, except in the situations provided for in paragraph a) of paragraph 2 and in paragraphs a) and b) of paragraph 2. 3 of Article 2
4. In the case provided for in subparagraph c) of paragraph 3 of Article 2, the user may exercise the right of option, by signing the medical prescription, when he wants a medicine at a lower price than the medicine prescribed, being forbidden, in pharmacy, if any substitution is made for a medicine with a higher price than the prescribed medicine.

# J. Extracts from court decisions

## I. *Novartis v Sanofi (zoledronic acid)*[6] 47

### Grounds for the decision

Novartis Pharma AG is the holder of the European patent EP 1296689 (EP'869), related to the zoledronic acid.

The court concluded that the patent protects a specific method of administration for the zoledronic acid, exclusively applicable to the therapeutic indication of osteoporosis, i.e. is a second use patent. The generic company made an amendment to its label and its generic medicine is exclusively indicate for the treatment of the Paget disease, although from a medical perspective the medicine may be used for the treatment of both diseases.

Novartis argues that even a different therapeutic indication does not prevent the use for the protected indication and therefore the manufacture and commercialisation of said medicines will constitute an infringement of Novartis's IP rights and Sanofi should be sentenced not to import, manufacture, warehouse, launch in the market, sell or offer the generic medicines while EP'869 remains in force.

[6] Arbitration court, 13 May 2014.

However, according to the court since EP'869 solely protects the use of zoledronic acid for the treatment of osteoporosis, thus the generic medicine does not fall within the scope of protection of EP'869. Although there is a risk of the medicine being used for the treatment of osteoporosis, since it does not have said indication in its label, there is no infringement of EP'869. EP'869 is not a product patent and it solely protects the use of the substance zoledronic acid.

The possible use of the generic medicine for the protected indication may arise from the prescription system in Portugal (based on the mandatory prescription of the DCI) which may lead to liability of the Portuguese State, but not the generic company.

**Costs of the proceedings**

The arbitrators' fees and secretariat fees were determined to be € 70,000.

Since all the claims filed by Novartis were dismissed, the court sentenced Novartis in the payment of all the court fees.

48

## II. *Novartis v Fair-med Healthcare (zoledronic acid)*[7]

**Grounds for the decision**

Novartis Pharma AG is the holder of the European patents EP 1296689 (EP'869) and EP 1591122, related to the zoledronic acid.

The court concluded that the relevant scope of protection of the patents is the use for the treatment of osteoporosis, i.e. is a second use patent. The generic medicine is exclusively indicate for the treatment of the Paget disease. The Portuguese mandatory prescription system for the DCI raises the risk of cross-label use of the generic medicine for the treatment of osteoporosis. In Portugal the number of patients with Paget disease are between 2000 and 3000.

The court also concluded that there is a collision of rights since the claim aimed at the prohibition of manufacture or commercialisation of the generic medicine cannot be applicable to the use for the Paget disease, but it may be applicable for the use of the medicine for the treatment of osteoporosis.

Since the court cannot prohibit a company from carrying out a legal activity, the limitation of commercialisation of the generic medicine will ensure that the generic company is free to sell its medicine for the treatment of Paget and also ensure Novartis' IP rights.

In view of that, the court sentenced Fair-med to refrain from commercialising in Portugal, importing, manufacturing, warehousing, launching in the market, sell, or offer the generic medicine beying 6000 units per year.

**Costs of the proceedings**

The arbitrators' fees and secretariat fees were determined to be € 70,000.

Since the claims filed by Novartis were solely partially granted, the court sentenced Novartis in the payment of 70 % of the court costs and Fair-me in the payment of 30 % of the court costs.

49

## III. *Pfizer v Pharmakern (pregabalin)*[8]

**Grounds for the decision**

According to the court, Pfizer is the holder of the European patent EP 934061 (E'061), related to pregabaline. EP'061 is a second use patent which protects the use of pregabalin for

[7] Arbitration court, 31 December 2014.
[8] Lisbon Court of Appeal, 6 December 2017.

the treatment of pain. The generic medicine is not indicated for the treatment of pain, but it has been prescribed for the treatment of pain due to conducts from third parties and not the Defendant itself.

The Defendant has the right to commercialise the generic medicine but said commercialisation cannot lead to sales for the protected use of pregabalin.

The court concluded that the use of the generic medicine for the treatment of pain may be a responsibility of the users themselves or the pharmacists and doctors, ie third parties unrelated to the Defendant. Thus, there are no grounds to sentence the Defendant in the payment of a licence to Pfizer, since the Defendant never showed interest in commercialising the pregabalin product for the treatment of pain.

However, the court also concluded that there is a collision of rights, which is a rule that although it is subsidiary, it is the only possible rule to be applied to this case.

In view of that, the court sentenced the Defendant to the payment of a compensation for damages based on the sales of the pregabalin product which were effectively used for the treatment of pain and based on the profits obtained by the Defendant.

### Costs of the proceedings

The decision does not refer the total amount of the court costs.

Since the claims filed by Pfizer were solely partially granted, the court sentenced Novartis in the payment of 90 % of the court costs and Fair-me in the payment of 10 % of the court costs.'

## IV. *Novartis v Non-identified generic company (everolimus)*[9] 50

### Grounds for the decision

Novartis is the owner of the European patent EP 2269604 (EP'604) related to everolimus.

In the decision it is concluded that EP'604 is a second use patent, i.e. the scope of protection of the patent is limited to everolimus for the treatment of solid tumours other than lymphatic cancer, wherein the solid tumour is a kidney tumour. And everolimus has other uses other than the protected use.

The court concluded that it needs to protect both the Defendant's right to competition and use the product for the uses that are not protected and, also, Novartis' IP rights.

During the proceedings, the Defendant informed the court that it carried out a carve-out and removed the indication for the treatment of kidney tumours.

The court considered that it is necessary to assess a possible indirect infringement of Novartis' rights, but the mere knowledge that the medicine may be used for the protected indication is not sufficient to conclude that there is an infringement of the IP rights. It could only be deemed proven an infringing conduct if it was shown that the Defendants instruct, recommend, advise leading to the use of the generic medicine for the protected use.

In view of that, the court acquitted the Defendants from the claims filed by Novartis.

### Costs of the proceedings

The decision does not refer the total amount of the court costs.

Although the claims were dismissed, since the proceedings were initiated under a mandatory enforcement system, the court sentenced Novartis in the payment of 70 % of the court costs and Fair-me in the payment of 30 % of the court costs.

---

[9] Arbitration court, 1 July 2021.

# § 11
# Spain

## A. Executive summary

1 At present, there is still insufficient case law in Spain on skinny labelling to be able to consider the issue a settled matter. The two patent courts which have so far adjudicated on the matter reached different conclusions:

1. A first line of reasoning, supported by older rulings from the Madrid Court of Appeal (also followed, *obiter dicta*, by the Granada Court of Appeal), found that skinny labelling was sufficient per se to exclude patent infringement, so no additional measures needed be taken by the alleged infringer to avoid risks of off-label prescription and/or dispensing (other than abstaining from actively offering or promoting the use of its medicines for the patented indications) (*'passive approach'*).
2. A second line of reasoning, supported by more recent rulings from the Barcelona Court of Appeal, found, on the other hand, that skinny labelling was *not* sufficient per se to exclude patent infringement when off-label prescription and/or dispensing appear to be de facto likely,[1] and the alleged infringer would have had to undertake proactive measures (including information campaigns aimed at customers and entities to whom the products are offered, and refrain from supplying the medicines in those cases where off-label use is specifically suspected) to avoid such off-label prescription and/or dispensing in order to be exempted from liability (*'active approach'*)

2 As a result, until the case law evolves further, and the Supreme Court or the Appeal Courts themselves unify these diverging positions, just relying on skinny labelling seems a risky strategy for a generic/biosimilar if an off-label use appears to be possible. Including express warnings in all the product literature and all promotional materials and communications is thus recommended.

3 If only a passive approach is adopted by the generic/biosimilar producer, a finding of infringement appears to be quite possible. This finding of infringement may entail litigation costs, partial injunctions and orders to undertake information campaigns, and awards of damages if loss and damage are eventually caused and can be attributed to the alleged infringer's passivity.

4 Conversely, if a sufficiently active approach is adopted to prevent off-label prescription and dispensing, liability for patent infringement is not likely according to current case law.

5 Although there are no precedents of unconditional injunctions (i.e. orders not to market the product at all) being granted against medicines properly skinny-labelled, this is something that could be warranted in the future depending on the specific circumstances of the case (e.g. if the alleged infringer knows that the cases of non-patented use will be purely anecdotic or marginal and that, de facto, all, or virtually all, of the prescriptions will be made for the patented indication). Spanish courts tend to assess legal disputes on a case-by-case basis.

[1] In the case of biosimilars, this cannot be taken for granted, and the real likelihood of off-label prescription will need to be assessed on a case-by-case basis.

## B. Scope of protection and interpretation of second medical use claims

As seen in the introductory section, Swiss-type claims in particular were important in the past, as a way (recommended by the European Patent Office itself, following the practice of the Swiss Patent Office) of protecting first and second medical use inventions (i.e. new therapeutic uses of known compounds) without falling under the ban on patentability of therapeutic methods included in the EPC (and in the Spanish Patents Act – *Ley 24/2015 de Patentes*). 6

Additionally, in the case of Spain, Swiss-type claims were commonly used whilst the reservation that Spain entered when it joined the EPC was in force (i.e. until 7 October 1992[2]), precisely thanks to the fact that Swiss-type claims were treated as process claims rather than product claims. See, for example, the ruling of the Barcelona Court of Appeal (15th Chamber) no. 59/2018 of 16 May 2018: 7

> 22. Literally the reservation only refers to 'European Patents, insofar as they confer protection to chemical or pharmaceutical products as such'. It does not include first use claims, even though the question would be more arguable (product claims limited by use), but it certainly does not include Swiss-type claims, as we have defined them, which limit their scope to the use of X for the manufacture of a medicine for the treatment of a disease Y. These only protect the use of the product for a specific therapeutic indication, but do not provide absolute protection. It should be noted that in Spain the protection of the procedures for obtaining a pharmaceutical product was allowed, but what was prohibited was the absolute protection of the pharmaceutical product itself.[3]

Also, the ruling of the Barcelona Court of Appeal (15th Chamber) no. 127/2016 of 5 July 2016: 8

> 69. We have said that a Swiss-type claim confers on its owner protection similar to a process claim. In our case, it protects the use of pregabalin or a pharmaceutically acceptable salt thereof, for the preparation of a pharmaceutical composition for the treatment of pain. As we have said, it protects the use of pregabalin in the manufacture of a medicine for the treatment of pain.

When the new EPC2000 format was adopted by the EPO, this was also incorporated to the Spanish case law. This is explained for example in Judgment no. 71/2013 of 4 March 2013 issued by the 28th Chamber of Madrid Court of Appeal: 9

> The issue was finally resolved with the revision of the EPC 2000, which since 2007 has allowed claims for second and subsequent pharmaceutical indications, just as it had previously allowed claims for the first pharmaceutical indication (purpose-limited product claims). These are claims of the type: 'Compound X for the treatment of disease Y' or 'Compound X for use in the treatment of disease Y'.
>
> And regarding the possibility of drafting Swiss-type claims as an alternative or additionally, already recognised earlier (G 5/83, EISAI/Second medical indication, OJ 1985, 64), the Enlarged Court of Appeal has held since its decision G 2/08 that, where the claim is for a new therapeutic use of a medicinal product, such claims cannot have the format of a Swiss-type claim as instituted by the decision of G 5/83. As Article 54(5) EPC 2000 now allows purpose-limited product claims

---

[2] Upon joining the European Patent Organisation, the Kingdom of Spain entered a reservation under Article 167(2)(a) EPC, providing that European patents were ineffective in Spain in so far as they conferred protection on chemical or pharmaceutical products as such.

[3] Quotes from passages from Spanish court rulings and legal provisions are only 'official' in its original (Spanish) wording. The translations included in this chapter are provided for informative purposes only. Italics have been added by the author for emphasis.

for any further specific use of a known drug, the loophole in the provisions of the EPC 1973 has been filled. In this respect the decision has no retroactive effect in relation to Swiss-type patents.

10 The current Guidelines for Examination of the Spanish Patent and Trademark Office (SPTO) admit in fact use claims both in EPC2000 format and in *Swiss-type* format (at p. G-126):

The following table summarises the different types of wording of product claims and their patentability according to the regulations:

| Cases | Claims | Patentable? | Article |
|---|---|---|---|
| A | Use of product X for the treatment of asthma | NO | 5.4 |
| B | 1. Product X for use as a medicine [X is known as a herbicide]<br>2. Product according to R1 for use in the treatment of asthma. | YES (even if product X is known but not its use in medicine) | 6.4 |
| C | Product X for the treatment of cancer | YES (even if case B is state of the art, provided that the claim is inventive with respect to case B) | 6.5 |
| D | Product X for use in the treatment of leukaemia | YES (even if cases B and C are prior art, provided that case D is inventive with respect to B and C, because leukaemia is a specific type of cancer) | 6.5 |

Corresponding use claims with Swiss-type wording are also admissible for cases C and D. This wording would be 'Use of product X for the preparation of a drug for the treatment of cancer/leukaemia'.

11 The nature of use claims as an autonomous claim type was also confirmed by the Supreme Court judgment (Civil Chamber) no. 766/2011 of 11 November 2011, which stated:

The ground of appeal is dismissed for lack of consistency.
The European patent system admits, in addition to patents for the manufacturing process of a product and product patents, patents for use or utilisation – Article 63. 2 b) of the Munich Convention on the Grant of European Patents of 5 October 1973 (Instrument of Accession of 10 July 1986, BOE 30 September), in the wording of the Revision Act of 17 December 1991 (Ratified by Spain on 21 March 1997); and also Article 29.2 ('product, procedure, device or use'… 'b), different uses of a product or device') of the Implementing Regulation, of the Act of Revision of the EPC of 29 November 2000 in force since 13 December 2007, approved by Decision of the Administrative Council of 12 December 2002 –, which are characterised by the 'use' for a specific purpose of a certain known substance or compound. This purpose or objective of the method, and not the materiality or physical entity of the product, is the distinctive and limiting characteristic of the claim. *The existence of the autonomy of the use patent in the European patent regime has been admitted by this Chamber* in the recent judgment of 27 October 2011.

12 The scope of protection of use claims was dealt with by the Barcelona Court of Appeal in its two rulings of 24 January 2008 and 17 March 2008. The latter (the one leading to the Supreme Court judgment referred to in the preceding paragraph) stated as follows:

We have recently had the opportunity to pronounce on this matter (Judgment 24 January 2008 RA 127/07), drawing attention to the fact that the EPC expressly provides for claims of use or utilisation of a product, i.e., certain technical applications of a known product whose utility, efficacy or advantages were not known until the research culminating in the patent was carried out. Thus,

> Article 63.2.b) EPC contemplates as the subject matter of the invention not only a product, or a process for the manufacture of a product, but also 'a use of a product', and Article 167.2.a) refers to the protection conferred by the patent insofar as it refers to a process for the manufacture 'or use of a chemical product'. Consistent with this, the Convention's Implementing Regulations of 5 October 1973, in Rule 29.2, concerning the 'Form and content of claims', after establishing as 'categories' of claims those of 'product, process, apparatus or application', provide that a European patent application may include 'different applications of a product or apparatus' ('uses' or 'utilisations' in the English, German and French versions).
> Utilisation or use claims, in addition to being admissible, are different in their conception, effects and in particular as regards the scope of protection they confer, from product claims. In the latter, protection is absolute, since they protect the product regardless of the production process and regardless of its use; whereas claims relating to an activity (manufacturing process and use claims) confer relative protection, limited to the claimed activity, but not to the product or device per se when it is used outside the claimed activity. Thus, the exclusivity conferred by the claim of use is limited to the application that defines the claim, but does not extend to the mere existence of the product. *Any infringement, therefore, will require proof not only of its manufacture or sale, but also that it is intended to be used for the purpose and under the conditions expressed in the claim.*

Despite the autonomous character of use claims proclaimed by the Supreme Court, some later decisions from lower courts have in practice continued treating Swiss-type claims as process claims. Order from Commercial Court No. 5 of Barcelona no. 169/2017 of 12 July 2017 explicitly states that 'the Spanish case law considers this type of claims as process claims' and the more recent judgment of Commercial Court No. 4 of Barcelona no. 230/2022 of 7 March 2022 specifies more particularly that Swiss-type claims are purpose-limited process claims. Conversely, judgment 288/2016 of the Barcelona Court of Appeal considers an EPC 2000 claim as a product claim. 13

In any event, for the purposes of infringement and when dealing with patents not subject to the Spanish reservation, whether the second medical use claim is rather drafted or construed as a product claim or as process claim seems irrelevant in cases where the only 'process' consists of using a given active ingredient for the treatment of a given disease, when it is clear from the circumstances (and in particular from the Summary of Product Characteristics) that the contested product includes the claimed active ingredient and is indicated for the treatment of the claimed illness. 14

And, in the particular case of Swiss-type claims (which require the claimed compound to be used for the preparation of a medicine), if interpreted like process claims, it is immaterial that the defendants are not the actual manufacturers of the infringing products. According to Article 69(1) Spanish Patents Act, 'when a product is introduced in Spain in respect of which there is a process patent for the manufacturing of such product, the patentee will have, with regards to the introduced product, the same rights that the present law affords in relation to the products manufactured in Spain'. It must also be remembered that the scope of protection granted by process claims to the holder not only covers the process itself, but also covers the products directly obtained from the patented use of the given active ingredient (Article 59(1)(b) and (c) Patents Act and Article 64(2) EPC). Note in this regard that the 2008 ruling from the Barcelona Court of Appeal above requires evidence of the 'manufacture or sale' in order to verify the infringement of a second medical use claim. 15

## C. Direct and indirect infringement of second medical use claims

16 Spanish law does not contain a specific regulation regarding the infringement of second medical use patents, so the same general rules apply.

17 What is beyond discussion is that, for direct infringement to exist, the all elements-rule must be satisfied, which means that all claim features must have been performed by the infringer, either literally or by equivalents. In the field of second (of subsequent) medical use claims, the claimant for infringement must therefore prove in particular that the feature 'for use' (EPC 2000 format) / 'use…for' (Swiss-type format) has been met by the infringer when manufacturing, offering for sale, marketing or using the patented product, or importing or possessing it therefor.[4]

18 In the case of indirect infringement, the claimant for infringement needs to prove that the infringer has supplied or offered to supply means that are essential to the invention to persons that are not authorised to exploit it, knowing (or being expected to know) that such means are suitable for reducing the invention to practice and that are destined to (intended for) that purpose.[5]

19 In both cases (either under direct or indirect infringement), it is commonly understood that it is not enough that the medicinal product is 'suitable for' treating the indication subject to patent protection, but it must be 'destined' to (intended for) that purpose.

20 The difficulty with these cases lies on determining where this 'destined' element has been fulfilled (especially when both infringing and non-infringing uses concur), and what is the standard of evidence required from the claimant. It is undisputed that, when the alleged infringer seeks authorisation for (inter alia) the patented indication, so that the patented indication is included in the Summary of Product Characteristics (SmPC) among the approved therapeutical indications of the medicine, then such 'destined' feature is deemed met (and, absent any other valid non-infringement defence, the patent shall be considered infringed). The same conclusion can be reached if the infringing defendant has actively advertised, offered or promoted its medicine for the indication that is still subject to patent protection (irrespective of whether such indication has been approved by the health authorities, or rather an off-label use is being promoted).

21 Up to this point, case law and legal opinions on this topic seem to be in alignment. Where differences arise is when the alleged infringer *carves out* the patented indication from the SmPC, leaving only specific off-patent indications on it (i.e. what we know as *skinny labelling*)[6], but however the medicine is de facto prescribed by doctors and/or dispensed by pharmacies for other indications that are patented (i.e. off-label prescription and/or dispensing, often referred to in this context as cross-label, because in contrast to other types of off-label use, the active ingredient is here indeed authorised for the other indication, though only under the market authorisation obtained by the patentee or its licensees).

22 The key question arising in these cases is whether a skinny labelling is sufficient to exclude liability, or rather the defendant can be required to take other measures to avoid

---

[4] Article 59 Patents Act (Law 24/2015). In the event of method claims, direct infringement will exist when any of those exploitation acts are performed with the product directly obtained from the patented process, as well as when the patented process is used or offered (knowing, or being expected to know, that such procedure infringes the patent).

[5] Article 60 Patents Act (Law 24/2015); → mn. 55.

[6] This is permitted by Article 37 of Royal Decree 1345/2007 → mn. 65.

infringement and whether it can be held liable for patent infringement if those measures are not taken. We will discuss this in the next section.

## D. Infringement of second medical use claims and skinny label products

Spanish law does not address the particular issue of skinny labelling, so this assessment is left to case law, which so far is meagre, divergent and generally confined to the particular facts of the case in question, such as the behaviour of the parties, the precise wording of the claims, or the market circumstances and the regulatory framework at any given point in time. **23**

Court decisions issued to date in these situations reveal markedly different positions regarding the scope of protection of second medical use patents in these circumstances. Until the Spansih Supreme Court takes a position on this issue, we have to rely on the two main judicial precedents that expressly deal with the second medical use claims and the potential risk of patent infringement in the event of skinny labelling, which constitute the two landmark cases in Spain so far: **24**

### I. Madrid courts – *Venlafaxine* (2006–2010)

The pharmaceutical company Wyeth sued several generics companies for placing in the market medicines including the active ingredient venlafaxine. The asserted patents were the Spanish validations of EP 797991 (which protects a sustained release pharmaceutical composition of venlafaxine) and of EP 639374 (which covers the use of venlafaxine to prepare a medicament for the treatment of generalised anxiety disorder). **25**

The first instance courts (Commercial Court No 3, in relation to the complaint filed against the generics companies Arafarma and Qualitec, and Commercial Court No. 2, in relation to the complaint filed against the generics company Uso Racional) originally granted preliminary injunctions. They placed an unconditional ban on putting the contested generics on the market (note: this is because a formulation patent was also being asserted). They also prohibited the defendants from putting on the market any other venlafaxine generics 'indicated for the treatment of generalised anxiety disorder'. **26**

The generics companies filed their respective appeals before the 28$^{th}$ Chamber of the Court of Appeal (the one in charge of patent disputes). With its orders 128/2008 and 12/2010, the Court of Appeal upheld the appeals filed by the generics companies and lifted the preliminary injunctions imposed by the first instance courts, ordering Wyeth to pay the damages and legal costs caused to the defendants. **27**

The Court of Appeal found, on the one hand, that the sustained release composition patent was not likely to be infringed. Additionally, in what is relevant for the purposes of the present book, the Court rejected the request for precautionary measures based on the new medical use patent because the generic medicine was authorised with a skinny labelling (only for the treatment of depression and social anxiety, which were not indications protected by the second medical use patent) and therefore the Court considered they did not meet the requirements for patent infringement. However, the Court stated that patent infringement would have occurred if the defendants had marketed the generic medicine having requested and obtained administrative approval for the new patented **28** therapeutic indication, or if they had carried out other actions aimed at promoting the use of the same for said new indication:

> What could justify the adoption of the precautionary measure is that the defendant had infringed the patent for the new therapeutic indication, and *such infringement would have occurred if the defendant had marketed its generics having requested and obtained the administrative approval of the same for the new patented therapeutic indication, or had carried out other conduct aimed at promoting the use of the same for said new indication. Once it is established that there is no evidence of this fact, there has been no infringement of the patent and no precautionary measure can be adopted in this regard. If the plaintiff considers that 'measures must be adopted to inform doctors and pharmacists of the existence of said patents*, otherwise, doctors could prescribe and pharmacists could dispense a generic medicine for the treatment of the generalised anxiety disorder covered by the WYETH patent', *it is free to initiate as many information campaigns as it considers relevant – respecting the laws–, but it cannot obtain a preliminary injunction against the defendant* because it is a necessary condition that the patent infringement has occurred. If the mere marketing of drugs containing an active ingredient that is already in the public domain, authorised for an indication that is not protected by a new therapeutic treatment patent, as is the case of the appellant's generics, is considered as an infringement (actual or potential) of the new therapeutic treatment patent, the scope of the patent protected by the new therapeutic treatment patent is being extended to the point of turning it into an extension or reactivation of the patent of the active ingredient that has already expired, which is in direct conflict with the regulation of the patent, specifically with regard to the time limitation of the same.

**29** The same findings were confirmed in the main proceedings. In its judgment 228/2010, Commercial Court No. 2 dismissed Wyeth's claim as regards the new medical use patent on the grounds that the potential off-label use 'is not attributable to [the defendant] but rather to a common practice of physicians, who prescribe medicines beyond the indications that can be read in the summary of product characteristics'. Wyeth's appeal was then dismissed by the Court of Appeal, which pointed out in its judgment 405/2012 that no infringing conduct was attributable to the respondent, and that the appellant 'just intended to make the respondent accountable for consequences that are simply derived from a given regulatory framework that Wyeth deems harmful to its interests'. A further appeal was filed by Wyeth before the Supreme Court, but (unfortunately from the legal certainty aspect) the appeal was limited to the sustained release patent only.

**30** Order no. 115/2011 of 14 October 2011 of the Granada Court of Appeal (*Docetaxel*[7]) came to a similar conclusion:

> since the patent refers to new therapeutic indications for an active ingredient, which is already in the public domain, we must reject that the mere commercialisation of the active ingredient is protected by the second medical use patent. Therefore, such activity, relating only to the active ingredient, does not justify the exploitation required for the plaintiff and the infringement alleged against the defendant. *The plaintiff's second medical use patent can only be considered infringed, and exploited by itself, if the parties have marketed docetaxel, the active ingredient, having applied for and obtained the administrative authorisation of the new patented therapeutic indication for the active ingredient, or have carried out other conduct aimed at promoting the use of the same for the new indication.*

---

[7] This case did not actually concern a *skinny labelling* case, but rather a case where the SmPC explicitly instructed the physicians on the use of the allegedly infringed product in a combo therapy that was part of the patent claims, which led the court to find that there was infringement.

## II. Barcelona courts – *Pregabalin* (2015–2016)

A very different approach was adopted by the Barcelona courts in the Spanish part of the famous *Pregabalin* case. 31

The plaintiffs (Warner Lambert and Pfizer) claimed that the defendants (several generics companies) were infringing their patent rights (the Spanish part of EP 934061, which protected the use of pregabalin for the preparation of a pharmaceutical composition for the treatment of pain) by marketing a generic medicine that, although indicated for epilepsy and generalised anxiety disorder only, the defendants knew would de facto be prescribed and dispensed also for the patented indication. This is because the general rule under Spanish law is the prescription by active ingredient, and the dispensing of the cheapest medicine available with the same active ingredient, strength, dosage form and administration route, which means that quite often a generic will be dispensed, irrespective of the reason (therapeutic indication) for which pregabalin was prescribed by the doctor.[8] 32

The claimants invoked both direct patent infringement, indirect patent infringement, unfair competition and the law of torts. 33

Notably, the requests for preliminary injunctions did not include a request for an unconditional order of cessation, but merely the adoption of informative measures to the acquirers of the medicines and to different stakeholders in the Spanish National Health System in order to avoid an off-label prescription of the generics (the Medicines Agency, the Ministry of Health and the equivalent regional bodies, the General Council of Physicians and the General Council of Pharmacists). It must be taken into account that, unlike the venlafaxine case, no other patent protecting the active ingredient per se or a given formulation thereof was being asserted. 34

The court of first instance (Commercial Court No. 4) ruled out the existence of both direct and indirect infringement. 35

As regards direct infringement, the Court considered that there were no elements that could prove the defendants' infringing intention. There were no references in the generic products to the patented indication, nor were there any promotional activities aimed at committing the infringement. Neither had the alleged risk of prescription of the generic medicine for the patented indication been proved in the case at hand (this is mostly because the court of first instance understood that Lyrica® – and, it seems, skinny-labelled medicines in general – qualified as a medicine that could be included in the exception of non-replaceable medicines, which enabled its prescription by brand; and because the plaintiff had already undertaken information campaigns aimed at the relevant stakeholders to avoid off-label prescription of pregabaline) . 36

As for the assertion of indirect infringement, the Court also dismissed this because: (i) although the generics at hand are suitable for putting the invention into practice, it has not been proven that they are destined to this purpose, based on what has been said above; and (ii) it has not been proven either that the person to whom the medicines are supplied actually put the claims into practice (this would require the pharmacist or distributor to use Pregabalin to manufacture a pharmaceutical compound, which was not the case). 37

The Court also denied that the behaviour of the defendants could constitute an unlawful act of unfair competition or otherwise generate out-of-contract liability under 38

[8] At the time of the *Pregabalin* case, this dispensing of generics was even more likely because there was a rule that gave preference to the dispensing of generics (and biosimilars of biological medicines) if they were the same price as the reference medicine (which is what occurred in the case of Lyrica®, the reference pregabaline medicine). This preference was removed by Article 87 of the Medicines Act as from 1 January 2016, and now either the reference medicine or the generic can be dispensed if both are the same price.

the general law of torts (no damage attributable to the defendants was proven or could be expected).

39 The Court of Appeal partially overturned the first instance judgment. It considered that the risk of off-label prescription was a real risk (the electronic prescription system allows the prescription by active ingredient, and this enabled the dispensing of pregabaline generics). Moreover, doctors are incentivised, including with regard to their salary, to prescribe generics, and the data submitted by the plaintiff suggest that they lost 20 % market share since the launch of the generics.

40 Once this risk is considered to exist, the Court of Appeal examined whether marketing generics without the adoption of measures capable of avoiding the risk can be considered to constitute an infringement.

41 As regards direct infringement, the Court of Appeal considered that the skinny labelling allowed the conclusion that the defendants did not manufacture or market the generic medicine with the purpose of using it for the patented indication, so the 'for the treatment of pain' feature was not fulfilled.

42 However, the Court does admit the possibility of indirect infringement, since it considers that the defendants are providing the essential elements for pregabalin to ultimately be prescribed, at least in part, for the patented indication, and that this is tantamount to the practice of the invention. In this sense, the Court concluded that 'if the defendants want to market pregabalin they must contribute fairly to avoid the prohibited result, i.e. that their pregabalin ends up being used for the treatment of pain [patented indication]'.

43 As a result, the Court of Appeal imposed an obligation on the defendants to inform the third parties to whom they offer their products that they cannot be dispensed or prescribed for the patented indication, and to refrain from supplying them if they have *prima facie* evidence that the medicine will be directly used for that indication. The other informative measures sought are dismissed.

## E. Infringement of second medical use claims and biosimilar products

44 It is worth mentioning that all cases so far on skinny labelling in Spain related to generic medicines. From a regulatory perspective, biological medicines, including biosimilars, should in principle be prescribed by brand name,[9] and should not be subject to substitution by a cheaper medicine when dispensed at pharmacies.[10] Therefore, a skinny-labelled biosimilar seems *a priori* less prone to off-label use, and this may well have influenced the court's assessment. However, to the extent that it can be established that doctors may de facto prescribe, or the pharmacist may de facto dispense, the biosimilar for the patented use in a meaningful degree (that is, beyond anecdotic, isolated cases), the same reasoning applied in *Pregabaline* might be applied here.[11]

---

[9] Article 87(3) Spanish Medicines Act (→ mn. 62), Order SCO/2874/2007 and Commission Implementing Directive 2012/52/EU of 20 December 2012 laying down measures to facilitate the recognition of medical prescriptions issued in another Member State.

[10] Order SCO/2874/2007.

[11] This may happen in particular if the commission responsible for therapeutical protocols at the hospital or relevant public administration in question supports so, and the doctors justifies its clinical decision to prescribe the alternative medicine with the consent of the patient (Article 13 of Royal Decree 1015/2009, which however expressly stipulates that such off label use must be exceptional and 'shall be limited to cases where there are no authorised therapeutic alternatives for a given patient').

## F. Strategies and considerations

As can be seen from the above discussion, the contents of the SmPC is crucial in determining whether there is patent infringement of second medical use claims. It is in particular sufficient to establish the fulfilment of the 'destination' requirement (leading to direct or indirect patent infringement) when the patented indication is included in the generic's SmPC. But, conversely, the carving out of this indication may not be sufficient (for some courts) to exclude liability, at least for indirect infringement. 45

Therefore, in light of current case law, it is not advisable to rely on skinny labelling alone. Express and specific warnings that the product cannot be prescribed and dispensed for the patented indication should be included in the product literature and in all promotional materials and communications. Information letters to the holders of pharmaceutical databases and medical associations is also recommended in order to minimise risks, as well as refraining from supplying the medicines when there are reasonable indications that they will be used for the patented indication. 46

## G. Legal remedies

The Spanish Patents Act enables the patentee to take any measures which are necessary for safeguarding its patent rights. Although this includes an open catalogue of remedies, typically the patentee will seek an order of prohibition of future acts of infringement and cessation of past acts of infringement (injunction), as well as compensation for loss and damage caused. The law also makes provision for seizure of the infringing goods and their subsequent destruction, transformation or adjudication to the patentee, as well as the publication of the judgment in the media or its notification to interested addressees. 47

For infringement to be declared, it is not sufficient that the owner of the generic or biosimilar medicine has applied for or obtained marketing authorisation, but rather it is required that it has conducted one of the infringement acts referred to in Articles 59 and 60 Patent Act (e.g. that it has manufactured, offered for sale, used, or imported or possessed therefor the infringing products). However, even if none of these acts has yet taken place, the patentee is entitled to prevent future acts of infringement, and it may request preliminary injunctions to remain provisionally in force pending main infringement proceedings. 48

These preliminary injunctions may be granted even before hearing the defendant (i.e. *ex parte*), if doing so may render the measures useless (e.g. if holding the prior hearing would mean that the preliminary injunctions will not be in place in time to prevent the launch of the infringing medicine to the market). In those cases, the interim measures will be provisionally adopted, and then the defendant will be able to file an opposition if it wishes to do so. In any case, the generic or biosimilar company that fears being subject to an *ex parte* preliminary injunction application can file a protective letter in order to make sure that, once such application is filed by the patentee, its arguments (i.e. the defendant's arguments against the grant of the preliminary injunction which were included in the protective brief) are considered by the court before a decision is made. 49

With regard to the specific scenario of skinny labelling, as commented, skinny labelling has been considered sufficient by some courts to exclude indirect/contributory patent infringement, whilst others expect further active efforts from alleged infringers 50 to avoid off-label prescription and/or dispensing. We would like to note though that even those other courts, which take a stricter approach, have limited the remedies granted to imposing proactive informative obligations on the alleged infringers (which could lead to having to pay damages if the alleged infringers did not act sufficiently diligently according to the court's criterion). However, no unconditional injunctions have been granted so far by any Spanish court in cases of skinny labelling, and all the existing judicial decisions seem to implicitly agree on the idea that the alleged infringer cannot be completely deprived of the possibility of marketing a product which, as such, is in the public domain, and whose commercialisation for certain indications is not covered by patent protection. In other words, it is consistently implied through all the rulings issued so far that there must be some way the competitor can sell its product for the indications it is entitled to (and this should apply regardless of whether it is a generic, biosimilar or an alternative full-dossier, reference medicine).

51 However, courts generally take into account the specific circumstances of each case. It is yet to be seen if an unconditional injunction could be granted in exceptional cases where, for example, the alleged infringer knew that the patented indication would take nearly 100 % of the prescriptions in practice, despite the information campaigns.

## H. Statutory provisions

### I. Law 24/2015 of 24 July on Patents[12]

52 **Article 5**
**Exceptions to patentability**

The following shall not be the subject matter of a patent:

[…]

(4) Methods of surgical or therapeutic treatment of the human or animal body, and diagnostic methods applied to the human or animal body. This provision shall not apply to products, in particular substances or compositions, or to inventions of apparatus or instruments for putting such methods into practice.

[…]

53 **Article 6**
**Novelty**

(1) An invention is considered to be new when it is not comprised in the state of the art.

(2) The state of the art is constituted by everything which, prior to the filing date of the patent application, has been made available to the public in Spain or abroad by written or oral description, by use or by any other means.

(3) The content of Spanish patent or utility model applications, European patent applications designating Spain and PCT international patent applications that have entered the national phase in Spain, as originally filed, whose filing date is prior to that mentioned in the preceding paragraph and which have been published in Spanish on that date or on a later date, shall also be understood to be included in the state of the art.

---

[12] Consolidated version. See: https://www.boe.es/buscar/act.php?id=BOE-A-2015-8328.

(4) The provisions of paragraphs 2 and 3 shall not exclude the patentability of any substance or composition comprised in the prior art for use in any of the methods referred to in Article 5.4, provided that its use for any of those methods is not comprised in the prior art.

(5) Paragraphs 2 and 3 shall not exclude the patentability of a substance or composition referred to in paragraph 4 for a particular use in any of the methods referred to in Article 5(4) provided that such use is not comprised in the prior art.

## Article 59 54
## Prohibition of direct exploitation of the invention

(1) The patent shall confer on its owner the right to prevent any third party who does not have its consent from:

(a) Manufacturing, offering for sale, introducing into commerce or using a product which is the subject matter of the patent, or the importation or possession thereof for any of the aforementioned purposes.
(b) Using a process which is the subject matter of the patent or the offer of such use, where the third party knows, or the circumstances make it obvious, that the use of the process is prohibited without the consent of the patent owner.
(c) Offering for sale, introducing into commerce or using the product directly obtained by the patented process, or the importation or possession of such a product for any of the aforementioned purposes.

## Article 60 55
## Prohibition of indirect exploitation of the invention

(1) The patent shall also confer on its owner the right to prevent any third party from delivering or offering to deliver, without its consent, means for putting the patented invention into practice relating to an essential element thereof to persons not entitled to exploit it, where the third party knows, or the circumstances make it obvious, that such means are suitable for putting the invention into practice and are destined to that purpose.

(2) The provisions of the foregoing paragraph shall not apply where the means referred to therein are products that are commonly available on the market, unless the third party incites the person to whom it makes the delivery to commit acts prohibited under the foregoing article.

(3) Persons who carry out the acts provided for in paragraphs (a) to (d) of the following Article shall not be regarded as persons entitled to exploit the patented invention within the meaning of paragraph 1.

## Article 61(4) 56
## General limits and exhaustion of the patent right

The rights conferred by the patent shall not extend to:

(a) Acts done in a private sphere and for non-commercial purposes.
(b) Acts done for experimental purposes relating to the subject matter of the patented invention.
(c) The performance of the studies and trials necessary to obtain the marketing authorisation for medicinal products in Spain or outside Spain, and the resulting practical requirements, including the preparation, procurement and use of the active ingredient for these purposes.
(d) The preparation of medicinal products in pharmacies extemporaneously and per unit, in execution of a medical prescription, and to acts relating to the medicinal products thus prepared.

[...]

57 **Article 69**
**Scope of protection in process patents**

(1) Where a product is introduced into Spain in relation to which a process patent exists for the manufacture of the said product, the owner of the patent shall have the same rights in respect of the product introduced as are granted under this Law in relation to products manufactured in Spain.

(2) Where a patent relates to a process for the manufacture of new products or substances, it shall be presumed, in the absence of proof to the contrary, that any product or substance having the same characteristics has been obtained by the patented process.

(3) In the taking of the steps for the proof to the contrary provided for in the foregoing paragraph, the legitimate interests of the defendant in the protection of its manufaturing and business secrets shall be taken into consideration.

## TITLE VII

## Remedies against the infringement of patent rights

58 **Article 70**
**Defence of rights**

The owner of a patent may bring before the courts the appropriate actions, of whatever kind and nature, against those who infringe its right, and may demand the necessary measures to safeguard it.

59 **Article 71**
**Civil actions**

(1) The owner whose patent The owner whose patent rights have been harmed may, in particular, seek:

(a) The cessation of the acts infringing his right, or their prohibition if they have not yet occurred.
(b) Indemnification for damages and prejudice suffered.
(c) The seizure of the objects produced or imported in violation of its right, and of the means exclusively intended for such production or for carrying out the patented process.
(d) The attribution in ownership of the objects or means seized pursuant to the provisions of the preceding paragraph when this is possible, in which case the value of the goods affected shall be imputed to the amount of the compensation for damages. If the aforementioned value exceeds the amount of the compensation awarded, the patent owner shall compensate the other party for the excess.
(e) The adoption of the necessary measures to prevent further infringement of the patent and, in particular, the transformation of the objects or means seized under paragraph (c), or their destruction where this is indispensable to prevent further infringement of the patent.
(f) Exceptionally, the court may also, at the request of the owner of the patent and at the expense of the infringer, order the publication of the judgment finding against the infringer of the patent, by means of notices and notifications to the persons concerned.

(2) The measures referred to in subparagraphs (a) and (e) of the preceding paragraph may also be requested, where appropriate, against intermediaries whose services are used by a third party to infringe patent rights, even if the acts of such intermediaries do not in themselves constitute an infringement, without prejudice to the provisions of Law 34/2002 of 11 July 2002 on information society services and electronic commerce. Such measures shall be objective, proportionate and non-discriminatory.

## II. Royal legislative decree 1/2015, of 24 July, approving the recast of the law on guarantees and rational use of medicines and medical devices[13]

### Article 3(1) 60
### Guarantees of supply and dispensation.

Pharmaceutical laboratories, distribution entities, importers, pharmacies, hospital pharmacy services, health centres and other health care structures are obliged to supply or dispense the medicines and medical devices requested to them under the conditions established by law and regulations

### Article 24 61
### Guarantees of availability of medicines in specific situations and special authorisations.

[...]

The head of the Ministry of Health, Social Services and Equality shall establish the conditions for the prescription of authorised medicinal products when they are used under conditions other than those authorised, which shall in any case be exceptional.

### Article 87 62
### Prescription of medicines and medical devices.

(1) The prescription of medicinal products and medical devices in the National Health System shall be carried out in the most appropriate manner for the benefit of patients, while protecting the sustainability of the system.

(2) In the National Health System, prescriptions for medicines included in the reference price system or homogeneous groups not included therein shall be made in accordance with the following scheme:

a) For acute processes, the prescription shall be made, in general, by active ingredient.
b) For chronic processes, the first prescription, corresponding to the establishment of the first treatment, shall be made, in general, by active ingredient.
c) For chronic processes whose prescription corresponds to the continuity of treatment, it may be made by brand name, provided that the latter is included in the reference price system or is the lowest priced within its homogeneous group.

(3) However, prescription by brand name of medicinal products shall be possible provided that the principle of greater efficiency for the system is respected and in the case of medicinal products considered to be non-replaceable.

(4) When prescribing by active ingredient, the pharmacist shall dispense the lowest-priced medicinal product in its homogeneous group.

(5) In any case, the prescription of a medicinal product for use in conditions other than those established in its summary of product characteristicas shall be authorised in advance by the committee responsible for therapeutic protocols or equivalent collegiate body in each Autonomous Community

### Article 89 63
### Substitution by the pharmacist

(1) The pharmacist shall dispense the medicinal product prescribed by the medical practitioner.

[13] Consolidated version. See: https://www.boe.es/buscar/act.php?id=BOE-A-2015-8343.

(2) Exceptionally, when the prescribed medicinal product is not available in the pharmacy due to shortage of stock or when there is an urgent need to dispense it, the pharmacist may substitute it for the lower priced product. In any case, it must have the same composition, pharmaceutical form, route of administration and dosage. The pharmacist shall in all cases inform the patient of the substitution and ensure that he/she is aware of the treatment prescribed by the doctor.

(3) In such cases, the pharmacist shall note, in the appropriate place on the prescription, the dispensed medicinal product of the same composition, pharmaceutical form, route of administration and strength, the date, signature and stamp.

(4) Exempt from this possibility of substitution shall be those medicinal products which, due to their bioavailability and narrow therapeutic range, are determined by the Ministry of Health, Social Services and Equality.

(5) When the prescription is made by brand name, if the prescribed medicinal product has a price higher than the 'minor price' in its homogeneous group, the pharmacist shall replace the prescribed medicinal product by the lowest-priced in its homogeneous group. In the case of biosimilar medicinal products, the rules in force according to specific regulations on substitution and interchangeability shall be respected

## III. Order sco/2874/2007, of 28 September, establishing the medicines that constitute an exception to the possible substitution by the pharmacist in accordance with Article 86.4 of Law 29/2006, of 26 July, on guarantees and rational use of medicines and health products[14]

64 **Sole Article. Non-replaceable medicines.**

(1) In accordance with the provisions of Article 86.4 of Law 29/2006 of 26 July, on guarantees and rational use of medicines and health products[15], the following medicines may not be substituted in the act of dispensing without the express authorisation of the prescribing doctor:

(a) Biological medicinal products (insulins, plasma derivatives, vaccines, biotechnological medicinal products).
(b) medicinal products containing any of the active substances considered to have a narrow therapeutic range as listed in Annex I, except when administered intravenously.
(c) Medicinal products containing active substances which are subject to special medical supervision or which require specific monitoring measures for safety reasons and which are listed in Annex II.
(d) Medicinal products for the respiratory system administered by inhalation.

(2) The Spanish Agency for Medicinal Products and Health Products shall draw up a list of non-substitutable medicinal products, which shall be publicly accessible.

(3) Exceptionally and for reasons of risk to health, the Ministry of Health and Consumer Affairs may establish, by means of a reasoned decision which shall be duly publicised, that a medicinal product not included in paragraph 1 is not substitutable at the time of dispensing

[14] Consolidated version. See: https://www.boe.es/buscar/act.php?id=BOE-A-2007-17420.
[15] This law was repealed and this reference now should correspond to Articles 87(3) and 89(4) of Royal Legislative Decree 1/2015.

## IV. Royal decree 1345/2007, of 11 October, regulating the procedure for the authorisation, registration and the conditions for dispensing of industrially manufactured medicines for human use[16]

**Article 37** 65

**Ommission of therapeutical indications**

The Spanish Agency of Medicines and Medical Devices may decide to omit certain therapeutic indications from the patient information leaflet or the summary of products characteristics, particularly when the applicant for a generic medicine communicates that these indications were protected by patent or data exclusivity rights at the moment in which the generic medicine is authorised.

## V. Royal decree 1015/2009, of 19 June, regulating the availability of medicines in special circumstances[17]

[...]

Article 24(3) of Law 29/2006, of 26 July, also states that the Minister of Health and Consumer Affairs shall establish the conditions for the prescription of authorised medicinal products when they are used in conditions other than those authorised, which in any case shall be exceptional. 66

This precept originates from the fact that there are some circumstances in which the clinical data supporting a particular therapeutic use for an already authorised medicinal product are not included in the summary of product characteristics of the medicinal product. This may be particularly relevant in therapeutic areas where research activity is very intense and the pace of evolution of scientific knowledge may precede the necessary steps to incorporate such changes in the summary of product characteristics of the medicinal product. There are also conditions of use established in clinical practice but not included in the product authorisation, often due to the absence of commercial interest in conducting the necessary studies to obtain authorisation from the Spanish Agency for Medicines and Medical Devices.

These exceptional uses of medicinal products under conditions other than those authorised fall within the sphere of clinical practice, and therefore within the responsibility of the prescribing physician, and do not require authorisation on a case-by-case basis. However, there are certain situations in which it is advisable for the Spanish Agency for Medicines and Medical Devices to issue a recommendation based on the available evidence on efficacy and safety.

To date, use under conditions other than those authorised in the hospital setting has been subject to the regime established for the compassionate use of investigational medicinal products, and it is therefore necessary to establish a differentiated procedure for these two situations.

[...]

[16] Consolidated version. See: https://www.boe.es/buscar/act.php?id=BOE-A-2007-19249.
[17] Consolidated version. See https://www.boe.es/buscar/act.php?id=BOE-A-2009-12002.

## CHAPTER III

### Access to medicinal products other than under authorised conditions

67 **Article 13**

**Requirements for access to medicinal products under conditions other than those authorised in Spain**

(1) The use of authorised medicinal products under conditions other than those established in their summary of product characteristics will be exceptional and will be limited to situations in which there are no authorised therapeutic alternatives for a given patient, respecting, where appropriate, the restrictions that have been established in relation to the prescription and/or dispensing of the medicinal product and the therapeutic protocol of the healthcare centre. The doctor responsible for the treatment must duly justify in the clinical history the need for the use of the medicine and inform the patient of the possible benefits and potential risks, obtaining the patient's consent in accordance with Law 41/2002, of 14 November.

(2) The Agency may draw up recommendations for use when it can reasonably foresee a risk to patients arising from the use of a medicinal product under conditions not contemplated in the summary of product characteristics, when the medicinal product is subject to restricted medical prescription, in accordance with Royal Decree 1345/2007, of 11 October, or when the use of the medicinal product under these conditions would have a significant healthcare impact.

The use of authorised medicinal products under conditions other than those set out in their summary of product characteristics, following the recommendations for use issued by the Agency, shall in all cases comply with the requirements set out in the previous section.

(3) The recommendations issued by the Agency shall be taken into account when drawing up therapeutic protocols for healthcare centres.

68 **Article 14**

**Actions of the Agency**

(1) The Agency, in the access to medicinal products under conditions other than those authorised, shall be responsible for:

(a) Drawing up recommendations for use in the cases specified in Article 13. These recommendations shall be based on the efficacy and safety data available, also reviewing the results of the clinical trials of which it is aware and the risk management plan for the medicinal product. In drawing up these recommendations, the Agency may rely on its network of experts and seek information from the marketing authorisation holder.

(b) Establishing a system for the exchange of information with the competent authorities of the Autonomous Communities.

(c) Revising the recommendations when new data so advise.

(d) Informing the marketing authorisation holder about the recommendations for use.

(e) Notifying suspected adverse reactions to the marketing authorisation holder, in accordance with the provisions of Royal Decree 1344/2007, of 11 October, which regulates the pharmacovigilance of medicinal products for human use.

69 **Article 15**

**Obligations of the doctor responsible for treatment**

The doctor responsible for treatment shall be obliged to:

(a) Inform the patient, in comprehensible terms, of the nature of the treatment, its importance, implications and risks, and obtain his or her consent in accordance with Law 41/2002, of 14 November.

(b) Notify suspected adverse reactions in accordance with the provisions of Royal Decree 1344/2007, of 11 October.
(c) Respect, where applicable, the restrictions that have been established in relation to prescription and/or dispensing and the healthcare therapeutic protocol of the healthcare centre.

**Article 16** 70
**Obligations of the holder of the marketing authorisation for the medicinal product**

The holder of the marketing authorisation for the medicinal product shall be obliged to:
(a) Notify suspected adverse reactions of which it is aware in accordance with Royal Decree 1344/2007, of 11 October.
(b) Not to promote the use of the medicinal product under conditions other than those authorised, nor distribute any type of material that could indirectly encourage its use.
(c) Provide the Agency with any information relating to the medicinal product that could have an impact on the recommendations for use.

## VI. Royal decree 1718/2010 of 17 December 2010 on prescriptions and dispensing orders[18]

**Article 3** 71
**Common formats and data for medical prescriptions**

(1) The prescriber shall enter on the prescription and on the patient information sheet the following mandatory basic data, which are essential for the validity of the prescription, as indicated below:

[...]

b) Details of the medicinal product:
1.º Name of the active ingredient(s).
2.º Name of the medicine if it is a biological medicine or if the prescribing health professional considers it necessary from a medical point of view, always in accordance with the provisions of Law 29/2006, of 26 July, on guarantees and rational use of medicines and health products. In this case, the prescription shall briefly justify the use of the brand name.

# J. Extracts from court decisions

## I. General decisions on medical use claims

### 1. Barcelona Court of Appeal – *Atorvastatin*[19] 72

[...] FOURTH: The complaint considers that P1 is partially void for lack of novelty. Specifically, it considers invalid:

Claim 1, which would be the product itself of atorvastatin calcium: 'Hemi-calcium salt of [R-(R ,R)]-2-(4-fluorophenyl)-ß-d-dihydroxy-5-(1-methylethyl)-3-phenyl-4[(phenylamino)-carbonyl]-1H-pyrrole-1-heptanoic acid'.

[18] Consolidated version. See https://www.boe.es/buscar/doc.php?id=BOE-A-2011-1013.
[19] $15^{th}$ Chamber, no. 100/2008 of 17 March 2008.

The 2nd, which would relate to a pharmaceutical composition incorporating this active ingredient and a pharmaceutically acceptable carrier; and

and the 3rd, which would cover, as a first therapeutic use claim, 'the use of the compound of the first claim for the preparation of a pharmaceutical composition useful in the treatment of hypercholesterolemia or hyperlipidaemia ' .

[...] TENTH. On the nullity of claims 1, 2 and 3 of P1 for protecting matter not patentable in Spain

The applicant and now appellant justifies the invalidity of the first three claims of P1 on the ground that they protect a pharmaceutical chemical product, and at the time the patent was applied for (20 July 1990), the patentability of chemical and pharmaceutical products was expressly prohibited in Spain, as a result of Spain's reservation made in the Instrument of Accession to the European Patent Convention [...].

The defendant does not deny that R1 and R2 are product claims, the former to a chemical product and the latter to a pharmaceutical product, but it does deny such classification to R3, which is considered to be a use claim.

In the claimants' view, R3 conceals a product claim, namely the pharmaceutical composition claimed in R2, useful for treating hypercholesteremia or hyperlipidaemia. Underlying this argumentation is a misunderstanding: claiming the use of a product, in this case a pharmaceutical product, implies protecting the product to some extent, and therefore falls within the exclusionary effects of the reservation formulated by our country in the instrument of accession to the EPC. Apart from the fact that the product itself is already the object of protection by R2, it is important to clear up the confusion and clarify that for the purposes of asserting the reservation, the use patent cannot be equated with a product patent.

We have recently had the opportunity to pronounce on this matter (Judgment 24 January 2008, appeal 127/07), drawing attention to the fact that the EPC expressly provides for claims of use or utilisation of a product, i.e., certain technical applications of a known product whose utility, efficacy or advantages were not known until the research culminating in the patent was carried out. Thus, Article 63.2.b) EPC contemplates as the subject matter of the invention not only a product, or a process for the manufacture of a product, but also 'a use of a product', and Article 167.2.a) refers to the protection conferred by the patent insofar as it refers to a process for the manufacture 'or use of a chemical product'. Consistent with this, the Convention's Implementing Regulations of 5 October, 1973, in Rule 29.2, concerning the 'Form and content of claims', after establishing as 'categories' of claims those of 'product, process, apparatus or application', provide that a European patent application may include 'different applications of a product or apparatus' ('uses' or 'utilisations' in the English, German and French versions).

Utilisation or use claims, in addition to being admissible, are different in their conception, effects and in particular as regards the scope of protection they confer, from product claims. In the latter, protection is absolute, since they protect the product regardless of the production process and regardless of its use; whereas claims relating to an activity (manufacturing process and use claims) confer relative protection, limited to the claimed activity, but not to the product or device per se when it is used outside the claimed activity. Thus, the exclusivity conferred by the claim of use is limited to the application that defines the claim, but does not extend to the mere existence of the product. Any infringement, therefore, will require proof not only of its manufacture or sale, but also that it is intended to be used for the purpose and under the conditions expressed in the claim. [...]

## 73 2. Supreme Court – *Atorvastatin*[20]

[...] SEVENTH – The second ground of appeal alleges infringement of Articles 4 of the Patents Act and 52 EPC in that it contravenes the case law defining what is meant by patent-

[20] 1st Chamber, no. 766/2011 of 11 November 2011.

able process in interpreting the scope of the reservation made by Spain in the Instrument of Accession to the EPC of 10 July 1986, which is also infringed by non-application.

The approach is summarised in that the claimant-appellant claimed that claim 3 of P1 protected a pharmaceutical product, i.e. a pharmaceutical composition of atorvastatin calcium for the treatment of hypercholesterolaemia or hyperlipidaemia, and the judgment under appeal considers that the said claim protects 'a process for the use of a chemical process', so that, in its view, the claim would not be affected by the statutory prohibition [of the Reservation]. The Court of Appeal's assessment would then infringe upon the doctrine of the case law which has held that a patentable process (as opposed to a chemical-pharmaceutical product, which was not patentable before 7 October 1992 [given the Reservation]) is to be understood as 'a succession of operations aimed at obtaining an industrial result or product ', which is something very different from the mere use of a product for a given function, without specification of the mode, phases or operations to be carried out. In this regard, Judgments of 16 October 1987, 22 January 1996, and 28 April 2005.

The ground of appeal is dismissed for lack of consistency.

The European patent system admits, in addition to patents for the manufacturing process of a product and product patents, patents for use or utilisation –Article 63.2 b) of the Munich Convention on the Grant of European Patents of 5 October 1973 (Instrument of Accession of 10 July 1986, BOE September 30), in the wording of the Revision Act of 17 December, 1991 (Ratified by Spain on 21 March 1997); and also Article 29.2 ('product, procedure, device or use'... 'b), different uses of a product or device') of the Implementing Regulations, of the Act of Revision of the EPC of 29 November 2000 in force since 13 December 2007, approved by Decision of the Administrative Council of 12 December 2002–, which are characterised by the 'use' for a specific purpose of a certain known substance or compound. This purpose or objective of the method, and not the materiality or physical entity of the product, is the distinctive and limiting characteristic of the claim. The existence of the autonomy of the use patent in the European patent regime has been admitted by this Chamber in the recent judgment of 27 October 2011. [...]

## 3. Madrid Court of Appeal – *Finasteride – Paricalcitol*[21] 74

[...] The issue was finally resolved with the revision of the EPC 2000, which since 2007 has allowed claims for second and subsequent pharmaceutical indications, just as it had previously allowed claims for the first pharmaceutical indication (purpose-limited product claims). These are claims of the type: 'Compound X for the treatment of disease Y' or 'Compound X for use in the treatment of disease Y'.

And regarding the possibility of drafting Swiss-type claims as an alternative or additionally, already recognised earlier (G 5/83, EISAI/Second medical indication, OJ 1985, 64), the Enlarged Court of Appeal has held since its decision G 2/08 that, where the claim is for a new therapeutic use of a medicinal product, such claims cannot have the format of a Swiss-type claim as instituted by the decision of G 5/83. As Article 54(5) EPC 2000 now allows purpose-limited product claims for any further specific use of a known drug, the loophole in the provisions of the EPC 1973 has been filled. In this respect the decision has no retroactive effect in relation to Swiss-type patents.[...]

[21] 28th Chamber, no. 71/2013 of 4 March 2013.

## 75 4. Barcelona Court of Appeal[22]

[...] 25.- It is appropriate to reproduce literally claim 24: 'A compound as defined in any one of claims 1 to 9, for treating primary or secondary hyperparathyroidism'.

[...]

In the present case claim 24 refers to the first indication, the primary indication.

In the light of that criterion, the appeal brought by Warfy AbbVie's representatives in respect of claim 24 must be dismissed on the ground that claim 24 is, in reality, a claim to a product per se.

It is not a Swiss-type claim, but a claim limited by its use, though a product claim, since, if the formulation of this type of claim to circumvent the reservation made by Spain to the EPC were allowed, the consequences of the reservation for all types of product patents would be avoided, since they are all principally indicated to treat a specific disease or condition.

The appeal must be dismissed on this point, without this implying that we have modified the criterion already expressed in our Judgment of 17 March 2008.'

## 76 5. Commercial Court No. 5 of Barcelona – *Rosuvastatin*[23]

[...] SIXTH.- On swiss-type claims

6.1 Swiss-type claims are one of the types of claims that have been used to protect second medical use patents. They have traditionally been worded as follows: 'use of compound X for the preparation of a medicinal product for the treatment of disease Y'.

6.2 Their origin lies in the need to protect inventions that are considered to be valuable, without at the same time running afoul of the prohibition on patenting methods of treatment set out in Article 52(4) EPC (1973 version).

6.3 They involve the use of a specific chemical compound to create a medicinal product with a new therapeutic indication. They are justified by the fact that the chemical compound in question is no longer new, so that it is the new therapeutic application that gives it its novelty.

6.4 In T 138/02, the EPO stated that the structure of a swiss-type claim must contain elements: a) for the use of a compound or substance; b) for the manufacture of a medicinal product; and c) for a therapy.

6.5 Along the same lines, Spanish case law considers swiss-type claims to be process claims. In this regard, and further analysing this type of claim, the Barcelona Provincial Court, section 15, 5 July 2016, prebagalin case (rapporteur: Mr Rodríguez Vega) [...]

7.6 R16 uses the Swiss-type format to protect the second use:

'Use according to claim 15 wherein the pharmaceutical composition is for the treatment of hypercholesterolaemia, hyperlipoproteinaemia and atherosclerosis'. Use of pharmaceutical compound X for the treatment of disease Y.

7.7 The novelty in R16 derives from the new therapeutic characteristics of the already known product (rosuvastatin): in our case, from the discovery of its therapeutic efficacy in the treatment of hypercholesterolaemia, hyperlipoproteinaemia and atherosclerosis.

7.8 Consequently, R16 must be considered as a second use claim in Swiss-type format and we must consider and classify it as a process claim, as concluded by the national and foreign case law set out above.[...]

[22] No. 288/2016 of 19 December 2016.
[23] No. 169/2017 of 12 July 2017.

## 6. Barcelona Court of Appeal – *Rosuvastatin*[24] 77

[…] 9. Spain, by acceding to the Convention of 5 October 1973 on the Grant of European Patents (EPC) by Instrument of 10 July 1986, made the following reservation:

'Pursuant to the provisions of Article 167(2)(a), European Patents, insofar as they confer protection to chemical or pharmaceutical products as such, shall have no effect in Spain'.

This reservation, in accordance with the provisions of Article 167.3 EPC, took effect until 7 October 1992.

[…] 22. Literally the reservation only refers to 'European Patents, insofar as they confer protection to chemical or pharmaceutical products as such'. It does not include first use claims, even though the question would be more arguable (product claims limited by use), but it certainly does not include Swiss-type claims, as we have defined them, which limit their scope to the use of X for the manufacture of a medicine for the treatment of a disease Y. These only protect the use of the product for a specific therapeutic indication, but do not provide absolute protection. It should be noted that in Spain the protection of the procedures for obtaining a pharmaceutical product was allowed, but what was prohibited was the absolute protection of the pharmaceutical product itself. […]

## 7. Commercial Court No. 4 of Barcelona – *DHA*[25] 78

[…] **3.17** The above claims are Swiss-type second medical use claims (Swiss-type claim). Without dwelling on doctrinal expositions on this type of invention (as they are sufficiently well known to the parties), it should be pointed out that the scope of protection of a Swiss-type claim is that of a process claim, as it is a purpose-limited process claim. This means that the Swiss-type claim provides protection only for the product obtained directly from the claimed method of manufacture.

**3.18** The EPO in Decision T 138/02 said that the structure of a swiss-type claim should contain three elements, namely: a) the use of a compound or substance; b) for the manufacture of a medicinal product; and c) for a therapy.

**3.19** This implies that the elements of R1 are:

(a) use of docosahexaenoic acid (or DHA); and
(b) for the preparation of a medicinal product (pharmaceutical composition or nutraceutical);
(c) for (the purpose of being used in) the treatment of a neurodegenerative pathology, or an ocular pathology, or an ischaemic pathology or atherosclerosis.

[…]

**7.3** We shall now transcribe the provision that regulates direct infringement of a patent in Spain, for easier understanding, as we shall refer to the different letters it uses. Said rule is Article 59 section 1 of the LP which reads as follows:

'1. The patent shall confer on its owner the right to prevent any third party who does not have its consent from:
   (a) Manufacturing, offering for sale, introducing into commerce or using a product which is the subject matter of the patent, or the importation or possession thereof for any of the aforementioned purposes.
   (b) Using a process which is the subject matter of the patent or the offer of such use, where the third party knows, or the circumstances make it obvious, that the use of the process is prohibited without the consent of the patent owner.
   (c) Offering for sale, introducing into commerce or using the product directly obtained by the patented process, or the importation or possession of such a product for any of the aforementioned purposes.'

[24] 15th Chamber, No. 59/2018 of 16 May 2018.
[25] No. 230/2022 of 7 March 2022.

**7.4** It is worth starting this section by making it clear and insisting that R 1 and 13 are Swiss-type second medical use claims and that they are considered and treated as process claims limited by purpose (as the EPO has reiterated in countless decisions).

**7.5** In Spain, unlike in other neighbouring countries, the little case law that has dealt with this type of claim considers that direct infringement must be analysed from the perspective of points b) and c) of the aforementioned provision, and that a subjective or intentional element must be required of the manufacturer in order for direct infringement to be attributed to him. These factors are decisive for the following finding of direct infringement. […]

## II. Specific decisions on skinny labelling

### 79 1. Madrid Court of Appeal – *Venlafaxine*[26]

[…] FIRST. The plaintiff, WYETH, which brought proceedings against the now appellants ARAFARMA GROUP, S.A. (hereinafter ARAFARMA) and QUALITEC EUROPA LA GESTIÓN TÉCNICA DE LA EMPRESA, S. (hereinafter QUALITEC), as well as against other entities, simultaneously made an application for interim measures aimed essentially at preventing the defendants, during the proceedings, from carrying out what the applicant considered to be acts of marketing generic medicinal products (GMPs) of venlafaxine sustained-release capsules on the grounds that the generic pharmaceutical products in respect of which the defendants were carrying out such acts infringed their patents ES 2.210,454 (from the validation in Spain of European patent EP 797,991), which claims a sustained-release pharmaceutical composition of the active ingredient venlafaxine, and ES 2,174,864 (from the validation in Spain of European patent EP 639,374), which claims new therapeutic indications for that active ingredient, specifically its use in the preparation of medicinal products for the treatment of generalised anxiety disorder.

The Commercial Court found that there was an appearance of good title in the plaintiff's application in that 'the coincidence between the active ingredient and the excipients that make up both the WYETH spheroids and those of ARAFARMA and QUALITEC and the fact that the function of the excipients and the form of the product is, both in one and the other, to obtain the prolonged release effect of the active ingredient, constitute sufficient evidence of the appearance of good title'; and also found a danger of delay, essentially that arising from the fixing of the reference price for the GMPs with the active ingredient venlafaxine and the difficulty for the plaintiff to regain the market lost due to competition with the GMPs. As a result of the foregoing, it partially granted the application for interim measures in respect of the said ARAFARMA and QUALITEC.[…]

In the light of the foregoing, and also taking into account the structural differences between the two products referred to in the previous ground of law, the Chamber considers that there is no appearance of good title on the part of the applicant for interim measures as regards infringement of patent ES 2 210 454, and therefore, without prejudging the outcome of the dispute in the main proceedings, the appeal brought by the appellants ARAFARMA and QUALITEC must be allowed on this point.

EIGHTH.- The appellants ARAFARMA and QUALITEC also question the precautionary measures adopted in respect of patent ES 2.174.864, which claims the use of phenethyl derivatives, including venlafaxine, to prepare a medicinal product for the treatment of generalised anxiety disorder, and which is a translation of European patent 2174864. It is therefore a patent for a pharmaceutical product for a new therapeutic indication, as venlafaxine was previously only used for the treatment of depression.

The appellants argue that the GMPs in respect of which the interim measures have been sought have not been authorised for the treatment of generalised anxiety disorder, but only for

[26] 28th Chamber, no. 128/2008 of 16 April 2018.

the treatment of depression, in the case of ARAFARMA, and for the treatment of depression and social anxiety disorder, in the case of QUALITEC, and therefore do not infringe that patent for a new use or new therapeutic indication.

The order under appeal does not contain any specific consideration regarding the infringement of this patent, but, referring to the two patents whose infringement is alleged by WYETH, states that 'such circumstances give an indication that there is a clear plan and capacity on the part of the defendants, at least on the part of ARAFARMA and QUALITEC, to market in Spain GMPs of the active ingredient VENLAFAXINE which could be covered by WYETH's patents'. Infringement of that patent would therefore result from the mere fact that the defendants were about to market pharmaceutical products containing the active ingredient venlafaxine.

That conclusion cannot be accepted. Since it is accepted that the applicant's patent on that active ingredient, venlafaxine, has expired and is therefore in the public domain, the argument put forward by the order under appeal would amount to granting patents for new uses or new therapeutic indications the effect of prolonging or resuming the effectiveness of patents on expired active ingredients, which is not admissible.

For its part, the respondent WYETH does not dispute that the Spanish Medicines Agency approvals obtained by the defendants do not contain an indication for the treatment of generalised anxiety disorder for those EFGs. However, it argues that, if that is the case, 'the injunction granted by the Court can in no way prejudice [the defendants]', since 'regardless of the fact that the ARAFARMA [and QUALITEC] GMPs are not indicated for the treatment of generalised anxiety disorder, measures must be taken to inform the doctor and the pharmacist of the existence of these patents, otherwise the doctor could prescribe and the pharmacist could dispense a GMP for the treatment of the generalised anxiety disorder that is the subject of the WYETH patent'.

The argument is not accepted. What can justify the adoption of an interim injunction against ARAFARMA and QUALITEC is that they have infringed the plaintiff's patent for a new therapeutic indication, and such infringement would have occurred if the defendants had marketed their GMPs having requested and obtained administrative approval for them for the new patented therapeutic indication or had carried out other conduct aimed at promoting their use for that new indication. Once it is established that there is no proof that this has occurred, there has been no infringement of the patent and no precautionary measure can be adopted in this regard. If the plaintiff considers that 'measures must be taken to inform the doctor and the pharmacist of the existence of these patents, otherwise the doctor could prescribe and the pharmacist could dispense a GMP for the treatment of the generalised anxiety disorder covered by the WYETH patent', it is free to initiate any information campaign it deems appropriate and in accordance with the legal regulation of the matter, but it cannot obtain an interim injunction against the defendants because it is a prerequisite for this that the patent has been infringed. If the mere marketing of medicinal products containing an active ingredient which is already in the public domain, authorised for an indication which is not protected by a patent for a new therapeutic treatment, as is the case with the appellants' GMPs, is to be regarded as infringing (actually or potentially) the patent for a new therapeutic treatment, then the scope protected by the aforementioned patent is being extended to the extent that it becomes an extension or reactivation of the patent on the active ingredient which has already expired, which is in direct conflict with the patent regulation, specifically with regard to the limitation in time of the patent[27].

This plea in law in ARAFARMA's and QUALITEC's actions must therefore also be upheld, and the corresponding plea in law in WYETH's challenge seeking the extension of the

[27] NB: This paragraph containing the *ratio decidendi* of the decision is repeated almost verbatim in the later order no. 12/2010 of 22 January 2010 of the same court, adjudicating on the parallel proceedings initiated by Wyeth against another defendant, Uso Racional SLU. This other order has not been reproduced here, for the sake of avoiding unnecessary repetition, but the relevant paragraph is quoted in → mn. 28.

interim measures adopted on the basis of the alleged infringement of the second patent must accordingly be dismissed. [...]

80 ## 2. Granada Court of Appeal – *Docetaxel*[28]

[...] FOURTH: In assessing the infringement by the defendant, on the basis of the scope of protection of the patents indicated above, examining at the same time the applicant's compliance with the requirement to exploit the patent, as required by Article 133 of the Patent Act, and in line with the assessment made by the Order of 16 April 2008, section 28, AP Madrid, handed down in precautionary seat, since the patent refers to new therapeutic indications for an active ingredient, which is already in the public domain, we must reject that the mere commercialisation of the active ingredient is protected by the second medical use patent. Therefore, such activity, relating only to the active ingredient, does not justify the exploitation required for the plaintiff and the infringement alleged against the defendant. The plaintiff's second medical use patent can only be considered infringed, and exploited by itself, if the parties have marketed docetaxel, the active ingredient, having applied for and obtained the administrative authorisation of the new patented therapeutic indication for the active ingredient, or have carried out other conduct aimed at promoting the use of the same for the new indication. [...]

81 ## 3. Barcelona Court of Appeal – *Pregabalin*[29]

[...] FIRST. Terms in which the conflict appears to be determined at this instance

(1) Warner-Lambert and Pfizer filed an application for interim relief on 2 March 2015, anticipating the filing of the corresponding declaratory proceedings against the defendants, to ensure the effectiveness of the judgment that will be handed down in due course. The former acts as the holder of patent ES 2,200,184 (ES'184), which protects the use of the active ingredient pregabalin for the preparation of a pharmaceutical composition for the treatment of pain, and PFIZER SLU does so as a company that markets pregabalin-based medicines in Spain with its authorisation and under the brand name LYRICA. The purpose of this application is for the Court to order reasonable precautionary measures to prevent generic pregabalin medicines, for which the defendants have obtained marketing authorisation and a price for their inclusion in the national health system, from being prescribed and dispensed for the treatment of pain, an indication patented by Warner-Lambert. The defendants entered an appearance to oppose that application, which was dismissed by the court of first instance by the contested order.

(2) The claimants contest the rejection of that application and insist on their arguments, while the defendants seek confirmation of the contested decision.

SECOND. Relevant and uncontested facts in this instance. [...]

h) Warner-Lambert claims that 77.76 % of sales are for the treatment of pain (patented indication) and 22.24 % for the treatment of epilepsy, GAD and other pathologies not assigned to a specific indication (off-patent indications), although the defendants deny these percentages.

i) The defendants have obtained the corresponding authorisation from the Spanish Medicines and Health Products Agency (AEMPS) and market pregabalin compounds in different presentations for two indications, epilepsy and GAD (generalised anxiety disorder), for which pregabalin is not protected.

[28] No. 115/2011 of 14 October 2011.This case concerns a 'fat label' where the patented indication had not been *carved out*; however, we find this decision interesting to the extent that it explicitly refers to the ruling from the Madrid court previously quoted and, with it, seems to rule out infringement in a case of *skinny labelling* when no promotional acts are made in favour of the patented indication.

[29] 15th Chamber, no. 127/2016 of 5 July 2016.

j) Neither the data sheets nor the package leaflets of generic pregabalin medicines include pain management as an indication, nor have the holders of these authorisations made any advertising campaign to link their pregabalin to this latter indication.
k) The generic pregabalin drugs, once marketed, in their various forms of presentation, form part of the same homogeneous grouping of drugs as Lyrica, so that Pfizer, in order to compete with the new drugs, had to reduce the price to match the price of the generics. [...]

SIXTH. The practice of the prescription and dispensing regime

[...](39) Taking into account the legal regime for prescribing and dispensing medicines, as well as the practice of prescribing and dispensing by ICS physicians, we can conclude that there is a real likelihood that generic pregabalin medicines are prescribed and dispensed for the treatment of pain. [...]

(46) Counsel [...] defending the defendants, both in the opposition to the measures and in his opposition to the appeal, argued that the actual data on pharmacy sales of Lyrica and the generics do not allow it to be deduced that generics are being prescribed for the treatment of pain.

(47) In support of its allegations it has provided data from IMS Health SA [...] We can only conclude that the plaintiff has lost 20 % of market share; from the 100 % it had in January 2015, in seven months it has lost 20 %, even though it had reduced its price to the same level as generics. [...]

EIGHTH: Direct infringement of the patent. [...]

(69) We have said that a Swiss-type claim confers on its owner protection similar to a process claim. In our case, it protects the use of pregabalin or a pharmaceutically acceptable salt thereof in the preparation of a pharmaceutical composition for the treatment of pain. As mentioned above, it protects the use of pregabalin in the manufacture of a medicinal product for the treatment of pain. [...]

(76) If, as we have said, this third element is to be understood as the expression of the purpose of the user of the medicinal product, i.e. the purpose of its use in the treatment of pain, when the manufacturer of the pregabalin compound does not produce it for that purpose, it does not reproduce that third element and does not directly infringe the patent. In this case, the defendants have obtained authorisation to market the drug for two other, unpatented therapeutic indications, epilepsy and GAD. Therefore, neither their manufacturer produces nor they market pregabalin for the purpose of pain treatment, so do not reproduce all the features of the claim.

(77) The proprietor of the patent, Warner-Lambert, maintains that the defendants, who refuse to take any additional measures to avoid the effects of the prescription system, produce and market pregabalin for those indications, but intentionally take advantage of what might be called the side-effects of the system. The plaintiff does not allege that the defendants have a hidden agenda in marketing their pregabalin for the treatment of pain, but that they simply take advantage of those side effects, which is why it is not asking for the cessation of marketing, but for what it understands to be proportionate measures to avoid or reduce those side effects. Consequently, the defendants do not directly infringe the patent by not reproducing the third of the technical elements of the claim.

NINTH: Indirect or contributory infringement

[...] (79) As mentioned above, in order to analyse this second option, we have to start from the assumption that the public prescription and dispensing system makes the use of a part of the generic pregabalin drugs for the treatment of pain possible and likely. The manufacturers and marketers of these generics are aware or must be aware of this situation, so it must be concluded that there is at least a risk of contributory patent infringement if they do nothing to prevent their pregabalin from being used for the treatment of pain. The defendants use pregabalin for the preparation of a pharmaceutical composition which, due to the current prescribing and dispensing conditions, is likely to be intended for the treatment of pain.

(80) The defendants offer pregabalin compounds to the public health system which, at least in part, may ultimately be prescribed by the system's physicians for the treatment of pain. In this way the defendants are providing essential elements, the pregabalin compounds, to be ultimately prescribed for the treatment of pain, thus putting the invention into practice.

(81) If the defendants want to market pregabalin, they must contribute fairly to avoid the prohibited result, i.e. that their pregabalin ends up being used for the treatment of pain. To prevent this, the plaintiff, for its part, has reduced the price of the drug by more than 50 % and has tried to get the defendants and the health authorities to warn doctors not to prescribe generic pregabalin for the treatment of pain. However, the defendants have limited themselves to not including the patented indication in the data sheet or package leaflet of their medicines and to refrain from any campaign that might link their pregabalin to the patented indication. However, as we have repeated, the defendants know that, under the current system of prescription and dispensing of medicines, some of their pregabalin will end up being used for the treatment of pain.

(82) In relation to the possible contributory infringement, as well as in particular the role of doctors in relation to the execution of the patented invention, the Supreme Court has ruled in judgment 182/2015, 14 April (ROJ: STS 1703/2015). In its 15th ground, it describes the role attributed by the Court, stating that:

'The appeal no longer disputes that the marketing of the drug Docetaxel Hospira, which contains the active ingredient docetaxel, provides the doctor with sufficient information, with the patient information leaflet or summary of product characteristics of the drug (apart from its other purposes), for the implementation of the patented invention (EP 745). What is at issue is that, on the basis that the judgment under appeal understands that doctors are not considered to be "persons not entitled to exploit the invention", they would not infringe the patent and therefore there could be no contributory infringement'.

The Court concludes as follows:

'The judgment under appeal does not state that the doctors for whom the drug marketed by Hospira is intended would not directly infringe the patent, but limits itself to reasoning that in the case in question it was not a matter of examining the 'alleged infringing conduct of the doctors, or of conjecturing about it, but of verifying an infringing action of a third party, which provides the means for a person not qualified, in the terms of Article 51 LP, to put 'into practice the patented invention'.

Therefore, the High Court accepts that doctors are, in the sense required in a case of contributory infringement, those who put the patent into practice, even though they are not persons entitled to exploit it.

(83) It should be remembered that contributory infringement does not require direct infringement. The aim is to avoid the risk of the patented invention being carried out by an unauthorised person, whether or not the latter is guilty of direct infringement. This is clear from the wording of Article 51.1 PL, which does not require direct infringement. The same can be deduced from the third paragraph of the aforementioned Article 51 PL, which refers to acts to which the patent right does not extend, in which the unauthorised person who executes the invention does not incur in any infringement whatsoever, since he carries out acts to which the patent right does not extend.

(84) The defendants should have taken reasonable measures to modify that situation and thus avoid, in the words of the aforementioned Article 51.1 PL, the circumstances which make it obvious that such means are suitable for putting the invention into practice. Under these conditions, we can state that there is a risk of infringement which justifies the adoption of precautionary measures, since there is a real likelihood that part of generic pregabalin is intended for the treatment of pain.

TENTH. The specific measures proposed and those granted

(85) The applicant seeks the adoption of various measures, the first of which consists of:

'Order the defendants, as a precautionary measure, to inform the persons and bodies to whom they have offered their generic medicinal products and, in particular, the purchasers of the said medicinal products, that, as long as patent ES 2 200 184 is in force, the said medicinal products may not be prescribed or dispensed for the treatment of pain, and to refrain from supplying them with the said medicinal products unless they guarantee that they are not prescribed and/or dispensed for the treatment of pain'.

(86) The measures that can be taken must be reasonable and proportionate to the risk to be avoided. In this first group of measures, the plaintiff asks the defendants for two things, firstly, to inform the purchasers of the medicines that these medicines cannot be prescribed or dispensed for the treatment of pain until the patent expires on 16 July 2017. We believe that this measure is reasonable to avoid the risk of generic medicines being used for the treatment of pain, and at the same time it is proportionate, as it does not seem to involve excessive cost or effort, provided that we understand that the measure does not in any case refer to the patient-consumer.

(87) The second of the measures in this first group consists of ordering the defendants to refrain from supplying their medicinal product if the purchasers [do not] guarantee that it will not be used for the treatment of the patented indication. Once the defendants inform the purchasers of their product of that limitation, the defendants cannot be ordered to make their supply conditional on their guaranteeing something that we do not know they are able to guarantee. We can order the defendants to refrain from supplying their product when they have reasonable grounds to believe that their product will be 'directly' intended to treat pain, which logically excludes the usual system of prescribing and dispensing medicines, but nothinh beyond that.

(88) The second group of measures concerns supplementary measures addressed to the Spanish Agency for Medicines and Health Products and the Ministry of Health [...].

(89) This Court is competent to adopt supplementary measures to make the measures adopted effective, against the defendants and even to request the collaboration of the Public Administrations to execute them, but this is not the case, as the measures requested have nothing to do with the measures granted. We can impose on the defendants to inform their purchasers of the limitations of the product, as we have ruled, and even to refrain from selling to them in certain circumstances, but the transcribed measures have nothing to do with those orders. This is not the competent jurisdiction to impose obligations on the Administration, which has not even been heard in these proceedings.

(90) The same applies to similar measures requested for the Autonomous Communities and the Medical and Pharmaceutical Associations. [...]

FOURTEENTH – Unfair competition and non-contractual liability

(97) The applicant has sought the same relief on several legal grounds, patent law, unfair competition and tort, but neither of these two grounds entitles it to seek the specific relief rejected. The measures have been granted partly on the basis of Warner-Lambert's patent rights, so that its interest in these measures is exhausted by this decision. The plaintiff does not offer, on the basis of those two headings, any special justification to adopt the dismissed measures [...].

# § 12
# Türkiye

## A. Executive summary

1 In Türkiye, compositions, products, or substances belonging to the technical field of pharmacology can be patented by stipulating some exceptions in accordance with the Turkish Industrial Property Law No. 6769 (*Sinai Mülkiyet Kanunu* – IPL), which came into force on 10 January, 2017. Although subparagraph (3)(c) of Article 82 IPL states that 'methods of treatment, including diagnostic methods to be applied to the body of humans or animals, cannot be patented', as an exception, Article 82(6) IPL states that 'the provision in subparagraph (c) of the third paragraph does not apply to the products, especially the substances and compositions used in any of the methods listed in the same subparagraph'. Therefore, the compositions, products or substances belonging to the technical field of pharmacology can be the subject of a patent (→ mn. 51).

2 Indication patents for primary or secondary uses of products, molecules and substances belonging to the technical field of pharmacology can be patented thanks to Türkiye's explicit acceptance of the European Patent Convention (EPC) 1973[1], EPC 2000[2] and G5/83[3] decisions in order to comply with EPC provisions despite the fact that the patentability of pharmacological products as indication patents is not explicitly stated as 'patentable' or 'non-patentable' in the IPL.[4]

3 With regard to infringement, Article 141 IPL deals with acts considered as direct infringement (→ mn. 55), while the concept of 'indirect infringement' is not specifically defined in the IPL. However, Article 86 IPL regarding prohibition of indirect use of the invention asserts the right of a patentee to prohibit others from supplying to unauthorised persons the critical means for the implementation of the patented invention relating to an essential element thereof. There is also no specific provision in the IPL regarding direct or indirect infringement of second medical use patents. Finally, the doctrine of equivalents is also addressed in Article 89(5) IPL (→ mn. 54) and, at the time of the alleged infringement, equivalents of the elements cited in the claims are also considered.

4 In the case of a skinny label product, such a product is unlikely to infringe a second medical use patent, provided that its manufacturer does not encourage the prescription of its product for a patented indication. The risk of infringement is even lower for biosimilar products than for skinny label products, as the prescription of a biosimilar product instead of a reference product is not common in Türkiye. In any case, generic companies should especially alert the relevant stakeholders including physicians and pharmacists, to ensure that their product is prescribed only for the indications listed in their skinny labels and not for carved-out indications.

5 In the case of patent infringement disputes, Article 149 IPL provides that a prevailing plaintiff in a main infringement action may be entitled to remedies such as compensation

---

[1] Decision EPC 1973.

[2] European Patent Office Official Journal, 1985, p. 60: G1/83 German, G5/83 English, G6/83 French.

[3] Decision EPC 2000.

[4] Article 82(6) IPL.

for damages, including moral, material and reputational damages, destruction of the infringing products, seizure of the equipment used to manufacture the infringing products and publication of the final judgment of the court.

## B. Scope of protection and interpretation of second medical use claims

The Grand National Assembly of Türkiye ratified the EPC 1973 with all its decisions published in the Official Gazette on 12 July 2000[5]. It also ratified EPC 2000 upon its publication in the Official Gazette on 13 December 2007. There was a debate in Türkiye that since Article 52(4) of the EPC 1973 does not explicitly mention the patentability of subject matters relating to second medical use, such subject matters granted before that date should not benefit from patent protection. However, since the Grand National Assembly of Türkiye has adopted the EPC 1973 with all its decisions and published it in the Official Gazette, this means that it also accepts the G5/83 decisions concerning the secondary medical use of products, substances and articles belonging to the technical field of pharmacology. This debate arose as a result of a court decision, as explained in detail below. 6

In 2014, the Istanbul IP Court decided that second medical use patents granted before 13 December, 2007 were not patentable under Article 52(4) EPC 1973, as the Article did not specifically mention their patentability. The court also held that EPC 1973 did not cover the protection of second medical use patents. The patent holder appealed this decision to the Supreme Court, which overturned the lower court's decision, stating that second medical use patents were not exempt from patentability, and that the patent's novelty and inventive step should be evaluated. Despite this, the First Instance Court upheld its previous ruling, adding that the Enlarged Board of Appeal decisions (which include the G5/83 decision stating that a known substance's use for a new and inventive therapeutic application is patentable) are not binding on member countries. In its final ruling, the Supreme Court insisted that any patent, including second medical use claims, could only be invalidated after a proper assessment of novelty, inventive step and industrial applicability. The Turkish Patent and Trademark Office (TURKPATENT), despite this legal wrangling, has always accepted both international and national second medical use patents, even those granted before 13 December 2007. 7

In the light of the above, second medical use patents meeting the conditions of Articles 82 and 83 IPL are acceptable and enforceable in Türkiye. 8

## C. Direct and indirect infringement of second medical use claims

### I. Direct infringement

While there is no specific provision in the IPL regarding infringement of patents relating to second medical use, Article 141 IPL deals with acts considered as direct in- 9

[5] Official Gazette No. 24107 dated 2 July 2000, available from; http://www.resmigazete.gov.tr.

fringement. The article states that imitation of the patented product as a result of partial or complete manufacture without the consent of the patent owner constitutes infringement of the patent right. In addition, it is an infringement to use, sell, distribute or otherwise place on the market or import infringing products for these purposes, to store such products for commercial purposes or to make an offer to enter into a contract for infringing products, provided that it is known or ought to be known that the products in question are manufactured in whole or in part by imitation. The same applies to process patents and products manufactured by patented processes.

10 Accordingly, the use of the known substance for a novel medical indication protected by a second medical use patent is a direct infringement of a patent right in Türkiye.

11 On the other hand, Article 85(3) IPL lists acts to be excluded from patentability. These include:

a) practices which do not involve industrial or commercial purposes and are confined to special purposes;
b) trial practices involving the invention subject to a patent;
c) trial practices involve the performances of the invention subject to a patent in order to register drugs including necessary tests and experiments needed for this purpose;
d) using the drugs prepared in pharmacies without a mass production in order to prepare only one prescription and practices regarding drugs prepared this way;

12 Accordingly, Article 85(3)(b) IPL deals with the exemption for experimental use, while Article 85(3)(c) IPL deals with the so-called Bolar exemption (→ mn. 52). Therefore, a clinical trial carried out by a generic company to obtain marketing authorisation benefits from the experimental use and Bolar exemptions and is therefore not liable for patent infringement. The purpose of these articles is to promote technological progress, particularly in the pharmaceutical field, and to allow cheaper generic medicines to enter the market.

13 The doctrine of equivalents is also contained in Article 89(5) IPL. According to this article, when assessing the scope of protection, consideration shall also be given to elements which, at the time of the alleged infringement, were considered equivalent to those specified in the claims. An element is considered to be equivalent to an element expressly mentioned in the claims if it operates in the same way, fulfils the same functional requirements and leads to the same result.

14 In patent infringement proceedings, the plaintiff must prove that the defendant has committed at least one of the acts described. The burden of proof rests primarily on the plaintiff. However, in cases involving patents for a process leading to a specific substance or product, the court has the discretion to require the defendant to prove that the substances or products with identical properties were produced without infringing the patented process. In cases involving a patent for a process leading to a novel substance or product, any substance or product with matching properties is legally presumed to have been produced by the patented process. Those who argue otherwise must provide evidence to support their claim.

## II. Indirect infringement

15 While a direct infringement constitutes an unauthorised usage of the patent, indirect infringement is not directly tied to the patent's usage, but rather it involves deliberate contribution to the infringement of the patent right. An indirect infringer offers necessary tools to facilitate infringement and encourages it. While the concept of indirect infringement is not specifically defined in the IPL, Article 86 IPL states that the patent also confers

on its owner the right to prevent any third party from delivering or offering to deliver means for the implementation of the patented invention relating to an essential element thereof to persons not authorised to exploit it without the patent owner's consent, when the third party knows or the circumstances make it evident that such means are suitable to put the invention into practice and are intended for it. The provisions of Article 85 IPL are not applicable when the means to which it refers are products that are found habitually in trade, i.e. staple products, unless the third party incites the person to whom the delivery is made to commit acts prohibited in Article 85 IPL.

16 Article 86 IPL contains conditions that, if met, indicate that a patent has been indirectly infringed. For the indirect use of the patented product to be prohibited, the following conditions must be met cumulatively:

1. The elements used must be essential elements of the invention.
2. The supplier must know the following:
   a) These elements or tools are sufficient to enable the patented use, and
   b) The invention will be used for this purpose, or this must be clear from the surrounding circumstances.
3. If the product is found habitually in trade, i.e. is a staple commercial product, 'unauthorised use' of the patented invention cannot be claimed unless third parties encourage the unauthorised individuals in question to act in a way that falls within the scope of protection of the patent.[6]

17 Generic pharmaceutical companies in Türkiye can limit their Marketing Authorisation (MA) applications to specific indications and market their products with skinny labels by carving out the indications still protected by second medical use patents from the Summary of Product Characteristics (SmPC) and Product Information Leaflet (PIL) of the products. By doing so, generic pharmaceutical companies declare their intention not to use patented indications and in this way they avoid themselves the likelihood of direct or even indirect infringement actions.

18 Under Turkish law, for a patent infringement to occur, it is generally accepted that the product should be supplied solely for infringement purposes and there must be an 'incentive' to use the product in a way protected by the patent. If the supplier does not personally commit the infringement but encourages, promotes, assists third parties to commit the infringement, the supplier is deemed an infringer.[7] In the same vein, if a supplier counsels or suggests to an infringer how to implement an invention, this action is enough to make the supplier culpable for indirectly infringing the patent.[8] In instances where the disputed elements or tools are *staple commercial products*, the patent owner cannot assign liability to the supplier unless evidence shows that the supplier encouraged individuals to whom the product was presented to conduct an act that falls under the patent's protective scope.[9]

19 If the supplier initially lacks the knowledge that the supplied product is intended for executing the patent, a claim cannot be made against the supplier. However, once the supplier gains knowledge (or is informed by the rights holder) about the unauthorised use, the rights holder can take steps to prevent the supplier from supplying the product. On

[6] Yusufoğlu, Indirect Infringement of Second Medical Use Patents, Galatasaray Üniversitesi Hukuk Fakültesi Dergisi 2022, 1797.

[7] Köker/Yalçiner, Uzman Gözüyle Patent ve Faydalı Modelden Kaynaklanan Uyuşmazlıklar, Ankara 2020, p. 295; Şehirali, Patent Hakkinin Korunmasi, Ankara 1998, p. 111.

[8] Güneş, Sinai Mülkiyet Kanunu Işiğinda Uygulamali Patent ve Faydali Model Hukuku, Ankara 2019, p. 269; Saraç, Patentten Doğan Hakka Tecavüz ve Hakkin Korunmasi, Ankara 2003, p. 165; Suluk/Arasu/Nal, Fikri Mülkiyet Hukuku, Ankara 2017, p. 294.

[9] Tekinalp, Fikri Mülkiyet Hukuku, Istanbul 2012, p. 605.

the other hand, even if the supplier is unaware of the unauthorised use but the situation makes it apparent, the rights holder can still prohibit the supply.

20 In a recent legal case, a generic drug manufacturer initiated a non-infringement action against an original drug company, involving a patent related to a second medical-use claim. In response, the originator company requested the application of Article 86. After filing the action, the generic company carved out the patented indication from SmPC and patient information leaflet documents to avoid patent infringement. Despite modifying the SmPC and PIL, the originator company argued that the generic product still infringed the patent due to its identical formulation and expected effect. The court ruled that the generic company neither directly nor indirectly infringed the patent under Article 86 IPL, and handed down a non-infringement verdict. The court's final judgment has not yet been issued. Once issued, both parties will have the opportunity to appeal the decision at the district court. This case sets a precedent in Turkish IP practice, providing the first interpretation of Article 86 IPL in relation to second medical-use claims.

## D. Infringement of second medical use claims and skinny label products

21 Generic drug manufacturing companies may make abbreviated marketing authorisation (MA) Applications for generic pharmaceutical products that are substantially similar to the original pharmaceutical product previously authorised, by referring to the data of the original product in question when the data exclusivity period, if any, provided to the original pharmaceutical product, which also varies from country to country, expires. Marketing Authorisation applications may be made for one or more indications of the pharmaceutical product. Thus, generic drug companies may limit MA applications for certain indications of their pharmaceutical products and may remove indications of pharmaceutical products still protected by second medical use patents from the SmPC and PIL of pharmaceutical products by a method called carve-out. As a result, generic drug manufacturers have the opportunity to remove the patented indication from MA applications for their pharmaceutical products to be processed by the Ministry of Health of the Republic of Türkiye using the carve-out method in order not to violate the patented indications.[10]

22 As mentioned in the third section of this chapter, generic-original pharmaceutical product substitution is legal in Türkiye and supported by the authorities. In addition, the MEDULA system, established by the Social Security Institution (SSI), the reimbursement institution for the use of health stakeholders including pharmacies, technically allows this substitution. Public and private health institutions under contract with the SSI use the e-prescription system, which includes the indications of pharmaceutical products. Accordingly, pharmacists should know the indications of pharmaceutical products so as to prevent, where appropriate, substitution of original products for patented indications with generic products covering the same indications.[11]

23 In some cases, in Türkiye, physicians can prescribe pharmaceutical products only with their original name in the prescriptions, that is, without providing any information regarding their indications. In cases where the pharmacy is authorised to replace the orig-

[10] Acar/Yeğenoğlu, Türkiye'de İlaçta Patent, Ankara Üniversitesi Eczacilik Fakültesi Dergisi 2004.

[11] Suluk, Türkiye'de İlaçlarin Patent ve Diğer Fikri Mülkiyet Haklari ile Korunmasi, Terazi Hukuk Dergisi 2014, 9 (100).

inal pharmaceutical product with the generic pharmaceutical product, the pharmacy may give the patient the generic pharmaceutical product instead of the original pharmaceutical product. Therefore, it may be possible to use the generic pharmaceutical product in the patented indication area instead of the original pharmaceutical for which the indication information is not shared. In fact, in a system in which the original product patented for the indication for which it is prescribed and not indicated in the prescription can be replaced by a generic product by the pharmacist, pharmacies do not know for sure for what indication the drug is prescribed.[12]

Considering the fact that generic drugs are cheaper than the originals, it is quite common for the pharmacy to substitute the original product with the generic drug, and it is even supported by health authorities in order to reduce health expenditures.[13] 24

For the substitution of some specific products subject to different reimbursement rules according to the legislation, the MEDULA system stipulates full indication eligibility as well as a clear reference to the indication specified in the prescription. For such products, it is not technically possible to use skinny labelled products interchangeably within the system. In this way, such products may be limited to indications; otherwise reimbursement is refused by the SSI. However, if there is no information sharing on the indication of pharmaceutical products contained in the prescriptions, it can happen that pharmacies substitute original products with generic pharmaceutical products that are not approved for a patented indication.[14] 25

It is debatable whether the above-mentioned scenarios may constitute a violation of the second medical use patents under the current legislation in Türkiye. It suggests that a generic drug manufacturer has declared its intention to manufacture its pharmaceutical product only for non-patentable indications by removing the patented indications from the label by using the carve-out method. To determine whether there is any violation, it needs to be determined whether the activities of the generic pharmaceutical company, despite the limited indications, encourage the use of the original pharmaceutical products for their patented indications. 26

According to Articles 85 and 86 IPL, it is possible to connect the acts of physicians and pharmacists with infringement only in certain cases which are as follows: 27

1. whether physicians and pharmacies are writing prescriptions for skinny labels products in the patented indication area;
2. whether the skinny labels product is defined as the generic of the original pharmaceutical product in the MEDULA system;
3. whether physicians provide information in the prescription on the indication of the original pharmaceutical product;
4. whether the SSI, which provides reimbursement, provides information on the 'indication suitability' of the skinny labels product;
5. whether an e-prescription is used and in which cases pharmacies pay attention to the indications for pharmaceutical products.[15]

Nonetheless, in Türkiye, even if liability is established, legal action against physicians and pharmacies is not a common practice within the pharmaceutical industry.[16] 28

---

[12] Bkz dipnot 12.

[13] Çetin/Arıcıoğlu, 'Orijinal İlaç, Eşdeğer İlaç Tartişmalari Üzerine', Klinik Psikofarmakoloji Bülteni 2009, 19 (3).

[14] Bkz dipnot 14.

[15] Düğer, Sektörünün Düzenlenmesinin İdare Hukuku Açısından Değerlendirilmesi, Tıp Hukuku Dergisi 2016, 5 (10).

[16] https://www.corp-intl.com/news/newsitem.aspx?ID=39.

29 In case no. 2020/156, the defendant was a generic drug manufacturer of a drug containing the active ingredient vildagliptin, whose patent protection had expired, which drug was used in the treatment of type 2 diabetes. The defendant's SmPC and PIL was also in the form of a skinny label. The plaintiff, on the other hand, had protection for the active substance vildagliptin when used in combination with antidiabetic agents (metformin, sulfonyl urea derivatives and insulin) in its three patents in Türkiye. The plaintiff claimed that the doctors prescribed the defendant's drug with the active substance vildagliptin in combination with metformin, sulfonyl urea derivatives and insulin drugs already being marketed by the plaintiff, and thus infringed its patents protecting the prescribed combination.

30 Having considered all evidence, the opinion of the court-appointed expert panel was as follows:

- the defendant's placing on the market of its product with the active substance vildagliptin fulfils the conditions for the prohibition of indirect use of the invention in the plaintiff's patents within the scope of Article 86(1) IPL;
- the product with the active substance vildagliptin falls within the scope of 'products that are always available in the market' within the scope of Article 86(2) IPL;
- that the defendant did not encourage unauthorised persons to commit the specified acts; and
- the acts of the defendant do not fall within the scope of indirect use of the invention subject of the plaintiff's patents.[17]

## E. Infringement of second medical use claims and biosimilar products

31 A biosimilar is a biologic that has been developed to be substantially similar to an existing biologic. Biosimilar products are not the same as generic pharmaceutical products, which have simpler chemical structures and are considered to be the same as reference products. Since the production process of the biosimilar product will be different, it is predicted that it is not possible to reproduce exactly the same biological drug.[18]

32 As one of the countries that recognised the problems that may arise in the evaluation and licensing of biosimilar products early on, Türkiye created a biosimilar guideline in 2008 by adopting to a large extent the approach of EMA and this guideline was updated in 2021 in the light of the latest developments and the requirements of the country. The updated draft guideline is available on the website of the Turkish Medicines and Medical Devices Agency.[19]

33 It is possible to use biosimilar products instead of reference products in non-patented indications. However, as in all countries of the world, biosimilar products are not easy to substitute for reference biological products as generic pharmaceuticals are. For this reason, we are of the opinion that infringement cases related to the use of generic phar-

---

[17] This case file was closed as a result of the parties' withdrawal from the case. If this had not been the case and the case had continued, we believe that the judge would most likely have reached a decision in line with the opinion of the expert committee. It is also highly probable that disputes similar to this case will be decided in line with the approaches and opinions in the expert report.

[18] Karadoğan/Sezer, Biyobenzerler: Kavramlar ve Ruhsatlandrima Süreçleri, Marmara Pharmaceutical Journal 2015, 19.

[19] https://titck.gov.tr.

maceutical products in patented indications as in skinny labels products may not be very common. In Türkiye, the use of biosimilar products instead of reference products is not a process that pharmacies perform frequently and without consulting physicians. Infringement may of course occur with the use of biosimilar products in patented indications, but the potential of this is quite low compared to skinny labels products.[20]

## F. Strategies and considerations

The most common reason for infringement in relation to the use of biosimilar and generic pharmaceutical products in patented indications in Türkiye is that physicians do not provide information about the indication of the pharmaceutical product in the prescriptions, allowing pharmacists to substitute the original pharmaceutical product with the generic pharmaceutical product. To prevent this happening, steps must be taken to ensure that physicians and pharmacists are informed by generic drug manufacturers through drug sales representatives.[21] **34**

To prevent the use of biosimilar and generic pharmaceutical products for patented indications in Türkiye, the Ministry of Health of the Republic of Türkiye can make regulations about the appropriate indications that can be used for skinny labels products in their systems. This can be achieved when generic drug and biosimilar product manufacturers help update the systems of the Ministry of Health.[22] **35**

When a generic drug or biosimilar drug manufacturer claims to have declared its intention to manufacture their drug only for unpatented indications by carving out the patented indications from their label, the generic manufacturer should, to determine whether there is any infringement, be able to show that they do not encourage and promote the use of their drug for patented indications. On the contrary, they should be prohibited from doing so.[23] **36**

Through clear labelling and instructions, generic or biosimilar drug manufacturers should also identify their target patients and groups to be treated in non-patented indications. **37**

The generic or biosimilar drug manufacturers must continue to monitor safety and effectiveness of their products after they are placed on the market. This continuous surveillance can help to detect any instances of unsafe practices and infringement of intellectual property rights which may arise, and to take swift action when necessary.[24] **38**

---

[20] Iskit, 'Key concepts in biosimilar medicines: What physicians must know', North Clin Istanb. 2022, 86.

[21] Cetin/Arıcıoğlu, 'Orijinal İlac, Eşdeğer İlac Tartışmaları Uzerine', Klinik Psikofarmakoloji Bulteni 2019, 211.

[22] Yusufoğlu, Jenerik İlaç ve Jenerik İlaç Ruhsat Başvurusunun Patente Tecavüz Çerçevesinde Değerlendirilmesi, Galatasaray Üniversitesi Hukuk Fakültesi Dergisi 2014, 1155.

[23] Cetin/Arıcıoğlu, 'Orijinal İlac, Eşdeğer İlac Tartışmaları Uzerine', Klinik Psikofarmakoloji Bulteni 2019, 211.

[24] ibid.

## G. Legal remedies

39 If the defendant has committed at least one of the acts of infringement described in Article 141 IPL, the patentee may, in accordance with Article 149 IPL (→ mn. 56), seek the following remedies from the courts

- determination of the existence of infringement,
- prevention of possible infringement,
- the cessation of the infringing acts,
- compensation for damages, including moral, material and reputational damages,
- destruction of the infringing products,
- seizure of the infringing products and equipment used to manufacture the infringing products,
- ownership of the seized products and equipment; and
- publication of the final judgment of the court.

40 Each item of Article 149 IPL will be explained in some more detail below.

41 Even where the infringement of the patent right has not yet occurred, in cases where there is convincing evidence and risk that it will occur, the right holder may file an action for the determination of evidences and prevention of possible patent infringement. If the actions that violate the patent right have commenced and are ongoing; then the right holder may file an action to cease the existing infringement.[25]

42 When patent infringement is identified by the court, the patentee can seek compensation for the losses. Damages can be calculated based on the following:

- Potential profits the patent holder could have made without the infringer's competition. Court experts review both the patentee's and the infringer's financial records to estimate lost profits.
- The income the infringer made from using the patent. This involves an expert review of the infringer's financial records.
- What the infringer would've paid to use the patent legally under a licence agreement.

43 Claimants should judiciously select one of these methods, bearing in mind the specifics of the infringement.

44 In the event of poor-quality production by the infringer such as using sub-standard material, the patentee may also file a reputational compensation action against infringing party.[26]

45 The patentee can also ask the court to order the destruction of infringing products. A fast destruction process for such products exists under Article 163 IPL (→ mn. 60). Additionally, the patent owner can ask for the confiscation of goods produced in violation of patent rights, as well as associated equipment and machinery, ensuring non-infringing products aren't affected. The patentee can also request the transfer of ownership rights of confiscated violating items to them. If there's a valid reason, the patent owner can ask the court to publicise the final judgment in full or as a summary in daily media and inform the relevant parties. Recall directives are also applicable for items posing public health risks or those not in proper condition.

46 According to Article 159 IPL, the patentee may also request the relevant courts to issue an interim injunction to prevent the indirect and direct use by third parties before or dur-

---

[25] Suluk, Fikri Mülkiyet Yazilari I – Mütalaalarim (2001-2020), Ankara 2021.

[26] Yusufoğlu, Jenerik İlaç ve Jenerik İlaç Ruhsat Başvurusunun Patente Tecavüz Çerçevesinde Değerlendirilmesi, Galatasaray Üniversitesi Hukuk Fakültesi Dergisi 2014, 1155.

ing legal proceedings. Of course, the applicant is obliged to gather and submit to the court the evidence or grounds that substantiate the granting of an interim injunction for the subject of the invention.[27] The court has the power to grant an *ex parte* injunction. However, it is quite rare in Türkiye. Therefore, injunctions are usually granted in *inter partes* proceedings. In these cases, the court sets a date for the assessment of the application and can either refer the case to a panel of experts for a detailed report or decide directly on the application. To protect the rights of the defendant and any third parties who might be adversely affected by the preliminary injunction, a fair deposit might be mandated.

Infringement actions can be brought from the date of publication of a patent application, whereas the court considers the decision to grant the patent as a prejudicial question and therefore renders its decision only after the patent is granted. **47**

Türkiye has a three-tier court system including the courts of first instance, district courts and court of appeal. IP related disputes are initially heard in the courts of first instance. These courts are located in every district of Türkiye. If one of the parties is dissatisfied with the decision of the court of first instance, they can appeal the decision to a district court. District courts have jurisdiction over appeals of decisions made by the courts of first instance within their geographical region. If one of the parties is still dissatisfied with the decision of the district court, they can appeal to the Court of Appeal. The Court of Appeal will review the decision and any evidence presented, and may affirm, reverse, or modify the decision. It should also be noted that the Court of Appeal only examines whether the law has been correctly applied and does not go into the merits of the decision. In addition to the courts of first instance, Türkiye has specialised IP courts, which are located in Ankara, Istanbul, and Izmir. These courts have exclusive jurisdiction over IP related disputes. The decisions of the specialised IP courts can be appealed to the district court and then to the Court of Appeal. **48**

The IP courts are presided over by a single judge, who, while lacking technical expertise, is well-versed in IP law. As regards main stages of patent infringement proceedings, after the submission of the action petition and its subsequent notification to the defendant, the defendant is allowed to submit a defence petition. Once both sides have responded to each other's claims with two respective petitions, the court conducts an initial review hearing. During this hearing, the court identifies each party's claims and demands, clarifying the core issues in dispute. Given the judge's technical knowledge limitations in patent enforcement cases, a panel of court-appointed experts is engaged after the pleadings have been completed. The court's panel of experts consists mainly of three experts, including a patent attorney and technical experts from the relevant technical field, such as academics or senior professionals. This expert review can be reiterated multiple times to address party objections. Typically, the IP court judge will make a decision by the third review at the latest. Hence, the conclusion of patent enforcement cases heavily relies on the findings of the court-designated expert review. **49**

If the court determines that an ongoing separate action is a prejudicial question, it might hold off on its decision in the current case, deeming it reliant on the outcome of that separate action. A frequent strategy employed by defendants aiming to postpone proceedings is to initiate a counter-action challenging the patent's validity. Given that an invalidation action bears retrospective implications, local courts typically suspend the ongoing proceedings until the validity dispute is resolved. **50**

[27] Yildirim, Sinai Mülkiyet Kanunu Kapsamında Patent Tecavüzü Davaları İhtiyati Tedbirler, FMR Dergisi 2018, 87.

## H. Statutory provisions

# Industrial Property Law No. 6769

51 **Article 82**
**Patentable inventions and exceptions to patentability**

(1) A patent shall be granted to the inventions in all fields of technology providing that the invention is new, involves an inventive step and is susceptible to industry.

(2) Below mentioned shall not be considered as inventions. In case the application for a patent or the patent itself are involved in the subjects or activities mentioned below, this subject only or the activity itself shall stay out of patentability.

a) Discoveries, scientific theories and mathematical methods;
b) mental acts, business activities or game related plans, rules and methods;
c) computer programs;
ç) products with aesthetical creations , belles-lettres, artworks and treatise;
d) presentation of the information.

(3) Below mentioned inventions shall not be granted a patent:

a) inventions violating public order or public moral;
b) biological processes relating to plant varieties or animal races; or intending to generate plant varieties or animal races with the exception of microbiological processes or products obtained in the result of such processes;
c) all treatment modalities including the diagnosis methods which are intended to be applied to human or animal bodies and surgical methods;
ç) discovering only one of the parts of human body including human body and a gene sequence or a partial gene sequence in the various phases of their generation and evolution;
d) the human cloning processes, the changing processes of genetic identity of human sextinked inheritance, using human embryos for industrial or commercial purposes, changing processes of genetic identity in a way that may agonise the animals without providing any significant medical avails for human or animals and animals that are obtained in the result of such operations.

(4) Within the scope of subparagraph (a) of paragraph three, commercial use of the invention being prohibited by legislation shall not necessarily mean that this use is violating public order or public moral.

(5) The microbiological process that is specified in subparagraph (b) of paragraph 3 expresses any operation which includes microbiological materials, processed with microbiological materials or in the result of which microbiological materials are formed; plant or animal production procedures that are consisting of basically biological processes, hybridisation or selection that are completely natural.

(6) The provision mentioned in subparagraph (c) of paragraph 3 shall not be applied to the products, especially the substances and compositions which are used in any methods that are mentioned in the same option.

52 **Article 85**
**Scope of a patent right and its limits**

(1) The patentee avails himself of the patent right without any exceptions of where the invention was made, its technological area and whether the products are imported or are domestic.

(2) The patentee has a right to claim the prevention of the practices mentioned below in case that they are performed without his consent:

a) producing, selling, using or importing the goods subject to a patent or keeping those at hand for such purposes and for other reasons than personal needs;
b) using a process that is subject to a patent;
c) offering others to use the process patent the use of which is known or should be known to be prohibited;
ç) selling, using or importing the goods which are directly obtained by the process subject to a patent or keeping them at hand for such purposes and for other reasons than personal needs.

(3) The practices mentioned below shall be out of the scope of the rights provided by a patent:

a) practices which do not involve industrial or commercial purposes and are confined to special purposes;
b) trial practices involving the invention subject to a patent;
c) trial practices involve the performances of the invention subject to a patent in order to register drugs including necessary tests and experiments needed for this purpose;
ç) using the drugs prepared in pharmacies without a mass production in order to prepare only one prescription and practices regarding drugs prepared this way;
d) using the invention subject to a patent in making and running ships, space vehicles, airplanes or land transport vehicles for party countries of Paris Convention or in meeting the needs of such vehicles; using the mentioned vehicles provided that they are within the borders of Republic of Türkiye temporarily or accidentally.
e) provisions of Article 27 of International Civil Aviation Agreement which is approved by the Law dated 06.05.1945 and numbered 4749 and practices regarding aircrafts of a country in which the provisions of this Article are being applied.

(4) A small farmer whose definition is made in the Law on Protection of Breeder's Rights for New Plant Varieties dated 01.08.2004 and numbered 5042 has the right, in his own land which they operate, to use the reproduction material that derived from the product in the result of the production made by a patented product provided from the patentee; or sold by his permission; or obtained by another commercial way, in order to do new productions in their own land which they operate. This tenancy shall be subject to the provisions of the Law number 5042.

(5) The farmer has a right to use the patented breeding or other animal reproduction material provided from the patentee; or sold by his permission; or obtained by another commercial way for agricultural purposes. This tenancy covers the use of animals or other animal reproduction material in order to maintain their own agricultural strength. The procedure and rules regarding the use of this right shall be determined by regulations.

(6) The subject of the patent shall not be used in a way that will cause harm for the law, morals, and public order. This use shall also be bound up with current or future definite or indefinite-statutory prohibitions and restrictions.

## Article 86 53
## Preventing the indirect use of the invention

(1) The patentee has a right to prevent the factors or equipment regarding a part which makes the practice of the invention subject to a patent possible and constitutes the basis of the invention from being released third parties to parties who do not have an authority to use the invention subject to a patent. In order to implement this provision, the subject third parties must be aware that such factors or equipment are sufficient to use the invention and must be aware of using them for this purpose; or the situation must be clear enough.

(2) If the factors or equipment mentioned in the paragraph 1 are products which can be found anytime in the market, the provision of the paragraph 1 shall not be implemented in case the third parties do not induce the subject unauthorised parties to perform such practices.

(3) The performers of the practices specified in the subparagraph (a), (b), (c) and (ç) of the paragraph 3 of Article 85 shall not be considered as those who are unauthorised to use the patent according to the provision of paragraph 1.

54

## Article 89
## Scope of the protection

(1) The extent of the protection provided by the patent application or the patent itself shall be determined by claims. However, the description and the drawings shall be used in interpreting the claims.

(2) The claims shall not be interpreted based on the limits of the meaning of the words used. However, when determining the extent of the protection, the claims shall not be extended in way covering the ideas that had been thought of by the inventor but had not been demanded in the claims, and also in a way to cover the features which are expected to arise by interpretation of the description and the drawings by a skilled person in the art.

(3) The claims are interpreted in a way that the application or the patentee shall be provided with the protection they deserve; and the third parties shall be provided with a situation displaying positive assertion in a reasonable level in terms of the extent of the protection.

(4) The extent of the protection provided by the patent application shall be determined by the published claims of the application for the time passed until the patent is granted. But the situation of the patent when granted or its situation after the objection or invalidity procedures shall determine the protection provided from the application retroactively on condition that the protection scope is not extended.

(5) The factors which are equivalent to the factors mentioned in the claims by the time in which the violation was alleged to be existing are considered, too, in determining the extent of the protection provided by the patent application or the patent itself. A factor, in essence, shall be considered as equivalent to the factor which is generally demanded in the claims if it is functioning the same way as the factor demanded in the claims; it is fulfilling the function requirements in the same way and it is leading to the same conclusion.

(6) During the procedures which are required to determine the extent of the claims regarding granting the patent or during the validity of the patent, the patent application or the patentee's statements shall be considered in order to determine the extent of the protection.

(7) If the patent includes samples regarding the invention, the claims shall not be interpreted as limited to such samples. The product or the method shall not be left out of the extent of the protection provided by the claims especially in cases that the additional features of the product or method do not exist among the samples mentioned in the patent; do not cover the features of such samples; or cannot reach every objective or feature specified in such samples.

55

## Article 141
## Actions deemed as infringement on patent utility model right

(1) The following acts shall be considered as an infringement on patent or utility model right.

a) To imitate partially or completely the product forming the subject of invention as a result of production without the consent of owner of patent or utility model.
b) To sell, distribute or release to commercial area the products forming the subject of invention with other ways or to import it for these purposes, to keep it for commercial purposes, to use it by means of making applicable or to make suggestion draw up contract related to the product through infringement action, although it is known or it is required to know that product in question is partially or completely produced through imitation.
c) To use the method forming the subject of invention without receiving the consent of patent owner or to sell the products produced directly by method forming the subject of invention, to distribute or release to commercial area them or to import

them for these purposes, to keep them for commercial purposes, to use them by means of making applicable or to make suggestion to draw up contract related to these products, although it is known or it is required to know that this method is used without permission.

ç) To seize the patent or utility model right.

d) To expand the rights granted by owner of patent or utility model through contractual license or compulsory license without permission or to transfer these rights to third parties.

(2) In the event that the subject of the patent becomes a method related to obtaining of a product or material, the court may request the defendant to prove that the method related to obtaining of the same product or material is different from the method forming the subject of patent. In case that product or material obtained by method forming the subject of patent is new, the same product or material produced without permission of patent owner is deemed to have been obtained by the method forming the subject of patent. Anyone who claims otherwise shall be obliged to prove it. In such a case, the legitimate interests of the defendant shall be considered to protect the production and business secrets of the defendant.

(3) Starting from the date of publication of patent application or utility model application according to Article 97, the owner of the patent application or utility model application shall be authorised to institute a legal proceeding due to infringements carried out against invention. If person who infringes on patent rights are informed about application or the scope of application, whether application is published or not shall not be taken into consideration. If court decides that person who infringes on patent rights has malicious intent, the existence of the infringement will be accepted before the publication.

(4) Prior to the publication made in accordance with third and seventh paragraph of Article 99 and the tenth or twelfth paragraph of Article 143, the court shall not decide about the validity of the claims alleged.

### Article 149 56
### Claims that can be made by right owner whose industrial property right is infringed

(1) Right owner whose industrial property right is infringed can claim the following from the court:

a) To determine the existence of infringement.

b) To prevent the possible infringement.

c) To stop the infringing actions.

ç) To remedy infringement and compensate material and moral damages.

d) To seize the products causing infringement or requiring penalty, as well as instruments, such as devices and machine exclusively used in their production, without preventing the production of products other than infringing products.

e) To be granted property right on products, devices and machines seized in accordance with subparagraph (d).

f) To take measures to prevent the continuity of infringement, in particular at the expense of the infringer to change the shapes of products and instruments such as device and machine seized according to subparagraph (d), to erase the trademarks on them or to destroy them if it is inevitable for preventing the infringement of industrial property rights.

g) If there is any justified reason or interest, announcement of the final judgment at the expense of the opposite party fully or in summary through the daily newspapers or other means or notification to relevant parties.

(2) In case of acceptance of the claim specified in subparagraph (e) of first paragraph, the value of devices and machines shall be deducted from amount of compensation. If this value

exceeds the amount of agreed compensation, exceeding portion shall be paid to opposite party by right owner.

57 **Article 150**
**Compensation**

(1) Those who commit acts deemed as infringement on industrial property right shall be obliged to compensate the damage of right owner.

(2) Where the industrial property right is infringed, additional compensation may be claimed if reputation of industrial property right suffers damage because the products or services forming the subject of the right are used or produced in an inferior manner; or such products produced in this way are made available or launched to the market in an improper manner.

(3) The right owner, before instituting a legal proceeding for compensation related to infringement of industrial property right, in order to determine the evidences or if a legal proceeding for compensation has been instituted, in order to determine the amount of damages, may ask the court to order the person responsible for compensation to submit to the court the documentation related to the use of industrial property right.

58 **Article 151**
**Loss of revenue**

(1) Damage suffered by the right owner includes actual loss and loss of revenue.

(2) Loss of revenue, depending on the choice of the right owner who suffered damages, shall be calculated according to one of the following evaluation methods:

a) The potential revenue to be gained by right owner if the competition by the person infringing the industrial property right had not existed.
b) The net revenue obtained by the person infringing the industrial property right.
c) License fee to be paid by the person who infringed the industrial property right, if this person used this right through a license agreement in accordance with the law.

(3) In calculation of loss of revenue; factors such as economic importance of industrial property right in particular or the number, time and type of licenses related to industrial property right during infringement action and the nature and size of violation shall be taken into consideration.

(4) In calculation of loss of revenue; in the event that one of the evaluation methods specified in the subparagraph (a) or (b) of the second paragraph is selected and if court reaches the conclusion that industrial property right has been the determinant factor in creating the demand to that product, then the court shall decide that an equitable share be added in the calculation of revenue.

(5) In case of infringement of patent rights; if the court reaches the conclusion that the patent owner did not fulfil the obligations to use the patent as foreseen by this Code, loss of revenue shall be calculated according to the subparagraph (c) of the second paragraph.

(6) The provisions of this Article shall not be applied in case of infringement of geographical sign or traditional product name.

59 **Article 159**
**Request for interlocutory injunction and the scope of interlocutory injunction**

(1) Persons who have the right to institute a legal proceeding under this Code, on the condition that they prove that the action forming the subject of the legal proceeding violates the industrial property right within the country or serious and effective undertakings are performed to that end, may request the court to order an interlocutory injunction to ensure the effectiveness of judgment to be delivered.

(2) Interlocutory injunctions should especially cover the following measures:

a) To prevent and stop the actions, which constitute infringement of plaintiff's industrial property right.
b) To seize and store at their location anywhere within territories of Republic of Türkiye including areas such as customs and free port or zone, the products infringing the industrial property right that were produced through infringing the industrial property right or imported; without preventing the production of products other than infringing products, instruments exclusively used in the production of infringing goods or instruments used in performing a patented method.
c) To submit a security in terms of compensation for any damage.

(3) In the matters for which there are no provisions in this Code regarding interlocutory injunctions, the provisions of Code of Civil Procedure dated 12/01/2011 and numbered 6100 shall apply.

**Article 163** 60
**Fast destruction procedure**

(1) If the infringing goods, seized or placed under protection due to the crimes mentioned under this Code cannot be preserved at the custodial office due to quantity, size or character; after taking sufficient samples from the goods, which are suitable for collection of samples, in line with the instructions of the public prosecutor, the remaining goods shall be sent to the financial organisation of the locality. The official record including all information such as quantity, type, and size related to the goods seized together with samples shall be delivered to the office of the prosecutor.

(2) In case there is a risk that the infringing goods delivered to the financial organisation of the locality, after taking sample as per the first paragraph, would be damaged or fundamentally lose value or the preservation thereof provides a significant burden; after the expert examination is completed, based on the request of the public prosecutor at the investigation phase the judge or at the prosecution stage the court shall decide on the destruction of those goods before the verdict. The destruction shall be performed at the presence of a committee comprised of three persons established by the financial organisation under the chairmanship of the public prosecutor and a report shall be prepared.

# J. Extracts from court decisions

## I. Infringement of second medical use patent for literal infringement and infringement under doctrine of equivalents[28] 61

**Summary of the Claimant's arguments:** The plaintiff argues that the molecule can be used in the treatment of idiopathic pulmonary fibrosis, that the use of the molecule is open to everyone since the patent has expired, that the client intends to launch a drug whose active ingredient is pirfenidone, that indication patents are the most controversial patents in terms of protection, although there is no patent protecting the pirfenidone molecule, the defendant company was found to have some 'indication patents', the drug that the plaintiff intends to put on the market does not violate the rights of the defendant's patents, another drug has been developed to treat idiopathic pulmonary fibrosis (IPF) …

**Summary of the defendant's arguments:** In its reply, the defendant stated that the drug that the plaintiff intends to put on the market infringes the patent rights of the defendant, and

[28] Istanbul 2nd IP Court, Case No. 2016/119 from 13 January 2021.

that it is understood that the product subject to the lawsuit infringes the defendant's patent rights according to the SmPC and PIL information …

**Summary of the court decision based on the court expert report:**

*Literal infringement examination with respect to patent numbered…*

'…As a result of the technical evaluation made by the expert committee in the light of the explanations in the description, it has been determined that the drug defined in the SmPC and PIL of the … product contains elements (i) and (iv) of claim 2, but does not contain elements (ii) and (iii), therefore, it has been concluded that the plaintiff's … product does not fall within the scope of claim 2 of the defendant's patent numbered …, and finally, the plaintiff's … product does not fall within the scope of the defendant's patent numbered…'

*Literal infringement examination for patent numbered…*

'… is based on the discovery that the activity of CYPs is significantly increased in patients who smoke compared to non-smokers. The specification states that the invention is based on the discovery of an adverse reaction in patients who smoke and take pirfenidone at the same time…'

'…Although the plaintiff claimed that there was no warning about smoking in the SmPC of the product, the expert committee concluded that 'the statement that smoking reduces the exposure to … and may cause changes in the effect profile of pirfenidone is within the scope of the expression 'avoiding the use or co-administration of concomitants' of the indices defined in the claim (cigarette smoke, cigarette smoking) in order to avoid reduced exposure to pirfenidone in claim 1'. Therefore, the plaintiff's … product falls within the scope of claim 1 of the defendant's patent numbered …. As a result, it has been concluded that the plaintiff's … product falls within the scope of the defendant's patent numbered …'

*Infringement examination in terms of the doctrine of equivalents*

'…It has been found in the invention subject to the patent that even patients exhibiting abnormal liver function can continue to receive the original full target dose of pirfenidone after briefly discontinuing pirfenidone or taking pirfenidone at low doses, thus providing the advantage of maximising the time to the full target dose of the drug and the potential for a beneficial therapeutic effect through this delivery regimen. This administration regimen is limited to the patient group specified in the claim…'

'…The SmPC and PIL of the claimant's product, on the other hand, do not define such a dosing regimen. In the plaintiff's product, the drug administration regime is not consciously determined by monitoring according to AST and ALT values. Therefore, as a result of the evaluation made by the experts in terms of the conditions of being accepted as equivalent, which are to perform the same function – to perform in the same way – to produce the same result, '… cannot be said to give results for the specific patient group mentioned in the claim, … … will not produce the same result with the element specified in the claims, therefore, based on the definition of 'mild' and 'moderate' hepatitis disorder in the SmPC, it is concluded that … cannot fall within the scope of equivalent infringement of the claim of the patent due to the possibility of administering this drug to patients with AST and ALT values mentioned in the claim.'…'

## 62 II. Patentability of second medical use patent[29]

**Summary of the plaintiff's arguments:** … the plaintiff summarised in the petition; …. is the owner of the patent registered before the TURKPATENT with the number …. , that the nasal drops and spray subject to the patent are also exported to Türkiye, that the main substance of this nasal spray and the patent subject … are used by the defendant company in their own products, that they put imitation products on the market and sell them…

[29] Istanbul District Court, Case No. 2021/680 from 2 December 2021.

**Summary of the defendant's arguments:** ... the patent of the plaintiff is not related to the substance ... as claimed, this substance has been widely used in the world since the 1970s in terms of upper respiratory tract and oral and dental health, so it is not possible to grant the plaintiff a patent on the substance ..., when evaluated within the framework of the plaintiff's claims subject to the patent, it does not constitute an infringement of the plaintiff's patent right, ..., sodium chloride, sodium bicarbonate, grapefruit seed extract and glycerin, whereas the content of the plaintiff's 31 separate claims subject to the patent is different, therefore there is no infringement, and furthermore, it is not possible to register the second medical use as a patent in terms of pharmaceutical patents in the Decree Law No. 551...

**Summary of the first instance court decision:**...It has been decided that the patent of the plaintiff subject to the lawsuit is related to secondary medical use, and until the entry into force of the EPC 2000 in Türkiye in 2007, the second medical use claims cannot be accepted even if they are in Swiss type format, and therefore the patent of the plaintiff is invalidated.

**Summary of the district court judgment:** The patent is related to secondarx medicale use, and although there was nich explicit regulation for 'secondary medical use' in the pre-amendment text of the EPC (EPC 1973) which entered into force in 2007, in the decision numbered G/5-83 of the European Patent Office Extended Board of Appeal (EPO EBoA), it was accepted by the EPO that a patent may be granted for secondary use if the claims in the patent application are written in a form referred to as 'Swiss-type', Since the decisions of the extended Board of Appeal, including Decision No. G5/83, were published as an annex to the Convention in the Türkiye's Official Gazette No. 24107 of 12 July 2000, it was necessary to decide that these decisions should be taken as a basis for the interpretation of the provisions of the Convention and that the judgment of the court of first instance should be set aside.

## III. Indirect use[30] 63

**Summary of plaintiff arguments:** ... the plaintiffs made inventions protecting the combination of vildagliptin with metformin, the combination of vildagliptin with sulfonylurea and the combination of vildagliptin with insulin, these inventions were granted with three Turkish Patents, the defendant made an abbreviated licence application by referring to the plaintiff's drug licence files named ... and thus obtained the manufacturing and sales licence for their generic product named . ..., it was seen that the defendant removed the explanations that the product could be used in combination with metformin, insulin and sulfonylurea from the defendant's documents, however, the defendant's reference to the original marketing authorisation files of ... with the active substance vildagliptin, whose effectiveness and safety as a combined treatment with metformin, insulin and sulfonylurea has been proven by the plaintiff. ... with the active substance vildagliptin, which is intended for use in the treatment of type 2 diabetes, is mostly used in combination with metformin or insulin or sulfonylurea, and the use of the active substance vildagliptin alone in treatment is extremely rare, ... ... tablet drug on the website of ..., it is stated on the page containing the indication information of the drug that 'if deemed necessary by the physician ..., it can be used together with insulin and other oral diabetes medicines', thus causing patent infringement pursuant to Article 141 of the IPL, it was requested to determine the indirect use of the patents subject to the lawsuit pursuant to Article 86 of the IPL and to decide to prevent infringement and indirect use...

**Summary of the defendant's arguments:** The protection period of the patent numbered ... containing the active substance ... of the plaintiff expired on ..., the defendant company made an abbreviated licence application by referring to the plaintiff's drug licence file named ... containing this active substance, and obtained a licence and sales permit for the generic product named ..., both drugs are used in the monotherapy treatment of Type 2 diabetes ac-

[30] Istanbul 1st IP Court, Case No. 2016/156 from 13 April 2022.

cording to ... and ... documents, the plaintiff's vildagliptin and metformin, vildagliptin and sulphate ... and ... documents, both drugs are used in the monotherapy treatment of Type 2 diabetes, the Plaintiff cited three patents containing a combination of two active substances as vildagliptin and metformin, vildagliptin and sulfonylurea, vildagliptin and insulin, whereas ... contains only one active substance, vildagliptin, the Defendant's... is only used in the monotherapy treatment of Type 2 diabetes, the defendant is not the person who uses this drug, but the person who supplies it to the market with the permission of the health authority, and from this supply, 'drug use', in other words, 'prescription, pricing, etc. ' is under the supervision and control of the relevant Ministry in accordance with the health legislation, the Constitutional Court's decision dated ..., ... is an independent product and the defendant is the authorised person who has the right to sell this drug, there is no data and guidance on combined use in the SmPC information and it is not recommended, physicians and pharmacists will not be considered among the 'unauthorised persons' within the framework of the provision of IPL 86, and requested the dismissal of the lawsuit...

**Summary of the Report Prepared by the Expert Panel Appointed by the Court:** The defendant was a generic drug manufacturer of a drug containing the active ingredient vildagliptin, whose patent protection had expired, which drug was used in the treatment of type 2 diabetes. The defendant's SmPC and PIL was also in the form of a skinny label. The plaintiff, on the other hand, had protection for the active substance vildagliptin when used in combination with antidiabetic agents (metformin, sulfonyl urea derivatives and insulin) in its three patents in Türkiye. The plaintiff claimed that the doctors prescribed the defendant's drug with the active substance vildagliptin in combination with metformin, sulfonyl urea derivatives and insulin drugs already being marketed by the plaintiff, and thus infringed its patents protecting the prescribed combination.

Having considered all evidence, the opinion of the court-appointed expert panel was as follows:

- the defendant's placing on the market of its product with the active substance vildagliptin fulfils the conditions for the prohibition of indirect use of the invention in the plaintiff's patents within the scope of Article 86(1) IPL
- the product with the active substance vildagliptin falls within the scope of 'products that are always available in the market' within the scope of Article 86(2) IPL
- that the defendant did not encourage unauthorised persons to commit the specified acts,
- the acts of the defendant do not fall within the scope of indirect use of the invention subject of the plaintiff's patents

Annotation: This case file was closed as a result of the parties' withdrawal from the case. If this had not been the case and the case had continued, we believe that the judge would most likely have reached a decision in line with the opinion of the expert committee. It is also highly probable that disputes similar to this case will be decided in line with the approaches and opinions in the expert report.

# § 13
# United Kingdom

## A. Executive summary

Under UK law Swiss-form claims are treated as purpose-limited process claims and EPC 2000 claims as purpose-limited product claims. Direct infringement of these claims is therefore dealt with under different sections of the Patents Act 1977. 1

The key judicial guidance on direct infringement of second medical use claims by 'skinny label' products comes from the Supreme Court in *Warner-Lambert v Generics*, where the majority of the court preferred the 'outward presentation' test. Based upon this test, the physical characteristics of the product (including the patient information leaflet identifying the indiciations that the product is intended to treat) are determinative of the issue of infringement, except in situations where the outward presentation of the product is deemed to be a 'charade'. While the Supreme Court guidance was addressed to Swiss-form claims, the direct infringement of claim in EPC 2000 form is expected to be approached in the same way. 2

Although the Supreme Court confirmed there to be no scope for asserting indirect infringement of a Swiss-form claim, the same cannot be said for an EPC 2000 claim. Indirect infringement of several EPC 2000 claims was recently addressed in *Akebia v Fibrogen* in respect of off-label indictations, before the product in question was on the market. While indirect infringement of an EPC 2000 claim by a 'skinny label' product is not yet the subject of any case law, such a claim is likely to involve a detailed assessment of prescribing and dispensing practices, as well as the conduct of the supplier. 3

Although the case law to date on infringement of second medical use claims has related to small molecule pharmaceuticals, the treatment of biosimilar products is not expected to be any different. 4

## B. Scope of protection and interpretation of second medical use claims

Under UK law a Swiss-form claim is recognised to be a purpose-limited process claim (see *Generics (UK) Ltd v Warner-Lambert Co LLC*[1]), and an EPC 2000-form claim as a purpose-limited product claim. As such, they have a different scope of protection, which is consistent with the position arising from several cases before the Technical Boards of Appeal of the European Patent Office.[2] 5

---

[1] [2018] UKSC 56, [2019] Bus LR 360 at [2], [63]; → mn. 36.

[2] See T 1373/11 GENZYME/Treatment of Pompe's Disease [2016] EPOR 33 at [21] cited in Case Law of the Boards of Appeal at p. 522.

# C. Direct and indirect infringement of second medical use claims

## I. Bringing an infringement claim

6 There are several examples of *quia timet* claims for infringement being allowed to proceed in pharmaceutical cases before the UK courts. In such cases it must be demonstrated that there is a sufficiently strong probability that an injunction would be required (to prevent harm to the claimant) to justify the proceedings being brought[3]. In considering whether such actions should be allowed to proceed, the following principles have emerged in the case law[4]:

1. Starting a patent revocation action in the UK infers a rebuttable presumption that the party seeking to revoke the patent intends to launch an infringing product before patent expiry;
2. Not having a marketing authorisation does not necessarily mean that no threat of infringement is posed;
3. Starting a patent revocation action outside the UK may not be enough to infer a threat of infringement in the UK; and
4. Conduct and plans of the alleged infringer are of key relevance, including whether the alleged infringer is prepared to give adequate notice of an intention to launch.

7 In the context of a second medical use case, it is likely to be difficult for the Court to make substantive determinations regarding the issue of infringement without adequate detail regarding the product label being sought by the applicant of the marketing authorisation and/or without some meaningful evidence regarding likely clinical practice in relation to the allegedly infringing product.

8 In *Akebia Pharmaceutics v Fibrogen*[5], which concerned *inter alia* infringement of several patents with claims in EPC 2000 form, the claimant brought a *quia timet* claim for infringement before the product in suit was on the market, rather than waiting to see what would happen if and when the product was marketed. The claim was allowed to proceed and the Court considered whether on the evidence before it at that point in time, the defendants were threatening to infringe the patents-in-suit. Although there was found to be no threat of infringement at that time, it would have been open to the claimants to file a further infringement claim in the face of a material change in circumstances.

9 It is also possible to seek a declaration of non-infringement under section 71 of the Patents Act 1977 and/or under the inherent jurisdiction of the Court. In such a situation, it would be open to the claimant to ask the Court to consider the issue of infringement by reference to different forms of a product label.

## II. Direct patent infringement

10 As Swiss-type claims are purpose-limited process claims, direct infringement is concerned with the manufacture of the medicament (including questions about what it is

[3] *Merck Sharp Dohme Corp v Teva Pharma BV* [2013] EWHC 1958 (Pat), [2014] FSR 13 at [56]-[59].
[4] *Teva UK Limited v Chiesi Farmaceutici SpA* [2020] EWHC 1311 (Pat).
[5] [2020] EWHC 866 (Pat).

manufactured 'for') along with the handling of the resultant product. This is governed under sections 60(1)(b) and 60(1)(c) Patents Act 1977 (→ mn. 35).

Section 60(1)(b) provides that, where the invention is a process, a person infringes the patent where, amongst other things, they use the process or offer it for use. In the common scenario in which the manufacture of the product takes place outside the UK, section 60(1)(b) does not apply. This was the case in *Warner-Lambert v Generics*. If the interpretation of the Supreme Court in *Warner-Lambert v Generics* is followed, then a Swiss-type claim will be infringed where the product emerges from the process of manufacture (no matter where manufacture takes place) formulated, packaged and labelled for the patented use. 11

Section 60(1)(c) entitles the patentee to prevent the sale or offer for sale, use or importation of a product obtained directly by means of that process. Therefore, where the manufacture of a product covered by a patentee's Swiss-type claim takes place outside of the jurisdiction, it will be an infringement to import the product in situations where manufacture amounts to an infringement of the Swiss-type claim. The Supreme Court also confirmed in *Warner-Lambert v Generics* that for Swiss-form claims, the invention is the process identified in the claim i.e. the actual act of manufacture, and does not extend to acts downstream of manufacture (such as the affixing of a sticker to the packaging by the pharmacist). 12

The infringement of EPC 2000 claims, being purpose-limited product claims concerns the product itself (rather than the process) and is governed by section 60(1)(a) Patents Act 1977, which provides that where the invention is a product, a person infringes the patent for the invention where they make, disposes of, offer to dispose of, use or import the product. It is therefore expected that a pharmaceutical product formulated, packaged and labelled in a form suitable for use in the treatment of the patented indication (i.e. a 'full label' product) will infringe an EPC 2000 claim. In contrast, where a 'skinny label' is used to carve out the patented indictation(s), the mere manufacture of such a product should not be encompassed by an EPC 2000 claim. 13

## III. Indirect patent infringement

Indirect infringement is set out in section 60(2) Patents Act 1977, which covers the acts of supplying and offering to supply any means relating to an essential element of the invention for putting the invention into effect when the person knows, or it is obvious to a reasonable person in the circumstances, that those means are suitable for and intended to put the invention into effect in the United Kingdom. 14

For a process claim, the 'invention' in section 60(2) is the process identified in the relevant claim (*Menashe Business Mercantile Ltd v William Hill Organisation Ltd*[6]). Thus for Swiss-form claims, which are claims to processes of manufacture, putting the invention into effect necessarily entails the act of manufacturing the medicament. The Supreme Court therefore held in *Warner-Lambert v Generics* that there cannot be indirect infringement by reason of the supply of the generic product to third parties, as all subsequent acts do not fall within the process of manufacturing.[7] However, no such problem arises in the case of EPC 2000 claims. 15

With regard the knowledge and intention requirements of section 60(2), the key principles from *Grimme Landmaschinenfabrik GmbH v Scott*[8], which remains a key 16

[6] [2003] 1 WLR 1462.
[7] See [87]–[88]; → mn. 36.
[8] [2010] EWCA Civ 1110, [2011] FSR 7.

authority on indirect infringement, were summarised as follows in *Akebia Pharmaceutics v Fibrogen*[9]:

1. The required intention is to put the invention into effect. The question is what the supplier knows or ought to know about the intention of the person who is in a position to put the invention into effect – the person at the end of the supply chain, [109].
2. It is enough if the supplier knows (or it is obvious to a reasonable person in the circumstances) that some ultimate users will intend to use or adapt the 'means' so as to infringe, [107(i)] and [114].
3. There is no requirement that the intention of the individual ultimate user must be known to the defendant at the moment of the alleged infringement, [124].
4. Whilst it is the intention of the ultimate user which matters, a future intention of a future ultimate user is enough if that is what one would expect in all the circumstances, [125].
5. The knowledge and intention requirements are satisfied if, at the time of supply or offer to supply, the supplier knows, or it is obvious to a reasonable person in the circumstances, that ultimate users will intend to put the invention into effect. This has to be proved on the usual standard of the balance of probabilities. It is not enough merely that the means are suitable for putting the invention into effect (for that is a separate requirement), but it is likely to be the case where the supplier proposes or recommends or even indicates the possibility of such use in his promotional material, [131]

**17** Therefore, for EPC 2000 claims, in order to satisfy the requirements of section 60(2), it is sufficient that a proportion of users will intend to use the means so as to infringe. Even if the majority of users will not intend to use the means to infringe, that is only relevant to remedies, and in particular financial remedies.[10] However, 'speculative, maverick or unlikely use' of the means should be disregarded.[11] Such use must be established in the usual way, on the balance of probabilities.

**18** Indirect infringement was considered in *Akebia v Fibrogen* in relation to a product that was not yet on the market. The assessment was therefore based on the current state of the clinical evidence and whether is was foreseeable that clinicians would prescribe the medicament in question for the patent-protected uses that were the subject of certain EPC 2000 claims. In the case of *Akebia v Fibrogen*, those uses were off-label. Based on the evidence of clinicians who assessed the state of clinical knowledge on the effect of the claimed compounds (HIF prolyl hydroxylase inhibitors; HIF-PHIs) on iron parameters that were the subject of the claims, there was found to be no risk that the product-in-suit, vadadustat (a HIF-PHI), would be marketed in circumstances where Akebia would know, or it would be obvious to a reasonable person in the circumstances, that vadadustat is suitable for putting and intended to put the claimed inventions into effect in the United Kingdom.

---

[9] [2020] EWHC 866 (Pat).
[10] *Grimme v Scott* [2010] EWCA Civ 1110 at [134]–[137].
[11] ibid. at [116], [124], [127] and [129]–[130] and *KCI v Smith & Nephew* [2010] EWHC 1487 at [47].

## D. Infringement of second medical use claims and skinny label products

The most significant guidance on the direct infringement of second medical use claims in the context of 'skinny label' products comes from *Warner-Lambert v Generics*[12]. Addressing questions regarding the patentability and infringement of Swiss-type claims in the litigation concerning pregabalin, the Supreme Court considered the meaning of 'for' in second medical use claims and were divided three ways as to the correct approach to the mental element required for direct infringement of a Swiss-form claim. The primary contenders were whether the test should be one of subjective intention (i.e. where the generic manufacturer deliberately targets the patented market), or whether intention is irrelevant and what actually matters is the physical characteristics of the product itself (termed the 'outward presentation' test). 19

The majority preferred the 'outward presentation' test. Thus, for a Swiss-type claim (i.e. a purpose-limited process claim), the Supreme Court has indicated that the badge of purpose is the physical characteristics of the product as it emerges from the relevant process, including its formulation and dosage, packaging and labelling and the patient information leaflet which will identify the conditions for whose treatment the product is intended. Although there is no case law or guidance in respect of EPC 2000 claims (i.e. purpose limited product claims), in the context of direct infringement, the same test of 'outward presentation' is also likely to be applied. 20

Based upon the application of the *'outward presentation'* test from *Warner Lambert v Generics*, a 'skinny label' should normally suffice to avoid infringement, subject to the outward presentation of the product being a mere 'charade' (→ mn. 25). In such circumstances, prescribing practices will not be of relevance. 21

In relation to indirect infringement of an EPC 2000 claim under section 60(2), it will be necessary to establish whether a proportion of users intend to use the means so as to infringe, whereby such use is not speculative maverick or unlikely (→ mn. 17). While there is no case law on indirect infringement of an EPC 2000 claim by a 'skinny label' product, as demonstrated by the detailed assessment in *Akebia v Fibrogen*, which concerned off-label prescribing, any such assessment will be a highly factual assessment taking into account prescribing and dispensing practices, as well as any measures taken to avoid or target the patent-protected market. 22

## E. Infringement of second medical use claims and biosimilar products

The *'outward presentation'* test was developed in the context of a case relating to a small molecule pharmaceutical. Whilst there is no case law that has addressed the position regarding biosimilar products, given the legal approach in terms of direct infringement is a function of claim construction there is no reason why biosimilar products should be treated any differently. The categories of information included in the product label of biosimilar products (i.e. Summary of Product Characteristics and Product Information 23

---

[12] See also § 19 mn. 47 et seq.

Leaflet) is also the same as for small molecule pharmaceuticals. Therefore, the expectation is that biosimilar products will be treated in the same way.

24 As regards indirect infringement of an EPC 2000, the way in which a biosimilar is prescribed and dispensed will be key to the issue of intention. The usual test will be applied under section 60(2) whereby it will be necessary to establish whether a (non-trivial) proportion of users intend to use the biosimilar so as to infringe.

## F. Strategies and considerations

25 Based upon the application of the '*outward presentation*' test from *Warner-Lambert v Generics*, a 'skinny label' should normally suffice to avoid infringement. The Supreme Court recognised, however, that there may be remote situations in which the outward presentation of the product is merely a 'charade' (for example, because generic manufacture is supplying in quantities exceeding the non-patented market or encouraging dealers and pharmacists to supply the drug for the patented indication).[13] In considering circumstances constituting such a charade, the Supreme Court referred to the potential scenario of encouraging dealers and pharmacists.

26 The Supreme Court has effectively left the position open regarding what the courts should do if faced with such a situation. However, when dealing in any generic or biosimilar 'skinny label' products, it would be advisable to ensure that the amount of 'skinny label' generic or biosimilar product supplied into the UK market does not exceed the percentage of the market attributable to the 'skinny label' indication(s). It would also be important to ensure that no positive steps are taken actively to target the 'skinny label' generic or biosimilar product to the patent protected market.

## G. Legal remedies

### I. Injunctions

27 Injunctions are a discretionary remedy that are generally available in cases involving a finding of patent infringement. A general injunction prohibiting further infringement is ordinarily granted by the court unless there are good reasons not to do so (for example, if the granting of an injunction would be against the public interest). In recent years, there have also been cases of patentees choosing not to seek an injunction where they recognise the life-saving nature of the product in question.

28 The appropriateness of a general prohibitory injunctions in second medical use cases was considered by the various courts in *Warner-Lambert v Generics*, largely as a consequence of the patentee's proposed test for infringement (i.e. foreseeability that the drug will be used for the patented indication). If infringement was found on this basis (which, given the prescribing and dispensing regime in the UK, would be almost inevitable), all of a manufacturer's product would be infringing as it would be impossible to differentiate between batches where infringement was foreseeable and those where it was not. However,

---

[13] *Warner-Lambert v Generics* [2018] UKSC 56 at [86]; → mn. 36.

the Supreme Court having rejected the foreseeability test, did not need to consider the position further.

The High Court in *Warner-Lambert Company, LLC v Actavis Group PTC EHF & Others* [14] issued a mandatory injunction requiring NHS England to issue guidance to Clinical Commissioning Groups regarding the prescription of medicaments for either patented or unpatented indications. In requiring that such guidance be issued, the court also ordered that Warner-Lambert give a cross-undertaking in damages to certain interested parties, namely various NHS entities and generic manufacturers, entitling them to whatever relief the court might order in the event that the guidance caused loss to those interested parties. Following the decision of the Supreme Court in *Warner-Lambert v Actavis*, it is not clear whether patentees will seek the issuance of similar guidance in the future. 29

## II. Damages

Under UK law, damages are intended to be compensatory. The measure of damages is, as far as possible, a sum that will put the claiming party in the same position as they would have been had they not sustained the wrong. 30

Awarding damages in respect of infringement of a second medical use patent is a complicated assessment. For example, in the face of a finding of infringement by generic suppliers, what level of compensation will be appropriate for a patentee that has been forced to lower the price of its product because of the presence of a generic alternative which was legitimately on the market for the non-patented indications? Establishing the split in the market between patented and non-patented indications to attempt to distinguish legitimate, non-infringing sales from infringing sales is likely to be relevant, but the court may also need to find a creative way of arriving at an outcome which provides adequate compensation for patentees without unduly penalising generic competitors from accessing the legitimate, non-patented market. It may be of relevance that the Supreme Court in *Warner-Lambert v Generics* acknowledged, in the context of direct infringement, the imperfect nature of the protection conferred by an outward presentation test, which it considered to arise from a limitation inherent in a Swiss-form patent. In this regard the court observed that '[a] person's exposure to liability for infringement depends on the purpose for which the patent-protected product was manufactured. The patentee's protection is therefore necessarily incomplete'. Such a limitation would also seem inherent in an EPC 2000 patent. 31

In what is the largest damages inquiry in the history of the Patents Court, several generic pharmaceutical manufacturers, and the NHS are seeking compensation for damages caused by Warner-Lambert's various interim injunctions, agreements, and groundless threats occurring prior to the Supreme Court's decision on liability, in the final stages of the *Warner-Lambert v Generics* litigation. 32

While a number of the parties have reached a settlement with Warner-Lambert, the initial phases of the inquiry have demonstrated the immense complexity of the claims. So far, there have been several case management hearings and a trial dealing with a preliminary issue trial concerning the counterfactual assumptions that should be applied to the various claims. 33

In the preliminary issue trial, the Court held that the inquiry will, in principle, proceed on the basis of a single hypothetical 'counterfactual' in which it is to be assumed that none of the interim injunctions, agreements or threats were ever made, but that the patent was 34

[14] [2015] EWHC 485 (Pat).

not known to be invalid[15]. The first substantive trial in the claims is scheduled to take place in 2023.

## H. Statutory provisions

## Patents Act 1977

35 **Section 60**

(1) Subject to the provisions of this section, a person infringes a patent for an invention if, but only if, while the patent is in force, he does any of the following things in the United Kingdom in relation to the invention without the consent of the proprietor of the patent, that is to say –

(a) where the invention is a product, he makes, disposes of, offers to dispose of, uses or imports the product or keeps it whether for disposal or otherwise;

(b) where the invention is a process, he uses the process or he offers it for use in the United Kingdom when he knows, or it is obvious to a reasonable person in the circumstances, that its use there without the consent of the proprietor would be an infringement of the patent;

(c) where the invention is a process, he disposes of, offers to dispose of, uses or imports any product obtained directly by means of that process or keeps any such product whether for disposal or otherwise.

(2) Subject to the following provisions of this section, a person (other than the proprietor of the patent) also infringes a patent for an invention if, while the patent is in force and without the consent of the proprietor, he supplies or offers to supply in the United Kingdom a person other than a licensee or other person entitled to work the invention with any of the means, relating to an essential element of the invention, for putting the invention into effect when he knows, or it is obvious to a reasonable person in the circumstances, that those means are suitable for putting, and are intended to put, the invention into effect in the United Kingdom.

## J. Extracts from court decision

## *Warner-Lambert Company LLC v Generics (UK) Ltd t/a Mylan and another*[16]

36 (61) Patent infringement is a statutory tort. Section 60 of the Patents Act 1977 (so far as is relevant) provides as follows:

*[see s. 60 provisions → mn. 35]*

(62) Some general points should be made at the outset about section 60 of the Patents Act. First, although liability for infringement is often said to be strict, section 60 of the Patents Act distinguishes between those heads of infringement which require proof of a mental element

[15] *Dr Reddy's Laboratories v Warner-Lambert* [2021] EWHC 2182 (Ch).
[16] [2018] UKSC 56.

and those which do not. In short, under section 60(1)(a) and (c), there is no mental element. Liability, as Lord Hoffmann observed in *Merrell Dow Pharmaceuticals Inc v HN Norton & Co Ltd* [1996] RPC 76, 92, is absolute. 'It depends upon whether the act in question falls within the claims and pays no attention to the alleged infringer's state of mind.' On the other hand, an allegation of infringement under section 60(1)(b) (at any rate by offering the process for use in the United Kingdom), or an allegation of indirect infringement under section 60(2), on the other hand, requires proof of knowledge. In both cases, the knowledge required is encapsulated in the phrase 'when he knows, or it is obvious to a reasonable person in the circumstances …'. Secondly, section 60 uses a consistent conceptual approach to the relationship between the words product, process and invention. Invention is a class with only two members, product and process, and the invention in question is the subject matter of one or more claims in the patent. Thus, for the purposes of section 60, phrases about using the process, product or invention, or working the invention or putting the invention into effect need to be understood and applied by reference to the claim (or claims) in the patent alleged to be infringed.

## Direct infringement: section 60(1)(c)

(63) It is common ground that Swiss-form claims are purpose-limited process claims. Claim 3 of the patent in suit is not a product claim, because the product is not novel. It is a process claim because it protects the process of 'preparation' (or manufacture) of a medicament containing pregabalin. It is purpose-limited because it only protects that process so far as it is undertaken 'for' treating neuropathic pain. The monopoly claimed is a monopoly of preparation or manufacture of the product for the designated purpose. It is not a monopoly of the subsequent use of the product for that purpose. This is the basis on which Claim 3 is consistent with the prohibition of patents for methods of treatment or diagnosis. It follows that Warner-Lambert's allegation of direct infringement is and must be based on section 60(1)(c).

(64) Section 60(1)(c) is concerned with cases where a product is obtained directly by means of the patented process. Infringement occurs whenever a person disposes of that product, offers to dispose of it, uses or imports it, or keeps it, whether for disposal or otherwise. The infringer may be, but need not be, the same as the person who makes the product. The section also applies to anyone in the downstream generic market, including wholesalers and pharmacists. Liability is strict. Provided only that the product has been obtained directly by means of the process, it extends to subsequent dealings with all and every such product irrespective of knowledge.

## Paragraphs 84 – 88

(84) In my opinion, in a purpose-limited process claim, the badge of purpose is the physical characteristics of the product as it emerges from the relevant process, including its formulation and dosage, packaging and labelling and the patient information leaflet which in EU (and other) countries will identify the conditions for whose treatment the product is intended. I shall call this, for want of a better phrase, the 'outward presentation' test. I adopt it for the following reasons. First, it provides an objective test, which is not dependent on proof of the internal cogitations of the manufacturer. The patient information leaflet is not just a public statement of the use for which the product is made, but one which is directly addressed to the potential user, ie to those persons whose acts are potentially within section 60(1)(c), namely importers, distributors, pharmacists and patients. Accordingly, it avoids the unacceptable anomalies associated with a test based on the manufacturer's subjective intention. Secondly, as the EPO has recognised, in a purpose-limited claim, the designated purpose is an inherent characteristic of the invention. The outward presentation test is consistent with this notion. A test based on intention is not. This is because the manufacturer's state of mind in exploiting the process is not a characteristic of the invention. It is a characteristic of the inventor, coming into being after (usually long after) the invention has been made and the patent granted. Likewise, the market conditions which may make some consequence of manufacture

objectively foreseeable are not a characteristic of the invention. They arise from subsequent facts. Third, the outward presentation test properly reflects the critical feature of Swiss-form patents, namely that the patent is for the process of manufacture, not for the subsequent use that may be made of the product. The physical presentation of the product is generally part of the process of manufacture. Subsequent activities of the manufacturer in marketing the product are not. Fourth, it provides legal certainty, in particular for those downstream of the manufacturer who deal in the product. Fifth, and critically, it strikes a fair balance between the public interest in rewarding the invention by allowing the patentee to exploit his monopoly and the public interest in the free use of the invention for therapeutic uses which do not have, or no longer have, patent protection. In my opinion, it satisfies all four policy objectives governing the interpretation of patent claims which I summarised at para 82 above. Finally, the outward presentation test derives some support from the case law of the EPO Technical Board of Appeal. The Board does not of course deal with infringement claims, but it has construed purpose-limited claims as referring to the purpose identified by reference to the characteristics of the product. In T 1673/11 *GENZYME/Treatment of Pompe's disease* [2016] EPOR 33, the patent claimed use of human acid alpha glucosidase in the manufacture of a medicament for the treatment of infantile Pompe's disease. In opposition proceedings, the Board (para 9.1) defined the scope of the claim as limited to

'the manufactured medicament which contains as an active substance human acid alpha glucosidase in the 100-110 kD form *and which is packaged and/or provided with instructions for use in the treatment of infantile Pompe's disease.*' (Emphasis added)

(85) 'Outward presentation' is a rough paraphrase of the German 'sinnfällige Herrichtung' which is the major part of the test of infringement applied to purpose-limited patent claims by the German courts: see Antivirusmittel (Case X ZR 51/86) (Bundesgerichthof, 16 June 1987), (1987) GRUR 794, at para 18; Chronische Hepatitis C – Behandlung/Ribavirin I (Case 4a O 145/12) (Landgericht Düsseldorf, 24 February 2004); Chronische Hepatitis C – Behandlung/ Ribavirin II (Case 4a O 145/12) (Landgericht Düsseldorf, 14 March 2013); Cistus Incanus (Case I-2 U 53/11) (Oberlandesgericht Düsseldorf, 31 January 2013). This is why Floyd LJ associated what he called the 'only packaging will do' test with German law. It is, however, important to guard against the over-ready transfer of concepts from one legal system to another, in which the legal context may be different. For the purpose of determining infringement, German law does not distinguish between product and process claims in the clear-cut way that the United Kingdom Patents Act does. In either case, the monopoly claimed may be treated as extending to the use made of the product after its manufacture: Patentgesetz, section 9 and Dexmedetomidin (Case I-2 U 30/17) (Oberlandesgericht Düsseldorf, 1 March 2018), (BeckRS 2018, 2410, at paras 41-43). Moreover, many of the anomalies considered above are avoided in German law by the limitation of monetary remedies for infringement to cases of deliberate or negligent infringement, although negligence will readily be assumed: Patentgesetz, section 139(2). This background explains why the German courts, while applying an objective test, have been prepared on appropriate facts to find infringement of purpose-limited claims on a wider basis than the mere presentation of the product: see Östrogenblocker (Case I-2 W 6/17) (Oberlandesgericht Düsseldorf, 5 May 2017) at para 39, and Dexmedetomidin (Case I-2 U 30/17) (Oberlandesgericht Düsseldorf, 1 March 2018) at para 44.

(86) However, whether or not it is soundly based on German law, Floyd LJ's objection to the 'only packaging will do' test deserves to be considered on its merits. His main point was that once it was accepted (as it was, by both parties before him) that there was a mental element in a purpose-limited claim, there was no reason to limit the evidence of the manufacturer's intention to the physical presentation of the product. As he pointed out (para 191), 'packaging may be a means of demonstrating the necessary mental element, whatever that is, but it cannot possibly be the only means of doing so.' I accept that there is force in this point, which is one reason why I reject the importation of a mental element in the claim. It falls away if the mental element is discarded. More pertinent is Floyd LJ's objection that an outward presentation test gives insufficient protection to the patentee. One can imagine circumstances

in which the labelling and the patient information leaflet of a generic manufacturer might be regarded as a charade. He might, for example, manufacture pregabalin with the intention of supplying an unexceptionable label and patient information leaflet but then encouraging dealers and pharmacists to supply it for the treatment of pain. To the extent that this is a realistic scenario, the outward presentation test may be imperfect. But I cannot regard the existence of such imperfections as decisive, for two reasons. In the first place, the patentee's interest, although important, is not the only consideration. As I have pointed out by reference to the Protocol on the interpretation of EPC Article 69, the interpretation of a claim requires the court to take account both the reasonable protection to which the patentee is entitled and the need for legal certainty for third parties. Broader policy objectives, including the public interest in the free exploitation of a product for a patent-expired use, are also relevant. This may involve, as it does in this case, a compromise between opposing and incommensurate factors. It may be thought anomalous that the manufacturer of the generic product should be free of liability if he markets it for a patent-protected use provided that he labels it as being for a non-protected use. But to my mind it is a far greater anomaly that in a 'charade' case the generic manufacturer's intention exposes to liability not just himself but any pharmacist who handles his product even if he scrupulously supplies it only for a non-protected use. Secondly, the imperfect nature of the protection conferred by an outward presentation test arises, as it seems to me, from a limitation inherent in a Swiss-form patent. A person's exposure to liability for infringement depends on the purpose for which the patent-protected product was manufactured. The patentee's protection is therefore necessarily incomplete. A test which treated the claim as extending to the promotion of the product after its manufacture appears on the face of it to ignore this limitation. There is no perfect solution to this problem in the absence of a general defence of good faith available to third parties, such as exists in Germany in the case of claims to monetary remedies. But we are not in a position to add such a defence to the UK Patents Act. I consider that the outward presentation test is less imperfect than any other. The evidence does not enable us to say how serious the problem identified by Floyd LJ really is. The legislation was not drafted with purpose-limited products in mind, and if it proves to be serious it must be for the legislature to address it.

### Indirect infringement: section 60(2)

(87) Warner-Lambert's alternative case of infringement, based on section 60(2) can be shortly dealt with. Section 60(2) is concerned with indirect infringement, ie with cases where a person incurs liability for infringement by knowingly supplying to a primary infringer the means of putting the invention into effect. There is a mental element in indirect infringement, for knowledge is expressly required. But it is unnecessary on this appeal to explore what that entails. Lecaent is manufactured by Balkanpharma in Bulgaria to the order of Actavis, which then imports and markets it in the United Kingdom. This case has proceeded at all levels on the basis that Actavis can be treated as if they were the manufacturer. The infringement case under section 60(2) is that, in supplying Lecaent in the United Kingdom, Actavis are knowingly 'supply[ing] in the United Kingdom a person … with … means, relating to an essential element of the invention, for putting the invention into effect'. The argument is that 'the invention' is the use of pregabalin to treat neuropathic pain, and that it is 'put into effect' when a pharmacist dispenses a pack of Lecaent against a prescription written by a doctor for neuropathic pain. Therefore by supplying Lecaent (directly or indirectly) to pharmacists Actavis supply them with the means for putting the invention into effect.

(88) The short answer to this is that the invention protected by Claim 3 is the manufacture of pregabalin for the designated use, and not the subsequent use of the product for treating patients. This is what the Court of Appeal decided, correctly in my view, in *Menashe Business Mercantile Ltd v William Hill Organisation Ltd* [2003] 1 WLR 1462: see para 24 (Aldous LJ). It was the ground on which the judge struck out the indirect infringement claim on the interlocutory application of Actavis. It was re-instated by the Court of Appeal as arguable.

At trial, Arnold J held that the argument was bad. In the Court of Appeal, Floyd LJ adhered to his earlier view. He accepted that *Menashe* was authority for the proposition that the 'invention' in section 60(2) was the process identified in the relevant claim. But he considered that the 'preparation' referred to in the claims might still not be put fully into effect until the pharmacist had dispensed the medicament and affixed a sticker with the patient's name on it. He warned against the danger of translating section 60(2) into infringement limited to acts upstream of manufacture. In my view Arnold J was right about this. The whole purpose of the Swiss-form for purpose-limited medical use claims is to avoid the problem of lack of novelty associated with product claims and the statutory provision which makes a method of treatment unpatentable. It is well understood that the degree of protection available from a Swiss-form claim may be more limited than that available from standard product claims. These essential features of purpose-limited patents are fatal to any attempt to construe Claim 3 as extending to steps taken by the pharmacist.'

# § 14
# European Unified Patent Court and Unitary Patent

## A. Introduction to the new European system[1]

The creation of the the Unified Patent Court (UPC) and the Unitary Patent heralds the beginning of a new era in patent law in Europe. The Agreement on a Unified Patent Court (UPCA) entered into force on 1 June 2023 when the new UPC finally began operations. The opening of the UPC also coincides with the introduction of a new 'Unitary Patent'. From now on, innovative companies will no longer have to apply for, maintain and, in the event of a dispute, enforce patents in court individually for all European Union Member States in order to protect their technical inventions. The new system provides a uniform court procedure with direct effect of the decisions for all participating EU Member States. 1

The Unified Patent Court (UPC) is an entirely new patent court for EU Member States, in which the UPCA is in force. 25 of the current 27 EU Member States participate in the so-called Enhanced Cooperation (Spain and Croatia have so far declined to participate). All states participating in the Enhanced Cooperation, with the exception of Poland, signed the UPCA on 19 February 2013 (hereinafter also referred to as 'contracting member states'). Of these 24 contracting member states, 17 have meanwhile ratified the UPCA and deposited their instrument. With the deposit of its ratification instrument by Germany on 17 February 2023, the new system entered into force as of 1 June 2023. After ratification of the UPCA by all contracting member states, there will be a total of 24 countries. The remaining EU Member States could still accede to the Agreement at any time. 2

The implementation of the reform is a particular example of successful European cooperation. The introduction of the unitary patent creates a new set of instruments from which innovative industry and especially small and medium-sized enterprises will benefit as they can save considerable effort and costs. All entities dealing with European patents, be they patent owners, licensees or technology research companies now need to take action. They need to weigh up the advantages and disadvantages of filing a request for unitary effect in respect of pending and future patent applications. 3

## B. Structure of the UPC

The Court's panels are multinational with a completely new judiciary to be appointed by the Administrative Committee. Since the UPC has to deal with both infringement and validity of a patent or SPC, the UPC comprises both legally and technically qualified judges.[2] So far, a total of 105 judges (34 legally qualified judges and 51 technically qualified 4

---

[1] Cf. Analysis by Stief/Röder-Hitschke, Einheitspatent und einheitliches Patentgericht – Vorstellung des neuen europaweiten Patent- und Gerichtssystems, PharmR 2022, 649.

[2] Cf. Augenstein, BeckOK Patentrecht, 31st edn, 15.1.2024, EPGÜ Art. 15 mn. 1-4.

judges) have been appointed by the UPC.[3] All appointed judges belong to a 'pool of judges', from which the panels of judges are filled in addition to the local legally qualified judges already assigned to the Local and Regional Divisions.

## I. The Court of First Instance

5 The UPC Court of First Instance comprises three different types of divisions – Central Division, Local Divisions and Regional Divisions – at different locations.[4]

### 1. Central Division

6 The Central Division has its seat in Paris and a division in Munich. Its panels are staffed multi-nationally with two legally qualified judges from different contracting Member States and one technically qualified judge from the pool of judges. This makes it very difficult to predict the composition of the respective panels. Cases heard by the Central Division are assigned according to the main classes of the International Patent Classification (IPC) Classification Code (see UPCA, Annex II). The Paris division is responsible for sections B, D, E, G, H and thus, among others, for e-tech cases, while the Munich division is responsible for section F (mechanical engineering, lighting, heating, weapons, blasting). The originally planned London division was supposed to be responsible in particular for the field of life science and thus also for pharmaceutical products (sections A and C). However, after the United Kingdom withdrew its ratification of the UPCA on 20 July 2020, the presidium of the UPC decided that actions pending before the Central Division related to patents in IPC section A shall be assigned to the seat in Milan while actions related to patents in IPC section C shall be assigned to the section in Munich.[5]

### 2. Local and Regional Divisions

7 The Local and Regional Divisions are generally composed of three legally qualified judges. A technically qualified judge may be called in at the request of one of the parties and must be called in if the division is also deciding on an annulment action. Although in principle also staffed on a multinational basis, the Local Divisions are nevertheless intended to enable and guarantee a local connection. Therefore, at least one, and possibly also a second judge from the country of the seat of the litigant(s) is assigned to them. The remaining judges are drawn from the pool of judges.

8 Each contracting member state may apply for one to a maximum of four[6] Local Divisions or, together with one or more other contracting member states, for a Regional Division. The establishment of the divisions as well as the respective number of legally qualified local judges was decided by the Administrative Committee of the UPC as follows:[7]

---

[3] For the complete list, see 'Unified Patent Court judicial appointments and Presidium elections' under <https://www.unified-patent-court.org/en/news/unified-patent-court-judicial-appointments-and-presidium-elections> (last accessed 23 April 2024).

[4] Cf. Schoenen in: Hasselblatt, MAH Gewerblicher Rechtschutz, § 36 Europäisches Patentrecht mn. 270 et seq.

[5] Cf. https://www.unified-patent-court.org/sites/default/files/upc_documents/decision-d_ac_03_26062023_-amendment-upca.pdf (last accessed 23 April 2024) and Augenstein, BeckOK Patentrecht, 31st edn, 15.1.2024, EPGÜ Art. 7 mn. 1-11.

[6] Depending on the number of patent proceedings initiated in the respective country per year: one additional Local Division per 100 proceedings, Art. 7(4) UPCA.

[7] Decision of 8 July 2022, document AC/13/08072022_D.

Local divisions: Austria: Vienna (1); Belgium: Brussels (1); Denmark: Copenhagen (1); Finland: Helsinki (1); France: Paris (2); Germany: Düsseldorf (2), Hamburg (2), Mannheim (2), Munich (2); Italy: Milan (2); Portugal: Lisbon (1); Slovenia: Ljubljana (1); Netherlands: The Hague (2). **9**

Regional Division for the Nordic-Baltic region (Sweden, Estonia, Latvia, Lithuania): Stockholm (2). **10**

The panels of the Local Divisions of the most active patent litigation countries to date, namely France, Italy, the Netherlands and especially Germany, will each be staffed with two experienced local judges. It is hoped that this will have a positive influence on the popularity and good reputation of these Local Divisions from whom litigants expect high-quality decisions. **11**

## II. Court of Appeal

The Court of Appeal is the sole appellate court; a further appeal on point of law is not possible. Only on questions of interpretation of applicable EU law can the Court of Justice of the European Union (CJEU) be called upon as a 'further instance' in preliminary ruling proceedings. Appeals may be lodged against disputed final decisions (comparable to an appeal under German law), but also against procedural decisions (also comparable to an appeal under German law). **12**

An appeal against a final decision may be lodged by any party who has been unsuccessful in whole or in part within two months of notification of the decision and must be substantiated within four months. It has no suspensive effect, and the procedure is in principle comparable to the first instance procedure. The appeal must be filed within three months; the *Rules of Procedure* do not provide for any further deadlines.[8] **13**

The panels of the Court of Appeal are multinational with three legally qualified judges from different contracting Member States and two technically qualified judges from the pool of judges. The language of the proceedings of the appellate instance is usually that of the first instance or, by agreement between the parties, the language of the grant of the patent; further exceptions are possible (Article 50 UPCA). **14**

# C. Jurisdiction

The UPC has exclusive jurisdiction not only for future unitary patents (a new legal title created by EU Regulation No. 1257/2012, enjoying a unitary effect throughout the Enhanced Cooperation territory) but also for all 'classic' European bundle patents, European patent applications and SPCs based thereon. Its jurisdiction does not extend to national IP rights. Article 32 UPCA conclusively lists the types of actions and proceedings that are admissible before the UPC.[9] **15**

The local jurisdiction of the Divisions of the Court of First Instance essentially depends on the type of action: infringement actions, summary proceedings, actions for damages **16**

---

[8] Cf. Schoenen in: Hasselblatt, Munchener Anwaltshandbuch Gewerblicher Rechtsschutz, 6th edn, Munich 2022, § 36 Europaisches Patentrecht mn. 293.

[9] → mn. 41. Note: actions for vindication and actions based on a licence agreement, e.g. for payment of a licence fee, are not included and must still be brought before the national courts; cf. Tochtermann in Benkard, PatG, 12th edn, Munich 2023, PatG, vor § 1 mn. 170 et seq.

or compensation or in connection with rights of prior use are to be brought before the respective Local/Regional Division depending on the place of the offence, i.e. the place of the actual or threatened infringement, or at the defendant's place of residence or place of business.[10] If the defendant's place of residence is outside the contracting Member States, the Central Division is also available as an alternative to the place of infringement. In this respect, the plaintiff is to a certain extent able to engage in 'forum shopping'.[11] If no Local or Regional Division is maintained in the country of the offence or seat, the above-mentioned actions must always be filed with the Central Division.

17 Actions for a declaration of non-infringement[12] as well as isolated nullity actions must always be filed with the Central Division. What is new and noteworthy is that the isolated nullity action, unlike the nullity action before the German Federal Patent Court, can be filed independently of an opposition before the EPO. Also, the UPC is not obliged to suspend this nullity action until the conclusion of the opposition proceedings ('overtaking nullity action').

18 If an infringement action is already pending before a Local or Regional Division, invalidity can only be asserted by way of a counterclaim.[13] The UPCA permits (and requires) the raising of objections against the patent-in-suit in the context of an invalidity counterclaim in ongoing infringement proceedings; mere objections to the body of law are irrelevant. The Division before which the infringement action is pending is competent. If this is not the Central Division, but a Local or Regional Division, this Division, after hearing the parties, has three options for further proceedings. It can (i) deal with the invalidity counterclaim itself with the mandatory assistance of a technically qualified judge or (ii) hand it over to the Central Division (with or without suspension of the infringement dispute) ('bifurcation') or (iii) refer the entire legal dispute to the Central Division.[14]

19 During a transitional period of seven years from the entry into force of the UPCA, the applicant/holder of European patents (and SPCs based thereon) has the right to 'opt out' from this automatic competence of the UPC. As an independent court, the UPC initially takes its place alongside the national courts, which continue to deal with both infringement and invalidity of the national part of an EP for their respective national jurisdiction.

20 Under the new system, once a European patent has been granted by the European Patent Office (EPO), it can, at the request of the patent proprietor, be declared a '*Unitary Patent*' for the participating contracting member states. This means that the entire territory of these states is covered by only one patent, renewal fees are only payable for this one patent and both infringement and invalidity of this patent are judged with uniform effect for all contracting member states by the exclusively responsible UPC. In this scenario, the European patent offers in future combined protection from the unitary patent with unitary effect in the contracting member states and the 'bundle' of conventional national parts of the EP in all other EPC contracting states in which it has been validated.

21 The legal framework for the new patent and court system is essentially set by the following legal sources: the Unitary Patent Regulation (EU) No. 1257/2012 is the basic substantive legal source for the unitary patent. It is supplemented (amongst others) by Regulation (EU) No. 1260/2012 regarding applicable translation arrangements, the Rules relating to Unitary Patent Protection and the Rules relating to Fees for Unitary Patent

---

[10] Cf. Article 33(1) UPCA.

[11] Cf. for more details on this: Schröer, Einheitspatentgericht – Überlegungen zum Forum-Shopping im Rahmen der alternativen Zuständigkeit nach Art. 83 Abs. 1 EPGÜ, GRUR Int. 2013, 1102.

[12] However, this is suspended if an infringement action is brought before a Local/Regional Division within three months of receipt of the negative declaratory action, Article 33(6) UPCA.

[13] Cf. Rule 61 of the Rules of Procedure of the Unified Patent Court.

[14] Cf. Schoenen in: Hasselblatt, Munchener Anwaltshandbuch Gewerblicher Rechtsschutz, 6th edn, Munich 2022, § 36 Europaisches Patentrecht mn. 290.

protection. As an international treaty, the UPCA contains comprehensive regulations on the structure and functioning of the EPC, but also substantive and procedural regulations. In addition, there are the Rules of Procedure, which serve to implement the UPCA, the Rules of Court and the EPC.

The UPC presents with no doubt an opportunity for the harmonisation of case law regarding skinny labelling and second medical indication patents amongst the contracting UPC states and – if the CJEU delivers a relevant preliminary ruling – possibly within the EU. 22

This raises the question what relevance the legal traditions of the UPC contracting member states will play for the interpretation of direct and indirect infringement under Articles 25 and 26 UPCA by the UPC.[15] It is safe to assume that skinny labelling may ultimately land before the CJEU for a preliminary ruling, although the drafters of the UPCA silently intended to circumvent the CJEU's jurisdiction on matters of substantive patent law.[16] The CJEU's jurisdiction could be based on the general primacy of EU law echoed by Article 20 UPCA and the fact that the practice of skinny labelling can be based on EU legislation such as Article 11(2) of Directive 2001/83/EC (→ mn. 42) and Article 3(3)(b) Regulation No. 726/2004 (→ mn. 43).[17] Others may however interpret that these provisions of EU law, which just relate to regulatory requirements for the obtaining of a market authorisation (namely, the information that must be included in the Summary of Product Characteristics), can hardly be a sufficient basis for a finding by the CJEU on questions of patent infringement, as it is at least not immediately apparent how a national legislation or case law on patent infringement could conflict with those EU regulatory requirements. 23

## D. Direct and indirect infringement under the UPC

Articles 25 and 26 UPCA regulate the direct and indirect infringement of a patent. Based on these provisions, the UPC will decide whether and on what conditions the practice of skinny labelling infringes a second-medical-use patent: 24

**Article 25 – Right to prevent the direct use of the invention**

A patent shall confer on its proprietor the right to prevent any third party not having the proprietor's consent from the following:

(a) making, offering, placing on the market or using a product which is the subject matter of the patent, or importing or storing the product for those purposes;

(b) using a process which is the subject matter of the patent or, where the third party knows, or should have known, that the use of the process is prohibited without the consent of the patent proprietor, offering the process for use within the territory of the Contracting Member States in which that patent has effect;

(c) offering, placing on the market, using, or importing or storing for those purposes a product obtained directly by a process which is the subject matter of the patent.

[15] Cf. Sonntag in Bopp/Kircher, Handbuch Europäischer Patentprozess, 2nd edn, Munich 2023, § 13 Verletzungsklage mn. 150 et seq.

[16] Cf. Haedicke/Timmann, PatR-HdB, 2nd edn, Munich 2020, § 1. Einführung, mn. 62 et seq.

[17] Cf. Cuonzo/Ampollini, Generic Medicines and Second Medical Use Patents: Litigation or Regulation? An Overview of Recent European Case Law and Practice, IIC 2018, 895 (897).

**Article 26 – Right to prevent the indirect use of the invention**

(1) A patent shall confer on its proprietor the right to prevent any third party not having the proprietor's consent from supplying or offering to supply, within the territory of the Contracting Member States in which that patent has effect, any person other than a party entitled to exploit the patented invention, with means, relating to an essential element of that invention, for putting it into effect therein, when the third party knows, or should have known, that those means are suitable and intended for putting that invention into effect.

(2) Para. 1 shall not apply when the means are staple commercial products, except where the third party induces the person supplied to perform any of the acts prohibited by Article 25.

(3) Persons performing the acts referred to in Article 27(a) to (e) shall not be considered to be parties entitled to exploit the invention within the meaning of para. 1.

## E. Applicable law regarding infringement of second-medical-use patents and cross-label-use

25 To predict how the UPC will possibly decide on second medical use patents and the skinny labelling practice, one must first determine which law is applicable. Article 20 UPCA stresses the primacy of EU law and requires that the UPC applies it in its entirety (→ mn. 36). Article 24(1) UPCA reaffirms this and further enlists other sources of law, while setting Union law (including the Unitary Patent Regulation (EU) No. 1257/2012) on top of the hierarchy (lit.a) (→ mn. 37). Amongst the legal sources enlisted in Article 24(1) UPCA, such as the UPCA (b), the EPC (c) and other international treaties applicable to patents and binding on all the Contracting Member States (d) like the TRIPS Agreement and the PCT, 'national law' is mentioned in lit.e. To determine which national law is applicable, Article 24(2)(b) UPCA refers to 'directly applicable provisions of Union law containing private international law rules'. Regarding European patents with unitary effect, such a rule can be found in Articles 5(3) and 7 Unitary Patent Regulation.[18]

26 Article 7 Unitary Patent Regulation (→ mn. 45), which Article 5(3) regarding infringement of the unitary patent refers to, determines the applicable national law according to the seat of the applicant, and when the applicant is not seated in a UPC contracting state, on the seat of the European Patent Organisation, thus German law is applicable in the latter case.[19] In both cases, however, the UPC contracting states have incorporated Article 25 et seq. UPCA in their legal regime. In principle, Article 25 et seq. UPCA regulate the unitary scope of protection and its limitations exhaustively, thus there is little room for the application of national law.[20] However, there is an exception for the right of prior use according to Article 28 UPCA.[21] Regarding European patents (with no unitary effect) that fall under the jurisdiction of the UPC (no opt-out), a conflict-of-laws rule within the meaning of Article 24(2)(a) is found in Article 8(1) Rome II Regulation that renders *lex*

---

[18] Drexl in Münchener Kommentar zum Bürgerlichen Gesetzbuch: BGB (MüKo BGB) Bd. 13, 8th edn, Munich 2021, Rom II-VO Art. 8 mn. 153; Müller-Stoy/Paschold, Europäisches Patent mit einheitlicher Wirkung als Recht des Vermögens, GRUR Int. 2014, 646 (649); Nieder, Vindikation europäischer Patente unter Geltung der EPatVO, GRUR 2015, 936.

[19] Cf. Osterrieth, Patentrecht, 6th edn, Munich 2021, mn. 208.

[20] Drexl in Münchener Kommentar zum Bürgerlichen Gesetzbuch: BGB (MüKo BGB) Bd. 13, 8th edn, Munich 2021, Rom II-VO Art. 8 mn. 153; Augenstein in: BeckOK PatR, 32nd edn, 15.4.2024, EPGÜ Art. 24 mn. 7.

[21] Ann, Patentrecht, 8th edn, Munich 2022, § 30a, Europäisches Patent mit einheitlicher Wirkung und Einheitliches Patentgericht mn. 35.

*loci protectionis* applicable (→ mn. 46).[22] In this case, the national law of the state where protection is sought is applicable. For example, if protection for a European patent is sought in a UPC contracting member state, Article 25 et seq. of the UPCA would equally apply. Regarding skinny labelling in the context of second medical indication patents, direct and indirect infringement are exhaustively regulated in Articles 25 and 26 UPCA, respectively, so that even if national law was indirectly applicable, which is not the case, it could only have marginal importance.[23] However, one could argue that the applicable law and its relevant jurisprudence could influence how the UPCA provisions are interpreted.[24]

For example, a generics company infringes in France a second-medical-indication unitary patent of a patent owner who is based in Germany: in this case, Articles 7 and 5(3) Unitary Patent Regulation renders German law applicable if the patentee had its residence or principal place of business in Germany on the date of filing of the application for the European patent. German law has incorporated Articles 25 and 26 in its national jurisdiction. Does this mean that the German case law regarding skinny-labelling considering e.g. the mandatory substitution practice according to § 129(1) SGB V (Social Code, Book V) has to be applied?[25] Not necessarily. In a case of an infringement taking place in France, the concrete circumstances of the case must be taken into account to establish both the subjective and objective elements of infringement. As such, the circumstances regarding the treatment of skinny label in the French public healthcare system would be relevant despite German law being in principle applicable. The case could notably become more complex in cross-border infringement cases. 27

The new European patent system generally exists as a comprehensive and autonomous legal system that is basically independent of the national law of the UPC contracting member states. Even those provisions which expressly refer to national law (Article 7(1) Unitary Patent Regulation, Article 28 UPCA) have only complementary relevance. However, one can predict that local and regional chambers will not turn a blind eye to their own legal tradition.[26] *Haedicke* argues that the UPC consisting of various first instance local and regional chambers should take into account the relevant legal traditions of all UPC contracting member states.[27] In *Haedicke's* opinion, the UPC should employ means of comparative interpretation while autonomously developing the unitary patent system on the basis of the unitary patent law package as enlisted by Article 24(1) UPCA.[28] As he rightly points out, 'Union law cannot look back on a tradition in patent law from which it could develop further'.[29] In contrast to this, *Osterrieth* argues that previous national case law can only be 'a source of inspiration, but not an authoritative, further legal basis 28

---

[22] Augenstein in BeckOK PatR, 32nd edn, 15.4.2024, EPGÜ Art. 24 mn. 5. It is also supported that Article 8(2) Rome II Regulation determines the applicable national law for European patents with unitary effect, thus the applicable law in this case should be the law of the state where the infringing act has taken place (Cf. Augenstein at mn. 6). However, Art. 8(2) Rome II Regulation only applies 'for any question that is not governed by the relevant Community instrument'. In this case, Article 7 Unitary Patent Regulation provides for an exhaustive conflict-of-laws rule, so that Article 8(2) Rome II Regulation is not applicable.

[23] Cf. Ullrich, Patent Dependency under European and European Union Patent Law – A Regulatory Gap, GRUR Int. 2023, 1107 (1108).

[24] Smielick in Hasselblatt, Münchener Anwaltshandbuch Gewerblicher Rechtsschutz, 6th edn, Munich 2022, § 36 Europäisches Patentrecht mn. 248.

[25] Cf. Schacht, Objektive Eignung und finales Element, GRUR 2022, 1017 (1018–1019).

[26] Augenstein in BeckOK PatR, 32nd edn, 15.4.2024, EPGÜ Art. 24 mn. 2 et seq.

[27] Haedicke, Rechtsfindung, Rechtsfortbildung und Rechtskontrolle im Einheitlichen Patentsystem, GRUR Int 2013, 609 (611).

[28] ibid., 611.

[29] ibid., 614: 'Das Unionsrecht kann im Patentrecht auf keine Tradition zurückblicken, aus der es sich weiterentwickeln könnte.': 'In the field of patent law, Union law cannot look back on any tradition from which it could develop further.'

for future decisions of the European Patent Court'.[30] *Haedicke* also stresses that the UPC should use its own autonomous legal regime as its main reference when using comparative interpretation.[31] Considering the above, it is safe to assume that the UPC will have to form but not reinvent its own autonomous understanding regarding the legality of skinny labelling. Practically, this would inevitably reflect a synthesis of previous European jurisprudence.[32]

## F. Skinny label under UPC: a delicate balance

29 However, even if a common legal approach is possible, the concrete circumstances of infringement must be determined specifically for all the countries where allegedly infringing acts take place. *England*[33] rejects in this regard a one-size-fits-all approach, as the UPC will have to calculate damages and apportion costs accordingly. *England*[34] provides some practical guidance for generics manufacturers that may characterise a unified approach to the infringement of second-medical-use claims under the UPC:

1. make it clear during the tendering process, and in any resulting supply agreement, that the generic supplied is only to be used for non-patented purposes, and
2. cooperate with healthcare providers by supplying as much information as possible to enable them, where permitted by national rules, to issue the appropriate guidance on prescribing for doctors and dispensing for pharmacists.

30 The skinny label practice under UPC undoubtedly presents a daunting task for the newly established court as it should find a common denominator between diverging national jurisdictions and settle conflicting interests between originators and generics manufacturers, thereby exerting a political impact on the various public healthcare systems of the contracting UPC states. Allowing the evolution of different standards may risk the demarcation of the scope of protection contrary to the UPC's fundamental aim to foster the integration of the EU internal market.[35]

## G. Procedure and duration of proceedings

31 Proceedings before the UPC are essentially conducted according to the Rules of Procedure of the United Patent Court. To ensure fast and efficient processing, the first instance proceedings are tightly structured and stick to a rigid time frame. Proceedings are divided into three parts (written proceedings, interlocutory proceedings, oral proceedings) to be completed within one year in the 'basic case' (infringement/non-infringement

---

[30] Osterrieth, Patentrecht, 6th edn, Munich 2021, mn. 319–321.

[31] Haedicke, "Rechtsfindung, Rechtsfortbildung und Rechtskontrolle im Einheitlichen Patentsystem', GRUR Int 2013, 609 (611).

[32] Cf. England, Infringement of second medical use patents in Europe and the UPC', GRUR Int. 2016, 714(719): 'The UPC must therefore make its own way, drawing such guidance from national models.'

[33] ibid., 720.

[34] ibid.

[35] Cf. Preamble to UPCA.

proceedings without counterclaims).[36] As far as possible, pleadings are to be submitted electronically.

32 For example, in infringement actions, the parties usually exchange two written pleadings each in the written procedure (a statement of claim or a statement of defence which may include a counterclaim for revocation and a reply to the statement of defence or rejoinder to the reply by the defendant), which takes five to nine months depending on the case. The very short deadlines, which can only be extended in exceptional cases, will be a challenge for the parties and their representatives. If a request for revocation has been filed, the panel will decide on the further handling of the case ('bifurcation') at the end of the written procedure. Both the written proceedings and the interim proceedings, which usually take three months, are conducted by the reporting judge.[37] In the interim proceedings, the reporting Judge prepares the oral proceedings, clarifies any existing ambiguities with the parties, if necessary in the context of an interim conference, and schedules the oral proceedings with at least two months' notice. In the final stage, the presiding Judge takes over the management of the proceedings and, after the public oral hearing has (ideally) been completed within one day, the written judgment issues within six weeks.

33 The UPC may also issue interim injunctions to prevent an imminent infringement or stop an existing infringement (Article 62 UPCA). The order is issued after conducting a two-step (written and oral) summary procedure.[38] In justified cases, interim measures may also be issued *ex parte*. Unfortunately, neither the UPCA nor the Rules of Procedure make any specific statements on the duration of proceedings. Especially in the initial period of the new court, it seems likely that the national courts, which are already well tried and tested in this respect, will act comparatively faster in preliminary injunction proceedings.

34 Potential addressees of an urgent application can file a protective brief in the language of the patent. As already known from e.g. the German procedure, the protective brief will be kept in the court's custody for six months and can be extended upon request.

35 Interim measures are to be revoked at the request of the defendant if the applicant does not initiate proceedings on the merits before the UPC within 31 calendar days or 20 working days.

# H. Statutory provisions

## I. Agreement on a Unified Patent Court (UPCA)

### Article 20 – Primacy of and respect for Union law 36

The Court shall apply Union law in its entirety and shall respect its primacy.

### Article 24 – Sources of law 37

1. In full compliance with Article 20, when hearing a case brought before it under this Agreement, the Court shall base its decisions on:
   (a) Union law, including Regulation (EU) No 1257/2012 and Regulation (EU) No 1260/2012;

---

[36] Cf. Tochtermann in: Benkard, PatG, 12th edn, Munich 2023, PatG, vor § 1 mn. 188.

[37] Cf. Grabinski, Der Entwurf der Verfahrensordnung für das Einheitliche Patentgericht im Überblick, GRUR Int 2013, 310 (312 et seq).

[38] See Rules 205 to 213 of the Constitution.

(b) this Agreement;
(c) the EPC;
(d) other international agreements applicable to patents and binding on all the Contracting Member States; and
(e) national law.

2. To the extent that the Court shall base its decisions on national law, including where relevant the law of non contracting States, the applicable law shall be determined:
   (a) by directly applicable provisions of Union law containing private international law rules, or
   (b) in the absence of directly applicable provisions of Union law or where the latter do not apply, by international instruments containing private international law rules; or
   (c) in the absence of provisions referred to in points (a) and (b), by national provisions on private international law as determined by the Court.
3. The law of non-contracting States shall apply when designated by application of the rules referred to in paragraph 2, in particular in relation to Articles 25 to 28, 54, 55, 64, 68 and 72.

38 **Article 25 – Right to prevent the direct use of the invention**

A patent shall confer on its proprietor the right to prevent any third party not having the proprietor's consent from the following:

(a) making, offering, placing on the market or using a product which is the subject-matter of the patent, or importing or storing the product for those purposes;
(b) using a process which is the subject-matter of the patent or, where the third party knows, or should have known, that the use of the process is prohibited without the consent of the patent proprietor, offering the process for use within the territory of the Contracting Member States in which that patent has effect;
(c) offering, placing on the market, using, or importing or storing for those purposes a product obtained directly by a process which is the subject-matter of the patent.

39 **Article 26 – Right to prevent the indirect use of the invention**

1. A patent shall confer on its proprietor the right to prevent any third party not having the proprietor's consent from supplying or offering to supply, within the territory of the Contracting Member States in which that patent has effect, any person other than a party entitled to exploit the patented invention, with means, relating to an essential element of that invention, for putting it into effect therein, when the third party knows, or should have known, that those means are suitable and intended for putting that invention into effect.
2. Paragraph 1 shall not apply when the means are staple commercial products, except where the third party induces the person supplied to perform any of the acts prohibited by Article 25.
3. Persons performing the acts referred to in Article 27(a) to (e) shall not be considered to be parties entitled to exploit the invention within the meaning of paragraph 1.

40 **Article 28 – Right based on prior use of the invention**

Any person, who, if a national patent had been granted in respect of an invention, would have had, in a Contracting Member State, a right based on prior use of that invention or a right of personal possession of that invention, shall enjoy, in that Contracting Member State, the same rights in respect of a patent for the same invention.

41 **Article 32 – Competence of the Court**

1. The Court shall have exclusive competence in respect of:
   (a) actions for actual or threatened infringements of patents and supplementary protection certificates and related defences, including counterclaims concerning licences;

(b) actions for declarations of non-infringement of patents and supplementary protection certificates;
(c) actions for provisional and protective measures and injunctions;
(d) actions for revocation of patents and for declaration of invalidity of supplementary protection certificates;
(e) counterclaims for revocation of patents and for declaration of invalidity of supplementary protection certificates;
(f) actions for damages or compensation derived from the provisional protection conferred by a published European patent application;
(g) actions relating to the use of the invention prior to the granting of the patent or to the right based on prior use of the invention;
(h) actions for compensation for licences on the basis of Article 8 of Regulation (EU) No 1257/2012; and
(i) actions concerning decisions of the European Patent Office in carrying out the tasks referred to in Article 9 of Regulation (EU) No 1257/2012.

2. The national courts of the Contracting Member States shall remain competent for actions relating to patents and supplementary protection certificates which do not come within the exclusive competence of the Court.

## II. Directive 2001/83/EC

### Article 11 42

The summary of the product characteristics shall contain the following information:

1. Name of the medicinal product.
2. Qualitative and quantitative composition in terms of the active substances and constituents of the excipient, knowledge of which is essential for proper administration of the medicinal product. The usual common name or chemical description shall be used.
3. Pharmaceutical form.
4. Pharmacological properties and, in so far as this information is useful for therapeutic purposes, pharmacokinetic particulars.
5. Clinical particulars:
   5.1. therapeutic indications,
   5.2. contra-indications,
   5.3. adverse reactions (frequency and seriousness),
   5.4. special precautions for use and, in the case of immunological medicinal products, any special precautions to be taken by persons handling such products and administering them to patients, together with any precautions to be taken by the patient,
   5.5. use during pregnancy and lactation,
   5.6. interaction with other medicaments and other forms of interaction,
   5.7. posology and method of administration for adults and, where necessary, for children,
   5.8. overdose (symptoms, emergency procedures, antidotes),
   5.9. special warnings,
   5.10. effects on ability to drive and to use machines.
6. Pharmaceutical particulars:
   6.1. major incompatibilities,
   6.2. shelf life, when necessary after reconstitution of the medicinal product or when the immediate packaging is opened for the first time,
   6.3. special precautions for storage,
   6.4. nature and contents of the immediate packaging,
   6.5. special precautions for disposal of unused medicinal products or waste materials derived from such medicinal products, if appropriate.

7. Name or corporate name and permanent address of the marketing authorization holder.
8. For radiopharmaceuticals, full details of internal radiation dosimetry.
9. For radiopharmaceuticals, additional detailed instructions for extemporaneous preparation and quality control of such preparation and, where appropriate, maximum storage time during which any intermediate preparation such as an eluate or the ready-to-use pharmaceutical will conform with its specifications.

## III. Regulation No. 726/2004

43

### Article 3

1. No medicinal product appearing in the Annex may be placed on the market within the Community unless a marketing authorisation has been granted by the Community in accordance with the provisions of this Regulation.
2. Any medicinal product not appearing in the Annex may be granted a marketing authorisation by the Community in accordance with the provisions of this Regulation, if:
   (a) the medicinal product contains a new active substance which, on the date of entry into force of this Regulation, was not authorised in the Community; or
   (b) the applicant shows that the medicinal product constitutes a significant therapeutic, scientific or technical innovation or that the granting of authorisation in accordance with this Regulation is in the interests of patients or animal health at Community level.

   Immunological veterinary medicinal products for the treatment of animal diseases that are subject to Community prophylactic measures may also be granted such authorisation.
3. A generic medicinal product of a reference medicinal product authorised by the Community may be authorised by the competent authorities of the Member States in accordance with Directive 2001/83/EC and Directive 2001/82/EC under the following conditions:
   (a) the application for authorisation is submitted in accordance with Article 10 of Directive 2001/83/EC or Article 13 of Directive 2001/82/EC;
   (b) the summary of the product characteristics is in all relevant respects consistent with that of the medicinal product authorised by the Community except for those parts of the summary of product characteristics referring to indications or dosage forms which were still covered by patent law at the time when the generic medicine was marketed; and
   (c) the generic medicinal product is authorised under the same name in all the Member States where the application has been made. For the purposes of this provision, all the linguistic versions of the INN (international non-proprietary name) shall be considered to be the same name.
4. After the competent committee of the Agency has been consulted, the Commission may adapt the Annex to technical and scientific progress and may adopt any necessary amendments without extending the scope of the centralised procedure. Those measures, designed to amend non-essential elements of this Regulation, shall be adopted in accordance with the regulatory procedure with scrutiny referred to in Article 87(2a).

## IV. Regulation (EU) No. 1257/2012 (Unitary Patent Regulation)

44

### Article 5 – Uniform protection

1. The European patent with unitary effect shall confer on its proprietor the right to prevent any third party from committing acts against which that patent provides protection throughout the territories of the participating Member States in which it has unitary effect, subject to applicable limitations.

2. The scope of that right and its limitations shall be uniform in all participating Member States in which the patent has unitary effect.
3. The acts against which the patent provides protection referred to in paragraph 1 and the applicable limitations shall be those defined by the law applied to European patents with unitary effect in the participating Member State whose national law is applicable to the European patent with unitary effect as an object of property in accordance with Article 7.
4. In its report referred to in Article 16(1), the Commission shall evaluate the functioning of the applicable limitations and shall, where necessary, make appropriate proposals.

**Article 7 – Treating a European patent with unitary effect as a national patent** **45**

1. A European patent with unitary effect as an object of property shall be treated in its entirety and in all the partici pating Member States as a national patent of the participating Member State in which that patent has unitary effect and in which, according to the European Patent Register:
   (a) the applicant had his residence or principal place of business on the date of filing of the application for the European patent; or
   (b) where point (a) does not apply, the applicant had a place of business on the date of filing of the application for the European patent.
2. Where two or more persons are entered in the European Patent Register as joint applicants, point (a) of paragraph 1 shall apply to the joint applicant indicated first. Where this is not possible, point (a) of paragraph 1 shall apply to the next joint applicant indicated in the order of entry. Where point (a) of paragraph 1 does not apply to any of the joint applicants, point (b) of paragraph 1 shall apply accordingly.
3. Where no applicant had his residence, principal place of business or place of business in a participating Member State in which that patent has unitary effect for the purposes of paragraphs 1 or 2, the European patent with unitary effect as an object of property shall be treated in its entirety and in all the participating Member States as a national patent of the State where the European Patent Organisation has its headquarters in accordance with Article 6(1) of the EPC.
4. The acquisition of a right may not be dependent on any entry in a national patent register.

## V. Regulation (EC) No. 864/2007 (Rome II)

**Article 8 – Infringement of intellectual property rights** **46**

1. The law applicable to a non-contractual obligation arising from an infringement of an intellectual property right shall be the law of the country for which protection is claimed.
2. In the case of a non-contractual obligation arising from an infringement of a unitary Community intellectual property right, the law applicable shall, for any question that is not governed by the relevant Community instrument, be the law of the country in which the act of infringement was committed.
3. The law applicable under this Article may not be derogated from by an agreement pursuant to Article 14.

# J. Extracts from court decisions

No applicable case law. **47**

# PART II
# UNITED STATES OF AMERICA

## § 15
## United States of America

### A. Introduction and executive summary

As of 2020, the median cost to develop a novel pharmaceutical agent was estimated to be about US$ 985 million.[1] While some 'blockbuster' drugs rapidly earn that investment back, drugs directed to disease indications having smaller patient populations may take longer to provide a return on a pharma company's investment. In an effort to combat slow return or to expand market share for blockbusters, pharma companies often work to identify, patent, and obtain approval for second (and sometimes third and fourth) uses for their already approved medicines. These so-called second medical uses provide an opportunity for pharma companies to expand their revenue without the extreme cost and uncertainty associated with developing a new Active Pharmaceutical Ingredient (API) from scratch. 1

Nevertheless, obtaining approval from the FDA for new indications for previously approved actives is not without risks for branded pharma companies, particularly when the patents protecting the original indication will expire well before the patents for the second indication. Early expiration of the patents covering the original indication provides generic companies with an opportunity to avoid the patents for the approved second indication via 'skinny labeling.' Skinny labeling, also referred to as a 'section viii carve-out,' involves omitting the patented indication from the generic's label and seeking approval from the FDA only for the original indication that is no longer patent protected. 2

Although skinny labeling offers generics an opportunity to avoid infringing branded pharma's patents, generic entrants must exercise caution to be certain that their product label appropriately removes all instructive language that could potentially be viewed as inducing infringement of a branded company's method of treatment patents directed to the second approved indication. Likewise, recent rulings from the Federal Circuit have raised questions about what actions a generic can take once it has excised patented indications from its label. 3

Skinny labeling may also provide opportunities for biosimilar entrants, but the statutory regime governing biosimilars differs significantly from the statutory regime governing small molecules. Although the general framework for skinny labeling is the same for biologic products as for small-molecule drugs, differences in how biologic drugs are approved and marketed may create increased opportunities for induced infringement in the context of biologic drugs, even when a given indication has been carved out of the label. But the legal landscape for biosimilars is largely unlitigated; therefore, whether the 4

[1] Wouters/McKee/Luyten, Estimated Research and Development Investment Needed to Bring a New Medicine to Market, 2009-2018, JAMA 2020, 844–853.

marketing of biosimilars will in fact result in an increased risk of infringement liability remains to be seen.

## B. Scope of protection and interpretation of second medical use claims

### I. Legislative background and statutory framework

5 Unlike in Europe, the U.S. patent statute explicitly permits claims to methods of treating a disease or condition in a human.[2] Accordingly, it is permissible in U.S. patent practice to directly claim a method of treating a disease or condition and it is not necessary, or permissible, to employ the 'use' construction commonly used throughout the rest of the world (i.e. 'use of compound X for treating disease Y'). Method of treatment claims are typically filed concurrently with compound and composition claims. But method of treatment claims, particularly claims to new uses of old compounds, can be filed at any time, including well after the expiration of patents directed to the original API and its formulations. And just as with any other purported invention, these new method of treatment claims must meet the requirements of 35 U.S.C. §§ 101, 102, 103, and 112.

### II. Abbreviated new drug applications, the section viii carve-out, and skinny labeling

#### 1. The Hatch-Waxman Act and abbreviated new drug applications

6 The 'Drug Price Competition and Patent Term Restoration Act of 1984' (Pub. L. 98-417) – a more commonly known as the 'Hatch-Waxman Act,' in honor of its principal sponsors in Congress – provides the statutory framework for generic drug competition in the United States. Generic applicants can file an Abbreviated New Drug Application (ANDA), which allows them to rely on the safety and efficacy data of the branded drug, thereby avoiding the need to repeat expensive clinical trials to demonstrate the safety and efficacy of their proposed generic drug products.[3] Instead, an ANDA applicant must generally show that its proposed drug product will be 'bioequivalent' to the branded drug, meaning that there is no significant difference in the rate and extent to which the active ingredient becomes available at the site of drug action.[4]

7 Innovator companies with patents that cover a drug, formulations comprising the drug, or use of either the drug itself or its formulation for treating a particular disease or condition, can list those patents in the FDA's 'Orange Book,' which is formally entitled *Approved Drug Products with Therapeutic Equivalence Evaluations*. The Orange Book[5] contains, among other things, a list of patents the branded company would consider infringed if the generic product were marketed before the expiration date of the listed

[2] See 35 U.S.C. §§ 101 (permitting patents for any 'new and useful process' and any 'improvement thereof') and 100 (defining 'process' as 'process, art or method, and includes a new use of a known process, machine, manufacture, composition of matter, or material').

[3] See 21 U.S.C. § 355(j)(2)-(4); → mn. 47.

[4] 21 C.F.R. § 320.21.

[5] See https://www.accessdata.fda.gov/scripts/cder/ob/index.cfm.

patents.[6] The Orange Book likewise provides physicians, pharmacists, and patients with information on when therapeutically equivalent generic drugs can be substituted for brand-name products once a generic product has been approved.

When submitting an ANDA, generics must make one of four certifications concerning each Orange Book-listed patent for the approved drug: 8

1. That no patent information is listed in the Orange Book;
2. That the patent has expired;
3. The generic drug will not be marketed until after the expiration of the patent; or
4. That the patent is invalid or will not be infringed by the manufacture, use, or sale of the generic drug.[7]

The fourth option is known as a 'Paragraph IV' certification because it is found in subparagraph IV of the statute (21 U.S.C. § 355(j)(2)(A)(vii)(IV)). When a Paragraph IV certification has been filed, the ANDA applicant must notify the patent owner *and* the holder of the FDA approval for the branded drug[8] about the certification and about the legal and factual basis for the ANDA applicant's opinion that the patent is invalid or will not be infringed.[9] The filing of an ANDA with a Paragraph IV certification is deemed to be an act of infringement,[10] and notification of such a filing generally results in a patent-infringement lawsuit against the ANDA applicant. 9

## 2. The section viii carve out

Ordinarily, an ANDA must include 'information to show that the conditions of use prescribed, recommended, or suggested in the labeling proposed for the new drug have been previously approved for a [listed drug].'[11] In practice, this typically means that an ANDA filer is obligated to copy the FDA approved label for the pertinent branded drug product. But a generic filer is *not* obligated to seek approval for every indication for which the branded drug is approved. Instead, where a drug is approved for more than one use, the ANDA applicant can omit or 'carve out' from its proposed label a patent-protected method to avoid infringing patents covering that use. This type of carve-out is sometimes called a 'section viii' carve-out because it is authorized by subsection viii of the statute (21 U.S.C. § 355(j)(2)(A)(viii)).[12] It is also sometimes referred to as 'skinny labeling' because it narrows the scope of the label. 10

Because the FDA considers the label to limit the approved uses of the generic drug product, in the eyes of the agency, carving a use out of generic's label suffices to allow the generic drug product to be marketed without interfering with the brand's exclusivity on the patented use. The FDA does not perform any substantive patent-infringement analysis and instead merely checks to see whether each patent listed in the Orange Book has an 11

---

[6] 21 U.S.C. § 355(c)(2).

[7] 21 U.S.C. § 355(j)(2)(A)(vii); → mn. 47.

[8] The patent owner may be different from the holder of the FDA approval when, for example, the patent owner has exclusively licensed the patent to third party who is responsible for marketing the approved product. In that case, the third party will be listed as the approval holder, though both the patent owner *and* the approval holder must be notified.

[9] 21 U.S.C. § 355(j)(2)(B).

[10] 35 U.S.C. § 271(e)(2)(A); → mn. 46.

[11] 21 U.S.C. § 355(j)(2)(A)(i); → mn. 47.

[12] 21 U.S.C. § 355(j)(2)(A)(viii) ('[I]f with respect to the listed drug referred to in clause (i) information was filed under subsection (b) or (c) for a method of use patent which does not claim a use for which the applicant is seeking approval under this subsection, a statement that the method of use patent does not claim such a use.'); see also 21 C.F.R. § 314.94(a)(8)(iv) (permitting 'omission of an indication or other aspect of labeling protected by a patent').

appropriate certification or carve-out by the ANDA applicant. As discussed below, it is possible that carve-outs allowed by the FDA will not be sufficient to avoid liability for patent infringement by the ANDA applicant.

## C. Direct and indirect infringement of second medical use claims

### I. Direct infringement

12 Submitting an ANDA containing a Paragraph IV certification is an act of constructive infringement that permits a branded drug company to sue an ANDA applicant on at least the branded company's Orange Book listed patents, long before the applicant's proposed generic product comes to market.[13] In such a suit, the plaintiff must prove that 'if a particular drug were put on the market, it would infringe [the claims of the patents in suit].'[14] If a patent in suit claims an API or, for example, a formulation, then then proving infringement involves demonstrating that the API or formulation of the proposed generic product falls within the scope of the claims. If so, then the ANDA applicant is liable for *directly* infringing the relevant claims because it is the ANDA applicant itself that 'makes, uses, offers to sell, or sells [the] patented invention, within the United States'[15] without the authority of the patent holder.

13 But ANDA applicants rarely directly infringe method of treatment claims because ANDA applicants are typically not the sole actor[16] carrying out all of the steps of the branded company's claimed method.[17] Rather, the direct infringer is most often the prescribing physician or even the patient or person administering the drug. Such direct infringers have not traditionally been targets for infringement lawsuits for obvious reasons: No drug company wants to sue its customers. Instead, branded drug companies sue generic companies on method of treatment patents for a type of *indirect* infringement – namely, actively inducing infringement by the direct infringers – usually because the drug's label instructs prescribing physicians and others to use the drug in an infringing manner. The standard for inducement is discussed below.

### II. Inducement standard, generally

14 'Whoever actively induces infringement of a patent shall be liable as an infringer.'[18] 'Induced infringement 'requires knowledge that the induced acts constitute patent infringement.''[19] In the context of inducement, 'actively' means that the inducer knows,

---

[13] 35 U.S.C. § 271(e)(2)(A); → mn. 46.

[14] *Vanda Pharms. Inc. v West-Ward Pharms. Int'l Ltd.*, 887 F.3d 1117, 1129-30 (Fed. Cir. 2018).

[15] 35 U.S.C. § 271(a); → mn. 46.

[16] Where all of the steps of a claimed method are not infringed by a single entity, the issue of divided infringement arises. A detailed discussion of divided infringement is beyond the scope of this paper. But for a discussion of the relevant standard see, for example, *Limelight Networks, Inc. v Akamai Tech., Inc.*, 572 U.S. 915, 921-26 (2014).

[17] See *Eli Lilly & Co. v Teva Parenteral Meds., Inc.*, 845 F.3d 1357, 1364 – 68 (Fed. Cir. 2017).

[18] 35 U.S.C. § 271(b); → mn. 46.

[19] *Commil USA, LLC v Cisco Systems*, 720 F.3d 1361, 1366 (Fed. Cir. 2013) (quoting *Global-Tech Appliances, Inc. v SEB S.A.*, 563 U.S. 754 (2011)), *rev'd on other grounds* 135 S. Ct. 1920 (2015).

or should know, about the infringement and acts to 'bring about the desired result.'[20] In other words, the alleged inducer (i.e. the generic defendant) must have 'possessed specific intent to encourage another's infringement.'[21] 'While proof of intent is necessary, direct evidence is not required; rather, circumstantial evidence may suffice.'[22] And 'direct infringement is a necessary predicate for a finding of induced infringement in the usual patent infringement case.'[23]

Proof of the prevalence of direct infringement of the patented method is not necessary for the specific intent element or the direct infringement element of inducement.[24] A plaintiff 'can satisfy its burden to prove the predicate direct infringement by showing that if the proposed ANDA product were marketed, it would infringe the [] patent.'[25] 'In the context of patent infringement litigation involving pharmaceuticals, the Federal Circuit has held that 'the sale of a product specifically labeled for use in a patented method constitutes inducement to infringe that patent.''[26] **15**

Proving inducement also requires establishing specific intent to cause infringement. 'When a plaintiff relies on a drug's label accompanying the marketing of a drug to prove intent, "[t]he label must encourage, recommend, or promote infringement."'[27] Where a label encourages both infringing and non-infringing methods, induced infringement is proven as long as at least some prescribers will follow the infringing method.[28] But 'vague label language cannot be combined with speculation about how physicians may act to find inducement.'[29] Infringing labels must 'specifically direct' that the 'particular [claimed] action, or series of [claimed] actions be taken.'[30] The existence of substantial non-infringing uses for a drug can sometimes be used to demonstrate a lack of specific intent to induce infringement.[31] **16**

---

[20] *Global-Tech*, 563 U.S. at 760.

[21] *DSU Med. Corp. v JMS Co.*, 471 F.3d 1293, 1306 (Fed. Cir. 2006) (en banc in relevant part) (internal quotation marks omitted).

[22] ibid. (internal quotation marks omitted).

[23] *Vanda*, 887 F.3d at 1129.

[24] See *Eli Lilly.*, 845 F.3d at 1368.

[25] ibid.; see also, e.g., *Pernix Ireland Pain v Alvogen Malta Operations*, 323 F.Supp.3d 566, 585 (D.Del. 2018).

[26] *Pernix*, 323 F. Supp. 3d at 585 (quoting *Eli Lilly & Co. v Actavis Elizabeth LLC*, 435 F. App'x 917, 926 (Fed. Cir. 2011)).

[27] *GlaxoSmithKline LLC v Teva Pharmaceuticals USA, Inc.*, 7 F.4th 1320, 1327 (Fed. Cir. 2021) (quoting *Takeda Pharm. USA, Inc. v West-Ward Pharm. Corp.*, 785 F.3d 625, 631 (Fed. Cir. 2015)) (citations omitted); → mn. 49.

[28] See *Eli Lilly*, 845 F.3d at 1369; *AstraZeneca LP*, 633 F.3d at 1060; see also *GlaxoSmithKline*, 7 F.4th at 1329-1330 (rejecting argument that inducement cannot be found where a label 'encourage[s] both infringing and noninfringing uses.').

[29] *Takeda Pharms. U.S.A., Inc. v West-Ward Pharm. Corp.*, 785 F.3d 625, 632 (Fed. Cir. 2015).

[30] *Otsuka Pharm. Co., Ltd. v Torren Pharms. Ltd., Inc.*, 99 F. Supp. 3d 461, 493 (D.N.J. 2015); *see also Shire LLC v Amneal Pharms., LLC*, 2014 WL 2861430 (D.N.J. June 23, 2014) (holding that a label can 'describe' claimed steps as long as it does not require or encourage performing them).

[31] See *Warner-Lambert Co. v Apotex Corp.*, 316 F.3d 1348, 1365 (Fed. Cir. 2003).

## D. Infringement of second medical use claims and skinny label products

### I. Careful generic labeling can usually (but not always) avoid liability for induced infringement

17 'FDA acceptance of the carve-out label allows the generic company to place its drug on the market (assuming the ANDA meets other requirements), but only for a subset of approved uses, i.e., those not covered by the brand's patents.'[32] To the extent the approved uses are not covered by a patented method of use claim, the generic company will, most likely, not induce infringement and thus escape liability.

18 But even in instances where a label includes a carve-out and the ANDA is filed with a Section viii statement, the carve-out alone may not be sufficient to avoid inducement. In *AstraZeneca v Apotex*, for example, Apotex submitted a label to the FDA that *excluded* a patent-protected once-daily approved use present in AstraZeneca's label, but the FDA would not permit Apotex to remove language related to unpatented twice-daily dosing, including instructions regarding downward titration of the dose.[33] The Federal Circuit concluded that because Apotex retained the downward titration instructions, the label *instructed* at least some users to move to a once-daily dosing regimen that would result in at least some patients and physicians infringing AstraZeneca's Orange Book listed patents. Thus, despite carving out the patent-protected method of use in AstraZeneca's label, Apotex still induced infringement because its label contained instructive language, i.e. a requirement for downward titration, that would cause at least some physicians and patients to infringe if they followed the instructions on Apotex's label.[34]

### II. The Federal Circuit's latest (confusing) pronouncement on skinny labels: *GSK v Teva*

19 Prior to 2021, the case law regarding skinny labeling and inducement was relatively well settled, and generic ANDA filers and branded companies alike generally understood the nuances of when and how a skinny label could be effectively employed to reduce the likelihood that the generic would infringe. But the Federal Circuit appeared to shift the paradigm significantly—even calling into question the viability of skinny labeling as a tactic for avoiding infringement—in its decision in *GSK v Teva*, where it held that carving-out a patented indication from a generic's label was *not* sufficient to absolve the generic manufacturer of infringement liability.[35]

---

[32] *Caraco Pharm. Labs., Ltd. v Novo Nordisk A/S*, 566 U.S. 399, 406 (2012).

[33] *AstraZeneca*, 633 F.3d at 1045.

[34] The result in *AstraZeneca* stands in contrast to the result in *HZNP Medicines LLC v Actavis Laboratories UT, Inc.*, 940 F.3d 680 (Fed. Cir. 2019). Unlike *AstraZeneca*, the Federal Circuit in *HZNP* concluded that a generic's label (that did not include a carve out) did not induce infringement because while the label included a warning to 'wait until the treated area [was] dry before covering it or applying another substance,' the label did not *instruct* users to specifically apply another substance. ('[Plaintiff's] evidence [of a warning that constitutes an otherwise absent step in a patented method]...establishes that some users might infringe. Th[at] evidence, however, does not establish that "the proposed label *instructs* users to perform the patented method."' (emphasis added)).

[35] See generally *GlaxoSmithKline LLC v Teva Pharms. USA, Inc.*, 7 F.4th 1320 (Fed. Cir. 2021); → mn. 49.

GSK developed a drug called carvedilol, which it marketed under the brand-name Coreg. Coreg is a beta-blocker approved for three indications: hypertension, congestive heart failure ('CHF'), and left ventricular dysfunction following myocardial infarction ('post-MI LVD'). 20

At the time Teva filed an ANDA for its generic carvedilol product, GSK still held a patent on use of carvedilol for treating CHF. To avoid infringing that patent, Teva carved the CHF indication out of its label. GSK nevertheless sued Teva for inducing infringement of the CHF treatment patent. Upon launching its product, Teva's press releases and catalogs described it as 'indicated for treatment of heart failure and hypertension,' the 'generic version of GSK's cardiovascular agent, Coreg,' and an 'AB-rated generic equivalent of GSK's Coreg tablets.'[36] At trial, the jury found that Teva willfully induced infringement during its skinny-label period and awarded GSK $235 million in damages. The district court subsequently granted Teva's motion for judgment as a matter of law, reversing the jury verdict. 21

GSK appealed, arguing that substantial evidence supported the jury's finding of induced infringement. The Federal Circuit agreed with GSK, reversed the district court's judgment of no infringement, and reinstated the jury's verdict. According to the Federal Circuit panel majority, expert testimony from both GSK and Teva provided substantial evidence for the jury's finding that although Teva's label carved out the patented CHF indication of use, the remaining label still instructed methods of use taught in GSK's active patent.[37] The panel majority also ruled that Teva's marketing and promotional material supported the jury's finding of Teva's specific intent to induce infringement.[38] The panel majority's opinion seemed to raise the possibility that describing a generic drug product as an 'AB-rated generic equivalent' to a branded drug might provide a basis for finding infringement liability even if an infringing method of treatment had been carved out of the generic drug product's label. 22

Teva, supported by a number of *amici curiae*, petitioned for rehearing by both the panel and by the full *en banc* court. The panel granted the petition and withdrew its original opinion. On rehearing, the panel majority again held that substantial evidence supported the jury's verdict of infringement and entered judgment against Teva and in favor of GSK, but painted the case as a narrow holding, limited to its facts. The panel majority said, 'this narrow, case-specific review of substantial evidence does not upset the careful balance struck by the Hatch-Waxman Act re section viii carve-outs.'[39] 23

In its revised holding, the panel's majority emphasized that Teva's purported skinny label was insufficiently skinny because the language in the 'Indications' portion of label regarding post-MI LVD – an unpatented indication – partially aligned with GSK's patent claims. Relying on GSK's cardiology expert, and admissions from Teva's cardiology expert, the majority further concluded that the 'Clinical Study' section of Teva's label and the 'Dosage and Administration' section of the label (which immediately followed the Indication section), provided the remaining elements of GSK's claim. Although Teva argued that GSK's reading of its label required cobbling together disparate portions of the label to arrive at instructions to treat CHF, the Federal Circuit's majority disagreed. 24

[36] ibid. at 1324; → mn. 49.

[37] See *Lucent Techs., Inc. v Gateway, Inc.*, 580 F.3d 1301, 1309 (Fed. Cir. 2009) ('Infringement is a question of fact, reviewed for substantial evidence when tried to a jury.'); see also *DSU Med Corp v JMS*, 471 F.3d 1293, 1306 (Fed. Cir. 2006) (Inducement requires establishing that 'defendant possessed specific intent to encourage another's infringement.').

[38] See *GlaxoSmithKline*, 7 F.4th at 1334 ('When a product is sold with an infringing label or infringing instruction manual, such a label is evidence of intent to induce infringement.'); also ('The content of the label… permits the inference of specific intent to encourage infringing use.'); → mn. 49.

[39] ibid. at 1326; → mn. 49.

Consequently, the panel majority held, a reasonable jury could find, on the specific facts in this case, that Teva's label, press releases, and catalogs had the effect of encouraging use of Teva's generic carvedilol product for CHF.[40]

25 The Federal Circuit's decision was not, however, unanimous. And Judge Prost, in her dissent, attacked the majority's reasoning, alleging that it unreasonably 'glean[ed] intentional encouragement from a label specifically designed to avoid infringement' and that, among other things, it 'creat[ed] confusion for generics, leaving them in the dark about what exposes them to liability…throw[ing] a wrench into Congress's design for enabling quick public access to generic versions of unpatented drugs with unpatented uses.'[41]

26 Thus, despite the panel majority's efforts to cabin its holding in the case to the particular facts at issue, the effect of *GSK v Teva* has been to raise questions about the continued viability of skinny-label strategies. Given the importance of this question to generic companies generally, and Teva specifically—the Federal Circuit's holding cost Teva $235 million—Teva filed a Petition for a Writ of Certiorari on July 11, 2022, asking the U.S. Supreme Court to overturn the Federal Circuit's revised holding.

27 On May 16, 2023, the U.S. Supreme Court denied Teva's Petition for Writ of Certiorari without comment, leaving the Federal Circuit's revised opinion intact. And although at least three Federal District Courts[42] have considered and applied *GSK v Teva* to cases involving a carveout–each finding that the generic's labels and/or actions did *not* induce infringement–these decisions are not binding on other trial courts and thus provide, at most, a suggestion for how courts may apply the *GSK* precedent in the future. Accordingly, generics employing a carve-out strategy must exercise extreme caution and make certain that their label and actions are sufficiently distinguishable from the facts of *GSK*.

## E. Infringement of second medical use claims and biosimilar products

28 Skinny labeling and the use of carve-outs has yet to be litigated in the context of biosimilars, but as more biologics and biosimilars enter the market, carve-outs with respect to biosimilars will surely become a point of dispute.

29 In 2010, Congress enacted the Biologics Price Competition and Innovation Act ('BPCIA'), establishing an abbreviated pathway for biosimilar approvals, similar to the ab-

---

[40] 'GSK presented evidence that Teva's partial label did not successfully carve out the patented use, and thus, Teva was selling its generic with a label which infringed the method claim. GSK presented evidence that doctors read and consider labels, that Teva's marketing materials guided doctors to the label and to its website promoting the patented use, that Teva issued press releases encouraging doctors to prescribe carvedilol for the patented use, that Teva's own employees expected doctors to prescribe carvedilol during the partial label period for the patented uses, and expert testimony that Teva's actions encouraged doctors to do so. This is substantial evidence from which a reasonable jury could conclude that Teva intentionally encouraged the practice of the claimed method.' *GlaxoSmithKline*, 7 F.4th at 1338; → mn. 49.

[41] ibid. at 1343; → mn. 49.

[42] *See, Amarin Pharma, Inc. v Hikma Pharms. USA Inc.*, 578 F. Supp. 3d 642 (D. Del. 2022) (holding that Hikma's actions were sufficiently distinguishable from Teva's actions such that a finding of inducement was not warranted); *Genentech, Inc. v Sandoz, Inc.*, 592 F. Supp. 3d 355, 368 (D. Del.), appeal dismissed, No. 2022-1595, 2022 WL 2165992 (Fed. Cir. June 16, 2022), and aff'd, 55 F.4th 1368 (Fed. Cir. 2022) (concluding that Genentech did not show that Sandoz's label or actions evinced a specific intent to induce infringement of the relevant patents); and *Lundbeck v Lupin Ltd.*, No. CV 18-88-LPS, 2021 WL 4944963, at *106 (D. Del. Sept. 30, 2021) (concluding that Lupin's label would not 'encourage, recommend, or promote infringement.')

breviated pathway for small-molecule generic drugs established in the Hatch-Waxman Act.[43] An important difference between small-molecule generic drugs and biosimilar drugs is that the former are more likely to be automatically substituted for their branded counterparts. As a result, there is generally little marketing of generic products beyond announcing their availability. In contrast, as of May 2023, there were 41 FDA-approved biosimilar products on the market, of which only four had been granted interchangeable status allowing pharmacists to substitute them automatically for the corresponding branded biologic product.[44] Consequently, biosimilar products do need to be marketed, and biosimilar companies will need to pay careful attention to avoid encouraging infringement of method of treatment patents in their marketing materials. Future cases will need to clarify how far a biosimilar company can go in promoting its drug as a biosimilar without crossing the line into inducing infringement.

## I. Legislative background and abbreviated pathway for biosimilars

Section 351(k) Public Health Service Act[45], included in the BPCIA, sets forth require- 30
ments for the approval of a biosimilar.[46] The branded biologic drug for which biosimilarity is to be demonstrated is referred to as the 'reference product.' Biosimilars are defined as a biological product that is 'highly similar to the reference product notwithstanding minor differences in clinically inactive compounds' and with 'no clinically meaningful differences between the biological product and reference product in terms of safety, purity, and potency of the product.'[47] Approval of a biosimilar is obtained by filing an abbreviated Biologics License Application ('aBLA'), which must contain data demonstrating biosimilarity between the proposed biosimilar and reference product based on analytical studies, animal studies, and clinical studies; however, the FDA determines on a case-by-case basis which studies, if any, are unnecessary.[48] Like generic manufacturers, biosimilar manufacturers are not required to generate the full profile of nonclinical and clinical data, as the reference drug manufacturer would need in order to demonstrate the safety and efficacy of the product.[49]

As in the small molecule space, the FDA maintains a published database—the so-called 31
'Purple Book'—that contains information about biologics, their indications, biosimilar and interchangeable products, as well as a list of potentially relevant patents.[50] And aBLA

---

[43] Implementation of the Biologics Price Competition and Innovation Act of 2009, Food and Drug Admin., available from https://www.fda.gov/ (content current as of February 12, 2016).

[44] Biosimilar Product Information, Food and Drug Admin., https://www.fda.gov/drugs/biosimilars/biosimilar-product-information (last updated May 25, 2023). See also Hagen, 'An Interchangeable Biosimilar vs. Authorized Biologics Battle May be Looming' (October 2021), available from https://www.centerforbiosimilars.com/ and Arthur,' FDA approves Cimerli as the first interchangeable biosimilar to Lucentis for all indications', available from https://www.biopharma-reporter.com/ (last updated August 4, 2022).

[45] 42 U.S.C. 262(k); → mn. 48.

[46] Draft Guidance for Industry: Biosimilars and Interchangeable Biosimilars: Licensure for Fewer than All Conditions of Use for Which the Reference Product Has Been Licensed, February 2020 (found at fda.gov).

[47] PHS Act section 351(i)(2).

[48] Draft Guidance for Industry: Biosimilars and Interchangeable Biosimilars: Licensure for Fewer than All Conditions of Use for Which the Reference Product Has Been Licensed, February 2020 (found at fda.gov).

[49] Biosimilar Development, Review, and Approval, Food and Drug Admin. (content current as of October 20, 2017).

[50] Purple Book: Lists of Licensed Biological Products with Reference Product Exclusivity and Biosimilarity or Interchangeability Evaluations, Food and Drug Admin., available from https://www.fda.gov/ (last visited July 16, 2022).

applicants seeking approval for a biosimilar drug must provide notice to the branded biologic drug manufacturer 180 days before the first commercial marketing.[51]

32 Unlike generics, where the API used in a generic formulation is structurally identical to the API used in the approved product, biosimilars vary structurally from the reference drug because biosimilars are derived from different strains of living cell than the approved biologic product.[52] As a result, the abbreviated pathway for biosimilar approvals is slightly different from the abbreviated pathway for generic approvals.[53] One key difference is that in order for a biosimilar to be deemed interchangeable with its reference biologic drug, a biosimilar must meet additional requirements, including establishing that the biosimilar provides the 'same clinical result as the reference product in any given patient[.]'[54] While it is more expensive and time consuming to demonstrate that the biosimilar meets the FDA's requirements for interchangeability, an interchangeable biosimilar can be substituted at the pharmacy for its corresponding brand name biologic without the intervention of a prescribing healthcare professional.[55]

33 Another difference between the generic and biosimilar approval pathways is the concept of extrapolation, which applies when the reference biologic drug is approved for multiple indications. If the totality of evidence supports biosimilarity for one approved indication, then the biosimilar manufacturer can use the same data to justify approval for other approved indications that it did not directly study.[56] Extrapolation is based on 'all available data and information in the biosimilar application, FDA's previous finding of safety and efficacy for other approved indications for the reference product, and knowledge and consideration of various scientific factors for each indication.'[57] However, extrapolation must be accompanied by scientific justification, which includes factors such as knowledge of the mechanism(s) of action, pharmacokinetics, pharmacodynamics, efficacy, safety, and immunogenicity of the reference drug in each of its approved indications.[58] Once these factors show no meaningful clinical differences between the biosimilar and reference drug, the FDA can, at its discretion, extrapolate the results to other indications for which the reference drug was approved.[59]

## II. Carve-outs in biosimilar skinny labeling

34 In 2020, the FDA issued a non-binding draft guidance for labeling biologic products. The draft guidance instructs the biosimilar applicant to draft a label that incorporates the data and information from the reference drug label relevant to the proposed indication(s) of use, with appropriate modifications.[60] Additionally, the draft guidance instructs the

---

[51] BPCIA section 262(I)(8)(A).

[52] Dye, 'Extrapolation Explained' (October 30, 2017), available from https://www.gene.com/.

[53] Biosimilars Info Sheet, Food and Drug Admin., https://www.fda.gov/media/154912/download (last visited July 15, 2022).

[54] PHS Act section 351(k)(4)(A).

[55] Biosimilar and Interchangeable Biologics: More Treatment Choices, Food and Drug Admin., available from https://www.fda.gov/ (content current as of October 12, 2021)

[56] Biosimilar Development, Review, and Approval, Food and Drug Admin., https://www.fda.gov/ (content current as of October 20, 2017); Dye, 'Extrapolation Explained' (October 30, 2017), https://www.gene.com/.

[57] ibid.

[58] ibid.

[59] Dye, 'Extrapolation Explained' (October 30, 2017), https://www.gene.com/.

[60] Shea, Jr., FDA Issue Biosimilar Guidance for Label Carve-Outs and Supplements (February 13, 2020), available from https://www.jdsupra.com/.

biosimilar applicant to 'carefully scrutinize the content of all sections of the labeling to ensure that relevant information is included.'[61]

With respect to carve-outs, the draft guidance states that the FDA does not consider the applicability of patents to a proposed biosimilar product (e.g., the validity or enforceability of patents or potential infringement) in its review of the application. If a biosimilar manufacturer seeks licensure of fewer than all of the reference drug's indications of use (i.e., a carve-out), they are instructed to submit a supplement to inform the FDA's review of the draft labeling in light of the carve-out. Here, the biosimilar manufacturer can submit a justification as to why the label meets the requirement for approval, considering the indications of use.[62] 35

As previously mentioned, skinny labeling and the use of carve-outs has yet to be litigated in the context of biosimilars.[63] Broadly speaking, the same analysis and considerations should apply to skinny labels on biosimilar products as to skinny labels on small-molecule generics. Biosimilar manufacturers are likely to face allegations of actively inducing direct infringement by prescribing physicians or patients due to statements that the biosimilar manufacturers make in their FDA-approved labels or in press releases, catalogs, or other marketing materials. Particularly for biosimilars that have not been approved as interchangeable with a biologic product, it will be necessary to market the biosimilar to encourage physicians to prescribe the biosimilar in lieu of the reference product. Biosimilars that have indications carved out of their labels will need to take care to ensure that, in promoting their drug, they do not encourage its use for indications that have been carved out of the label. 36

Relying on extrapolation in seeking approval may limit a biosimilar manufacturer's ability to omit information from its label or from its promotional materials. A biosimilar manufacturer may have good reasons to conduct its biosimilarity studies in patients suffering from a particular condition rather than another: For instance, because the patient population is larger, or because the drug's effects are more easily measured in patients with that condition, or because patients having that condition are more sensitive to the drug. If the biosimilarity studies are done in a population of patients suffering from a given condition, then the FDA may require the data from the biosimilarity studies to remain in the label even if the indication itself is carved out. Suppose, for example, that a reference product is approved to treat rheumatoid arthritis and certain types of lymphoma. And suppose that a biosimilar manufacturer has carried out its biosimilarity studies in patients with rheumatoid arthritis, and the FDA has extrapolated the results of those studies to grant approval for the lymphoma indication as well as for rheumatoid arthritis. In those circumstances, even if the biosimilar manufacturer carves the rheumatoid arthritis indication out of its label, the FDA may well require data from the rheumatoid arthritis studies to remain in the label, and the biosimilar manufacturer may need to reference those studies in order to try to convince physicians to prescribe its biosimilar for lymphoma. 37

In these circumstances, the branded biologic drug maker may well argue that the inclusion in the biosimilar's label or marketing materials of data demonstrating biosimilarity for rheumatoid arthritis constitutes encouraging the use of the biosimilar to treat rheumatoid arthritis (and hence of actively inducing infringement of patents covering the use of the drug to treat rheumatoid arthritis), even if the rheumatoid arthritis indication is carved out of the label. No such case has yet been litigated, and the result will depend 38

---

[61] ibid. (quoting Guidance at 5-6).

[62] Guidance at 6.

[63] Williams McKeon/Abele Isaacson, *GSK v. Teva:* The Skinny on Induced Infringement and Label Carve-Outs, (January 13, 2021), available from https://kilpatricktownsend.com.

critically on the particular facts of the case and the precise statements and data at issue. But, particularly given the uncertainty that *GSK v Teva* has introduced into the law, the outcome of such a case is far from clear.

## F. Strategies and considerations

39 The Patent Act, as amended by the Hatch-Waxman Act and the BPCIA, explicitly sets forth the remedies available for filing an ANDA or aBLA that is held to be an act of infringement.[64] Briefly, these are (A) an automatic order prohibiting FDA approval of the drug before expiration of the patent that has been infringed; (B) a possible injunction preventing commercial manufacture, use, offer to sell, sale, or importation of the generic or biosimilar product.

### I. Brand strategy for reducing the likelihood of a successful carve-out

40 Branded pharmaceutical companies must consider the prospect of a skinny label when planning for second and subsequent indications and should, to the best of their ability, stagger patent filings for the first approved indication in a way that maximizes patent term. While this is a best practice regardless of the prospects of a second indication, staggering filings to provide maximum patent life is often easier said than done, particularly in view of the U.S. double-patenting prohibition and the potential effect of a branded company's earlier filings (and intervening third party disclosures) as prior art.

41 Where staggered filings are not possible, branded pharmaceutical companies should be prepared to initiate testing for second and subsequent indications as soon as possible to maximize the overlap between patents covering the first indication and patents covering the follow-on approvals. The shorter the overlap, the shorter the period of exclusivity for both approved indications. Once a substitutable product having a skinny label is available on the market, branded companies should expect sales for *all indications* drop significantly as pharmacies shift patients to the equivalent generic.

42 In addition to the strategies noted above, branded pharma companies should closely monitor the contents of their label and make certain that when they submit their label for the second or subsequent indication, that, to the extent possible, and to the extent permitted by the FDA, they include instructive language in portions of the label that will be difficult to modify or omit. Further, and in order to make sure the language retained in the label is sufficient, the regulatory and patent teams must work together to make sure that the language in the claims covering the second indication mirrors (or mirrors as closely as possible) the language in the label, or vice versa.

### II. Generic strategy for increasing the likelihood of a successful carve-out

43 For generic pharmaceutical companies planning to launch a product with a skinny label, much of the advice discussed above applies, only in reverse. That is, generics en-

[64] See generally 35 U.S.C. § 271(e)(4).

trants should monitor their branded competitors, understand when these companies plan to launch patent protected second indications, and evaluate the timing for entering the market with a product that opportunistically avoids the patents for the first indication. Further, generic entrants should analyze branded labels carefully to ensure that their proposed skinny label is truly 'skinny enough' and that their further business activities including the contents of their promotional materials, their marketing strategies, and other external communications avoid referencing language that could be construed as instructing a patient or physician to infringe.

## G. Legal remedies

The filing of an ANDA or aBLA is deemed an act of infringement, so patent infringe- **44**
ment litigation can commence in response to such a filing without the need to wait for the commercial launch of a generic or biosimilar product.[65] If a lawsuit is commenced in response to an ANDA filing, then final FDA approval of the generic drug is automatically stayed for 30 months after the commencement of the suit, in the hope that the court can reach a decision on patent infringement liability before the generic comes to market.[66] Although there is no corresponding automatic stay of FDA approval in the BPCIA, biosimilar manufacturers must give branded companies notice at least 180 days before the date of first commercial marketing of the biosimilar product, thus making it likely that litigation will commence before the biosimilar product is on the market.[67]

Until the product has been launched, money damages for infringement are not availa- **45**
ble as a remedy. Instead, if a patent in suit is held to be valid and infringed, then the court will enter an injunction preventing the FDA from granting final approval to the generic or biosimilar drug until the expiration of the patent at issue.[68] This preserves the branded company's market exclusivity while its patents are in force. A generic or biosimilar whose attempt to avoid patent infringement liability with a skinny label turns out to be unsuccessful will therefore not be able to market its product until the expiration of the method of treatment patent at issue.

## H. Statutory provisions

### I. 35 U.S.C. § 271. Infringement of patent **46**

(a) Except as otherwise provided in this title, whoever without authority makes, uses, offers to sell, or sells any patented invention, within the United States or imports into the United States any patented invention during the term of the patent therefor, infringes the patent.

(b) Whoever actively induces infringement of a patent shall be liable as an infringer.

…

[65] 35 U.S.C. § 271(e)(2); → mn. 46.

[66] 21 U.S.C. § 355(j)(5)(B)(iii); → mn. 47.

[67] 42 U.S.C. § 262(I)(8)(A). Such notice of commercial marketing can be given even before FDA approval of the aBLA. See *Sandoz Inc. v Amgen Inc.*, 137 S.Ct. 1664 (2017)

[68] 35 U.S.C. § 271(e)(4)(A).

(e)(2) It shall be an act of infringement to submit–

(A) an application under section 505(j) of the Federal Food, Drug, and Cosmetic Act or described in section 505(b)(2) of such Act for a drug claimed in a patent or the use of which is claimed in a patent,

(B) an application under section 512 of such Act or under the Act of March 4, 1913 (21 U.S.C. 151-158) for a drug or veterinary biological product which is not primarily manufactured using recombinant DNA, recombinant RNA, hybridoma technology, or other processes involving site specific genetic manipulation techniques and which is claimed in a patent or the use of which is claimed in a patent, or

(C)(i) with respect to a patent that is identified in the list of patents described in section 351(l)(3) of the Public Health Service Act (including as provided under section 351(l)(7) of such Act), an application seeking approval of a biological product, or

(ii) if the applicant for the application fails to provide the application and information required under section 351(l)(2)(A) of such Act, an application seeking approval of a biological product for a patent that could be identified pursuant to section 351(l)(3)(A)(i) of such Act,

if the purpose of such submission is to obtain approval under such Act to engage in the commercial manufacture, use, or sale of a drug, veterinary biological product, or biological product claimed in a patent or the use of which is claimed in a patent before the expiration of such patent.

47

## II. 21 U.S.C. § 355. New drugs

**(j) Abbreviated new drug applications**

(1) Any person may file with the Secretary an abbreviated application for the approval of a new drug.

(2)(A) An abbreviated application for a new drug shall contain–

(i) information to show that the conditions of use prescribed, recommended, or suggested in the labeling proposed for the new drug have been previously approved for a drug listed under paragraph (7) (hereinafter in this subsection referred to as a 'listed drug');

(ii)(I) if the listed drug referred to in clause (i) has only one active ingredient, information to show that the active ingredient of the new drug is the same as that of the listed drug;

(II) if the listed drug referred to in clause (i) has more than one active ingredient, information to show that the active ingredients of the new drug are the same as those of the listed drug, or

(III) if the listed drug referred to in clause (i) has more than one active ingredient and if one of the active ingredients of the new drug is different and the application is filed pursuant to the approval of a petition filed under subparagraph (C), information to show that the other active ingredients of the new drug are the same as the active ingredients of the listed drug, information to show that the different active ingredient is an active ingredient of a listed drug or of a drug which does not meet the requirements of section 321(p) of this title, and such other information respecting the different active ingredient with respect to which the petition was filed as the Secretary may require;

(iii) information to show that the route of administration, the dosage form, and the strength of the new drug are the same as those of the listed drug referred to in clause (i) or, if the route of administration, the dosage form, or the strength of the new drug is different and the application is filed pursuant to the approval of a petition filed under subparagraph (C), such information respecting the route of administration, dosage form, or strength with respect to which the petition was filed as the Secretary may require;

(iv) information to show that the new drug is bioequivalent to the listed drug referred to in clause (i), except that if the application is filed pursuant to the approval of a petition filed under subparagraph (C), information to show that the active ingredients of the new drug are of the same pharmacological or therapeutic class as those of the listed drug referred to in clause (i) and the new drug can be expected to have the same therapeutic effect as the listed drug when administered to patients for a condition of use referred to in clause (i);

(v) information to show that the labeling proposed for the new drug is the same as the labeling approved for the listed drug referred to in clause (i) except for changes required because of differences approved under a petition filed under subparagraph (C) or because the new drug and the listed drug are produced or distributed by different manufacturers;

(vi) the items specified in clauses (ii) through (vi) of subsection (b)(1)(A);

(vii) a certification, in the opinion of the applicant and to the best of his knowledge, with respect to each patent which claims the listed drug referred to in clause (i) or which claims a use for such listed drug for which the applicant is seeking approval under this subsection and for which information is required to be filed under subsection (b) or (c)–

(I) that such patent information has not been filed,

(II) that such patent has expired,

(III) of the date on which such patent will expire, or

(IV) that such patent is invalid or will not be infringed by the manufacture, use, or sale of the new drug for which the application is submitted; and

(viii) if with respect to the listed drug referred to in clause (i) information was filed under subsection (b) or (c) for a method of use patent which does not claim a use for which the applicant is seeking approval under this subsection, a statement that the method of use patent does not claim such a use.

The Secretary may not require that an abbreviated application contain information in addition to that required by clauses (i) through (viii).

## III. 42 U.S.C. § 262. Regulation of biological products 48

**(k) Licensure of biological products as biosimilar or interchangeable**

(1) In general

Any person may submit an application for licensure of a biological product under this subsection.

(2) Content

(A) In general

(i) Required information

An application submitted under this subsection shall include information demonstrating that–

(I) the biological product is biosimilar to a reference product based upon data derived from–

(aa) analytical studies that demonstrate that the biological product is highly similar to the reference product notwithstanding minor differences in clinically inactive components;

(bb) an assessment of toxicity (which may rely on, or consist of, a study or studies described in item (aa) or (cc)); and

(cc) a clinical study or studies (including the assessment of immunogenicity and pharmacokinetics or pharmacodynamics) that are sufficient to demonstrate safety, purity, and potency in 1 or more appropriate conditions of use for which the reference product is licensed and intended to be used and for which licensure is sought for the biological product;

(II) the biological product and reference product utilize the same mechanism or mechanisms of action for the condition or conditions of use prescribed, recommended, or suggested in the proposed labeling, but only to the extent the mechanism or mechanisms of action are known for the reference product;

(III) the condition or conditions of use prescribed, recommended, or suggested in the labeling proposed for the biological product have been previously approved for the reference product;

(IV) the route of administration, the dosage form, and the strength of the biological product are the same as those of the reference product; and

(V) the facility in which the biological product is manufactured, processed, packed, or held meets standards designed to assure that the biological product continues to be safe, pure, and potent.

**(ii) Determination by Secretary**

The Secretary may determine, in the Secretary's discretion, that an element described in clause (i)(I) is unnecessary in an application submitted under this subsection.

**(iii) Additional information**

An application submitted under this subsection–

(I) shall include publicly-available information regarding the Secretary's previous determination that the reference product is safe, pure, and potent;

(II) may include any additional information in support of the application, including publicly-available information with respect to the reference product or another biological product; and

(III) may include information to show that the conditions of use prescribed, recommended, or suggested in the labeling proposed for the biological product have been previously approved for the reference product.

**(B) Interchangeability**

An application (or a supplement to an application) submitted under this subsection may include information demonstrating that the biological product meets the standards described in paragraph (4).

**(l) Patents**

**(8) Notice of commercial marketing and preliminary injunction**

**(A) Notice of commercial marketing**

The subsection (k) applicant shall provide notice to the reference product sponsor not later than 180 days before the date of the first commercial marketing of the biological product licensed under subsection (k).

**(B) Preliminary injunction**

After receiving the notice under subparagraph (A) and before such date of the first commercial marketing of such biological product, the reference product sponsor may seek a preliminary injunction prohibiting the subsection (k) applicant from engaging in the commercial manufacture or sale of such biological product until the court decides the issue of patent validity, enforcement, and infringement with respect to any patent that is–

(i) included in the list provided by the reference product sponsor under paragraph (3)(A) or in the list provided by the subsection (k) applicant under paragraph (3)(B); and

(ii) not included, as applicable, on–

(I) the list of patents described in paragraph (4); or

(II) the lists of patents described in paragraph (5)(B).

**(C) Reasonable cooperation**

If the reference product sponsor has sought a preliminary injunction under subparagraph (B), the reference product sponsor and the subsection (k) applicant shall reasonably cooperate to expedite such further discovery as is needed in connection with the preliminary injunction motion.

**(9) Limitation on declaratory judgment action**

**(A) Subsection (k) application provided**

If a subsection (k) applicant provides the application and information required under paragraph (2)(A), neither the reference product sponsor nor the subsection (k) applicant may, prior to the date notice is received under paragraph (8)(A), bring any action under section

2201 of Title 28 for a declaration of infringement, validity, or enforceability of any patent that is described in clauses (i) and (ii) of paragraph (8)(B).

**(B) Subsequent failure to act by subsection (k) applicant**

If a subsection (k) applicant fails to complete an action required of the subsection (k) applicant under paragraph (3)(B)(ii), paragraph (5), paragraph (6)(C)(i), paragraph (7), or paragraph (8)(A), the reference product sponsor, but not the subsection (k) applicant, may bring an action under section 2201 of Title 28 for a declaration of infringement, validity, or enforceability of any patent included in the list described in paragraph (3)(A), including as provided under paragraph (7).

**(C) Subsection (k) application not provided**

If a subsection (k) applicant fails to provide the application and information required under paragraph (2)(A), the reference product sponsor, but not the subsection (k) applicant, may bring an action under section 2201 of Title 28 for a declaration of infringement, validity, or enforceability of any patent that claims the biological product or a use of the biological product.

## J. Extracts from court decisions 49

### *GlaxoSmithKline LLC v Teva Pharmaceuticals USA, Inc.*[69]

**Background:** Owner of patent directed to method of using beta-blocker for treatment of mild to severe congestive heart failure brought induced infringement action against manufacturer of generic beta-blocker, alleging that manufacturer had caused physicians to prescribe the generic drug to treat congestive heart failure. After jury trial resulting in verdict of infringement and no invalidity of the patent, manufacturer filed renewed motion for judgment as a matter of law or, in the alternative, new trial. The United States District Court for the District of Delaware, Leonard P. Stark, Chief Judge, 313 F.Supp.3d 582, granted motion for judgment of non-infringement. Parties cross-appealed.

On rehearing, the Court of Appeals held that sufficient evidence supported finding inducement to infringe.

[...]

#### Opinion

Dissenting opinion filed by Circuit Judge Prost.

**Per Curiam.**

***1323** GlaxoSmithKline LLC and SmithKline Beecham (Cork) Ltd. (collectively, GSK) sued Teva Pharmaceuticals USA, Inc. in the United States District Court for the District of Delaware for infringement of claims of GSK's Reissue Patent No. RE40,000. After the jury's verdict of infringement and its award of damages, the district court granted Teva's renewed motion for judgment as a matter of law of noninfringement. GlaxoSmithKline LLC v. Teva Pharm. USA, Inc., 313 F. Supp. 3d 582 (D. Del. 2018) (Dist. Ct. Op.). GSK appeals the JMOL, and Teva conditionally cross-appeals the jury's damages award. We have jurisdiction under 28 U.S.C. § 1295(a)(1).

For the reasons below, we vacate the grant of JMOL, reinstate the jury's verdict and damages award, and remand for appropriate further proceedings.

GSK markets and sells the medicinal product carvedilol, a beta-blocker, under the brand name Coreg®. The Food and Drug Administration (FDA) has approved carvedilol for three

[69] United States Court of Appeals, Federal Circuit, August 5, 2021.

indications of use. By 1997, the FDA had approved carvedilol for treatment of hypertension and congestive heart failure (CHF). Then, in 2003, the FDA approved carvedilol for a third use: to reduce cardiovascular mortality in patients suffering from left ventricular dysfunction following a myocardial infarction, i.e., the 'post-MI LVD' indication.

When GSK began investigating carvedilol's use for treating CHF, beta-blockers were contraindicated for that use. This was because beta-blockers slow the heart rate and reduce the heart's ability to pump blood, a potentially deadly combination for patients with heart failure. Very few doctors or companies, therefore, saw the potential for investigating beta-blockers for treating CHF. Despite this skepticism, GSK spent years investigating, and conducting trials of, carvedilol for the treatment of heart failure. And at the time, the only known treatment for improving mortality rates in CHF patients was with angiotensin-converting enzyme (ACE) inhibitors. Still, even with ACE inhibitors, patients continued to die from heart failure at high rates. It was not until the FDA approved GSK's Coreg® that using a beta-blocker to treat CHF became the standard of care for reducing mortality in heart failure patients.

The carvedilol compound was patented in 1985. See U.S. Patent No. 4,503,067, expiration date March 5, 2007. In 1998, U.S. Patent No. 5,760,069 issued, which claimed a method of administering a combination of carvedilol and one or more of an ACE inhibitor, a diuretic, and digoxin to decrease mortality caused by CHF in a patient.

In March 2002, Teva filed an Abbreviated New Drug Application (ANDA) for FDA approval of its generic carvedilol for all three indications. It certified, under Paragraph III of the Hatch-Waxman Act,[1] that it would not launch its product until the '067 patent on the carvedilol compound expired in March 2007. See s. Teva also certified, under Paragraph IV, that the '069 patent was 'invalid, unenforceable, or not infringed.' ***1324** See 21 U.S.C. § 355(j)(2)(A)(vii)(IV). On May 24, 2002, Teva sent GSK a Paragraph IV notice stating that the claims of the '069 patent are anticipated or would have been obvious. GSK did not sue Teva upon receipt of the notice, and on November 25, 2003, GSK applied for reissue of the '069 patent under 35 U.S.C. § 251. Teva received FDA 'tentative approval' for its ANDA in 2004, 'for treatment of heart failure and hypertension.' J.A. 7437. The approval was to become effective when the '067 patent expired in 2007.

On January 8, 2008, the PTO issued Reissue Patent No. RE40,000, and GSK notified the FDA on February 6, 2008. See J.A. 6880–82. The '000 patent, asserted in this case, claims a method of decreasing mortality caused by CHF by administering carvedilol with at least one other therapeutic agent. See, e.g., '000 patent, col. 1, ll. 17–25. Claim 1 recites:

1. A method of decreasing mortality caused by congestive heart failure in a patient in need thereof which comprises[:]

administering a therapeutically acceptable amount of carvedilol in conjunction with one or more other therapeutic agents, said agents being selected from the group consisting of an angiotensin converting enzyme inhibitor (ACE), a diuretic, and digoxin,

*wherein the administering comprises administering to said patient daily maintenance dosages for a maintenance period to decrease a risk of mortality caused by congestive heart failure, and said maintenance period is greater than six months.* (emphasis in original).

The '000 patent is listed in the FDA's publication 'Approved Drug Products with Therapeutic Equivalence Evaluations,' commonly known as the Orange Book, as a patent claiming a method of using Coreg®.

Just before Teva launched its generic carvedilol in 2007, it certified to the FDA that its label 'will not include the indication defined in use code U-233' until the expiration of the '069 patent. J.A. 6176; see 21 U.S.C. § 355(j)(2)(A)(viii) (section viii). Patent use code U-233 corresponded to 'decreasing mortality caused by congestive heart failure.' J.A. 7833. Teva's label dated '8/2007' thus included only two indications: the post-MI LVD indication and the hypertension indication. J.A. 5506, 5508. Teva's press releases and marketing materials, how-

[1] Drug Price Competition and Patent Term Restoration Act of 1984, Pub. L. 98–417, 98 Stat. 1585 (1984).

ever, touted its generic carvedilol as 'indicated for treatment of heart failure and hypertension,' as the 'Generic version of [GSK's] cardiovascular agent Coreg®,' and as an 'AB-rated generic equivalent of [GSK's] Coreg® Tablets.'[2] J.A. 6347, 6353.

In 2011, following GSK's delisting of certain patents from the Orange Book, including the '069 patent and U.S. Patent No. 5,902,821, the FDA instructed Teva to 'revise [its] labeling to include the information associated with patent '821 (delisted) and the associated Use Code (U-313).' J.A. 5557. It told Teva to submit labeling 'that is identical in content to the approved [GSK Coreg®] labeling (including the package insert and any patient package insert and/or Medication Guide that may be required).' J.A. 5557. The FDA also requested Teva 'provide information regarding ***1325** [its] position on [the '000 patent].' Id.

Teva amended its label to include the indication for treating patients with chronic heart failure by administering carvedilol to increase survival and to reduce the risk of hospitalization. J.A. 5532. In addition, the post-MI LVD and hypertension indications remained on the label. In response to the FDA's request for information regarding its position on the '000 patent, Teva told the FDA it believed it need not 'provide certification to [the '000 patent]' because it received final approval of its ANDA before the '000 patent issued. J.A. 5554.

On July 3, 2014, GSK sued Teva and Glenmark Pharmaceuticals USA, the two largest suppliers of generic carvedilol, in the District of Delaware, alleging that each had induced infringement of the '000 patent. The action against Glenmark was severed and stayed.

During a seven-day jury trial, Teva argued the asserted claims of the '000 patent were invalid and not infringed. Teva argued it could not have induced infringement, at least prior to 2011, because it had 'carved out' the indication and prescribing information for treatment of congestive heart failure in its 2007 label under section viii. Teva also argued that it could not be liable for inducement for any time period because it did not cause others to infringe the method claimed in the '000 patent.

The district court instructed the jury to assess whether Teva induced infringement during two distinct time periods: the 'partial label' period and the 'full label' period. J.A. 171. The partial label period was from January 8, 2008, through April 30, 2011, when Teva's label had the post-MI LVD and hypertension indications but not the chronic heart failure indication. Id. The full label period was from May 1, 2011, through June 7, 2015, when Teva's label had all three indications, including the chronic heart failure indication. Id.

The jury found the '000 patent was not invalid, that Teva induced infringement of claims 1–3 during the partial label period, and that Teva induced infringement of claims 1–3 and 6–9 during the full label period. The jury assessed damages based on a combination of lost profits and a reasonable royalty and found Teva's infringement willful.

The district court granted Teva's renewed motion for JMOL, stating that substantial evidence did not support the verdict of induced infringement because GSK failed to prove that Teva's alleged inducement, as opposed to other factors, actually caused physicians to directly infringe by prescribing generic carvedilol for the treatment of mild to severe CHF. Dist. Ct. Op. at 591. The district court explained that '[w]ithout proof of causation, which is an essential element of GSK's action, a finding of inducement cannot stand.' Id.

The district court also determined no reasonable juror could have found induced infringement based on the post-MI LVD indication in Teva's partial label, which GSK had argued instructed practice of the claimed method. Id. at 592 n.9. Although the district court acknowledged there is some overlap with CHF patients and post-MI LVD patients, it reasoned 'the two indications are distinct and require different clinical testing and different FDA approvals to treat.' Id. It further reasoned infringement required carvedilol be 'prescribed to treat the risk

---

[2] The FDA assigns an 'AB rating' for a drug that is considered therapeutically equivalent to another drug. FDA, Orange Book Preface § 1.7 (41st edn. current as of January 21, 2021), https://www.fda.gov/drugs/development-approval-process-drugs/orange-book-preface. A therapeutically equivalent drug is one that 'can be expected to have the same clinical effect and safety profile when administered to patients under the conditions specified in the labeling.' Ibid. § 1.2 (emphasis added); see also 21 C.F.R. § 314.3(b) (same).

of mortality *caused by CHF.*' Id. (emphasis in original). The district court concluded a reasonable juror could not have found Teva's post-MI LVD indication 'caused or even encouraged direct infringement' of this claimed use. Id.

***1326** GSK appealed, arguing that substantial evidence supported the jury's finding of induced infringement and that its verdict should be reinstated. We agreed. Teva petitioned for en banc rehearing, which we construed as also requesting panel rehearing. Teva argued our October 2, 2020 decision could be broadly read to impose liability on ANDA filers that carve out patented uses under section viii when seeking approval to market generic drug products, in direct contravention of the Hatch-Waxman Act. Amici curiae raised concerns about lack of clarity of our decision when the patented uses are carved out of the FDA-approved label. On February 9, 2021, we granted the petition for panel rehearing, vacated the October 2, 2020 judgment, and withdrew the October 2, 2020 opinions.

Amici were concerned that our prior decision could be read to upset the careful balance struck with section viii carve-outs. The Novartis Brief explained, 'Generics could be held liable for actively inducing infringement if they marketed a drug with a label describing a patented therapeutic use or if they took active steps to encourage doctors or patients to use the drug in an infringing manner. But generics could not be held liable for merely marketing and selling under a 'skinny' label omitting all patented indications, or for merely noting (without mentioning any infringing uses) that FDA had rated a product as therapeutically equivalent to a brand-name drug.' Novartis Br. at 1–2. We agree that Novartis accurately stated the law, and we agreed to rehear this case to make clear how the facts of this case place it clearly outside the boundaries of the concerns expressed by amici. As this record reflects, in both time periods, substantial evidence supports that Teva actively induced by marketing a drug with a label encouraging a patented therapeutic use. They did not 'omit[] all patented indications' or 'merely note[] (without mentioning any infringing uses) that FDA had rated a product as therapeutically equivalent to a brand-name drug.' Novartis Br. at 1–2. This is a case in which substantial evidence supports a jury finding that the patented use was on the generic label at all relevant times and that, therefore, Teva failed to carve out all patented indications. This narrow, case-specific review of substantial evidence does not upset the careful balance struck by the Hatch-Waxman Act regarding section viii carve-outs.

## Discussion

We apply regional circuit law for review of a district court's grant of JMOL. *Lucent Techs., Inc. v. Gateway, Inc.*, 580 F.3d 1301, 1309 (Fed. Cir. 2009). The Third Circuit reviews those grants *de novo. Curley v. Klem*, 499 F.3d 199, 205–06 (3d Cir. 2007). Following a jury trial, a district court should grant JMOL 'sparingly' and 'only if, viewing the evidence in the light most favorable to the nonmovant and giving it the advantage of every fair and reasonable inference, there is insufficient evidence from which a jury reasonably could find liability.' *Marra v. Phila. Hous. Auth.*, 497 F.3d 286, 300 (3d Cir. 2007). 'To prevail on a renewed motion for JMOL following a jury trial, a party must show that the jury's findings, presumed or express, are not supported by substantial evidence or, if they were, that the legal conclusion(s) implied by the jury's verdict cannot in law be supported by those findings.' *Power Integrations, Inc. v. Fairchild Semiconductor Int'l, Inc.*, 843 F.3d 1315, 1326 (Fed. Cir. 2016).

## I

## Induced Infringement

'Whoever actively induces infringement of a patent shall be liable as an infringer.' 35 U.S.C. § 271(b). 'Infringement ***1327** is a question of fact, reviewed for substantial evidence when tried to a jury.' *Lucent,* 580 F.3d at 1309. A finding of inducement requires establishing 'that the defendant possessed specific intent to encourage another's infringement.' *DSU Med. Corp. v. JMS Co.,* 471 F.3d 1293, 1306 (Fed. Cir. 2006) (*en banc* in relevant part) (internal quotation marks omitted). This requires a plaintiff to show 'that the alleged infringer's actions induced infringing acts and that he knew or should have known his actions would induce actual infringements.' Id. (internal quotation marks omitted). 'While proof of intent is necessary, direct evidence is not required; rather, circumstantial evidence may suffice.' Id. (internal quotation marks omitted). When a plaintiff relies on a drug's label accompanying the marketing of a drug to prove intent, '[t]he label must encourage, recommend, or promote infringement.' *Takeda Pharm. USA, Inc. v. West-Ward Pharm. Corp.,* 785 F.3d 625, 631 (Fed. Cir. 2015) (citations omitted).

GSK argues that substantial evidence supports the jury's verdict of induced infringement. Throughout the trial and on appeal, GSK argued there are two indications on the labels that instruct doctors to prescribe carvedilol for uses that directly infringe the '000 patent claims: the post-MI LVD indication and the congestive heart failure indication. Thus, GSK argues both the partial label and the full label encourage infringement. We first address the partial label period and then turn to the full label period.

### The Partial Label Period

A generic producer may exclude a patented use from its label, by way of a 'section viii carveout' as provided by 21 U.S.C § 355(j)(2)(A)(viii):

(2)(A) An abbreviated application for a new drug shall contain—

(i) information to show that the conditions of use prescribed, recommended, or suggested in the labeling proposed for the new drug have been previously approved for a drug listed under paragraph (7) (hereinafter in this subsection referred to as a 'listed drug');

* * *

(viii) if with respect to the listed drug referred to in clause (i) information was filed under subsection (b) or (c) for a method of use patent which does not claim a use for which the applicant is seeking approval under this subsection, a statement that the method of use patent does not claim such a use.

The applicant must also submit its proposed label to the FDA omitting or carving out all methods of use claimed in a patent. 21 C.F.R. § 314.94(a)(8)(iv). 'FDA acceptance of the carve-out label allows the generic company to place its drug on the market (assuming the ANDA meets other requirements), but only for a subset of approved uses—*i.e.,* those not covered by the brand's patents.' *Caraco Pharm. Labs., Ltd. v. Novo Nordisk A/S,* 566 U.S. 399, 406, 132 S.Ct. 1670, 182 L.Ed.2d 678 (2012).

GSK argues that, despite Teva's section viii certification purporting to carve out one heart failure indication and its deletion of the indication from its partial label, substantial evidence supports the jury's finding that Teva induced doctors to infringe the method of use claimed in the '000 patent. GSK argues that substantial evidence supports the jury's verdict that Teva's partial label encouraged an infringing use (via the post-MI LVD indication) and that Teva's marketing materials encouraged prescribing carvedilol in a manner that would cause infringement of the '000 patent. We agree.

### *1328 A

The parties dispute whether Teva effected a section viii carve-out of GSK's patented methods of use, making Teva's label a so-called 'skinny label.' Since the jury found infringement, we must assume it decided that question in GSK's favor. *Williamson v. Consol. Rail Corp.,* 926 F.2d 1344, 1348 (3d Cir. 1991) ('When reviewing the jury's finding ..., we give [plaintiff], as verdict winner, the benefit of all logical inferences that could be drawn from the evidence presented, resolve all conflicts in the evidence in his favor and, in general, view the record in the light most favorable to him.'). And as a quintessential fact question, we must uphold the jury's verdict on that point so long as substantial evidence supports it. GSK provided substantial evidence that Teva's partial label instructed the method of use claimed in the '000 patent and thus was not a skinny label.

At the outset, GSK's cardiology expert, Dr. McCullough, explained that doctors, the alleged direct infringers, receive information about generic drug products from a variety of sources, including the drug labels. J.A. 10612:1–9. He then walked through each element of claim 1 of the '000 patent and compared it to Teva's partial label. He relied on the post-MI LVD indication in Teva's partial label, which stated:

Carvedilol is indicated to reduce cardiovascular mortality in clinically stable patients who have survived the acute phase of a myocardial infarction and have a left ventricular ejection fraction of ≤ 40 % (with or without symptomatic heart failure) (see CLINICAL STUDIES [14.1]).

J.A. 5508 (emphasis and brackets in original). Dr. McCullough testified this description satisfied the 'decreasing mortality caused by congestive heart failure in a patient' limitation. See J.A. 10623:6–17; see also J.A. 10629:19–10630:6, 10630:16–20. He also explained that post-MI LVD 'is intertwined with heart failure.' J.A. 10673:23–10674:1. Teva's cardiology expert, Dr. Zusman, agreed that a patient who has a left ventricular ejection fraction of less than or equal to 40 % with symptomatic heart failure (as recited on Teva's partial label) would be diagnosed as suffering from congestive heart failure under the district court's construction. J.A. 11226:14–19.

GSK presented evidence that Teva's partial label also satisfied the remaining claim limitations. Dr. McCullough testified that the Dosage and Administration section of the partial label disclosed administering particular dosages that satisfied the 'administering a therapeutically acceptable amount of carvedilol' and administering 'daily maintenance dosages' limitations. See J.A. 10624:12–18, 10624:24–10625:3, 10626:9–19, 10626:23–10627:1. The post-MI LVD indication, the portion of the label Dr. McCullough testified satisfied the CHF limitation, explicitly directs the reader to Clinical Studies § 14.1 of Teva's label. J.A. 5508. The Clinical Studies § 14.1 showed that patients taking carvedilol in the study had background treatment of ACE inhibitors and diuretics. Dr. McCullough explained this satisfied the claim limitation of administering carvedilol in conjunction with one or more other therapeutic agents selected from the group consisting of ACE inhibitors, a diuretic, and digoxin. J.A. 10625:4–19, 10625:24–10626:8; see also J.A. 5523 (CAPRICORN study in which 47 % of patients receiving carvedilol had symptoms of heart failure, 97 % also had background treatment of ACE inhibitors or angiotensin receptor blockers, and 34 % had background treatment of diuretics); *Sanofi v. Watson Labs. Inc.*, 875 F.3d 636, 645 (Fed. Cir. 2017) (Indication section referencing clinical study section 'expressly direct[ed] the reader to that section ***1329** for elaboration of the class of patients for whom the drug is indicated to achieve the stated objective'). Finally, Dr. McCullough testified that Figure 1 in Clinical Studies § 14.1 showed treatment for longer than six months, which satisfied the 'maintenance period is greater than six months' limitation. J.A. 10627:9–21, 10629:15–18, 10630:21–10631:6, 10631:12–15; see also J.A. 5524 (Fig. 1).

Teva characterizes GSK's argument as a 'cobbl[ing] together' of disparate portions of the partial label. Teva Principal and Resp. Br. at 48, 50. The dissent appears to adopt Teva's characterization, arguing that a jury would have to 'piece[] together' the partial label to arrive at the infringing use. Dis. at 1350–52; *see also id.* at 1359. All of the claim limitations were contained in the Indication section (which amounted to a single sentence), the Clinical Study section (to which doctors were directly referred by the Indication section), and the Dosage and Administration section (which immediately follows the Indication section and which says how much and how often to give the carvedilol). The jury was entitled to credit expert testimony regarding the label's instructions on who should take what drug, when, why, and how, and to reject the argument that certain portions of the label were disjointed from others.

Teva relies on our decision in *Bayer Schering Pharma AG v. Lupin, Ltd.*, 676 F.3d 1316 (Fed. Cir. 2012). In *Bayer Schering,* the patented method of use required achieving three simultaneous effects in the body. Id. at 1320. The defendant's drug product label contained an indication for only one of those effects, with no discussion of safety or efficacy for the other two claimed effects. Id. at 1322. Thus, we held the label failed to recommend or suggest achieving the claimed combination of effects. Id. at 1324. Here, however, as discussed above,

Dr. McCullough marched through Teva's label explaining how it met the limitations of claim 1. Unlike the absence of information in the label of *Bayer Schering*, Dr. McCullough provided testimony that Teva's partial label instructed the claimed treatment and use.

Teva never genuinely challenged Dr. McCullough's testimony regarding the contents of Teva's partial label. Teva cites portions of Dr. Zusman's testimony as purporting to contradict that the post-MI LVD indication means treating heart failure. Teva relies on Dr. Zusman's testimony that treating patients to help them survive heart attack is not treating heart failure. Teva Principal and Resp. Br. at 53 (citing J.A. 11183). But Dr. Zusman also agreed the post-MI LVD patients with symptomatic heart failure would be diagnosed as suffering from congestive heart failure under the district court's construction of that term (which has not been appealed). J.A. 11226:14–19. It was within the province of the jury to weigh the testimony presented by both sides and make its finding. *See Dardovitch v. Haltzman*, 190 F.3d 125, 140 (3d Cir. 1999) ('Credibility determinations are the unique province of a fact finder, be it a jury, or a judge sitting without a jury.'); *MobileMedia Ideas LLC v. Apple Inc.*, 780 F.3d 1159, 1168 (Fed. Cir. 2015) ('[W]hen there is conflicting testimony at trial, and the evidence overall does not make only one finding on the point reasonable, the jury is permitted to make credibility determinations and believe the witness it considers more trustworthy.').

We also do not agree with Teva's argument that its partial label's recitation of treating patients 'with or without symptomatic heart failure' precludes inducement since this may encourage both infringing and noninfringing uses. Teva relies on ***1330** *HZNP Medicines LLC v. Actavis Laboratories UT, Inc.*, 940 F.3d 680 (Fed. Cir. 2019), and *Grunenthal GmbH v. Alkem Laboratories Ltd.*, 919 F.3d 1333 (Fed. Cir. 2019). According to Teva, when its generic carvedilol is used to treat patients without symptomatic heart failure, there is no infringement, and thus, the label's recommended use on both types of patients somehow obviates infringement. We do not find this argument persuasive, and neither of the cases cited by Teva is analogous to these facts.

In *HZNP*, the claimed method of use required three steps: applying a topical medication, waiting for the treated area to dry, and then applying a second topical product. 940 F.3d at 702. Actavis' generic label, however, only required the first applying step. The district court examined the label and held, at summary judgment, it did not induce the claimed use. Id. We agreed given the lack of evidence that the label encouraged, recommended, or promoted users to perform two of the three claimed steps. Id. In contrast, substantial evidence in this case supports the jury's determination that Teva's partial label contained information encouraging each claimed step and the preamble. Dr. McCullough's testimony that the partial label met each claim limitation and represented to doctors that the treatment decreased mortality caused by CHF supports the jury's finding. See J.A. 10623:6–17, 10629:19–10630:6, 10630:16–20.

In *Grunenthal*, the claimed method of use was treating polyneuropathic pain. 919 F.3d at 1336. The defendants filed section viii statements carving out treatment of diabetic peripheral neuropathy (DPN), a type of polyneuropathic pain. Id. at 1339. The generic labels nonetheless maintained an indication to broadly treat severe pain requiring around-the-clock treatment. Yet evidence supported that this severe pain would not necessarily be polyneuropathic, but could also be mononeuropathic or nociceptive. Id. In that case, the district court made a factual determination that this label did not instruct the claimed method. We found no *clear error* in the district court's finding of no inducement because the generic labels did not 'implicitly or explicitly encourage or instruct users to take action that would inevitably lead to … treatment of polyneuropathic pain.' Id. at 1340.[3] Here, a jury found inducement. The combination of Teva's partial label, Dr. McCullough's element-by-element testimony that the partial label explicitly instructs administering carvedilol for the claimed use of decreasing mortality

[3] Moreover, in contrast to this case, we recognized in *Grunenthal* that the partial label was the only evidence of inducement and that we could not conclude on those facts that the district court clearly erred.

caused by CHF, and Dr. Zusman's admission that the post-MI LVD indication falls within the definition of congestive heart failure is substantial evidence that supports the jury's finding.

Critically, the district court erred by treating this fact question—whether the post-MI LVD indication instructs a physician to prescribe carvedilol for a claimed use—as though it were a legal one for it to decide *de novo*. In a footnote of the district court's JMOL decision, it decided the post-MI LVD portion of Teva's label was insufficient to find that the label instructed an infringing use. *Dist. Ct. Op.* at 592 n.9. The district court erred at JMOL by making a fact finding, namely, '[w]hile there may be some overlap between populations of patients suffering from CHF – the treatment of which is within the scope of the '000 patent's claims – and those suffering from post-MI LVD – whose treatment is outside the scope of the claims – the two indications ***1331** are distinct and require different clinical testing and different FDA approvals to treat.' Id. Whether treating post-MI LVD patients with symptomatic heart failure with carvedilol was within the scope of the claims was a fact question. It was for the jury, not this court or the district court, to resolve. 'In determining whether the evidence is sufficient to sustain [the jury's finding of] liability, the court may not weigh the evidence, determine the credibility of witnesses, or substitute its version of the facts for the jury's version.' *Lightning Lube, Inc. v. Witco Corp.*, 4 F.3d 1153, 1166 (3d Cir. 1993). The district court erred in reweighing the evidence and finding against GSK following the jury's verdict in its favor.

**B**

To be sure, the record was not devoid of contrary or equivocal evidence. Teva argues that GSK's submissions to the FDA for Orange Book listing associated with the '000 patent is such evidence. If a new drug application (NDA) has already been approved when the applicant obtains a patent, the applicant must notify the FDA of such patent within 30 days of it issuing. 21 C.F.R. § 314.53(c)(2)(ii). Under penalty of perjury, GSK submitted information for the '000 patent, which issued after carvedilol was FDA-approved, declaring it claimed a method of use for carvedilol. J.A. 6880–87 (Form FDA 3542). GSK was required in part 4.2a of its declaration to 'identify the use with specific reference to the approved labeling for the drug product.' J.A. 6881. It listed: 'treatment of mild-to-severe heart failure of ischemic or cardiomyopathic origin, usually in addition to diuretics, ACE inhibitor, and digitalis, to increase survival.' Id. GSK did not mention the post-MI LVD indication in this submission to the FDA. This, however, does not appear to be the information listed in the Orange Book.

The FDA further required, in part 4.2b of the Form, that GSK '[s]ubmit the description of the approved indication or method of use that [it] propose[d] FDA include as the 'Use Code' in the Orange Book.' J.A. 6882. GSK answered: 'Decreasing Mortality Caused By Congestive Heart Failure.' Id. The FDA accepted that representation and listed the corresponding use code in the Orange Book as describing what is covered by the '000 patent.

There are two ways in which GSK's failure to identify the post-MI LVD use in its part 4.2a statement could be relevant to inducement in this case. First, that failure is relevant to whether the post-MI LVD use infringes. Second, at least for the partial label period, that failure is relevant to intent to induce infringement.[4] On both points, the jury decided against Teva.

As Teva acknowledged, GSK's submissions to the FDA are 'not absolutely dispositive of infringement.' See *GlaxoSmithKline LLC v. Teva Pharm. USA, Inc.*, No. 18-1976 (Feb. 23, 2021), Oral Arg. at 55:49–57:07, available at http://oralarguments.cafc.uscourts.gov/default.aspx?fl=18-1976_02232021.mp3. As we have observed, 'the FDA is not the arbiter of patent infringement issues.' *AstraZeneca LP v. Apotex, Inc.*, 633 F.3d 1042, 1061 (Fed. Cir. 2010). In fact, the FDA has made clear that use codes in the Orange Book 'are not meant to substitute for the [ANDA] applicant's review of the patent and the approved labeling.' ***1332** Applications for FDA Approval to Market a New Drug, 68 Fed. Reg. 36,676, 36,683 (June 18, 2003) (to be

[4] It is hard to imagine how GSK's failure to identify that the '000 patent claims the post-MI LVD use has any bearing on the full label period, as during the full label period, Teva's listed all three indications without regard for GSK's assertions in the Orange Book or its FDA declaration.

codified at 21 C.F.R. pt. 314). The FDA further concluded that it has no expertise in patent law and that a court is the appropriate forum for determining the scope of patent rights. Id.; see also Trial Tr. at 525:12–526:15 (GSK's regulatory expert, Prof. Lietzan, discussing the FDA's statements). Teva's FDA expert, Mr. Karst, agreed that a generic may not rely upon the Orange Book use codes provided by the brand for patent infringement purposes and that ANDA applicants have a separate obligation to analyze the scope of the patents themselves:[5]

Q. And FDA has also stated that [use codes listed in the Orange Book provided by the patentee] are not meant to substitute for the applicant's review of the patent and the approved labeling. Correct?

A. That is what FDA said, correct.

Q. And that is something that you understand in your line of work; is that correct?

A. Yes, I do.

[...]

Q. You believe there's a separate obligation by ANDA applicants to analyze the scope of patents listed in the Orange Book to determine how to prepare their Section viii carve-out label; is that correct?

A. It's correct that FDA said the statement you just had up there. I guess it's gone now, where FDA provides a statement to that effect. That is correct.

Trial Tr. at 1057:13–1058:10. Both FDA experts agreed that the FDA plays no role in determining patent infringement. The jury heard this evidence and the evidence discussed above as to GSK's claim that the post-MI LVD indication infringed the '000 patent. Thus, substantial evidence supports the jury's finding that the post-MI LVD indication infringed the '000 patent.

At oral argument on rehearing, Teva suggested that GSK's FDA submission for the Orange Book listing for the '000 patent, which according to Teva is at odds with GSK's infringement allegations, creates equitable estoppel. See Oral Arg. at 53:56–55:28. There are serious consequences for filing false or incomplete information to the FDA. See id. at 55:28–56:04 (Teva explaining the consequences including rejection of the NDA); see also 18 U.S.C. § 1001 (it is a criminal act to file a false declaration under penalty of perjury). Teva argues one such consequence ought to be equitable estoppel, which should preclude GSK's assertion of the '000 patent against Teva at least as to the post-MI LVD use. GSK's representations regarding the Orange Book listing of the '000 patent, Teva's reliance, and fairness go directly to an equitable estoppel defense, which has not yet been tried to the district court. The district court acknowledged that Teva raised this defense, but decided that it was 'reserved to be tried to the Court at a later date.' J.A. 29.

There are factual disputes regarding the estoppel issue that the district court has not yet had an opportunity to decide. For example, GSK argued on appeal that the use code that was listed in the Orange Book—'decreasing mortality caused by congestive heart failure'—covers all heart failure patients including post-MI LVD patients and that Teva's assertion that the use code covers only the CHF indication is wrong. GSK Resp. and Reply Br. at 30. GSK further argues that 'the use code is ***1333** not tied to any particular indication, and the FDA tells generics that the use code 'is not meant to substitute for the applicant's review of the patent and the approved labeling.' ' Id. (quoting 68 Fed. Reg. at 36,683). And Dr. McCullough testified that the post-MI LVD indication satisfied the first claim limitation, i.e., decreasing mortality caused by congestive heart failure. J.A. 10623:6–10623:23. It is also not clear from this record whether Teva had access to GSK's declaration (which was marked confidential and is not included in the Orange Book). Teva responds that it modified the label exactly as the FDA instructed it to in accordance with the GSK-provided use code. See J.A. 6908–10 (FDA mark-up of Teva label). As acknowledged above, Teva's own FDA expert, Mr. Karst, explained that an ANDA filer must perform its own analysis for patent infringement purposes. Trial Tr. at 1057:13–1058:10

[5] In fact, an ANDA filer can omit from its label 'an indication or other aspect of labeling protected by patent,' whether that patent is contained in the Orange Book or not. See 21 C.F.R. § 314.94(a)(8)(iv).

(testimony of Mr. Karst). Issues of fact remain as to GSK's representations and Teva's reliance on those representations that have been 'reserved to be tried' by the district court. J.A. 29.

The dissent proposes that this court leapfrog that normal process and resolve these questions of law, equity, and fact on appeal without any trial. We decline to do so. The dissent claims it is not focused on estoppel, but rather on whether 'the law' permits an inference of intent from a label in light of GSK's representations to the FDA. See Dis. at 1351. The dissent would hold that GSK's representations to the FDA in its declaration bar a finding of intent by the jury *as a matter of law* regardless of the remainder of the record. But intent is itself a question of fact, and this record contained substantial evidence from which the jury could find Teva intended to infringe despite GSK's representation to the FDA. This rule of law the dissent seeks is exactly the estoppel case made by Teva, which the district court has yet to try.

The issues before us are the issues that were tried to the jury and decided in the district court. We conclude substantial evidence supports the finding that Teva's partial label was evidence Teva instructed physicians to use its carvedilol in an infringing way. Dr. McCullough explained where Teva's partial label met each claim limitation and discussed other materials that would lead physicians to the partial label, culminating with his conclusion that Teva took action that it 'intended would encourage or assist actions by another, i.e., the physician.' J.A. 10644:15–19. Dr. McCullough did not testify that Teva's actions merely describe infringement; he testified that Teva's actions encouraged infringement.

The dissent's suggestion that there were only three pieces of evidence (the partial label plus the two press releases) on which the jury could have relied to find intent is equally inaccurate. The jury received Teva's partial label, extensive expert testimony, Teva's product catalogs, Teva's advertising and promotional activities, Teva's Monthly Prescribing References for doctors, and testimony from Teva's own company witnesses, all of which the jury could have relied on to find Teva intended to encourage, recommend, or promote infringement.

As the Supreme Court explained in *Grokster:*

Evidence of active steps taken to encourage direct infringement such as advertising an infringing use or instructing how to engage in an infringing use, show an affirmative intent that the product be used to infringe, and a showing that infringement was encouraged overcomes the law's reluctance to find liability when a defendant merely sells a commercial product suitable for some lawful use.

***1334** *Metro-Goldwyn-Mayer Studios Inc. v. Grokster, Ltd.*, 545 U.S. 913, 936, 125 S.Ct. 2764, 162 L.Ed.2d 781 (2005) (citation and alterations omitted). In this case, we must presume the jury found that Teva sold carvedilol with a label that instructed physicians to use it in an infringing manner. Our precedent has consistently held that, when a product is sold with an infringing label or an infringing instruction manual, such a label is evidence of intent to induce infringement. *See Vanda Pharm. Inc. v. West-Ward Pharm. Int'l Ltd.*, 887 F.3d 1117, 1130–31 (Fed. Cir. 2018) (no clear error in the district court's finding that the label instructions constituted a recommendation to infringe the claimed use); *Sanofi v. Watson Labs. Inc.*, 875 F.3d 636, 646 (Fed. Cir. 2017) ('The content of the label in this case permits the inference of specific intent to encourage the infringing use.'); *Eli Lilly and Co. v. Teva Parenteral Med., Inc.*, 845 F.3d 1357, 1368 (Fed. Cir. 2017) ('When the alleged inducement relies on a drug label's instructions, '[t]he question is not just whether [those] instructions describ[e] the infringing mode, … but whether the instructions teach an infringing use such that we are willing to infer from those instructions an affirmative intent to infringe the patent. The label must encourage, recommend, or promote infringement.' ') (citation omitted) (quoting Takeda, 785 F.3d at 631); *AstraZeneca*, 633 F.3d at 1060 ('The pertinent question is whether the proposed label instructs users to perform the patented method. If so, the proposed label may provide evidence of … affirmative intent to induce infringement.'); *Arthrocare Corp. v. Smith & Nephew, Inc.*, 406 F.3d 1365, 1377 (Fed. Cir. 2005) (affirming jury's induced infringement determination when defendant distributed marketing material and manuals that instructed how to use the product in an infringing manner).[6]

We assume, as we must, that the jury found the post-MI LVD use infringes the '000 patent, and that Teva's label contained instructions encouraging prescribing carvedilol in a manner that infringes the '000 patent. Throughout, the dissent claims that there was not substantial evidence upon which the jury could conclude that Teva's label would encourage doctors to prescribe Teva's carvedilol for the labeled uses. That is because, according to Teva (and the dissent), there is no evidence that doctors read labels or prescribe according to those labels. But the jury was presented expert testimony from Dr. McCullough (GSK's expert), from Dr. Zusman (Teva's expert), and from Teva's own documents to the contrary. First, Dr. McCullough testified that doctors do read labels. See J.A. 10612:7–9 ('Q. Two, that doctors don't read labels? Do you agree that that is the case? A. No, I disagree with that.'). Second, Teva's own Monthly Prescribing References, which were 'intended solely for use by the medical professional,' explained that '[t]he clinician must be familiar with the full product labeling provided by the manufacturer or distributor of the drug, of every product he or she prescribes, as well as the relevant medical literature.' J.A. 6196 (Teva's 2012 Monthly Prescribing Reference); see also J.A. 10611:19–25 (Dr. McCullough); Trial Tr. at 1253:15–23, 1254:23–1255:9 (Dr. Zusman agreeing that Teva's MPR indicates that the MPR 'has been produced to provide an easily accessible reminder ***1335** of basic information useful to review when prescribing medications' and that physicians should verify any questions against the labelling). In other words, the literature Teva provided to doctors told them to read labels and to prescribe according to them. While Teva's Monthly Prescribing References were published during the full label period, they powerfully refute Teva's claim that doctors do not and need not read labels in conjunction with their prescribing practices. Teva's own Monthly Prescribing References merely confirm the quite logical proposition that doctors read labels and that the labels are intended to affect prescribing decisions. We cannot conclude that it would be unreasonable for the jury to think that, in 2007 or 2011, Teva believed doctors did not and need not read labels and only then wisened to the idea in 2012. In fact, Teva's own Director of National Accounts, Mr. Rekenthaler, testified to his belief that doctors would prescribe carvedilol according to the package insert (the label). Trial Tr. at 590:15–17 ('I guess my expectation is, like any drug, that it would be used as detailed in the package insert.'); id. at 592:5–8 ('I mean my assumption would be, unless something specific was brought up, that it would be used, that the physicians would use it as they should use it, again which is detailed in our insert.').

This is record evidence that Teva intended its label to affect physician's prescribing practices, and the jury was entitled, as our caselaw has repeatedly held, to rely upon that to determine Teva's intent. But it is not the only evidence.

GSK also presented extensive expert testimony along with Teva's marketing efforts, catalogs, press releases, and testimony from Teva's own witnesses, showing that Teva encouraged carvedilol sales for CHF despite its attempted carve-out. This is evidence supporting the jury's finding that Teva induced infringement.

The jury was presented with evidence of Teva's marketing materials. Teva's Spring 2008 and Spring 2009 Product Catalogs described Teva's carvedilol as an AB rated therapeutic equivalent to Coreg®. J.A. 6221, 6270. Teva and amici agree that an AB rating means the generic product is therapeutically equivalent to the brand product under the conditions specified in the generic's label. As explained above, substantial evidence supports the jury's presumed conclusion that the partial label's indication for post-MI LVD did not effectively carve out the use claimed in the '000 patent. Thus, Teva's AB rated representations under these limited circum-

[6] Consistent with all of these cases, when a label instructs or teaches an infringing use, it can be considered evidence of intent to encourage that use. The jury was entitled to credit expert testimony regarding the label's instructions on who should take what drug, when, why, and how, and to reject the dissent's claim that the label describes rather than instructs as to an infringing use.

stances, when substantial evidence supports the jury's presumed determination regarding the label's contents, are further affirmative evidence supporting the jury's inducement finding.[7]

GSK also presented evidence that, prior to the '000 patent's issuance, Teva issued two relevant press releases: one in 2004 and another in 2007. In its 2004 press release, Teva announced that the FDA granted it 'tentative approval' for its carvedilol tablets, with final approval 'anticipated upon expiry of patent protection for the brand product on March 5, 2007.' J.A. 6347. It noted its 'Carvedilol Tablets are the AB rated generic equivalent of GlaxoSmithKline's Coreg® Tablets and are indicated ***1336** for treatment of heart failure and hypertension.' Id. (emphasis added). The dissent suggests that Teva's 'reference to heart failure' is not evidence that supports the jury's finding that Teva intended to encourage infringement of GSK's claimed method. The entire purpose of this press release is to announce its approval as a substitute for GSK's Coreg® Tablets, and it expressly says that the Teva generic 'tablets are the AB-rated generic equivalent of GlaxoSmithKline's Coreg® Tablets and are indicated for treatment of heart failure and hypertension.' J.A. 6347. The press release's use of 'heart failure' does not parse between congestive heart failure or post-MI LVD. This is not an errant reference to 'heart failure'; it is Teva in a press release telling the world that its generic is a substitute for GSK's Coreg® tablets to treat congestive heart failure in the same manner as Coreg® (which is a method that infringed the '000 patent). The dissent criticizes our analysis, claiming that we have weakened intentional encouragement because 'simply calling a product a 'generic version' or 'generic equivalent'—is now enough.' Dis. at 1359–60. That is not our holding or the facts.

Though the dissent seems to think the press release is not evidence of encouragement, it seems self-evident that a jury could conclude that Teva's intent in issuing a press release telling the world it could use Teva's tablets as a substitute for GSK's Coreg® tablets to treat congestive heart failure was to encourage that use. Moreover, Dr. McCullough testified that he saw the 2004 press release and that it indicates physicians should prescribe generic carvedilol for heart failure. J.A. 11656:1–10; J.A. 11657:6–10 (testifying that Teva's press release informed doctors that 'it certainly *should* be' prescribed for the treatment of heart failure); J.A. 11659:11–19 (Teva's press release indicates that doctors *should* be able to prescribe generic carvedilol for heart failure). Dr. McCullough also testified that doctors consider press releases so they 'know when drugs are going generic.' J.A. 11655:9–24.

Teva issued a second press release in 2007 in which it stated that it had received final approval 'to market its Generic version of GlaxoSmithKline's cardiovascular agent Coreg® (Carvedilol) Tablets.' J.A. 6353. Dr. McCullough testified that the 2007 press release's use of 'cardiovascular agent' indicated to doctors they could use Teva's carvedilol 'for all indications,' including heart failure. J.A. 11660:3–13. Dr. McCullough also testified that he believed that this press release would encourage doctors to prescribe Teva's generic carvedilol for the infringing indications. J.A. 10644:15–19 ('Q. And so this element that Teva took action and failed to take action, what Teva intended would *encourage* or assist actions by another party, i.e., the physician. In your expert opinion, has that requirement been met? A. Yes.' (emphasis added)) (Dr. McCullough discussing the impact of the press releases on doctors). On appeal, we review the jury's verdict for substantial evidence based upon the record; we cannot hunt outside the record to find evidence to try to contradict the verdict. The dissent claims there is no intentional encouragement because the word cardiovascular is '[a] well-understood adjective' that means 'relating to the heart,' and as such Teva's press release could simply be read to encourage use for non-patented heart related conditions. Dis. at 1353. First, the dissent goes outside the record to make up this definition, something the district court explicitly told the jury it could not do. See Trial Tr. at 264 ('During the course of the trial, you must not conduct any independent research about the case … In other words, you should not consult

[7] We do not hold that an AB rating in a true section viii carve-out (one in which a label was produced that had no infringing indications) would be evidence of inducement. In this case, Teva's representation of AB rating would point physicians to its partial label, which, for the reasons above, the jury was free to credit as evidence of induced infringement.

dictionaries or reference materials.'). Second, there was actual testimony ***1337** in the record about how the word cardiovascular in this press release would be understood by skilled artisans. See J.A. 11660:3–13 (McCullough testifying that a skilled artisan would understand the word cardiovascular in this press release to indicate that the generic could be used for all indications including heart failure). Third, Teva did not merely say its drug is a cardiovascular agent, leaving the world to wonder about its uses. It said its product is a generic equivalent of GSK's cardiovascular agent Coreg®. It was reasonable for the jury to conclude, especially in light of the prior press release that expressly mentioned heart failure, that Teva was again encouraging the substitution of its product for all of Coreg's® cardiovascular indications, including as claimed in the '000 patent.

We have acknowledged that, as a matter of law, affirmative acts taken before a patent issues cannot violate § 271(b). *Nat'l Presto Indus., Inc. v. W. Bend Co.,* 76 F.3d 1185, 1196 (Fed. Cir. 1996). Consistent with this rule, the jury was instructed GSK needed to prove by a preponderance of the evidence:

> that Teva took some affirmative action, or that Teva continued to take an action that began before the '000 patent issued, after the '000 patent was issued on January 8, 2008, intending to cause the physicians to directly infringe by administering Teva's carvedilol product[.]

J.A. 168. In this case, the jury was presented with evidence from which it could infer that Teva's press releases remained on Teva's website until at least 2015. J.A. 6353 (2007 press release date stamped '4/14/2015'). Teva's Director of Marketing testified that Teva added carvedilol product information to the Teva website as part of its 2007 launch. J.A. 10991:13–22 (Suzanne Collier, Teva's Director of Marketing Communications and Trade Dress). The 2007 press release given to the jury contains a directory path showing it was stored on the Teva website as follows: 'Home page>Media>Latest News.' And GSK demonstrated the 2007 Teva press release was available on the Teva website as late as 2015. The press releases were extensively and repeatedly presented before the jury, with at least five witnesses discussing them. See J.A. 10643:2–10644:14, 11656:4–11657:5, 11659:11–11660:17 (discussed with Dr. McCullough); J.A. 11238:10–11241:14, Trial Tr. at 1241:15–1243:5 (discussed with Dr. Zusman); J.A. 10533:16–23, 10542:1–25 (discussed with Prof. Lietzan); Trial Tr. at 445:9–447:10, J.A. 10973:15–10974:23, Trial Tr. at 974:24–975:4 (discussed with Teva's Senior Director of Regulatory Affairs, Jill Pastore); Trial Tr. at 1619:9–18 (discussed with Teva's damages expert, Dr. Sumanth Addanki). Teva neither provided contrary evidence nor argued to the jury that the press releases, at least one of which could be found on the Teva website even at the time of trial, were not available on Teva's website throughout the alleged infringement period. Under these circumstances, the jury could infer, from Teva's placement of information on its website and from its press releases, that Teva intended its website to be a source of information for prescribing doctors and that its website promoted the infringing use throughout the period of infringement.[8] Teva had encouraged ***1338** in its labels, press releases, product catalogs, and marketing materials. Substantial evidence supports the jury's verdict that Teva induced infringement.

### C

GSK presented evidence that Teva's partial label did not successfully carve out the patented use, and thus, Teva was selling its generic with a label which infringed the method claim. GSK presented evidence that doctors read and consider labels, that Teva's marketing materials guided doctors to the label and to its website promoting the patented use, that Teva issued

---

[8] The jury was even presented evidence that Teva encouraged doctors to visit its website for information about its generic drugs when prescribing them. Trial Tr. at 1245:16–19 (Teva's expert, Dr. Zusman, acknowledging that Teva advised doctors to 'visit its website' to obtain product information); Trial Tr. at 1249:12–15 (same); Trial Tr. at 1251:8–11 (same); Trial Tr. at 1258:12–20 (same). Though the evidence comes from Teva's 2012 and 2013 Monthly Prescribing References for doctors (during the full label period), it was reasonable for the jury to conclude that Teva intended for doctors to visit its website for prescribing information about the Teva's products.

press releases encouraging doctors to prescribe carvedilol for the patented use, that Teva's own employees expected doctors to prescribe carvedilol during the partial label period for the patented uses, and expert testimony that Teva's actions encouraged doctors to do so. This is substantial evidence from which a reasonable jury could conclude that Teva intentionally encouraged the practice of the claimed method. Accordingly, substantial evidence supports the jury's finding of induced infringement for the partial label period.

### The Full Label Period

Beginning on May 1, 2011, Teva's carvedilol label contained all three indications present in the Coreg® label. That is, in addition to the post-MI LVD and hypertension indications, Teva's label contained the 'Heart Failure' indication. Specifically, it added the following indication:

1.1 Heart Failure. Carvedilol tablets are indicated for the treatment of mild-to-severe chronic heart failure of ischemic or cardiomyopathic origin, usually in addition to diuretics, ACE inhibitors, and digitalis, to increase survival and, also, to reduce the risk of hospitalization [see Drug Interactions (7.4) and Clinical Studies (14.1)].

J.A. 5532 (brackets in original, italics omitted). Dr. McCullough testified that the addition of the heart failure indication also met all the claim limitations of the '000 patent. J.A. 10623:24–10625:3, 10625:20–10626:11, 10626:20–10627:8, 10628:15–10629:20, 10630:7–23, 10631:7–21. Substantial evidence supports the jury's presumed finding that Teva's full label contains all of the claim limitations, which Teva does not dispute.

In addition to the information Teva placed in its press releases and on its websites, Teva sent marketing materials and catalogs to healthcare providers during the full label period. For example, Teva's 2012 Monthly Prescribing Reference, which explained a 'clinician must be familiar with the full product labeling … of every product he or she prescribes, as well as the relevant medical literature,' contained a listing for carvedilol with the heart failure indication. J.A. 6196, 6200. Dr. McCullough testified that the 2012 MPR was intended for prescribing doctors and that he and doctors across the country receive the MPR 'on a regular basis.' J.A. 10607:9–10608:1, 10609:19–22. He also testified that the 2012 MPR was telling doctors to 'verify any questions against the labeling or contact the company marketing the drug,' that the label 'provides the base information that flows to doctors,' and that Teva is 'clearly telling doctors they should read the labels.' J.A. 10610:3–21.

Teva's 2013 MPR contained the same information, same instructions to doctors, and same carvedilol listing with the heart failure indication. J.A. 6205, 6208. Dr. Zusman agreed that one could interpret the ***1339** 2013 MPR as being a part of the educational materials Teva provided to doctors and that Teva wanted the MPR to be a part of a treating doctor's toolbox. Trial Tr. at 1250:18–23, 1252:5–1253:9. He also agreed that the 2013 MPR was instructing doctors to verify the information in the MPR by referring to the product labeling or contacting the company marketing the drug, here Teva. Trial Tr. at 1254:24–1255:9, 1256:1–10. He also acknowledged that the 2013 MPR instructed doctors to visit Teva's website for more information. Trial Tr. at 1258:8–20.

Substantial evidence supports the finding that Teva encouraged physicians to use its carvedilol for an infringing purpose during the full label period. The jury was entitled to credit the full label itself containing the infringing use, Dr. McCullough's testimony that the full label contained each claim limitation, and Teva's marketing materials as demonstrating Teva specifically intended to encourage, recommend, or promote the use of carvedilol in an infringing manner. The dissent confronts none of this evidence. To be clear, the dissent would overturn a jury verdict, finding Teva's full label encouraged doctors to prescribe an infringing manner, as not supported by substantial evidence where the label undisputedly encourages an infringing uses (CHF) and when Teva tells doctors to read its label for prescribing information. To do so would be a major change in our precedent.

### Causation

To establish inducement, a patent owner must show that the accused inducer's actions actually induced the infringing acts of another and knew or should have known that its actions would induce actual infringement. *DSU Med.*, 471 F.3d at 1304. The jury was instructed 'GSK must prove that Teva's alleged inducement, as opposed to other factors, actually caused physicians to directly infringe the '000 patent.' J.A. 173. Teva could only be found liable for induced infringement if GSK showed 'Teva successfully communicated with and induced a third-party direct infringer and that the communication was the cause of the direct infringement by the third-party infringer.' Id. The jury was also instructed 'GSK must prove that Teva's actions led physicians to directly infringe a claim of the '000 patent, but GSK may do so with circumstantial – as opposed to direct – evidence.' Id.

Teva argues that it did not cause doctors to actually prescribe generic carvedilol. Teva argues that, at all relevant times, doctors were prescribing carvedilol for CHF based on information they had received for GSK's Coreg®. Teva points to guidelines from the American College of Cardiology (ACC), the American Heart Association (AHA), medical textbooks, and treatises to argue doctors already knew to treat CHF using carvedilol long before Teva launched its generic. Teva argues that this information, not its actions, made physicians aware of all the benefits of carvedilol for heart failure patients. The district court accepted Teva's argument as sufficient to overcome the jury's verdict in GSK's favor. *Dist. Ct. Op.* at 594. We do not agree.

The jury had before it Teva's partial label, full label, various marketing materials, and press releases. It heard from the expert witnesses that doctors read labels and that Teva's labels satisfied all of the claim limitations. *See* J.A. 10612:7–9 (testimony of Dr. McCullough: 'Q. Two, that doctors don't read labels? Do you agree that that is the case? A. No, I disagree with that.'). It also heard that doctors received marketing materials from Teva, that these materials directed doctors to prescribe according to the labels, and that ***1340** these materials told doctors to visit Teva's website for more information regarding its products. Teva tried to convince the jury that doctors do not read labels even after its own marketing material, which was sent directly to doctors, explicitly instructed them to read the labels.

Despite all of this evidence, Teva asks us to supplant the role of the jury and reweigh evidence in its favor. But it was for the jury to decide—not us, the district court, or the dissent—whether Teva's efforts actually induced infringement. It was fair for the jury to infer that when Teva distributed and marketed a product with labels encouraging an infringing use, it actually induced doctors to infringe.[9] 'Indeed, we have affirmed induced infringement verdicts based on circumstantial evidence of inducement (e.g., advertisements, user manuals) directed to a class of direct infringers (e.g., customers, end users) without requiring hard proof that any individual third-party direct infringer was actually persuaded to infringe by that material.' *Power Integrations,* 843 F.3d at 1335; *see also Arthrocare,* 406 F.3d at 1377 ('There was also strong circumstantial evidence that Smith & Nephew's probes were used in an infringing manner, and that Smith & Nephew induced users to employ the probes in that way.'). Given Teva distributed other materials in addition to its labels, we do not have to decide in this case whether the labels alone are enough to establish causation. The dissent criticizes the presence of circumstantial evidence, but as the jury was correctly instructed, '[i]t is your job to decide how much weight to give the direct and circumstantial evidence. The law makes no distinction between the weight that you should give to either one, nor does it say that one is any better evidence than the other.' J.A. 147 (Jury Instruction 1.4). The jury had sufficient circumstantial evidence, in the form of labels, marketing materials, catalogs, press releases, and expert

[9] The dissent acknowledges that an example of when a jury might reasonably infer causation is when a product's user manual encourages an infringing use. Dis. at 1358–59 (collecting cases). But the dissent would hold, nonetheless, that a jury cannot infer causation from the full label, which undisputedly contains all of the claim limitations, despite the evidence showing the full label instructs doctors to infringe, just as a user manual.

testimony, for it to conclude that Teva succeeded in influencing doctors to prescribe carvedilol for the infringing use. We thus vacate the district court's grant of JMOL of no induced infringement and reinstate the jury verdict, which was supported by substantial evidence.

II

**Damages**

The Patent Act provides: 'the court shall award [the patent owner] damages adequate to compensate for the infringement, but in no event less than a reasonable royalty for the use of the invention by the infringer.' 35 U.S.C. § 284. To recover lost profit damages, 'the patent owner must show 'causation in fact,' establishing that 'but for' the infringement, he would have made additional profits.' *Grain Processing Corp. v. Am. Maize-Prod. Co.,* 185 F.3d 1341, 1349 (Fed. Cir. 1999).

GSK's damages expert testified that 17.1 % of Teva's generic carvedilol sales during the period of infringement were for the method claimed in the '000 patent. Teva does not dispute this calculation. The jury assessed damages of $234,110,000 based on lost profits, plus a reasonable royalty payment of $1,400,000. The verdict amount is about half of that presented by GSK's damages expert. Teva argues that, if the jury had been properly instructed, it ***1341** would have assessed no damages or at most only a reasonable royalty.

Teva argues the jury should have been instructed that GSK must prove that, for every infringing sale Teva made, the direct infringer would have purchased Coreg® rather than another generic producer's carvedilol. The district court declined to present that instruction, explaining:

The undisputed evidence is that [Teva's] generic carvedilol is interchangeable with the generic carvedilol of the non-party manufacturers; therefore, the generic carvedilol of these non-party manufacturers is an *infringing alternative* – and *not* a non-infringing alternative. These non-parties' products, thus, would not exist in the but-for world, which must be constructed to include 'likely outcomes with *infringement factored out of the economic picture.*' *Grain Processing Corp. v. Am. Maize-Prods. Co.,* 185 F.3d 1341, 1350 (Fed. Cir. 1999) (emphasis added).

J.A. 222 (Memorandum Order (June 9, 2017) (emphasis in original)). The district court recognized that '[i]t is undisputed that, at all times relevant to the lost profits analysis, there were generic carvedilol tablets available from at least eight different generic manufacturers,' J.A. 222 n.3, and stated that '[i]t doesn't matter whether the *sales* by other generic suppliers would be non-infringing, because the ultimate **use** of those products by doctors *would* be infringing and thus not a permissible consideration.' J.A. 223 (emphasis in original).

Teva argues that it was incorrect to instruct the jury that '[t]he use of the acceptable substitutes also must not infringe the patent because they did not include all the features required by the patent. For example, the use of generic carvedilol supplied by companies other than Teva was not an acceptable non-infringing substitute.' J.A. 195 (Jury Instruction 6.3.3). Teva argues that this instruction ignores the reality of the marketplace because other carvedilol producers who had not been sued for infringement would have made the sales Teva made, in part because pharmacies would automatically substitute generic carvedilol for Coreg® prescriptions. Teva's argument is in conflict with long-standing precedent that the presence of noninfringing alternatives precludes an award of lost profits, but the presence of other infringers does not.

The district court correctly instructed the jury that the availability of carvedilol from other generic producers is not a 'non-infringing substitute.' GSK's expert's analysis accounted for Teva's sales for the infringing use, amounting to 17.1 % of Teva's total carvedilol sales. Had another generic producer made those sales, those uses too would have been infringing. The other generic carvedilol producers were, therefore, not noninfringing alternatives. See Grain Processing, 185 F.3d at 1350 ('The 'but for' inquiry therefore requires a reconstruction of the market, as it would have developed absent the infringing product, to determine what the patentee would have made.') (internal quotations and alterations omitted); *Micro Motion, Inc.*

*v. Kane Steel Co.*, Inc., 894 F.2d 1318, 1322 (Fed. Cir. 1990) ('There is precedent for finding causation despite an alternative source of supply if that source is an infringer.'). Accordingly, the damages verdict, which is not otherwise challenged, is sustained.

**Conclusion**

Because substantial evidence supports the jury's verdict of induced infringement, we vacate the district court's grant of JMOL. Because the district court did not err in its jury instructions on damages, we ***1342** affirm on the cross-appeal. We remand for appropriate further proceedings.

**VACATED-IN-PART, AFFIRMED-IN-PART, AND REMANDED**

Costs

Costs are awarded to GSK.

**Prost, Circuit Judge, dissenting.**

GSK's patent on carvedilol expired in 2007. At the time, however, it still had a patent on one of carvedilol's three FDA-approved uses. Because the FDA cannot authorize a generic version of a drug that would infringe a patent, this one remaining patented use could have prevented a less-expensive, generic carvedilol from coming to market altogether—even though the drug *itself* and other uses of it were unpatented. Congress saw this problem coming. It wanted to make sure that one patented use wouldn't prevent public access to a generic version of a drug that also has unpatented uses. *See Caraco Pharm. Labs. Ltd. v. Novo Nordisk* A/S, 566 U.S. 399, 415, 132 S.Ct. 1670, 182 L.Ed.2d 678 (2012). So it created rules for just this situation.

These rules, embodied in the so-called skinny-label provisions of the Hatch-Waxman Act, are straightforward. If a brand drug company (here, GSK) has a patent on one of a drug's uses, it tells the FDA which use is patented. In fact, it tells the FDA exactly what language from its label is covered by its patents. The FDA will then permit a generic version of that drug to come to market if the manufacturer 'carves out' such use from its drug label by omitting the language that the brand drug company identified. That's what happened here. GSK's sworn FDA filings identified just one use as patented. So Teva carved out that use and came to market with its 'skinny' label. It played by the rules, exactly as Congress intended. It sold its generic for years without controversy.

And then, in the seventh year, GSK finally sued. It alleged that, even though Teva's skinny label carved out the very use—indeed, the *only* use—that GSK said was patented, the label showed that Teva intended to encourage an infringing use. GSK also supported its inducement case by pointing to two cursory, pre-patent press releases that announced Teva's drug's approval (or 'tentative' approval) and called it the generic equivalent of GSK's brand drug Coreg. The evidence of inducement—i.e., that Teva had culpable intent to encourage infringement and that its skinny label or press releases caused doctors' prescribing practices—was thin to nonexistent. But a jury found Teva liable all the same. This sometimes happens. And when it does, there is a remedy: a court will reverse a jury's verdict if there is insufficient evidence to support it. The experienced trial judge sensibly did just that.

The majority, now on its second try, again reinstates the verdict nonetheless. Its first try prompted widespread criticism concerning the troubling implications for skinny labels. This effort is no better. With reasoning sometimes labored, sometimes opaque, the majority strains to prop up a jury verdict that is unsupportable. For example, based on language that remained on the skinny label after Teva's carve-out, the majority finds it reasonable to infer that Teva *intentionally encouraged* infringement. It finds this reasonable even though Teva, by carving out everything that GSK said would infringe, was trying to *avoid* having its label encourage infringement. The majority then indulges the inference that doctors, as a class, *relied* on

Teva's skinny label to infringe, even though every expert cardiologist at trial said he *didn't even read* the label to make prescribing decisions. And, most ***1343** troubling, the majority is willing to see culpable intent behind a generic's describing its product as the 'equivalent' of a brand drug—in a system that requires generic drugs to be equivalent, and in which everyone understands that generic drugs are equivalent.

I write in this case because far from being a disagreement among reasonable minds about the individual facts, this case signals that our law on this issue has gone awry. I am particularly concerned with three aspects of the majority's analysis. First, even setting aside the majority's willingness to glean intentional encouragement from a label specifically designed to avoid encouragement, the majority further weakens the intentional-encouragement prong of inducement by effectively eliminating the demarcation between describing an infringing use and encouraging that use in a label. Second, the majority defies basic tort law by eviscerating the causation prong of inducement. The upshot of these two moves is that a plaintiff now has to show very little for a jury to speculate as to the rest. Third, the majority creates confusion for generics, leaving them in the dark about what might expose them to liability. These missteps throw a wrench into Congress's design for enabling quick public access to generic versions of unpatented drugs with unpatented uses.

## I. Background

### A. Hatch-Waxman: Congress's Compromise

With the Hatch-Waxman Act, Congress contemplated this case. Indeed, Congressman Waxman himself agrees.[1] When Congress passed the Act, it enacted a complex statutory framework to balance generic and brand interests. See Drug Price Competition and Patent Term Restoration Act of 1984, Pub. L. No. 98-417, 98 Stat. 1585.[2] One effect was to bolster patent terms for brand companies. *Eli Lilly & Co. v. Medtronic Inc.,* 496 U.S. 661, 669, 110 S.Ct. 2683, 110 L.Ed.2d 605 (1990). Another was to 'speed the introduction of low-cost generic drugs to the market,' *Caraco,* 566 U.S. at 405, 132 S.Ct. 1670, in part by permitting immediate market entry for drugs with at least one unpatented FDA-approved use.[3]

Under Congress's design, the FDA regulates the manufacture, sale, and labeling of prescription drugs. See *Caraco,* 566 U.S. at 404–05, 132 S.Ct. 1670. The process begins when a brand manufacturer submits a new drug application ('NDA'). The NDA must include a proposed label describing ***1344** the specific uses—called indications—for the drug. Id. at 404, 132 S.Ct. 1670; see 21 U.S.C. § 355(b)(1); 21 C.F.R. § 314.50(a)(1), (e)(2)(ii). See generally 21 C.F.R. pt. 201.

Once the FDA has approved a brand drug, another company may seek permission to market a generic version by filing an abbreviated new drug application ('ANDA'). Because the Act is designed to minimize the barriers to entry for generic drugs, the generic doesn't have to rehash the brand's safety-and-efficacy trials. It must, however, show that what it manufactures is bioequivalent to the brand drug. 21 U.S.C. § 355(j)(2)(A)(iv), (j)(4)(F); 21 C.F.R.

---

[1] See Brief of Amicus Curiae Former Congressman Henry A. Waxman in Support of Petition for Rehearing En Banc 3–8, ECF No. 170 ('Waxman Br.').

[2] See generally Brief of Amici Curiae Fifty-Seven Law, Economics, Business, Health, and Medicine Professors in Support of Cross-Appellant's Petition for Rehearing En Banc, ECF No. 171 ('57 Law Professors Br.'); Waxman Br.; Brief of Amicus Curiae Association for Accessible Medicines in Support of Defendant-Cross-Appellant in Support of Affirmance 1–9, ECF No. 69; Brief for the Association for Accessible Medicines as Amicus Curiae in Support of Rehearing En Banc 5–7, ECF No. 164.

[3] See also *Warner-Lambert Co. v Apotex Corp.*, 316 F.3d 1348, 1358 (Fed. Cir. 2003); H.R. Rep. No. 98-857, pt. 1, at 14–15 (1984) ('The purpose … is to make available more low cost generic drugs by establishing a generic drug approval procedure …'); id. at 22 (explaining that a 'listed drug may be approved for two indications. If the [generic] applicant is seeking approval only for Indication No. 1, and not Indication No. 2 because it is protected by a use patent, then the applicant must make the appropriate certification and a statement explaining that it is not seeking approval for Indication No. 2').

§ 314.94(a)(7)(i).[4] And the generic's proposed labeling must essentially copy the brand drug's label. See 21 U.S.C. § 355(j)(2)(A)(i), (v), (j)(4)(G); *Caraco,* 566 U.S. at 406, 132 S.Ct. 1670. Thus, by congressional design, generic approval is a comparison of equivalence between the generic and a specific brand drug.

Often a generic wants to launch while patents remain on a drug or its uses. Anticipating this, Congress provided two pathways for generics to show that a proposed label will not infringe.

The first pathway is to file a certification explaining why the generic label will not infringe any patent that a brand has identified to the FDA as covering the drug. The commonly used 'paragraph IV' certification states that a generic label will not infringe because the patent 'is invalid or will not be infringed by the manufacture, use, or sale of the [generic] drug.' 21 U.S.C. § 355(j)(2)(A)(vii)(IV). Paragraph IV often prompts litigation. If a generic, armed with a good-faith paragraph IV argument, files an ANDA with a brand's full label, the Hatch-Waxman Act allows the brand to sue and entitles it to an automatic 30-month stay of final FDA approval of the generic drug while the underlying patent issues are worked out in court. See 35 U.S.C. § 271(e)(2)(A); 21 U.S.C. § 355(j)(5)(B)(iii); *Eli Lilly,* 496 U.S. at 670–71, 676, 110 S.Ct. 2683. This first pathway, then, has parties sort things out up front if infringement or validity are in legitimate dispute.

The second pathway—and the one relevant here—is available if at least one brand-labeled use is unpatented. If that's so, the generic can just 'carve out' the patented uses from its label. *See* 21 U.S.C. § 355(j)(2)(A)(viii) ('section viii'); 21 C.F.R. § 314.94(a)(8)(iv); Caraco, 566 U.S. at 404–07, 132 S.Ct. 1670; *Takeda,* 785 F.3d at 630 ('Congress intended that a single drug could have more than one indication and yet that an ANDA applicant could seek approval for less than all of those indications.' (cleaned up)). The result, an exception to 'the usual rule that a generic drug must bear the same label' as the brand, *Caraco,* 566 U.S. at 406, 132 S.Ct. 1670, is commonly called a 'skinny' or 'partial' or 'carve-out' label.

Because the skinny-label pathway's availability depends on at least one brand-labeled use being unpatented, the FDA needs to know whether any labeled uses are unpatented—and which. More pragmatically, because the FDA 'cannot authorize a generic drug that would infringe a patent,' *Caraco,* 566 U.S. at 405, 132 S.Ct. 1670, it needs assurance that a generic's ***1345** skinny label has carved out the patented brand-labeled uses, leaving behind only unpatented ones. But because the FDA is not an arbiter of patent issues,[5] how can it know whether the skinny-label pathway is available and whether it can approve a given label?

The solution that worked—before today, at least—was for the FDA and generics to rely on what brands say their patents cover. See *Caraco,* 566 U.S. at 407, 132 S.Ct. 1670 ('[W]hether section viii is available to a generic manufacturer depends on how the brand describes its patent.'); see also 21 U.S.C. § 355(b), (c) (requiring submission of patent information with NDA). In particular, a brand submits under penalty of perjury a declaration identifying 'each pending method of use or related indication and related patent claim' and 'the specific section of the proposed labeling for the drug product that corresponds to the method of use claimed by the patent submitted.' 21 C.F.R. § 314.53(c)(2)(O) (2008).[6] This declaration also contains a brand-crafted, 240-character 'use code.'[7] 68 Fed. Reg. at 36,683, 36,686, 36,697; see also 21

---

[4] 'Bioequivalence is the absence of a significant difference in the rate and extent to which the active ingredient or active moiety in pharmaceutical equivalents or pharmaceutical alternatives becomes available at the site of drug action when administered at the same molar dose under similar conditions in an appropriately designed [bioequivalence] study.' 21 C.F.R. § 314.3(b). That is, two drugs are 'bioequivalent' if they would be expected for all practical purposes to be the same.

[5] Indeed, it routinely disclaims expertise on that front. See, e.g., 68 Fed. Reg. 36,676, 36,683 (2003) ('[W]e have long observed that we lack expertise in patent matters.'); *Caraco,* 566 U.S. at 406–07, 132 S.Ct. 1670.

[6] Subsequent amendments to the FDA's regulations now require even more detail, underscoring the critical public-notice function of patent declarations. See, e.g., 21 C.F.R. § 314.53(c)(2)(O) (2020).

[7] The majority quotes a portion of the Federal Register saying that use codes 'are not meant to substitute for the [ANDA] applicant's review of the patent and the approved labeling' and relies on testimony concerning the same. Maj. 1331–32 (alteration in original) (quoting 68 Fed. Reg. at 36,683); see also id.

C.F.R. § 314.53(c). This 'use code' appears in the Orange Book,[8] a reference in which brands list the patents on their drugs and the covered uses to provide notice to generics and the FDA. The FDA relies on what the brand says: 'In determining whether an ANDA applicant can 'carve out' the method of use, ... we will rely on the description of the approved use provided by the NDA holder or patent owner in the patent declaration and listed in the Orange Book.' 68 Fed. Reg. at 36,682; see also *Caraco*, 566 U.S. at 406, 132 S.Ct. 1670 (in assessing a proposed skinny label, the FDA looks to what the brand says, takes it 'as a given,' and approves the label only if there is no perceived overlap).

The point is clarity. Hatch-Waxman is designed to resolve patent disputes as early as possible.[9] And to know whether there ***1346** is a dispute, the FDA and generic manufacturers rely on a brand's representations of which labeled indications are patented. *See, e.g.*, 68 Fed. Reg. at 36,682.

### B. Carvedilol

Carvedilol, the drug here, is well studied and well understood. By 2007, the compound itself was no longer patented, nor were most uses of it.

Carvedilol is a beta blocker, a class of drugs used since the 1960s to treat heart conditions. Carvedilol in particular was developed in the 1980s and was covered by U.S. Patent No. 4,503,067, which issued in 1985 and claimed the compound itself.

By the early 1990s, research from various groups revealed that beta blockers could be useful for treating a condition called congestive heart failure ('CHF'), which prevents the heart from being able to deliver enough oxygenated blood to the body. By 1995, GSK had already received approval for an NDA under the brand name Coreg for hypertension. A supplement to that NDA added the CHF indication to the label in 1997. After the approval of the CHF labeling, GSK received U.S. Patent No. 5,760,069, relating to a particular manner of using carvedilol with other drugs to treat CHF. GSK listed the '069 and '067 patents in the Orange Book. Eventually, and well before any generic launched, carvedilol became the standard of care for CHF. This standard was incorporated into the official guidelines of the American College of Cardiology and American Heart Association (as well as numerous medical textbooks and journals) and taught to medical students around the country.

As the 2007 expiration of GSK's carvedilol compound patent approached, interest grew among generics. Upon this expiration, generics would be able to market carvedilol in one of two ways: either with an all-indications label (by challenging GSK's method patent under a paragraph IV certification) or by simply omitting any patented uses from the label (with a section viii statement). Teva first chose the former, reasoning—correctly, as it turned out—that GSK's '069 method patent was invalid. And so in mid-2002 Teva filed its ANDA with a proposed full label directed to hypertension and CHF, certifying that it would wait for GSK's compound patent to expire but that GSK's '069 method patent was invalid. J.A. 3003–19,

---

at 21–23. It bears emphasizing that this statement refers specifically to the 240-character use code (given its length limitations and particular notice role), as distinct from other parts of the declaration (e.g., part 4.2a) identifying the label language corresponding to the claimed method. The full context of the passage makes this clear: Use codes are intended to alert ANDA applicants to the existence of a patent that claims an approved use. They are not meant to substitute for the applicant's review of the patent and the approved labeling. We understand that in some cases 240 characters may not fully describe the use as claimed in the patent. The declaration, which includes the complete description of the method-of-use claim and the corresponding language in the labeling of the approved drug, will be publicly available after NDA approval. 68 Fed. Reg. at 36,683.

[8] U.S. Food & Drug Admin., Approved Drug Products with Therapeutic Equivalence Evaluations (40th edn, 2020).

[9] See Brief of Amici Curiae Novartis Pharmaceuticals Corporation and Sandoz Inc. in Support of Rehearing En Banc 7, ECF No. 168 ('Novartis & Sandoz Br.') ('Both branded and generic pharmaceutical companies require stable, predictable legal environments to operate effectively. Patent litigation inherently entails some uncertainty, but the governing legal framework should be as predictable as possible and consistent with Congress's intent.').

5463. GSK did not sue or seek to block Teva's approval. Instead it sought reissue of its '069 patent, admitting invalidity of the original and adding narrowing limitations to overcome validity challenges.

In 2003, GSK got approval to add another indication to its label: post-MI LVD.[10] This entailed a discrete new set of label text, with new underlying clinical studies and new instructions. Teva likewise updated the label accompanying its pending ANDA to include all three indications. In 2004, the FDA determined that Teva had shown its product to be bioequivalent to GSK's and granted it tentative approval pending resolution of any exclusivity issues.

But by 2007—the year GSK's compound patent was set to expire—it was apparent that other generic manufacturers had opted for skinny labels instead. So Teva did ***1347** too, informing the FDA that it now intended to carve out from GSK's label the uses GSK said were patented.

Again, GSK's label contained three sets of instructions for three distinct indications: CHF, post-MI LVD, and hypertension:

| **INDICATIONS AND USAGE** |
|---|
| **Congestive Heart Failure:** COREG is indicated for the treatment of mild to severe heart failure of ischemic or cardiomyopathic origin usually in addition to diuretics, ACE inhibitor, and digitalis, to increase survival and, also to reduce the risk of hospitalization (see CLINICAL TRIALS). |
| **Left Ventricular Dysfunction Following Myocardial Infarction:** COEG is indicated to reduce cardiovascular mortality in clinically stable patients who have survived the acute phase of a myocardial infarction and have aleft ventricual ejection fraction of ≤40 % (with or without symptomatic heart failure) (see CLINICAL TRIALS). |
| **Hypertension:** COREG is also indicated for the management of essential hypertension. It can be used alone or in combination with other antihypertensive agents, especially thiazide-type diuretics (see PRECAUTIONS Drug Interactions). |

J.A. 7992. And according to GSK's sworn declaration to the FDA (which appropriately tracked the label's language), only one of these three was patented—CHF:

| | | |
|---|---|---|
| 4.2.a | If the answer to 4.2 is "Yes" identify with specificity the use with reference to the proposed labeling for the drug product. | Use: *(submit indication or method of use information as identified specifically in the approved labeling)*<br>Treatment Of Mild-To-Severe Heart Failure Of Ischemic Or Cardiomyopathic Origin, Usually In Addition To Diuretics, ACE Inhibitor, And Digitalis, To Increase Survial |

J.A. 6895. Faithful to GSK's declaration, the FDA forwarded Teva a redlined label for use that omitted everything GSK had said the '069 method patent covered:

| **1 INDICATIONS AND USAGE** |
|---|
| **1.1 Heart Failure** |
| COREG is indicated for the treatment of mild to severe heart failure of ischemic or cardiomyopathic origin, usually in addition to diuretics, ACE inhibitor, and digitalis, to increase survival and, also, to reduce the risk of hospitalization (*see CLINICAL STUDIES* [14.1]). |

[10] This condition concerns patients who have recently suffered a heart attack (a 'myocardial infarction,' or 'MI') and whose hearts have trouble pumping blood ('left ventricular dysfunction,' or 'LVD').

| **1.1 Left Ventricular Dysfunction following Myocardial Infarction** |
|---|
| Carvedilol is indicated to reduce cardiovascular mortality in clinically stable patients who have survived the acute phase of a myocardial infarction and have a left ventricular ejection fraction of ≃40 % (with or without symptomatic heart failure) (see *CLINICAL STUDIES [14.1]*). |
| **1.2 Hypertension** |
| Carvedilol is indicated for the management of essential hypertension. It can be used alone or in combination with other antihypertensive agents, especially thiazide-type diuretics (see *DRUG INTERACTIONS [7.2]*). |

J.A. 6913. It instructed Teva to use that label, which Teva did—with the same carve-out as the other seven generic manufacturers that launched at that time.

After the generics launched, GSK's '069 method patent reissued as U.S. Patent No. RE40,000, the patent relevant here. GSK added several narrowing limitations to the '000 patent to save it from invalidity. ***1348** With the reissue process now completed, GSK delisted its '069 method patent from the Orange Book and listed the '000 patent in its stead—again submitting a sworn declaration identifying *only* the CHF indication as covered. J.A. 6880–87. Consistent with this representation, GSK did not sue the generics, whose skinny labels included everything but CHF.

Years later in 2011, the FDA directed Teva to revise its label to include the CHF indication. Teva complied. The skinny-label period thus ended and the full-label period began. Teva did not issue a press release or otherwise notify doctors of the change to its label. Indeed, Teva did not change anything about how it marketed its generic carvedilol; it continued to sell its product in the same manner since approved. And, to little surprise, nothing changed in the market: Teva and GSK maintained their respective market shares, and no doctor's prescribing habits changed.

### C. This Litigation

GSK did not sue in 2004 when Teva made its full-label paragraph IV certification. Nor in 2007 when Teva launched its skinny-label generic. Nor in 2008 when GSK's '000 patent emerged from reissue. Nor even in 2011 when Teva transitioned to the full label. It sued instead in 2014, just before the '000 patent expired.

The lawsuit ultimately led to a seven-day jury trial in 2018. The jury was asked to determine whether Teva induced infringement of the '000 patent based on the skinny-label period and the full-label period separately. It found that Teva induced infringement of the '000 patent based on both labels. It also found that GSK was entitled to $234.1 million in lost profits and $1.4 million in reasonable-royalty damages.

After the verdict, Teva filed a renewed motion for JMOL, arguing that GSK had not presented legally sufficient evidence to support a finding of inducement. The district court agreed and granted Teva's motion. *See GlaxoSmithKline LLC v. Teva Pharms. USA, Inc.*, 313 F. Supp. 3d 582 (D. Del. 2018). GSK appealed, and Teva cross-appealed as to damages.

The case was argued to us in September 2019. In October 2020, the majority issued a first opinion reversing the district court's JMOL. That opinion prompted widespread consternation and confusion, as described in Teva's petition for rehearing and the eight amicus briefs in support. Among these amici: both generics *and* brands, fifty-seven law professors, and Congressman Waxman. See Novartis & Sandoz Br.; 57 Law Professors Br.; Waxman Br.

Following these submissions, the majority vacated its first opinion and ordered another round of oral argument. Order, ECF No. 181. The majority now issues a second opinion reaching the same result as before, but with new reasoning. In particular, it now declares that this is not a 'true' skinny-label case. E.g., Maj. 1326–27, 1335 n.7. But this remains a skinny-label case, the record remains the record, and inducement liability remains unsupportable.

## II. Discussion

Although the JMOL standard is well settled, two points bear emphasizing. First, while we give the verdict winner the benefit of 'every favorable and reasonable inference,' *Dun & Bradstreet Software Servs., Inc. v. Grace Consulting, Inc.*, 307 F.3d 197, 205 (3d Cir. 2002), the operative word here is 'reasonable.' Indeed, 'only all *reasonable*' inferences need be drawn in GSK's favor, not '*all* possible inferences.' See *Villiarimo v. Aloha Island Air, Inc.*, 281 F.3d 1054, 1065 n.10 (9th Cir. 2002). Second, if too many inferences must be strung together to support the ***1349** verdict, the verdict is likely unsupportable. See *Roebuck v. Drexel Univ.*, 852 F.2d 715, 736 (3d Cir. 1988) ('Although we believe that each of the inferences that we have discussed [is] individually logically sound, we recognize that at some point too many inferences become[s] mere speculation ...'); *cf. United States v. Weber*, 923 F.2d 1338, 1345 (9th Cir. 1990) ('Each of these inferences standing alone may be reasonable. But with each succeeding inference, the last reached is less and less likely to be true.').

As to induced infringement under 35 U.S.C. § 271(b), GSK bore the burden at trial to prove two things relevant here. First, GSK had to prove that, more likely than not, Teva engaged in 'culpable conduct, directed to encouraging another's infringement.' *DSU Med. Corp. v. JMS Co.*, 471 F.3d 1293, 1306 (Fed. Cir. 2006) (en banc in relevant part); see *Metro-Goldwyn-Mayer Studios Inc. v. Grokster*, 545 U.S. 913, 937, 125 S.Ct. 2764, 162 L.Ed.2d 781 (2005) ('The inducement rule ... premises liability on purposeful, culpable expression and conduct ...'). In other words, not only must Teva have 'possessed specific intent to encourage another's infringement,' *DSU*, 471 F.3d at 1306, it must have taken 'affirmative steps to bring about [that] desired result,' *Global-Tech Appliances, Inc. v. SEB S.A.*, 563 U.S. 754, 760, 131 S.Ct. 2060, 179 L.Ed.2d 1167 (2011).

Second, GSK had to prove that, more likely than not, Teva's affirmative steps actually *caused* the infringement it wanted to bring about. *DSU*, 471 F.3d at 1304 (plaintiff must show that 'the alleged infringer's actions induced infringing acts'); see *Grokster*, 545 U.S. at 936–37, 125 S.Ct. 2764 (when defendant takes 'affirmative steps' to 'foster infringement, [it] is liable for the *resulting* acts of infringement by third parties' (emphasis added)); *Sanofi v. Watson Labs. Inc.*, 875 F.3d 636, 644 (Fed. Cir. 2017) (noting the 'purposeful-causation connotation' of the Supreme Court's characterization of inducement).

The discussion that follows has three parts. Part A addresses the lack of inducement during the skinny-label period, as well as the flaws in the majority's analysis. Part B does the same for the full-label period. Part C addresses more broadly why the majority's analysis has troubling implications for skinny labels and inducement law generally.

### A. The Skinny-Label Period

For the skinny-label period—that is, from Teva's skinny-label launch in 2007 to its full-label amendment in 2011—the majority relies on three key pieces of evidence to conclude that substantial evidence supports the verdict: the skinny label itself (in particular, the post-MI LVD indication on that label) and two press releases distributed before the '000 patent issued—one from 2007, another from 2004. I discuss each in turn, followed by the majority's supposedly substantial other evidence of intent. From them, alone or combined, no reasonable jury could have found (1) culpable intent to encourage infringement or (2) causation, much less both.

#### 1. The Skinny Label Itself

Before discussing what the skinny label said, recall what it didn't say—and why. The label omitted the CHF indication (and only the CHF indication) because GSK's sworn FDA filings asserted patent coverage of the CHF indication (and only the CHF indication). Analogizing to a typical patent case, it's as though Teva had drafted a potentially infringing user manual and then, abiding by the patentee's clear guidance, deleted all the pages that might be viewed as encouraging infringement of a patented method. Ironically, everything ***1350** about this process signals that, far from intending to encourage infringement, Teva very much intended *not* to encourage infringement with its skinny label.

Of course, this will likely be true of most generics that get approved via the Hatch-Waxman section viii skinny-label pathway. Indeed, inferring intentional encouragement to infringe a method—from a label that has intentionally omitted everything that the brand said covers that method—is a lot to ask of a reasonable factfinder. Only once has this court upheld an inducement finding involving a putative skinny label, and that case had a crucial, additional fact: the generic knew it had an infringement problem. *AstraZeneca LP v. Apotex, Inc.*, 633 F.3d 1042, 1060 (Fed. Cir. 2010); see *Grunenthal GmbH v. Alkem Labs. Ltd.*, 919 F.3d 1333, 1340 (Fed. Cir. 2019) ('[*AstraZeneca*] held that specific intent could be inferred because the defendant proceeded with a plan to distribute the generic drug knowing that its label posed infringement problems.'). By contrast, GSK put on no similar evidence here. Indeed, the facts surrounding Teva's skinny label are simple and undisputed.

The majority nonetheless manufactures a factual dispute, all on its own. It surmises that: maybe, just maybe, GSK's declarations were confidential, hidden from Teva's view—the implication being that Teva *couldn't* have relied on them.[11] Maj. 1332–33. Of course, GSK itself has never made this argument, despite having every incentive to do so (given how Teva featured the declarations and their significance to the jury, the district court, and this court). It's easy to guess why: the FDA confirms that the declarations are available to the public. 68 Fed. Reg. at 36,683.

At any rate, the majority's confidentiality conjecture is a red herring. Even if it were true that Teva never laid eyes on GSK's exact documents, it wouldn't matter. As no one disputes, Teva asked to carve out GSK's patented uses, and the FDA in return used GSK's representations to provide Teva with a carved-out label. The FDA itself took no non-infringement position; GSK did. And so by accepting the FDA-provided skinny label, which hewed to GSK's patent declarations, Teva relied on GSK's representations of patent scope.[12] See, e.g., Cross-Appellant's Br. 12–13, 51–52; J.A. 12475 (Teva's JMOL motion).

Everything that follows must be assessed against the carve-out backdrop. With that in mind, I turn to what remained of the label *after* it was carved out. For a drug label to induce, it must 'encourage, recommend, or promote infringement.' *Takeda*, 785 F.3d at 631. 'Merely describing an infringing use' in a label 'will not suffice.' ***1351** *HZNP Meds. LLC v. Actavis Labs. UT, Inc.*, 940 F.3d 680, 702 (Fed. Cir. 2019); *Takeda*, 785 F.3d at 631.

The majority supports the verdict with GSK's expert testimony concerning the post-MI LVD indication. Again, this indication remained on the label because GSK's sworn declarations never said it was patented. Dr. McCullough did walk through claim 1 of the '000 patent and compare each limitation to somewhere on the skinny label. Maj. 1328–29 (citing testimony at J.A. 10623–31). But he never testified that the skinny label encouraged, recommended, or promoted practicing the claimed method.[13] Rather, in response to a series of questions about

---

[11] The suggestion appears to be based on the word 'confidential' at the bottom of the declarations' pages in our appendix. See Maj. 1333. The majority's reliance on this branding seems misplaced. Among documents similarly branded 'confidential': (1) the American College of Cardiology/American Heart Association Guidelines, published in the Journal of American College of Cardiology, J.A. 3245; and (2) Teva's 2012 Monthly Prescribing Reference, J.A. 6192, a circulation that the majority says doctors received 'on a regular basis,' Maj. 1338 (quoting J.A. 10607–08).

[12] To that end, the declarations also belie GSK's insistence that the 240-character use code was 'not tied to any particular indication.' See Appellant's Reply Br. 30. GSK submitted a patent declaration identifying only one indication. E.g., J.A. 6895. From that declaration came the use code. GSK's use-code argument is therefore wrong as a matter of law here. And regardless, GSK's problem remains part 4.2a of the declarations, which required GSK to '[s]ubmit indication or method of use information *as identified specifically in the approved labeling.*' E.g., J.A. 6895 (emphasis added).

[13] The majority suggests otherwise, via a misleading cite to a snippet of testimony. See Maj. 1333 (citing J.A. 10644). While Dr. McCullough did testify that Teva 'took action' intended to encourage, none of the evidence he was referencing included the skinny label itself. His earlier skinny-label testimony concerned underlying direct infringement. E.g., J.A. 10631. But after moving to the *intent* element of inducement,

whether certain portions of the label 'met' the claim limitations, he testified that some limitations were met (or 'mentioned') in the Indications and Usage section, others in the Dosage and Administration section, and still others in the Clinical Studies section. J.A. 10623–31. At most, a reasonable jury could have found that the skinny label *described* the infringing use (if pieced together just right), in the context of post-MI LVD patients. Describing is not enough.

This failure of proof alone should end the intentional-encouragement inquiry as to the skinny label here. But when we also consider the backdrop as to how the skinny label arose—i.e., that Teva took out the only indication GSK said was patented—the lack of inducement based on this label is beyond dispute. *See Vita-Mix Corp. v. Basic Holding, Inc.*, 581 F.3d 1317, 1329 n.2 (Fed. Cir. 2009) ('[The question] is whether [defendant's] instructions teach an infringing use … *such that we are willing to infer* from those instructions an affirmative intent to infringe the patent.' (emphasis added)); *see also Grokster*, 545 U.S. at 937, 125 S.Ct. 2764 ('The classic instance of inducement is by advertisement … that broadcasts a message *designed to* stimulate others to commit violations.' (emphasis added)). The law simply does not permit an inference of culpable, intentional encouragement from the label on this record.[14]

All of that is just the intentional-encouragement prong though; GSK also had to show causation. At a minimum, it had to prove that doctors would have read the skinny label, then pieced together the disparate ***1352** portions just like Dr. McCullough did at trial, then viewed that pieced-together description as an encouragement to prescribe carvedilol for CHF according to the specific limitations of the claimed method, and *then relied* on that pieced-together message to make that prescribing decision.

Dr. McCullough certainly didn't connect these dots. Indeed, he would have been a poor choice for that task. A question arose at trial as to whether he had even *read* the label before making his prescribing decisions. To survive a pre-verdict JMOL motion on causation, GSK's counsel promised the trial judge that if given another chance, Dr. McCullough would 'absolutely' testify that he did so. J.A. 10959; see also J.A. 10959 (counsel insisting that 'obviously, he always reads the label'). But when given the chance, he testified that no, he *didn't* read the label before making his prescribing decisions. J.A. 11662–63. Not that Dr. McCullough was alone in this regard; the other two expert cardiologists at trial testified that they didn't do so either. J.A. 11151 (Dr. Zusman); J.A. 11296–97 (Dr. Rosendorff).

Nothing else connected these dots. In fact, evidence from both sides showed that doctors relied primarily on medical guidelines, experience, education, and journals when making their prescribing decisions. E.g., J.A. 10668, 10676–77 (Dr. McCullough), 11151–52, 11164–68 (Dr. Zusman), 11296–97 (Dr. Rosendorff). Evidence from both sides also showed that pharmacies substituted generics for the brand version automatically, as all fifty states allow or even require. See, e.g., J.A. 10678–79 (Dr. McCullough), 10750–51 (Dr. Reisetter), 11038 (Mr. Karst), 11076–77 (Ms. Kinsey). The majority, however, disregards this uncontroverted, direct evidence of causation in favor of letting unsupported inferences bridge GSK's evidentiary gap. It starts with the label's contents and that they were perhaps 'read'—then ends up at causation.

---

where the majority finds this testimony, the label did not come up again—neither directly nor indirectly. J.A. 10634–44. This may explain why GSK never cited this testimony to show that the skinny label encouraged. Had GSK done so, Teva would have had an opportunity to contest the characterization the majority now adopts.

[14] Despite the majority's characterization, this is not a contention that estoppel arose from GSK's FDA filings. Maj. 1332–33. Rather, the issue concerns what intent could be reasonably gleaned from the skinny label, given the way that label came about and the absence of other evidence of intent. Intent is a required element of inducement—and, as the majority itself acknowledges, GSK's failure to list the post-MI LVD indication in its FDA filings 'is relevant to intent to induce infringement.' Id. at 1331. Estoppel is a separate issue based on a different legal standard that the district court may resolve in the first instance. The majority's charge that I seek to 'leapfrog' and resolve estoppel here on appeal is therefore disturbingly off-base. Id. at 1333. I am instead addressing what a reasonable jury could find Teva's intent to be. I do not understand the majority to be suggesting that the potential availability of a different type of relief (i.e., estoppel) forecloses the court from considering the main issue in this appeal (i.e., inducement) if resolution of the two issues might involve some of the same facts.

Maj. 1339–40. I disagree with the majority that this inferential leap is 'fair,' id. at 1339–40, particularly here, where direct evidence across the board points to medical texts and expertise as being the main influence. In my view, 'fair' would be ensuring that causation means something. See infra Part II.C.2.

Before turning to the press releases, one last, critical point bears mentioning. The majority confines its reliance on the skinny label to the post-MI LVD indication. In particular, its skinny-label inducement path starts with 'encouragement' from the post-MI LVD indication, and ends in direct infringement when a doctor prescribes carvedilol for any post-MI LVD patient who *also* happens to have CHF (assuming that the rest of the claim limitations are met when so prescribing). See Maj. 1327–29, 1330–31. Notably, however, as both sides acknowledge, the damages award in this case was *not* confined to just the appropriate subset of infringing prescriptions to post-MI LVD patients who also had CHF—it encompassed CHF patients more broadly. Cross-Appellant's Br. 54; see Appellant's Reply Br. 31–32. GSK's damages testimony was not predicated on, nor did it quantify, the subset of uses that would infringe under the majority's skinny-label-based inducement theory.

Recognizing the problem, GSK leans on the press releases to save the full damages award; it says they 'encouraged the infringing use for all … symptomatic heart failure patients.' Appellant's Reply Br. 31. But, as I explain below, that's far too much weight for these press releases to bear. Accordingly, even if the majority's upholding the verdict on the basis of the skinny label were appropriate, we would have to remand this case for a proper damages calculation. But Teva's argument on this ***1353** important issue goes unacknowledged in the majority's opinion.

### 2. The 2007 Press Release

Beyond the skinny label itself, the majority also supports the verdict with a 2007 Teva press release that announced final FDA approval for Teva to market its '[g]eneric version of [GSK's] cardiovascular agent Coreg® (Carvedilol) Tablets.' Maj. 1336 (citing J.A. 6353). From this press release—which was distributed before the '000 patent issued but apparently appeared on Teva's website during the patent's term—the majority permits inferences of intentional encouragement and causation. Neither is reasonable.

As to intentional encouragement, the majority interprets Teva's 2007 press release as saying that its product is a 'generic equivalent of GSK's cardiovascular agent Coreg®,' id. at 1337—and, from this, permits the inference that Teva intended to encourage substitution of its product for *all* of Coreg's indications, including CHF, id. at 1336–37. In other words, the majority holds that a generic can be deemed liable for inducement for saying that its product is a 'generic version' or 'generic equivalent' of a brand drug. This is a drastic holding. And it makes little sense. Essentially *all* ANDA generics are the 'generic version' or 'generic equivalent' of a brand drug; the law *requires* them to be. To come to market, such a generic must demonstrate that its product is bioequivalent to a brand drug. 21 U.S.C. § 355(j)(2)(A)(iv), (j)(4)(F); 21 C.F.R. § 314.94(a)(7)(i); see also 21 C.F.R. § 314.92(a) (noting that, with limited exceptions not relevant here, ANDAs are suitable only for '[d]rug products that are the same as a listed drug,' and that 'the same as' includes drugs with label modifications made for patent carve-outs). See generally supra Part I.A. The system is inherently comparative. I therefore find it highly unlikely that Congress intended to make generics liable for simply stating what the law requires.

The majority also sees culpable intent in Teva's describing its product as a 'cardiovascular' agent. See Maj. 1336–37. A well-understood adjective, 'cardiovascular' means relating to the heart. Carvedilol is a heart-related drug; it's used to treat CHF, post-MI LVD, and hypertension—all heart-related conditions. I cannot see how using the word 'cardiovascular' to describe a heart-related drug could *reasonably* be viewed as evidencing culpable intent to encourage practicing the specific claimed CHF method in particular here—or how this adjective does anything beyond what 'generic version' or 'generic equivalent' do in terms of intent.

And still there remains causation. The majority never explains how a reasonable jury could have found that this press release (as it later appeared on Teva's website) affected doctors' prescribing practices so as to cause their infringement. Indeed, outside of testimony that doctors 'get' press releases, J.A. 11655, and that it's 'possible' doctors read them, J.A. 11239, GSK supplied no evidence that any doctor read this one before the litigation—much less accessed it from Teva's website, and was then so moved by it that it caused him or her to prescribe carvedilol in an infringing manner, trumping every medical text along the way.

We simply have a press release that describes a generic version of a cardiovascular brand drug as a *'generic version'* of a *'cardiovascular'* brand drug. From that alone, the majority permits inferences of culpable intent to encourage and causation. I fail to see how those inferences are reasonable.

### *1354 3. The 2004 Press Release

The majority's final key piece of evidence is the 2004 press release, which announced Teva's 'tentative [FDA] approval' to market its product, described as 'the AB-rated generic equivalent of [GSK's] Coreg® … indicated for treatment of heart failure and hypertension.' J.A. 6347.

Before turning to whether these statements could show intentional encouragement to infringe, some undisputed facts must be acknowledged. First, this press release was distributed several years before the '000 patent issued, at a time when Teva was pursuing a different pathway to regulatory approval. At that time, Teva's product *was* indicated for treatment of CHF. But Teva ultimately pursued the section viii pathway. Second, the press release announced the product's *'tentative* approval,' which has a specific, legal meaning—namely, that a patent or regulatory exclusivity stands in the way of final approval. 21 U.S.C. § 355(j)(5)(B)(iv)(II)(dd)(A); 21 C.F.R. § 314.3(b); see J.A. 10533. In other words, this 'approval' had conditions.

With that in mind, the question remains: what is there in this press release to suggest intent to encourage infringement of the (future-issued) '000 patent? Like the 2007 press release, the majority sees culpable intent in Teva's describing its product as the 'AB-rated generic equivalent' of Coreg. Maj. 1336. But, for the reasons described above, this cannot plausibly support liability within Congress's framework in this area. And although the press release does reference 'heart failure,' given the circumstances here—i.e., that the press release was distributed years before the patent issued (under materially different regulatory circumstances) and announced 'tentative' approval—inferring culpable intent from this press release exceeds the bounds of reasonableness.

And again: causation. To prove it, GSK first had to show that Teva made this years-old press release available on its website during the patent's term. This should have been a crucial showing—after all, this press release is one of the three key pieces of evidence the majority relies on. Once again, though, direct evidence is missing. And once again, the majority is untroubled. It simply calls up some inferences to bridge the gap. In particular, the majority suggests the inference that, because the 2007 press release was on Teva's website, and because Teva had a website with some information about carvedilol, the 2004 press release must have been there too. Maj. 1336–37. GSK, for its part, never argued any of these inferences to the jury. And while the majority faults Teva for not showing that the 2004 press release was not there, id. at 1337, this is GSK's case and its burden—and besides, it's hard to blame Teva for not rebutting a fact that GSK never even tried establishing.

But, for argument's sake, let's assume the jury could have reasonably found that GSK carried its burden on this point. A further question remains: what is there to suggest that any doctor saw it—years later on the website—then relied on *that* as the basis for his or her infringing prescribing decisions? The answer: nothing. At least, that's the answer the majority gives. See id. at 1339–40. Nothing in the record suggested that doctors were in the habit of searching a generic's website for old press releases to help them make life-or-death prescribing decisions. The most we have is that Dr. McCullough saw the 2004 press release (timing unspecified) and that it said what it said. The rest is left to sheer possibility.

***1355** And indeed, it's possible that things panned out this way. Maybe a doctor *did* search Teva's website for old press releases, found this one (assuming it was there), and then relied on that press release to make his or her prescribing decision (at least three years after the date of this press release), trumping every medical text along the way. Maybe every relevant doctor did. Many things are possible. But '[m]ere speculation' is not substantial evidence.' *OSI Pharms., LLC v. Apotex Inc.*, 939 F.3d 1375, 1382 (Fed. Cir. 2019) (quoting *Intell. Ventures I LLC v. Motorola Mobility LLC,* 870 F.3d 1320, 1331 (Fed. Cir. 2017)).

In sum, the 2004 press release's description of Teva's product as the 'AB-rated generic equivalent' of Coreg, along with its reference to 'heart failure,' would be a slender enough reed upon which to rest culpable intent, given that this communique was distributed years before the patent issued (under materially different regulatory circumstances) and announced an approval that was only 'tentative.' But it's the causation that truly vexes me. It's the notion that, instead of the various medical texts (and experience, and education), all along it was really the 2004 press release, found years later on the website, that caused doctors' CHF prescribing decisions. In the face of uncontroverted evidence of the former, some evidence of the latter should be necessary. But there's none.

### 4. The Supposedly Substantial Other Evidence of Intent

The majority calls it 'inaccurate' to observe that it relies on only three key pieces of evidence as to culpable intent during the skinny-label period. Maj. 1333–34. It says there's additional evidence too.[15] But while the majority discusses the three pieces above in some detail, it only gestures to the rest without much meaningful discussion. Such references can hardly be enough to sustain a verdict, and they return us to the uncertainty concerns plaguing the first, vacated version of the majority's opinion. At bottom, however, this other evidence just relates back to the three key pieces.

There was 'extensive expert testimony,' the majority first insists without elaboration. Maj. 1333. As best I can tell, the majority is referring to Dr. McCullough and Dr. Zusman, see id. at 1334–35—Dr. McCullough saying that doctors read labels, and Dr. Zusman agreeing that Teva's circulations suggested reading labels if doctors have questions. So, we're back to the skinny label—the first of the three key pieces of evidence. And if the skinny label doesn't show intent, then neither does suggesting that doctors should read it.[16]

Teva's 'Monthly Prescribing References' get some attention elsewhere. See id. at 1334–35. But, like the 'extensive' expert testimony discussed above, that's just for the proposition that Teva intended doctors to read its labels. Again, back to the skinny label.

The majority adds to the list Teva's 'product catalogs' and 'advertising and promotional activities.' Id. at 1333. I presume it means Teva's catalogs discussed shortly afterward. But the only thing for ***1356** which *that* evidence was relied on was to show that Teva described its drug as the 'AB rated' equivalent to Coreg. See id. at 1335 (discussing 2008 and 2009 catalogs at J.A. 6221 and J.A. 6270). Statements of equivalence were discussed with respect to the two press releases—the other two key pieces of evidence. So it's unclear what this adds to the intent calculus. And as before, if this is evidence of intent, we should be disturbed.

Finally, the majority notes 'testimony from Teva's own company witnesses.' Id. at 1333. Maybe this means Teva's marketing director (who the majority says 'added carvedilol product information to the Teva website' in 2007) and regulatory-affairs director (who the majority says 'discussed' the press releases with the jury). See id. at 1337. Whatever the case, this discussion just concerns the press releases—well-trodden ground. Or maybe instead the majority means Mr. Rekenthaler, who it quotes as having 'expected' or 'assum[ed]' that doctors would use drugs as labeled. *Id.* at 1335. But this just brings us back to the skinny label.

---

[15] Much of this evidence comes in the form of trial testimony that was not included in the record on appeal—which means it's testimony that GSK didn't rely on, and to which Teva therefore had no occasion to respond. Anything the majority cites as 'Trial Tr.' references such testimony.

[16] Of course, because causation is an element, what matters in the end is whether doctors *did* in fact not only read but also *rely* on this label. See supra pp. 1351–52. Recall too that every relevant witness testified that he *hadn't* read this label before prescribing.

The bottom line is that, to the extent that this evidence is relevant, its relevance depends on finding culpability from the three key pieces of evidence—i.e., the skinny label or the two press releases, particularly their statements of equivalence.

### B. The Full-Label Period

As with the skinny-label period, JMOL of no inducement was necessary for the full-label period. The reason is simple: nothing about doctors' prescribing practices changed when Teva amended its label to the full version. Both GSK and its experts confirmed as much. Appellant's Br. 21 ('Doctors continued to administer Teva's accused product for infringing use during [the full-label] period *(without change from the partial label period)* ...' (emphasis added)); J.A. 12204–05 (GSK's counsel conceding that any market impact as a result of the amendment was 'minimal'); J.A. 10699 (Dr. McCullough agreeing that, in his practice, there was 'no difference in [his] prescribing habits from when Teva had its skinny label to after Teva amended to have its full label'); J.A. 10754 (different GSK expert testifying that his survey of 200 doctors indicated no change in prescription patterns from pre- to post-amendment).

The majority, for its part, identifies nothing about doctors' prescribing practices that changed after Teva amended its label. Maj. 1338–40. If nothing about this changed, then nothing Teva did during the full-label period could have caused anything beyond whatever caused direct infringement during the skinny-label period. And because the record lacks evidence that Teva caused direct infringement during the skinny-label period, Teva cannot have caused direct infringement during the full-label period—and therefore cannot have induced.

### C. Why the Majority's Flawed Analysis Matters

In reinstating the jury's unsupportable verdict, the majority commits several errors—some legal, some practical, and all spelling trouble for skinny labels specifically and inducement law generally. Below are three main concerns with the majority's approach.

#### 1. The Majority Weakens the Intentional-Encouragement Requirement as to Labels

Direct infringement is strict liability; induced infringement is not. And when it comes to inducement's intentional-encouragement requirement, the law draws a line between encouraging, recommending, or promoting an infringing use and merely ***1357** describing that use. E.g., *Takeda,* 785 F.3d at 631. This line is important because while the former provides evidence of intent, the latter does not. See id. (collecting cases); *HZNP,* 940 F.3d at 702 ('Merely describing an infringing use ... will not suffice ...'). The majority blurs this line beyond recognition.[17]

Take the skinny label here. GSK's expert Dr. McCullough, despite having *never read* the label himself before making prescribing decisions, walked through it and found piecemeal language that he could say 'met' or 'mentioned' each claim limitation in isolation. Supra pp. 1350–51. That was the extent of it. There was no testimony or other evidence that this label language encouraged practicing the patented method, or that it even came with a wink or nudge. At most, then, a reasonable jury could have found that the skinny label *described* the infringing use.

The majority somehow ends up at encouragement but fails to justify how it got there. In particular, it never meaningfully engages with the legal distinction between encouraging, recommending, or promoting an infringing use and describing it. Nor does it explain how a reasonable jury could have found the former from the latter on this record. If a jury can simply infer culpable intent to encourage from a mere description, the legal distinction is meaningless. Description would *always* suffice to infer inducement.

[17] GSK would have us ignore this line entirely. Appellant's Reply Br. 28 ('It is doubtful whether such a distinction actually exists ...'); see id. at 16 ('Teva's partial label encouraged doctors to infringe GSK's patent because it described every limitation of the claimed method.').

That's a problem. '[S]howing that infringement was encouraged' is necessary to 'overcome[] the law's reluctance to find liability when a defendant merely sells' a product with legitimate non-infringing uses, like carvedilol. *Grokster*, 545 U.S. at 936, 125 S.Ct. 2764; see id. at 937, 125 S.Ct. 2764 (acknowledging 'the need to keep from trenching on regular commerce or discouraging the development of technologies with lawful and unlawful potential'). 'This requirement of inducing acts is particularly important in the Hatch-Waxman Act context because the statute was designed to enable the sale of drugs for non-patented uses even though this would result in some off-label infringing uses.' *Takeda*, 785 F.3d at 631 (citing *Caraco*, 566 U.S. at 414–15, 132 S.Ct. 1670).

On that note, I emphasize that this criticism is all about how the majority treats what was left of the skinny label *after* the carve-out. That Teva first carved out exactly what GSK said would infringe should settle the question of what intent could be reasonably inferred from the label itself on these facts. It's also a circumstance that distinguishes every case the majority relies on to support its holding.

### 2. The Majority Eviscerates the Causation Requirement

Patent infringement is a tort. E.g., *Wordtech Sys., Inc. v. Integrated Networks Sols., Inc.*, 609 F.3d 1308, 1313 (Fed. Cir. 2010); *see Carbice Corp. of Am. v. Am. Pats. Dev. Corp.*, 283 U.S. 27, 33, 51 S.Ct. 334, 75 L.Ed. 819 (1931). Accordingly, liability attaches only to one who causes the injury—here, practice of the patented method. Legal cause, not simply but-for cause, is required. Restatement (Second) of Torts § 9 cmt. a.

Traditional tort principles inform how a plaintiff proves, or fails to prove, causation:

As on other issues in civil cases, the plaintiff is required to produce evidence ***1358** that the conduct of the defendant has been a *substantial factor* in bringing about the harm he has suffered, and to sustain his burden of proof by a preponderance of the evidence. ... *A mere possibility of such causation is not enough; and when the matter remains one of pure speculation and conjecture, or the probabilities are at best evenly balanced, it becomes the duty of the court to direct a verdict for the defendant.*

Id. § 433B cmt. a (emphasis added); see also id. § 876 cmt. d (noting that if 'encouragement or assistance is a substantial factor in causing [a] resulting tort, the one giving it is himself a tortfeasor'). Therefore, to prove causation, GSK had to show that Teva's conduct (apart from simply being on the market) was a substantial factor in causing doctors to prescribe its carvedilol in an infringing way. A mere possibility wouldn't do; rather, a reasonable jury must have been able to find that it was more likely than not. Here it could not.

To start, the majority identifies no direct evidence of causation by Teva. And it casts aside the direct evidence from both sides pointing to the same things—things other than Teva—as the cause. *Supra* pp. 1351–52, 1353–55. Instead, it says that it was 'fair' for the jury to 'infer' causation from the existence of the skinny label itself and the two press releases. Maj. 1339–40. This conclusion relies on a passing observation in one case saying: '[W]e have affirmed induced infringement verdicts based on circumstantial evidence of inducement (e.g., advertisements, user manuals) directed to a class of direct infringers (e.g., customers, end users) without requiring hard proof that any individual third-party direct infringer was actually persuaded to infringe by that material.' Id. (quoting *Power Integrations, Inc. v. Fairchild Semiconductor Int'l, Inc.*, 843 F.3d 1315, 1335 (Fed. Cir. 2016)). But this observation is not a license to substitute speculation for proof. The evidence-to-conclusion link must always make sense.

In some inducement cases, a jury might reasonably infer causation based solely on circumstantial evidence. One example might be where a product's user manual encourages an infringing use, and where the user had no familiarity with the product *other than* the manual. A reasonable jury might infer that the manual caused the user, otherwise unfamiliar with the product's intricacies, to use the product that way, and we have upheld inducement verdicts on this basis. E.g., *Golden Blount, Inc. v. Robert H. Peterson Co., 438 F.3d 1354, 1362–63 (Fed. Cir. 2006)* (causation evidence included an instruction sheet teaching infringement and packaged with each product); *ArthroCare Corp. v. Smith & Nephew, Inc.*, 406 F.3d 1365, 1377 (Fed. Cir. 2005) (causation evidence included 'sales literature accompanying one of the accused devices' and other instruction manuals recommending an infringing use); *Moleculon Rsch. Corp. v. CBS, Inc.*, 793 F.2d 1261, 1272 (Fed. Cir. 1986) (causation evidence included 'dissemination of an instruction sheet teaching' the infringing method). Although purely circumstantial, the inferential hops are few and short. In those cases, what else but the user manual might have caused the user to use the product in an infringing way? *Cf. Golden Blount*, 438 F.3d at 1363 ('[N]othing in the record suggests that either [defendant] or any end-user ignored the instructions ...').

In other inducement cases, inferential leaps are too many and too great, and evidence of a different cause too strong, for the circumstantial evidence that is offered to carry the day. Take this case. To accept that Teva's skinny label was a substantial ***1359** factor in causing doctors to infringe, one would have to infer doctors read it to make prescribing decisions (even though all three testifying expert cardiologists said they didn't); infer those doctors pieced together the portions of the label to uncover a description of the infringing use (maybe); infer those doctors interpreted that description as an encouragement (no evidence); and then infer those doctors relied on that description to make their prescribing decisions (no evidence). Supra pp. 1351–52. As to the press releases, one would have to infer Teva made them available during the relevant time period (maybe); infer doctors read them during that time (no evidence); and then infer doctors relied on some inducing message therein to make prescribing decisions affecting their patients' health (no evidence).[18] Supra pp. 1353–55.

Unlike the prototypical user-manual case, in which we might permit the inference that a user relied on the manual without requiring testimony to that effect, the inference might not hold up as well in this context—with highly educated users and well-studied products. And whatever strength the inference has in a context such as this, it crumbles when, as here, we *have* users who testified, and they either (1) failed to say they relied or (2) affirmatively said they *didn't* rely on the allegedly inducing materials.

Moreover, unlike the prototypical user-manual case, it's not as though the record here was wanting for another cause. Both sides' expert cardiologists said under oath and without contradiction that medical texts, education, and experience caused their prescribing decisions. *Supra* pp. 1351–52. Under these circumstances, would accepting the Teva-caused version of events amount to anything more than speculation, given the chain of inferences required—not all of them reasonably grounded in the record evidence?

The most troubling part of all this is that the majority never explains how a reasonable jury could have come out this way on this record. Given the size of the infringing doctor class here, it should have been easy to present testimony of causation if that theory had a basis in fact. *Cf. TransUnion LLC v. Ramirez*, --- U.S. ----, 141 S. Ct. 2190, 2212, --- L.Ed.2d ---- (2021) (pointing to evidence that could have been sought and citing *Interstate Circuit, Inc. v. United States*, 306 U.S. 208, 226, 59 S.Ct. 467, 83 L.Ed. 610 (1939), for the proposition that '[t] he production of weak evidence when strong is available can lead only to the conclusion that the strong would have been adverse'). But not a single doctor testified as to causation by Teva, and in fact, the most on-point testimony shows the *absence* of causation.

As a doctrinal matter, the majority's opinion suggests that there is no independent causation element for inducement; intentional encouragement might always suffice to infer causation too. Add that to the majority's weakening of intentional encouragement (where describing an infringing use piecemeal—or simply calling a product a 'generic version' or 'generic equivalent'—is now enough), and finding inducement becomes possible based largely on speculation. The law requires more from a plaintiff.

[18] This is to say nothing of the causal implications of pharmacies' ubiquitous automatic-substitution practices—where, for example, a doctor might write 'Coreg,' but a generic is dispensed nonetheless. See J.A. 10750–51.

### 3. The Majority Creates Confusion About Skinny Labels

The majority's opinion will create confusion for everyone. Under its analysis, the ***1360** difference is indiscernible between this case and one in which the generic is safe. Indeed, it's unclear what Teva even did wrong—or, put another way, what another generic in its shoes should do differently.

Initially, the majority suggests that this is not a skinny-label case. Nothing to see here, the majority reassures concerned amici: the Act remains intact. See Maj. 1326–27. But it's hard to see how. As a matter of law, this is a skinny-label case about the skinny-label provisions. The Act's text makes that much clear: section viii by its own terms references the brand-submitted patent 'information' (i.e., patent declaration). 21 U.S.C. § 355(j)(2)(A)(viii); see 21 C.F.R. § 314.53(c)(2)(O) (patent 'information' includes portions of label covered by method patent). This patent information dictates whether a generic label is a section viii label. If a generic omits the uses the brand has said are patented, the label is skinny. The FDA understands that. See supra Part I.A (discussing brand-dependent regulatory framework). So does the Supreme Court. *Caraco,* 566 U.S. at 404–07, 132 S.Ct. 1670. So should we.

What's more, the background facts here will seemingly persist in most skinny-label cases. Under the Act, '[g]eneric copies' are essentially 'the same as the original drug.' See H.R. Rep. No. 98–857, pt. 1, at 14–15; *accord* 21 U.S.C. § 355(j)(2)(iv); 21 C.F.R. § 314.92(a)(1). Thus, bioequivalence; comparison to a brand drug; duplication of a brand's label (at least in part); reliance on a brand's clinical-trial data; references to a drug's therapeutic class; cursory press releases announcing a generic's regulatory approval; doctors' assumptions about what going generic means; pharmacies' generic substitution; a generic's knowledge that some sales may occur from off-label, infringing uses—all of that will generally be there whether there is inducement or not. See, e.g., *AstraZeneca Pharms. LP v. Apotex Corp., 669 F.3d 1370, 1380 (Fed. Cir. 2012)* (discussing 'market realities' of substitution that do not implicate infringement). Those facts cannot sort inducement from non-inducement.

So where did Teva go wrong in this case? Should it not have followed the brand's sworn representations as to what was patented? The majority offers no principled division between this and what it suggests would be a true skinny label. For decades, everyone has assumed they could rely on what brands said about what their patents covered. The FDA's skinny-label approval pathway and regulations are expressly predicated on that. As far as adherence to Congress's framework, this was about as faithful as it gets.

Or is the takeaway, instead, that Congress meant to expose ANDA generics to liability for simply describing themselves as the 'generic version' or 'generic equivalent' of a brand drug? Given that the Hatch-Waxman Act's framework requires ANDA generics to be the same as a brand drug, and that doctors understand what being a generic means, this seems a dubious proposition.

One of amici's key criticisms of the first version of the majority's opinion was that it was unclear what among the muddled mass of evidence actually formed the basis of liability. So too here. It's unclear whether the skinny label was enough—or whether the press releases were, or some of the other ancillary evidence in the record, 'all of which' the majority suggests the jury 'could have relied on.' Maj. 1333.

The lack of clarity extends to the majority's characterization of its holding as 'case-specific.' See id. at 1326–27. For example, the majority's new opinion relies on the post-MI LVD indication remaining on the skinny label as a potentially 'case-specific' circumstance. See id. Not only is this reliance problematic (for the reasons ***1361** described above), it's a mirage. If the majority were truly relying on this circumstance to distinguish this case, it would accept Teva's argument that the damages should be confined to the appropriate subset of infringing prescriptions to post-MI LVD patients who also had CHF. See supra pp. 1352–53. But, given that this argument goes unacknowledged in the majority's opinion, the implication is that the press releases alone—with their references to 'generic version' or 'generic equivalent'—suffice to support the *entire* verdict, encompassing CHF patients more broadly. And if that's so, then it's unclear why the majority's analysis of the skinny label itself is relevant. Under the majority's holding, a brand can just rely on statements of equivalence to capture even that portion of the market that was specifically carved out.

The only clear thing now is that no generic can know until hit with the bill whether it's staying within the confines of the law. Being unable to predictably rely on use codes and patent declarations 'throws a wrench' into Congress's skinny-label design. See *Caraco,* 566 U.S. at 419, 132 S.Ct. 1670.

### III. Conclusion

Before today, there was an equilibrium to the skinny-label system—one that allowed companies to make informed, responsible decisions in this area. If a generic wanted to avoid patented uses, it had the simple expedient of omitting from its label the uses the brand identified. And if a brand wanted to block a skinny label containing a use it thought was patented, it had the simple expedient of including that use in its FDA patent declaration. That equilibrium is no more.

So, what's next? We are now on the majority's second opinion in this case. The first was vacated in light of Teva's petition for rehearing and the eight amicus briefs in support. This new opinion does little to assuage, and even exacerbates, concerns raised by the original.

I respectfully dissent.

# PART III
# AUSTRALIA

## § 16
## Australia

### A. Executive summary

Similarly to other parts of the world, in recent years Australia has increasingly seen pharmaceutical patent strategies focusing on second or subsequent indications for known compounds or active pharmaceutical ingredients (APIs). As API patents for 'blockbuster' products expire, 'second medical use' claims have come to the fore, often the only remaining barrier to generic entry. This offers not only significant commercial potential for generic manufacturers but also substantial negative financial consequences for originators, who face major price decreases on sales of their products through the Australian government subsidised medicine scheme, the Pharmaceutical Benefits Scheme (PBS) on generic entry.[1] 1

Within this landscape, the Australian courts (in particular the Federal Court of Australia (FCA) and the Full Court of the Federal Court of Australia (FCFCA) which hears appeals from the FCA) have dealt with a number of second medical use patent revocation and/or infringement claims, requiring them to construe such claims and consider strategies by generic companies to 'carve out' patented indications from their regulatory approval in an attempt to avoid patent infringement. It cannot be said in general terms whether such strategies will always be successful or not. The courts have emphasised the need to assess all of the circumstances of such a case. In addition, the outcome may depend on the form of the claims at issue, which in Australia may include method of treatment claims, Swiss-style claims and/or 'EPC 2000' claims. 2

Cases analysing second medical use claim infringement to date in Australia have related to small molecule generic products. In principle, there is no reason to think that biosimilar products would be subjected to any different legal standard to that applicable to generic products. However differences in the regulatory environment, PBS processes and requirements, and prescribing, dispensing and administration practices are all matters which may be relevant in practice to infringement of a second medical use claim. 3

[1] In Australia, reference products (including biologicals) that comprise new active components enjoy a five-year data exclusivity period for regulatory purposes. However data exclusivity is not available for new indications.

## B. Scope of protection and interpretation of second medical use claims

4 Second medical use claims in Australia may take three forms: method of treatment claims, Swiss-style claims or EPC 2000 claims. The construction of each of these claim forms differs, and these construction issues have implications for infringement requirements.

### I. Method of treatment claims

5 Unlike in Europe, methods of medical treatment of human beings, including surgery and the administration of therapeutic drugs, may be the subject of patent claims.

6 Section 18(1)(a) of the Patents Act 1990 (Cth) (Patents Act) provides that an invention is patentable if it is a 'manner of manufacture within the meaning of section 6 of the Statute of Monopolies'. The English Statute of Monopolies 1624 forms the basis for patent law in Australia, and manner of manufacture is the cornerstone of patentability, a common law concept which has consistently evolved with the development of modern patent law. While early Australian cases suggested that methods of medical treatment did not fall within the conception of a patentable invention, in 1992 the Federal Court found a method for treating obstructive sleep apnoea to be patentable in *Rescare Ltd v Anaesthetic Supplies Pty Ltd.*[2] In *Apotex Pty Ltd v Sanofi-Aventis Australia Pty Ltd.*[3] (Sanofi), the High Court put the matter beyond doubt, confirming that such methods are patentable.

7 Method of treatment claims generally take the form *'A method of treating [condition Y] comprising administering [compound X]'* and are directed to a method, generally performed by a clinician in the treatment of a patient. In *Sanofi,* the High Court confirmed that a method of treatment claim is limited to the specific purpose of treating the specified condition, and is confined to the deliberate administration of the compound for that purpose.[4]

### II. Swiss-style claims

8 Swiss-style claims in Australia refer to the same claim form as the European Swiss-type claim deriving from the European Patent Office's decision in G5/83,[5] in the form *'Use of [compound] X in the manufacture of a medicament for the treatment of [condition Y]'.* Although Swiss-type claims were developed to overcome the prohibition on method of medical treatment claims in Europe, which as explained in section I. above is not the position in Australia, Swiss-type claims are common in Australia particularly given the number of patents drafted elsewhere in the world before entering Australia via the PCT system.

---

[2] [1994] FCA 1065.
[3] [2013] HCA 50.
[4] Per Hayne J at [172].
[5] EPO Enlarged Board of Appeal G5/83, dated 5 December 1984.

The FCFCA has confirmed that Swiss-type claims are properly characterised as method or process claims: *Mylan Health Pty Ltd v Sun Pharma ANZ Pty Ltd*[6] (Mylan). However as emphasised by the FCFCA, Swiss type claims are not method of treatment claims. The monopoly obtained by a Swiss-type claim is in respect of the method or process of making a medicament, and that process is complete upon manufacture.[7] Further, Swiss-type claims are purpose-limited in the sense that the medicament resulting from the method or process is characterised by the therapeutic purpose for which it is manufactured, as specified in the claim.[8] Given that the novelty of a Swiss-type claim is rooted in the specified therapeutic purpose, the claim is limited to the achievement of that purpose and not any other therapeutic purpose. In particular, a Swiss-type claim does not claim a medicament that is merely useful, or can be used, for the specified therapeutic purpose. 9

## III. EPC 2000 claims

For similar reasons to those explained above in relation to Swiss-type claims, EPC 2000 claims in the form *'[Compound X] for use in the treatment of [condition Y]'* also commonly form part of claim sets entering Australian PCT national phase. 10

Traditionally the Australian Patents Office (APO) has taken the view in examination that in EPC 2000 claim format, the words '*for use*' will generally be equivalent to '*suitable for*', which is not considered limiting under Australia law. In other words, such a claim was generally considered by the APO to relate to the claimed compound per se.[9] 11

Because EPC 2000 claims were often rejected by the APO for lack of novelty and/or inventiveness given that they are not construed as being limited by indication, Federal Court cases involving granted EPC 2000 claims are limited. However in *Biogen International GmbH v Pharmacor Pty Ltd*[10] (Biogen), the proper construction of EPC 2000 claims (which included additional features relating to the pharmaceutical form) was considered by the Court in the context of an interlocutory injunction application.[11] The Court reviewed the relevant case law in relation to Swiss-type claims confirming that the specified therapeutic purpose is limiting, and concluded that EPC 2000 claims were not dissimilar. On that basis the Court considered that '*at least on a provisional view*' (as the interlocutory injunction application did not finally decide the matter), there was a sufficiently strong prospect that the specified therapeutic purpose was an essential (and limiting) feature of the claim. The case subsequently settled before a final hearing and the issue has not subsequently been determined by a Court. Since the decision in *Biogen*, the APO's position on EPC 2000 claims is not entirely clear. Its relevant Practice Note suggests that the general rule is that 'for use' is not limiting but that the context of the claim may mandate a different interpretation. It cites Swiss-style claims as an example, but EPC 2000 claims are not mentioned at all.[12] 12

---

[6] [2020] FCAFC 116; → mn. 71. See also *Otsuka Pharmaceutical Co., Ltd v Generic Health Pty Ltd (No 4)* [2015] FCA 634 *(Otsuka FCA)* at [120]; → mn. 72.

[7] *Mylan* at [195].

[8] ibid. at [196]; → mn. 71.

[9] Note that the APO takes a different approach to Swiss-style claims in line with the case law discussed above → mn. 9.

[10] [2021] FCA 1591.

[11] An argument made in defence of the interlocutory injunction application was that the patent term extension which had been granted was invalid, because the claims were not to a pharmaceutical substance per se.

[12] See Patent Manual of Practice and Procedure, section 5.5.4.7.

# C. Direct and indirect infringement of second medical use claims

## I. Introduction

13 The requirements for infringement of second medical use claims will depend on the form of the claim in question, and in particular whether the question involves a method of treatment claim, Swiss-type claim or an EPC 2000 claim, each of which are discussed above.

14 Swiss-type claims are directed to the process of manufacture and as such, direct infringement claims may be brought against a pharmaceutical party manufacturing a relevant product. Similarly EPC 2000 claims are directed at a pharmaceutical product and so will be directly infringed by relevant exploitation of that product.

15 Because method of treatment claims are directed to the activity of treating a condition, a clinician or other person administering the treatment will generally be the party directly infringing the claim. Since patent proceedings in respect of second medical use claims will generally be brought against a pharmaceutical company or companies involved in the manufacture and supply of the relevant pharmaceutical product, the issue is generally one of indirect infringement.

16 Indirect infringement allegations may also arise in relation to parties involved in the manufacture and/or supply of infringing products but which have not directly undertaken an infringing act of exploitation.

## II. Direct patent infringement

### 1. Infringing acts

17 The exclusive rights given to the patentee pursuant to section 13 of the Patents Act are the right to exploit the invention and to authorise another person to exploit the invention. Undertaking these acts in relation to a claimed product or process without the permission of the patentee will amount to patent infringement. *Exploitation* in relation to an invention is not defined exhaustively but includes:

1. where the invention is a product: making, hiring, selling or otherwise disposing of the product, offering to make, sell, hire or otherwise dispose of it, using or importing it, or keeping it for the purpose of doing any of those things; and
2. where the invention is a method or process: using the method or process or doing any act mentioned in paragraph (a) in respect of a product resulting from such use.

### 2. Swiss-type claims

#### a) Products manufactured outside of Australia

18 In general, importation, sale or other commercial acts of exploitation, of a product manufactured outside of Australia which falls within the scope of the claims, will be within the exclusive rights of the patentee and so amount to infringement of the patent.

19 Because Swiss-type claims are to a method or process, being the process of manufacture, the question has arisen as to whether importation and/or commercial exploitation in Australia of a pharmaceutical product manufactured outside of Australia is an infringe-

ment of such a claim. The Federal Court and FCFCA have now confirmed on several occasions that such acts infringe an Australian patent.[13] The definition of exploitation includes acts of exploitation *in respect of a product resulting from use of the patented method.* It is the acts of exploitation in respect of such products which must take place in Australia, but there is no territorial restriction in such circumstances on the place where the method is used.

#### b) Medicament must be for the specified therapeutic purpose

In *Mylan*, the FCFCA was required to consider the level of knowledge or intention required of a manufacturer with respect to the claimed therapeutic purpose of the medicament in order to establish infringement. **20**

The Court held that a Swiss-type claim does not include as an essential feature the manufacturer's intention in making the medicament. Rather, a single factual question arises: as the product of the claimed method or process, is the medicament *for* the specified therapeutic purpose? This question is to be determined with regard to the characteristics of the manufactured product, having regard to all the circumstances of the case. **21**

In making such an assessment, the Court set out a number of matters which may be relevant to ascertaining whether a medicament is for a particular purpose: **22**

1. The physical characteristics of the medicament including its formulation and dosage, packaging and labelling and patient information. This is 'a most important' consideration.
2. Direct evidence of the manufacturer's intention may be relevant, but not determinative.
3. The reasonably foreseeable use or uses to which the medicament would be put after manufacture. However the fact that it is reasonably foreseeable, or even likely, that a medicament would be used extensively for non-patented purposes is not determinative. It can be reasonably foreseeable that a product will be put to particular use, even where the product, as manufactured, is not for that use.
4. Evidence of suitability for use is ambiguous and cannot alone answer the relevant question.

### 3. EPC 2000 claims

Since an EPC 2000 claim is directed to a product, it will be infringed if any of the relevant acts of exploitation are carried out in relation to a product which falls within the claim. As noted above (→ mn. 10 et seq.) no Australian cases have yet finally considered the requirement to establish that a product is 'for' a use for the purposes of an EPC 2000 claim. However if the Courts determine that the relevant use is limiting in a similar way to that of a Swiss-type claim, the Courts may approach infringement in a similar manner. **23**

---

[13] *Warner-Lambert Company LLC v Apotex Pty Limited (No 2)* [2018] FCAFC 26 at [167]-[168] and *Mylan Health Pty Ltd (formerly BGP Products Pty Ltd) v Sun Pharma ANZ Pty Ltd (formerly Ranbaxy Australia Pty Ltd)* [2019] FCA 28 at [93].

## III. Indirect patent infringement

### 1. Section 117 Patents Act

24 Section 117 Patents Act provides for a statutory form of indirect patent infringement based on the supply of a product which is used for an infringing purpose. In particular, unauthorised supply of a product is an infringement if the use of the product by a person would infringe a patent. There are three ways in which the 'use' of the product in this context is to be determined:

1. if the product is capable of only one use having regard to its nature or design, then that is the use of the product;
2. if the product is not a staple commercial product, any use of the product which the supplier had reason to believe the product would be put to is a relevant 'use'. 'Staple commercial product' is not defined in the Patents Act, but case law provides some guidance. In particular, the High Court has confirmed that a staple commercial product is a product that is generally available and supplied commercially for a variety of uses.[14] No pharmaceutical product has yet been found to be a staple commercial product in Australia;[15]
3. if instructions are provided to use the product in a particular way, then that is a relevant use.

25 A second medical use claim in the form of a method of treatment claim may be infringed by a supplier of a medicament, with respect to the use to be made of the medicament by a person administering it to patients.

26 It is not necessary for the purposes of section 117 to prove actual use falling within the scope of the claim, nor it is necessary to identify a person or persons who will use it in an infringing manner.[16] The inquiry relates to the use of the product, when considered within the above three categories.

27 In the case of pharmaceutical patent claims, category (2) (reason to believe it will be put to an infringing use) and/or (3) (instructions for infringing use) are generally at issue. Where a skinny label strategy is employed (→ mn. 29), there will usually be no instruction for infringing use and so it will usually be asserted that there is reason to believe (notwithstanding the skinny label) that the product will be used for an infringing use. The Court has also confirmed that if such reason to believe exists, it is not necessary that the product is actually supplied for that purpose.[17]

### 2. Common law indirect infringement

28 Under Australian common law, procuring or inducing another person to engage in patent infringing activity, or joining in a common design with another person to undertake conduct that infringes an Australian patent, also amounts to infringement of a patent.

[14] *Northern Territory of Australia v Collins & Anr* (2008) 235 CLR 619; [2008] HCA 49.

[15] The argument was put in *AstraZeneca AB v Apotex Pty Ltd* [2014] FCAFC 99 *(AstraZeneca FCFCA)*, and was rejected on the basis that there were a number of specific indications for the product. It also failed in *Otsuka FCA*. However note that in *Hood v Down Under Enterprises International Pty Ltd* [2022] FCAFC 69, an essential oil was considered a staple commercial product.

[16] *AstraZeneca FCFCA* at [433].

[17] *Otsuka FCA* at [172]; → mn. 72.

# D. Infringement of second medical use claims and skinny label products

In Australia, a 'skinny label product' is understood as a generic product which has been registered on the Australian Register of Therapeutic Goods (ARTG) for more limited indications than the reference product, and in particular which excludes a patented indication. The registered indications will be listed in the product information leaflet which is approved by the Therapeutic Goods Administration (TGA) and must accompany the product. There is provision for variations to be made to the details of registration,[18] and this has been employed in some cases in response to litigation. It should be noted that in one case, a request to vary the registration to add a positive disclaimer that a product was not to be used for a particular indication was refused by the TGA.[19] 29

Brand substitution for a prescription is permitted in Australia unless the prescriber has noted on the prescription that no substitution is permitted. Where multiple bioequivalent brands of a particular medication are listed on the PBS, they will be 'a-flagged' on the PBS, indicating that they have been deemed bioequivalent. 30

The legal analysis applied to skinny label products in the context of infringement of second medical use patent claims will depend on the form of the claim as discussed above (→ mn. 13 et seq.). However recent Australian cases in respect of both method of treatment claims and Swiss-type claims have demonstrated that the success of a skinny label in avoiding patent infringement (where a patent claim relates to an indication which is not listed on the registration), will depend on the circumstances of the case. The courts have been unwilling to lay down any general rule. It seems clear that actual prescribing and dispensing practice will likely be very relevant to this analysis. It also seems likely that method of treatment claims will be more difficult for a generic party to overcome by way of a skinny label strategy due to the Court's consideration of 'off-label' use, which has less significance in the context of a Swiss-type claim. 31

## I. Method of treatment claims

### 1. Relevant cases

In *Sanofi* the High Court considered a claim in respect of the supply of ApoLeflunomide for infringement of patent claims covering the treatment or prevention of psoriasis. ApoLeflunomide was registered on the ARTG as indicated for rheumatoid arthritis (RA) and psoriatic arthritis (PsA). The High Court accepted that a person suffering RA or PsA may have psoriasis, and that administration of ApoLeflunomide to treat the RA or PsA would be likely to inevitably relieve the patient's psoriasis. However the product was supplied with a product information leaflet stating that ApoLeflunomide is 'not indicated for the treatment of psoriasis that is not associated with manifestations of arthritic disease'. 32

The High Court accepted that a proper construction of the claim confined it to the deliberate administration of the compound to prevent or treat psoriasis. It found that Apotex had no reason to believe that ApoLeflunomide would be put to the use of preventing or treating psoriasis, and so did not infringe. 33

---

[18] Section 9D, Therapeutic Goods Act 1989 (Cth).

[19] → mn. 48.

34 The *Sanofi* case concerned a specific disclaimer of the patented indication, and did not deal with a situation where the indications were limited to exclude the patented indication, with no express disclaimer. The question of infringement of method of treatment claims in those circumstances arose in *Warner-Lambert Company LLC v Apotex Pty Ltd* (Warner-Lambert),[20] which brought to the fore issues of whether or not medicines are permissibly prescribed and dispensed in Australia for indications for which they are not registered on the ARTG, a practice known as 'off-label' prescribing or use, and the significance of this for patent infringement claims under section 117 of the Patents Act.

35 The *Warner-Lambert* case concerned a generic equivalent of Pfizer's pregabalin product, Lyrica. Lyrica was registered on the ARTG for use for the treatment of neuropathic pain (neuropathic pain indication) and for seizures (seizure indication). Warner-Lambert Company's patent covered use of pregabalin for the neuropathic pain indication, but not the seizure indication. Pfizer promoted Lyrica in Australia for the neuropathic pain indication, but not for the seizure indication and Lyrica was listed on the PBS only for neuropathic pain refractory to other medications. Apotex obtained ARTG registration for Apotex-Pregabalin, limited to the seizure indication. Warner-Lambert Company sought an interlocutory injunction which would prevent Apotex from selling this product for any indication, including the unpatented seizure indication, relying on the 'reason to believe' arm of the section 117 test (section 117(2)(b) Patents Act). Since an interlocutory injunction was sought, Warner-Lambert Company only needed to make out a *prima facie* case of infringement.

36 Warner-Lambert Company argued that notwithstanding the skinny label, Apotex had reason to believe that its product would be used for the neuropathic pain indication, particularly given the market for the seizure indication was very limited. The evidence established that regardless of whether a brand name medicine was specified on the prescription or not, a pharmacist could substitute any other ARTG registered equivalent brand (as long as it was not marked as not for substitution). However there was conflicting expert evidence as to whether pharmacists would dispense a product registered only for the seizures indication for neuropathic pain. There was evidence that many doctors would routinely prescribe pharmaceuticals, including pregabalin, without specifying an indication on the prescription. However the experts differed on the question of whether it would be ethical to prescribe a bioequivalent product knowing it was to be used for an off-label use.

37 The trial judge found that Warner Lambert Company had not made out a *prima facie* case of infringement. He relied in particular on data which had been submitted by Pfizer in support of a PBS application to have Lyrica listed on the PBS for the seizure indication, and also Apotex's own sales projections, as evidence of a genuine market for the seizures indication. On appeal, the FCFCA overturned this finding, concluding that the evidence before the trial judge had provided strong support that the seizure market was very small (potentially less than 0.25 % of the total market) so that there was essentially no market for pregabalin in Australia as an anti-seizure medication. The FCFCA also considered that the conflict between the experts in relation to off-label use could not be resolved until a full trial.

38 Apotex also indicated that it would circulate relevant 'promotional materials', including (a) a pro forma letter to medical practitioners informing them that Apotex-Pregabalin was not indicated for the treatment of neuropathic pain and stating that when prescribing Apotex-Pregabalin for the treatment of seizures, that indication should be shown on the prescription, and (b) a pro forma letter to pharmacists informing them that if a prescription did not specify the indication for which pregabalin had been prescribed, or if

---

[20] [2014] FCAFC 59.

it was a PBS prescription, then they should not offer Apotex-Pregabalin to patients. The FCFCA found that there was no evidence whether clinicians or pharmacists would heed these instructions.

Accordingly, the question of whether or not the absence of a pain related indication for Apotex-Pregabalin from the relevant ARTG registrations, coupled with the information and directions to be given to doctors and pharmacists by means of the Apotex promotional material, should lead to the same result as in *Sanofi* (where there was an express disclaimer of the relevant indication) was not something that could be resolved before trial. On that basis, a *prima facie* case had been made out and the status quo should be maintained until trial through the grant of an interlocutory injunction. **39**

Following *Warner-Lambert*, it seemed clear that a skinny label strategy was not a guarantee of success in avoiding patent infringement of a method of treatment claim, and that the question of infringement would depend on all the circumstances. **40**

A further example supporting that conclusion, akin to skinny labelling, was the FCFCA decision in *Astrazeneca FCFCA*. One of the patent claim sets covered the administration of rosuvastatin products in a 10 mg dose. The question arose as to whether a generic product sold in 20 mg doses infringed these claims. **41**

It was noted that a patient directed by a doctor to take a 10 mg dose would have a financial incentive to purchase a pack of 20 mg tablets and split them into 10 mg dosages. Evidence was given from a pharmacist as to the widespread availability of 'tablet splitting' devices used by patients in relation to many different kinds of prescription medicines, and from clinicians aware that some patients split their statin tablets and who were willing to prescribe a higher dosage of statin to permit tablet splitting in order for the patient to save money. **42**

The FCFCA found it established that the generic parties had reason to believe that some consumers would put the generic parties' 20 mg products to an infringing use and had therefore infringed the relevant patent under section 117. **43**

### 2. Potential significance of authority prescriptions under PBS

There are many medicines listed on the PBS which require a medical practitioner to obtain authority from the Department of Human Services to prescribe them with PBS subsidy. These include medicines which have particular features relating to clinical use, including the requirement for additional monitoring or tests, and high cost medications. **44**

The processes for obtaining authority for an authority prescription and dispensing are such that it appears that additional arguments may be available in the case of an authority prescription medicine, that it will not be used off label. This would appear to be a factor relevant to the question of whether a manufacturer has reason to believe a product will be used for an off-label indication. Such arguments have not yet been tested by the Australian Courts, however it may be that it will be more difficult to show a 'reason to believe' in such cases. **45**

## II. Swiss-type claims

The position of skinny labelling in relation to Swiss-type claims came to be considered in *Mylan*. The FCFCA considered in some detail the decision of the UK Supreme Court in *Generics (UK) v Warner-Lambert*.[21] However as noted (→ mn. 20 et seq.), it ultimately **46**

---

[21] [2018] UKSC 56.

proposed a different test in Australia, finding the crucial question to be whether the medicament is *for* the specified therapeutic purpose having regard to the characteristics of the manufactured product, and all the circumstances of the case.

47 The question in that case was whether the allegedly infringing products (the Ranbaxy Products) were 'for' diabetic retinopathy, as claimed. On the facts of the case, the FCFCA found that the amended product information for the Ranbaxy Products presented the products as having a substantial therapeutic use in the treatment of hypercholesterolaemia, various types of dyslipidaemia, and dyslipidaemia associated with type 2 diabetes. The product information for the Ranbaxy Products also referred to them as bioequivalent to Lipidil, the patentee's product, Lipidil being indicated for diabetic retinopathy. However the Court concluded that reference to bioequivalence with a product which was indicated for the patented indication did not point persuasively to a conclusion that the Ranbaxy Products were medicaments for that indication, especially since that statement was made in the context of simply referring to the bioequivalence that had been found in clinical trials. The Court also took account in this regard of evidence that clinicians do not typically read product information leaflets for generic products.

48 The fact that the product information for the Ranbaxy Products did not contain a disclaimer of use for the specified purpose of the claims in suit was also a relevant consideration. But the absence of a disclaimer was not proof that, as manufactured, a medicament is one for a therapeutic use that has *not* been disclaimed, when the medicament's therapeutic use *has* been clearly stated. Notably there was also evidence that Sun Pharma applied to the TGA to amend the product information to add an express disclaimer that the Ranbaxy Products are not indicated for the prevention or treatment of retinopathy (including diabetic retinopathy) and the TGA refused the request on the basis this would be not be permitted under section 9D(2) of the Therapeutic Goods Act 1989 (Cth).

49 In the present case, the indications stated in the product information were found to inferentially indicate the therapeutic uses they serve as medicaments, which did not include the patented uses.

50 Mylan also argued that Sun Pharma could have written to medical practitioners and pharmacists asking or instructing them not to prescribe or provide the Ranbaxy Products for the treatment or prevention of diabetic retinopathy. The FCFCA considered that this strayed from the question of whether the Swiss-type claims were infringed, which focuses on the characteristics of the medicament as it emerges as the product of the claimed method or process. The argument raised was more relevant to the question of indirect infringement of the method of treatment claims. Note also that an undertaking to the Court that a party would not advertise or otherwise promote the relevant products specifically for patented use, where it was registered for such indication, was not sufficient to avoid infringement in *Otsuka FCA*[22] given that the question is an objective one.

51 It is notable that in *Mylan* the first instance judge had found equivalent method of treatment claims infringed and this finding was not appealed. The end result therefore was that in respect of the same product and same patent claims, the method of treatment claims were infringed but the Swiss-type claims were not. This difference arises due to the focus for Swiss-type claims on evidence of the use of the product as manufactured, as opposed to method of treatment claims which are focused on the 'downstream' use of the product and so take into account matters such as the likelihood of off-label use of a medicine. As a result method of treatment claims appear to present a greater difficulty for generic parties in implementing a skinny label strategy due to the difficulties for the generic party in controlling use of the product downstream once introduced to the market.

[22] At [173]; → mn. 72.

### III. EPC 2000 claims

As noted (→ mn. 23), no infringement claim has yet been finally determined by the Australian Courts in relation to an EPC 2000 claim. However if they are determined to be limited by the specified use, it seems likely that the requirements for infringement, and position of a skinny label, will be similar to that in relation to a Swiss-type claim. 52

## E. Infringement of second medical use claims and biosimilar products

### I. Biosimilar products in Australia

As of March 2023 there were over 120 biological active ingredients listed on the PBS,[23] accounting for many of the top PBS-subsidised medicines by expenditure. Nine of these include 'a-flagged' substitutable brands (→ mn. 30). 53

The Australian Government has implemented various initiatives to encourage the use of biosimilars, recognising the opportunity for cost savings in the health system. In 2015, the Australian Government committed AU$20 million to a three-year awareness campaign to support the increased use of biosimilar medicines by patients, pharmacists and specialists (subsequently extended).[24] In 2017 the Government further reached agreement to implement certain 'biosimilar uptake drivers', the encouragement of prescription of a biosimilar brand rather than the reference biological brand for treatment naïve patients; and providing for streamlined approval process for prescribing biosimilar brands.[25] 54

The TGA has largely adopted the European approach to regulatory approval of biosimilars.[26] Regulatory approval for a biosimilar requires that no clinically meaningful differences exist and that the biosimilar molecule is therapeutically equivalent to the reference medicine. To obtain TGA approval, each biosimilar must be evaluated using clinical, pre-clinical and laboratory-based comparability studies to generate evidence of similar quality, safety and efficacy of each new biosimilar. Once biosimilarity is established in relation to a particular indication, it may be possible for a biosimilar to be approved for other indications by 'indication extrapolation' from the reference product's data. 55

### II. Patent infringement by biosimilar products

The Australian Courts have not yet had occasion to issue a judgment substantively considering the requirements for establishing infringement of a second medical use claim relating to a biosimilar product.[27] However there is no reason to believe that the Courts 56

---

[23] https://www.pbs.gov.au/info/browse/biological-medicines-currently-listed-on-the-pbs (last accessed 9 July 2024).

[24] https://sussanley.com/pharmaceutical-benefits-scheme-to-be-reformed/ (last accessed 9 July 2024).

[25] https://www.pbs.gov.au/general/biosimilars/biosimilar-uptake-drivers-q-and-a.pdf (last accessed 9 July 2024).

[26] https://www.tga.gov.au/resources/resource/guidance/biosimilar-medicines-regulation (last accessed 9 July 2024).

[27] In *F. Hoffman-La Roche AG v Sandoz Pty Ltd* [2018] FCA 874 the Federal Court determined an interlocutory injunction application in relation to method of treatment claims for rituximab, however the

will depart from the same general principles as are set out above (→ mn. 13 et seq.), both in relation to method of treatment claims and Swiss-type claims.

57 However it is to be noted that most biologic products listed on the PBS are subject to the authority prescription process discussed above (→ mn. 44 et seq.). As noted there, the Courts have not yet considered a case involving an authority prescription product, and in particular the significance of this for off-label use, which has been found to form the basis for at least a *prima facie* case of infringement of a method of treatment claim under section 117 Patents Act. This question may well come to be considered in the context of a biosimilar case in the future.

## F. Strategies and considerations

58 As is apparent from the above, on the basis of the current case law in Australia there is no clear strategy which will ensure non-infringement of a skinny label product, and an assessment will be undertaken of all of the facts of the case. However the following measures may be taken into account and so have the potential to reduce the risk of infringement:

1. Inclusion of a specific disclaimer of the patented indication on the ARTG registration;
2. Provision of information to medical practitioners and pharmacists emphasising the limited indication(s) of the generic product and directing that it not be used for the patented purpose (particularly for method of treatment claims);
3. Ensuring that there is in fact a viable market for the non-patented indication(s);
4. Not taking any steps to actively market the product for the patented indication(s).

## G. Legal remedies

### I. Interlocutory injunctions

59 Interlocutory injunctions are available in appropriate cases in Australia to protect the status quo pending a final trial to determine infringement. The injunction will only be in place until final judgment is delivered. Interlocutory injunction applications are generally heard on notice to the respondent. *Ex parte* injunctions can be sought in extremely urgent circumstances but will generally only be in place until the respondent is put on notice and has an opportunity to make its case. Where an interlocutory injunction is granted, the patentee will be required to provide '*the usual undertaking as to damages*' which requires it to undertake to compensate any affected party caused damage by the injunction if it is ultimately that it should not have been granted (i.e. there was no infringement or the patent(s) in suit are found invalid).

60 To obtain an interlocutory injunction, the patentee must show a *prima facie* case of infringement, as well as that the balance of convenience supports the grant of the injunction. Until recently the fact that generic entry to the market will cause an immediate price drop in the price of the reference product, as well as further ongoing price reductions, has generally been sufficient to establish that if an interlocutory injunction is not

relevant generic products were ARTG registered for the patented indications and Sandoz did not dispute there was a *prima facie* case of infringement, instead relying on arguments of invalidity.

granted, the patentee will suffer irreparable harm, which the Courts have considered ought be protected against. However recent cases in which generic manufacturers (and the Commonwealth Government) have made claims pursuant to the undertaking as to damages mentioned above have demonstrated the highly complex nature of establishing damage in such a circumstance, due to the need to prove the 'counterfactual' scenario of what would have occurred in the relevant market had the injunction not been granted.[28] In *Mylan Health Pty Ltd v Sun Pharma ANZ Pty Ltd* (No 2),[29] the Court noted in the context of refusing an application for an interim injunction pending appeal that the calculation of compensation under an undertaking as to damages can impose burdens and raise uncertainties that are far greater than the burdens and uncertainties involved in assessing damages for infringement.

## II. Permanent injunctions

Although the grant of an injunction is a discretionary matter for the Court, in general terms where infringement of a valid patent claim is established at a final trial, the Court will make a permanent injunction without the need for any additional justification. **61**

However, it is apparent from the above analysis that infringement may be found under section 117 Patents Act even where there is likely to be non-infringing use of the product in question, and perhaps even very substantial non-infringing use. In *AstraZeneca FCFCA*, the Court noted[30] that in such circumstances it may be undesirable to impose a blanket restraint upon a supplier who has reason to believe that only some consumers, perhaps a very small minority, may put the product that is or may be supplied to them to an infringing use. **62**

The Court suggested that, all other things being equal, the more difficult it is for the patentee to establish that there is a likelihood of widespread infringing use, the more difficult it should be for the patentee to obtain injunctive relief in the broad terms restraining *any* supply of the relevant product. This suggestion was also noted in *Otsuka FCA* at [247], however to date, the Australian Courts have not had to consider the question of appropriate relief in such circumstances since in the relevant cases the patent claims have been found invalid. It seems likely that this question will be addressed by Australian Courts in the future. **63**

## III. Monetary compensation

Where infringement is established a patentee will be entitled to elect for an award of damages or an account of the infringer's profits attributable to the infringement. **64**

For the reasons discussed above in relation to interlocutory injunction applications, many pharmaceutical patent cases are brought before the generic product enters the market (to prevent such entry) and so damages/account of profits are not in issue. However where compensation is at issue, generally early on in a patent infringement proceeding an order will be made separating the question of liability from that of compensation. This means that damages/account of profits will only be dealt with at a later stage once judgment has been delivered on liability, and only if liability is established. A further **65**

---

[28] See, for example, *Commonwealth of Australia v Sanofi (formerly Sanofi-Aventis)* [2023] FCAFC 97.
[29] [2019] FCA 505.
[30] At [444]; → mn. 74.

stage of the proceeding will then follow at which time the patentee is required to make its election and there will be further evidence, discovery and a hearing to quantify the amount of compensation/damages payable.

## IV. Other remedies

66 Other remedies commonly sought and awarded in patent infringement cases include declarations of infringement and patent validity and an order for delivery up of any infringing goods.

# H. Statutory provisions[31]

**Patents Act 1990 (Cth)**

67 **Section 13: Exclusive rights given by patent**

(1) Subject to this Act, a patent gives the patentee the exclusive rights, during the term of the patent, to exploit the invention and to authorise another person to exploit the invention.

(2) The exclusive rights are personal property and are capable of assignment and of devolution by law.

(3) A patent has effect throughout the patent area.

68 **Section 18: Patentable inventions**

Patentable inventions for the purposes of a standard patent

(1) Subject to subsection (2), an invention is a patentable invention for the purposes of a standard patent if the invention, so far as claimed in any claim:

(a) is a manner of manufacture within the meaning of section 6 of the Statute of Monopolies; and

...

69 **Section 117: Infringement by supply of products**

(1) If the use of a product by a person would infringe a patent, the supply of that product by one person to another is an infringement of the patent by the supplier unless the supplier is the patentee or licensee of the patent.

(2) A reference in subsection (1) to the use of a product by a person is a reference to:

(a) if the product is capable of only one reasonable use, having regard to its nature or design—that use; or

(b) if the product is not a staple commercial product—any use of the product, if the supplier had reason to believe that the person would put it to that use; or

(c) in any case—the use of the product in accordance with any instructions for the use of the product, or any inducement to use the product, given to the person by the supplier or contained in an advertisement published by or with the authority of the supplier.

[31] All legislative extracts sourced from the Federal Register of Legislation, pursuant to https://creativecommons.org/licenses/by/4.0/: https://www.legislation.gov.au/Details/C2017C00045.

**Schedule 1 – Dictionary** 70

*exploit*, in relation to an invention, includes:

(a) where the invention is a product—make, hire, sell or otherwise dispose of the product, offer to make, sell, hire or otherwise dispose of it, use or import it, or keep it for the purpose of doing any of those things; or

(b) where the invention is a method or process—use the method or process or do any act mentioned in paragraph (a) in respect of a product resulting from such use.

# J. Extracts from court decisions

## I. *Mylan Health Pty Ltd v Sun Pharma ANZ Pty Ltd*[32] 71

(194) 'As explained in Otsuka at [100] – [115], Swiss type claims derived from the need to accommodate and satisfy particular requirements for patentability which, formerly, applied under the European Patent Convention. These particular requirements are not, nor have they been, part of the Australian legal landscape. Nevertheless, patentees have sought Swiss type claims in their Australian patents. They have, perhaps, been motivated to do so because such claims provide an avenue, in addition to indirect infringement under section 117(1) of the Act, for suing to restrain the supply of competitive pharmaceutical products rather than seeking to restrain medical practitioners who prescribe, and patients who use, those products for medical treatment.

(195) It is also important to bear steadily in mind that, while Swiss type claims are method or process claims, they are not method of treatment claims. The monopoly obtained through a Swiss type claim is in respect of the method or process of making a medicament. That process is complete upon manufacture. A Swiss type claim does not, in and of itself, create a monopoly that extends to a method of treatment using, for example, the medicament once made. This is the province of method of treatment claims.

(196) Further, Swiss type claims are purpose-limited claims in the sense that the medicament resulting from the method or process is characterised by the therapeutic purpose for which it is manufactured, as specified in the claim. Claim 1 of the 711 patent is typical of such claims. It claims the use of fenofibrate (or a derivative thereof) for the manufacture of a medicament for the prevention and/or treatment of retinopathy, in particular diabetic retinopathy: see [37] above.

(197) The specification of a therapeutic purpose imposes an important limitation on the scope of the claim. In theory, it is this limitation which supports the novelty, and hence the patentability, of the invention. Without this limitation, the claim would be invalid because its scope would be broadened to include old subject matter (bearing in mind that Swiss type claims are directed to methods or processes whose products are for second or later therapeutic uses). It is appropriate, therefore, to consider this purpose as one that confines the use of the method or process to the achievement of one end and one end only—a medicament for the specified therapeutic purpose; not a medicament for any other therapeutic purpose. Put another way, a Swiss type claim does not claim the invention in terms of a medicament that is useful for, or can be used for, the specified therapeutic purpose and other therapeutic purposes. In order to support its patentability, and preserve its validity, the invention, as claimed through a Swiss type claim, is necessarily more limited in scope.

[32] [2020] FCAFC 116. All judgment extracts obtained from AustLII: www.austlii.edu.au.

(198) The characterisation of the medicament by specification of the therapeutic purpose is, therefore, an essential feature of the invention as claimed. Like any other essential feature, it must be proved in order for infringement of the claimed method or process to be established.

...

(221) Australian patent law does not provide a fiat by reference to which patent claims are to be construed. Patent claims are construed by reference to common law principles applicable to patent specifications as documents created in a particular setting and serving particular ends. There is no requirement to construe patent claims by reference to stated policy objectives such as those contained in the Protocol.

(222) As a matter of claim construction, we do not read Swiss type claims, such as those in this proceeding, as adding a further essential feature to the invention, namely the manufacturer's intention in making the medicament. We disagree, therefore, with the primary judge's finding at [102] that the crucial question for infringement is whether the manufacturer has made (or will make) the relevant medicament with the intention that it be used in the treatment of the specified condition. Infringement arises from the taking of the essential features of the invention as claimed. Therefore, infringement of a Swiss type claim is concerned with what the allegedly infringing manufacturer has done, not what it intended to do. Bearing in mind the limited scope of such claims, a single factual question is presented when considering infringement: as the product of the claimed method or process, is the medicament for the specified therapeutic purpose? This question is directed to the characteristics of the manufactured product. It is answered having regard to all the circumstances of the case. We are satisfied that Ground 2 of the notice of appeal is established because the primary judge proceeded on an incorrect basis in addressing the question of infringement by fixing on the manufacturer's intention. As a consequence of this conclusion, Ground 3 of the notice of appeal does not arise.

(223) Plainly, one badge of therapeutic purpose (to adopt Lord Sumption's expression) is the physical characteristics of the medicament as it emerges as a product of the manufacturing process, including its formulation and dosage, packaging and labelling, and its patient information. This is a most important consideration. But it does not represent the only evidence that could rationally affect, directly or indirectly, the determination of the question of medicament's therapeutic purpose. Although we do not read the Swiss type claims as adding the manufacturer's intention as an essential feature of the invention, we do not reject the relevance of direct evidence of the manufacturer's actual intention in making the medicament, where that evidence is available. This is not to say that such evidence would be determinative. If such evidence is available, it would form part of the circumstances of the case to be taken into account with all the other circumstances. Such evidence was not available in the present case.

(224) Further, we would not reject consideration of the reasonably foreseeable use or uses to which the medicament would be put after manufacture. Such consideration would also form part of the circumstances of the case. However, we agree with the primary judge that, where a medicament would be used extensively for purposes that fall outside the monopoly of a Swiss type claim, the fact that it is reasonably foreseeable, or indeed likely, that a substantial portion of the manufactured medicament would also be used for the claimed therapeutic purpose will not be determinative of infringement: it might be reasonably foreseeable that a product might be put to a particular use, but it does not necessarily follow that the product, as manufactured, is for that use. Thus, we reject Mylan's submission that the primary judge acted inconsistently by rejecting the case on infringement of the Swiss type claims whilst nevertheless finding infringement under section 117(1) of the Act with reference to section 117(2)(b) in respect of the method of treatment claims. Different considerations inform the question of infringement arising under section 117(1). Ground 4 of the notice of appeal fails.

(225) We also agree with the primary judge that mere suitability of a medicament for a claimed purpose cannot be determinative of the question of infringement of a Swiss type claim. We have already touched on this consideration when discussing the limited scope

of these claims. The fact that the patent has been granted on the basis of a second or later therapeutic use necessarily means that there are multiple uses to which, potentially, the medicament can be put. Thus, evidence of suitability for use is ambiguous and cannot alone answer the question whether the medicament, as manufactured, is one for the specified therapeutic purpose.

(226) Turning to the facts of the present case, there was a substantial therapeutic use for the Ranbaxy Products in the treatment of hypercholesterolaemia, various types of dyslipidaemia, and dyslipidaemia associated with type 2 diabetes. This is how the amended product information, in evidence before the primary judge, presented these products to the market. We accept that it is relevant to consider, as part of the circumstances of the case, the fact that the product information for the Ranbaxy Products refers to them as bioequivalent to Lipidil. It is also relevant to consider that, separately, the product information for Lipidil states that Lipidil is indicated for the reduction in the progression of diabetic retinopathy. But, the conjunction of these facts does not point persuasively to a conclusion that the Ranbaxy Products are medicaments for the specified therapeutic purpose, especially when it is recognised that the statement that is made with respect to Lipidil in the product information for the Ranbaxy Products is in the context of simply referring to the bioequivalence that has been found in the majority of clinical trials that have been conducted. Mylan's point is diminished further by its acceptance of the primary judge's finding (at [117]) that medical practitioners do not typically read the product information for generic products.

(227) The fact that the product information for the Ranbaxy Products does not contain a disclaimer of use for the specified purpose of the claims in suit is also a relevant consideration. But the absence of a disclaimer is hardly proof that, as manufactured, a medicament is one for a therapeutic use that has not been disclaimed, when the medicament's therapeutic use has been clearly stated. If anything, the making of such a disclaimer might, in a given case, bolster the position of a manufacturer who is alleged to have infringed a Swiss type claim.

(228) In the present case, the product information for the Ranbaxy Products states the indications for which they are registered and thus, inferentially, the therapeutic purpose they serve as medicaments. Those indications are hypercholesterolaemia; types II, III, IV and V dyslipidaemia; and dyslipidaemia associated with type 2 diabetes, in each case as an adjunct to diet. The evidence discloses that Sun Pharma applied to the Therapeutic Goods Administration (*TGA*) to amend the product information by adding an express disclaimer that the Ranbaxy Products are not indicated for the prevention or treatment of retinopathy (including diabetic retinopathy) or for the reduction in the progression of diabetic retinopathy in patients with type 2 diabetes. The TGA refused that request because it did not consider that such an amendment would be sanctioned by *section 9D(2)* of the *Therapeutic Goods Act 1989* (Cth).

(229) In oral submissions, Mylan argued that, in the face of that rejection, Sun Pharma might have pursued other avenues to obtain the disclaimers it had sought. The suggestion seems to be that, somehow, Sun Pharma's application to the TGA to amend was made half-heartedly or was, perhaps, a pretence. That seems to be an unlikely interpretation of events. It begs the Court's acceptance of an elaborate feint rather than acceptance of what Sun Pharma's application most obviously was—a request to amend the product information, on which the TGA was asked to act.

(230) Mylan also argued that Sun Pharma could have written to medical practitioners and pharmacists asking or instructing them not to prescribe or provide the Ranbaxy Products for the treatment or prevention of diabetic retinopathy. It submitted that Sun Pharma had proffered undertakings to this effect, but only if it be found at trial that supply of the Ranbaxy Products infringed the 711 patent. No doubt, Sun Pharma could take such steps, independently of the outcome of Mylan's infringement case. But this seems to stray from the question of whether the Swiss type claims are infringed, which focuses on the characteristics of the medicament as it emerges as the product of the claimed method or process. The argument that Mylan raises is one that seems to be more relevant to a consideration of downstream activity, and thus the question of indirect infringement of the method of treatment claims, which the

primary judge found would have been infringed by dint of section 117(1) of the Act read with section 117(2)(b), had the method of treatment claims been valid.

(231) Had the Swiss type claims been valid—in particular, claim 5 advanced in this appeal—we are not persuaded that the evidence establishes that, as manufactured, the Ranbaxy Products are medicaments for the treatment of retinopathy, in particular diabetic retinopathy. For this reason Ground 1 of the notice of appeal fails. Although Ground 2 of the notice of appeal has been established, it does not lead to the granting of any relief by this Court.'

72 ## II. *Otsuka Pharmaceutical Co., Ltd v Generic Health Pty Ltd* (No 4)[33]

(120) 'In my view, an invention defined by a Swiss type claim is appropriately characterised as method or process. For the purpose of this analysis, no useful distinction exists between the words 'method' and 'process'. In the Act, the words 'method' and 'process' are not defined. In my view, neither word has a meaning that is different from its ordinary English signification. My conclusion reflects, therefore, what I consider to be an apt use of the words 'method' and 'process' when applied as ordinary English words to describe the content and subject matter of the generalised form of the claim to which I have referred.

...

(172) For the purpose of determining infringement of a Swiss type claim, does it matter that the alleged infringer does not actually advertise or promote the medicament specifically for the therapeutic use defined in the claim? I do not think it necessarily does. The question is whether, objectively ascertained, the medicament that results from the claimed method or process is one that has the therapeutic use defined in the claim. The question is not really about how the alleged infringer markets its product, although, plainly, its conduct in that regard may well assist in determining, objectively, whether the accused product has the claimed therapeutic use.

(173) In the present case, I am not persuaded that an absence of advertising or promotion by the respondent of the GH products for the therapeutic use defined in claim 1 would change the objective characterisation of those products as ones that are, nevertheless, 'effective in the treatment' defined in claim 1.

...

(247) Having considered all the evidence, I am satisfied that the applicants have discharged the onus of establishing that the respondent has reason to believe that, if supplied in Australia, the GH products would be put to a use that would infringe claim 7 of the 772 patent. That is enough to establish infringement under section 117(1) of the Act. Infringement under that provision cannot be avoided by establishing that the product will also be put to non-infringing uses, although this may influence, for example, the scope of injunctive relief that might be granted: AstraZeneca 226 FCR 324 at [444]. I am satisfied, therefore, that the case on infringement of claim 7 would have been established, had the claim been valid.'

73 ## III. *Warner-Lambert Company LLC v Apotex Pty Limited*[34]

(39) 'Dr Jackson is an experienced pharmacist who gave evidence for Warner-Lambert. He said he was well aware of Lyrica and that he had dispensed it frequently in the past. He said that in his experience medical practitioners (except those working in hospitals) mostly prescribed pregabalin using the brand name Lyrica and that the overwhelming majority of

---

[33] [2015] FCA 634.
[34] [2014] FCAFC 59.

prescriptions for Lyrica are PBS prescriptions indicated for neuropathic pain. Dr Jackson said that he could not recall ever seeing a prescription for Lyrica for seizures.

(40) In his first affidavit Dr Jackson gave evidence that Schedule 4 medicines (which include pregabalin) can be prescribed for a non-ARTG registered indication (ie. 'off-label') so long as the prescription is made by a medical practitioner or any other health professional legally capable of making a prescription. He said that medical practitioners commonly rely on other sources of information and their own clinical experience when prescribing medicines for off-label uses. Dr Jackson also said:

If a medical practitioner writes a prescription, whether PBS or non-PBS, for a particular pharmaceutical substance (whether or not a particular brand is specified), and the pharmacist is aware that there is an alternative brand of the same pharmaceutical substance registered on the TGA and available to the pharmacist, the pharmacist is entitled to supply that alternative brand. In doing so, the pharmacist would be expected to satisfy himself or herself that, as well as having the same active pharmaceutical ingredient, the medicine is the same dosage and that there is no evidence of a lack of bioequivalence to the prescribed brand. The active ingredient and dosage are recorded on the label and ordinarily also in the pharmacist's dispensing software. Pharmacists are regularly visited by representatives of generic suppliers who inform them when bioequivalent products are available, and most pharmacists also have dispensing software that specifically identifies bioequivalent products. It is a requirement under professional guidelines that patient consent is gained when generic substitution occurs.

(41) Dr Jackson went on to state that a pharmacist may legally dispense and supply a generic medicine to a patient holding a private prescription for the originator product. He added that in his experience pharmacists usually do so only after having consulted with the patient by, for example, asking whether the patient would like a cheaper or alternative brand.

(42) In his second affidavit, responding to evidence of Mr McEvoy (discussed below), Dr Jackson reiterated that it was his belief that there was no professional or legal obligation preventing a medical practitioner from prescribing, or a pharmacist dispensing, a medicine that is ARTG listed for an 'off-label' indication if the medicine is registered on the ARTG. He sought to support his opinion by reference to relevant professional standards including the 'Guidelines for dispending of medicines' issued by the Pharmacy Board and the National Competency Standards Framework for Pharmacists in Australia issued by the Pharmaceutical Society of Australia (the Competency Standards). Dr Jackson is the former chair of the committee which developed the Competency Standards. Dr Jackson said:

[i]f a product is bioequivalent with a prescribed brand, and there are no contraindications, substitution is completely acceptable within the Competency Standards without any need to have reference to the TGA approved indications.

...

(66) Mr McEvoy is an experienced pharmacist who gave evidence for Apotex. He is the National Merchandise Manager, for Health, for the Terry White chain of pharmacies. Relevantly, Mr McEvoy gave evidence as to whether a pharmacist would dispense a medicine to a patient for an indication in respect of which the medicine is not registered. He said:

In the context of offering an alternative bioequivalent product to a patient instead of the brand specified on a valid script issued by a prescriber, in my experience, a pharmacist cannot, and would not, dispense a medicine to a patient for an indication when the pharmacist knows that that medicine is not approved for that indication on the ARTG ... In my opinion, it is not sufficient that a medicine is registered on the ARTG for 'something'; a product must be approved for a particular use in order for that product to be dispensed for that use ... If the TGA has registered a medicine on the ARTG as only being approved for a given indication, than I would consider the TGA only to have approved that medicine (which includes an assessment of the medicine's relevant safety and efficacy data) to be used in the treatment of humans for that specific indication. In my opinion, a pharmacist is not entitled to, and would not risk their professional standing and registration by proceeding to, dispense a substituted product that they know is not approved on the ARTG for the treatment of the same condition as the product which the prescriber has issued the script for.

(67) This evidence from Mr McEvoy is expressly directed to a situation in which the script issued by the prescriber specifies a particular brand of drug. Whether or not the ethical issue to which he alluded in this evidence would also arise if the prescriber used the generic name of the drug (eg. pregabalin) is not clear. In any event, the effect of this evidence (which is directly contrary to that given by Dr Jackson) is that a pharmacist would not be entitled to substitute Apotex-Pregabalin for Lyrica for the treatment of pain even with the patient's consent.

...

(74) Warner-Lambert argued that the primary judge erred in principle in his assessment of the strength of their case by rejecting (in the sense of discounting entirely) relevant evidence. In particular, it submitted that there was clear evidence that the seizure indication for which Lyrica is registered could account for a very small percentage of the total market for pregabalin only and that it was likely that Apotex-Pregabalin would be dispensed by retail pharmacists for the treatment of pain much more often than it would be dispensed by them for the treatment of seizures.

(75) As to Pfizer Australia's 2005 application for PBS listing for Lyrica in respect of the seizure indication (see [70](a) of the primary judge's reasons), it was submitted that his Honour's reliance upon this evidence was misplaced. Warner-Lambert submitted that the 2005 application did not contain any market or prescribing data, that the forecasts included in the application were nearly 10 years old, and that they were given on the assumption that Lyrica would be listed on the PBS with a seizure indication and be promoted by Pfizer Australia accordingly. Warner-Lambert also relied on the fact that the Pharmaceutical Benefit Advisory Committee (PBAC) rejected the claim, apparently advanced in support of the application for PBS listing, that pregabalin was significantly more effective than a comparable treatment for seizures which was already listed on the PBS.

(76) As to the primary judge's reliance on the CMI and the API for Lyrica (see [70](c) of his reasons), Warner-Lambert submitted that his Honour was wrong to give any weight to the fact that the CMI and the API describe the seizure indication. Warner-Lambert submitted that these documents say nothing about the extent to which Lyrica is used for that indication.

(77) As to the primary judge's reliance upon Apotex's sales forecasts, and his conclusion (see [70](d) of his reasons) that there was no 'demonstrated reason to doubt the genuineness of Apotex's own assessment that there is a viable non-PBS market for the use of pregabalin in the treatment of seizures', Warner-Lambert submitted that there was no evidence to indicate that Apotex had undertaken such an assessment or at least not one based upon any identified information or experience as to the size of the seizure market. In particular, it was submitted the assessment referred to by the primary judge reflected no more than an unsupported and, in any event, erroneous assumption made by Mr Millichamp as to the size of the seizure market.

(78) Apotex submitted that it was open to the primary judge to conclude that Warner-Lambert had not made good their claim that there was essentially no market in Australia for pregabalin for the seizure indication. In support of this submission particular reliance was placed on Pfizer Australia's 2005 PBS application which Apotex submitted was cogent evidence, on which the primary judge was entitled to rely, that directly contradicted the argument that there was no market for Lyrica for the treatment of seizures. Apotex also placed considerable reliance on Apotex's three year sales forecasts exhibited to Mr Millichamp's affidavit, the genuineness of which was not put in issue by Warner-Lambert at the interlocutory hearing.

(79) In our view the evidence before the primary judge provided strong support for Warner-Lambert's argument that Lyrica is only rarely prescribed for the treatment of seizures and that the seizure market is very small even to the point where it might be said (with sales quite possibly accounting for less than 0.25 % of the market) that there was essentially no market for pregabalin in Australia as an anti-seizure medication.

(80) As is apparent from our summary of the evidence, Mr Dimopoulos' evidence, supported by evidence from Professor Schug and Dr Jackson, provided strong support for Warner-Lambert's argument that there was essentially no market, or at least only a very small market for pregabalin in the treatment of seizures. None of the witnesses called by Apotex directly contradicted Mr Dimopoulos' evidence on this issue. In particular, Mr McEvoy was conspicuously silent on the issue. He did not respond in his affidavit to Dr Jackson's evidence that he (Dr Jackson) had never seen a prescription for Lyrica for use in the treatment of seizures. We do not know, for example, whether Mr McEvoy has ever knowingly dispensed Lyrica for treatment of seizures.

(81) As to Pfizer Australia's 2005 PBS application, we do not consider that it demonstrates the existence of a significant market for the use of Lyrica in the treatment of seizures. In particular, we do not understand it to contradict the clear evidence given by Mr Dimopoulos in 2014 to the effect that Lyrica is only rarely prescribed for the treatment of seizures. Apart from the fact that Pfizer Australia's 2005 application was almost 10 years old, it is important to recognise that the projected market referred to in the document was based upon two implicit assumptions, first, that Lyrica would receive a PBS listing for the seizure indication, and second, that Pfizer Australia would promote the sale of Lyrica to doctors for that particular indication. Another relevant fact is that Pfizer Australia's 2005 PBS application was put forward on the basis that pregabalin (600 mg) was significantly more effective than gabapentin (1800 mg) (the relevant comparator), a claim that the PBAC did not accept.

(82) Nor do we think the Apotex forecasts upon which the primary judge relied should have been given any weight. We say this in circumstances where neither the relevant document (Exhibit Confidential RM-12) nor Mr Millichamp's evidence indicated the basis for the assumption made as to the size of the seizure market. This is not a matter of questioning the genuineness of the Apotex's forecasts, but merely recognising that the evidence does not disclose any basis for this key assumption. If it was based on empirical evidence of some description, one would still need to know whether it was further assumed that there would be a PBS listing for Apotex-Pregabalin for the seizure indication. The primary judge's reasons suggest that the forecast was not predicated on a PBS-listing for the seizure indication but whether or not it was prepared on that basis is not apparent from the evidence.

(83) In our view, Warner-Lambert's submissions on this issue should be accepted. In particular, we consider the primary judge erred in finding that the evidence relied upon by Warner-Lambert was insufficient to demonstrate, on a prima facie basis, that the market for pregabalin for the treatment of seizures was virtually non-existent or (as we would prefer to express it) extremely small. In our view the evidence from Mr Dimopoulos, which found support in the prescribing data upon which he relied, as well as Dr Jackson's and Professor Schug's evidence, was sufficient to establish, to a prima facie level, that the seizure market for pregabalin was indeed extremely small. It is important to note that none of the evidence relied upon by Apotex contradicted Mr Dimopoulos' evidence, supported by the other witnesses to whom we have referred, that Lyrica was rarely prescribed for seizures. We include here not only the evidence from Mr Millichamp but also the evidence of Mr McEvoy who might reasonably be expected to have at least some knowledge as to the extent to which Lyrica is dispensed for the treatment of seizures by pharmacists working in the Terry White group of pharmacies.

...

(88) We have already set out the passages from the primary judge's reasons ([72]-[73]) which explain the significance which his Honour attached to the Apotex promotional materials. At [72] of his reasons, the primary judge noted that prescribers will be informed (by the letter to doctors) that Apotex-Pregabalin is not indicated for the treatment of neuropathic pain and that when prescribing Apotex-Pregabalin for the treatment of seizures, that indication should be shown on the prescription. Specifically, the letter to doctors states under the heading 'Action Required' that '[w]hen prescribing APOTEX-PREGABALIN for the treatment of seizure disorders, please ensure that you include the indication on the prescription.' There

was no evidence at all to indicate what notice, if any, doctors would pay to such a direction from Apotex, a company with which, as we understood the evidence, doctors have little, if any, direct contact. There was evidence before the primary judge to show that many doctors who prescribe drugs (including pregabalin) routinely do so without specifying any indication on the prescription. Moreover, there does not appear to us to be any reason to think that doctors are likely to write prescriptions for Apotex-Pregabalin (as opposed to Lyrica or pregabalin) unless perhaps they are prompted to do so by the letter to doctors itself.

(89) The primary judge also found that pharmacists were to be informed (by the letter to pharmacists) that if a prescription does not specify the indication for which pregabalin has been prescribed, or if it is a PBS prescription, then they should not offer Apotex-Pregabalin to patients. His Honour did not make any explicit finding that pharmacists would comply with Apotex's requests although it is implicit in his Honour's reasoning that he considered a pharmacist who had read and considered the letter would not supply Apotex-Pregabalin unless the relevant prescription indicated that the medication was to be used in the treatment of seizures.

(90) The primary judge dealt expressly with the argument by Warner-Lambert based upon Dr Jackson's evidence that pharmacists would not be deterred from substituting Apotex-Pregabalin based upon their knowledge that it is bioequivalent to Lyrica. As is apparent from [73] of his reasons, the primary judge rejected this argument on the ground that it was 'unsupported by any evidence and is based on mere speculation and assertion'. In our respectful opinion, this was an error by the primary judge. Dr Jackson's evidence included his reasoned expert opinion (apparently admitted into evidence without objection) as to why a pharmacist would not be deterred for legal or ethical reasons from substituting Apotex-Pregabalin for Lyrica. In particular, his evidence included a detailed response to Mr McEvoy's evidence to the contrary effect, in which Dr Jackson referred to the Competency Standards which he considered supported his opinion that if Apotex-Pregabalin is bioequivalent to Lyrica, it would not be unethical for a pharmacist to substitute one for the other with the patient's consent.

(91) The primary judge was confronted with a clear conflict of expert evidence from Dr Jackson and Mr McEvoy on what seems to us to be a critical matter. In our opinion, it was not a conflict that could be resolved on the basis that Dr Jackson's evidence was 'mere speculation and assertion'. Consistent with the reasoning in Shercliff, the conflict was one that could be resolved at a final hearing only.

(92) Apotex relied on the recent decision of the High Court in Apotex Pty Ltd v Sanofi-Aventis Australia Pty Ltd [2013] HCA 50; (2013) 304 ALR 1 in support of a submission that Apotex is entitled to sell Apotex-Pregabalin indicated for a condition outside the 'limited novelty' possessed by the pain patent. We were referred in particular to the reasons of Hayne J at [169]-[172] and Crennan and Kiefel JJ at [293]-[304]. For present purposes it is sufficient for us to refer to the reasons of Crennan and Kiefel JJ (with whom French CJ and Gageler J agreed at [51] and [316] respectively). Their Honours said at [304]:

For the purposes of the application of section 117(2)(b), it was not shown, nor could it be inferred, that Apotex had reason to believe that the unpatented pharmaceutical substance, which it proposes to supply, would be used by recipients in accordance with the patented method, contrary to the indications in Apotex's approved product information document.

(93) The finding recorded in [304] involved a question of fact. In that case, the High Court was not satisfied that Apotex had the requisite 'reason to believe'. The matters relied on by their Honours in support of that conclusion included the fact that the approved production information document for the relevant pharmaceutical product (Apo-Leflunomide) disclosed that it was not indicated for the method of treatment to which the claims of the patent in suit were directed. Whether or not the absence of a pain related indication for Apotex-Pregabalin from the relevant ARTG registrations, the API and the CMI, coupled also with the information and directions given to doctors and pharmacists by means of the Apotex promotional material, should lead to the same result in this case is not something that can be resolved before trial.

### CONCLUSIONS ABOUT PRIMA FACIE CASE

(94) We consider that the primary judge erred in rejecting important aspects of Warner-Lambert's evidence in circumstances where the factual disputes to which the evidence gave rise could not properly be resolved before final hearing. Once that evidence is taken into account as required for the purpose of assessing whether interlocutory relief should be granted, it becomes apparent that his Honour's conclusion that Warner-Lambert had not established a prima facie cannot be accepted. His Honour's alternative assumption that, if he was wrong about no prima facie case being established, then the case was a weak one, is inseparable from his primary conclusion that there was no prima facie case established at all. Accordingly, and as explained below, that assumption undermines his Honour's assessment of the balance of convenience.'

## IV. *AstraZeneca AB v Apotex Pty Ltd*[35] 74

(431) 'We are not satisfied that rosuvastatin is a staple commercial product. The fact that it may be used for both infringing and non-infringing purposes is not conclusive. There are many products capable of being used for both infringing and non-infringing purposes that cannot be characterised as either raw materials or basic products commonly used for a variety of purposes. The uses to which rosuvastatin may be put appear to us to be limited to the prevention or treatment of cardiovascular disease and its associated risk factors (e.g., high cholesterol). This is apparent from the evidence of Dr Wilson, a cardiologist called by AstraZeneca, who said that he does not prescribe rosuvastatin (or any other statin) for any indication other than cardiovascular disease or its associated risk factors. It is true that Dr Hay, a general practitioner called by AstraZeneca, gave evidence that he also prescribes rosuvastatin for the treatment of conditions such as cerebrovascular disease, chronic renal disease and diabetes. However, as we read his evidence, rosuvastatin is prescribed by Dr Hay in order to prevent or treat cardiovascular disease in situations where there is increased risk of it occurring due to the existence of these conditions.

...

(434) The second argument relied upon by the generic parties in relation to section 117(2)(b), which was accepted by the primary judge, raises what is primarily a question of fact. In short, the primary judge was not satisfied, on the evidence, that any of the generic parties had reason to believe that consumers would engage in tablet splitting and use the generic parties' 20 mg or 40 mg products in a manner that would infringe the claims of the 051 or low dose patent.

(435) So far as the economic incentive to engage in tablet splitting is concerned, the evidence showed that AstraZeneca's rosuvastatin product (whether it is in 5 mg, 10 mg or 20 mg dosages) comes in the same size pack and (at least for patients with PBS prescriptions) at the same price. This means that a patient who is directed by a doctor to take 10 mg dosages will have a financial incentive to purchase a pack of 20 mg tablets which he or she may then split into 10 mg dosages.

(436) There was evidence from Mr Sanghvi, a pharmacist from Melbourne called by AstraZeneca, as to the widespread availability of 'tablet splitting' devices used by patients in relation to many different kinds of prescription medicines. There was also evidence from Dr Wilson who said he was aware that some of his patients split their statin tablets. He said that he regularly agrees to requests from patients to prescribe a higher dosage of statin to permit them to engage in tablet splitting in order to save money. Dr Hay also gave evidence to much the same effect, although he was more specific in his evidence as to his prescribing practices in such situations than was Dr Wilson. Dr Hay said that if he wanted to prescribe a 10 mg

35 [2014] FCAFC 99.

dose of rosuvastatin to a patient who wants to split tablets (to save money) he would always write '20 mg, take half a tablet' on the script.

(437) Market research data relied upon by AstraZeneca indicated that only a small percentage (2.75 %) of prescriptions written by medical practitioners directed patients to take half a 20 mg tablet. AstraZeneca submitted that there are likely to be more patients who engage in tablet splitting who do so in circumstances where there is no relevant direction on their prescription. However, this submission is not supported by the evidence. It seems doubtful that doctors would prescribe rosuvastatin in 20 mg tablets to a patient who was to be treated in 10 mg dosages without taking the same precautions taken by Dr Hay. One can see why a doctor would feel the need to guard against the patient taking more than the prescribed dosage by making it clear on the prescription that the patient was to take half a tablet in order to ensure the patient received the correct dosage.

(438) On the primary judge's analysis of the evidence, AstraZeneca established that the generic parties were aware (or, objectively, should have been aware) that there was a risk that consumers would split the generic parties' 20 mg tablets in order to save money. However, her Honour stopped short of holding that they had reason to believe that consumers would engage in such a practice.

(439) It is difficult to draw any precise conclusions as to how widespread the practice of 20 mg tablet splitting might become (at the time of trial the generic parties' products were not yet on sale) without knowing what developments might occur in the market place with respect to the pricing of both the generic parties' 20 mg products and AstraZeneca's 10 mg product. The more AstraZeneca's 10 mg product costs relative to the generic parties' 20 mg products, the more likely it is that consumers would buy and split the generic parties' 20 mg products. However, in our view, contrary to the finding of the primary judge, the evidence established that the generic parties had reason to believe that some consumers would put the generic parties' 20 mg products to an infringing use.

…

(444) It may be undesirable to impose a blanket restraint upon a supplier who has reason to believe that only some consumers, perhaps a very small minority, may put the product that is or may be supplied to them to an infringing use. This is because the effect of such an injunction may be to deny a supplier access to a market, and consumers' access to a product, in circumstances where the supplier could have no reason to believe that the majority of consumers would put the product to an infringing use. It seems to us that, all other things being equal, the more difficult it is for the patentee to establish that there is a likelihood of widespread infringing use, the more difficult it should be for the patentee to obtain injunctive relief in the broad terms restraining any supply of the relevant product. In the present case, even if AstraZeneca established that the generic parties had reason to believe that some consumers would engage in infringing use, the likely scale of that activity, were it to occur, was not shown to be such as would justify the grant of the wide injunction that AstraZeneca sought. Given our conclusion in relation to the validity of claims of the 051 or low dose patent, it is not necessary for us to consider what other injunctive relief, if any, might have been appropriate in lieu of that sought by AstraZeneca.'

# PART IV
# ASIA

## § 17
## China

### A. Executive summary

A medical use invention is protected in China by using a form of 'Swiss-type claim', which is drafted as 'use of compound X in the manufacture of a medicament for treating disease Y'. Such kind of claim is usually interpreted as a process claim, the protection of which not only covers the process itself, but also extends to the products directly obtained by the patented process, i.e., it is prohibited to use the process of manufacturing the medicament, to use, to offer to sell, to sell, or to import the medicament without authorisation from the patentee. It also has seen a precedent case interpreting the claim based on the nature of the medical use invention, i.e., construing the scope as 'prohibiting the use of the drug in the patented new medical use' without authorisation from the patentee. 1

According to the precedent cases, acts which are highly likely to be deemed infringing include, but are not limited to, explicitly indicating in written materials such as drug labels and packaging that the generic drug can be used for the patented indication, and selling, offering to sell, and importing the infringing generic drug. 2

Infringement risks still exist if the generic company clearly indicates that the drug can be used for the patented medical use in other forms, even if a skinny label is already used. Generic companies are advised to avoid any acts connecting the generic drug with the patented use, and even may try to use a disclaimer if necessary. 3

If infringement is established, the infringer will be liable for stopping the infringing acts and damages. The patentee can seek remedies through administrative and judicial routes. Administrative remedies by the patent administrative department include confirmation of infringement, order to cease infringement, and mediation. Judicial remedies by the court include injunctions before and during litigation, order to cease infringing acts, and damages. 4

There are no specific provisions on biosimilar infringement in China. The relevant laws and legal precedents on chemical generic infringement serve as important references. 5

### B. Scope of protection and interpretation of second medical use claims

When a substance or composition is used to treat disease for the first time, it is generally designated as 'first medical use', and as 'second medical use' when a known substance 6 or composition already used for treating one disease is used to treat a different disease. However, there is no distinction in Chinese patent practice between first and second medical uses, both are referred to as medical use, including not only new use of a new substance but also new use of a known substance.

7 Medical use claims should be drafted in the format of a Swiss-style claim, i.e., 'use of compound X in the manufacture of a medicament for treating disease Y', according to the *Guidelines of Patent Examination*.

8 As prescribed by the relevant legislation.

> [i]f the medical use of a substance is claimed as 'for treating disease', 'for diagnosing disease', 'application as a medicament' etc., it falls under 'methods for diagnosis and treatment of diseases' as stipulated in Article 25.1(3) of the Chinese Patent Law, and cannot be granted patent rights; however, since drugs and their preparation methods can be patented, medical use inventions claimed as drug claims or Swiss-style claims such as 'use in the manufacture of medicaments' and 'use in the manufacture of medicaments for treating disease X' can be granted patent rights without violating Article 25.1(3). The Swiss-style claims can be drafted as 'use of compound X in the manufacture of a medicament for treating disease Y' or similar formats.

9 Medical use patents actually protect the medical use of a drug, although they are drafted as claims to the preparation of a drug for that use. Chinese courts usually interpret medical use claims as process claims when determining the scope of protection i.e. in addition to directly using the patented process constitutes infringement, the scope of protection also extends to the products (i.e., drugs) obtained directly from the patented process. Therefore, using, offering for sale, selling and importing the drug with/for the patented use also constitute infringement. In early cases, there were also judgments construing the scope of the claims as prohibiting the use of the drug in the patented medical use, i.e. any act concerning the use of the drug in the new medical use constitutes infringement.

10 An example of the prevailing interpretation is the *AstraZeneca v Huapont* case[1] where the Supreme Court found the claim at issue to be a Swiss-type claim. A Swiss-type claim relates to a medical use invention essentially directed to a new medical use of a substance to be claimed in a process claim format. The product obtained directly from the patented process in this case was the drug anastrozole. Therefore, provisions relating to process claims can be applied, and the courts at the place of seller and where the infringing acts take place have jurisdiction.

11 Although this civil ruling concerns jurisdiction disputes, the Supreme Court expressly construed the Swiss-style medical use claim as a process claim and applied relevant provisions on process claims. Since the drug was obtained directly through the patented process, the scope of protection of the process claim can extend to the product itself. Therefore, infringing acts of the medical use patent also include the use, offering for sale, sale and importing the drug.

12 Another interpretation example is *Yichang Sanxia Pharma v Nanning Yongjiang Pharma* case[2]. The claim at issue reads: 'Use of L-lysine hydrochloride in the manufacture of medicaments for treating traumatic brain injury'. The court of second instance held that the scope of protection of the patent claim prohibits the use of L-lysine hydrochloride for the new use of treating traumatic brain injury and associated syndromes without authorisation. The first alleged infringer's drug label stated that the drug can be used as '*auxiliary treatment for brain diseases*', which falls within the scope of protection of the patentee's patent. The second alleged infringer is the seller of the drug the subject of the dispute in China, having reproduced the content of the patentee's patent specification on

[1] (2019) Supreme People's Court's Civil Final Judgment No. 319; → mn. 64.

[2] (2004) Gui-Civil-San-Final No. 13; → mn. 65.

its website and written promotional materials to indicate the drug is suitable for brain trauma conditions. These acts were deemed to constitute selling and offering for sale infringing products.

It can be seen from this case that the court established infringement based on the nature of the invention. The medical use claim was construed as 'prohibiting (third parties) from using the drug in the patented medical use without authorisation'. Potentially infringing acts include listing the medical use on drug labels as an indication, and promoting the drug as suitable for the patented use through its website, written materials, and the like. 13

## C. Direct and indirect infringement of second medical use claims

### I. Direct infringement

The basis for determining direct infringement of a medical use claim is Article 11 Chinese Patent Law: after the granting of a patent on an invention, unless it is otherwise prescribed by this law, no entity or individual is entitled, without authorisation of the patentee, to exploit the patent, that is, to make, use, offer for sale, sell or import the patented product, or use the patented process, or use, offer for sale, sell or import the product obtained directly through the patented process, for a commercial purpose. 14

It can be seen from this provision that direct infringement of a medical use patent in China includes the acts of using the patented process, and acts concerning the using, offering for sale, selling and importing products obtained directly through the process. Each act can individually constitute an infringing act of the medical use claim. 15

In *Hunan Warrant v Nanjing Sanhome*[3], the claim at issue reads: 'Use of levofloxacin in the manufacture of medicaments for treating anaerobic infections'. The infringer appealed that the lower court erred in ordering it to cease infringement generally, arguing that the court should only order it to cease indicating the patented medical use on the label of the product the subject of the dispute, rather than broadly ordering it to cease infringing all of its activities in relation to the patent. This argument shows that the infringer considered that only indicating the patented use on the drug label represented an infringing act. 16

The Supreme Court took the view that the ways the infringer exploited the patent not only included indicating the medical use on the label, but also included offering to sell the infringing drug through exhibitions, advertisements and so on. Evidence shows the product manufactured, sold and offered for sale by the infringer specified the patented indication. Therefore, the Supreme Court upheld the lower court's order for the infringer to immediately cease infringement of the patent and dismissed the infringer's appeal. 17

From this case it seems that the key to determining infringement is whether the act explicitly indicates that the generic drug is used for the patented medical use. The acts associate the drug with the patented medical use and clearly indicate that the drug is used for that medical use, for example, including content related to the patented medical use on drug labels, packaging, and other materials, promoting the drug for the patented medical 18

[3] (2020) Supreme People's Court's Civil Final Judgment No. 1158.

use in any form, offering for sale based on the above promotion, and thus constitute direct infringement of the medical use claim.

## II. Indirect infringement

19 Chinese law does not treat indirect infringement as a distinct type of infringement and it is only established in the Judicial Interpretations[4]. There are two types of indirect patent infringement: contributory infringement by supplying specialised means, and induced infringement by inducing infringement. Both are regulated under joint infringement provisions in the Chinese Civil Code, bearing joint liability.

20 In judicial practice, indirect patent infringement disputes are also mostly handled by applying joint infringement rules. For example, Articles 116–122 of the Beijing High Court's Guidelines for Patent Infringement Determination (2017) list many scenarios that are all considered joint patent infringement.

21 Article 118 provides that 'knowingly instigating or assisting another person's acts that constitute patent infringement as provided in Article 11 of the Patent Law shall be deemed joint infringers bearing joint liability.'

22 Articles 119–122 further enumerate specific scenarios that constitute contributory infringement and induced infringement. Contributory infringement includes: (i) supplying specialised means to others for production or business purposes without the patentee's authorisation; (ii) facilitating conditions such as venue, storage, transportation and so on to assist infringement. Induced infringement includes: (i) actively inducing others to perform specific technical solutions for production or business purposes by providing drawings, product descriptions, technology solutions, demonstrations; (ii) assigning a technology while knowing it would infringe another's patent rights.

23 According to the above judicial interpretations and practice, determination of indirect patent infringement requires subjective fault of the actor, who knows or should have known of the existence of the patent rights and the nature of his acts, and his assistance or inducement objectively facilitates or promotes the occurrence of direct infringement. At the same time, indirect infringement is premised on the occurrence of direct infringement, so evidence proving the infringing acts have been committed is also crucial. If one has intent to induce or instigate another to infringe a patent, but no direct patent infringement occurs, there is no induced infringement.[5] Therefore, it also needs to be proven that a third party has completed the infringing acts when determining whether a generic company has indirectly infringed a patent.

24 There have been very few indirect infringement cases in China. It is believed issues concerning the application of indirect infringement theories will gain more attention going forward.

---

[4] → mn. 48.

[5] Xu, China Patent Infringement Litigation Practice, IP Publishing House 2017, p. 79.

## D. Infringement of second medical use claims and skinny label products

Drug categorisation and labelling information must be submitted to the NMPA for marketing of a generic drug. The label should list the approved indications and other information. Although there are no express provisions on 'skinny labelling' in Chinese law, generic companies have used it for risk-avoiding purposes. 25

Generics companies may still face risks of infringement even through skinny labelling by carving out the patented indication from the list of approved indications in the label. The Court reached this conclusion in a series of preliminary injunction cases involving the same plaintiff but filed against different generic companies (*Novartis v Hansoh*[6] and *Novartis v Chaitai*[7]). 26

Gilvec is a tyrosine kinase inhibitor developed by Novartis containing the active ingredient imatinib mesylate for first line treatment of Philadelphia chromosome positive chronic myeloid leukemia (CML). The patent on the imatinib compound and CML indication expired in 2013 in China. It was later found to be also suitable for treating Gastrointestinal Stromal Tumor (GIST). The GIST medical use patent in form of a Swiss-type claim, which expired in 2021 in China, reads: 'Use of imatinib and other pharmaceutically acceptable salts thereof in the manufacture of a medicament for treating gastrointestinal stromal tumor (GIST)'. 27

In 2013, after expiration of the imatinib compound patent in China, Hansoh Pharma (hereinafter: Hansoh) obtained approval for a generic version for the indication of CML, and Chaitai Pharma (hereinafter: Chaitai) also obtained approval for a generic version for CML. 28

In the same year, Novartis sued Hansoh for infringement of its GIST medical use patent, on the basis that Hansoh's generic drug label mentions GIST in the pharmacokinetics section. In this case, Novartis applied for a pre-trial injunction against Hansoh's manufacturing, selling, offering for sale of the generic drug, requesting Hansoh to cease use of labels containing GIST-related information in the pharmacokinetics section. Upon review, the court held that since the alleged infringing acts were ongoing and the generic drug was already widely sold in the market, failure to immediately stop such acts would cause irreparable harm to Novartis. Consequently, the court granted a preliminary injunction. It is notable that although GIST was not listed in the Hansoh generic drug's approved indications, the court still ordered the defendant to cease using labels containing GIST-related information in the pharmacokinetics section. 29

In the same year, Novartis sued Chaitai for infringement. Similarly, although GIST was not listed in Chaitai's generic drug's approval indications in its actual label, its pharmacokinetics section still mentioned GIST. Moreover, Chaitai further listed GIST as an approved indication in the electronic drug label on its website, and also mentioned in the pharmacokinetics section that the drug can be used to treat this indication. The drug was also being sold by distributors. In this case, Novartis also applied for a preliminary injunction during the lawsuit, demanding Chaitai to cease using the label containing GIST-related information in the 'Indications' and 'Pharmacokinetics' sections in its manufacturing, selling, offering for sale of the generic drug. Upon review, the court ruled to grant a preliminary injunction. Likewise, Chaitai was ordered to stop using labels 30

[6] (2014) Beijing Intermediate Civil No. 7639; → mn. 66.

[7] (2013) Beijing Intermediate Civil No. 16629.

containing GIST information in the 'Indications' and 'Pharmacokinetics' sections in its manufacturing, selling, offering for sale of the generic drug.

31 Moreover, off-label use may still occur in the event even if the patented indication is completely removed from the label. There are two reasons for off-label use. One is professional medical users, usually doctors, may deduce that the generic drug can treat indications beyond the label, based on the known information on the original drug. The other is induced by the generic company, e.g. through channels like the internet, seminars and so on, the generic company may promote or imply the generic drug's unapproved uses, leading to off-label use.

32 Off-label use harms the patentee's interests, especially when induced by the generic company's active promotion. Although the skinny label is used by the generic company, the acts may still be deemed to be infringing according to the precedent cases when it actively and directly informs users that the generic drug can be used for the patented medical use through other means.

## E. Infringement of second medical use claims and biosimilar products

33 'Biosimilar' refers to a therapeutic biological product which is similar to an approved original biological drug (reference drug) in terms of quality, safety and efficacy. Biosimilars are not generics and have 'similarity' but not identicalness to the reference drug, which is different from chemical generics.

34 The indications of a biosimilar cannot be directly determined from those of the reference medicine. According to the 'Technical Guidelines for the Evaluation of Similarity and Extrapolation of Indications for Biosimilar Drugs' issued by the Center for Drug Evaluation of the National Medical Products Administration (hereinafter NMPA) in 2021, for a biosimilar drug, based on the overall similarity with the reference drug, if a direct comparative clinical trial can demonstrate similarity of the candidate drug to the reference drug in terms of at least one indication, it may be supported for direct use of the candidate drug in other approved indications of the reference drug in China, through scientific demonstration of research data and information related to the extrapolated indications. If indication extrapolation cannot be directly obtained, considerations need to be made on a case-by-case basis based on characteristics of the drug's mechanism of action, similarities and differences in pathogenesis and pathophysiology between studied and extrapolated indications, and adequacy of the similarity studies.

35 Since the development of biosimilars is more recent, there have been no cases concerning biosimilar infringements. There are no specific provisions on biosimilar infringement in China, but existing patent infringement laws and cases concerning chemical generics may serve as important references.

## F. Strategies and considerations

36 It can be seen from the cases discussed above that once a medical use patent infringement case enters trial, the courts tend to determine infringement based on the nature of

the medical use invention, that is, any act that uses the drug in the scope of the patented use is prohibited. Therefore, the generic company needs to be careful not to associate the generic drug with the patented medical use in any explicit or implied, verbal or written manner in manufacturing, using, selling, offering for sale, e.g., not only by avoiding indicating the patented use in the generic drug labelling, but also by omitting any content related to the patented medical use from packaging, insert labels and other related materials. It is also not advisable to promote the drug based on the patented use, in order to minimise infringement risks.

As to off-label use occurring in practice, the generic manufacturer can make a disclaimer that the approved indications do not include the patented use. For authorising third party marketing and distribution, the generic company should specify before authorisation that any promotion indicating that the generic drug can be used for the patented use is prohibited. 37

## G. Legal remedies

Pursuant to Article 65 Chinese Patent Law[8], the patentee could enforce its patent via the administrative or judicial route, also called as administrative remedies and judicial remedies. 38

### I. Administrative remedies

Administrative remedies for patent infringement by the patent administrative department in China include confirmation of infringement, order to cease infringement, and mediation. 39

The patent administration department can mediate disputes between the parties, and also has the right to determine whether infringement exists. It can order the infringer to immediately cease the infringing acts and take certain measures to stop the acts, such as ordering the infringer to immediately cease use, destroy dedicated equipment, molds used in implementation of the patented process, destroy the infringing products, destroy or seal relevant promotional materials, and may apply to the court for compulsory execution. Upon request of the parties, the patent administrative department may also organise mediation between the parties on the amount of damages, but the mediation has no compulsory execution power. To obtain compulsory execution power, the parties need to apply to the court for judicial confirmation. Additionally, if a patent infringement dispute has already been brought before a court, the patent administrative department will not accept the request for handling the dispute. 40

### II. Judicial remedies

Judicial remedies for patent infringement by the court in China include injunctions before and during litigation, order to cease infringing acts, and damages. 41

[8] → mn. 51.

42 Patent infringement litigation typically can go through multiple rounds from filing to final judgment, taking anywhere from six months to several years. In cases of serious infringement that could cause irreparable harm to the patentee, the patentee can apply to the court for a preliminary injunction prohibiting certain acts before instituting the lawsuit or before the judgment/ruling takes effect, to stop the infringement promptly and mitigate losses. Urgency is one of the factors considered in granting a preliminary injunction. Examples are the pre-trial injunction in *Novartis v Hansoh* and injunction during litigation in *Novartis v Chaitai* in the section of skinny label.

43 The patentee can request the court to order the infringer to cease infringing acts and claim damages. The most recent 2020 Patent Law amendments[9] increased the statutory damages range (from 'not less than RMB 10,000 but not more than RMB 1 million' to 'not less than RMB 30,000 but not more than RMB 5 million') and the punitive damages multiples (from '1 to 3 times' to '1 to 5 times'), and added an infringer burden of proof clause in cases where the right holder has made reasonable efforts in providing evidence. In addition to damages, the patentee can also claim reasonable expenses paid to stop the infringing acts by the infringer. Moreover, for direct infringement, infringement determination does not consider the infringer's subjective fault, but the patentee bears the burden of proof concerning the infringer's 'intent to infringe' when claiming punitive damages for intellectual property rights.

## H. Statutory provisions

### I. Provisions about medical use patent

44

#### Article 2(2) Patent Law

'Invention' means any new technical solution relating to a product, a process or the improvement thereof.

45

#### Section 4.5.2 of Chapter 10, Part II of the Guidelines of Patent Examination

4.5.2 Claim of Medical Use of Substance

If the medical use of a substance is claimed as 'for treating disease', 'for diagnosing disease', 'application as a medicament' etc., it falls under 'methods for diagnosis and treatment of diseases' as stipulated in Article 25.1(3) of the Chinese Patent Law, and cannot be granted patent rights; however, since drugs and their preparation methods can be patented, medical use inventions claimed as drug claims or Swiss-style claims such as 'use in the manufacture of medicaments' and 'use in the manufacture of medicaments for treating disease X' can be granted patent rights without violating Article 25.1(3).

The Swiss-style claims can be drafted as 'use of compound X in the manufacture of a medicament for treating disease Y' or similar formats.

---

[9] → mn. 57.

## II. Provisions about direct infringement

### Article 11(1) Patent Law 46

After the grant of the patent for an invention or an utility model, except where otherwise provided for in this Law, no entity or individual may, without the authorisation of the patentee, exploit the patentee's patent, that is, for production or business purposes, manufacture, use, offer to sell, sell or import the patented product, or use the patented process, and use, offer to sell, sell or import the product directly obtained by the patented process.

## III. Provisions about indirect infringement

### Article 1169(1) Civil Code 47

A person who aids or abets an actor in the commission of a tortious act shall assume joint and several liability with the actor.

### Article 21 of Interpretations (II) of the Supreme People's Court on Several Issues Concerning the Application of Law in the Trial of Cases Involving Patent Infringement Disputes 48

Where a party has clear knowledge that certain products are the materials, equipment, parts and components, intermediate items, etc. specifically for the exploitation of a patent, and yet still provides, without the licensing from the relevant patentee and for the purpose of production and business operation, such products to another party committing the patent infringement, the competent people's court shall uphold the claim by the right holder that the party's provision of such products is an act of assistance for infringement as prescribed by Article 1169 of the Civil Code.

Where a party has clear knowledge that certain products or methods have been granted patent, and yet still actively induces, without the licensing from the relevant patentee and for the purpose of production and business operation, another party committing the patent infringement, the competent people's court shall uphold the claim by the right holder that the inducing act of the party is an act of abetting another party to commit infringement as prescribed by Article 1169 of the Civil Code.

## IV. Provisions about legal remedies for infringement

### Article 1167 Civil Code 49

Where a tortious act endangers another person's personal or property safety, the infringed person has the right to request the tortfeasor to bear tort liability such as cessation of the infringement, removal of the nuisance, or elimination of the danger.

### Article 1185 Civil Code 50

In case of an intentional infringement of another person's intellectual property rights, where the circumstances are serious, the infringed person has the right to request for corresponding punitive damages.

### Article 65 Patent Law 51

Where a dispute arises as a result of the exploitation of a patent without the authorisation of the patentee, that is, the infringement of the patentee's patent right, it shall be resolved through consultation between the parties. Where the parties are unwilling to consult with each other or where the consultation fails, the patentee or any interested party may file a lawsuit in the people's court, or request the departments in charge of patent-related work to deal with the dispute. When the department in charge of patent-related work dealing with the dispute considers that the infringement is established, it may order the infringer to stop the infringing act immediately. If the infringer refuses to accept the order, he may, within 15 days from the date of receipt of the notification of the order, file a lawsuit in the people's court in accordance with the Administrative Procedure Law of the People's Republic of China. If the infringer neither files a lawsuit nor stops the infringing act at the expiration of the period of time, the department in charge of patent-related work may file an application with the people's court for compulsory execution. At the request of the party concerned, the department in charge of patent-related work dealing with the dispute may carry out mediation concerning the amount of compensation for the patent right infringement. If the mediation fails, the parties may file a lawsuit in the people's court in accordance with the Civil Procedure Law of the People's Republic of China.

52

### Article 66(1) Patent Law

Where a patent infringement dispute involves a patent for an invention for a manufacturing process of a new product, the entity or individual manufacturing the identical product shall provide evidence to prove that the manufacturing process used in the manufacture of its or his product is different from the patented process.

53

### Article 67 Patent Law

In a patent infringement dispute, if the alleged infringer has evidence to prove that the technology or design exploited by it or him forms part of the prior art or prior design, such exploitation shall not constitute an infringement of the patent right.

54

### Article 68 Patent Law

Where any person counterfeits a patent of another person, he shall, in addition to bearing his civil liabilities in accordance with law, be ordered by the department in charge of patent enforcement to make rectifications, and the department shall make the matter known to the public. His illegal earnings shall be confiscated and, in addition, he may be imposed on a fine of not more than five times his illegal earnings. If there are no illegal earnings or the illegal earnings are less than RMB 50,000 Yuan, a fine of not more than RMB 250,000 Yuan may be imposed on him. Where the infringement constitutes a crime, he shall be investigated for his criminal responsibility in accordance with law.

55

### Article 69 Patent Law

When investigating and handling the suspected act of counterfeiting a patent, the department in charge of patent enforcement shall have the right to take the following measures based on the evidence obtained:

(1) to inquire the parties concerned, and investigate the circumstances related to the suspected illegal act;
(2) to carry out an on-the-spot inspection of the site where the party's suspected illegal act is committed;
(3) to consult and duplicate the contracts, invoices, account books and other relevant materials related to the suspected illegal act;
(4) to examine the products related to the suspected illegal act;
(5) to seal up or detain the products proved to be produced by the counterfeited patent.

When dealing with the patent infringement disputes at the request of the patentee or the interested party, the department in charge of patent-related work may take measures listed in Subparagraph (1), (2) and (4) of the preceding paragraph.

When the department in charge of patent enforcement or the department in charge of patent-related work exercises its functions and powers as stipulated in the preceding two paragraphs in accordance with law, the parties concerned shall provide assistance and cooperation and shall not refuse to do so or create obstacles.

**Article 70 Patent Law** 56

The patent administration department under the State Council may, at the request of the patentee or any interested party, deal with patent infringement disputes that have a major impact throughout the country.

When dealing with patent infringement disputes at the request of the patentee or any interested party, the department in charge of patent-related work of the local people's government may deal with the cases of infringement of the same patent right within its administrative area in a combined manner; for cases infringing the same patent right across administrative areas, it may request the department in charge of patent-related work of the local people's government at a higher level to deal with the matter.

**Article 71 Patent Law** 57

The amount of compensation for patent right infringement shall be determined on the basis of the actual losses suffered by the right holder as a result of the infringement or the profits earned by the infringer as a result of the infringement. Where it is difficult to determine the losses suffered by the right holder or the profits earned by the infringer, the amount shall be reasonably determined by reference to the multiple of the amount of the royalties for the patent license. For intentional infringement of a patent right, if the circumstances are serious, the amount of compensation may be determined at not less than one time and not more than five times the amount determined in accordance with the above-mentioned method.

Where it is difficult to determine the losses suffered by the right holder, the profits earned by the infringer and the royalties for the patent license, the people's court may determine the amount of compensation, which is not less than RMB 30,000 Yuan and not more than RMB 5,000,000 Yuan, in light of such factors as the type of the patent right, the nature and the circumstances of the infringing act.

The amount of compensation shall also include the reasonable expenses of the right holder paid for putting an end to the infringement.

In order to determine the amount of compensation, under the circumstance that the right holder has tried its or his best to provide evidence, and the account books or materials related to the patent infringement are mainly at the hands of the infringer, the people's court may order the infringer to provide such account books or materials. Where the infringer refuses to provide the account books or materials, or provides false account books or materials, the people's court may determine the amount of compensation by reference to the right holder's claims and the evidence provided.

**Article 72 Patent Law** 58

Where the patentee or any interested party has evidence to prove that another person is infringing or is about to infringe its or his patent right or hinders the realisation of the right, which, unless being stopped in time, may cause irreparable damage to his lawful rights and interests, it or he may, before filing a lawsuit, apply to the people's court for adopting measures for property preservation, ordering to do certain acts or to prohibit certain acts in accordance with the law.

**Article 73 Patent Law** 59

In order to stop patent infringement, in cases where the evidence might be destroyed or where it would be difficult to obtain in the future, the patentee or the interested party may, before filing a lawsuit, apply to the people's court for evidence preservation in accordance with the law.

60 **Article 74 Patent Law**

The period of limitation for action against the infringement of a patent right is three years, beginning from the date on which the patentee or interested party knows or should have known of the infringing act and the infringer.

Where an appropriate royalty is not paid for exploiting an invention during the period from the publication of the application to the grant of the patent right, the limitation period for taking legal action by the patentee for requesting the payment of royalties is three years, beginning from the date on which the patentee knows or should have known of the exploitation of his or its invention by another person. However, where the patentee knows or should have known of the exploitation of the invention before the patent right is granted, the period of limitation for action shall begin from the date when the patent right is granted.

61 **Article 75 Patent Law**

None of the following shall be deemed as infringement of the patent right:

(1) where, after the sale of a patented product or a product acquired directly in accordance with a patented process by the patentee or any entity or individual authorised by the patentee, any other person uses, offers to sell, sells, or imports that product;
(2) where, before the filing date of the patent application, any person who has already manufactured the identical product, used the identical process, or made necessary preparations for its manufacturing or using, continues to manufacture or use it only within the original scope;
(3) where any foreign means of transport, which temporarily passes through the territory, territorial waters or territorial airspace of China, uses the relevant patent in its devices or installations for its own needs in accordance with the agreements concluded between the country to which the foreign means of transport belongs and China, or in accordance with the international treaties to which both countries are parties, or on the basis of the principle of reciprocity;
(4) where the relevant patent is used specially for the purposes of scientific research and experimentation; or
(5) where for the purposes of providing information needed for the administrative examination and approval, any person manufactures, uses, or imports patented drugs or patented medical apparatus and instruments, or any other person manufactures or imports patented drugs or patented medical apparatus and instruments especially for that person.

62 **Article 76 Patent Law**

In the review and approval process before the marketing of a pharmaceutical product, where the applicant for marketing approval of the pharmaceutical product has any disputes over the relevant patent right associated with the pharmaceutical product applied for registration with the relevant patentee or interested party, the party concerned may file a lawsuit before the People's Court and request a judgment on whether the technical solution related to the pharmaceutical product that is applied for registration falls within the protection scope of any pharmaceutical product patent right owned by others. The medical product regulatory department under the State Council may, within a prescribed time limit, make a decision on whether to suspend the marketing approval of the pharmaceutical product according to the effective judgment or written order of the People's Court.

The applicant for marketing approval of the pharmaceutical product, the relevant patentee or the interested party may also petition the patent administration department under the State Council for an administrative adjudication on the disputes over the patent right associated with the drug applied for registration.

The medical products regulatory department under the State Council shall, in conjunction with the patent administration department under the State Council, formulate specific cohesive measures for patent right dispute resolutions at the stages of pharmaceutical product marketing license approval and pharmaceutical product marketing license application, which shall be implemented after the approval of the State Council.

**Article 77 Patent Law** 63

Any person who, for production and business purposes, uses, offers to sell or sells a patent-infringing product, without knowing that it is manufactured and sold without the authorisation of the patentee, may not be liable for compensation provided that he can prove the legitimate source of the product.

# J. Extracts from court decisions

## I. *AstraZeneca v Huapont*[10] 64

**Cause of action:** Appeal of jurisdiction objection over infringement of invention patent right

**Appellant** (the defendant in the first instance): Chongqing Huapont Pharmaceutical Co., Ltd.

**Appellee** (the plaintiff in the first instance): AstraZeneca (Sweden) Co., Ltd.

**Defendant in the first instance:** Suzhou Renhe Pharmacy Jiade Medical Technology Co., Ltd.

'The appellant Chongqing Huapont Pharmaceutical Co., Ltd. (hereinafter: Huapont) dissatisfied with the ruling of (2019)-Su-05-IP-First Trial No. 334 issued by the Intermediate People's Court of Suzhou Municipality on July 29, 2019, in the infringement dispute of patent right with Appellee AstraZeneca (Sweden) Co., Ltd. (hereinafter: AstraZeneca), Defendant in the first instance Suzhou Renhe Pharmacy Jiade Medical Technology Co., Ltd. (hereinafter: Jiade).

**Appellant request:**

To revoke the ruling issued by the first instance and transfer the case to the First Intermediate People's Court of Chongqing Municipality of the People's Republic of China.

Facts and reasons are as follows: the original ruling misunderstood the protection scope of the use patent in a process patent. The patent at issue belongs to the use patent in a process patent, and the act of exploiting the patent can only be the act of using the patented process, rather than the act of selling and offering for sale. The patent at issue is different from the traditional manufacturing and processing method, and the use of the patented process itself cannot produce the product in the sense of patent law. The subject constituting infringement only can be Huapont, who acts the preparation of the drug. Jiade is a drug seller, and it is impossible to use the patented process, and its location is not the place where the infringing act occured. Jiade is not the eligible defendant in this case, and its domicile cannot be used as the connecting point of the case. Since the domicile of Huapont is located in Chongqing Municipality, the domicile of the defendant and the place where the infringement occurred is located in Chongqing. The First Intermediate People's Court of Chongqing Municipality of the People's Republic of China has jurisdiction over the case according to the laws.

[10] Supreme People's Court's Civil Final Judgment No. 319, 30 October 2019.

**AstraZeneca argues:**

Jiade is an eligible defendant in this case and that the ground of the jurisdictional objection by Huapont cannot be sustained. It belongs to the scope of substantive trial for Huapont's claims that the infringement act of the patent at issue can only be using, but cannot be selling and offering for sales, rather than the scope of trial of jurisdiction objection.

Jiade did not make any statement.

The Court found that the patent at issue is titled with 'use of anastrozole in the manufacture of a medicament for postmenopausal women with early breast cancer', and the claim at issue is as follows: '1. Use of anastrozole or its pharmaceutically acceptable salt in the manufacture of a medicament for reducing the rate of cancer recurrence in postmenopausal women with early breast cancer,...'.

After examination, the court opines that this case is an appeal case on the jurisdiction dispute in the infringement of invention patent right.

The patent at issue is a method (or process) patent. According to Article 5 of the Provisions of the Supreme People's Court on the Application of Law to the Trial of Patent Dispute Cases, a lawsuit brought for infringement of patent right shall be under the jurisdiction of the people's court at the place where the infringement occurs or the place where the defendant has his domicile. The place of infringement includes the place of implementation of the use of a patented method, and the place of implementation of the use, offer for sale, sale or import of the product directly obtained in accordance with the patented method.

In this case, the claim at issue belongs to the use claim in a form of process for manufacturing a drug, which is a special kind of claims used in the patent application in the field of chemistry. In order to protect the inventor's innovative contribution over the existing technology and realise the purpose of protection innovation and encourage invention, the patent administrative department under the State Council allows the invention which essence is new use invention to be drafted as a kind of process for manufacturing a drug for obtaining patent right, such as 'use of compound X in the manufactured of a medicament for treating Y disease' or similar forms, and its essence is a kind of the special provisions for medical use of substance. Accordingly, the product directly obtained by the patented process at issue is anastrozole in this case, Jiade, as a seller of the accused infringing anastrozole tablet, both of its domicile and the place where an infringing act is committed are in Suzhou, Jiangsu province. According to the Reply of the Supreme People's Court on Approving the Intermediate People's Court in Nanjing, Suzhou, Wuhan and Chengdu to Set up Special Judicial Bodies and to Administer Some Intellectual Property Cases Across Regions, the first instance intellectual property civil case occurred in the jurisdiction of Suzhou shall be under the jurisdiction of the Intermediate people's court of Suzhou, Jiangsu Province of China. Therefore, the original trial court has jurisdiction over this case.

To sum up, the reasons for Huapont's appeal cannot be established, and this court rejects it. The original ruling is not improper and should be upheld.'

## 65 II. *Yichang Sanxia Pharma v Nanning Yongjiang Pharma*[11]

**Cause of action:** Patent infringement dispute

**Appellant (the defendant in the first instance):** Yichang Sanxia Pharmaceutical Co., Ltd.

**Appellee (the plaintiff in the first instance):** Guangxi Nanning Yongjiang Pharmaceutical Co., Ltd.

**Defendant in the first instance:** Wuhan Tongyuan Pharmaceutical Co., Ltd.

**Defendant in the first instance:** Nanning Shenzhou Pharmaceutical Co., Ltd.

---

[11] The High People's Court of Guangxi Zhuang Autonomous Region, (2004) Gui-Civil-San-Final No. 13, September 2004.

**Medical use claim at issue:** 'Use of L-lysine hydrochloride in the manufacture of medicament for treating traumatic brain injury'

……

**The court of the second instance found that:**

'On March 16, 1993, the appellee, Guangxi Nanning Yongjiang Pharmaceutical Co., Ltd. (hereinafter: Nanning Yongjiang Pharma), applied an invention titled with 'Use of L-lysine hydrochloride in the manufacture of medicament for treating traumatic brain injury' before the SIPO (now the CNIPA), which was granted on July 5, 1996. The patent number is ZL93102915.5, and it is currently valid (…).

The claim of the patent at issue reads: 'use of L-lysine hydrochloride in the manufacture of medicament for treating traumatic brain injury'…

The appellant, Yichang Sanxia Pharmaceutical Co., Ltd. (hereinafter: Yichang Sanxia Pharma), began to produce the drug named as 'shulang Lysine Chloride Injection' (hereinafter: SHULANG) in June 2003. The main ingredient of the drug is lysine hydrochloride. The external packaging box of the drug, the label of the drug and the glass bottle of the injection bottle column indicated as follows: 'this product can improve the permeability of the blood and brain barrier, help the drug into the brain cells, can be used as an auxiliary treatment of encephalopathy(…).'

The original defendant, Wuhan Tongyuan Pharmaceutical Co., Ltd. (hereinafter: Tongyuan Pharma), is the general distributor of SHULANG manufactured by Yichang Sanxia Pharma in China. For selling the drug, Tongyuan Pharma published some materials of SHULANG manufactured by Yichang Sanxia Pharma on its Internet webpage, to propaganda SHULANG can be used to treat brain injury. Tongyuan Pharma also produced a written promotional material of SHULANG, the content of which specifies the 'indications' in the section of SHULANG prescription data as follows: 'this product is used for the treatment of brain injury, chronic brain tissue ischemia, hypoxic diseases brain protection (…).'

After comparison, the above promotional materials basically copied the contents of the patent specification of the appellee.

……

**The key issues to be addressed in the second instance is as follows:**

Does the drug SHULANG produced by Yichang Sanxia Pharma fall within the scope of the claim at issue 'use of L-lysine hydrochloride in the manufacture of medicament for treating traumatic brain injury' of Nanning Yongjiang Pharma? Does it constitute an infringement?

**The court of second instance opines that:**

According to paragraph 1 of Article 56 of the Patent Law of the People's Republic of China, 'the scope of protection of the patent right for an invention or utility model shall be subject to the contents of the claim, and the specification and attached drawings may be used to interpret the claim.' The patent of the appellee, which is 'use of L-lysine hydrochloride in the manufacture of medicament for treating traumatic brain injury'.

According to the claim, the scope of protection of the patent at issue is: the new use of L-lysine hydrochloride in the treatment of traumatic brain injury…

Yichang Sanxia Pharma manufactured the drug SHULANG… Among the materials, the expression of 'as an auxiliary treatment of encephalopathy' in materials falls within the scope of protection of the L-lysine hydrochloride invention patent of Nanning Yongjiang Pharma. The reasons are as follows:

(1) …

(2) From the claim of patent at issue, 'use of L-lysine hydrochloride in the manufacture of medicament for treating traumatic brain injury', the scope of protection of patent at issue is to prohibit any other entity or individuals to use L-lysine hydrochloride in the treatment of traumatic brain injury and syndrome.

……

Tongyuan Pharma, as the general distributor of SHULANG manufactured by Yichang Sanxia Pharma in China, in order to sell the drug, indicated clearly SHULANG could be used in brain trauma symptoms on its website and in the written promotional materials.

Considering that Yichang Sanxia Pharma and Tongyuan Pharma have a clear responsibility in the production and sales of SHULANG, It can be concluded that, Yichang Sanxia Pharma should has clear knowledge about that, Yichang Sanxia Pharma and Tongyuan Pharma have the common purpose of using L-lysine hydrochloride for the treatment of brain injury...

To sum up, SHULANG manufactured by Yichang Sanxia Pharma falls within the scope of the invention patent of 'use of L-lysine hydrochloride in the manufacture of medicament for treating traumatic brain injury', which constitutes infringement...

**The judgment is as follows:**

....

(2) ... the appellant Yichang Sanxia Pharma is prohibited from using SHULANG, produced by the appellant Yichang Sanxia Pharma, for the treatment of cranial trauma. The packaging box, instructions for use, and bottle label of SHULANG, produced by the appellant Yichang Sanxia Pharma, shall not contain the *statements 'this product can increase blood-brain barrier permeability, facilitate the entry of drugs into brain cells, and can be used as an adjuvant therapy for brain diseases.'*

(3) The appellant, Yichang Sanxia Pharma, the defendant in the first instance Tongyuan Pharma, and the defendant in the first instance Shenzhou, are immediately ordered to cease the sales of SHULANG manufactured by Yichang Sanxia Pharma.'

66

## III. *Novartis v Hansoh*[12]

**Cause of action:** Patent infringement dispute

**Applicant:** Shanghai Novartis Trading Co., Ltd.

**Respondent:** Jiangsu Hansoh Pharmaceutical Co., Ltd.

**Respondent:** Beijing JingweiYuanhua Pharmaceutical Technology Co., Ltd.

**Medical use claim at issue:** 'use of imatinib and other pharmaceutically acceptable salts thereof in the manufacture of a medicament for treating gastrointestinal stromal tumor (GIST)'

### Facts:

'The applicant, Shanghai Novartis Trading Co., Ltd. (hereinafter: Novartis Shanghai), said that Novartis Co., Ltd. is one of the co-owners of the invention patent No. ZL01817895.2 titled with 'treatment of gastrointestinal stromal tumors'. According to the Patent Implementation Agreement between Novartis Co., Ltd. and other patent co-owners, and the Patent License Agreement between Novartis Co., Ltd. and Novartis Shanghai, Novartis Shanghai could separately enforce the patent rights in China without the participation of any co-owner of the patent right.

Novartis Shanghai found that the generic drug 'XINWEI imatinib mesylate' (hereinafter: XINWEI) was manufactured, offered to sell and sold by Jiangsu Hansoh Pharmaceutical Co., Ltd. (hereinafter: Hansoh), and some information on its packaging box and in the drug instructions indicated that the drug could be used for the treatment of patients with gastrointestinal stromal tumors (GIST)[13]. Accordingly, Novartis Shanghai believes that the above Hansoh's behaviour constituted an infringement of its patent rights at issue. At the same time, since the current drug procurement and bidding system in China only involves the common name of active ingredients, and does not distinguish between indications and manufacturers, so once the generic drug XINWEI containing infringement information enters the drug list

[12] Beijing Intermediate Civil No. 7639, 7 October 2014.

[13] The GIST was not listed in the Hansoh generic drug's approved indications.

stipulated by the medical insurance, it will bring irreparable losses to the legitimate interests of Novartis. In addition, the respondent Beijing JingweiYuanhua Pharmaceutical Technology Co., Ltd. (hereinafter: JWYH) sold, offered to sell the drug, and also constituted the infringement of the patent at issue. Once the patients take the drug generally for a long time, JWYH's behaviour may cause irreparable damage to Novartis Shanghai's rights and interests.

In conclusion, Novartis Shanghai requested the court to order Hansoh and JWYH to stop using such statements in the 'pharmacokinetics' part as 'give the same dose (400 mg / day), GIST patients its steady state drug exposure is 1.5 times that of CML patients. Based on the preliminary population pharmacokinetic study of GIST patients, there were three statistically significant changes of imatinib pharmacokinetics (albumin, WBC, and bilirubin). Low albumin levels decrease clearance, as with higher WBC levels. However, these effects are not sufficient to determine that the dose needs to be adjusted', when Hansoh manufactures, sells, offers to sell XINWEI and when JWYH manufactures, sells, offers to sell XINWEI. For the above application, Novartis Shanghai has provided the corresponding guarantee to the court.

The court opines that the request of Novartis Shanghai is in accordance with the legal provisions and uphold it. The ruling is as follows:

When Hansoh manufactures, sells, offers to sell XINWEI and when JWYH sells, offers to sell XINWEI, both of them are prohibited to use such statements in the 'pharmacokinetics' part as 'give the same dose (400 mg / day), GIST patients the steady-state drug exposure is 1.5 times that of CML patients. Based on the preliminary population pharmacokinetic study of GIST patients, there were three statistically significant changes of imatinib pharmacokinetics (albumin, WBC, and bilirubin). Low albumin levels decrease clearance, as with higher WBC levels. However, these effects are not sufficient to determine that the dose needs to be adjusted."

# § 18
# Japan

## A. Executive summary

1 In Japan, there is no specific standard for claim interpretation for second medical use, and therefore the standard for claim interpretation for general 'use inventions' is applied. To determine whether medical use is novel, consideration is given to the mechanism of action and the efficacy of known pharmaceuticals.

2 Direct infringement and indirect infringement are applicable to second medical use claims. Indirect infringement includes 'dedicated product type indirect infringement' and 'non-dedicated product type indirect infringement.' The latter occurs more commonly.

3 Infringement of second medical use claims may occur in the case of skinny label products. The 'label theory' is applied to determine whether a medical use claim has been infringed. In other words, infringement is determined on the basis of the descriptions in the package insert, and interview forms. Therefore, the duplication of descriptions on a package insert and interview form, when comparing between originals and generics, is an aspect that needs to be monitored. Even in the absence of duplication, off-label use will result in infringement.

4 Biosimilar products are handled in the same manner as generic pharmaceuticals. However, skinny labels for biosimilar products need to be handled more carefully, as the preadjustment required for patent linkage may not be performed on biosimilars.

5 To reduce the liability risk of skinny-label products, it is necessary to carefully check the expiry of the patent term of the original pharmaceutical for each indication. It is also important to prevent off-label use.

6 In the event of an infringement, patentees can obtain an injunction, claim compensation for damages, claim for unjust enrichment, etc. In order to facilitate claims for damages, the Japanese Patent Act has provisions for calculating the amount of damages, and presumes that there was negligence in the act of infringement.

## B. Scope of protection and interpretation of second medical use claims

### I. Introduction: skinny labelling of generic and biosimilar products in Japan

7 In Japan, as in other countries, there are constant battles between original pharmaceutical manufacturers and generic pharmaceutical manufacturers. Generic pharmaceutical manufacturers make thorough preparations so that they can introduce their generic pharmaceuticals or biosimilars onto the market as soon as the original pharmaceutical manufacturers' substance patent expires. Original pharmaceutical manufacturers try to prevent generic pharmaceutical manufacturers from entering the market by acquiring

patents on manufacturing methods, formulations, and uses (including second medical uses) while staggering the filing dates. On the other hand, generic pharmaceutical manufacturers use skinny labelling (known in Japan as 'basic efficacy application' or 'worm-eaten application,' introduced in 2009) to avoid potentially infringing patents and obtain approval for only selected indications of the original pharmaceutical.

During this time, patent infringement lawsuits may arise, and in many cases, this is due **8**
to different interpretations of the expiry term of the patent, and the scope of rights for the original pharmaceutical products and the generic pharmaceutical products.

In Japan, the conditions for generic pharmaceutical manufacturers to manufacture **9**
and market generic pharmaceuticals and biosimilars are that:

(i) the term of the original pharmaceutical manufacturer's patent has expired,
(ii) the reexamination period for pharmaceutical efficacy (equivalent to the data protection period) has passed, and
(iii) there is no patent linkage problem.

Regarding (i), since extension of the term is granted separately for each efficacy in **10**
the same patent, there is a complication that even for the same patent, the expiry term of the patent differs for each indication. In addition, due to revisions to the Examination Guidelines, dosage regime patents are now possible, and even if the efficacy is the same, if the dosage or regime is different, a different patent can be granted. Therefore, careful study is needed in order to determine when and for which indications skinny label applications are possible.

The following is a brief explanation of the term of a patent: If there is a period during **11**
which the patented invention cannot be used due to regulatory approval (marketing authorisation), patent terms will be extended for up to five years ('registration of extension'). In Japan, even for a singular patent, multiple extensions can be granted for each individual pharmaceutical approval. In other words, a singular patent may have a plurality of patent rights with different terms. Regarding the requirements of regulatory approval in registration of extension, the Supreme Court has issued two judgments.[1] In the past, it was judged in terms of efficacy. If another regulatory approval with 'identical efficacy + different dosage/regimen' was obtained at a later date, a patent term extension was not obtained for this subsequent regulatory approval. However, currently, if regulatory approval is later obtained for pharmaceuticals with 'identical efficacy + different dosage/regimen', patent term extension is possible for this subsequent regulatory approval.

Concerning (i), there are cases where generic pharmaceutical manufacturers have **12**
decided to manufacture and distribute pharmaceuticals which are not identical to the original pharmaceuticals but are covered by the original pharmaceutical manufacturer's patents, knowing that they may pay a large amount of licensing fees. Such cases occur when the original pharmaceutical is expected to become a blockbuster drug, and production begins before the original manufacturer's patent expires (e.g. *Ono v MSD*[2]).

Regarding (ii), if generic pharmaceutical manufacturers spend time and money to **13**
submit their own clinical data, an application for marketing authorisation may be accepted even during the reexamination period, which renders it as no longer being a generic pharmaceutical application.

Regarding (iii), it is not stipulated by law in Japan, but is based on the notification from **14**
the Ministry of Health, Labour and Welfare (Ministry of Health, Labour and Welfare section manager notification dated 5 June 2009, hereinafter abbreviated as 'notification').

---

[1] 2009 (Gyo Hi) No. 326; 2014 (Gyo Hi) No. 356, → mn. 82.

[2] Ono Pharmaceutical and Professor Tasuku Honjo filed a patent infringement lawsuit against MSD, who obtained manufacturing and marketing approval for KEYTRUDA (generic name: pembrolizumab, MK-3475) in 2016. A settlement was later reached.

In terms of procedure, a two-step review is required, which places a heavy burden on generic pharmaceutical manufacturers. This procedure treats generic pharmaceuticals and biosimilars differently.

15 The follownig is a brief explanation of patent linkage in Japan: The notification states that if a patent (substance patent or use-invention patent) for the active ingredient in the original pharmaceutical is active, regulatory approval for generic pharmaceuticals will not be issued for the active ingredient and efficacy. The Ministry of Health, Labour and Welfare requires the original pharmaceutical manufacturers to report substance patents and use-invention patents. Information other than substance patents and use-invention patents is not required. In contrast, the US Orange Book describes patent information on all substances, uses, formulations, and dosage forms of original pharmaceuticals.[3] Generic pharmaceutical manufacturers cannot distribute generic pharmaceuticals or biosimilars on the market until these are listed on the NHI (National Health Insurance) price listing, after obtaining manufacturing approval. After manufacturing approval is granted, preadjustments are made between the parties concerned, regarding patents other than substance patents and use-invention patents, and only those that can be stably supplied to the market (in other words, those that are not at risk of patent litigation) are listed in the pharmaceutical price list. Since the period for preadjustment is limited, if the preadjustment cannot be made within that period, generic pharmaceutical manufacturers will be required to submit a memorandum of understanding that they will not discontinue the supply even if an infringement lawsuit is filed. In this way, decisions are made in two stages (manufacturing approval stage and preadjustment stage), placing a heavy burden on generic pharmaceutical manufacturers. In the case of biosimilars, there seems to be no preadjustment in practice, and the burden on biosimilar manufacturers seems to be even greater than for generics.

16 As explained above (→ mn. 11), the expiration date is different for each efficacy, even for a singular patent and even after the expiration of the substance patent, various patents related to second medical use and dosage regime are filed by original pharmaceutical manufacturers. As a result, applications for skinny labels by generic pharmaceutical manufacturers are complex, and there are cases where lawsuits are filed due to differences in interpretation.

## II. Claim format

17 Patents for second medical use are allowed in Japan. However, even if the content of the invention is the same, such patents will be assessed as lacking novelty depending on the wording of the claims and, therefore, much caution should be exercised in deciding on the format of the claims.

18 In Europe, 'substance X for use in the treatment of disease Y' is a recognised format for a claim in second medical use inventions. However, when X is a pure substance (a single compound), this format is interpreted as lacking novelty in Japan. A phrase such as 'substance X for treating disease Y' only indicates the usefulness of substance X. If 'substance X' or 'substance X for treating disease Z' are already known, 'substance X for treating disease Y' is assessed as lacking novelty. An 'agent claim' is often used in order to avoid such an assessment. A typical claim format would be 'Y-disease treating agent comprising substance X as an active ingredient.' In the case of a composition rather than a pure substance, the claim format 'Y-disease treating composition for use in the treatment

[3] → § 17 mn. 5.

of disease Y, the composition comprising substance X' is acceptable. Even in this case, it is recommended to draft an 'agent claim' such as 'Y-disease treating agent consisting of a composition comprising substance X as an active ingredient.'

Dosage regimen claimare understood to be a type of medical use claim, are now permissible according to revisions made in 2019 to the Examination Guidelines. For example, the claim can recite 'An antiasthmatic agent comprising the compound "A" characterised in that the compound "A" is administered orally in an amount of 30 to 40 µg/kg of body weight, once every three months to a human patient.' This claim is novel and inventive because, conventionally, 1 µg/kg body weight of compound 'A' was orally administered daily for the treatment of asthma, but the effect of the treatment soon dissipated between doses and side effect B occured, however, the new dosage regimen resolved these problems. **19**

Regarding concomitant medical products, a claim expression for example 'A diabetic pharmaceutical product combining, compound A and compound B' has been accepted, but this can be also expressed as a dosage regimen type claim, e.g. 'A pharmaceutical product comprising compound A characterised by being used together with compound B.' **20**

## III. Claim interpretation for second medical use

In Japan, there is no specific standard exclusively for the interpretation of second medical use claims. Since a second medical use invention is considered to be a type of 'use invention', the standard for interpreting a 'use invention' is applied. A use invention is defined as 'an invention based on (a) discovering an unknown property of a specific substance, and (b) determining whether the substance is suitable for a novel use based on this property'[4]. Both 'property' and 'use' should be regarded as novel. If at least one of these characteristics is proven not to be novel, then the product itself is not considered to be novel. **21**

When comparing (i) a known medical use and (ii) another medical use, if (ii) can be derived from an action mechanism of (i), or if a medical effect of (ii) necessarily occurs due to a close pharmacological effect of (i) and (ii), (ii) is not considered to be a novel use. For example, when the known medical use is 'bronchodilator', 'asthmatic agent' is not considered a novel use because the medicinal use of 'asthmatic agent' can be derived from an action mechanism of 'bronchodilator', and when the known medical use is 'anti-inflammatory agent','analgesic' is not considered a novel use because the medicinal effect of 'analgesic' necessarily occurs due to the close pharmacological effect of 'anti-inflammatory agent' and'analgesic'. **22**

Therefore, a 'second medical use' in a second medical use claim shall be construed as distinguishable from other known uses according to the above criteria. **23**

---

[4] 1998 (Gyo-Ke) No. 401, → mn. 82; Examination Guidelines.

## C. Direct and indirect infringement of second medical use claims

### I. Legal requirement for a patent infringement

24 In Japan, there are no legal requirements for infringement solely for second medical use inventions. The requirements applied to all other types of inventions are also applied to second medical use inventions. Patent infringement relating to a second medical use invention requires that the pharmaceutical is 'used' for the second medical use. In this case, the 'label theory' is applied to determine whether it is 'used.' Specifically, the contents described in the 'package insert' and 'interview form' attached to the pharmaceutical serves as evidence that the pharmaceutical product has been used for a second use.

25 Package insert here refers to a document for medical professionals such as physicians and pharmacists, which is attached to pharmaceutical products and medical devices, and describes the composition, product, dosage and administration, warnings, contraindications, and the like. The interview form is an explanation of the pharmaceutical product for medical professionals such as physicians and pharmacists, and contains comprehensive information provided by pharmaceutical companies to supplement the information on the package insert.

26 Determinations of infringement are based on the labelling of the documents attached to the pharmaceutical product. However, even if a product is not sold with a direct and explicit indication of its use, an infringement of a pharmaceutical use invention is recognised if it can be determined that the product is sold for that use in consideration of the specific circumstances.[5]

27 Regarding the scope of injunctions, if the defendant's product has multiple uses and some are covered by the plaintiff's patent, the manufacture and distribution of the defendant's product could be suspended unless some of the uses are explicitly excluded.[6]

28 In the Ketotifen Fumarate Case, the defendant argued that the their product was non-infringing because it was a therapeutic agent, not a prophylactic agent. However, the court found that the defendant's product was an asthma preventive agent (plaintiff's patented invention), and the defendant's entire product was suspended because the therapeutic agent and prophylactic agent were not manufactured and distributed separately.

### II. Direct patent infringement

29 Direct infringement occurs when an unauthorised third party 'works' (e.g. produces) a patented invention comercially. Here, the term 'working' is defined in Article 2(3) of the Patent Act (*Tokkyoho*; → mn. 71): producing, using, assigning, exporting, importing, offering for assignment (including displaying for the purpose of assignment) fall under 'working'. A non-exclusive licensee or an exclusive licensee is an authorised third party.

30 Recently, infringement (direct infringement) was disputed with respect to antibody pharmaceutical products described in functional claims.[7] The plaintiff's invention did

[5] 2005 (Ne) No. 10125 – *Cilostazol*; → mn. 83.
[6] 1990 (Wa) No. 12094 – *Ketotifen Fumarate*; → mn. 84.
[7] 2017 (Wa) 16468, 2019 (Ne) No. 10014 – *Sanofi v Amgen*; → mn. 85.

not specify any amino acid sequence of the antibody, and was described as blocking and 'neutralising' binding between PCSK9 and LDLR, and 'competing' with reference antibodies for binding to PCSK9. The defendant argued that the patent should be limited to antibodies having the specific amino acid sequences described in the specification, but the court denied this and found infringement.

Under current Japanese patent practice, an antibody may be described by specifying an antigen recognised by the antibody and cross-reactivity. In particular, a monoclonal antibody may be described by specifying an antigen recognised by the monoclonal antibody, a hybridoma which produces the monoclonal antibody, cross-reactivity, and an amino acid sequence of CDR in the monoclonal antibody. The plaintiff in *Sanofi v Amgen* utilised this practice to make the functional claim. 31

In a situation where the substance patent expired but the process patent was still in effect, a court ruled that a generic pharmaceutical manufacturer directly infringed the manufacturing process patent, according to an equivalent infringement.[8] 32

Maxacalcitol was developed as a new substance by Chugai Pharmaceutical. A substance patent was filed in 1985, and a patent application was filed in 1986 for a use invention relating to a therapeutic agent for psoriasis. The substance patent extension expired in December 2010, and the patent extension for the use invention expired in September 2012. In December 2012, the defendants started to distribute generic pharmaceutical products. Among the five requirements for equivalent infringement, the defendant denied infringement, reasoning that the fifth requirement (i.e., that the defendant's product or manufacturing process was not intentionally excluded from the scope of claims) was not met. That is, the defendant argued that their manufacturing process was intentionally excluded from the patent, but the Supreme Court did not accept this argument. 33

Equivalent infringement in Japan is briefly explained below. Even if there is no literal infringement of a patent claim, equivalent infringement is recognised if the product in question is substantially identical to the structure of the patented invention. In 1998, the Supreme Court issued a judgment indicating the standards for equivalent infringement.[9] 34

According to this judgment, equivalent infringement occurs when the following five requirements are met. 35

1. Even if the claim has a part which is different from the product in question, the differing part of the claim is not essential.
2. Even if the differing part in the claim is replaced by the corresponding part in the product in question, the objective of the patented invention can be achieved and the same effect can be obtained.
3. A person skilled in the art could have easily conceived the idea of replacing the differing part at the time the product in question was manufactured.
4. The product in question is not the same as the prior art at the time of filing of the patent application for the patented invention, nor could a person skilled in the art have easily deduced it from the prior art at the time of filing.
5. The product in question was not intentionally excluded from the claims in the patent application procedure for the invention.

---

[8] 2016 (Ju) No. 1242 – *Maxacalcitol.*

[9] 1994 (O) No. 1083 – *Ball Spline*; → mn. 86.

## III. Indirect Infringement

36 In Japan, indirect infringement is divided into 'dedicated product type indirect infringement' (Article 101(1) and (4) Patent Act) and 'non-dedicated product type indirect infringement' (Article 101(2) and (5) Patent Act).[10]

37 In the case of 'dedicated product type indirect infringement', the infringement is recognised when a product that is used only to manufacture the patented product is manufactured. However, since the requirement for 'dedicated' tends to be narrowly determined, 'non-dedicated product type indirect infringement' is often applied.

38 Where a patent is granted for an invention of a product, the following requirements are necessary for 'non-dedicated product type indirect infringement.'

1. The product in question is one that must be used in the production of the patented product.
2. The product in question must be not widely distributed in Japan.
3. The product in question must be indispensable for solving the problem of the invention.
4. The infringer knows that alleged product will be used to implement the patented invention.
5. Alleged infringer implements (e.g. produces) the product in question commercially.

39 Regarding indirect infringement, there is an issue as to whether direct infringement must occur in order for indirect infringement to occur. In connection with this, there are opposing theories reasoning that direct infringement is necessary for indirect infringement (dependent theory) and that it is not necessary (independent theory). The dependent theory is divided into two positions: (i) it is necessary to prove direct infringement, and (ii) it is sufficient if there is a probability of direct infringement. As for the situations where the patented invention is used overseas, when it is used for personal or family purposes and for experimental research, the independent theory may need to be applied since direct infringement does not occur in these cases. According to current academic theories and court decisions, there is no need to choose between the independent theory and the dependent theory. Instead, the theory often adopted is that which reasons it necessary to determine direct infringement on a case-by-case basis (compromise theory).

40 There are cases where indirect infringement was discussed regarding inventions related to combinations of two diabetes pharmaceutical products with different mechanisms of action.[11]

41 In this case, the claim in the plaintiff's patent was written as 'A medicine combining pharmaceutical product "A" and pharmaceutical product "B"'. Pharmaceutical products A and B are known compounds and their efficacies are also known. The plaintiff's patent for pharmaceutical product A had expired, so the defendant started distributing pharmaceutical product A (not a combination of pharmaceutical products A and B) as a generic product. Furthermore, the a package insert was identical to the plaintiff's package insert, showing a use of pharmaceutical products A in combination with pharmaceutical product B.

42 The defendant's product (pharmaceutical product A) is first (a) manufactured by the defendant, subsequently (b) delivered to a hospital, where (c) a physician writes a prescription for 'combining pharmaceutical products A and B, (d) a pharmacist 'places pharmaceutical product A and B in one container,' and (e) the patient consumes pharmaceutical products A and B.

---

[10] → mn. 75.

[11] 2011 (Wa) No. 7576 and 7578, 2011 (Wa) No. 19435 and No. 19436 – *Pioglidazone*; → mn. 87 et seq.

The plaintiff claimed there was 'non-dedicated product type indirect infringement,' and argued that the requirement (i) was implemented in the situations (c), (d), and (e). The plaintiff also argued that requirements (ii), (iii), (iv), and (v) were satisfied when the defendant manufactured and sold their product. This case was heard by the Osaka District Court and the Tokyo District Court – the Osaka District Court considered requirement (i), whereas the Tokyo District Court considered requirement (iii). 43

The court ruled as follows: regarding requirement (i), in order to be a 'production' it is necessary to use the supplied goods as materials and modify them in some way. The act of merely using materials according to their original purpose is not included in the 'production'. Each of the defendant's products was simply 'used' (prescribed, consumed) and did not fall under 'items used in the production.' The plaintiff argued that 'combining' included combining separately formulated products for administration to the patient, but the court held that 'combining' in the claim means producing a novel product by combining two or more active ingredients. The act of a pharmacist placing both pharmaceutical products into the same container and then both active ingredients being mixed inside the patient's body do not fall under 'combining'. 44

Regarding the requirement of (iii) 'indispensable for solving the problem of invention', the court interpreted this as 'those that directly bring about the unique configuration or component'. Subsequently, the court ruled that pharmaceutical product 'A' did not fall under this category, which means pharmaceutical product 'A' is not indispensable for solving the problem of the invention. 45

## D. Infringement of second medical use claims and skinny label products

Infringement of second medical use claims may occur in the case of skinny label products. As mentioned, in Japan, the label theory is applied to determine whether or not a claimed medical use invention is implemented. In other words, infringement is determined based on the descriptions in the package inserts and interview forms. 46

However, skinny label products may be used off-label in actual medical practices, and in such circumstances, infringement may be acknowledged. In relation to this, there is a case in which the dosage regimen patent became a problem.[12] Dosage regimens are different from second medical uses, but these are handled similarly. 47

In this case, the plaintiff's claim is as follows (the disclaimer is omitted): 'A Meniere's disease treating medicinal product comprising isosorbitol, characterised in that the medicinal product is orally administered in the dosage 0.15 to 0.75 g/kg body weight of isosorbitol per adult per day.' 48

The defendant manufactures and distributes medicinal products for treating Meniere's disease. The description of dosage and administration for Meniere's disease in the package insert and interview form of the defendant's product states: 'The standard dosage is 1.5 to 2.0 mL/kg of body weight per day, and the normal daily dosage for adults is 90 to 120 mL after each meal. It will be administered orally in divided doses. The dose is adjusted according to the symptoms.' This administration is equal to 1.05 to 1.4 g/kg body weight. 49

The plaintiff alleged that the physician reduced the dosage to 0.15 to 0.75 g/kg body weight by referring to the package insert, and that the MR (Medical Representative) pro- 50

[12] 2016 (Ne) No. 10023 – *Meniere's disease*; → mn. 89.

vided information that the patented range can be used from the beginning of treatment. However, the court held that the dosages in the package insert and interview form for the defendant's product differed from those of the plaintiff's patent, and that there is insufficient evidence that the defendant's product was used at the dosage in the plaintiff's patent. The defendant's products were therefore found to be non-infringing.

51 The court confirmed that the patent claim meant that 0.15-0.75 g/kg body weight was used from the beginning of treatment. Even if the initial amount was 1.05 to 1.4 g/kg body weight and was later changed to 0.15 to 0.75 g/kg body weight, this situation is not covered by the claim. However, if there had been sufficient evidence of off-label use (e.g. sufficient evidence that the MR had provided information that the medicinal product should be administered within the patented range from the beginning of treatment), the conclusion would have been different.

52 This case demonstrates that the label theory is effective for medicinal use inventions, but generic pharmaceutical manufacturers need to be cautious concerning off-label use. If the facts regarding off-label are substantiated by sufficient evidence, the label theory may prove to be ineffective.

## E. Infringement of second medical use claims and biosimilar products

53 The interpretation of second medical use claims, the requirement for direct or indirect infringement of second medical use claims, and the possibility of infringement of skinny-labeled products for generic pharmaceutical products also apply to biosimilar products.

54 However, as mentioned, the 'preadjustment' for patent linkage is not required for biosimilars in some cases. Thus, with regarding skinny labelling, biosimilars require more careful handling than generic pharmaceutical products, and inadequate handling increases the risk of litigation.

55 As for the first infringement lawsuit against a biosimilar product in Japan, there was a case in which the lawsuit was filed more than half a year before the biosimilar product was approved for manufacturing, which was closed due to a waiver immediately after approval (Herceptin case).[13]

56 According to the press release from the parties involved, the details of this case are as follows. Chugai Pharmaceutical is the exclusive licensee of the patent (Patent No. 5818545) by Genentech relating to 'Dosage for treatment with anti-ErbB2 antibody'.

57 Claim 1 of Patent No. 5818545 is as follows: (i) A container containing a pharmaceutical composition for treating breast cancer characterised by the overexpression of HER2, by the intravenous administration of the anti-ErbB2 antibody huMab4D5-8 at an initial dose of 8 mg/kg, and multiple subsequent doses of 6 mg/kg with each dose separated from each other by three weeks and (ii) a package comprising a package insert associated with said container.

58 On 17 August 2017, Genentech and Chugai Pharmaceutical requested an injunction before the Tokyo District Court against Nippon Kayaku Co., Ltd., who is an applicant for manufacturing and marketing approval of biosimilars. Normally, the original pharmaceutical manufacturer is not aware of the facts contained in the application for approval of

[13] No court decision was issued since Chugai withdrew the case. Information is only available in Japanese under: https://www.chugai-pharm.co.jp/news/detail/20180411153000_31.html.

the generic pharmaceutical manufacturer until the generic pharmaceutical or biosimilar product is approved but, in this case, it seemed that the defendant's press release revealed the facts.

Genentech and Chugai Pharmaceutical learned that manufacturing and marketing approval was granted for the defendant's product on 23 March 2018, for the indication of 'unresectable advanced or recurrent gastric cancer with confirmed HER2 overexpression'. Since breast cancer was no longer covered, they submitted a waiver to close the case on 10 April 2018. **59**

## F. Strategies and considerations

In order to reduce the liability risk associated with skinny-label products, it is necessary to carefully determine the expiry of the patent term of the original pharmaceutical product for each indication. It is also important to prevent off-label use. There is a case in which an original pharmaceutical manufacturer sued a generic pharmaceutical manufacturer, claiming that even though the number of patients for a generic pharmaceutical product is small, its sales volume is high (Linezolid case). **60**

Pfizer filed a lawsuit before the Tokyo District Court against Meiji Seika Pharma, which distributes generic medicinal products for the antibacterial medicinal product 'Zyvox', seeking an injunction against distribution, as well as compensation for damages, claiming that the exclusive license of the patent on methicillin-resistant Staphylococcus aureus (MRSA) infections had been infringed. Pfizer's Zyvox is indicated for MRSA and vancomycin-resistant enterococci (VRE), whereas Meiji Seika Pharma's indication is for VRE only. **61**

Although the estimated number of patients with VRE infections is only a few dozen per year in Japan, generic pharmaceutical products with only VRE indications were sold in larger quantities. This could be one reason for Pfizer deciding to file the lawsuit. **62**

To prevent generic pharmaceutical manufacturers from being sued for off-label use, manufacturers of generic pharmaceuticals or biosimilars need to provide sufficient guidance to physicians, and to explain the risk of an infringement lawsuit. In the Linezolid case, the Japanese Society for Infectious Diseases, the Japanese Society of Chemotherapy, and the Japanese Society of Clinical Microbiology seem to have called on the medical field to use generic pharmaceuticals appropriately. To reduce the risk of liability, a warning through academia such as from the organisations above should also be considered. **63**

## G. Legal remedies

It is possible for patentees to obtain an injunction, claim compensation for damages, claim for unjust enrichment, and request credit recovery as remedies through civil proceedings before the court. Criminal penalties are also applicable. **64**

## I. Injunction

65 Requests with the following contents can be made (Article 100 Patent Act).

(i) Demand a party infringing the patent right or exclusive license to cease such infringement.

(ii) Demand a party likely to infringe the patent right or exclusive license to prevent such infringement.

(iii) Request disposal of products constituting infringement, and the removal of facilities used for the infringement or other measures necessary to prevent infringement.

66 Of these, only (iii) be claimed along with (i) or (ii). In seeking an injunction, it is not a requirement that the infringer has intent to infringe or be negligent in infringing. When urgent, it is effective to apply to the court for a provisional injunction to suspend the infringing act.

## II. Claim for damages

67 It is possible to claim damages against a party who manufactures, distributes, or imports infringing goods (Article 709 Civil Code). In order to facilitate claims for damages, the Patent Act has provisions for calculating the amount of damages (Article 102 Patent Act; → mn. 76). In addition, negligence is presumed in the infringing act (Article 103 Patent Act, → mn. 77).

## III. Claim for unjust enrichment

68 It is also possible to file a claim for the return of unjust enrichment with respect to profits obtained by the perpetrator through acts that constitute patent infringement (Articles 703 and 704 Civil Code). However, some alternatives are claims for damages or for the return of unjust enrichment.

## IV. Measures to restore credibility

69 A court may, at the patentee's request, order a person who has damaged the patentee's business credibility to take measures to restore credibility (e.g., posting an apology advertisement) (Article 106 Patent Act, → mn. 78).

## V. Pursuing criminal liability

70 A person who infringes a patent right shall be punished by imprisonment with labour for not more than 10 years or a fine of not more than 10 million yen (Article 196 Patent Act, → mn. 78). It is also possible to impose both imprisonment and a fine. In addition to the punishment of perpetrators, corporations can also be fined (Article 201 Patent Act, → mn. 80).

# H. Statutory provisions

## Patent Act

### Article 2 (Definitions) 71

(3) 'Working' of an invention in this Act means the following acts:

(i) in the case of an invention of a product (including a computer program, etc., the same shall apply hereinafter), producing, using, assigning, etc. (assigning and leasing, and in the case where the product is a computer program, etc., including provision through an electric telecommunication line, the same shall apply hereinafter), exporting or importing, or offering for assignment, etc. (including displaying for the purpose of assignment, etc., the same shall apply hereinafter) thereof;

(ii) in the case of an invention of a process, the use thereof; and

(iii) in the case of an invention of a process for producing a product, in addition to the action as provided in the preceding item, acts of using, assigning, etc., exporting or importing, or offering for assignment, etc. the product produced by the process.

### Article 68 (Effect of patent right) 72

A patentee shall have the exclusive right to work the patented invention as a business; provided, however, that where an exclusive license regarding the patent right is granted to a licensee, this shall not apply to the extent that the exclusive licensee is licensed to exclusively work the patented invention.

### Article 68-2 (Effect of patent right in the case of duration extension) 73

Where the duration of a patent right is extended (including the case where the duration is deemed to have been extended under Article 67-2(5)), such patent right shall not be effective against any act other than the working of the patented invention for the product, which was the subject of the disposition designated by Cabinet Order under Article 67(2), which constituted the reason for the registration of extension (where the specific usage of the product is prescribed by the disposition, the product used for that usage).

### Article 100 (Right to seek injunction) 74

(1) A patentee or exclusive licensee may demand a person who infringes or is likely to infringe the patent right or exclusive license, to cease or prevent such infringement.

(2) In making a demand under the preceding paragraph, the patentee or exclusive licensee may demand measures necessary for the prevention of such infringement; including the disposal of products constituting such act of infringement (including, in the case of a patented invention of a process of producing products, products produced by the act of infringement; the same shall apply in Article 102(1)) and the removal of facilities used for the act of infringement.

### Article 101 (Acts Deemed to constitute infringement) 75

The following acts shall be deemed to constitute infringement of a patent right or an exclusive license:

(i) where a patent has been granted for an invention of a product, acts of producing, assigning, etc., importing or offering for assignment, etc. any product to be used exclusively for the production of the said product as a business;

(ii) where a patent has been granted for an invention of a product, acts of producing, assigning, etc., importing or offering for assignment, etc. any product (excluding those widely distributed within Japan) to be used for the production of the said product, and indispensable for the resolution of the problem by the said invention as a business, knowing that the said invention is a patented invention and the said product is used for the working of the invention;

(iii) where a patent has been granted for an invention of a product, acts of possessing the said product for the purpose of assigning, etc., or exporting it as a business;

(iv) where a patent has been granted for an invention of a process, acts of producing, assigning, etc., importing or offering for assignment, etc., any product to be used exclusively for the use of the said process as a business; and

(v) where a patent has been granted for an invention of a process, acts of producing, assigning, etc., importing or offering for assignment, etc., any product (excluding those widely distributed within Japan) to be used for the use of the said process, and indispensable for the resolution of the problem by the said invention, knowing that the said invention is a patented invention and the said product is used for the working of the invention as a business;

(vi) where a patent has been granted for an invention of a process of producing a product, acts of possessing the product produced by the said process for the purpose of assigning etc., or exporting it as a business.

76 **Article 102 (Presumption of Amount of Damage, etc.)**

(1) If a patentee or exclusive licensee files a claim against an infringer for compensation, for damage sustained as a result of the intentional or negligent infringement of their patent right or exclusive license, and the infringer has transferred articles that constitute the act of infringement, the amount of damage sustained by the patentee or exclusive licensee may be established to be the total of the amount set forth in each of the following items.

(i) The amount arrived at when the amount of profit per unit for the articles that the patentee or exclusive licensee would have been able to sell if the infringement had not taken place, is multiplied by that part of the quantity of articles that the person infringing the patent right or exclusive license has transferred (referred to as the 'quantity transferred' in the following item), which does not exceed the quantity covered by the patentee's or exclusive licensee's ability to work the patented invention (referred to as the 'workable quantity' in the following item) if there are circumstances that render the patentee or the exclusive licensee unable to sell a quantity of products equivalent to all or part of the workable quantity, the workable quantity deducted from the quantity not sellable due to those

(ii) if applicable, an amount equivalent to the amount of money that is to be received in exchange for the working of the patented invention under the patent right or exclusive license, for any quantity exceeding the workable quantity, which is part of the quantity transferred, or for any specified quantity which is part of the quantity transferred (unless it is not found that the patentee would have been able to establish an exclusive license or grant a non-exclusive license under the patentee's patent rights, or that exclusive licensee would have been able to grant a non-exclusive license under the exclusive licensee's exclusive license).

(2) If a patentee or exclusive licensee files a claim for compensation for damage that the patentee or licensee personally incurs due to infringement, against a person that, intentionally or due to negligence, infringes the patent or exclusive license, and the infringer has profited from the infringement, the amount of that profit is presumed to be the value of damage incurred by the patentee or exclusive licensee.

(3) The patentee or exclusive licensee may fix the value of the damages that the patentee or licensee has personally incurred as being equivalent to the amount of money the patentee

or exclusive licensee would have been entitled to receive for the working of the patented invention, and may claim compensation for this against a person that, intentionally or due to negligence, infringes the patent or violates the exclusive license.

(4) When a court determines the amount equivalent to the amount of money to be received for the working of a patented invention as provided in paragraph (1) item (ii) or the preceding paragraph, the court may take into consideration the consideration that the patentee or exclusive licensee would hypothetically obtain if they reached an agreement with the infringer, based on the premise that the patent right or exclusive license had been infringed, concerning the consideration for the working of the patented invention that is covered by their patent right or exclusive license.

(5) The provisions of paragraph (3) do not preclude any claim to compensation for damages in excess of the amount provided for therein. In this case, the court may consider the absence of intent or gross negligence by the person that has infringed the patent or violated the exclusive license in fixing the amount of damages.

### Article 103 (Presumption of negligence) 77

An infringer of a patent right or exclusive license of another person is presumed negligent in the commission of the said act of infringement.

### Article 106 (Measures to Restore Credibility) 78

At the request of the patentee or exclusive licensee, the court may order a person that has harmed the business credibility of the patentee or exclusive licensee by intentionally or negligently infringing upon the patent right or exclusive license, to take measures necessary to restore the business credibility of the patentee or exclusive licensee in lieu of or beyond compensation for damages.

### Article 196 (The Crime of Infringement) 79

A person that infringes a patent right or exclusive license (other than a person committing an act that is deemed to constitute the infringement of a patent right or exclusive license pursuant to Article 101), is subject to punishment by imprisonment for a term not exceeding ten years or a fine not exceeding ¥10,000,000 (Yen), or a combination thereof.

### Article 201 (Dual Liability) 80

(1) If the representative of a corporation or an agent, employee or other employee of a corporation or an individual commits a violation of the provisions set forth in one of the following items, in connection with the business of that corporation or individual, beyond the offender being subject to punishment, the corporation is subject to punishment by a fine prescribed in the relevant item, and the individual is subject to punishment by a fine prescribed in the relevant Article referred to in the that item:

(i) Article 196, Article 196-2, or paragraph (1) of the preceding Article: a fine not exceeding 300 million yen; and
(ii) Article 197 or 198: a fine not exceeding 100 million yen.

(2) In a case as referred to in the preceding paragraph, a complaint as referred to Article 200-3, paragraph (2) which is filed against the offender, also has effect against the corporation or individual; and a complaint that is filed against the corporation or individual also has effect against the offender.

(3) If a fine is imposed on a corporation or individual pursuant to paragraph (1) in connection with a violation referred to in Article 196 or 196-2, or paragraph (1) of the preceding Article, the period of prescription is governed by the same rules as those for crimes in the provisions of those provisions.

# J. Extracts from court decisions

## 81 I. 2014 (Gyo-Hi) No. 356

It is construed that approval of manufacturing and sale of a pharmaceutical product under the provisions of the Pharmaceuticals and Medical Devices Act, makes it possible to manufacture and distribute the pharmaceutical product specified for each approval with regard to all the matters to be examined in relation to the pharmaceutical product, namely, its 'name, ingredients, quantity, dosage, administration, effectiveness, effect, side effects and other matters relating to the quality, efficacy and safety' (the main body of Article 14, paragraph (2), item (iii) of the Pharmaceuticals and Medical Devices Act).

Determination as to whether or not the scope of manufacturing and distribution of the pharmaceutical product subject to the prior disposition includes the manufacturing and distribution of the pharmaceutical product subject to the disposition stated as the reason for the application, should be made not by comparing these dispositions in form with regard to all those matters to be examined, but by comparing them with regard to the matters to be examined that would directly affect the substantial identity of the relevant products as pharmaceutical products, in light of the type or subject of the patent to which the application for registration of extension pertains.

According to the above, if the manufacturing and distribution of the pharmaceutical product that were the subject of a prior disposition are deemed to include the manufacturing and distribution of the pharmaceutical product subject to the disposition stated as the reason for the application, It is appropriate to understand that it is not recognised that it was necessary to receive a disposition on grounds for filing the application in order to practice the patented invention related to the application for extension registration.

## 82 II. 1998 (Gyo-Ke) No. 401

Since the gist of the present invention is '[a] flour for instant frozen noodles comprising 12 to 50 % by weight of tapioca starch and 88 to 50 % by weight of grain flour,' therefore, it can be said that it is an invention about blending this with other flours in a specific ratio, and using it for the purpose of flour for instant frozen noodles, and it can be said that it is a use invention in scholarly circles.

A use invention should be understood as an invention based on the discovery of an unknown property of a known substance, and the finding that the substance is suitable for use in a novel application due to this property. This is because, even if an unknown property is discovered in a known substance, unless the scope of application of the substance exceeds its conventional use, it cannot be said to be a creation of a technical idea. Unless it can be said that it is suitable for use in new applications, it is difficult to say that the scope of application has exceeded conventional applications.

## 83 III. 2005 (Ne) No. 10125 – *Cilostazo*

The defendant argued: 'Patented inventions related to pharmaceuticals should be evaluated as working only after they are manufactured and sold, with efficacy and effects approved under the Pharmaceutical Affairs Law. Even if a pharmaceutical product is used (off-label use) for the purpose of the use invention pertaining to the above, manufacturing and marketing of the pharmaceutical product cannot be considered as practice of the use invention.'

Certainly, it can be said that use inventions of pharmaceuticals are generally carried out after obtaining approval under the Pharmaceutical Affairs Law for the efficacy and effect associated with the use. However, in the case of a use invention of a pharmaceutical product, if the pharmaceutical product is sold as being used for that use, it can be said that the invention constitutes working. It should be said that this does not necessarily have a direct relationship with the presence or absence of approval under the Pharmaceutical Affairs Law. Even if the sale of the product may cause a problem under the Pharmaceutical Affairs Law, as long as the product is sold as being actually used for the purpose, it should be said that the use invention is being worked.

It can be said that a typical example of the implementation of a use invention for a pharmaceutical product is the case where the use is directly and explicitly indicated on the container or label of the product, and then the pharmaceutical product is manufactured and sold. However, even if the product is not necessarily sold with a direct and explicit indication of the use, it can be said that a use invention has been worked if it can be recognised that the product is being sold as being used for that purpose under specific circumstances.

## IV. 1990 (Wa) No. 12094 – *Ketotifen Fumarate* 84

Even if the defendants' preparations have uses other than as a preventive agent for allergic asthma, the defendants have not excluded the use of the defendants' preparations as a preventive agent for allergic asthma, and the product is not manufactured and sold with a clear distinction between its use as a prophylactic agent and other uses. It is unavoidable that the defendant's product, which is not used as a prophylactic agent for allergic asthma, is suspended.

## V. 2019 (Ne) No. 10014 – *Sanofi/Amgen* 85

Setting aside the question of whether each of the Inventions should be called a so-called functional claim, the technical scope of the patent invention must be determined on the basis of the recitation of the scope of claims, and should be construed on the basis of a technical idea disclosed therein, by taking the description of the specification and drawings into account. In addition, the appellant's allegation should be considered as a problem of support requirement or enablement requirement. A technical idea disclosed in each of the specifications is that an isolated monoclonal antibody competing with reference antibody 1 or 2, binds to PCSK9 in a location and/or a manner that prevents PCSK9 from binding to LDLR, blocks (neutralises) the binding between PCSK9 and LDLR, and reduces LDL level in a subject to exert an effect of causing the decrease of serum cholesterols in a subject. Further, as aforementioned, the defendant's monoclonal antibody and product fall within a technical scope of each of the inventions that are construed on the basis of the above technical idea.

Each of the inventions provides an isolated monoclonal antibody that neutralises the binding of PCSK9 and LDLR protein, and competes with each of the reference antibodies, and has constituent features of both blocking the binding between PCSK9 and LDLR for 'neutralisation', and 'competing' with the reference antibody with regard to the binding with PCSK9. Furthermore, it cannot be said that there is a description in each of the specifications that leads one to believe that each of the inventions is specified only by a function to compete with the reference antibody 1 or 2. The appellant's allegation that each of the inventions being limited to the example on the premise of that is not acceptable.

The inventions are not specified by amino acid sequences. Therefore, there is no reason to believe that the invention is limited to the specific antibody described in the specification or to an antibody having an amino acid sequence in which one or several amino acids at specific positions of the antibody are substituted.

## 86 VI. 1994 (O) No. 1083 – *Ball Spline*

In determining whether the product which a person produces or the means which this person uses in producing the product (hereinafter, 'the products') falls within the technical scope of the patented invention in an patent infringement action, the technical scope of the patented invention must be determined on the basis of the scope of the patent claim indicated in the patent specification attached to the patent application (Article 70(1) of the Patent Law). If there is a difference in the products in terms of configuration as indicated in the scope of the patent claims, the products cannot be regarded as falling within the technical scope of the patented invention. However, even if there is a part that is different from the products in terms of configuration as indicated in the claim in the patent specification, the products should be regarded as equivalent to the configuration as indicated in the scope of the patent claim and fall within the technical scope of the patented invention provided that (a) this part is not the essential part of the patented invention, (b) the purpose of the patented invention can be achieved by replacing this part with a part from the products, and an identical function and effect can be obtained, (c) a person skilled in the art pertaining to this invention could easily conceive the idea of such replacement at when manufacturing the products, (d) the products are not identical to the prior art at the time of filing the application for the patented invention or could have been easily conceived of at that time by a person skilled in the art pertaining to this invention, and (e) there were no special circumstances whereby the products had been intentionally excluded from the scope of the patent claim in the patent application process.

This is because (1) it is extremely difficult to foresee all kinds of infringements which may occur in the future and formulate the scope of the patent claim in the specification. If another person is able to easily avoid injunction and other exercise of rights by the proprietor by replacing part of the construction as indicated in the patent claim in the specification with the substance or technology which came to be known after the patent application, it will greatly reduce the incentive for invention in society in general, which is not only against the purposes of Patent Law, i.e., promotion of the development of industry through the protection and encouragement of invention, but would be contrary to social justice and ideas of fairness. (2) Taking this into account, the substantive value of the patented invention extends to the technology, which a third party can easily conceive of as being substantially the same in terms of configuration as indicated in the scope of patent claim in the specification, and third parties should be expected to foresee this. (3) On the other hand, concerning those technologies which were in the public domain or which a person skilled in the art pertaining to this invention could easily conceive at the priority date, such technologies cannot be found to be within the scope of the technical scope of the patented invention since no one could have obtained a patent (Article 29 Patent Law). (4) Furthermore, technology which the proprietor had once acknowledged as not belonging to the technical scope of the patent claim, or in relation to which they had behaved as if they had objectively acknowledged this to be the case, e.g., by intentionally excluding the technology from the scope of patent claim in the patent application process, the proprietor is not entitled to claim otherwise henceforth since this is against the doctrine of estoppel.

## 87 VII. 2011 (Wa) No. 7576 and No. 7578 – *Pioglidazone*

Production of a product in Article 101(2) of the Patent Law refers to the act of making a novel 'product that satisfies all of the constituent features of the invention' by using 'a product that does not satisfy the constituent features of the invention' as a raw material. In other words, although there are no restrictions on the mode of action such as processing, repair, assembly, and the like, it is necessary to use the supplied items as materials and to modify them in some way. This does not include the act of merely using such items according to the original purpose of the materials.

Each of the defendants' products is a complete pharmaceutical product by itself, and is not intended to be tampered with in any way. There is no dispute between the parties that the pharmaceutical product should be used (prescribed, taken) as it is according to its intended use as a pharmaceutical product for the prevention and treatment of diabetes or a diabetic patient.

Therefore, the defendants' products are not used for 'manufacturing'. In other words, the defendants' products are simply 'used' (prescribed, taken), and do not fall under 'items used in the production.'

The pharmacist merely delivers each of the defendants' product, which is a complete and individual medicine, to the patient according to the physician's prescription. At that time, even if there was an act of 'collecting' multiple medicines (such as putting them in a single container), it is difficult to say that the medicines are 'combined' by this act.

## VIII. 2011 (Wa) No. 19435 and No. 19436 – *Pioglidazone* 88

In Article 101(2) of the Patent Law, 'indispensable to solving the problem of the invention' is a different concept from the constituent elements (invention specifying matters) of the invention described in the claims. In addition to the constituent elements of the invention, tools and raw materials used in the production of goods may also be included. This does not apply to what has hitherto been required regardless of the problem to be solved by the invention. Thus, it corresponds to the case where the 'problem to be solved by the invention' is solved only by using it. In other words, with 'regard to the characteristic technical means newly disclosed by the invention, which are not found in the prior art, those that directly bring about the unique configuration or component characterising this means' correspond to this.

## IX. 2016 (Ne) No. 10023 – *Meniere's disease* 89

[S]ince the present invention is a use invention characterised by the creation of a novel use for a known substance called Isosorbitol, in order to conclude that the manufacture and distribution of the defendant's product falls under the 'working' of the present invention, the manufacture and distribution must have been made for this novel application. However, the dosage and administration in the package insert and interview form of the defendant's product is a standard dosage of 1.5 to 2.0 mL/kg of body weight per day, which is clearly different from the use of the present invention. There is also insufficient evidence that the defendant's product was manufactured and sold for the patented use. Therefore, the plaintiff's assertion lacks a correct understanding of the meaning of the use invention, is merely their own opinion, and cannot be adopted.

# § 19
# Singapore

## A. Executive summary

1 The Singapore Patents Act (Cap. 221) and the Patent Rules provides the legislative framework for the patent system in Singapore. The legislative framework provides the Registrar at the Intellectual Property Office of Singapore (IPOS) with authority to issue administrative decisions in relation to revocation and restoration of patents. Contentious matters may be brought before the High Court, and appeals from decisions of the High Court may be made to the Court of Appeal.

2 The Singapore Patents Act was enacted in 1994, and is modelled after the United Kingdom's Patent Act of 1977. Given the relatively young age of the legislation in relation to patents, Singapore's jurisprudence is not yet well developed in many areas of patent law. As a consequence, and because of the similarities between the Singapore Patents Act and UK Patents Act, the Singapore courts frequently cite UK and European patent cases, which are often viewed as persuasive but not binding. Guidance from the EPO is also often consulted, both from the courts and at a Patent Office level.

3 In Singapore, methods of treatment is statutorily excluded from patentability in section 16(2) of the Singapore Patents Act, which deems methods of treatment, practised on the human or animal body, to be incapable of industrial application (→ mn. 85).

4 However, section 16(3) provides that any product that was invented for use in the method of treatment is not caught by the exclusion. Thus, a medicinal product that is invented for use in the method of treatment may be patented provided it fulfils all the other patentability requirements in Singapore.

5 Hence, pharmaceutical products may be made the subject of medical or diagnostic use claims, and may be drafted in the form of a first medical use claim (e.g. X for use in therapy), or a Swiss-style second medical use claim (i.e. use of X in the manufacture of a medicament for the treatment of disease Y). This also extends to new dosage regimes.

6 There is no specific judicial guidance in Singapore on either direct or indirect infringement of second medical use claims in the context of 'skinny labelled' products. Although one could glean how a court may view such infringing activities from related UK and European authorities.

## B. Scope of protection and interpretation of second medical use claims

7 Second medical use claims may only be claimed in the form of 'Swiss-style' claims. Swiss-style claims are regarded as purpose limited process claims. Such claims are construed as directed to the use of the substance for the manufacture of a medicament for a specific medical use. Hence, Swiss-style claims are not restricted to second medical

uses of a substance or composition and may be used even when the first medical use of a compound is not previously known.

Swiss-style claims can only derive novelty from their intended use if the use is in a method of treatment practised on the human or animal body. The 'treatment' is used in a broad sense and thus the method of treatment may be a surgical method, therapeutic method or diagnostic method. This means that known substances when drafted in a Swiss-style claim format but are not directed to a method of treatment are not deemed to be novel. **8**

It should be noted that Singapore's practice of using a 'Swiss-type' claim format for second medical uses diverges from that of UK and Europe. While the medical provisions of the EPC 2000 has been implemented in the United Kingdom's Patent Act 2004, similar provisions were not introduced in the Singapore legislation. Accordingly, a clam in the form 'substance X for use in the treatment of disease Y' will be read as a first medical use claim. **9**

In Singapore, the question of how Swiss-style claims are to be interpreted has not directly arisen for consideration by the courts. In particular, the question as to whether a second medical use for a known substance is patentable has not arisen for consideration in Singapore. In *Warner-Lambert Company LLC v Novartis (Singapore) Pte Ltd*, the High Courts, in *obiter*, the problems and difficulties that arise with interpreting Swiss-style claims and hints that it will depend on the 'determination as to what is the technical contribution (or subject matter) that falls within the scope of the claim and protected by patent registration.[1] In *Warner-Lambert Company LLC v Novartis (Singapore) Pte Ltd*, the Court of Appeal notes, in *obiter*, that Swiss-style claims are 'merely a novel and perhaps questionable way of getting around what has been perceived to be the meaning of section 14(7) of the Patents Act'[2]. **10**

Until such a determination on second medical use claims is made by the Singapore courts, the construction of Swiss-style claims by the Patent Office (IPOS) is maintained. **11**

In this regard, the Examination Guidelines for Patent Applications at IPOS[3] states at 8.141: **12**

> Normally, 'for' is interpreted as 'suitable for'. However, in a 'Swiss-type' claim, 'for' is interpreted as 'suitable and intended for' treatment of the indication specified. In *Warner-Lambert Company, LLC v Actavis Group Ptc EHF & Ors (Rev 1)* [2015] EWHC 72, Arnold J. (citing *Actavis v Merck* and Birss J. in *Hospira UK Ltd v Genentech Inc.*), noted that a 'Swiss-type' claim is directed at the manufacturer and that the intention of the manufacturer in the production of the pharmaceutical product is key.

The Guidelines (at 8.157) also recognise that a new mode of administration may play a critical role in a medical treatment and can serve as a distinguishing feature over the prior art. **13**

The Guidelines also state however that the 'claim must be appropriately drafted such that the claimed mode of administration is directed at the manufacturer and not at the medical practitioner. If the claim is drafted such that it is deemed to be directed to a medical practitioner then it will be considered as a medical method of treatment and thus lack industrial application.' **14**

Furthermore the Guidelines cite with approval *Actavis v Merck*[4]. This UK case involved the use of finasteride at a new daily dosage of about 0.05 mg to 1.0 mg for the treatment of androgenic alopecia. Finasteride was a known drug for treating prostate **15**

[1] [2016] SGHC 106 at para. 86; the decision is summarised in → mn. 119 et seq.
[2] [2017] SGCA 45 at para. 96; → mn. 84 for section 14 of the Patents Act.
[3] October 2023 version.
[4] [2008] RPC 26.

conditions and had been previously proposed as a treatment for androgenic alopecia at a dosage of at least 5 mg. The new feature in the claim was a lowered dosage of finasteride for the treatment of androgenic alopecia. In this case, the Court of Appeal overturned the decision of the Patents Court in *Actavis v Merck*[5] and held that a second medical use claim in the form of a new dosage regime was allowable.

## C. Direct and indirect infringement of second medical use claims

16 The rights conferred on a patented process are infringed in the circumstances set out in section 61(1)(b) and (c) Singapore Patents Act which read:

> 66.—(1) Subject to the provisions of this Act, a person infringes a patent for an invention if, but only if, while the patent is in force, the person does any of the following things in Singapore in relation to the invention without the consent of the proprietor of the patent:
> (a) …
> (b) where the invention is a process, the person uses the process or the person offers it for use in Singapore when the person knows, or it is obvious to a reasonable person in the circumstances, that its use without the consent of the proprietor would be an infringement of the patent;
> (c) where the invention is a process, the person disposes of, offers to dispose of, uses or imports any product obtained directly by means of that process or keeps any such product whether for disposal or otherwise.

17 A granted Swiss-style claim would be infringed if a person uses or offers to use the disclosed compound in a process to manufacture the medicament for treating the disclosed disease in Singapore, when he knows, or is obvious to a reasonable person, that its use without consent is an infringement.

18 A granted Swiss-style claim would also be infringed if a person disposes, offers to dispose, uses or imports a product obtained directly from that manufacturing process.

19 The Court of Appeal in *Warner-Lambert Co LLC v Novartis (Singapore) Pte Ltd* considered the infringement of Swiss-style claims by referencing UK jurisprudence:

> It should, however, be noted that there are certain practical difficulties in recognizing Swiss-style claims and enforcing them in infringement actions. As observed by Floyd LJ in *Warner-Lambert Company LLC v Generics (UK) Ltd* (trading as Mylan) and others [2016] EWCA Civ 1006 at [187]: …[t]he law is struggeling on the one hand to give the patentee a proper reward for his contribution to the art by elucidating the new use for the drug, whilst at the same time not excluding the competing manufacturer from making and marketing the drug for its known purpose. The issue is complicated by the interaction with the law relating to, and the practices of the market in, prescription medicines. The solution adopted by this court in Warner-Lambert CoA was an attempt to strike the right balance by not placing insuperable obstacles in the path of the patentee, whilst at the same time recognising in very clear terms that the remedies available for infringement will have to be moulded so as to achieve fair and proportionate relief tailored to the very special circumstances of this type of case.[6]

20 In *Warner-Lambert Company LLC v Actavis Group PTC EHF* ('Warner Lambert CA') the English Court of Appeal held that the technical subject matter of the Swiss-style claim

---

[5] [2007] EWHC 1311.
[6] [2017] SGCA 45 at para. 94.

was the making of pregabalin for patients to whom it will be intentionally administered for treating pain but fell short of including the step of actually using pregabalin for treating pain.[7] The Singapore High Court in *Warner-Lambert Co LLC v Novartis (Singapore) Pte Ltd* cited this UK case with approval stating that the essential feature of the Swiss-style claim 'involves a link between the act of manufacture and the ultimate intentional use of the drug by the end-user, rather than the new therapeutic use of the drug itself'[8] (which is the construction properly given to method of treatment claims).

Section 66(2) sets out certain acts which would constitute an infringement of a patent 21
but is not an infringing act if:

(a) it is for purposes which are not commercial;
(b) it is done for experimental purposes;
(c) the pharmaceutical product which is produced by or with consent of the proprietor is imported, used, disposed, or offered to dispose of in Singapore; and
(d) it is solely to support an application for obtaining marketing approval for a pharmaceutical product.

However, a parallel import would be considered an infringement if the pharmaceutical 22
product is imported by an importer but the pharmaceutical product has not previously been sold or distributed in Singapore by or with consent of the proprietor, the import of which would result in a breach of contract between the proprietor and a licensee and the importer has actual or constructive knowledge of the contract.

Singapore has not legislatively provided for indirect or secondary patent infringement. 23
Such matters are to be governed by the common law position on joint tortfeasorship on proof of a common design to procure or actually participate in acts of infringement.[9]

## D. Infringement of second medical use claims and skinny label products

There is no specific judicial guidance on either direct or indirect infringement of 24
second medical use claims in the context of a 'skinny labelled' product in Singapore. To understand what may be considered to be a 'skinny labelled' product, patent infringement and related issues, one should consider the interplay between the Singaporean labelling regulations, the pharmaceutical regulatory approval process and patent linkage scheme, together with leading UK and European authorities.

The regulatory authority for pharmaceutical products in Singapore is the Health Ser- 25
vice Authority (HSA) which is under the auspices of the Singapore Ministry of Health.

As of November 2016, pharmaceutical products have been regulated as 'Therapeutic 26
Products' under the Health Products Act & Regulations, replacing the previous controls under the Medicines Act and the Poisons Act.

[7] [2015] EWCA Civ 556 at para. 118.
[8] [2016] 4 SLR 252 at para. 76.
[9] Leong, Intellectual Property Law of Singapore, Singapore 2013, mn. 19.054.

## I. Labelling requirements

27 Therapeutic products which are registered with the HSA are subject to labelling requirements that are either legislated by law or mandated as per HSA's administrative requirements. Legislated labelling requirements, under the Health Products (Therapeutic Products) Regulations, are subject to HSA's surveillance programme. Administrative labelling requirements, specified in the HSA's 'Guidance on Therapeutic Product Registration in Singapore', are included as part of the product registration application.

28 The requirements for the labelling and presentation of therapeutic products are set out under the Health Products Regulations. The requirements for the packaging and labelling of medicinal products are contained under Part 4 of the Medicines Act and the Medicines (Labelling) Regulations which includes:

> Where a medicinal product is a dispensed medicinal product, the container of the medicinal product shall be labelled to show the following particulars:
> (a) the name of the person to whom the medicinal product is to be administered;
> (b) the name and address of the medical or dental practice, registered pharmacy, hospital or any other institution where the medicinal product is supplied or dispensed and any other identification number or mark;
> (c) the date upon which the medicinal product is dispensed;
> (d) the direction for use of the medicinal product;
> (e) the name of the medicinal product being either the appropriate non-proprietary name or the proprietary designation; and
> (f) where the appropriate non-proprietary name is labelled, the appropriate quantitative particulars of the active ingredients of the medicinal product.

29 From a plain reading of Part 4(d) one cannot derive a requirement to list all known uses of the medicinal product.

30 With that said, the HSA can suspend or cancel the registration of a therapeutic product if it has reasonable grounds to believe that, among others:

- The registration has been obtained by fraud or misrepresentation.
- The registration has breached any provision in the Health Products Act or any condition for registration.
- The formulation, composition, design specification, quality, safety or presentation of the product has changed so that it is unsuitable to continue to be registered.

## II. Patent linkage

31 In *Millennium Pharmaceuticals, Inc v Zyfas Medical Co*[10] the Singapore High Court suggested that it is best for those seeking to register generic versions of pharmaceutical products to disclose *all potentially relevant patents* relating to those products, even if some or all of those patents do not cover the product as such. Disclosure is a requirement under Singapore's patent linkage scheme.

32 The case involved the anticancer proteasome inhibitory drug 'bortezomib'.

33 Millennium were the owner of only process patents directed to bortezomib, and Zyfas did not declare these patents in their patent linkage declaration to the HSA for the registration of a generic version of bortezomib. The registration was subsequently allowed.

34 Bortezomib was not covered by any existing *product* patents in Singapore and Zyfas admitted that they were of the view that only *product* patents had to be declared under

[10] [2020] SGHC 28, summarised in → mn. 125.

the patent linkage provisions of Regulation 23(2) of the Health Products (Therapeutic Products) Regulations 2016.

Millennium requested from the Court a declaration that Zyfas had made a misleading statement. This was granted. Zyfas filed an appeal. **35**

At stake in this case was the potential for Millennium to seek cancellation of Zyfas' product registration. **36**

As stated above the HSA has the discretion to cancel the registration of a therapeutic product if (among other things) it is satisfied that a Court has determined that the declaration made under Regulation 23(2) contains a statement that is false or misleading in a material particular or omits to disclose any matter that is material to the application. **37**

Zyfas conceded that the requirement under Regulation 23(2)(a) to disclose 'whether a patent under the Patents Act is in force in respect of a therapeutic product' included the disclosure of existing process patents in respect of the therapeutic product. This concession appears to have been made in light of the decision of the Court of Appeal in *Millennium Pharmaceuticals, Inc v Drug Houses of Australia Pte Ltd and another appeal*[11] ('*Drug House*'). **38**

Zyfas further accepted that the existence of the *process* patents was 'a matter that [was] material to the defendant's application' under Regulation 24(1)(a)(ii). **39**

Therefore, the only issue for the Court to consider was whether Zyfas had omitted to disclose the existence of the process patents. The answer to this turned on the following question of interpretation: whether an operative omission under Regulation 24(1)(a)(ii) requires that the defendant knowingly or intentionally omits to state the existence of relevant patents. **40**

From a normal reading of Regulation 24 the Court considered that there was nothing requiring mental elements of knowledge or intention. This interpretation was reinforced by the neighbouring provision of Regulation 25 (which deals with offences for making false patent declarations) which uses positive phrases such as 'person knows or has reason to believe is false' and 'intentional suppression'. Incidentally, contravention of Regulation 25 imposes criminal liability. **41**

The appeal was therefore ultimately dismissed with the Court granting Millennium the declaration sought. **42**

This highlights the fatal nature of making false or misleading declarations or omitting to disclose all matter *material* to the application. But what types of patents would be deemed 'material' and should be declared? This threshold test for materiality is somewhat clarified in the *Drug House* case which stated (in relation to the requisite patent linkage declaration): **43**

> he applicant for registration has to declare the patents and then state, among several possibilities, that the patents are invalid and will not be infringed by doing of the act for which the registration of its product is sought. It is then for HSA to decide whether to invoke Regulation 23(5) of the TPR to require the Respondent to serve the requisite notice on the Appellant.

From the above case it would appear that a conservative approach to declaring patents should be adopted, including declaring process, use (second-medical treatment), and formulation patents, which relate to the product to be registered. **44**

The ultimate take home message here is to ensure proper patent due diligence is performed to identify all *potentially* relevant patents and have these declared to the HSA. **45**

As of the writing of this Article the HSA product registration database no longer records the Zyfas registration. **46**

[11] [2019] SGCA 31.

## III. The UK approach to skinny labelling

47 As stated above, should the issue of skinny labelling be raised in a Court proceeding in Singapore, the Singapore Court is likely to seek guidance from UK and European judicial decisions. The leading authority in the UK comes from the Supreme Court in *Generics (UK) Ltd v Warner-Lambert Co LLC*[12], which involved the use of the drug Pregabalin.

48 In an *obiter* decision, the UK Supreme Court considered that there were potentially the following three ways of assessing infringement of Swiss-style use claims in the context of skinny labelling:

### 1. Consideration of the subjective intention

49 At the first instance Arnold J held that 'intention is a subjective state of mind, but it must be objectively assessed and may be inferred from appropriate facts'. In this earlier case the Court concluded there was no infringement because the generic company could not have reasonably foreseen that their generic product would be intentionally administered for the patentee's treatment, save in a small number of exceptional cases which were considered *de minimis*.

50 On Appeal, the two members of the Supreme Court, preferred this test which may be 'proved objectively by words, conduct or even inactivity'. This would include a skinny label as well as other factors demonstrating the manufacturer's actual intention. So in an actual trial one can see that the form of evidence as to the intention of the manufacturer would be important.

### 2. Consideration of the objective intention

51 On Appeal, one of the members of the Supreme Court, rejected the above test, instead favouring the following *objective test:* 'Does the manufacturer know (or could it reasonably foresee) that at least *some* of the medicament will intentionally be used to treat the patented indication?' The members went on to stipulate that the absence of the patented indication from the label cannot conceivably be sufficient to negate the intention, and that the generic manufacturer must take all reasonable steps within his power to prevent the infringing use. Those steps may include writing to pharmacists and doctors advising them to not to prescribe the generic for the patented indication, positively promoting the patentee's use of the drug for the patented use, and the like.

### 3. Consideration of the outward presentation

52 Two other members of the Supreme Court preferred an *'outward presentation test'*, which assesses the physical characteristics of the product as it emerges from the manufacturing process. This includes the dosage, formulation, packaging and labelling. Therefore, as long as the manufacturer ensures that the patented indication is absent from the product it will not infringe. That is, *a 'skinny label' is enough to avoid infringement.* Based upon this test, while the physical characteristics of the product are determinative of the issue of infringement, a Court will still carefully scrutinise for situations where the outward presentation of the product is deemed disingenuous (i.e., a 'charade').

53 Singapore Courts are likely to consider similar issues.

---

[12] [2018] UKSC 56; → § 13 mn. 19.

## E. Infringement of second medical use claims and biosimilar products

Whilst there is no case law that has addressed this position specifically to biosimilar products, we consider that biosimilar products are likely to treated in a similar manner to non-biological pharmaceuticals. The requirements for the packaging and labelling of medicinal products as contained under Part 4 of the Medicines Act and the Medicines (Labelling) Regulations which have been discussed above refers to all medicinal products which would include biosimilar products. 54

## F. Strategies and considerations

Generic or biosimilar manufacturers should steer clear of labelling pharmaceutical products for indications which are still validly protected via second medical use claims. For example, as part of the drug registration process in Singapore, under a patent linkage system, generic or biosimilar manufacturers are required to identify patents which are currently in force in Singapore. If patents with second medical use claims are in force, generic or biosimilar manufacturers should take precaution to not label their products with these indications. Additionally, generic or biosimilar manufacturers should ensure that their marketing materials do not mentions or suggests the patented use, and sales representatives should not to be marketing the pharmaceutical product for the patented use. 55

## G. Legal remedies

Under section 67(1) Singapore Patents Act, the following remedies are available in respect of a patent infringement: 56

(a) An injunction to stop the infringer from committing acts of patent infringement. This is a valuable tool to immediately restrain the alleged infringer from infringing your patent any further.
(b) An order to deliver up and destroy any patented product material or Article that infringe upon your patent.
(c) Damages from the infringement.
(d) An account of profits from the infringement, where the amount awarded takes into account the amount of profit the infringer has made from infringing your patent, rather than any loss suffered by you, as the patent owner.
(e) A declaration that the patent is valid and has been infringed by the alleged infringer. This provides the patent owner with certainty of his patent rights and a freedom to operate within the scope of the patent.

For the same infringement, the court can order either damages or an account for profits, but not both. The rationale for this is to prevent double recovery and to prevent recovery of more than what the patent owner had lost as a result of the infringement. 57

58 Apart from damages and an account of profits, the other remedies may be awarded jointly by the courts.

59 The standard of proof in such proceedings is the 'balance of probabilities' standard.

60 In infringement proceedings, the burden of proof is on the patent proprietor to prove infringement based on the above standard. However, the burden is reversed if the patent is a process for obtaining a new product. Thus the burden of proving that a product is new and not made by the process may lie with the alleged infringer if there is a substantial likelihood that the product was made by the process and the patent proprietor has been unable, through reasonable efforts, to verify the process actually used.

61 At the commencement of invalidity proceedings, the initial burden is on the party seeking invalidation to prove that the patent is invalid to the required standard. Mere assertions made by either an attorney and/or expert witness may be deemed insufficient to discharge the burden of proof to establish one or more grounds of invalidity.

62 Singapore courts typically deal with both infringement and validity together, unless one party applies to have separate proceedings. The validity of a patent is typically raised either as a counterclaim in infringement proceedings or in an action for a declaration of non-infringement. The damages inquiry is almost always heard separately, and only after patent infringement is established.

63 The defence of innocent infringement has consequences on the quantum of damages and account of profits, but not on liability for infringement.

64 Despite being statute-based, equitable defences, such as laches and estoppel, can be raised by a defendant.

65 Furthermore one may argue a 'prior user', either in the form of arguing the practice of the prior art (i.e. *Gillette* defence) or as part of a novelty attack.

66 One should also keep in mind that there is a six year statute of limitations calculated from the date of the *last* alleged act of infringement.

67 It is also possible for one to request that a Singapore Court or IPOS issue a declaration of non-infringement (whether on grounds of absence of factual or technical infringement, or by reason of invalidity or unenforceability of the subject patent).

## I. The patent litigation process

### 1. Overview

68 The proceedings in a patent trial are prescribed in Order 35 of the Rules of Court, which are designed to enable the parties to produce evidence (in the form of affidavits) in support of their respective claims.

69 Patent infringement proceedings are initiated by filing a writ of summons in a manner which follows UK procedures.

70 The claimant must also file a statement of claim, setting out its claims against the defendant. The defendant must then file its defence and any counterclaim against the claimant.

71 The process for discovery and exchange of affidavit evidence follows and once completed, parties and the court can set a trial date, where the matter will be substantively presented by the parties and examined by the Court. Disputed issues are decided by a judge, and not by jury. There is no independent patent court as there is usually only a handful of patent cases tried per year in Singapore.

72 A patent infringement trial typically lasts between 18 and 24 months, depending on the complexity of the case.

## 2. Preliminary injunctions and fast-track trials

The fast-tracking of the trial procedures are typically not available for patent proceedings. Nevertheless, one of the parties may apply for the proceedings to be heard on an expedited basis. An expedited trial is possible where *both* parties agree to resolve the issue of patent validity and infringement separately, or where the parties come to an agreement and proceed to trial on a limited set of disputed facts or law. **73**

A preliminary injunction shall granted if the following conditions are met: **74**

1. Existence of a serious question to be tried;
2. If the claimant subsequently succeeds in establishing a right to a permanent injunction, it would not be adequately compensated by an award of damages for the loss sustained in the meantime if a preliminary injunction is not awarded; and
3. The balance of convenience lies in favour of granting the injunction.

Thus in order to obtain a preliminary injunction, the claimant must satisfy the court that it has a serious issue to be tried, and that the balance of convenience favours the granting of an injunction. **75**

To establish that there is a serious issue to be tried, the claimant must demonstrate that it has a real and credible case. If there is a counterclaim for invalidity, the claimant must also address the defendant's invalidity arguments. **76**

In considering the balance of convenience, a court considers any harm which may be suffered by the claimant if the preliminary injunction is not granted relative to the harm that may be suffered by the defendant. One of the main factors which will be considered is whether any financial compensation will be an adequate remedy if infringement is later established. **77**

An application for the grant of an injunction can be made *ex parte* in cases of urgency. **78**

Preliminary injunction proceedings usually last between one and two months. **79**

# II. Alternative dispute resolution

While legal remedies are available to the patentee, Singapore encourages patentees and other involved parties to consider alternative dispute resolution such as negotiation, mediation, expert determination and arbitration as time and cost-effective alternatives to litigation. In fact, Singapore is increasingly being recognised as a hub for alternative dispute resolution, and in a 2021 survey, Singapore tied with London as a top location for arbitration globally.[13] **80**

In mediation, a mediator facilitates the discussions between the opposing parties. The mediator does not make a decision, but instead the parties will have to reach an agreement between themselves. In Singapore, mediation may be facilitated at the Singapore Mediation Centre or Singapore International Mediation Centre. **81**

In arbitration, an arbitrator decides on the issues in dispute based on the appropriate legal texts, and such a decision is binding on all parties in the arbitration. In Singapore arbitration may be conducted at the Singapore International Arbitration Centre. **82**

---

[13] 2021 International Arbitration Survey: Adapting arbitration to a changing world. White & Case LLP, Queen Mary University of London.

## H. Statutory provisions

## Singapore Patents Act 1994[14]

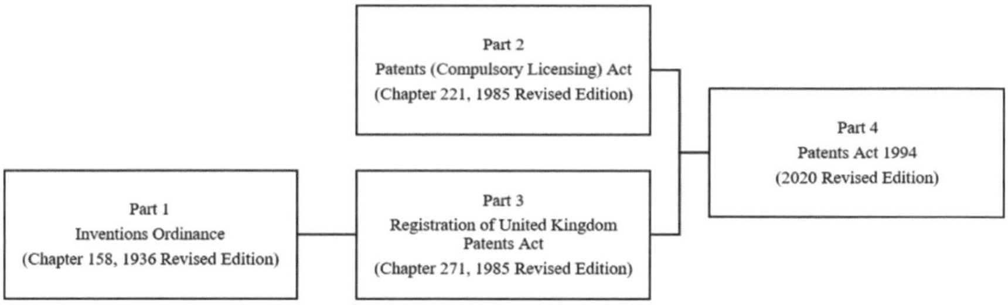


**Overview of Predecessor Acts**

83 **Section 13. Patentable inventions**

(1) Subject to subsection (2), a patentable invention is one that satisfies the following conditions:

(a) the invention is new;
(b) it involves an inventive step; and
(c) it is capable of industrial application.

(2) An invention the publication or exploitation of which would be generally expected to encourage offensive, immoral or anti-social behaviour is not a patentable invention.

(3) For the purposes of subsection (2), behaviour is not to be regarded as offensive, immoral or anti-social only because it is prohibited by any law in force in Singapore.

84 **Section 14. Novelty**

(1) An invention is taken to be new if it does not form part of the state of the art.

(2) The state of the art in the case of an invention is taken to comprise all matter (whether a product, a process, information about either, or anything else) which has at any time before the priority date of that invention been made available to the public (whether in Singapore or elsewhere) by written or oral description, by use or in any other way.

(3) The state of the art in the case of an invention to which an application for a patent or a patent relates is taken also to comprise matter contained in an application for another patent which was published on or after the priority date of that invention, if the following conditions are satisfied:

(a) that matter was contained in the application for that other patent both as filed and as published; and
(b) the priority date of that matter is earlier than that of the invention.

(4) For the purposes of this section, the disclosure of matter constituting an invention is to be disregarded in the case of a patent or an application for a patent if occurring later than the beginning of the period of 12 months immediately preceding the date of filing the application for the patent and either —

(a) the disclosure was due to, or made in consequence of, the matter having been obtained unlawfully or in breach of confidence by any person —
(i) from the inventor or from any other person to whom the matter was made available in confidence by the inventor or who obtained it from the inventor because

[14] Link to consolidated legal text: https://sso.agc.gov.sg/Act/PA1994.

the other person or the inventor believed that the other person was entitled to obtain it; or

(ii) from any other person (A) to whom the matter was made available in confidence by any person mentioned in sub paragraph (i) or in this sub paragraph or who obtained it from any person so mentioned because A or the person from whom A obtained it believed that A was entitled to obtain it;

(b) the disclosure was made in breach of confidence by any person who obtained the matter in confidence from the inventor or from any other person to whom it was made available, or who obtained it, from the inventor;

(c) the disclosure was due to, or made in consequence of, the inventor displaying the invention at an international exhibition;

(d) the disclosure was due to, or made in consequence of, the inventor describing the invention in a paper read by the inventor or another person with the inventor's consent or on the inventor's behalf before any learned society or published with the inventor's consent in the transactions of any learned society; or

(e) subject to subsections (6) and (7), the disclosure was made to the public by the inventor, or by a person who obtained the matter directly or indirectly from the inventor, in any circumstances not described in paragraphs (a) to (d)

(10) In the case of an invention consisting of a substance or composition for use in a method of treatment of the human or animal body by surgery or therapy or of diagnosis practised on the human or animal body, the fact that the substance or composition forms part of the state of the art does not prevent the invention from being taken to be new if the use of the substance or composition in any such method does not form part of the state of the art.

## Section 16. Industrial application 85

(1) Subject to subsection (2), an invention is taken to be capable of industrial application if it can be made or used in any kind of industry, including agriculture.

(2) An invention of a method of treatment of the human or animal body by surgery or therapy or of diagnosis practised on the human or animal body is not taken to be capable of industrial application.

(3) Subsection (2) does not prevent a product consisting of a substance or composition from being treated as capable of industrial application merely because it is invented for use in any such method.

## Section 36 A. Extension of term of patent 86

(1) The proprietor of a patent may apply to the Registrar to extend the term of the patent on any of the following grounds:

(a) that there was an unreasonable delay by the Registrar in granting the patent;

(b) where the patent was granted on the basis of any prescribed documents referred to in section 29(1)(d) relating to one corresponding application or related national phase application, that —

(i) there was an unreasonable delay in the issue of the corresponding patent or related national phase patent (as the case may be); and

(ii) the patent office that granted the corresponding patent or related national phase patent (as the case may be) has extended the term of the corresponding patent or related national phase patent (as the case may be) on the basis of such delay;

(c) where the subject of the patent includes any substance which is an active ingredient of any pharmaceutical product, that —

(i) there was an unreasonable curtailment of the opportunity to exploit the patent caused by the process of obtaining marketing approval for a pharmaceutical product, being the first pharmaceutical product to obtain marketing approval which uses the substance as an active ingredient; and

(ii) the term of the patent has not previously been extended on this ground.

(2) A delay by the Registrar in granting a patent is not treated as an unreasonable delay under subsection (1)(a) unless such requirements as may be prescribed are satisfied.

(3) Where the proprietor of a patent has made an application under subsection (1)(a) and has satisfied the Registrar that there was in fact a particular type of unreasonable delay by the Registrar in granting the patent, the Registrar must extend the term of the patent by such period as may be prescribed for that type of unreasonable delay.

(4) Where the proprietor of a patent has made an application under subsection (1)(b) and has satisfied the Registrar of the matters referred to in sub-paragraphs (i) and (ii) of subsection (1)(b), the Registrar may, if the Registrar thinks fit, extend the term of the patent by such period, not exceeding 5 years, as the Registrar may determine.

(5) A curtailment of the opportunity to exploit a patent, the subject of which includes a substance which is an active ingredient of any pharmaceutical product, caused by the process of obtaining marketing approval for a pharmaceutical product, being the first pharmaceutical product to obtain marketing approval which uses the substance as an active ingredient, is not treated as an unreasonable curtailment under subsection (1)(c) unless such requirements as may be prescribed are satisfied.

(6) Subject to subsections (7), (8) and (9), where the proprietor of a patent has made an application under subsection (1)(c) and has satisfied the Registrar that there was in fact an unreasonable curtailment of the opportunity to exploit the patent under subsection (1)(c), the Registrar must extend the term of the patent by such period as may be prescribed.

(7) The Registrar must not extend the term of the patent under subsection (6) unless the applicant has procured and submitted to the Registrar a certificate from the relevant authority stating such matters as may be prescribed.

(8) In determining the period by which to extend the term of the patent under subsection (6), the Registrar must rely on, and is not concerned to inquire into the truth of, the statements contained in the certificate from the relevant authority under subsection (7).

(9) Where the term of a patent has been extended under subsection (6), the protection conferred by the patent during the term of the extension applies only to the substance mentioned in subsection (1)(c).

87

## Section 66. Infringement of Patents

(1) Subject to the provisions of this Act, a person infringes a patent for an invention if, but only if, while the patent is in force, the person does any of the following things in Singapore in relation to the invention without the consent of the proprietor of the patent:

(a) where the invention is a product, the person makes, disposes of, offers to dispose of, uses or imports the product or keeps it whether for disposal or otherwise;

(b) where the invention is a process, the person uses the process or the person offers it for use in Singapore when the person knows, or it is obvious to a reasonable person in the circumstances, that its use without the consent of the proprietor would be an infringement of the patent;

(c) where the invention is a process, the person disposes of, offers to dispose of, uses or imports any product obtained directly by means of that process or keeps any such product whether for disposal or otherwise.

(2) An act which, apart from this subsection, would constitute an infringement of a patent for an invention is not an infringement of a patent if —

(a) it is done privately and for purposes which are not commercial;

(b) it is done for experimental purposes relating to the subject matter of the invention;

(c) it consists of the extemporaneous preparation of a medicine for an individual in accordance with a prescription given by a registered medical or dental practitioner or consists of dealing with a medicine so prepared;

(d) it consists of the use of a product or process in the body or operation of a relevant aircraft, hovercraft or vehicle which has temporarily or accidentally entered or is crossing Singapore (including the airspace above it and its territorial waters) or the use of accessories for such a relevant aircraft, hovercraft or vehicle;
(e) it consists of the use, exclusively for the needs of a relevant ship, of a product or process in the body of the ship or in its machinery, tackle, apparatus or other accessories, in a case where the ship has temporarily or accidentally entered the territorial waters of Singapore;
(f) it consists of the use of an exempted aircraft which has lawfully entered or is lawfully crossing Singapore as mentioned in paragraph (d) or of the importation into Singapore, or the use or storage, of any part or accessory for that aircraft;
(g) subject to subsections (3) and (6), it consists of the import, use or disposal of, or the offer to dispose of, any patented product or any product obtained by means of a patented process or to which a patented process has been applied, which is produced by or with the consent (conditional or otherwise) of the proprietor of the patent or any person licensed by the proprietor, and for this purpose 'patent' includes a patent granted in any country outside Singapore in respect of the same or substantially the same invention as that for which a patent is granted under this Act and 'patented product', 'patented process' and 'licensed' are to be construed accordingly;
(h) it consists of the doing of any thing set out in subsection (1) in relation to the subject matter of the patent to support any application for marketing approval for a pharmaceutical product, provided that any thing produced to support the application is not —
  (i) made, used or sold in Singapore; or
  (ii) exported outside Singapore,
  other than for purposes related to meeting the requirements for marketing approval for that pharmaceutical product; or
(i) subject to subsection (6), it consists of the import, disposal or offer to dispose of a patented pharmaceutical product for use by or on a specific patient in Singapore, or the use of that product by or on that patient, where
  (i) that product is required for use by or on that patient;
  (ii) the relevant authority has granted approval specifically for the import of that product for use by or on that patient; and
  (iii) that product was produced by or with the consent (conditional or otherwise) of the proprietor of the patent or any person licensed by the proprietor (and for this purpose 'patent' includes a patent granted in any country outside Singapore in respect of the same or substantially the same product and 'licensed' is to be construed accordingly).

(3) Subsection (2)(g) does not apply to the import of any patented pharmaceutical product by any person (called in this subsection and subsection (4) the importer) if —

(a) the product has not previously been sold or distributed in Singapore by or with the consent (conditional or otherwise) of the proprietor of the patent or any person licensed by the proprietor of the patent to sell or distribute the product in Singapore;
(b) the import of the product by the importer would result in the product being distributed in breach of a contract between —
  (i) the proprietor of the patent; and
  (ii) any person licensed by the proprietor of the patent to distribute the product outside Singapore; and
(c) the importer has actual or constructive knowledge of the matters referred to in paragraph (b).

88 **Section 67. Proceedings for infringement of patent**

(1) Subject to this Part, civil proceedings may be brought in the court by the proprietor of a patent in respect of any act alleged to infringe the patent and (without prejudice to any other jurisdiction of the court) in those proceedings a claim may be made —

(a) for an injunction restraining the defendant from any apprehended act of infringement;

(b) for an order for the defendant to deliver up or destroy any patented product in relation to which the patent is infringed or any Article in which that product is inextricably comprised or any material and implement the predominant use of which has been in the creation of the infringing product;

(c) for damages in respect of the infringement;

(d) for an account of the profits derived by the defendant from the infringement; and

(e) for a declaration that the patent is valid and has been infringed by the defendant.

(2) The court must not, in respect of the same infringement, both award the proprietor of a patent damages and order that the proprietor be given an account of the profits.

(3) In this Act, unless the context otherwise requires, any reference to a claimant includes a reference to the proprietor of the patent.

(6) Subject to this Part, in determining whether or not to grant any kind of relief claimed under this section and the extent of the relief granted, the court must apply the principles applied by the court in relation to that kind of relief immediately before 23 February 1995.

89 **Section 68. Reversal of burden of proof**

(1) In any proceedings for the infringement of a patent, where the subject matter of the patent is a process for obtaining a new product, the burden of proving that a product is not made by the process is on the alleged infringer if the product is new or a substantial likelihood exists that the product is made by the process and the proprietor of the patent has been unable through reasonable efforts to determine the process actually used.

(2) In considering whether a party has discharged the burden imposed upon the party by this section, the court is not to require the party to disclose any manufacturing or commercial secret if it appears to the court that it would be unreasonable to do so.

90 **Section 69. Restrictions on relief for infringement**

(1) In proceedings for infringement of a patent, damages must not be awarded and no order may be made for an account of profits against a defendant who proves that at the date of the infringement the defendant was not aware, and had no reasonable grounds for supposing, that the patent existed.

(2) A person is not to be taken to have been aware or to have had reasonable grounds for supposing by reason only of the application to a product of the word 'patent' or 'patented', or any word or words expressing or implying that a patent has been obtained for the product, unless the number of the patent accompanied the word or words.

(3) In proceedings for infringement of a patent, the court may, if the court thinks fit, refuse to award any damages, make an order for an account of profits or grant any other relief (including an injunction) in respect of an infringement committed during the period prescribed under section 36(3), but before the payment of the renewal fee and any additional fee prescribed for the purposes of section 36(3).

(4) Where an amendment of the specification of a patent has been allowed under any of the provisions of this Act, the court must not, in proceedings for an infringement of the patent committed before the decision to allow the amendment, award any damages, make an order for an account of profits or grant any other relief (including an injunction) unless the court is satisfied that the specification of the patent as published was framed in good faith and with reasonable skill and knowledge.

### Section 80. Power to revoke patents on application 91

(1) Subject to the provisions of this Act, the court or the Registrar may, on the application of any person, by order revoke a patent for an invention on (but only on) any of the following grounds:

(a) the invention is not a patentable invention;

(b) the patent was granted to a person who was not entitled (either alone or with other persons) to be granted that patent;

(c) the specification of the patent does not disclose the invention clearly and completely for it to be performed by a person skilled in the art;

(d) the matter disclosed in the specification of the patent extends beyond that disclosed —

(i) in the application for the patent, as filed; or

(ii) where the patent was granted on a new application filed under section 20(3) or 47(4) or section 116(6) of the Patents Act (Cap. 221, 1995 Revised Edition), or in accordance with section 26(11), in —

(A) the earlier application made under this Act;

(B) the application made under the United Kingdom Patents Act 1977; or

(C) the application under the European Patent Convention designating the United Kingdom filed at the European Patent Office,

(as the case may be) from which the filing date and the right of priority has been derived, as filed;

(e) an amendment or a correction has been made to the specification of —

(i) the patent; or

(ii) the application for the patent,

which should not have been allowed;

(f) the patent was obtained —

(i) fraudulently;

(ii) on any misrepresentation; or

(iii) on any non-disclosure or inaccurate disclosure of any prescribed material information, whether or not the person under a duty to provide the information knew or ought reasonably to have known of such information or the inaccuracy;

(g) the patent is one of 2 or more patents for the same invention having the same priority date and filed by the same party or the party's successor in title.

(2) On the application of any person for an order to revoke a patent on any of the grounds specified in subsection (1)(a), (c), (d) and (e), the court or the Registrar may, subject to subsection (3), cause the patent to be re-examined by an Examiner so as to determine whether the patent should be revoked on any of those grounds and require the applicant to pay the prescribed re-examination fee.

(3) The court or the Registrar must not cause a patent to be re-examined under subsection (2) where, within the prescribed period, the applicant for the revocation of the patent fails to give such security for the costs or expenses of the proceedings as the court or the Registrar may specify; in which case, the application for revocation is treated as having been abandoned.

(4) An application for the revocation of a patent on the ground mentioned in subsection (1)(b) —

(a) may only be made by a person found by the court in an action for a declaration or found by the court or the Registrar on a reference under section 47, to be entitled to be granted that patent or to be granted a patent for part of the matter comprised in the specification of the patent sought to be revoked; and

(b) may not be made if that action was commenced or that reference was made after the end of the period of 2 years beginning with the date of the grant of the patent sought to be revoked, unless it is shown that any person registered as a proprietor of the patent knew at the time of the grant or of the transfer of the patent to the person that the person was not entitled (either alone or with other persons, as the case may be) to the patent.

(5) An order under this section may be —

(a) an order for the unconditional revocation of the patent; or

(b) where one of the grounds mentioned in subsection (1) has been established, but only so as to invalidate the patent to a limited extent, an order that the patent should be revoked unless within a specified time the specification is amended under section 83 to the satisfaction of the court or the Registrar, as the case may be.

(6) A decision of the Registrar or on appeal from the Registrar does not estop any party to any civil proceedings in which infringement of a patent is in issue from alleging invalidity of the patent on any of the grounds mentioned in subsection (1), whether or not any of the issues involved were decided in the decision.

(7) An order under this section revoking a patent has effect from the date of the grant of the patent.

(8) Where an applicant for the revocation of a patent discontinues or withdraws the application, the applicant must pay such costs or expenses of the proceedings as the court or the Registrar may determine.

(9) An application to the Registrar for an order to revoke a patent must be —

(a) made in the prescribed form and filed at the Registry in the prescribed manner; and

(b) accompanied by the prescribed fee.

(10) Section 92 does not apply in relation to the decision of the Registrar to cause a patent to be re-examined under this section.

(11) Where an application is made to the Registrar under this section, the Registrar may at any stage of the proceedings refer the application to the court.

92 **Section 81. Registrar's power to revoke patents on own initiative**

If it appears to the Registrar that an invention for which a patent has been granted formed part of the state of the art by virtue only of section 14(3), the Registrar may on the Registrar's own initiative by order revoke the patent, but must not do so without giving the proprietor of the patent an opportunity of making any observation and of amending the specification of the patent so as to exclude any matter which formed part of the state of the art as aforesaid without contravening section 84.

93 **Section 82. Proceedings in which validity of patent may be put in issue**

(1) Subject to this section, the validity of a patent may be put in issue —

(aa) in a request for re-examination of the specification of a patent under section 38 A;

(a) by way of defence, in proceedings for infringement of the patent under section 67 or proceedings under section 76 for infringement of rights conferred by the publication of an application;

(b) in proceedings under section 77;

(c) in proceedings in which a declaration in relation to the patent is sought under section 78;

(d) in proceedings before the court or the Registrar under section 80 for the revocation of the patent; or

(e) in proceedings under section 56 or 58.

(2) The validity of a patent may not be put in issue in any other proceedings and, in particular, no proceedings may be instituted (whether under this Act or otherwise) seeking only a declaration as to the validity or invalidity of a patent.

(3) The only grounds on which the validity of a patent may be put in issue (whether in proceedings for revocation under section 80 or otherwise) are the grounds on which the patent may be revoked under that section.

(4) No determination may be made in any proceedings mentioned in subsection (1) on the validity of a patent which any person puts in issue on the ground mentioned in section 80(1)(b) unless —

(a) it has been determined in entitlement proceedings commenced by that person or in the proceedings in which the validity of the patent is in issue that the patent should have been granted to that person and not some other person; and

(b) except where it has been so determined in entitlement proceedings, the proceedings in which the validity of the patent is in issue are commenced before the end of the period of 2 years beginning with the date of the grant of the patent or it is shown that any person registered as a proprietor of the patent knew at the time of the grant or of the transfer of the patent to the person that he or she was not entitled (either alone or with other persons, as the case may be) to the patent.

(5) Where the validity of a patent is put in issue by way of defence or counterclaim, the court or the Registrar must, if the court or Registrar thinks it just to do so, give the defendant an opportunity to comply with the condition in subsection (4)(a).

(6) In subsection (4), 'entitlement proceedings', in relation to a patent, means a reference under section 47(1) on the ground that the patent was granted to a person not entitled (either alone or with other persons) to it or proceedings for a declaration that it was so granted.

(7) Where proceedings with respect to a patent are pending in the court under any provision of this Act mentioned in subsection (1), no proceedings may be instituted without the permission of the court before the Registrar with respect to that patent under section 80.

(8) For the purposes of this Act, the validity of a patent is not put in issue merely because the Registrar is considering its validity in order to decide whether to revoke it under section 81.

### Section 89. Proceedings before Court or Registrar 94

(1) Any proceedings before the court relating to patents and other matters under this Act are to be dealt with by a judge sitting alone or, if the judge thinks fit, with one or more scientific advisers selected by the judge from the panel appointed under subsection (2).

(2) Rules under this Act may make provision for the appointment of a panel of scientific advisers to assist the court and the Registrar in proceedings under this Act, for regulating the functions of such advisers and for remunerating such advisers.

### Section 90. Appeals from Registrar 95

(1) An appeal shall lie to the court from any decision of the Registrar under this Act or the rules except any of the following decisions:

(a) a decision falling within section 25(7);

(b) a decision under section 27(3) to omit any matter from a specification;

(c) a decision to give directions under section 33(1) or (2);

(ca) a decision under section 38 A(4) not to grant a request for re-examination;

(cb) a decision under section 38 A not to revoke a patent;

(d) a decision under the rules which is excepted by the rules from the right of appeal conferred by this section.

(2) For the purpose of hearing appeals under this section, the court may consist of one or more judges of the court in accordance with directions given by or on behalf of the Chief Justice.

(3) An appeal shall not lie to the appellate court from a decision of the court on appeal from a decision of the Registrar under this Act or the rules —

(a) except where the decision of the Registrar was given under section 20, 38, 47, 80, 81 or 83, or was a decision to revoke a patent given under section 38 A; or

(b) except where the ground of appeal is that the decision of the court is wrong in law, but an appeal shall only lie to the appellate court under this section if permission to appeal is given by the appellate court.

(4) In this section, 'appellate court' means the appellate court to which an appeal under subsection (3) is to be made under section 29C of the Supreme Court of Judicature Act 1969.

96 **Section 91. General powers of court**

(1) The court may, for the purpose of determining any question in the exercise of its original or appellate jurisdiction under this Act, make any order or exercise any other power which the Registrar could have made or exercised for the purpose of determining that question.

(2) In all proceedings before the court under this Act, the costs of the Registrar are in the discretion of the court, but the Registrar is not to be ordered to pay the costs of any other of the parties.

## J. Summaries of court decisions

### I. *V-Pile Technology (Luxembourg) SA & Ors v Peck Brothers Construction Pte Ltd*[15]

97 The courts applied the Windsurfer test for assessing inventive step, and this has been the test used by the courts ever since.

### II. *Merck & Co, Inc v Pharmaforte Singapore Pte Ltd*[16]

98 The courts applied the General Tire test for determining prior disclosure – 'planting the flag'.

### III. *Genelabs Diagnostics Pte Ltd v Institut Pasteur & Anor*[17]

99 The courts agreed that the assessment of inventive step is 'a qualitative not a quantitative test'.

100 With regard to an extent of sufficiency required for a patent specification, the courts have adopted a view that 'disclosure of an invention does not have to be complete in every detail, so that anyone, whether skilled or not, can perform it. Since the specification is addressed to the skilled man, it is sufficient if the addressee can understand the invention as described, and can then perform it. In performing the invention the skilled man does not have to be told what is self-evident, or what is part of common general knowledge, that is to say, what is known to persons versed in the art.'

---

15 [2000] 3 SLR 358.
16 [2000] 3 SLR 717; [2002] 2 SLR 515.
17 [2000] SGHC 53; [2001] 1 SLR 121.

## IV. *Bean Innovations Pte Ltd & Another v Flexon Pte Ltd*[18]

The courts clarified how the groundless threats provision can be applied. **101**

With regard to claim construction, the courts agrees that 'one must not adhere too strictly to the literal wordings of the claim. A purposive construction is to be adopted'. **102**

## V. *Ng Kok Cheng v Chua Say Tiong*[19]

The courts agree that 'commercial success is not conclusive of non-obviousness of invention, but goes some way towards establishing that the invention is not obvious'. **103**

The following indicators of a skilled person in the art have also been followed: **104**

- possesses common general knowledge of the subject matter in question;
- has a practical interest in the subject matter of the patent or is likely to act on the directions given in it; and
- whilst unimaginative is reasonably intelligent and wishes to make the directions in the patent work.

## VI. *Peng Lian Trading Co v Contour Optik Inc & Ors*[20]

The courts affirmatively agrees that 'ex post facto analysis can often be unfair to inventors'. **105**

## VII. *FE Global Electronics Pte Ltd and Others v Trek Technology (Singapore) Pte Ltd and Another Appeal*[21]

The courts relied on the following test to determine added matter: **106**

- To ascertain through the eyes of the skilled addressee what is disclosed, both explicitly or implicitly in the application.
- To do the same in respect of the patent as granted.
- To compare the two disclosures and decide whether any subject matter relevant to the invention has been added whether by deletion or addition. The comparison is strict in the sense that subject matter will be added unless such matter is clearly and unambiguously disclosed in the application either explicitly or implicitly.

The courts also clarified that 'misrepresentation must be material so as to revoke a patent'. **107**

Furthermore, in order to minimise issues during post-grant amendment requests, the courts suggests that 'a patentee ought to act expeditiously from the time he discovers the relevant prior art. The patentee seeking leave to amend must satisfy the court, based on the facts and circumstances, that the patentee acted reasonably and without undue delay'. **108**

---

18 [2001] 2 SLR (R) 116; [2001] SGCA 42.

19 [2001] 3 SLR 487.

20 [2002] SGHC 238; [2003] SGCA 25.

21 [2006] 1 SLR 874; [2005] SGCA 55.

## VIII. *Main-Line Corporate Holdings Limited v United Overseas Bank Limited and First Currency Choice Pte Ltd (First Currency Choice Pte Ltd, Third Party)*[22]

**109** The courts upheld the validity of a business method patent.

**110** However, this may not be binding in the future as during proceedings for the case, the issue of whether business methods fall within patentable subject matter was not raised for consideration by the courts.

## IX. *Muhlbauer AG v Manufacturing Integration Technology Ltd*[23]

**111** The courts expressed some scepticism with regard to experts' testimonies – 'one cannot be faulted for taking the views just expressed, with respect to an expert's duty to the court and to justice, with the proverbial pinch of salt, especially when one views this proposition through the lenses of practical reality.'

## X. *Dien Ghin Electronic (s) Pte Ltd v Khek Tai Ting (trading as Soon Heng Digitax)*[24]

**112** The courts highlighted the practice of defining claims scope using actual products to be undesirable, specifically mentioning that 'courts should therefore be critical of attempts by patentees to limit, ex post facto, the scope of their patent claims by conflating their actual manufactured products with their patent claims, in order to avoid invalidation on the ground of anticipation by the prior art'.

## XI. *Martek Biosciences Corporation v Cargill International Trading Pte Ltd*[25]

**113** The courts confirmed that a post-grant re-examination report is not binding.

## XII. *Main-Line Corporate Holdings Limited v DBS Bank Limited*[26]

**114** The courts clarified that 'at best, the reasons of the EPO for coming to a particular conclusion may only be said to be of persuasive value to our courts'.

**115** Further clarification in this regard was provided by the courts with the following statement – 'for all intents and purposes, decisions of the House of Lords (and now, the UK Supreme Court) continue to bind lower courts, regardless of any EPO decision. Likewise, in the present case, this court continues to be bound by the UOB Court of Appeal decision'.

---

[22] [2010] 1 SLR 189; [2009] SGHC 232.
[23] [2010] SGCA 6.
[24] [2011] SGHC 36.
[25] [2012] SGHC 35.
[26] [2012] SGHC 147.

## XIII. *Novartis AG and another v Ranbaxy (Malaysia) Sdn Bhd*[27]

The courts agree that 'patent attorneys with specialisations in relation to certain types of inventions are capable of assisting the court in relation to the disclosures made in patent specifications, on the construction of the ambit of the claims, and on their experience concerning the relevant art'. **116**

## XIV. *Ship's Equipment Centre Bremen GmbH v Fuji Trading (Singapore) Pte Ltd and others and another suit*[28]

The courts asked the following questions when deciding whether or not to allow post-grant amendments: **117**

- To determine if the patentee had disclosed all relevant matters pertaining to the desired amendment(s).
- To determine if the amendment(s) met requirements of the Act.
- To determine if the amendment(s) were sought promptly (no unreasonable delay).
- To determine if the patentee gained an unfair advantage by delaying the amendment(s).
- To determine if the conduct of the patentee was reasonable regardless of the merit of the invention.

## XV. *Warner-Lambert Company LLC v Novartis (Singapore) Pte Ltd*[29]

The courts made a determination on the allowability of post-grant amendments from claims of method of medical treatment to Swiss-style claims. **118**

The courts emphasised that an objection based on 'additional matter' was not the same as an objection based on 'extension of protection'. **119**

The courts concluded that an amendment from a method of treatment claim to a Swiss-style claim did not create or disclose any 'added matter'. **120**

The courts gave effect to the words in the Swiss-style claim 'in the preparation of a medicament' such that it was necessary to avoid the method of treatment exclusion. However, the courts considered that the manufacture/preparation of a medicament is not an activity which falls within the ambit of method of treatment claims and that the proposed amendments would therefore have the effect of extending the protection conferred by the patent and should not be allowed. **121**

## XVI. *National University Hospital (Singapore) Pte Ltd v Cicada Cube Pte Ltd*[30]*; Cicada Cube Pte Ltd v National University Hospital (Singapore) Pte Ltd*[31]

The dispute relates to who is the actual inventors and owners of the patent. The courts systematically addressed the issues as follows: **122**

[27] [2012] SGHC 253.
[28] [2015] SGHC 159.
[29] [2016] SGHC 106.
[30] [2017] SGHC 53.
[31] [2018] SGCA 52.

- identifying the inventive concepts;
- who contributed to the inventive concepts; and
- who is the rightful owner of the Patent.

123 The courts also highlighted that an application for post-grant challenges to patent entitlement should be applied to the High Court or at the Registrar within 2 years of the grant of the patent. Failing to do so will result in the application being time-barred, unless it could be shown that the registered proprietor knew at the time of the grant that it was not entitled to the patent.

## XVII. *Novartis (Singapore) Pte Ltd v Bristol-Myers Squibb Pharma Co*[32]

124 It was held that while there is no time-bar for making a request for correction of an error in a form, if the request is in relation to correction of a priority claim and is made after publication of the application, it will need to be supported by exceptional grounds.

## XVIII. *Millennium Pharmaceuticals, Inc v Zyfas Medical Co*[33]

125 The courts suggests that it is best for those seeking to register generic versions of pharmaceutical products to disclose all potentially relevant patents relating to those products, even if some or all of those patents do not cover the product as such.

## XIX. *IIa Technologies Pte Ltd v Element Six Technologies Ltd*[34]

126 The courts sets out the requirements for sufficiency of a patent specification. In particular, the burden of proving insufficiency rests on the party challenging the validity of a registered patent, and the assessment of sufficiency proceeds in two steps:

- identifying the invention and decides what it claims to enable a person skilled in the art (PSA) to do, and
- to ask whether the specification enables him to do it over the full breadth of the monopoly claimed.

---

[32] [2017] SGHC 322.
[33] [2020] SGHC 28.
[34] [2023] SGCA 5.

# § 20
# Taiwan

## A. Executive summary

Until now, patents on second medical use inventions in Taiwan could only be protected in the form of Swiss-type claims. Where the second medical use invention granted after 2013 is protected in the form of a product claim specified by use, the second medical use features do not have the effect of limiting the scope of the claim. 1

As stipulated in Chapter 4-1 'Patent Linkage of Drugs' of the Taiwan Pharmaceutical Affairs Act (→ mn. 59 et seq.), the Taiwan Food and Drug Administration (TFDA) would issue the generic drug permit provided the patented indication is carved out by means of a non-infringement declaration by the generic applicant. Such criteria also apply to biosimilar products. 2

However, in a recent Taiwan IP Court decision, it appears carve-outs allowed by TFDA will not be sufficient to avoid liability for patent infringement. The Taiwan IP Court held that where the patented indication carved out from the Summary of Product Characteristics (SmPC) is not medically logical, the SmPC does not substantially exclude the patented indication and thus constitutes patent infringement. The Taiwan IP Court also emphasised the therapeutic effect of the drug in question demonstrated by the results of the clinical trials cited in the SmPC. Even if the patented indication is carved out, the generic drug still infringes the patent right if the clinical trials data in the SmPC support its therapeutic efficacy on the patented medical use. 3

## B. Scope of protection and interpretation of second medical use claims

According to the provisions concerning inventions related to medicines and pharmaceuticals in the Taiwan Patent Examination Guidelines (Chapter 13 2.5.2, Part 2 of the Patent Examination Guidelines (2021); → mn. 58), Taiwan adopts the principle of absolute novelty for product claims, that is, whether the claimed technical features put any limitation on the claimed product per se is considered during examination. In detail, even if a known drug is found to have properties for a use which is not disclosed in the prior art, the new use will be deemed to be only a description of the product and will not be considered during examination with respect to novelty of the product claim specified by use whose subject matter is the 'drug' per se. 4

Furthermore, according to the provision in the section '2.7.1.2 explanation of a product claim specified by use' of the Taiwan Patent Infringement Verification Directions (2016), when explaining a product claim specified by use, if the use features do not affect or change the structure or composition of the claimed product per se, which merely describe the purpose or intended use of the product and do not imply that the product would have 5 a specific structure or composition, the use features do not have the effect of limiting the scope of the claim. For example, in a case in which the claim of the disputed patent states 'a composition X for use in treating cancers comprises compound A' while the challenged product is 'a composition X for use in treating heart diseases comprises compound A', the use features do not have the effect of limiting the scope of the claim because the use for treating cancers do not affect or change the structure or composition of composition X. Therefore, the challenged product falls within the scope defined by the claim of the disputed patent.

6 Therefore, according to the current provisions in Taiwan, a second medical use claim should be formulated as a use claim (rather than a product claim specified by use).

7 However, it is noted that, according to the Taiwan Patent Infringement Verification Directions (2004) and the Taiwan Patent Examination Guidelines before 2013, use features do have the effect of limiting the scope of the claim. Therefore, a scope defined by a 'product claim specified by use' granted based on Patent Examination Guidelines in Taiwan before 2013 should be explained as that limited by the use.

8 Article 24 of the Patent Act stipulates that a patent shall not be granted in respect of diagnostic, therapeutic and surgical methods for the treatment of humans or animals (→ mn. 50). The Taiwan Patent Examination Guidelines also clarify that a second medical use patent should be described as, for example, 'a use of compound A in preparing medicines for treating disease X' or 'a use of compound A which is used for preparing medicines for treating disease X' (also referred to Swiss-type claim). Such second medical use claim is explained as a method of preparing medicines, so it does not belong to diagnostic, therapeutic and surgical methods for treating humans or animals.

9 Furthermore, according to the provisions concerning inventions related to medicines and pharmaceutics in the Taiwan Patent Examination Guidelines (Chapter 13 5.2.3 and 5.3.3), in addition to indicated medical conditions or pharmacological effects, if technical features specific to a certain population of patients, specific body portion, dosage, route of administration, interval of administration and order of administrating different ingredients in a medical use claim can be distinguished from the prior art and are not obvious compared to the prior art, the medical use claim meets the requirements of novelty and non-obviousness. Accordingly, in patent examination in Taiwan, although a second medical use is in the form of Swiss-type claim to be explained as a method of preparing medicines to meet the requirements for patent eligibility, the claim per se is still an invention of a treatment application for a drug. Thus, technical features which are not related to the manufacturing process of the drug may still have a limitation on the claim and therefore will be taken into consideration when determining novelty and non-obviousness of the claim.

## C. Direct and indirect infringement of second medical use claims

10 Currently, unlike many other countries, there is no concept of 'indirect infringement' or 'contributory infringement' in Taiwan. The TIPO once tried to introduce corresponding concepts, but the attempt was eventually dropped.

11 On 23 October 2007, the Taiwan Intellectual Property Office (TIPO) announced its intention to amend the Taiwan Patent Act by introducing 'indirect infringement liability clauses' to clearly define the liability for indirect infringement. On 31 October 2007, a

consultation meeting was held, and in July 2009 experts from the US, Germany, Japan and Taiwan were invited to attend an international seminar focusing on patent indirect infringement held in Taiwan to discuss the subject. However, due to the strong opposition from many Taiwanese businesses, the amendment to the Taiwan Patent Act related to indirect infringement has until now not been passed.

So for the moment, anyone wishing to claim indirect infringement must resort to Article 185 Civil Code: 'If several persons have wrongfully damaged the rights of another jointly, they are jointly liable for the injury arising therefrom. The same rule shall be applied even if which one has actually caused the injury cannot be sure. Instigators and accomplices are deemed to be joint tortfeasors.' However, there are very few cases where patentees have won based on this clause. **12**

On the other hand, the handful of cases where indirect infringement was mentioned[1] are all predicated on the fact that 'there exists a direct infringer and an act of direct infringement', and 'the act of actively inducing or aiding shall to a certain extent be causally linked to the result of infringement for the instigator or accomplice to bear joint liability'. **13**

In summary, indirect infringement is not an offence in Taiwan. **14**

## D. Infringement of second medical use claims and skinny label products

The new Taiwan Pharmaceutical Affairs Act formally took effect on 20 August 2019 in Taiwan to implement the patent linkage system[2]. It stipulated indication carve-outs in Chapter 4-1 'Patent Linkage of Drugs' wherein if the valid patent(s) registered under a reference new drug of a generic drug is merely a patent for medical use, the applicant for the generic drug permit can exclude the indications corresponding to the patent for medical use and declare that the generic drug does not infringe said patent, after which the central competent health authority will issue the drug permit after examination.[3] The stay of drug permit issuance and the marketing exclusivity period do not apply to the application for generic drug permit under indication carve-outs. However, the procedure of patent declaration and notification to the patentee still need to be carried out. **15**

In 2021, the Taiwan Intellectual Property and Commercial Court (IP Court) established the legal criteria for deciding whether amending SmPC based on indication carve-outs can avoid patent infringement in two patent linkage-derived lawsuits for TSH Biopharm Corporation Ltd's Cretrol® (a new drug with a new therapeutic compound). **16**

Cretrol® developed by TSH Biopharm comprises active ingredients of Rosuvastatin calcium and Ezetimibe, which are identical to the ingredients of Crestor® of AstraZeneca (referred to as AZ) and EZETROL® of Merck Sharp & Dohme (referred to as MSD), respectively. Each of these two companies owns the patent rights for related indications. TSH Biopharm had excluded the said related indications with non-infringement declarations according to the provisions of Taiwan Pharmaceutical Affairs Act when applying for a drug permit. However, AZ and MSD still filed lawsuits against TSH Biopharm in an **17**

---

[1] *Takeda Pharmaceutical Company Limited v China Chemical & Pharmaceutical Co., Ltd.* (IP Court 2008 Minzhuansuzi No. 20 Judgment), *HSU v Panion & BF Biotech Inc.* (IP Court 2012 Minzhuanshangzi No. 1 Judgment), *Magic-Optimal-Service-Tech. Co. v Cyberlink Corp.* (IP Court 2011 Minzhuansuzi No. 69 Judgment), *Wu v The Walt Disney Company (Taiwan) Ltd.* (IP Court 2011 Minzhuansuzi No. 2 Judgment).

[2] Wisdom News Vol. 33 for introduction of patent linkage system in Taiwan, available from https://www.wisdomlaw.com.tw.

[3] → mn. 68.

attempt to prevent the issuance of a drug permit for Cretrol®. Nevertheless, the two court decisions for these two cases are different.

## I. *AstraZeneca v TSH Biopharm*

18 In *AstraZeneca v TSH Biopharm*[4], AZ is the patentee of Taiwan Invention Patent No. I238720 'Pharmaceutical Composition for use in the Treatment of Heterozygous Familial Hypercholesterolemia' ('720 patent), i.e., the corresponding patent of brand drug Crestor®.

19 Claim 1 of '720 is a product claim specified by use which claims 'a pharmaceutical composition for use in the treatment of heterozygous familial hypercholesterolemia in a patient suffering from heterozygous familial hypercholesterolemia', comprising a therapeutically effective amount of active ingredient Rosuvastatin and a pharmaceutically acceptable carrier. When explaining the claim, according to Patent Examination Guidelines in Taiwan before 2013, on the basis of which '720 was granted, the scope of claim 1 of '720 should be limited by the therapeutic use of 'heterozygous familial hypercholesterolemia'.

20 When TSH Biopharm applied to the TFDA for registration of Cretrol®, the indication listed in the original SmPC was 'primary hypercholesterolemia' which was amended into 'primary hypercholesterolemia (excluding heterozygous familial hypercholesterolemia)' during the examination. Therefore, the main issue in this case is whether Cretrol® does not infringe '720 because 'heterozygous familial hypercholesterolemia' has been specifically excluded from the SmPC.

21 First, regarding the definition of heterozygous familial hypercholesterolemia, primary hypercholesterolemia can be at least categorised into familial hypercholesterolemia (FH) associated with genetic inheritance and non-familial hypercholesterolemia caused by the interaction between several genes, dietary and other factors, wherein familial hypercholesterolemia can be further categorised into 'heterozygous familial hypercholesterolemia' (Heterozygous FH; He-FH) and 'homozygous familial hypercholesterolemia' (Homozygous FH; Ho-FH).

22 In this case, the court considered that judgment with regard to whether claim 1 of '720 literally reads on Cretrol® should be based on 'the therapeutic effect of Cretrol® per se represented by the human clinical trials results cited in the Cretrol®'s SmPC', rather than totally based on the 'amended SmPC of Cretrol®'. The SmPC is a guideline and an important reference for clinical or pharmaceutical personnel when prescribing a medicine. However, can the SmPC of Cretrol® still be deemed as a reliable reference after being amended by TSH Biopharm during the litigation? Consideration needs to be given to whether the therapeutic effect of Cretrol® per se can be supported by the clinical trials results cited in the SmPC thereby rendering the amendment medically logical.

23 The court considered that it was not medically logical to list the indication 'primary hypercholesterolemia (excluding heterozygous familial hypercholesterolemia)' in the amended SmPC, which was merely a deliberate attempt by TSH Biopharm to avoid giving a literal definition of '720, and that the indication cannot be evidence for judging infringement of a patent right. The court gave the following reasons:

1. *Inconsistency with clinical treatment practice*
   According to the provisions governing payment for hypolipidemic drugs in national health insurance and in the opinion of an expert witness, clinical treatment of pa-

[4] Taiwan Intellectual Property and Commercial Court, 2021 Min Zhuan Su Zi No. 9 Judgment; → mn. 70.

tients with primary hypercholesterolemia does not include purposely diagnosing the genotype of familial hypercholesterolemia before treating the patient. In addition, related evidence shows that even with genetic testing techniques, the patients with heterozygous familial hypercholesterolemia cannot be specifically identified. Therefore, it is difficult to apply the indication 'primary hypercholesterolemia (excluding heterozygous familial hypercholesterolemia)' listed in the amended SmPC of Cretrol® to treatment of patients in practice, which is thus obviously inconsistent with clinical treatment practice.

2. *Failure of the human clinical trials results cited in the amended SmPC to support the indication listed in the amended SmPC*
   Ho-FH is a rare disease. The prevalence of He-FH is approximately 2000 times that of Ho-FH. It can be reasonably inferred that the 11,308 patients with primary hypercholesterolemia recruited in the clinical trial of Cretrol® may include at least 100 He-FH patients and the other are all patients with non-familial primary hypercholesterolemia and would probably not include Ho-FH patients. Therefore, the results of the clinical trial of Cretrol® can support the treatment of 'non-familial primary hypercholesterolemia' and 'heterozygous familial hypercholesterolemia' by Cretrol® but fail to prove the therapeutic effect of Cretrol® for treating 'homozygous familial hypercholesterolemia'.
3. *Registration in Korea*
   Also, the clinical trial report submitted for registration of Cretrol® is identical with that submitted for registration in Korea and the drug with the market approval in Korea is granted for the indication 'heterozygous familial hypercholesterolemia', which also can prove that Cretrol® has indeed the therapeutic effect for treating 'heterozygous familial hypercholesterolemia'.

Accordingly, the court determined that Cretrol® fell within the literal scope of '720 and 24 constituted a literal infringement.

## II. *Merck Sharp & Dohme Corp. v TSH Biopharm*

In contrast, in *Merck Sharp & Dohme Corp. v TSH Biopharm*[5], the court held that TSH 25 Biopharm does not infringe the patent right of Merck Sharp & Dohme Corp. MSD is the patentee of Taiwan Invention Patent No. I337076 'The Use of Substituted Azetidinone Compounds for the Treatment of β-Sitosterolemia' ('076), i.e., the corresponding patent of brand drug EZETROL®.

Claim 1 of '076 is 'a pharmaceutical composition for the treatment of β-sitosterolemia', 26 comprising an effective amount of Ezetimibe in a pharmaceutically acceptable carrier. According to Patent Examination Guidelines in Taiwan before 2013, on the basis of which '076 was granted, claim 1 of '076 should be limited by the description of 'the treatment of β-sitosterolemia' in it.

According to the SmPC of Cretrol®, MSD considered that the medical use of Cretrol® 27 in the treatment of primary hypercholesterolemia must include the treatment of hypercholesterolemia in patients with sitosterolemia and thus claimed that '076 literally 'reads on' Cretrol®.

However, the court determined that '076 does not literally 'read on' Cretrol® because 28 treating 'β-sitosterolemia' was obviously different from treating 'primary hypercholester-

5 Taiwan Intellectual Property and Commercial Court, 2021 Min Zhuan Su Zi No. 4 Judgment.

olemia (excluding heterozygous familial hypercholesterolemia)'. The following reasons were given:

1. β-sitosterolemia is one of the causes of primary hypercholesterolemia. Patients with β-sitosterolemia show a normal or elevated level of plasma cholesterol concentration (e.g., LDL cholesterol) and elevated level of plasma phytosterol (e.g., β-sitosterol). Referring to the examples in the specification of '076, patients previously diagnosed with homozygous β-sitosterolemia were recruited for trials and efficacy of the treatment of β-sitosterolemia was evaluated by the reduction in the level of plasma phytosterol and LDL-C in the patients administered Ezetimibe.
   It was found that, in the clinical trials mentioned in the amended SmPC of Cretrol®, 11,308 patients with primary hypercholesterolemia were administrated with Ezetimibe combined with statin (the second active ingredient of Cretrol® is Rosuvastatin calcium which is a statin.) for treating excessive LDL-C. However, plasma phytosterol levels in the recruited patients were not evaluated, not to mention the efficacy of Cretrol® in reducing plasma phytosterol concentrations. Therefore, it was obvious that the amended SmPC of Cretrol® did not disclose that Cretrol® could treat β-sitosterolemia.
2. During reexamination, MSD claimed that 'β-sitosterolemia' is an indication different from 'hypercholesterolemia' to prove that '076 had an inventive step over the prior art.
3. Referring to the SmPC of brand drug EZETROL®, 'hypercholesterolemia' and 'homozygous sitosterolemia (phytosterolemia)' are listed as two indications and it can be seen that the evaluation indicators of the therapeutic effect of 'primary hypercholesterolemia' and 'homozygous β-sitosterolemia' are obviously different.

**29** The court further mentioned that there were no clinical trials specifically dealing with the treatment of β-sitosterolemia with Cretrol® in the amended SmPC of Cretrol® to support the assertion that β-sitosterolemia could be one of the indications of Cretrol®. In addition, clinical trials of Cretrol® did not recruit patients with β-sitosterolemia. Therefore, it could not be concluded that Cretrol® could be used to treat β-sitosterolemia. Accordingly, it could not be determined that Cretrol® could be used to treat β-sitosterolemia clinically based on the mechanism of the active ingredient, Ezetimibe, without the support of data from human clinical trials.

## E. Infringement of second medical use claims and biosimilar products

**30** According to provisions in Article 16(3) of the Taiwan Regulations for the Patent Linkage of Drugs[6], patent linkage system for generic drugs shall apply *mutatis mutandis* to the application for a biosimilar drug permit license. Therefore, the indication carve-outs mentioned above also apply to biosimilar products.

[6] → mn. 69.

# F. Strategies and considerations

Under the provisions in Article 48-20(2) of the Taiwan Pharmaceutical Affairs Act, infringement of pharmaceutical patents can be avoided by carve-outs of the patented indications (→ mn. 68). **31**

However, in *AstraZeneca v TSH Biopharm* mentioned above, despite a carve-out of a patented indication from the SmPC by TSH Biopharm, the Taiwan IP Court did not agree that the carve-out version of SmPC had substantially excluded the patented indication and concluded that the drug of TSH Biopharm infringed the patent right of AZ. **32**

The Taiwan IP Court adopts more elaborate steps and judging principles when determining whether an SmPC has substantially excluded the patented indication via carve-outs. Further, according to clinical treatment practice, the Taiwan IP Court established the requirement of being 'medically logical' when determining whether infringement comparison can be made based on the SmPC with carve-outs, which prevents the generic or biosimilar manufacturer from avoiding infringement by excluding patented indications in SmPC in form for a drug which infringes patent right substantially. It also corresponds to the legislative intention of carve-outs stipulated in the Taiwan Pharmaceutical Affairs Act and thereby keep the infringement comparison performed based on comparison between disputed drugs per se and claims of disputed patents. **33**

Accordingly, the Taiwan IP Court will not accept the content of an SmPC as the sole reference on which to determine whether a generic drug falls within scope of a patent even though the indications listed in the SmPC are highlighted. If the SmPC has been amended, reasons for amending the original SmPC and technical explanations will also be taken into consideration, especially the therapeutic effects demonstrated by clinical trials, to reach a conclusion on the particular case. **34**

Therefore, if a generic or biosimilar manufacturer wishes to adopt the strategy of omitting a patented indication from an SmPC, it should be carefully considered whether exclusion of the indication in the SmPC is medically logical and whether the clinical trials cited in the SmPC have demonstrated the therapeutic effect of the disputed drug for the patented indication in order to prevent the risk of infringement. **35**

# G. Legal remedies

In Taiwan, patent infringers shall bear civil liability. Civil remedies include injunctions and an award of damages. **36**

## I. Constitutive elements of patent infringement

### 1. Objective elements

To be regarded as infringing, a product or a process must fall within the scope of the claims of the plaintiff's patent and it must be proven that the defendant has carried out the infringing acts of exploiting the invention. **37**

38 Where the invention is a product, the exploiting of which means the acts of making, offering for sale, selling, using, or importing that product for the aforementioned purposes in Taiwan.

39 Where the invention is a process, the exploiting of which means the following acts:

1. Using the process; and
2. Using, offering for sale, selling or importing for these purposes the product obtained directly by that process in Taiwan.[7]

### 2. Subjective elements

40 If the plaintiff only desires to stop the infringing act, he does not need to prove that the infringer has acted intentionally or negligently[8]; however, if he also wants to be compensated for damages suffered as a result of the infringement, intention or negligence must be proven.[9]

41 In addition, Article 98 of the current Taiwan Patent Act stipulates that the patentee is obliged to mark the patented Article or its packaging with the patent certificate number to signal to the public that the product is under patent protection. Otherwise, if he claims damages, he will have to prove that the infringer knows or has reason to know that said product is patented.

## II. Remedies in civil litigation

42 The plaintiff in a patent infringement suit may claim the following:

1. Stopping of infringement;[10]
2. Prevention of imminent infringement;[11]
3. Compensation for damages suffered by the infringement;[12]
4. Destruction of infringing articles or the materials or implements used in the infringing act, or request for other necessary disposals;[13]
5. Where the inventor's right to be indicated as inventor is infringed, the inventor may request necessary disposition(s) to have his/her name indicated or his/her impaired reputation restored.[14]

## III. Limitation

43 The right to claim damages must be exercised within two years after the patentee has become aware of the damage infringement and the person liable for the resulting damages but the right may no longer be exercised if more than ten years have passed since the time of the infringement.[15]

---

[7] Art. 58 Patent Act; → mn. 51.
[8] Art. 96(1) Patent Act; → mn. 52.
[9] Art. 96(2) Patent Act.
[10] Art. 96(1) Patent Act.
[11] Art. 96(1) Patent Act.
[12] Art. 96(2) Patent Act.
[13] Art. 96(3) Patent Act.
[14] Art. 96(5) Patent Act.
[15] Art. 96(6) Patent Act.

## IV. Calculation of damages

Damages may be calculated according to any of the following methods. **44**

1. The patentee's losses as a result of infringement;
2. The difference between the reduced profit earned through patent exploitation after the infringement and the profit normally expected through the exploitation of the same patent;
3. The profit earned by the infringer as a result of patent infringement;
4. The amount calculated on the basis of reasonable royalties (license analogy).

In addition, where the infringement is found to have been intentionally committed, the **45** court may, at the request of the patentee and depending on the severity of the infringement, award punitive damages of up to three times the proven damages.[16]

## V. Sending warning letters and requesting preservation of evidence:

Patentees may send a warning letter when a potential infringer is identified. However, **46** since it may cause potential infringers to hide or destroy evidence in advance, rather than sending warning letters before initiating an action, patentees usually apply to the court for pre-action preservation of evidence according to Taiwan Civil Procedure Act[17], requesting search and seizure of the relevant evidence in the potential infringer's place of business or manufacturing facility. But patentees must initiate an action within 30 days after the court decision ordering preservation of evidence,[18] or the court may, on motion by an interested person, release the document or object retained for purposes of its perpetuation or take other appropriate measures.

Though patentees may apply for an injunction maintaining a temporary status quo **47** before initiating an action[19] in order to request for a ruling to stop the infringement, injunctions are seldom granted by courts. Therefore, the current situation is that patentees usually do not apply for injunctions.

## VI. Litigation procedure

In infringement litigation, the 'three levels and three instances' trial system is applied. **48** The IP Court is the first port of call in infringement litigation. A party dissatisfied with the judgment of the first instance may appeal to the second instance, which is also located within the IP Court, and may finally appeal to the Supreme Court. Usually, the first instance takes one and a half to two years, the second instance takes one to one and a half years, and the third instance takes about one year.

The party accused of infringement may apply various defense strategies, such as a **49** non-infringement defense, the defense that the alleged technical solution does not fall within the scope of the patent, the defense that the period of limitation has been exceeded or even the invalidity defence.[20] Moreover, as described above, the defendant can also initiate a parallel invalidation action with TIPO.

---

[16] Art. 97 Patent Act; → mn. 53.
[17] Art. 368 Code of Civil Procedure; → mn. 55.
[18] Art. 376-2 Code of Civil Procedure; → mn. 56.
[19] Art. 538 Code of Civil Procedure; → mn. 57.
[20] Art. 41(1) Intellectual Property Case Adjudication Act; → mn. 54.

## H. Statutory provisions

### I. Patent Act[21]

50 **Article 24**

**Statutory exclusion**

An invention patent shall not be granted in respect of any of the following:

1. animals, plants, and essential biological processes for the production of animals or plants, except for processes for producing microorganisms;
2. diagnostic, therapeutic and surgical methods for the treatment of humans or animals; or
3. inventions contrary to public order or morality.

51 **Article 58**

**Effects of invention patent right**

(1) Unless otherwise provided for in this Act, the patentee of an invention patent has an exclusive right to prevent others from exploiting the invention without the patentee's consent.

(2) Where the invention is a product, exploiting of which means the acts of making, offering for sale, selling, using, or importing that product for the aforementioned purposes.

(3) Where the invention is a process, exploiting of which means the following acts:

1. using the process; and
2. using, offering for sale, selling or importing for these purposes the product obtained directly by that process.

(4) The extent of the protection conferred by an invention patent shall be determined by the claim(s), and the description and drawing(s) may be considered as a reference when interpreting the claim(s).

(5) The abstract shall not be used for the purpose of interpreting claim(s).

52 **Article 96**

**Right to claim in the event of patent right infringement**

(1) A patentee of an invention patent may demand a person who infringes or is likely to infringe the patent right to stop or prevent such infringement.

(2) In case an infringement of invention patent occurs due to intentional act or negligence, the patentee may claim for damages suffered therefrom.

(3) When making a demand pursuant to Paragraph 1, the patentee may request for destruction of the infringing articles or the materials or implements used in the infringing act, or request for other necessary disposal.

(4) An exclusive licensee may, within the licensed scope, make demands in accordance with the preceding three paragraphs. However, if it is otherwise provided for in an agreement, such agreement shall prevail.

(5) Where the inventor's right to be indicated as such is infringed, the inventor may request for necessary disposition(s) to have his/her name indicated or to restore the impaired reputation.

(6) The rights to claim as set forth in Paragraph 2 and the preceding paragraph shall become extinguished if not exercised within two (2) years after the patentee has become aware of the damage and the person liable for damages. This right shall also become extinguished if it is not exercised within ten (10) years after the time of infringement.

---

[21] Version from 4 May 2022. Text available from: https://law.moj.gov.tw/eng.

**Article 97** 53
**Calculation of damages**

(1) The damages claimed pursuant to the preceding Article may be calculated according to any of the following methods:

1. the method as set forth in Article 216 of the Civil Code; if no method of proof can be produced to prove the damages suffered, a patentee may claim damages based on the difference between the profit earned through patent exploitation after infringement and the profit normally expected through exploitation of the same patent;
2. the profit earned by the infringer as a result of patent infringement; or
3. the amount calculated on the basis of reasonable royalties that may be collected from exploiting the invention patent being licensed.

(2) Subject to the preceding paragraph, where the infringement is found to be intentionally committed, the court may, upon request and on the basis of the severity of the infringement, award the damages greater than the loss suffered but not exceeding three (3) times of the proven loss.

## II. Intellectual Property Case Adjudication Act[22]

**Article 41** 54

(1) When a party claims or defends that an intellectual property right shall be cancelled or revoked, the court shall decide based on the merit of the case, and the Code of Civil Procedure, Code of Administrative Litigation Procedure, Trademark Act, Patent Act, Species of Plants and Seedling Act, or other applicable laws concerning the stay of an action shall not apply.

(2) Under the circumstances in the preceding paragraph, the holder of the intellectual property right shall not claim any rights during the civil action against the opposing party where the court has recognised the grounds for cancellation or revocation of the intellectual property right.

[…]

## III. Code of Civil Procedure[23]

### Item 6 Preservation of evidence

**Article 368** 55

(1) Where it is likely that evidence may be destroyed or its use in court may be difficult, or with the consent of the opposing party, the party may move the court for perpetuation of such evidence; where necessary, the party who has legal interests in ascertaining the status quo of a matter or object may move for expert testimony, inspection or perpetuation of documentary evidence.

(2) The perpetuation of evidence provided in the preceding paragraph shall be governed by the provisions of this Section relating to evidence-taking.

**Article 376-2** 56

(1) Where the action is not initiated after a thirty-day period has lapsed from the day following the conclusion of the perpetuation of evidence proceeding, the court may, on motion

[22] Version from 15 February 2023. Available from: https://law.moj.gov.tw/eng.
[23] Version from 8 December 2021. Available from: https://law.moj.gov.tw/eng.

by an interested person, release the document or object retained for purposes of its perpetuation or take other appropriate measures.

(2) Where the action is not initiated within the period provided in the preceding paragraph, the court may, on motion by an interested person, order the movant to bear the expenses for the proceeding.

(3) An appeal may be taken from the ruling provided in the two preceding paragraphs.

57 **Article 538**

(1) Where necessary for purposes of preventing material harm or imminent danger or other similar circumstances, an application may be made for an injunction maintaining a temporary status quo with regard to the legal relation in dispute.

(2) The ruling provided in the preceding paragraph may be issued only where the legal relation in dispute may be ascertained in an action on the merits.

(3) The injunction provided in the first paragraph may order certain prestation to be performed in advance.

(4) The court shall accord the parties an opportunity to be heard before issuing the rulings provided in the first paragraph and the preceding paragraph, except where the court considers it inappropriate to do so.

## IV. Taiwan Patent Examination Guidelines[24]

### Chapter 3

58 **2.5.2 Product Specified by Use**

If there is an expression specifying the product by use in a claim the product to be protected should be interpreted as suitable for the use specified. However, the actual limitation of the special use depends on whether the special use influences the product to be protected. In other words, it depends on whether the use implies that the claimed product has a certain specific structure and/or component which is (are) particularly suitable for the use. For example, if a claim refers to a 'mold for molten steel', a plastic ice cube tray disclosed in the prior art would not deprive the claim of novelty for that the use of molten steel renders the mold having structures and/or components to produce the properties for high melting point. In a further example, a claim is directed to 'a crane hook.' The use of crane implies that the hook has a structure with a specific size and intensity, and thus provides a limitation to the subject matter 'hook.' Although a fishing hook disclosed in the prior art has a similar shape, it would not come within the claims and not deprive the claim of novelty. In a further example, where a claim is directed to 'a Fe based alloy for a piano string,' the use 'for a piano string' implies that the Fe based alloy has a lamellar microstructure supporting high tension, and thus provides a limitation to the subject matter.' Therefore, a Fe based alloy without a lamellar microstructure disclosed in the prior art would not come within the claim and not deprive the claim of novelty.

If the use of a product specified in a claim merely describes the purpose of or the way to use the product, and fails to imply that the product would have a certain structure and/or component, the use does not furnish any effect for determining whether or not the claim involves novelty or an inventive step.

The following three conditions are provided:

(1) Compounds

The disclosure of compound X for use as a dye in the prior art takes away the novelty of the claimed invention directed to 'compound X for use as a catalyst' for that those chemical

[24] Version from 26 December 2022. Available from: https://www.tipo.gov.tw/eng.

structures determining the attributes of the compounds are identical, even if their stated uses are different.

(2) Compositions

The disclosure of an insecticidal composition comprising A + B in the prior art takes away the novelty of the claimed invention directed to 'a cleaning composition comprising A + B' for that their components determining the attributes are identical. The disclosure of a composition for treating influenza comprising A + B in the prior art takes away the novelty of the claimed invention directed to ' a composition for treating cardiac diseases comprising A + B' for that those components determining the attributes are identical.

(3) Articles

The disclosure of a U-shaped lock for a motorcycle in the prior art takes away the novelty of the claimed invention directed to ' a U-shaped lock for a bicycle' for that structures per se of them are identical, even if their stated uses are different.

[...]

## V. Pharmaceutical Affairs Act[25]

### Chapter 4-1 Patent Linkage of Drugs

#### Article 48-3 59

(1) If the holder of a new drug permit deems it necessary to submit the patent information regarding such drug, such holder shall submit relevant documents and information to the Central Competent Health Authority within 45 days after the next day to the receipt of the drug permit. If the holder fails to file such submission within the stipulated period, the regulations under this Chapter do not apply.

(2) The drug patent stipulated under Paragraph 1 hereof shall be limited to the following:

(1) Substance.
(2) Composition or Formulation.
(3) Medical use.

#### Article 48-9 60

(1) The applicant for a generic drug permit shall, with respect to the patent(s) of the approved new drug listed by the holder of said new drug permit, declare one of the following item(s) when applying for a generic drug permit:

1. No patent information of said new drug has been listed.
2. The patent(s) corresponding to said new drug has extinguished.
3. The Central Competent Health Authority will issue the generic drug permit after the patent(s) corresponding to said new drug extinguishes.
4. The patent(s) corresponding to said new drugs shall be revoked, or the patent(s) corresponding to said new drugs will not be infringed by the generic drug subject to the application for drug permit.

#### Article 48-12 61

(1) For the application for a generic drug permit that involves a declaration based on Item 4 of Article 48-9, the applicant shall, within 20 days after the next day to its receipt of the notification from the Central Competent Health Authority which indicates that all the documents required for an application of drug permit have been duly prepared, notify the holder of the new drug permit and the Central Competent Health Authority [of the declaration] in writing;

[25] Version from 31 Janunary 2018. Available from: https://law.moj.gov.tw/eng.

if the holder of said new drug permit is different from the patentee or the exclusive licensee, the patentee and the exclusive licensee shall also be notified.

(2) The applicant of a generic drug permit shall provide in the aforementioned notification an explanation and evidence regarding its allegation that that the patent shall be revoked or that there is no patent infringement.

(3) The Central Competent Health Authority shall dismiss the application for generic drug permit if the applicant fails to issue the notification in accordance with Paragraphs 1 and 2 hereof.

62 **Article 48-13**

(1) If the patentee or the exclusive licensee intends to file a patent infringement complaint on the basis of the listed patent(s) after its receipt of the notification stipulated by Paragraph 1 of Article 48-12, it shall file the complaint within 45 days after the next day to its receipt of said notification and notify the Central Competent Health Authority.

(2) The Central Competent Health Authority shall stay the issuance of the drug permit for twelve (12) months as of the next day to the new drug permit holder's receipt of the notification stipulated in Paragraph 1 of Article 48-12. However, if there is any of the following matters, the Central Competent Health Authority may issue the drug permit if [said application is] is examined to be in compliance with the regulations under this Act:

1. The patentee or the exclusive licensee, after its receipt of the notification stipulated by Paragraphs 1 of Article 48-12, fails to file an infringement complaint within the 45-day period.
2. The patentee or the exclusive license files an infringement complaint based on the patents which are not those listed before the date of the application for the generic drug permit.
3. The patent infringement complaint filed by the patentee or the exclusive licensee pursuant to Paragraph 1 hereof is overruled by the court according to Paragraph 1 or 2 of Article 249 of the Coded of Civil Procedure.
4. The court has determined that all of the patents pending in the infringement lawsuit shall be revoked, or a non-infringement judgment is obtained by the applicant for the generic drug permit.
5. All the patents under the declaration stipulated in Item 4 of Article 48-9 made by the applicant for the generic drug permit are determined as invalid by the Competent Patent Authority in a cancellation action.
6. A settlement or a mediation has been reached by the parties.
7. All the patents under the declaration stipulated in Item 4 of Article 48-9 made by the applicant for the generic drug permit have become extinguished.

(3) The period [for notification] stipulated in Item 1, Paragraph 2 hereof shall be commenced upon the receipt of the notification by the patentee(s) or the exclusive licensee(s), whichever is later.

(4) If the patentee or the exclusive licensee obtains a final and binding judgment confirming infringement of the listed patent(s) within the 12-month period stipulated in Paragraph 2 hereof, the Central Competent Health Authority shall issue the generic drug permit after said patent(s) extinguishes.

(5) Where the patent infringement complaint filed by the patentee or the exclusive licensee pursuant to Paragraph 1 hereof, if by reason of being improper exercise of patent right ab initio, the stay of drug permit issuance has caused damages to the applicant of a generic drug permit, [such patentee or the exclusive licensee] shall be held liable for compensation.

### Article 48-14 63

(1) For the applications for the generic drug permits filed by the same applicant for the same drug, the Central Competent Health Authority may only stay the issuance of the drug permit in accordance with Paragraph 2, Article 48-13 once.

### Article 48-15 64

(1) During the period of stay of drug permit issuance stipulated in Paragraph 2 of Article 48-13, if the examination for the application for a generic drug permit has been completed, the Central Competent Health Authority shall inform the same to the applicant for said generic drug permit.

(2) The applicant for a generic drug permit may apply for drug listing and reimbursement price with the National Health Insurance Administration after receiving the notification stipulated in Paragraph 1 hereof. However, no manufacture or importation [of the generic drug] is permitted before the Central Competent Health Authority's issuance of the generic drug permit.

### Article 48-16 65

(1) The application for a generic drug permit in accordance with Item 4 of Article 48-9 with application documents duly prepared at the earliest shall be granted a 12-month period of marketing exclusivity; the Central Competent Health Authority shall not issue other drug permits to other applicants for a generic drug permit before the expiration of the aforementioned period.

(2) For the aforementioned application for a generic drug permit with documents duly prepared under Item 4 of Article 48-9, upon occurrence of [vacancy due to] any of the following matters, the vacancy will be fulfilled by the subsequent applicant with application documents duly prepared:

1. During the period of drug permit examination, the declaration under Item 4 of Article 48-9 is amended.
2. The earliest applicant fails to obtain from the Central Competent Health Authority the notification that the examination of the application for generic drug permit has completed within 12 months after the next day to the date that all the application documents are duly prepared.
3. Any matter as stipulated in Paragraph 4 of Article 48-13 occurs.

(3) If more than one application for a generic drug permit in compliance with the requirements regarding the earliest duly prepared application documents is filed on the same date, such applications are jointly subject to the 12-month period of marketing exclusivity.

### Article 48-17 66

(1) The holder of a generic drug permit shall market the drug within 6 months after the next day to such holder's obtaining of said drug permit, and shall, within 20 days after the next day to the earliest marketing date, provide the evidence of the actual marketing date to the Central Competent Health Authority for its determination of the marketing exclusivity period granted and the commencement date and end date thereof.

(2) The marketing exclusivity period stipulated in Paragraph 1 hereof starts from the date of the actual marketing of the drug.

(3) If more than one application for the generic drug permit is jointly subject to the marketing exclusivity period, the commencement date thereof shall be the date on which any of such drugs are actually first marketed.

67 **Article 48-18**

(1) If any of the following matters occur to the applicant for generic drug permit subject to the marketing exclusivity period, the Central Competent Health Authority may issue generic drug permits to other applicants without being restricted by Paragraph 1 of Article 48-16:

1. Failure to collect the drug permit within the period prescribed by the Central Competent Health Authority.
2. Failure to abide by Paragraph 1 of Article 48-17.
3. All the patents declared under Item 4 of Article 48-9 have become extinguished.

[...]

68 **Article 48-20**

(1) The provisions under Articles 48-9 through 48-15 hereof related to the application for a generic drug permit shall apply mutatis mutandis to the new drugs not having a new ingredient.

(2) The provisions related to the stay of drug permit issuance and the marketing exclusivity period under Articles 48-13 to 48-18 are not applicable to the application for a generic drug permit set forth in Article 48-12 if the following circumstances are met:

1. The patent(s) registered under an approved new drug is still valid, and is a patent for medical use under Item 3, Paragraph 2 of Article 48-3.
2. The applicant of a generic drug permit excludes the indication corresponding to the patent for medical use referred to in Item (1) hereof, and declares that the generic drug does not infringe said patent.
   The exclusion of indication, declaration, and other matters shall be abided by in this regard as stipulated in Paragraph 2 hereof shall be promulgated by the Central Competent Health Authority.

## VI. Regulations for the patent linkage of drugs[26]

69 **Article 16**

(1) The new drug not having a new ingredient in Article 48-20 in the Act refers to drugs which are of the preparations having new compositions, new therapeutic compounds or new methods of administration.

(2) The provisions under Article 8 through 14 hereof shall be implemented in accordance with Paragraph 1 of Article 48-20 in the Act and shall apply mutatis to the new drugs not having a new ingredient.

(3) Except that the application for a biosimilar drug permit licence to execute clinical trials is approved before the enforcement date of Chapter 4-1 in the Act by the Central Competent Health Authority, provisions of Chapter 4-1 in the Act with respect to the regulations of the application for a generic drug permit license shall apply mutatis to the application for a biosimilar drug permit licence.

(4) The term 'biosimilar drug' as used in the preceding Paragraph refers to preparations that are similar to its reference biological new drug, have been made of biological sources and approved by the Central Competent Health Authority to manufacture and import.

[26] Version from 1 July 2019. Text available from: https://law.moj.gov.tw/eng.

# J. Extracts from court decision

## *AstraZeneca v TSH Biopharm*[27]

### Summary 70

Claim 1 of the disputed patent: 'a pharmaceutical composition for use in the treatment of heterozygous familial hypercholesterolemia in a patient suffering from heterozygous familial hypercholesterolemia...'

Accordingly, 'a product claim specified by use' refers to a claim with a product as its subject matter as well as technical features for defining the application field or purpose of the product in the claim. When explaining a product claim specified by use, judgement with regard to whether the use feature furnishes effect for limiting the scope of the claim should be based on whether the use feature affects or changes the structure or composition of the product. It is found that the description 'treatment of heterozygous familial hypercholesterolemia in a patient suffering from heterozygous familial hypercholesterolemia' in the claim 1 of the disputed patent had clarified the use for treatment and thus limited the scope of the claim.

The indication of the disputed drug amended by the defendant is 'primary hypercholesterolemia (excluding heterozygous familial hypercholesterolemia)'. However, according to the clinical trials results cited in the amended SmPC of the disputed drug, they still can support that the disputed drug can be used to treating heterozygous familial hypercholesterolemia.

Judgement with regards to whether the disputed drug falls into the literal scope of indication in the claim 1 of the disputed patent should be based on 'the therapeutic effect of the disputed drug per se represented by the human clinical trials results cited in the SmPC of the disputed drug', rather than totally based on the 'amended SmPC of the disputed drug'.

It was not medically logical to list the indication 'primary hypercholesterolemia (excluding heterozygous familial hypercholesterolemia)' in the amended SmPC of the disputed drug. Patent infringement could not be judged based on the indication listed in amended SmPC:

The indication 'primary hypercholesterolemia (excluding heterozygous familial hypercholesterolemia)' listed in the amended SmPC is inconsistency with clinical treatment practice:

According to the provisions of the National Health Insurance Act and payment for drugs in national health insurance and Exhibit 28, clinical treatment of patients with primary hypercholesterolemia does not include diagnosing whether they are patients with heterozygous familial hypercholesterolemia as the first step and, even with genetic testing techniques, the patients with heterozygous familial hypercholesterolemia cannot be specifically identified. Therefore, it is difficult to apply the indication 'primary hypercholesterolemia (excluding heterozygous familial hypercholesterolemia)' listed in the amended SmPC of the disputed drug to treatment of patients in practice, which is thus obviously inconsistent with clinical treatment practice.

According to the statement of the witness in the court, a person ordinarily skilled in the art to which the invention pertains would understand that when treating a patient with hypercholesterolemia, especially a patient with primary hypercholesterolemia, a clinician would not clarify whether the patient with primary hypercholesterolemia suffers from heterozygous familial hypercholesterolemia with genetic testing techniques. Therefore, the amended indication 'primary hypercholesterolemia (excluding heterozygous familial hypercholesterolemia)' of the disputed drug excludes patients with heterozygous familial hypercholesterolemia intentionally who would not be distinguished in the clinical treatment practice. Again, it is proved that the indication cannot be applied to clinical treatment in practice.

[27] Taiwan Intellectual Property and Commercial Court, 2021 Min Zhuan Su Zi No. 9 Judgment.

The human clinical trials results cited in the amended SmPC of the disputed drug fail to support listing indication 'primary hypercholesterolemia (excluding heterozygous familial hypercholesterolemia)' in the SmPC:

The results of the clinical trial of the disputed drug can support the treatment of 'non-familial primary hypercholesterolemia' and 'heterozygous familial hypercholesterolemia' by the disputed drug. However, there is no patients with homozygous familial hypercholesterolemia participating the clinical trial. Therefore, the human clinical trials results cited in the amended SmPC of the disputed drug fail to prove the therapeutic effect of the disputed drug for treating 'homozygous familial hypercholesterolemia'.

The disputed drug has therapeutic effect for treating 'heterozygous familial hypercholesterolemia':

The clinical trials results cited in the amended SmPC of the disputed drug represent that 'excessive LDL-C' can be treated, which shows that the disputed drug has therapeutic effect for treating heterozygous familial hypercholesterolemia. Also, according to the statement of the witness, it can be reasonably expected that the clinical trial included patients with heterozygous familial hypercholesterolemia. Regarding the evaluation result of successfully reducing LDL-C concentration, a person ordinarily skilled in the art to which the invention pertains would understand that the disputed drug has therapeutic effect for treating heterozygous familial hypercholesterolemia.

In addition, the clinical trial report (performed in Korea) submitted for registration of the disputed drug is identical with that submitted to Korean competent health authority for examination. Also, the disputed drug is made in Korea, granted with drug approval and marketed in Korea. The Korean health competent authority granted the indication 'heterozygous familial hypercholesterolemia' based on the same clinical trial. Again, it is proved that the disputed drug can be used for treating patients with heterozygous familial hypercholesterolemia indeed.

Accordingly, according to the provision of Paragraph 2, Article 48-20 of Taiwan Pharmaceutical Affairs Act, avoiding infringing other's patents for medical use by excluding the indications protected by those patents is allowed and indications and subject of treatment should be determined based on the indications listed in SmPC granted by Food and Drug Administration. However, in this special case, 'primary hypercholesterolemia (excluding heterozygous familial hypercholesterolemia)' of the disputed drug is not medically logical and thus the indication cannot be used to compare with the claim 1 of the disputed patent. Therefore, determination of whether the actual indication of the disputed drug falls into the scope of the claim 1 of the disputed patent should be based on the therapeutic effect for 'heterozygous familial hypercholesterolemia' of the disputed drug per se represented by the human clinical trials results cited in the SmPC of the disputed drug.